canadian edition

Marketing

the core

ROGER A. KERIN
Southern Methodist University

STEVEN W. HARTLEY
University of Denver

WILLIAM RUDELIUS
University of Minnesota

GERARD EDWARDS
Douglas College

CARLA GAIL TIBBO
Douglas College

McGraw-Hill Ryerson

Toronto   Montréal   Boston   Burr Ridge, IL
Dubuque, IA   Madison, WI   New York
San Francisco   St. Louis   Bangkok   Bogotá
Caracas   Kuala Lumpur   Lisbon   London
Madrid   Mexico City   Milan   New Delhi
Santiago   Seoul   Singapore   Sydney   Taipei

Marketing: The Core
Canadian Edition

ISBN: 0-07-092297-7

2 3 4 5 6 7 8 9 10 CTPS 0 9 8 7 6

Printed and bound in China

Statistics Canada information is used with the permission of the Minister of Industry, as Minister responsible for Statistics Canada. Information on the availability of the wide range of data from Statistics Canada can be obtained from Statistics Canada's Regional Offices, its World Wide Web site at <http://www.statcan.ca>, and its toll-free access number 1-800-263-1136.

Care has been taken to trace ownership of copyright material contained in this text; however, the publisher will welcome any information that enables them to rectify any reference or credit for subsequent editions.

Editorial Director and Vice President: Patrick Ferrier
Sponsoring Editor: Kim Brewster
Developmental Editors: Darren Hick / Andrew Simpson
Director of Marketing: Jeff MacLean
Sales Manager: Megan Farrell
Supervising Editor: Jaime Smith
Copy Editor: Mike Kelly
Production Coordinator: Paula Brown
Composition: Sharon Lucas
Cover Design/Interior Design: Sharon Lucas
Cover Image: © FoodPix/Brian Leatart
Printer: China Translation & Printing Services Ltd.

Library and Archives Canada Cataloguing in Publication

Edwards, Gerard,
    Marketing : The Core / Gerard Edwards, Carla Gail Tibbo. -- Canadian ed.

Include index.
ISBN 0-07-092297-7

    1. Marketing--Textbooks. I. Tibbo, Carla Gail II. Title.

HF5415.E43 2004   658.8   C2004-905752-9

AUTHOR PROFILES

Roger A. Kerin is the Harold C. Simmons Distinguished Professor of Marketing at the Edwin L. Cox School of Business, Southern Methodist University in Dallas, Texas. Professor Kerin holds a B.A. (magna cum laude), MBA, and Ph.D. from the University of Minnesota. His teaching and research interests lie in marketing planning and strategy, product management, financial aspects of marketing, and marketing research. Professor Kerin is a frequent participant in executive development programs and is also an active consultant on matters of marketing planning and strategy. Professor Kerin has published and authored several texts and many articles on marketing. He also serves on numerous journal editorial review boards and is currently a member of the Board of Governors of the Academy of Marketing Science.

Steven W. Hartley is Professor of Marketing in the Daniels College of Business at the University of Denver. He holds Bachelor of Mechanical Engineering, MBA, and Ph.D. degrees from the University of Minnesota. Dr. Hartley was formerly the chair of the Department of Marketing at the University of Denver, and has taught at the University of Colorado, the University of Minnesota, and in several executive development programs. His teaching interests include principles of marketing, marketing research, and marketing planning. Dr. Hartley's research has appeared in many leading marketing publications. He is an active consultant to several prominent U.S. corporations and is active in many professional organizations including the American Marketing Association, the Academy of Marketing Science, and the Marketing Educators' Association.

William Rudelius holds the Endowed Chair in Global Marketing at the Graduate School of Business of the University of St. Thomas in Minnesota. He holds a BS degree in Mechanical Engineering from the University of Wisconsin and an MBA in Marketing and Ph.D. in Applied Economics from the Wharton School of the University of Pennsylvania. Professor Rudelius has co-authored other marketing textbooks. His articles have appeared in leading academic journals. During the past ten years, he has taught extensively in Europe; he serves on the board of directors for several business and not-for-profit organizations.

Carla Gail Tibbo is chair of Marketing at Douglas College in British Columbia. Professor Tibbo holds a holds a B.Sc. from Acadia University, a B.Ed. from the University of Toronto, and an MBA from the University of British Columbia. Her teaching interests focus on marketing research, database marketing, and promotion. She has coauthored other texts for both students and instructors, and also writes for business audiences. She has developed extensive online learning resources and teaching methodologies. A former executive in both the government and private business sectors, she is an avid marketing practitioner and is the president of Incisive Marketing, a Vancouver-based firm of marketing consultants. Professor Tibbo holds the distinguished Certified Marketing Research Professional designation, is active in several professional organizations, and serves on the local board of the Professional Marketing Research Society chapter.

Gerard Edwards is an award-winning professor and past chair of Marketing at Douglas College in British Columbia. He holds an MBA in Management from Cranfield University in the United Kingdom, and also is a licensed professional electrical engineer. He worked extensively in the international telecommunications sector and held senior executive positions in engineering, marketing, and sales. He and Professor Tibbo have been business partners for over 10 years, and Professor Edwards specializes in consulting in the areas of marketing strategy, distribution, and sales. He is a sought-after and motivational sales educator in business and academia, and he serves as the Director of Education for Sales and Marketing Executives International, the global organization offering professional certification for sales and marketing practitioners in countries around the world. He holds the prestigious designations of Certified Marketing Executive and Certified Sales Executive from that organization.

BRIEF CONTENTS

DETAILED CONTENTS

Part 3 Targeting Marketing Opportunities 162

8 Turning Marketing Information into Action 164

PREFACE

Welcome to the exciting, dynamic, and challenging field of marketing! If you've been on the Web, in a store, working in a company, or a consumer of any of the thousands of products and services available in our marketplace, you are already involved with marketing, and you have probably already noticed many of the extraordinary changes taking place. Personalized advertising, multichannel retailing, cashless vending, customized products, online coupons, web-based surveys, and interactive media are just a few of the many indications that marketing is racing into a new era. At the same time, many traditional elements of the discipline such as segmentation, new product development, and pricing are growing in importance and use. The combination of the current and the traditional elements of marketing create a truly exceptional topic to study and understand. We are all marketed to, and we find marketing all around us, every day of our lives.

Marketing: The Core draws upon the content and highly successful approach we've used in seven editions of our other, longer, text entitled *Marketing*. Our goal with this new text is to present the concepts essential to an introductory marketing course, yet retain the pedagogy that has made *Marketing* a best-selling text.

What *is* our pedagogical framework? First, we use an active-learning approach that involves students in the text by combining facts, figures, information, cases, questions, exercises, and photos in an engaging, experiential fashion. Second, we incorporate many current examples using firms, products, and services that students recognize and may have purchased as consumers. Third, our in-chapter study aids and design elements—such as concept checks, discussion forums, and easy-to-read figures—are developed to match the learning styles of today's students.

We are gratified by the growing interest in our approach to the study of marketing. Feedback from students and instructors from around the world continues to reinforce our pedagogical style. Marketing and its translations and adaptations are now used extensively throughout the United States and Canada, and in Poland, Russia, China, and many Spanish- and Portuguese-speaking countries. We hope that you will find *Marketing: The Core* a key factor in your exploration of the knowledge, skills, and tools of the marketing discipline.

DISTINCTIVE FEATURES OF *THE CORE* FOR MARKETING STUDENTS

We have developed many important, student-focused features that are prominent in every chapter:

- **Engaging writing style.** Our easy-to-read writing style engages students through active-learning techniques, timely and interesting examples, and challenging applications.
- **Personal look at marketing professionals.** Our text provides vivid and accurate descriptions of contemporary marketing professionals in action—through cases, extended examples, and testimonials—that allow students to personalize marketing and identify possible career interests and role models.
- **Contemporary and classic real-world examples.** We use up-to-date examples that students are likely to recognize from their own experiences in the marketplace, plus classic examples that students of business and marketing can easily relate to text concepts and typical marketing decisions.
- **Built-in learning aids.** Learning objectives, concept checks, key terms, chapter summaries, Internet exercises, discussion forums, and application questions are used to reinforce learning and to allow students to assess their progress.

- **Outstanding support resources.** Each chapter also has a video segment that supplements the written case and adds an exciting visual perspective to the company, products, and marketing decision makers discussed in the case.
- **Marketing model.** We introduce a visual model that shows, simply and clearly, the world of marketing at a glance—the functions and interactions in marketing. We then use the model in each chapter to show the students what aspect of marketing the chapter covers, and how the contents of the chapter relate to the overall marketing process.

ORGANIZATION AND CONTENT OF *THE CORE*

Marketing: The Core is divided into four parts. Part 1, "Initiating the Marketing Process," looks first at what marketing is and how it creates customer value and customer relationships (Chapter 1). Then Chapter 2 provides an overview of the strategic marketing process that occurs in an organization, and provides a framework for the rest of the text. Appendix A provides a guide to preparing a marketing plan. Chapter 3 analyzes the major environmental factors in our changing marketing environment, and Chapter 4 provides a framework for including ethical and social responsibility considerations in marketing decisions.

Part 2, "Understanding Buyers and Markets," first describes, in Chapter 5, how individual consumers reach buying decisions. Next, Chapter 6 looks at industrial and organizational buyers and how they make purchase decisions. And finally, in Chapter 7, the nature and scope of world trade and the influence of cultural differences on global marketing practices are explored.

In Part 3, "Targeting Marketing Opportunities," the marketing research function and how information about prospective consumers is linked to marketing strategy and decisions are discussed in Chapter 8. The process of segmenting and targeting markets and positioning products appears in Chapter 9.

Part 4, "Satisfying Marketing Opportunities," covers the four Ps—the marketing mix elements. The product element is divided into the natural chronological sequence of first developing new products and services (Chapter 10) and then managing the existing products, services, and brands (Chapter 11). Pricing is discussed, focusing on the way organizations set prices (Chapter 12). Two chapters address the place (distribution) aspects of marketing: "Marketing Channels and Channel Logistics" (Chapter 13) and "Retailing and Wholesaling" (Chapter 14). Chapter 15 discusses integrated marketing communications and interactive marketing, topics that have grown in importance in the marketing discipline recently. The primary forms of mass market communication—advertising, sales promotion, and public relations—are covered in Chapter 16. Personal selling and direct marketing are covered in Chapter 17. The text concludes with a Postscript: a summary of the marketing voyage we have taken throughout the 17 chapters; a perspective on how the topics, tools, and techniques we have studied fit together for solid marketing; and a glimpse at the future of marketing as we foresee it today.

Chapter Highlights

- **The role of the Internet and technology in marketing today.** We recognize that the Internet and other digital technologies provide us with powerful new tools that can greatly enhance communication and commerce. From cover to cover, all chapters integrate coverage of e-commerce topics such as e-marketplaces, dynamic pricing, buzz marketing, viral marketing, personalization, multichannel retailing, eCRM, collaborative commerce, file sharing and peer-to-peer communication, cyberservices, Internet appliances, interactive television, online secondary data sources, and virtual advertising.

- **Emphasis on customer value.** Chapter 1 presents an enhanced emphasis on customer value, the role of brands and how they make firms accountable to consumers, new products, and the breadth of marketing and how it is used by many types of organizations.
- **Creating a successful marketing plan.** Following the discussion of marketing strategies in Chapter 2, we introduce how to actually craft an effective plan, with guidelines, checklists, contents, and organizational ideas.
- **Overview of the marketing environment.** Chapter 3 includes a discussion of the dramatic impact of file-sharing on the music industry; the shifting age distribution of the population; and the changing attitudes and roles of men and women. It also provides an introduction to current electronic business technologies, including the Internet, the World Wide Web, e-commerce, and the growth of collaborative commerce.
- **Ethics in marketing.** Chapter 4 is devoted to the topic of ethics and social responsibility in marketing. In addition, most chapters also integrate ethics coverage in the Ethics and Social Responsibility Alert boxes.
- **Consumer behaviour.** Chapter 5 includes current examples related to the stages of the consumer-decision process; it provides discussions of customer satisfaction and retention and looks at marketing strategies for high- and low-involvement products.
- **Organizational buying.** Chapter 6 features sections on online buying in organizational markets, e-marketplaces, and online auctions.
- **Global coverage.** Chapter 7 includes discussions of the emergence of a networked global marketspace and the influence of trade organizations on the global rules of trade between nations.
- **Market research technology.** Chapter 8 includes discussions of creative research techniques, such as hiring "cool hunters" to identify important cultural trends, and coverage of Internet and fax survey techniques, data mining, and the impact of research on marketing actions.
- **Brand equity.** Chapter 11 includes the customer-based brand equity pyramid, which helps explain the relationship between brand awareness and how consumers think and feel about a brand. This helps students understand how the added value of a brand name gives a product competitive and price advantage.
- **Channels coverage.** Chapter 13 includes examples related to multiple channels of distribution, strategic alliances, vertical marketing, exclusive distribution, slotting allowances, and satisfying buyer requirements. Current examples, such as Dell Computer Corporation and Wal-Mart are used to explain the role of supply chains and logistics management in marketing and how a firm balances distribution costs against the need for effective customer service.
- **Retailing and wholesaling coverage.** Chapter 14 chronicles the success of, and Canadians' love affair with, one of their favourite retailers; it also covers the global expansion of many retailers and e-tailers and popular retail formats such as franchising. This chapter also provides coverage of important new technologies, such as cashless vending systems, as well as new concepts such as everyday fair pricing and multichannel retailing.
- **Advertising coverage.** Chapters 15 and 16 discuss virtual advertising, interactive television, radio, and Internet advertising. Up-to-date examples of the latest forms of promotion, including sweepstakes, product placement, and online coupons, are also provided.
- **Interactive and multichannel marketing.** Chapter 15 presents ideas on marketing strategy in an Internet/Web-enabled marketspace. Emphasis is placed on interactive marketing practice and the growing application of multichannel marketing. Students will also find this chapter of interest because they will see how important it is for companies to forge collaborative channel relationships to improve their global market competitiveness.

ACKNOWLEDGMENTS

THE DEVELOPMENT PROCESS

Marketing: The Core is a Canadian first—a very "Canadian" introductory marketing text that is thorough, and at the same time, succinct and concise. The idea for *Marketing: The Core* was the result of many comments from McGraw-Hill Ryerson sales representatives, marketing instructors throughout the world, and students who had used other texts in their courses. We concluded that there is a need among some instructors and students for a comprehensive, but *concise*, marketing text. As the title suggests, our plan was to create a shorter text that would enable students to understand the *central* concepts of *Marketing*. This required reducing some coverage, enhancing some explanations, keeping the vocabulary manageable, and simplifying illustrations. We also used instructor feedback to match our pedagogical elements to the target audience. To determine exactly what content, design elements, and supplements would meet the needs of this segment, we conducted research in two phases: information solicitation and in-depth interviews.

Our cybrarian at Douglas College, Jean Cockburn, cheerfully helped us with the Marketing Newsnet about online and internet resources—with her relentless pursuit of cyber knowledge, she has enlightened and educated us over the past ten years, and we are very grateful to her. Our colleagues in the Marketing Department at Douglas College, Padma Vipat, Lorne Patterson and Mark Breedveld have supported and encouraged us, and we thank them for their confidence. Our students continually inspire us to produce marketing material that "speaks" to them and ignites their interest in marketing, and they are a major source of motivation behind our writing.

We appreciated the assistance and information provided to us by Peter Donato of Cervélo Cycles Inc., Scott Chandler of Padinox Inc., Bob Lyons of Terrapin Communications, Joanne Westwood of Vancouver City Savings Credit Union, Jason McPhail of Rogers Wireless, Hanna de Guzman and Sharon Jung of TIR Systems Ltd., Craig Cameron of Millward Brown Goldfarb; John Vavrik of ICBC, Peggy Tibbo-Cameron of the Nova Scotia Department of Tourism, Culture and Heritage, and Rhys Gibb and Steve Mossop of Ipsos-Reid. Brie Gowans of Rethink Advertising was particularly helpful in putting together information about advertising, and Rethink's role in the advertising world.

We appreciate the valuable comments, suggestions, and insights offered by the following reviewers of the first Canadian edition of *Marketing: The Core:*

Lesley Moffitt
Assiniboine Community College

Gordon McFarlane
Langara College

Deborah Reyner
Conestoga College

Dwight Dyson
Centennial College

Lee Ann Keple
Athabasca University

Linda Donville
Centennial College

Steve Janisse
St. Clair College

Diana Serafini
Dawson College

Paul Myers
St. Clair College

Robert Soroka
McGill University/Dawson College

Barry Mills
College of the North Atlantic

Megan Mills
Okanagan University College

George Dracopoulos
Vanier College

Bill Crowe
St. Lawrence College

Beth Pett
Niagara College

Jeff Schissler
Durham College

We are also deeply grateful to the reviewers of the U.S. first edition, which created such a strong foundation for us to work from. They include:

Chris Barnes *Lakeland Community College*	Rosemarie Houghton *Northwood University*
Pat Bernson *County College of Morris*	Jim Hutton *Fairleigh Dickinson University*
Al Brokaw *Michigan Tech*	Dennis Kimble *Northwood University*
Sergio Carvalho *Bernard Baruch College*	Anna Kwong *Santa Barbara City College*
John Crawford *Lipscomb University*	Donna Mayo *Tennessee State*
Charlene Davis *Trinity University*	Kevin McClean *Grand Canyon University*
Dexter Davis *Alfred State*	Susan Peterson *Scottsdale Community College*
Beth Elam *Western New England*	Donald Roy *Tennessee State*
Medhat Farooque *Central Arizona University*	Marvin Shapiro *South Mountain Community College*
Renee Foster *Delta State University*	Randy Stuart *Kennesaw State*
Hershey Friedman *Brooklyn College*	Lars Thording *Arizona State University—West*
Connie Golden *Lakeland Community College*	Sushila Umashankar *University of Arizona*
Susan Harmon *Middle Tennessee State*	Bill Wilkinson *Governor's State University*

Finally, we acknowledge the professional efforts of the McGraw-Hill Ryerson staff. Because this is the first Canadian edition of *Marketing: The Core*, the project required a team with a vision of a new and innovative product and a commitment to its timely completion. At McGraw-Hill, we appreciate the confidence placed in us by Pat Ferrier and James Buchanan in contracting us to do *The Core*; the advice and support of Kim Brewster, our Sponsoring editor; the creativity and insight of our developmental editors Darren Hick and Andrew Simpson; and the ongoing relationship we enjoy with Bruce McIntosh, i-learning sales specialist extraordinaire. We are truly grateful for the enthusiasm and support of all these exceptional people.

Gerard Edwards
Carla Gail Tibbo

A Student's Guide to
Marketing: The Core

Marketing: The Core offers an array of features to help you learn and apply the concepts.

Marketing Model

This unique feature is introduced at the beginning of each chapter; it is designed to guide you through your study of introductory marketing. We created this model to show the marketing process in a graphic way. It is used in *Marketing: The Core* to show the progression of topics as you move through the book. All of the topics covered in the text can be related to the model, and it demonstrates the dynamic interaction of all of the components of marketing.

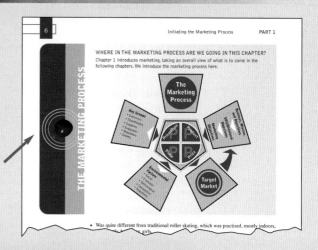

Chapter-Opening Vignettes

Chapter-opening vignettes introduce you to the chapter concepts ahead, using a recognizable and interesting company example. For instance, in Chapter 1, the authors use Rollerblade, a popular in-line skate, to grab your interest while introducing the concepts of marketing. The chapter opening story is then integrated into parts of the narrative and exhibits throughout the chapter.

| MARKETING MIX ELEMENT | MARKETING PROGRAM ACTIVITY TO REACH: | | RATIONALE FOR MARKETING PROGRAM ACTIVITY |
	RECREATIONAL SEGMENT	CHILDREN SEGMENT	
Product	Offer Fusion skates for beginning and intermediate skaters simply wanting fun and exercise	Offer the Mx 900, a skate for children that extends so that its length changes as the children grow	Use new-product research and the latest technology to offer high-quality skates to satisfy the needs of key customer segments
Price	Price up to $199 a pair	Price up to $99 a pair	Set prices that provide genuine value to the customer segment that is targeted
Promotion	Feature Rollerblade in sports competitions and magazines like Shape and Mademoiselle and local newspapers	Use gym classes to introduce children to in-line skating and place ads in local newspapers	Increase awareness to those new to the sport while offering ads and press releases for more advanced segments
Place	Distribute the lines through specialty and regular sporting goods stores and the Internet	Distribute the Mx 900 through sporting goods stores	Make it easy for buyers in the segment to buy at an outlet that is convenient and where they feel comfortable

FIGURE 1–4
Marketing programs for two of Rollerblade's skates, targeted at two distinctly different customer segments: recreational skaters and children

- *Aggressive segment.* Are you the kind of speed and stunt skater seen on XGames on TV? Then try the new TRS line, the Team Rollerblade Series, reflecting design suggestions from Rollerblade's skating team.
- *Fitness segment.* Do you skate often and are you serious about a good aerobic workout? Try the Lightning 05 (for women) or Lightning 07 (for men)—skates for people whose feet demand a good fit and shock dampening from Rollerblade's latest technology.
- *Recreation segment.* Skating ... the majority of in-li...

Dynamic Graphics
Tables, figures, and charts throughout the book have a fresh, new look with the addition of creative frames and drawings designed to present important information in an interesting and easy-to understand layout.

...Rollerblade case at the end of the chapter lets us look in greater depth at the marketing strategies that Rollerblade is developing for the twenty-first century.

Concept Check

1. An organization can't satisfy the needs of all consumers, so it must focus on one or more subgroups, which are its _____
2. What are the four marketing mix elements that make up the organization's marketing program?
3. What are uncontrollable factors?

Concept Checks
Found at the end of each major chapter section, these checkpoints offer critical thinking and memory recall questions, helping you reflect on the text and test your comprehension of the material before reading on.

---

customer value
Buyers' benefits including quality, price, convenience, on-time delivery, and before- and after-sale service

What is new, however, is a more careful attempt at understanding how a firm's customers perceive value. For our purposes, **customer value** is the unique combination of benefits received by targeted buyers that includes quality, price, convenience, on-time delivery, and both before-sale and after-sale service. Firms now actually try to place a dollar value on a loyal, satisfied customer.

Many successful firms have chosen to deliver outstanding customer value with one of three value strategies — best price, best product, or best service. Companies such as West-Jet and Zellers have been successful offering consumers the best price. Bombardier and Mountain Equipment Co-op claim to provide the best products on the market. Lee Valley Tools and Aldo Shoes pledge to provide the best service. What strategies do you think Canadian Tire employs?

Relationship Marketing and the Marketing Program

A firm achieves meaningful customer relationships by creating connections with its customers through careful coordination of the product, its price, the way it's promoted, and how it's placed.

relationship marketing
Linking the organization to its individual customers, employees, suppliers, and other partners for their mutual long-term benefit

Relationship Marketing: Easy to Understand, Hard to Do   The hallmark of developing and maintaining effective customer relationships is today called **relationship marketing**. Successful relationship marketing links an organization to its key groups (individual customers, employees, suppliers, and other partners—see Figure 1–2) for their mutual long-term benefit. In terms of selling a product, relationship marketing involves a personal, ongoing relationship between the organization and its individual customers that begins before and continues after the sale.

Major manufacturers find relationship marketing difficult to achieve. Today's information technology, along with cutting-edge manufacturing and marketing processes, have led to tailoring goods or services to the tastes of individual customers in high volumes at...

Helpful Margin Definitions
Brief definitions of the key terms contained in the text are placed in the margin for quick reference and review.

MARKETING NEWSNET

CREATING CUSTOMER VALUE THROUGH PACKAGING: PEZ HEADS DISPENSE MORE THAN CANDY

Customer value can assume numerous forms. For Pez Candy, Inc. (www.pez.com), customer value manifests itself in some 250 Pez character candy dispensers. Each refillable dispenser ejects tasty candy tablets in a variety of flavours that delight preteens and teens alike.

Pez was formulated in 1927 by Austrian food mogul Edward Haas III and successfully sold in Europe as an adult breath mint. Pez, which comes from the German word for peppermint, pfefferminz, was originally packaged in a hygienic, headless plastic dispenser. Pez first appeared in North America in 1953 with a headless dispenser, marketed to adults. After conducting extensive marketing research, Pez was repositioned with fruit flavours, repackaged with licensed character heads on top of the dispenser, and remarketed as a children's product in the mid-1950s. Since then, most top-level licensed characters and hundreds of other characters have become Pez heads. Consumers eat more than 3 billion Pez tablets annually, and company sales growth exceeds that of the candy industry as a whole.

The unique Pez package dispenses a "use experience" for its customers beyond the candy itself: namely, fun. And fun translates into a 98 percent awareness level for Pez among teenagers and 89 percent among mothers with children. Pez has not advertised its product for years. With that kind of awareness, who needs advertising?

Marketing NewsNet
This boxed feature provides exciting, current examples of marketing applications in action, organized around the following themes: technology & e-commerce, customer value, global, and cross functional.

ETHICS AND SOCIAL RESPONSIBILITY ALERT
STUDENT CREDIT CARDS: AN ULTIMATE BENEFIT OR A DISASTER IN THE MAKING?

Ethics and Social Responsibility Alert
These boxes increase your awareness and assessment of current topics of ethical and social concern.

If you are over 19, you have probably received a credit card application—or maybe you already have your own credit card or a supplementary card on your parents' account. Every year thousands of students across Canada apply for and receive their first credit card. The immediate benefit? Students can buy college necessities and purchase other amenities—clothes, perhaps, or a trip to Mexico? The long-term benefit may be that students establish a good credit rating, which they use for further financing later in their lives. But these benefits also mask a serious concern. Many students are drowning in credit card debt and student loans they have racked up over their period of studies.

According to the Canadian Federation of Students (CFS), student debt increased by as much as 30 percent between 1995 and 2000. Also, a 2004 Statistics Canada report indicates that students are increasingly having more difficulty repaying student debt. Increases in tuition fees will only make the situation worse. In that same time frame (1995–2000), the majority of students left the educational system burdened with a substantial debt load.

tion and related expenses.

Students fresh out of a post-secondary institution can face a huge financial problem. Think of the demands on them—credit card debt, outstanding student loans, rent, car payments, utilities, telephone costs, and other living expenses—these expenses often exceed the starting salaries of college graduates. For some students, their starting salaries barely permit them to make the minimum payments on their credit card debt, let alone pay back outstanding balances.

Some universities now offer on-site financial counselling. The federal government responded to the growing student debt problem by granting up to 5 years of interest relief and increasing the allowable time for students to repay their student loans from 10 to 15 years. This relief may help current students, but it does little to help those who have already graduated and are struggling under their past debt load.

What do you think should be done to help students

QUESTIONS: APPLYING MARKETING CONCEPTS AND PERSPECTIVES

1 What concepts of moral philosophy and social responsibility are applicable to the practices of VanCity, described in the introduction to this chapter? Why?

2 Compare and contrast moral idealism and utilitarianism as alternative personal moral philosophies. Which do you think sounds more like you?

3 How would you evaluate Milton Friedman's view of the social responsibility of a firm?

4 Cause-related marketing programs have become popular. Do you know of companies that use this technique? Why do you think the companies that you named have chosen the cause or causes they have?

5 Check out the corporate site for Sales and Marketing Executives International (www.smei.org), an organization committed to establishing standards for sales and marketing professionals around the world. Look for the organization's mission statement, its founding principles, and its published code of ethics. Research to find at least five other professional associations in other fields of business (e.g., accountants, engineers) and compare their approaches to ethics and standards.

6 In the section earlier in this chapter entitled "Corporate Culture and Expectations," we refer to the top 10 best Canadian corporate citizens. Three of these are financial institutions, and most of the others are manufacturing firms. Why do you think financial institutions are so focused on ethics and social responsibility? Compare and contrast the approach taken by manufacturing organizations to that of financial institutions. Which do you find more convincing and why?

7 Suppose you are a Canadian importer of spices and beans from southeast Asian countries. Develop a statement of ethics and a code of conduct for the company. How would you make sure that this is put into practice in your company?

DISCUSSION FORUM

Visit the Nike corporate website (www.nikebiz.com) and find the section called "Responsibility." Review the section on "Workers & Factories." There has been a lot of media attention in the past few years on Nike's treatment of and compensation to factory workers in foreign countries, and dealing with this is an ongoing challenge. Nike comments in its January 2004 report, "It is not a perfect record, and it never will be, but we're committed to the process." Discuss Nike's position, and then develop some counter arguments critiquing Nike's viewpoint and actions. What other companies with global manufacturing operations can you think of? How are they responding to similar challenges?

INTERNET EXERCISE

Bribery as a means to win and retain business varies widely by country. Transparency International, based in Germany, periodically polls employees of multinational firms and institutions and political analysts and ranks countries on the basis of their perceived level of bribery to win or retain business. To obtain the most recent ranking, visit the Transparency International website at www.transparency.org and click Info Center.

Scroll the Corruption Perceptions Index to find out where Canada stands in the worldwide rankings as well as its neighbours, the United States and Mexico. Any surprises? Which country listed in the most recent ranking has the highest ranking and which has the lowest ranking?

www.mcgrawhill.ca/college/thecore

Internet Exercises

These end-of-chapter exercises ask you to go online and think critically about a specific company's use of the Internet—helping you apply your knowledge of key chapter concepts, terms, and topics, as well as evaluate the success or failure of the company's efforts.

Questions and Discussion

At the end of each chapter, two features allow you to test your knowledge and your capability to apply the material covered in the chapter. *Questions: Applying Marketing Concepts and Perspectives* asks you to think about the marketing material and check yourself on your comprehension of it. *Discussion Forum* presents a thought-provoking scenario for you to discuss with other students. Understanding happens best when we **do**!

Video Case Studies

This end-of-chapter feature provides an up-close look at a company example—reinforcing the chapter content, while bringing the material to life. Rollerblade, Flyte Tyme, and Palm Inc. are just a few of the exciting video cases incorporated into *Marketing: The Core*.

VIDEO CASE 3

FLYTE TYME PRODUCTIONS, INC.: THE BEST IDEA WINS!

"Terry was looking for a keyboard player to be in the band he was just starting," remembers Jimmy Jam of Flyte Tyme Productions, Inc. "I had sort of rebelled because I had first thought of myself as a drummer," says Jam. But after he listened and heard how good the drummer was, he told Terry, "I'll be the keyboard player."

The conversation took place a few weeks after Terry Lewis and Jimmy Jam met at a summer math program for gifted junior high school students, sponsored by a local university. The two came to prominence in the early 1980s as members of the funk band "The Time" that appeared as the opener on many of Prince's early tours. The pair still credit Prince for much of their tenacious work ethic and eclectic musical tastes. After

accounts for 10 of their 16 No. 1 songs. Recently, they wrote and produced their fifth successive album for Janet Jackson,

Appendix A

Creating a Successful Marketing Plan

In this part of *The Core*, we have looked at all of the components of a marketing plan. Now in this appendix, we look at the actual crafting of a marketing plan, including some thoughts on making the plan work for an organization. You, as a marketing student, can create useful and interesting marketing plans, a skill that will benefit you throughout your business career. We have seen plans prepared by our marketing students that are as good if not better than some of those prepared by professional marketing firms. Marketing planning is part science, part art; it requires a few key skills: research capability, analytical competence, the ability to see the "big picture" of a firm and its future potential, and interpersonal connections to assist with getting input and insights from key stakeholders.

PURPOSE OF THE PLAN

Ensuring that a company's marketing orga[...]
requires a detailed and specific marketing [...]
to marketing success. There are different [...]
to create one:

- A marketing plan may communicate co[...] give them some guidelines about their [...]
- The company may require financing, a[...] company and its requirements to potent[...]
- Creating the plan may be the best stru[...] opportunities, and market or competitor[...]

Some marketers feel that the planning [...] creating an effective plan, a company und[...] this gives them information and market sa[...] their future. The planning process forces co[...] sions and identify priorities, and to face [...] weaknesses.

Appendix A: Creating a Successful Marketing Plan

At the end of Chapter 2, this guide to planning, researching, and writing a winning marketing plan is a resource that you can use in a number of ways, throughout your use of this text and beyond. It incorporates marketing plan rationale, detailed plan contents, effective design and execution of the plan, as well as checklists for implementing and evaluating the marketing plan.

HOW TO PLAN EFFECTIVELY

Many excellent marketing plans have been laboured over and written, only to sit on shelves. To make good use of the plan, it must be actionable, readable, and of a reasonable length. A few guidelines for effective planning include:

- Set goals and a time frame for developing the plan.
- Identify the target audience for the plan, that is, who is it intended for.
- Establish what you want to know and the time frame you have to undertake your research. Research can be a challenge, as there is so much information that you may have difficulty setting parameters about how much is enough, and when you should end your researching and go with the information you have
- Planning is *never* finished—a good marketing plan is a dynamic document, and it evolves, changes, and refocuses as the organization grows—so keep it current.
- Consider your audience and write to them. Avoid using jargon and complex explanations; some readers will not comprehend your language, and the plan will not have the desired effect on them.
- People absorb information in different ways: some like the written word, some see the message more clearly with a chart or graph, and some are pictorial learners. Craft your plan so that it has a mixture of ways of presenting information to ensure that you engage as much of your audience as possible.
- Involve different people with different perspectives, different skill sets, and different relationships to the company; solid teamwork with a variety of perspectives will result in the best plan.

BUSINESS VERSUS MARKETING PLANS

Business plans, marketing plans—what is the difference? Do we need both? Don't they overlap? The answers to these questions depend on the organization, who is doing the planning, and what the purpose of the plan is. The following chart shows the differences

COMPARING A BUSINESS PLAN TO A MARKETING PLAN	MARKETING PLAN	BUSINESS PLAN
Executive Summary	✓	✓
Table of Contents	✓	✓
Company Overview	✓	more detailed
Strategic Plan		✓
Situation Analysis	✓	✓
Mission Statement and Goals	✓	✓
Target Markets	✓	✓
Marketing Strategy	✓	✓
Research and Development Program		✓
Budget and Financials	✓	more detailed
Organizational Structure and Staffing		✓
Implementation	✓	✓
Control and Evaluation	✓	✓
Contingency Plans	✓	✓
Appendix A: Biographies of Key Personnel		✓
Other Appendixes: Details on Other Topics	✓	✓

An Instructor's Guide to Supplements

With this support package, you and your students receive everything from the basic supplements to the latest in educational technologies. Check it out for yourself.

LECTURE PREPARATION, ASSESSMENT, AND PRESENTATION TOOLS

Instructor's CD-ROM. The CD-ROM includes the print and electronic supplements, so you have access to all of the supplements on one CD-ROM.

Instructor's Manual. The thoroughly revised Instructor's Manual includes lecture notes; discussions of the Marketing NewsNet boxes, Ethics and Social Responsibility Alerts, and Internet Exercises; answers to the Applying Marketing Concepts and Perspectives and Discussion Forum questions; case teaching notes; in-class activities; supplemental lecture notes; teaching suggestions; and detailed information about integrating other supplements into the course and classroom.

PowerPoint presentations and digital assets. These incorporate a high-quality photo and art program, including figure slides, commercials, product shots, advertisements, marketing-in-practice shots, and video segments from the video package.

Computest program. This Brownstone Test Bank contains 3,000 questions categorized by topic and level of learning (definitional, conceptual, or application). The instructor-friendly format allows easy selection of questions from any part of the text, boxed materials and cases. The Brownstone program allows you to select any of the questions, make changes if desired, or add new questions—and quickly print out a finished set customized to your course.

Video case studies. A unique series of 17 contemporary marketing cases is available on VHS and DVD and from the Online Learning Centre. Each video case corresponds with chapter-specific topics and an end-of-chapter case in the text.

ONLINE TECHNOLOGY

Online Learning Centre

This robust book-specific website includes resources for both instructors and students. For the instructor, we offer downloadable supplement materials and continuous updates. Students have a 24–7 study centre to keep them up-to-date, to provide examples for application, and to prepare for tests.

Instructor Centre

- **"Ask the Authors"**
- **Instructor's Manual**
- **PowerPoint.** Includes concept screens, art from the text, and notes on other digital assets available in the PowerPoint Presentations.

Student Centre

- **Internet exercises**
- **Key term flash cards**
- **Self-quizzes with feedback**
- **Online video cases.** Includes video case text and several video clips.

PowerWeb (optional package)

- **Daily news feed.** Headlines with annotations from the leading periodicals and news sources—searchable by topic.
- **Weekly case updates.** Each week a new short case dealing with a company in the headlines is presented.
- **Readings in Marketing.** A collection of important articles selected by a team of marketing professors provides deeper topical study.
- **PowerSearch current journals and periodicals.** Search engine powered by Northern Lights.
- **Career resources**
- **Web research**
- **Study tips**

Online Course Options

The material in *Marketing: The Core* can be used with instructor-generated online learning sites. Any online platform, including WebCT, Blackboard, and eCollege, is compatible with the text's material. There are two basic options here: a course companion website or an online course where the course material is fully or partially delivered via a course website.

Companion website. McGraw-Hill's PageOut course website tool enables you to create a course website where you can post your syllabus, case solutions, course information updates, test results, and other key material. You can include links to the McGraw-Hill's Online Learning Centre or e-Book content, add links to important resources, and maintain student results in the online gradebook. A companion website can also be set up using other platforms.

Online course. Offering courses fully or partially online is increasingly popular, and definitely the way of the future for business learning. The content of *Marketing: The Core* has been prepared for ease of use in an online environment. You can customize the material, chapter by chapter, to your own teaching style and emphasis, or use it as the authors have designed it.

SUPERIOR SERVICE

Service takes on a whole new meaning with McGraw-Hill Ryerson and *Marketing: The Core*. More than just bringing you the textbook, we have consistently raised the bar in terms of innovation and educational research—both in marketing and in education in general. These investments in learning and the education community have helped us to understand the needs of students and educators across the country, and allowed us to foster the growth of truly innovative, integrated learning.

Integrated Learning

Your Integrated Learning Sales Specialist is a McGraw-Hill Ryerson representative who has the experience, product knowledge, training, and support to help you assess and integrate any of our products, technology, and services into your course for optimum teaching and learning performance. Whether it's using our test bank software, helping your students improve their grades, or putting your entire course online, your *i*-Learning Sales Specialist is there to help you do it. Contact your local *i*-Learning Sales Specialist today to learn how to maximize all of McGraw-Hill Ryerson's resources!

iLearning Services Program

McGraw-Hill Ryerson offers a unique iServices package designed for Canadian faculty. Our mission is to equip providers of higher education with superior tools and resources required for excellence in teaching. For additional information, visit www.mcgrawhill.ca/highereducation/iservices.

Teaching, Technology & Learning Conference Series

The educational environment has changed tremendously in recent years, and McGraw-Hill Ryerson continues to be committed to helping you acquire the skills you need to succeed in this new milieu. Our innovative Teaching, Technology & Learning Conference Series brings faculty together from across Canada with 3M Teaching Excellence award winners to share teaching and learning best practices in a collaborative and stimulating environment. Pre-conference workshops on general topics, such as teaching large classes and technology integration, will also be offered.

We will also work with you at your own institution to customize workshops that best suit the needs of your faculty at your institution. These include our **Teaching Excellence** and **Marketing Innovation** symposiums.

Research Reports into Mobile Learning and Student Success

These landmark reports, undertaken in conjunction with academic and private-sector advisory boards, are the result of research studies into the challenges professors face in helping students succeed and the opportunities that new technology presents to impact teaching and learning.

Marketing

the core

Initiating the Marketing Process

CHAPTER 1
Developing Customer Relationships and Value through Marketing

CHAPTER 2
Linking Marketing and Corporate Strategies

CHAPTER 3
Scanning the Marketing Environment

CHAPTER 4
Ethics and Social Responsibility in Marketing

The essence of the marketing process is developing customer relationships and value—we will talk about this in Part 1. Chapter 1 introduces the marketing process by describing the actions of Rollerblade as it faces the challenges of finding strategies to build on the phenomenal success of the product that created an entirely new industry. A dynamic marketing model that will be used through the text, to explain the interdependence and interaction of the various aspects of the marketing process, is also introduced in this chapter. Chapter 2 describes how organizations such as Ben & Jerry's utilize the strategic marketing process to better serve their customers. Chapter 3 scans the external business environment and identifies its important trends. The changes are described in terms of social, economic, technological, competitive, and regulatory forces. Finally, Chapter 4 provides a framework for including ethical and social responsibility considerations in marketing decisions.

Developing Customer Relationships and Value through Marketing

AFTER READING THIS CHAPTER YOU SHOULD BE ABLE TO:

- Understand and explain the process of marketing.

- Define marketing and explain the importance of discovering and satisfying consumer needs and wants.

- Understand marketing mix elements and environmental factors.

- Describe how organizations build strong customer relationships using current thinking about customer value and relationship marketing.

- Explain the meaning of ethics and social responsibility and how they relate to the individual, organizations, and society.

THINK ABOUT THIS WHILE YOU **WORKOUT.**

**Rollerblade®
makes serious
fitness serious fun**
with high performance
in-line skates for every
fitness level, Rollerblade
will help you burn as
many calories as running
with less than half the
impact to joints. Work
your hips, thighs and
shins in Rollerblade
comfort while working
your leg muscles longer
than possible with
running or cycling and
have more fun while
you do it! Get into the
new Lightning™ or
AERO™ skates from
Rollerblade and see
how much fun fitness
can be.

LIGHTNING™
Women's Lighting 05

AERO™
Men's AERO 9

ROLLERBLADE

www.rollerblade.com

AFTER HUGE SUCCESS...WHAT'S NEXT?

What do you do for the next act, for your encore, when you have created an entire industry?

That's the challenge facing the company featured here. It launched the in-line skate industry two decades ago. But such success attracts lots of competitors! So what does it do to provide exciting new products to build and maintain continuing, loyal customer relationships? A big part of the answer is its new Fusion™, Lightning™, and Mx 900™ lines of in-line skates. But that puts us ahead of the Rollerblade® story.

A New Idea That Wasn't So New In the early 1700s, a Dutch inventor trying to simulate ice skating in the summer created the first roller skates by attaching spools in a single row to his shoes. His "in-line" arrangement was the standard design until 1863 when the first skates with rollers set as two pairs appeared. This two-pair design became the new standard, and in-line skates virtually disappeared from the market.

In 1980, two Minnesota hockey-playing brothers found an old pair of in-line skates while browsing through a sporting goods store. Working in their garage, they modified the design to add hard plastic wheels, a moulded boot shell, and a toe brake. They sold their product, which they dubbed "Rollerblade skates," out of the back of their truck to off-season hockey players and skiers. In the mid-1980s, Rollerblade marketing executive Mary Horwath had to figure out how to market in-line skates to a broader range of customers.

Understanding the Consumer "When I came here," remembers Horwath, "I knew there had to be a change." By focusing only on hockey players and skiers who used in-line skates to train during the summer, Rollerblade had developed an image as a training product. Conversations with in-line skaters, however, convinced Horwath that using Rollerblade skates

- Was great fun.
- Was a great aerobic workout and made the skater stronger and healthier.

THE MARKETING PROCESS

WHERE IN THE MARKETING PROCESS ARE WE GOING IN THIS CHAPTER?

Chapter 1 introduces marketing, taking an overall view of what is to come in the following chapters. We introduce the marketing process here.

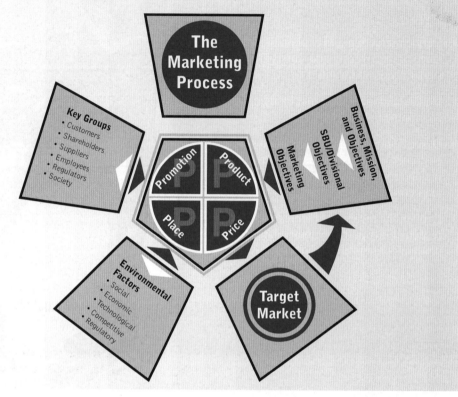

- Was quite different from traditional roller skating, which was practised, mostly indoors, and mostly by young girls.
- Would appeal to more than just off-season ice hockey skaters and skiers.

Horwath set out to reposition Rollerblade, to change the image in people's minds from in-line skating as off-season training to in-line skating as a new kind of fun and exercise that anyone could do.

It worked. As shown in Figure 1–1,[1] Horwath and Rollerblade succeeded in popularizing in-line skating—and actually launched an entirely new industry that by 1997 had more than 27 million in-line skaters.

Success Invites Imitation, Which Invites Innovation   The marketing problems of Rollerblade today are far different than those faced by Mary Horwath in the late 1980s. Rollerblade's success in launching a new industry brought its own challenges: major competition in terms of not only more than 30 other skate manufacturers but also competing sports such as skateboarding, biking, and snowboarding. Yet Rollerblade still has 35 percent of the industry sales, with no other competitor having more than 10 percent. Still, Figure 1–1 shows that the number of in-line skaters has declined from its 1997 peak, a concern for Rollerblade.

Fast forward to today to hear Jeremy Stonier, Rollerblade's current director of product marketing, describe a key challenge he faces: "How do you continue to innovate and perfect something that's already a pretty darn good device?" Stonier's answer focuses on innovation and customer benefits: "We make Rollerblade skates better year by year by providing benefits that are beyond what people are expecting to have."[2]

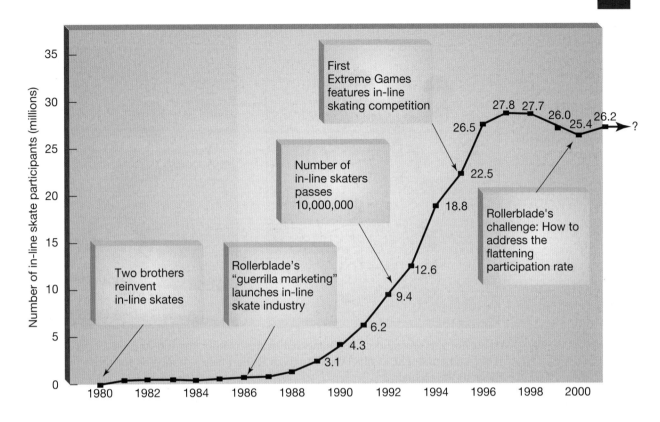

FIGURE 1–1

Number of in-line skaters in North America. Where is the trend headed?

Rollerblade's history presents a huge marketing lesson: Changing consumer tastes and changing competitive offerings require that organizations search continuously for ways to provide genuine value to customers, or sales will fall and the product will die.

Rollerblade Skates, Marketing, and You   What marketing strategy is the Rollerblade marketing team using today? By the time you reach the end of this chapter, you will know some of the answers to this question.

One key to how well Rollerblade succeeds lies in the subject of this book: marketing. In this chapter and in the rest of the book we'll introduce you to many of the people, organizations, ideas, and activities in marketing that have spawned the products and services that have been towering successes, shattering failures, or something in between. And who knows? Somewhere in the pages of this textbook you may find a career.

After you have finished all 17 chapters of this book, you'll have a good overview of the marketing process. Then read the Afterword near the end of this book, which offers a road map of what we have studied in The Core, as well as some insights into the future of the marketing industry. The Afterword also lists some websites and sources to research to keep up to date in this dynamic industry. Marketing is very vibrant, and it changes and evolves with amazing speed. Many industry specialists will tell you that the only predictable thing about marketing is change.

WHAT IS MARKETING?

Good marketing isn't always easy. In Rollerblade's case, it's easy to talk about making new and better skates for potential customers but not so simple to do. One of Rollerblade's strategies is to market skates designed for the special needs of different groups, or segments, of in-line skaters. What special features might Rollerblade build into an in-line

What special features might Rollerblade design into an in-line skate for the recreational segment? For children? Rollerblade's marketing programs for these two segments appear later in the chapter.

skate for the recreational segment that skates mainly for fun and the children segment? Give some thought to this. We'll analyze Rollerblade's strategies for these two segments later in the chapter.

Marketing: Using Exchanges to Satisfy Needs

marketing
The process of planning and executing the conception, pricing, promotion, and distribution of ideas, goods, and services to create exchanges that satisfy individual and organizational objectives

exchange
Trade of things of value between buyer and seller so that each is better off

Marketing is the process of planning and executing the conception, pricing, promotion, and distribution of ideas, goods, and services to create exchanges that satisfy individual and organizational objectives.[3] Many people incorrectly believe that marketing is the same thing as advertising or personal selling; this definition shows marketing to be a far broader activity. Further, this definition emphasizes the importance of beneficial exchanges that satisfy the objectives of both those who buy and those who sell ideas, goods, and services—whether they be individuals or organizations.

To serve both buyers and sellers, marketing seeks to discover the needs and wants of prospective customers and to satisfy them. These prospective customers include both individuals buying for themselves and their households, and organizations that buy for their own use (such as manufacturers) or for resale. The key to achieving these two objectives is the idea of **exchange**, which is the trade of things of value between buyer and seller so that each is better off.

The Diverse Factors Influencing Marketing Activities

Although an organization's marketing activity focuses on assessing and satisfying consumer needs, countless other people, groups, and forces interact to shape the nature of that activity. The marketing process begins with the organization itself, whose mission and objectives determine what business it is in and what goals it seeks to achieve. Within the organization, management is responsible for establishing these goals. The marketing department works closely with a network of other departments and employees to help provide the customer-satisfying products required for the organization to survive and prosper.

Figure 1–2 shows the key people, groups, and factors outside an organization that influence marketing activities. The marketing department is responsible for developing relationships with the organization's customers, shareholders, suppliers, and other organizations. Environmental factors, which consist of social, technological, economic, com-

[Handwritten notes in margin:] Four Factor ① customer Relationships. 12.B. 19. 5. 23 ② innovation. ③ Quality. ④ efficiency.

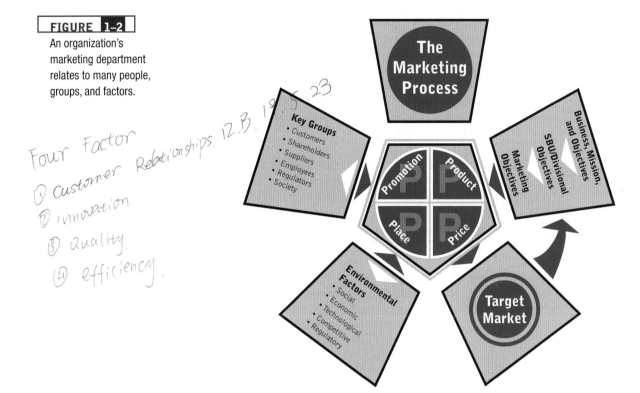

petitive, and regulatory factors, also shape an organization's marketing activities. Finally, an organization's marketing decisions are affected by and also impact society as a whole.

The organization must strike a continual balance among the sometimes differing interests of these individuals and groups. For example, it is not possible to simultaneously provide the lowest-priced and highest-quality products to customers and pay the highest prices to suppliers, highest wages to employees, and maximum returns to shareholders.

Concept Check

1. How would you define marketing in your own words?
2. Whose needs must be satisfied for effective marketing to take place?

HOW MARKETING DISCOVERS AND SATISFIES CONSUMER NEEDS

Good marketing focuses on the consumer! The importance of discovering and satisfying consumer needs is so critical to understanding marketing that we look at each of these two steps in detail next.

Discovering Consumer Needs

The first objective in marketing is discovering the needs of prospective consumers. Sound simple? Well, it's not.

Discovering consumer needs may look easy, but when you get down to the specifics of developing new products, problems crop up. For one thing, consumers may not always know or be able to describe what they need and want. When Apple built its first Apple II personal computer and started a new industry, consumers didn't really know what the benefits would be. So they had to be educated about those benefits and had to learn how to use personal computers. Also, knowing how to ask consumers the right questions to discover their real needs can be difficult. This is where effective marketing research, the topic of Chapter 8, can help.

Consumer Needs and Consumer Wants   Should marketing try to satisfy consumer needs or consumer wants? The answer is both. Marketers debate this question, depending on the definitions of needs and wants and the perceptions customers have about their requirements.

A *need* occurs when a person feels a lack of something that is important for physical or psychological well being. When you are hungry, your hunger could be interpreted as a need. A *want* is the way a person satisfies a need. Society, the people around us, and our individual tastes shape our wants. When you decide to satisfy your hunger by having your favourite meal—steak and potatoes—this is a want. Marketers work to position their products and services as preferred wants, which consumers will choose to satisfy their needs. There is ongoing debate about the definitions of wants and needs! Throughout the book we use these terms interchangeably.

Effective marketing can clearly shape a person's wants. At issue is whether marketing persuades prospective customers to buy the "wrong" things—say, a candy bar rather than an apple to satisfy hunger pangs. The Ethics and Social Responsibility Alert on the next page discusses student credit card debt: Is the marketing of credit cards encouraging students to consider that a credit card is a need, thus making high credit card debt a problem?.

Certainly, marketing tries to influence what we buy. A question then arises—at what point do we want government to step in to protect consumers? Most consumers would say they want government to protect us from harmful drugs and unsafe cars but not from candy bars. To protect students, should government limit the number of credit cards or amount of debt they can have? Such questions have no clear-cut answers.

Discovering needs involves looking carefully at prospective customers, whether they are children buying M&M's candy, college students buying Rollerblade in-line skates, or firms buying Xerox photocopying machines. The principal activities of a firm's marketing department involve obtaining information about consumers' needs and the trends and factors that shape them.

market
People with desire and ability to buy a specific product

What a Market Is   Potential consumers make up a **market**, which consists of people with both the desire *and* the ability to buy a specific product. All markets ultimately are people. Even when we say a firm bought a Xerox copier, we mean one or several people in the firm decided to buy it. People who are aware of their unmet needs may have the desire to buy the product, but that alone isn't sufficient. People must also have the ability to buy, such as the authority, time, and money. People may even "buy" an idea that results in an action, such as having their blood pressure checked annually or turning down their thermostat to save energy.

target market
Specific group of existing and potential consumers toward which an organization directs its marketing plan

Satisfying Consumer Needs

Marketing doesn't stop with the discovery of consumer needs. Because an organization obviously can't satisfy all consumer needs, it must concentrate its efforts on certain needs of a specific group of consumers. This is the **target market**—one or more specific groups of existing and potential consumers toward which an organization directs its marketing plan.

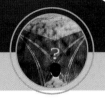

ETHICS AND SOCIAL RESPONSIBILITY ALERT
STUDENT CREDIT CARDS: AN ULTIMATE BENEFIT OR A DISASTER IN THE MAKING?

If you are over 19, you have probably received a credit card application—or maybe you already have your own credit card or a supplementary card on your parents' account. Every year thousands of students across Canada apply for and receive their first credit card. The immediate benefit? Students can buy college necessities and purchase other amenities—clothes, perhaps, or a trip to Mexico? The long-term benefit may be that students establish a good credit rating, which they use for further financing later in their lives. But these benefits also mask a serious concern. Many students are drowning in credit card debt and student loans they have racked up over their period of studies.

According to the Canadian Federation of Students (CFS), student debt increased by as much as 30 percent between 1995 and 2000. Also, a 2004 Statistics Canada report indicates that students are increasingly having more difficulty repaying student debt. Increases in tuition fees will only make the situation worse. In that same time frame (1995–2000), the majority of students left the educational system burdened with a substantial debt load. For those students with this kind of debt, the average estimated debt load reached $28,000. For some students, it was much higher.

In September 2003, CFS reported that some students rely on as much as $600 *per month* in student loans from the federally sponsored Canada Student Loan Program, and that 70 percent of all Canadian students are in debt upon graduation. Since the Canada Student Loan Program began, some 40 years ago, more than 3.8 million students have borrowed over $1.6 billion for their education and related expenses.

Students fresh out of a post-secondary institution can face a huge financial problem. Think of the demands on them—credit card debt, outstanding student loans, rent, car payments, utilities, telephone costs, and other living expenses—these expenses often exceed the starting salaries of college graduates. For some students, their starting salaries barely permit them to make the minimum payments on their credit card debt, let alone pay back outstanding balances.

Some universities now offer on-site financial counselling. The federal government has links on loan program sites offering students advice on how to manage their finances (check out www.canlearn.ca). In 2002, the federal government responded to the growing student debt problem by granting up to 5 years of interest relief and increasing the allowable time for students to repay their student loans from 10 to 15 years. This relief may help current students, but it does little to help those who have already graduated and are struggling under their past debt load.

What do you think should be done to help students manage their debt load? Is it ethical and socially responsible for financial institutions to make credit cards available to them, knowing the likelihood that they could lead to even higher debt upon graduation? [1]

[1] "About the Canada Student Loans Program (CSLP)," Human Resources and Skills Development Canada website (www.hrsdc.gc.ca/asp/gateway.asp?hr=en/hip/cslp/About/01_ab_MissionProgram.shtml&hs=cxp); *The Hill Times*, October 14, 2002, Issue 656; MacDonald, Isabel, *This Toronto*, Sept. - Oct. 2003, Vol. 37, Issue 2, p. 9; Canadian Federation of Students media release, Ottawa, April 26, 2004; Doherty-Delorme, Denise, *Briar Patch Regina*, April 2000, Vol. 29, Issue 3, p. 18; and Lexier, Roberta, *Briar Patch Regina*, May 2002, Vol. 31, Issue 4, p. 14.

The Four Ps: Controllable Marketing Mix Factors

Having selected its target market consumers, the firm must take steps to satisfy their needs. Someone in the organization's marketing department, often the marketing manager, must take action and develop a complete marketing plan to reach consumers by using a combination of four tools, often called the four Ps—a useful shorthand reference to them, first published by Professor E. Jerome McCarthy:[4]

marketing mix
The marketing manager's controllable factors—product, price, promotion, and place—that can be used to solve a marketing problem

- *Product*. A good, service, or idea to satisfy the consumer's needs.
- *Price*. What is exchanged for the product.
- *Promotion*. A means of communication between the seller and buyer.
- *Place*. A means of getting the product to the consumer.

We'll define each of the four Ps more carefully later in the book, but for now it's important to remember that they are the elements of the **marketing mix**. The marketing mix

Wal-Mart and Zellers (HBC) provide customer value using two very different approaches.

elements are called controllable factors because they are under the control of the marketing department. For example, when a company puts a product on sale, they are changing one element of the marketing mix—namely, the price.

The Uncontrollable, Environmental Factors   While marketers can control their marketing mix factors, other factors are mostly beyond their control (see Figure 1–2). These are the **environmental factors** in a marketing decision, the uncontrollable factors:

environmental factors
Uncontrollable marketing factors such as social, economic, technological, competitive, and regulatory forces

- *Social factors.* Consumer characteristics, culture, demographics
- *Economic factors.* State of the economy (unemployment rate, currency exchange)
- *Technological factors.* New inventions (e.g., HDTV), extent of use of certain technologies
- *Competitive factors.* Numbers of competitors and the actions they take
- *Regulatory factors.* Government laws and restrictions

These five environmental factors are discussed in Chapter 3.

THE MARKETING PROGRAM: HOW CUSTOMER RELATIONSHIPS ARE BUILT

A firm's marketing program connects the firm to its customers. To clarify this link, we shall first discuss the critically important concepts of customer value and relationship marketing and then illustrate these concepts with the marketing program at Rollerblade.

Customer Value: Developing Loyal Customers

Intense competition in today's fast-paced domestic and global markets has caused massive restructuring of many industries and businesses. Managers are seeking ways to achieve success in this new, more intense level of global competition.[5]

This has prompted many successful firms to focus on "customer value." The essence of successful marketing is gaining loyal customers by providing unique value to them.

customer value
Buyers' benefits including quality, price, convenience, on-time delivery, and before- and after-sale service

What is new, however, is a more careful attempt at understanding how a firm's customers perceive value. For our purposes, **customer value** is the unique combination of benefits received by targeted buyers that includes quality, price, convenience, on-time delivery, and both before-sale and after-sale service. Firms now actually try to place a dollar value on a loyal, satisfied customer.

Many successful firms have chosen to deliver outstanding customer value with one of three value strategies — best price, best product, or best service. Companies such as West-Jet and Zellers have been successful offering consumers the best price. Bombardier and Mountain Equipment Co-op claim to provide the best products on the market. Lee Valley Tools and Aldo Shoes pledge to provide the best service. What strategies do you think Canadian Tire employs?

Relationship Marketing and the Marketing Program

A firm achieves meaningful customer relationships by creating connections with its customers through careful coordination of the product, its price, the way it's promoted, and how it's placed.

relationship marketing
Linking the organization to its individual customers, employees, suppliers, and other partners for their mutual long-term benefit

Relationship Marketing: Easy to Understand, Hard to Do
The hallmark of developing and maintaining effective customer relationships is today called **relationship marketing**. Successful relationship marketing links an organization to its key groups (individual customers, employees, suppliers, and other partners—see Figure 1–2) for their mutual long-term benefit. In terms of selling a product, relationship marketing involves a personal, ongoing relationship between the organization and its individual customers that begins before and continues after the sale.

Major manufacturers find relationship marketing difficult to achieve. Today's information technology, along with cutting-edge manufacturing and marketing processes, have led to tailoring goods or services to the tastes of individual customers in high volumes at a relatively low cost. Thus, you can place an Internet order for a Dell or Apple computer and have it delivered in four or five days—in a configuration tailored to your unique wants. But with today's Internet purchases, you will probably have difficulty achieving the same personal, tender-loving-care connection that you once had with your own local computer store, bookstore, or other retailer.

FIGURE 1–3
Marketing's second task: satisfying consumer needs

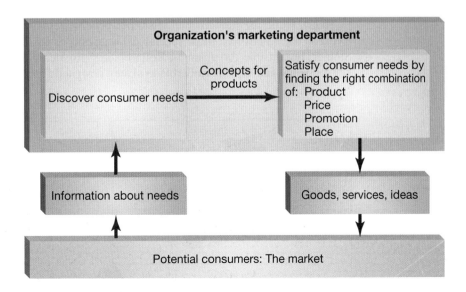

The Marketing Program   Effective relationship marketing strategies help marketing managers discover what prospective customers need. They must translate this information into concepts for products the firm might develop to satisfy these needs (Figure 1–3). These concepts must then be converted into a feasible **marketing program**—a plan that integrates the elements of the marketing mix to provide a good, service, or idea to prospective buyers. These consumers then react to the offering favourably (by buying) or unfavourably (by not buying), and the process is repeated. As shown in Figure 1–3, this process is continuous in a dynamic and successful organization: Consumer needs trigger product concepts that are translated into actual products that stimulate further discovery of consumer needs.

marketing program
Plan that integrates the elements of the marketing mix to provide a good, service, or idea to prospective buyers

A Marketing Program for Rollerblade

To see some specifics of an actual marketing program, let's return to the earlier example of Rollerblade and its in-line skates. Looking at the in-line skating horizon, Rollerblade's long-run strategy is to focus on three areas: listening to consumers to stay ahead of the trends, focusing its marketing program on four key market segments, and using the company's strengths in technology. These three areas are covered below.

Listening to Consumers to Stay Ahead of the Trends
Consumer tastes change—and quickly. This is the reason for Rollerblade's concerns that it stay ahead of trends in the marketplace. Competition is coming from directions never anticipated even two or three years earlier. Rollerblade has always had to compete with skateboards and mountain bikes. But now it also competes with other active sports, scooters, and Heelys, a sneaker with an embedded, detachable wheel in the heel.[6]

Today, Rollerblade uses careful marketing research to listen to what various segments of its customers want. For example, the website Rollerblade.com enables its marketing executives not only to obtain detailed information about what skate features customers want but also to link these wants to their individual characteristics, including age, sex, and lifestyle (such as hobbies and purchasing behaviours). Rollerblade's "skate selector" on its website not only helps consumers select the skate that's right for them but also provides timely data on consumer wants.

Focusing the Marketing Program on Four Key Market Segments
Three key benefits for customers remain the foundation for Rollerblade's marketing program: fun, fitness and health, and excitement.

Today, while the fundamental customer benefits remain the same, Rollerblade is now trying to reach narrower, more specialized segments of customers than in the past.[7] Jeremy Stonier, responsible for planning Rollerblade's product strategy, identifies four key market segments and typical Rollerblade skates designed for each segment:

Rollerblade in-line skate lines targeted at the recreational segment (left) and children segment (right).

Fusion Model

Mx 900 Model

retail trade .

MARKETING PROGRAM ACTIVITY TO REACH:

MARKETING MIX ELEMENT	RECREATIONAL SEGMENT	CHILDREN SEGMENT	RATIONALE FOR MARKETING PROGRAM ACTIVITY
Product	Offer Fusion skates for beginning and intermediate skaters simply wanting fun and exercise	Offer the Mx 900, a skate for children that extends so that its length changes as the children grow	Use new-product research and the latest technology to offer high-quality skates to satisfy the needs of key customer segments
Price ($99.00)	Price up to $199 a pair	Price up to $99 a pair	Set prices that provide genuine value to the customer segment that is targeted
Promotion	Feature Rollerblade in sports competitions and magazines like *Shape* and *Mademoiselle* and local newspapers	Use gym classes to introduce children to in-line skating and place ads in local newspapers	Increase awareness to those new to the sport while offering ads and press releases for more advanced segments
Place	Distribute the lines through specialty and regular sporting goods stores and the Internet	Distribute the Mx 900 through sporting goods stores	Make it easy for buyers in the segment to buy at an outlet that is convenient and where they feel comfortable

FIGURE 1–4

Marketing programs for two of Rollerblade's skates, targeted at two distinctly different customer segments: recreational skaters and children

- *Aggressive segment.* Are you the kind of speed and stunt skater seen on XGames on TV? Then try the new TRS line, the Team Rollerblade Series, reflecting design suggestions from Rollerblade's skating team.
- *Fitness segment.* Do you skate often and are you serious about a good aerobic workout? Try the Lightning 05 (for women) or Lightning 07 (for men)—skates for people whose feet demand a good fit and shock dampening from Rollerblade's latest technology.
- *Recreational segment.* Skating mainly for fun, like the majority of in-line skaters? Use a Fusion skate with the Total Fit System, a quick-closer mechanism that laces instantly by simply pulling up on a cord at the back of the boot.
- *Children segment.* Most parents can't afford to buy a new set of in-line skates each season as their children's feet grow. No problem now. Skates in the Mx 900 line extend up to four sizes with a simple push of a button.

Rollerblade has more than 20 lines of skates targeted to different market segments. As illustrated in Figure 1–4 for the Fusion and Mx 900 lines, most Rollerblade brands require a slightly different marketing program to reach their targeted segments of potential customers.

Exploiting Strengths in Technology   In 1995 Rollerblade was sold to the Benetton organization. This provided huge technology synergies for the two firms. Examples of exploiting tomorrow's technology include

- *CoolMax®.* A performance fabric used to keep a skater's feet dry and cool.
- *ABT®Lite.* A light, integral braking system that allows skaters to brake by sliding their heel downward, without compromising balance or performance.

Rollerblade's emphasis on the technology is reflected in the more than 200 patents it holds on key elements of its in-line skates.

The Rollerblade case at the end of the chapter lets us look in greater depth at the marketing strategies that Rollerblade is developing for the twenty-first century.

Concept Check

1. An organization can't satisfy the needs of all consumers, so it must focus on one or more subgroups, which are its _____.

2. What are the four marketing mix elements that make up the organization's marketing program?

3. What are uncontrollable factors?

HOW MARKETING BECAME SO IMPORTANT

To understand why marketing is a driving force in the modern global economy, let us look at the evolution of the market orientation, ethics and social responsibility in marketing, and the breadth and depth of marketing activities.

Evolution of the Market Orientation

Many manufacturers have experienced four distinct stages in the life of their firms. The first stage, the *production era*, covers the early years up until the 1920s. In North America, goods were scarce and buyers were willing to accept virtually any goods that were available and to make do with them. In the *sales era*, from the 1920s to the 1960s, manufacturers found they could produce more goods than buyers could consume. Competition grew. Firms hired more salespeople to find new buyers. This sales era continued into the 1960s for many firms.

marketing concept
Idea that an organization should strive to satisfy the needs of consumers while also trying to achieve the organization's goals

In the 1960s, marketing became the motivating force among many firms and the *marketing concept era* dawned. The **marketing concept** is the idea that an organization should strive to satisfy the needs of consumers while also trying to achieve the organization's goals. General Electric probably launched the marketing concept and its focus on consumers when its 1952 annual report stated: "The concept introduces . . . marketing . . . at the beginning rather than the end of the production cycle and integrates marketing into each phase of the business."[8]

market orientation
Focusing organizational efforts to collect and use information about customers' needs to create customer value

Firms such as General Electric, Marriott, and Toyota have achieved great success by putting huge effort into implementing the marketing concept, leading to today's *market orientation era*. An organization that has a **market orientation** focuses its efforts on continuously collecting information about customers' needs, sharing this information across departments, and using it to create customer value.[9]

This market orientation has led to *customer relationship management (CRM)*, the process of identifying prospective buyers, understanding them well, and developing favourable long-term impressions of the organization and its offerings so that buyers will choose them in the marketplace.[10] This requires the commitment of managers and employees throughout the organization.

Ethics and Social Responsibility: Balancing Interests

Standards of marketing practice have evolved over the past 40 years, and emphasis has gradually shifted from producers to consumers. Current marketing focuses on consumers' interests. In addition, organizations now increasingly consider the social and environmental consequences of their actions for all key groups.

Ethics   Many marketing issues are not specifically addressed by existing laws and regulations. For example, should information about a firm's customers be sold to other organizations? Should consumers be left on their own to assess the safety of a product? Questions such as these—and many more—raise difficult ethical issues. To respond to these issues, many companies, industries, and professional associations have developed codes of ethics to guide and assist managers.

societal marketing concept
View that organizations should satisfy the needs of consumers in a way that provides for society's well-being

Social Responsibility   While many ethical issues involve only the buyer and seller, others involve society as a whole. A manufacturer dumping toxic wastes into streams has an impact on the environment and society. This example illustrates the issue of social responsibility, the idea that individuals and organizations are accountable to society. The well-being of society at large should be recognized in an organization's marketing decisions. In fact, some marketing experts stress the **societal marketing concept**, the view that an organization should discover and satisfy the needs of its consumers in a way that also provides for society's well-being.[11] For example, Scotchbrite Never Rust Wool Soap Pads from 3M—which are made from recycled plastic bottles—are more expensive than competitors' (SOS and Brillo) but superior because they don't rust or scratch.

ultimate consumers
People who use the goods and services purchased for a household

The Breadth and Depth of Marketing

Marketing affects every person and organization. To understand this, let's analyze:

organizational buyers
Manufacturers, wholesalers, retailers, and government agencies that buy goods and services for their own use or for resale

- Who markets.
- What they market.
- Who buys and uses what is marketed.
- Who benefits from these marketing activities.
- How they benefit.

Marketing is used by nonprofit organizations, causes, and places, as well as businesses. Direct messages like that illustrated here can reach their target audiences very effectively.

Who Markets?   Every organization markets. It's obvious that business firms involved in manufacturing (McCain Foods), retailing (Loblaws), and providing services (Bell Canada) market their offerings. And nonprofit organizations such as your local hospital, your university, places (cities, provinces, countries), and even special causes (Stop Smoking!) also engage in marketing. Finally, individuals such as political candidates often use marketing to gain attention and preference.

What Is Marketed?   Goods, services, and even ideas are marketed. Goods are physical objects such as iron ore, apples, a computer, or an airplane. Services, a more complex category, include things as diverse as legal advice, a college education, a Toronto Maple Leafs game, and airline travel.

Ideas are most often marketed by nonprofit organizations or the government. For example, your local library may market the idea of developing improved reading skills. The Canadian Cancer Society markets the idea that it is worthwhile for you to donate money, and Mothers Against Drunk Driving (MADD) promotes the idea that drinking and driving is deadly.

Who Buys and Uses What Is Marketed?   Both individuals and organizations buy and use goods and services that are marketed. **Ultimate consumers** are the people—whether 80 years or 8 months old—who use the goods and services purchased for a household. In contrast, **organizational buyers** are units such as manufacturers, retailers, nonprofit organizations, or government agencies that buy goods and services for their own use or for resale. Although the terms *consumers, buyers,* and *customers* are sometimes used for both ultimate consumers and organizations, there is no consistency on this. In this book you will be able to tell from the example whether the buyers are ultimate consumers, organizations, or both.

Who Benefits?   Consumers who buy, organizations that sell, and society as a whole benefit from effective marketing. True competition between products and services in the marketplace ensures that consumers can find value from the best products, the lowest prices, or exceptional service. Providing choices leads to the consumer satisfaction and quality of life that we have come to expect from our economic system.

Organizations that provide need-satisfying products with effective marketing programs—for example, Sears, M.A.C cosmetics, and Hewlett Packard—have blossomed. But competition creates problems for ineffective marketers, such as Eatons and other retailers that have failed in the last few years.

Finally, effective marketing benefits society. It enhances competition, which, in turn, both improves the quality of products and services and lowers their prices. This makes countries more competitive in world markets and provides jobs and a higher standard of living for their citizens.

utility
Benefits or customer value received by users of the product

How Do Consumers Benefit?   Marketing creates **utility**, the benefits or customer value received by users of the product. This utility is the result of the marketing exchange process. There are five different utilities: form, information, place, time, and possession. The production of the good or service constitutes *form utility. Information utility* is providing consumers with knowledge they need to make informed purchases in the marketplace. *Place utility* means having the offering available where consumers need it, whereas *time utility* means having it available when needed. *Possession utility* is the value of making an item easy to purchase through accepting credit cards or other financial arrangements. Marketing creates its utilities by bridging space (place utility) and hours (time utility) to provide products (form utility) for consumers to own and use (possession utility) and background on those products (information utility).

Concept Check

1. What is the marketing concept?
2. What is the difference between goods and services?

SUMMARY

1   Marketing is the process of planning and executing the conception, pricing, promotion, and distribution of goods, services, and ideas to create exchanges that satisfy individual and organizational objectives. This definition relates to two primary goals of marketing: discovering the needs of consumers and satisfying them.

2   Because an organization doesn't have the resources to satisfy the needs of all consumers, it selects a target market of potential customers—a subset of the entire market—on which to focus its marketing program.

3   Four elements in a marketing program designed to satisfy customer needs are product, price, promotion, and place. These elements are called the *marketing mix*, the *four Ps*, or the *controllable variables* because they are under the general control of the marketing department.

4   Environmental factors, also called *uncontrollable variables*, are largely beyond the organization's control. These include social, technological, economic, competitive, and regulatory forces.

5 Building on customer value and relationship marketing concepts, successful firms develop mutually beneficial long-term relationships with their customers.

6 In marketing terms, business history is divided into four periods: the production era, the sales era, the marketing concept era, and the current market orientation era.

7 Marketing managers must balance consumer, organizational, and societal interests. This involves issues of ethics and social responsibility.

8 Profit-making and nonprofit organizations perform marketing activities. They market goods, services, and ideas that benefit consumers, organizations, and countries. Marketing creates utilities that give benefits, or customer value, to users.

KEY TERMS AND CONCEPTS

customer value p. 13
environmental factors p. 12
exchange p. 8
market p. 10
marketing p. 8
marketing concept p. 16
marketing mix p. 11
marketing program p. 14

market orientation p. 16
organizational buyers p. 17
relationship marketing p. 13
societal marketing concept p. 17
target market p. 10
ultimate consumers p. 17
utility p. 18

QUESTIONS: APPLYING MARKETING CONCEPTS AND PERSPECTIVES

1 What consumer wants (or benefits) are met by the following products or services? *(a)* Carnation Instant Breakfast, *(b)* Adidas running shoes, *(c)* Hertz Rent-A-Car, and *(d)* television home shopping programs.

2 Each of the four products, services, or programs in question 1 has substitutes. Respective examples are *(a)* a ham and egg breakfast, *(b)* regular tennis shoes, *(c)* taking a bus, and *(d)* a department store. What consumer benefits might these substitutes have in each case that some consumers might value more highly than those mentioned in question 1?

3 A university in a metropolitan area wishes to increase its evening-school offerings of business-related courses such as marketing, accounting, and finance. Who are the target market customers (students) for these courses?

4 Describe how each of the four marketing mix elements might be used to reach the target market in question 3.

5 What environmental factors (uncontrollable variables) must the university in question 3 consider in designing its marketing program?

DISCUSSION FORUM

Think back to the Rollerblade story at the beginning of this chapter. The company is now trying to expand into new markets and into other countries. Discuss these issues with your class and colleagues:

1 What are the advantages of trying to expand globally?

2 What problems or challenges may the company face in global markets?

3 Rollerblade could divide its market into two major categories: recreational and sport skating, the latter including roller hockey, speed skating, aggressive skating, and dance skating. How would the marketing mix elements differ for each of these two categories?

4 You or other students in your discussion group may have visited or lived in other countries. Discuss how marketing Rollerblade products there differs from marketing them in Canada.

INTERNET EXERCISE

"It!" "Ginger!" "Jetson's scooter!" These were early names given the revolutionary Segway™ Human Transporter (HT), a technology shrouded in secrecy until it was launched in 2001. The Segway HT relies on computers and gyroscopes to control its speed, balance, and direction. It can travel up to 15 miles on a six-hour battery charge. A commercial version is expected to sell for $5,000 to $6,000.

Go to the Segway HT website (www.segway.com/segway). View both the consumer and business models.

www.mcgrawhill.ca/college/thecore

1 What do you see as the advantages and disadvantages of the Segway HT?
2 For businesses, what applications could the Segway HT be used for?
3 Why would consumers want to buy a Segway HT?

VIDEO CASE 1

ROLLERBLADE®: BENEFITS BEYOND WHAT PEOPLE EXPECT

ABT, TRS, TFS . . . and SIS! Does this look like a spoonful of alphabet soup?

Perhaps. But it really refers to Rollerblade's technologies, programs, and commitment to providing in-line skaters with the best quality of skates and skating experiences possible. Or "by providing benefits beyond what people are expecting to have," as Jeremy Stonier, Rollerblade's director of product marketing describes it. In fact, Rollerblade's leading-edge technology is covered by more than 200 patents, with more on the way.

ROLLERBLADE'S LAUNCH

At Rollerblade's launch two decades ago only one in-line skate manufacturer existed—Rollerblade. The company had only a single skate line and there were few sales. No one had heard of in-line skating! So Rollerblade used a "guerrilla marketing" campaign to get the word out. It used a tiny budget to develop attention-getting promotions to make people aware of the skates and to try them. Promotions ranged from "Demo Vans" in supermarket parking lots, where prospects could try the skates for a half hour, to putting Rollerblade skates on cheerleaders at a football game or Arnold Schwarzenegger. Marketing research was almost limited to what skaters told the Demo Van drivers.

A SKATE LINE FOR EACH SEGMENT

From the outset, in-line skaters have been united by a common experience: the thrill and fun of the speed and freedom that comes from almost frictionless wheels on their feet. "As the market has matured, it has settled into four core groups of

users," says Stonier. Each requires a number of unique skate features.

"The trickiest segment we sell to is probably the 'aggressive' or 'stunt' skater—the 14- to 22-year-old in your neighbourhood who is doing tricks you might see on TV in XGames," says Stonier. Members of Team Rollerblade, a skating group that gives demonstrations around the country, suggest and test new technologies that find their way first into skates for this segment. The TRS—for Team Rollerblade Series—line of skates contains everything from a PFS Specialized form-fit memory foot liner gel insert for extreme shock absorption to CoolMax® fabric to keep the skater's feet cool and dry.

The "fitness" segment probably skates two or three times a week and may even aspire to skate in an in-line marathon. "The fitness user is going at high speeds and skating frequently, so we've developed the Lightning series of skates that are incredibly lightweight with an anatomical fit," says Stonier.

Most adult skaters are in the recreational segment, for which the Aero skate line is designed. All contain the Total Fit System (TFS) that incorporates a new shell, liner, and closure system. Don't want to waste time buckling the skates? Here you don't need to because you simply pull up on a cord at the back of the skate, giving you a customized fit in a matter of seconds. (That's Stonier in the photo demonstrating it to colleague Nicholas Skally.)

Parents are always concerned about having to buy their children new shoes or skates as their feet grow. Not only does the Mx 900 extendable skate adjust four sizes with a push of a button, but it also has a quick-pull lacing system, padded liner, and shell ventilation designed specifically for children.

The segments don't stop there. Besides its flagship Rollerblade brand marketed through sporting goods and skate specialty stores, Rollerblade has a lower-priced Bladerunner line sold through mass merchant and sporting goods chain stores. Finally, the global market has enormous potential. With China and South Korea showing high growth today, who knows what new segments could be next?

A FOCUS ON EACH CONSUMER

"One of the big differences between marketing today and in the future is that we will be able to reach each person, such as designing your own personal workout program," says Nicholas Skally, Rollerblade's manager of marketing and public relations. Rollerblade's website (www. rollerblade.com) is a step in that direction. "An important benefit of the website is our ability to acquire marketing research data on individual consumers inexpensively," says Skally. This enables Rollerblade to get feedback and ideas from users very inexpensively. Website topics include everything from helping you choose which skate is right for you (Skate Selector) to helping you brush up on your braking technique.

In the past, Rollerblade often sent out millions of direct-mail pieces or bought commercials on national TV networks. Today, Skally points out that Rollerblade now focuses more narrowly by selecting magazines that link directly to the user segments or grassroots programs like Skate-in-School (SIS) that offer physical education class options to students in more than 600 schools.

ROLLERBLADE'S FIRSTS

"If you're going to buy a pair of in-line skates, it only made sense to buy from us," says Stonier, "because we're the ones who started it, perfected it, and continue to push the innovation." As evidence of Rollerblade's innovation, he points to a number of firsts, such as the use of polyurethane boots and wheels, metal frames, dual bearings, and heel brakes. Other firsts include breathable liners, push-button adjustable children's skates, skates designed specifically for women, and the award-winning Advanced Braking Technology (ABT) that allows braking without raising the toe of the skate.

Questions

1   What trends in the environmental forces (social, economic, technological, competitive, and regulatory) identified in Figure 1–2 in the chapter (a) work for and (b) work against Rollerblade's potential growth in the twenty-first century?

2   Compare the marketing goals for Rollerblade (a) in 1986 when Rollerblade was launched and (b) today?

3   What kind of focused communication and promotion actions might Rollerblade take to reach the (a) recreational and (b) children market segments? For some starting ideas, visit rollerblade.com.

4   In searching for global markets to enter, (a) what are some criteria that Rollerblade should use to select countries to enter, and (b) what three or four countries meet these criteria best and are the most likely candidates?

Linking Marketing and Corporate Strategies

AFTER READING THIS CHAPTER YOU SHOULD BE ABLE TO:

- Describe how strategy is developed at the corporate, business unit, and functional levels in an organization.

- Explain the concepts of business, mission, culture, and goals and why they are important in organizations.

- Understand how organizations formulate their strategies.

- Describe the strategic marketing process and its three key phases: planning, implementation, and evaluation.

- Explain how the marketing mix elements are worked into a marketing program.

- Explain how companies evaluate and monitor the marketing plan.

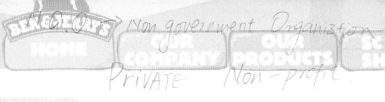

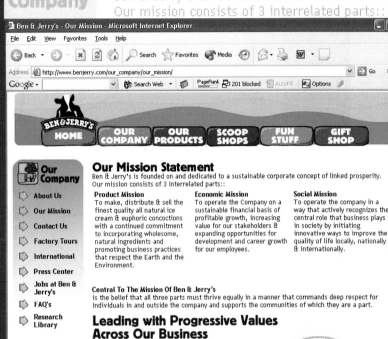

nuke [nju:k] 核武器

WHERE CAN AN "A" IN ICE CREAM MAKING LEAD?

These two entrepreneurs aren't just your typical Tom, Dick, or Harry! Consider some facts about the company they founded:

- It launched a program letting customers send "Ice Cream by Mail" via its website.
- It contributes 7.5 percent of its pretax profits to charities.
- Its PartnerShops help not-for-profit organizations provide training and job opportunities for people such as at-risk youth.[1]

By now you know the company: Ben & Jerry's, or more formally, Ben & Jerry's Homemade, Inc. Its website reflects its creative, funky approach to business—linked to a genuine concern for social causes. They even have a social mission!

Ben Cohen and Jerry Greenfield were grade school classmates in New York. In 1978 they headed north to Vermont and started an ice cream parlour in a renovated gas station.[2] Buoyed with enthusiasm, $12,000 they had

borrowed and saved, and ideas from the $5 they spent on a correspondence course in ice cream making (with perfect scores on their open-book tests!) they were off and running.[3]

Today, Ben & Jerry's Homemade, Inc., now owned by Unilever, the world's leading producer of ice cream,

Company founders Ben Cohen and Jerry Greenfield with their world-famous ice cream.

WHERE IN THE MARKETING PROCESS ARE WE GOING IN THIS CHAPTER?

Chapter 2 focuses on strategic planning and the role it plays in the marketing process.

has more than $200 million in annual sales worldwide—mainly from selling its incredibly rich ice cream[4]. Ben & Jerry's has also been a leader with its social mission. For example, the company is committed to improving "the quality of life locally, nationally, and internationally"[5] and "promoting business practices that respect the Earth and the environment."[6] Customers love Cherry Garcia and One Sweet Whirled ice cream flavours, but many also want to support Ben & Jerry's social mission, too. The company has international sales in Europe, the Middle East, and Asia.

Chapter 2 describes how organizations set their mission and overall direction and link these activities to marketing strategies. As consumers become more concerned about a company's impact on society, marketing strategy may need to be linked to the social goals of the company's mission statement.

ORGANIZATIONS AND THEIR LEVELS OF STRATEGY

Large organizations today are extremely complex. All of us deal in some way with huge organizations every day, so it is useful to understand the two basic kinds of organizations and the levels that exist in them and their link to marketing.

Today's organizations can be divided into business firms and not-for-profit organizations. A *business firm* is an organization that serves its customers in order to earn a profit. **Profit** is the excess of revenues over costs, the reward to a business for the risk it undertakes in offering a product for sale. In contrast to business firms, a *not-for-profit organization* is an organization that serves its customers but does not have profit as an organizational goal.

profit
The excess of revenues over costs, the reward to a business for the risk it undertakes in offering a product for sale

For simplicity in the rest of the book, however, the terms *firm, company, corporation,* and *organization* are used to cover both business and not-for-profit operations.

Levels in Organizations and How Marketing Links to Them

strategy
A plan of action to achieve specific goals

A **strategy** is a plan of action to achieve specific goals. All organizations should have a strategic direction—that is, they should have an idea of what they hope to achieve and how they plan to achieve it. Marketing not only helps set the direction but also helps the organization get there. Figure 2-1 illustrates the three levels of strategy in an optimal organization.

The *corporate level* is where top management directs overall strategy for the entire organization. Multimarket, multiproduct firms such as General Electric or Unilever really manage a group of different businesses, variously termed strategic business units (SBUs), strategic business segments, or product-market units (PMUs).[7] Each of these units markets a set of related products to a clearly defined group of customers. Management at the corporate level focuses on the interests of the shareholders of the firm, as measured by stock performance and profitability. The *business unit level* is where business unit managers set the direction for individual products and markets. Strategic direction is more specific at the business unit level of an organization. For less complex firms with a single business focus, the corporate and business unit strategies may merge.

At the *functional level*, each business unit has marketing and other specialized activities such as finance, manufacturing, or human resources. The name of a *department* generally refers to its specialized function, such as the marketing department or information systems department. At the functional level, the strategic direction becomes very specific and focused.

In a large corporation with multiple business units, marketing may be called on to assess consumer trends as an aid to corporate planning. At the business unit level, marketing may be asked to provide leadership in developing a new, integrated customer service program across all business units. At the *functional level*, marketing may implement an advertising campaign.

Strategy Issues in Organizations

Organizations need a reason for their existence—and a direction. This is where their business, mission, and goals converge. We'll discuss each below. As shown in Figure 2–1, business and mission apply to the corporate and business unit levels, while goals relate to all three levels.

The Business   Organizations like Ben & Jerry's, the Red Cross, and your university exist for a purpose—to accomplish something for someone. At the beginning, most organizations have clear ideas about what "something" and "someone" mean. But as the organization grows over time, often its purpose becomes fuzzy and continually unclear.

This is where the organization repeatedly asks some of the most difficult questions it ever faces: What business are we in? Who are our customers? What offerings should we provide to give these customers value? One guideline in defining the company's business: Try to understand the people served by the organization and the value they receive, which emphasizes the critical customer-driven focus that successful organizations have.

In a now-famous article, Harvard professor Theodore Levitt cited railroads as organizations that had a narrow, production-oriented statement of their business: "We are in the railroad business!" This narrow definition of their business lost sight of who their customers were and what their needs were. Railroads saw only other railroads as competitors and failed to design strategies to compete with airlines, barges, pipelines, trucks, bus lines, and cars. Railroads would probably have fared better over the past century by recognizing they are in "the transportation business."[8]

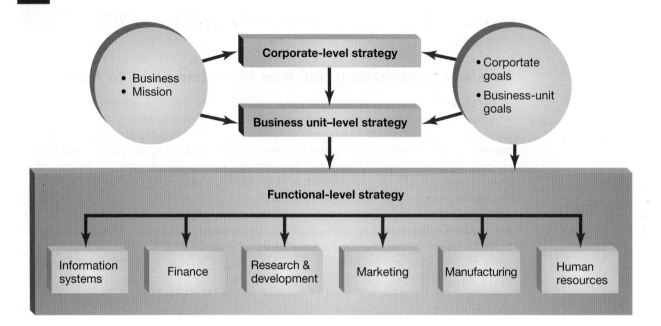

FIGURE 2–1

The three levels of strategy in organizations: corporate, business unit, and functional

With this focus on the customer, Disney is *not* in the movie and theme park business, but rather it *is* in the business of entertainment, creating fun and fantasy for customers. Similarly, as we'll see shortly, Medtronic is *the* world leader in developing, producing, and marketing heart pacemakers and other implantable medical devices. It would be a strategic error to say that Medtronic is in the medical device business; this is too limiting. It *is* in the business of alleviating pain, restoring health, and extending life. In this respect Medtronic's business somewhat overlaps its mission, the next topic.

The Mission   By understanding its business, an organization can take steps to define its **mission**, a statement of the organization's scope, often identifying its customers, markets, products, technology, and values. Today, often used interchangeably with "vision," the "mission statement" frequently has an inspirational theme — something that can ignite the loyalty of customers, employees, and others with whom the organization comes in contact.

mission
Statement of the organization's purpose and direction

> To explore strange new worlds, to seek out new life and new civilizations, to boldly go where no one has gone before.

This continuing mission for the starship *Enterprise*, as Gene Rodenberry wrote it for the *Star Trek* adventure series, is inspirational and focuses the advanced technology, strong leadership, and skilled crew of the *Enterprise* on what is to be accomplished.

This inspiration and focus appears in the mission of many organizations, such as the Canadian Red Cross:

> We help people deal with situations that threaten their survival and safety, their security and well-being, their human dignity, in Canada and around the world.

Or like this first sentence from Medtronic's mission statement:

> To contribute to human welfare by application of biomedical engineering in the research, design, manufacture, and sale of instruments or appliances that alleviate pain, restore health, and extend life.

Organizations must connect not just with their customers but with all their *stakeholders*. Stakeholders are the people who are affected by what the company does and how well it

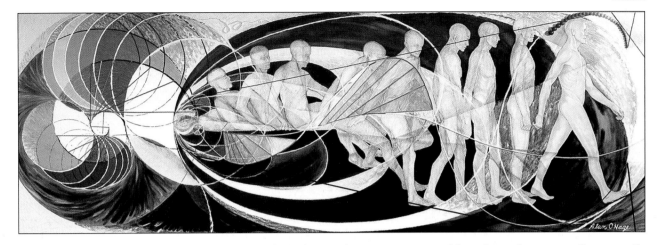

People see this "rising figure" mural in the headquarters of Medtronic, a world-class corporation. What does it suggest about its mission?

performs. This group includes employees, owners, and board members, as well as suppliers, distributors, unions, local communities, governments, society in general, and, of course, customers. Communicating the mission statement is an important corporate-level marketing function. Some companies publish their mission statement on their website or in their annual reports. One British Columbia company has its mission statement on a huge wall poster in their manufacturing facility, and every employee reads and signs it! Others take a more dramatic approach—like the "rising figure" wall painting at Medtronic's corporate headquarters, which powerfully communicates the inspiration and focus of its mission to employees, doctors, and patients alike.[9] Check them out at www.medtronics.com.

goals (objectives)
Targets of performance to be achieved within a specific time frame

Goals   **Goals** or **objectives** (terms used interchangeably in this book) take an organization's mission and translate it into targeted levels of performance to be achieved within a specific time frame. These goals measure how well the mission is being accomplished. As shown in Figure 2–1, goals exist at the corporate, business unit, and functional levels. All lower-level goals must contribute to achieving goals at the next higher level.

Business firms can pursue several different types of goals:

- *Profit.* Classic economic theory assumes a firm seeks to get as high a profit as possible.
- *Sales.* A firm may elect to maintain or increase its sales level even though profitability may not be maximized.
- *Market share.* A firm may choose to maintain or increase its market share, sometimes at the expense of greater profits if industry status or prestige is a desired goal. **Market share** is the ratio of sales revenue of the firm to the total sales revenue of all firms in the industry, including the firm itself.

market share
Ratio of a firm's sales to the total sales of all firms in the industry

- *Quality.* A firm may target the highest quality, as Medtronic does with its implantable medical devices.
- *Customer satisfaction.* Customers are the key to an organization's success, so their perceptions and actions are of vital importance. Their satisfaction can be measured directly with surveys or tracked with data such as number of customer complaints or percentage of orders shipped within 24 hours of receipt.
- *Employee welfare.* A firm may recognize the critical importance of its employees by having an explicit goal stating its commitment to good employment opportunities and working conditions.
- *Social responsibility.* A firm may seek to balance conflicting goals of consumers, employees, and stockholders to promote overall welfare of all these groups, even at the expense of profits. Firms manufacturing products abroad increasingly seek to be "good global citizens" by paying reasonable wages and reducing pollution from their manufacturing plants.

Many organizations (for example, museums, symphony orchestras, and private schools) do not seek profits as a primary goal. These organizations strive to serve consumers as efficiently as possible. Government agencies also perform marketing activities in trying to achieve their goal of serving the public good.

Concept Check

1. What are the three levels of organization in today's large corporations?

2. What is the purpose of an organization's mission?

3. How should an organization's goals relate to its mission?

SETTING STRATEGIC DIRECTIONS

Setting strategic directions involves answering challenging questions: Where are we now? Where do we want to go? How will we get there?

A Look Around: Where Are We Now?

Asking an organization where it is at the present time involves identifying its customers, competencies, and competitors. More detailed approaches of assessing "where are we now?" include SWOT analysis, discussed later in this chapter, and environmental scanning (Chapter 3). These may be done at each of the three levels in the organization.

Customers   Ben & Jerry's customers are ice cream and frozen yogourt eaters. But they are not all the same, because they have different flavour preferences, fat preferences, convenience preferences, and so on. Medtronic's "customers" are cardiologists and heart surgeons who serve patients.

Lands' End, a well-known North American retailer, provides an example of a clear focus on customers. Its stores, catalogues, and website give a remarkable statement about its commitments to customer relationships and quality of its products with these unconditional words:

> GUARANTEED. PERIOD.®

The Lands' End guarantee has always been an unconditional one and it has read: "If you are not completely satisfied with any item you buy from us, at any time during your use of it, return it and we will refund your full purchase price." But to get the message across more clearly to its customers, it put it in the two-word guarantee above. Check out "Our commitment to service" at www.landsend.com.

The crucial point: Strategic directions must be customer-focused and provide genuine value and benefits to existing and prospective customers.

Competencies   **"What do we do best?"** asks about an organization's competencies —an organization's special capabilities, including skills, technologies, and resources that distinguish it from other organizations. Exploiting these competencies can lead to success.[10] In Medtronic's case, its competencies include world-class technology plus training, service, and marketing activities that respond to both standard and urgent, life-threatening medical needs and wants. Competencies should be distinctive enough to provide a *competitive advantage*, a unique strength relative to competitors, often based on quality, time, cost, or innovation.[11] In the 1990s, Hewlett-Packard had a truly competitive advantage with its development time, which allowed it to bring innovative products to markets rapidly.[12]

*Lands' End's
unconditional guarantee
for its products highlights
its focus on its customers.*

Competitors   In today's global competition, the lines among competitive sectors are increasingly blurred. Lands' End started as a catalogue retailer. But defining its competitors simply as other catalogue retailers is a huge oversimplification. Lands' End now competes not only with other catalogue retailers of clothing but with traditional department stores, other online retailers, mass merchandisers, and specialty shops. Even well-known clothing brands like Liz Claiborne now have their own chain stores. Although only some of the clothing in any of these retailers competes directly with Lands' End products, many of the stores have websites for Internet selling. That's a lot of competition!

Sears purchased Lands' End in 2002.[13] To exploit its competencies, Lands' End now operates retail stores, and sells its goods in Sears stores in the U.S., complementing both its catalogue and Internet operations. Like all Internet retailers, it has a goal of increasing its "conversion rate," the percentage of browsers who actually buy something on visits to the website. Among big name e-tailers, Lands' End's conversion rate of 9.0 percent trails only L.L. Bean's 10.1 percent.[14] Successful firms continuously assess both who the competitors are and how they are changing in order to respond with their own strategies.

Growth Strategies: Where Do We Want to Go?

Knowing where the organization is at the present time enables managers to set a direction for the firm and commit resources to move in that direction. Two techniques to aid in these decisions are the business portfolio analysis and the market-product analysis.

Business Portfolio Analysis   Developed by the Boston Consulting Group (BCG), *business portfolio analysis* uses quantified performance measures and market growth to analyze a firm's strategic business units as though they were a collection of separate investments.[15] While used at the business unit level here, this so-called BCG analysis has also been applied at the product line or individual product or brand level. This kind of portfolio analysis is very popular; most large firms have used it in some form.

BCG, a leading management consulting firm, advises its clients to locate the position of each of its SBUs on a growth-share matrix (Figure 2–2). The vertical axis is the *market growth rate*, which is the annual rate of growth of the specific market or industry in which

FIGURE 2–2

Boston Consulting Group growth-share matrix for a strong, diversified firm showing some strategic plans

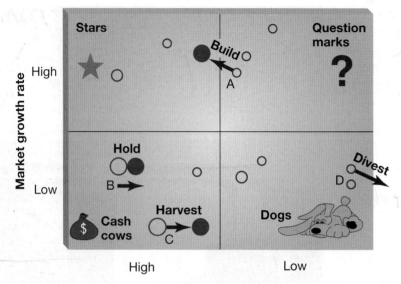

a given SBU is competing. The horizontal axis is the *relative market share*, defined as the sales of the SBU divided by the sales of the largest firm in the industry.

BCG has given specific names and descriptions to the four resulting quadrants in its growth-share matrix based on the amount of cash they generate for or require from the firm:

- *Cash cows* are SBUs that typically generate large amounts of cash, far more than they can invest profitably in their own product line. They have a dominant share of a slow-growth market and provide cash to pay large amounts of company overhead and to invest in other SBUs.

- *Stars* are SBUs with a high share of high-growth markets that may need extra cash to finance their own rapid future growth. When their growth slows, they are likely to become cash cows.

- *Question marks* or *problem children* are SBUs with a low share of high-growth markets. They require large injections of cash just to maintain their market share, and even more to increase it. Their name implies management's dilemma for these SBUs: choosing the right ones to invest in and phasing out the rest.

- *Dogs* are SBUs with a low share of low-growth markets. Although they may generate enough cash to sustain themselves, they do not hold the promise of ever becoming real winners for the firm. Dropping SBUs that are dogs may be required, except when relationships with other SBUs, competitive considerations, or potential strategic alliances exist.[16]

The circles in Figure 2–2 show the current SBUs in a strong, diversified firm. The area of each circle is proportional to the corresponding SBU's annual sales revenue.

Management often makes conscious decisions on what role each SBU should have in the future and either injects or removes cash from it. Four alternative strategies are available for each SBU. The firm can invest more in the SBU to *build* its share (SBU A in Figure 2–2), as Fujitsu has done with its tablet PC computer product lines. Or it can invest just enough to *hold* the SBU's share at about its current level (SBU B in the figure). Or it can *harvest* the SBU (SBU C in the figure), trying to milk its short-term cash flow even though it may lose share and become a dog in the longer run. Finally, the firm can *divest* the SBU (SBU D) by phasing it out or actually selling it to gain cash, as Procter & Gamble did by selling its Duncan Hines cake mix line to Aurora Foods.

The Stylistic® ST4000 Tablet PC Is Here.

Don't expect our Tablet PC to be like all the rest. It's not some OEM clone. Or a PDA on steroids. Or a stripped down notebook. Instead, it's powered by the latest Intel® processor. Runs any Window's application. Thrives with or without a keyboard and slips effortlessly into our optional Tablet Dock for instant desktop duty. It's thin, it's light, it's flat. In other words, it's everything 12 years of industry-defining experience said it could be: The most natural, mobile, productive and thoroughly thought out PC the world has ever seen.

12 YEARS.

12 YEARS OF DESIGNING, TESTING AND IMPLEMENTING PEN COMPUTING PRODUCTS.

OUR TABLET PC IS HERE.

12 YEARS AWAY FROM ORDINARY.

FUJITSU

THE POSSIBILITIES ARE INFINITE

The Stylistic® ST4000 is powered by an ultra low voltage Mobile Intel® Pentium® III Processor 800MHz – M which supports enhanced Intel® SpeedStep® Technology.

Learn how our Tablet PCs can give your company a competitive edge. Call us today at **1-877-372-3473** or visit **www.fujitsupc.com/12years**

Fujitsu recommends Microsoft® Windows® XP Professional for Mobile Computing.

You're Why I Bake A Duncan Hines Cake. You don't need a special occasion to bake a cake as moist and mouth-watering as a Duncan Hines cake. Just a special person.

*Strategies emerging from a business portfolio analysis: Fujitsu **builds** its tablet PC business while Procter & Gamble **divests** its Duncan Hines cake mix line to Aurora Foods.*

Market-Product Analysis   Firms can also view growth opportunities in terms of markets and products. Let's think of it this way: For any product there is both a current market (consisting of existing customers) and a new market (consisting of potential customers). And, for any market, there is a current product (what they're now using) and a new product (something they might use if it were developed). Four possible market-product strategies are shown in Figure 2–3.

As Unilever attempts to increase sales revenues of its Ben & Jerry's business, it must consider all four of the alternative market-product strategies shown in Figure 2–3. For example, it can try to use a strategy of *market penetration*—increasing sales of present products in its existing markets, in this case by increasing sales of Ben & Jerry's present ice cream products to consumers. There is no change in either the basic product line or the market served, but increased sales are possible—either by selling more ice cream (through better promotion or distribution) or by selling the same amount of ice cream at a higher price to its existing customers.

Market development, which here means selling existing Ben & Jerry's products to new markets, is a reasonable alternative. Australia, for example, is a good possible new market.

An expansion strategy using *product development* involves selling a new product to existing markets. When Ben and Jerry's launched sorbet and frozen yogourt products, the firm was following a product development strategy. Figure 2–3 shows that the firm could try leveraging the Ben & Jerry's brand by selling its own frozen yogourt in North America.

FIGURE 2–3

Four market-product
strategies: alternative ways
to expand sales revenues
for Ben & Jerry's

| Markets | PRODUCTS | |
	Current	New
Current	**Market penetration** Selling more Ben & Jerry's super premium ice cream in North America	**Product development** Selling a new product such as frozen yogourt under the Ben & Jerry's brand in North America
New	**Market development** Selling Ben & Jerry's super premium ice cream in Australia for the first time	**Diversification** Selling a new product such as breakfast cereal in China for the first time

Diversification involves developing new products and selling them in new markets. This is a potentially high-risk strategy for Ben & Jerry's—and for most firms—because the company has neither previous production experience nor marketing experience on which to draw. For example, in trying to sell a Ben & Jerry's brand of breakfast cereal in China, the company has expertise neither in producing cereals nor in marketing to consumers in China.

Which strategies will Ben and Jerry's follow? Keep your eyes, ears, and taste buds working to discover the marketing answers!

Concept Check

1. What are competencies and why are they important?

2. What is business portfolio analysis?

3. What are the four market-product strategies?

THE STRATEGIC MARKETING PROCESS

After an organization assesses where it's at and where it wants to go, it must work out how it will get there. Specifically, it must decide:

- How to allocate resources.
- How to convert plans into actions.
- How results compare with plans, and whether deviations (results that differ from expectations) require new plans and actions.

strategic marketing process
Approach whereby an organization allocates its marketing mix resources to reach its target markets and achieve its goals

This approach is used in the **strategic marketing process**, whereby an organization allocates its marketing mix resources to reach its target markets and achieve its goals. This process is divided into three phases: planning, implementation, and evaluation (Figure 2–4).

The strategic marketing process is so central to the activities of most organizations that they formalize it as a **marketing plan**, which is a road map for the marketing activities of an organization for a specified future period of time, such as one year or five years.

marketing plan
Road map for the marketing activities of an organization for a specified future period of time

The following section gives an overview of the strategic marketing process that puts Chapters 3 through 17 in perspective.

Strategic Marketing Process: The Planning Phase

As shown in Figure 2–4, the planning phase of the strategic marketing process

consists of the three steps shown at the top of the figure: situation analysis, market-product focus and goal setting, and the marketing program. Let's use the recent marketing planning experiences of several companies to look at each of these steps.

Step 1: Situation (SWOT) Analysis

The essence of **situation analysis** is taking stock of the firm or product's past performance, where it is now, and where it is headed in light of the organization's plans and the external factors and trends affecting it. The situation analysis box in Figure 2–4 is the first of the three steps in the planning phase.

A **SWOT analysis** describes an organization's appraisal of its internal **S**trengths and **W**eaknesses and its external **O**pportunities and **T**hreats. Both the situation and SWOT analyses can be done at the level of the entire organization, the business unit, the product line, or the specific product. As an analysis moves from the level of the entire organization to the specific product, it, of course, gets far more detailed. For small firms or those with basically a single product line, an analysis at the firm or product level is really the same thing.

The SWOT analysis is based on a detailed study of the four areas shown in step 1 of the planning phase of the strategic marketing process (Figure 2–4). Knowledge of these areas forms the foundation on which the firm builds its marketing program:

- Identifying trends in the firm's industry.
- Analyzing the firm's competitors.
- Assessing the firm itself.
- Researching the firm's present and prospective customers.

Let's assume you are the Unilever vice president responsible for integrating Ben & Jerry's into Unilever's business. You might do the SWOT analysis shown in Figure 2–5. Note that your SWOT table has four cells formed by the combination of internal versus external factors (the rows) and favourable versus unfavourable factors (the columns) that summarize Ben & Jerry's strengths, weaknesses, opportunities, and threats.

situation analysis
Taking stock of a firm or product's past performance, where it is now, and where it is headed

SWOT analysis
Organization's appraisal of its internal strengths and weaknesses and its external opportunities and threats

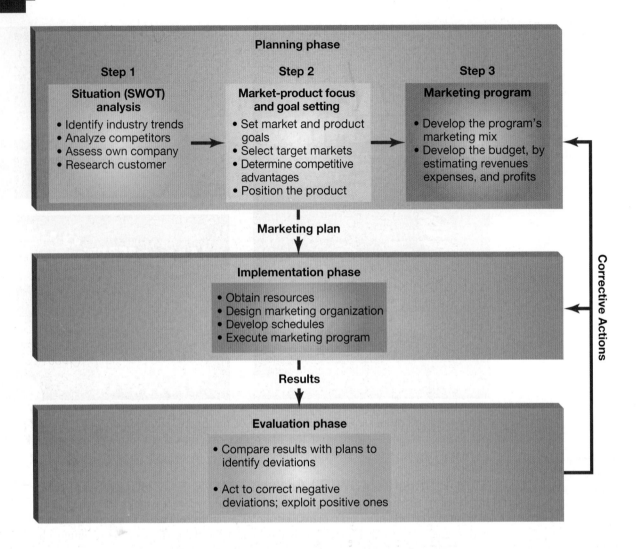

A SWOT analysis helps a firm identify the strategy-related factors in these four cells that can have a major effect on the firm. The goal is not simply to develop the SWOT analysis but to translate the results of the analysis into specific actions to help the firm grow and succeed. The ultimate goal is to identify the critical factors affecting the firm and then build on vital strengths, correct glaring weaknesses, exploit significant opportunities, and avoid or prepare for disaster-laden threats. That is a big order.

The Ben and Jerry's SWOT analysis in Figure 2–5 can be the basis for these kinds of specific actions. An action in each of the four cells might be:

- *Build on a strength.* Find specific efficiencies in distribution with Unilever's existing ice cream brands.
- *Correct a weakness.* Recruit experienced managers from other consumer product firms to help stimulate growth.
- *Exploit an opportunity.* Develop a new line of low-fat yogourts to respond to consumer health concerns.
- *Avoid or prepare for a disaster-laden threat.* Focus on less risky international markets, such as Mexico.

Step 2: Market-Product Focus and Goal Setting
Determining which products will be directed toward which customers (step 2 of the planning phase in Figure 2–4) is

FIGURE 2–5

Ben & Jerry's: a SWOT analysis

Location of Factor	TYPE OF FACTOR	
	Favourable	**Unfavourable**
Internal	**Strengths** • Prestigious, well-known brand name among North American consumers • Major share of the super premium ice cream market • Can complement Unilever's existing ice cream brands • Widely recognized for its social responsibility actions	**Weaknesses** • Danger that B&J's social responsibility actions may add costs, reduce focus on core business • Need for experienced managers to help growth • Flat sales and profits in recent years
External	**Opportunities** • Growing demand for quality ice cream in overseas markets • Increasing demand for frozen yogourt and other low-fat desserts • Success of many firms in extending successful brand in one product category to others	**Threats** • Consumer concern with fatty desserts; B&J customers are the type who read new government-ordered nutritional labels • Competes with giant Pillsbury and its Haagen-Dazs brand • International downturns increase the risks for B&J in European and Asian markets

market segmentation Sorting potential buyers into groups that have common needs and will respond similarly to a marketing action

essential for developing an effective marketing program (step 3). This decision is often based on **market segmentation**, which involves considering prospective buyers in terms of groups, or segments. These groups have common needs and will respond similarly to a marketing action. Ideally, a firm can use market segmentation to identify the segments on which it will focus its efforts—its target market segments—and develop one or more marketing programs to reach them.

Understanding the customer is essential. In the case of Medtronic, executives researched a potential new market in Asia by talking extensively with doctors in India and China. They learned that these doctors saw some of the current state-of-the-art features of heart pacemakers as unnecessary and too expensive. Instead, they wanted an affordable pacemaker that was reliable and easy to implant. This information led Medtronic to develop and market a new product, the Champion heart pacemaker, directed at the needs of this Asian market segment.

Goal setting involves setting measurable marketing objectives to be achieved. For a specific market, the goal may be to introduce a new product—such as Medtronic's Champion pacemaker in Asia or Toyota's launch of its hybrid car, the Prius. For a specific brand or product, the goal may be to create a promotional campaign or pricing strategy that will get more consumers to purchase. (Remember all those commercials touting the auto industry's popular 0 percent financing?) For an entire marketing program, the objective is often a series of actions to be implemented over several years.

Using the strategic marketing process shown in Figure 2–4, let's examine Medtronic's five-year plan to reach the "affordable and reliable" segment of the pacemaker market:[17]

• *Set marketing and product goals.* The chances of new-product success are increased by specifying both market and product goals. Based on their market research showing the need for a reliable yet affordable pacemaker, Medtronic executives set the following as their goal: Design and market such a pacemaker in the next three years that could be manufactured in China for the Asian market.

The Champion: Medtronic's high-quality, long-life, low-cost heart pacemaker for an Asian market segment

competitive advantages
Those characteristics of a product or service that make it superior to competing substitutes

- *Select target markets.* The Champion pacemaker will be targeted at cardiologists and medical clinics performing heart surgery in India, China, and other Asian countries.
- *Determine competitive advantages.* **Competitive advantages** are those characteristics of a product that make it superior to competing substitutes. For the Champion pace-maker, the key points of difference are not the state-of-the-art features that drive up production costs and are important to only a minority of patients. Instead, they are high quality, long life, reliability, ease of use, and low cost.
- *Position the product.* The pacemaker will be "positioned" in cardiologists' and patients' minds as a medical device that is high quality and reliable with a long, nine-year life. The name Champion is selected after testing acceptable names among doctors in India, China, Pakistan, Singapore, and Malaysia.

Details in these four elements of step 2 provide a solid foundation to use in developing the marketing program—the next step in the planning phase of the strategic marketing process.

Step 3: Marketing Program   Activities in step 2 tell the marketing manager which customers to target and which customer needs the firm's product offerings can satisfy—the *who* and *what* aspects of the strategic marketing process. The *how* aspect—step 3 in the planning phase—involves developing the program's marketing mix and its budget.

Figure 2–6 shows components of each marketing mix element that are combined to provide a cohesive marketing program. For the five-year marketing plan of Medtronic, these marketing mix activities include the following:

- *Product strategy.* Offer a Champion brand heart pacemaker with features needed by Asian patients at an affordable price.
- *Price strategy.* Manufacture Champion to control costs so that it can be priced below $1,000 (in U.S. dollars)—a fraction of the price of the state-of-the-art pacemakers offered in Western markets.

FIGURE 2–6
Elements of the marketing mix that comprise a cohesive marketing program

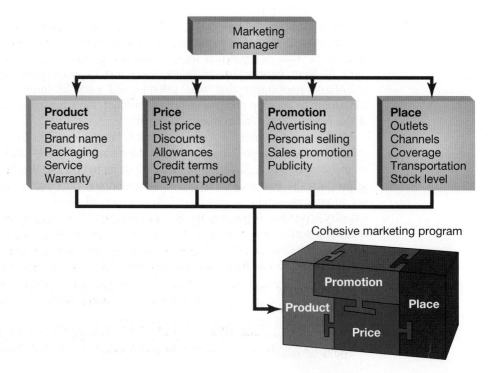

- *Promotion strategy.* Feature demonstrations at cardiologist and medical conventions across Asia to introduce the Champion and highlight the device's features and application.
- *Place (distribution) strategy.* Search out, utilize, and train reputable medical distributors across Asia to call on cardiologists and medical clinics.

Putting this marketing program into effect requires that the firm commit time and money to it, prepare a sales forecast, and establish a budget that must be approved by top management.

Concept Check

1. What is the difference between a strength and an opportunity in a SWOT analysis?
2. What is market segmentation?
3. What are competitive advantages and why are they important?

STRATEGIC MARKETING PROCESS: THE IMPLEMENTATION PHASE

A firm's marketing plan is the result of the many hours spent in the planning phase of the strategic marketing process. Implementation, the second phase of the strategic marketing process, involves carrying out the marketing plan that emerges from the planning phase. If the firm cannot put the marketing plan into effect—in the implementation phase—the planning phase was a waste of time. Figure 2–4 shows the four components of the implementation phase: obtaining resources, designing the marketing organization, developing schedules, and actually executing the marketing program designed in the planning phase. Eastman Kodak, the world's largest photography company, provides an example.[18]

Obtaining Resources   When chief executive officer (CEO) George Fisher arrived at Kodak in the mid-1990s, he observed, "There are textbook types of things that are wrong with this company. Decisions are too slow. People don't take risks."[19] So he pushed some revolutionary decisions that seemed obvious to him:

- Focus on Kodak's core business: imaging.
- Serve customer needs better, and stress quality.
- Shorten product-development cycles.
- Encourage a more dynamic, risk-taking, fast-decision culture.

Fisher needed money to implement these ideas, however, so he obtained $8 billion by selling off divisions not related to Kodak's core imaging business.

Designing the Marketing Organization   A marketing program needs marketing staff to implement it. Figure 2–7 shows the organization chart of a typical manufacturing firm, giving some details of the marketing department's structure. Four managers of marketing activities are shown to report to the vice president of marketing. Several regional sales managers and an international sales manager may report to the manager of sales. This marketing organization is responsible for converting marketing plans to reality.

Developing Schedules   In early 2000, Daniel Carp became Kodak's CEO. Carp immediately launched a strategy to move aggressively into digital camera and imaging

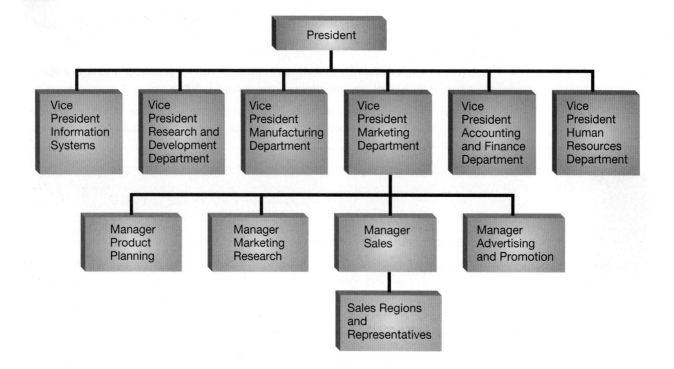

Organization of a typical manufacturing firm, showing a breakdown of the marketing department

technology while improving Kodak's traditional cash cow: film and film processing services. The emphasis on film came about because Kodak believed that a large majority of consumers were still happy using film cameras and Kodak's paper, chemicals, and technical savvy are needed to complete the picture and make great prints.[20] Carp set key deadlines for Kodak, such as:

- By the first quarter of 2001, launching the mc3 digital camera line ($250–$350), targeted at 18- to 28-year-olds, that combines still camera, video camera, and MP3 player.[21]
- Introduce a family of Easy Share digital cameras in the $400–$600 range, plus docking stations ($80), facilitating easy uploading of photos to a PC and the Internet.[22]

Executing the Marketing Program   Marketing plans are meaningless unless they are put into action. This requires attention to detail to both marketing strategies and marketing tactics. A **marketing strategy** is the means by which a marketing goal is to be achieved, usually characterized by a specified target market and a marketing program to reach it. Although the term strategy is often used loosely, it implies both the end sought (target market) and the means to achieve it (marketing program).

To implement a marketing program successfully, hundreds of detailed decisions are often required, such as writing ads or setting prices. These decisions, called **marketing tactics**, are detailed day-to-day operational decisions essential to the overall success of marketing strategies. Here are examples of both kinds of decisions at Kodak:

- *Marketing strategy decision.* Kodak saw the surprising success of cameras targeted at 18- to 28-year-olds (the Generation Y or Gen Y consumers) and teenagers: Nintendo's Game Boy digital camera that printed out tiny, grainy images on sticky paper and Polaroid's I-Zone Instant Pocket camera. Kodak's strategy decision: Launch a new product targeted at Gen Y.
- *Marketing tactics decision.* Concurrently, Kodak engineers were toying with the idea of hooking the computing power of digital cameras to digital MP3 music files. "We

marketing strategy
Means by which a marketing goal is to be achieved

marketing tactics
Detailed day-to-day operational decisions essential to the overall success of marketing strategies

proposed the technology of the product," recalled engineer Clay Dunsmore, "but we didn't have a clear idea of who we would sell it to!" Kodak's tactics decision: Form a cross-functional team to work on the gadget.

The result: the mc3 was introduced in February 2001, meeting Carp's target launch date.[23] Marketing strategies and marketing tactics go hand in hand. Effective marketing program implementation requires close attention to both.

Strategic Marketing Process: The Evaluation Phase

The evaluation phase of the strategic marketing process seeks to keep the marketing program moving in the direction set for it. Accomplishing this requires the marketing manager to compare the results of the marketing activities with the goals laid out in the marketing plans to identify deviations and to act on these deviations—correcting negative deviations and exploiting positive ones.

Comparing Results with Plans

In April of 2003, Carp hired Antonio Perez to be Kodak's new president and chief operating officer. After reviewing the results of the past years, Perez realigned the business for the second time in two years. The focus now is moving away from traditional film, and directed towards digital technology. These moves came after Perez observed the company's drop in the consumer film business, as well as increased price competition from Japan's Fuji Photo Film Company.

When a company sets goals and then compares them to actual results, it needs to research the reasons for the differences. Where plans are exceeded, the company determines the drivers of this success and identifies ways to build on them as it moves forward. When there is a shortfall (actual results less than planned—often referred to as the *planning gap*), the company has to "fill in" this planning gap with a revised marketing program and possibly new goals.

Acting on Deviations

Carp decided to focus on growth businesses after he saw the lower-than-expected results in consumer film. He and Perez reorganized the company into five operating groups instead of the existing three, adding a commercial printing group and separating out the fast-growing health-imaging division into a standalone unit. Now, Kodak's five SBUs are:

- Commercial printing (equipment to print colour posters and signs),
- Commercial imaging (image storage products for business and governments),
- Display and components (digital camera sensors and displays),
- Health imaging (X-ray film and image management software), and
- Digital and film imaging systems (consumer film and entertainment products).[24]

According to Carp, "We have implemented a structure and leadership team that will unlock the potential of our existing operations, and build entirely new businesses that will position us for growth. We will continue to invest in the most attractive areas of the business, and we will aggressively and intelligently manage our mature operations for long-term customer satisfaction, for market share, and for cash."[25]

Concept Check

1. How would you distinguish a marketing strategy from a marketing tactic?
2. How do the objectives set for a marketing program in the planning phase relate to the evaluation phase of the strategic marketing process?

SUMMARY

1 Today's large organizations, both business firms and not-for-profit organizations, are often divided into three levels: the corporate, business unit, and functional levels.

2 Marketing has a role in all three levels by keeping a focus on customers and finding ways to add genuine customer value. At the lowest level, marketing serves as part of a team of functional specialists whose day-to-day actions actually involve customers and create customer value.

3 Organizations exist to accomplish something for someone. To give itself focus, an organization continuously assesses its business, mission, and goals.

4 Setting strategic directions for an organization involves asking "Where are we now?" to assess the organization's customers, competencies, and competitors. It also involves asking "Where do we want to go?" and using techniques like portfolio analysis and market-product analysis, and asking questions like "How will we get there?" that uses marketing plans.

5 The strategic marketing process involves an organization allocating its marketing mix resources to reach its target markets using three phases: planning, implementation, and evaluation.

6 The planning phase of the strategic marketing process has three steps, each with more specific elements: situation (SWOT) analysis, market-product focus and goal setting, and marketing program.

7 The implementation phase of the strategic marketing process has four key elements: obtaining resources, designing the marketing organization, developing schedules, and executing the marketing program.

8 The evaluation phase of the strategic marketing process involves comparing results with the planned targets to identify deviations and taking actions to correct negative deviations and exploit positive ones.

KEY TERMS AND CONCEPTS

competitive advantages p. 36
goals p. 27
marketing plan p. 32
marketing strategy p. 38
marketing tactics p. 38
market segmentation p. 35
market share p. 27
mission p. 26

objectives p. 27
profit p. 24
situation analysis p. 33
strategic marketing process p. 32
strategy p. 25
SWOT analysis p. 33

QUESTIONS: APPLYING MARKETING CONCEPTS AND PERSPECTIVES

1 *(a)* Explain what a mission statement is. *(b)* Create a mission statement for your own career.

2 What competencies best describe *(a)* your university, *(b)* your favourite restaurant, and *(c)* the company that manufactures the computer you own or use most often?

3 Why does a product often start as a question mark and then move counterclockwise around BCG's growth-share matrix shown in Figure 2–2?

4 Many Canadian universities have traditionally offered an undergraduate degree in business (the product) to full-time 18- to 22-year-old students (the market). How might they use the four market-product expansion strategies to compete in the 21st century?

5 What is the main result of each of the three phases of the strategic marketing process? *(a)* planning, *(b)* implementation, and *(c)* evaluation.

6 The goal-setting step in the planning phase of the strategic marketing process sets quantified objectives for use in the control phase. What actions are suggested for a marketing manager if measured results are below objectives? Above objectives?

DISCUSSION FORUM

Imagine that you have just launched a new company called Escapade Travels, which is designed to organize trips to far-away, rarely-heard-of destinations with adventure-type activities, such as igloo building in Greenland and sand-dune racing in the desert in Dubai. You have just graduated with your marketing degree, so you want to make sure that you follow the strategic marketing process you learned. Think about what you want your company to be and discuss the following issues with your class/colleagues:

1 What should go into your mission statement? Draft one, limiting it to no more than 60 words.
2 What business units will your company have? Who will your company's stakeholders be?
3 What planning decisions will take place at the corporate level? At the business unit level? At the functional level?
4 Sketch out a SWOT analysis, a market-product focus, and at least six goals for your new company.
5 Choose an important target market for your company, and outline a suitable marketing mix.

INTERNET EXERCISE

www.mcgrawhill.ca/college/thecore

Ben & Jerry's markets its flavours of ice cream, frozen yo-gourt, sorbet, and novelty bars in response to both consumer tastes and important causes it supports, a practice continued even after being sold to Unilever in 2000. Recently, Ben & Jerry's teamed up with the award-winning Dave Matthews Band and SaveOurEnvironment.org to fight global warming by creating the One Sweet Whirled ice cream flavor in pints and novelty bars. But not all flavours last. The ones that don't, wind up in Ben & Jerry's Flavor Graveyard.

1   Go to www.benjerry.com to read Ben & Jerry's mission statement. What are the elements of its mission? Do you think all companies should have these elements in their mission statement, particularly the idea of "linked prosperity"? Why or why not?

2   Ben & Jerry's prides itself on being a socially responsible firm. Each year, it publishes a "social audit" that reviews its social responsibility in several areas. Check out Ben & Jerry's latest Social Performance Report by clicking the Company Info link and then the link for the latest social audit. Be sure to click on the Marketing & Sales link. What has Ben & Jerry's done in the areas of packaging, marketing and sales, and activism to be a socially responsible corporate citizen?
3   To see Ben & Jerry's current flavours and those "laid to rest" in the Flavor Graveyard, visit www.benjerry.com/product. Have any of your favourite flavours been laid to rest? If yes, what are they? Why do you think they were discontinued?

VIDEO CASE 2

SPECIALIZED BICYCLE COMPONENTS, INC.: RIDE THE RED "S"

The speaker leans forward with both intensity and pride in his voice. "We're in the business of creating a bike that delivers the customer the best possible ride," he explains. "When the customer sees our red 'S,' they say this is the company that understands the cyclist. It's a company of riders. The products they make are the rider's products." The speaker is Chris Murphy, director of marketing for Specialized Bicycle Components, Inc.—or just "Specialized" to serious riders.

THE COMPANY

Specialized was founded in 1974 by Mike Sinyard, a cycling enthusiast who sold his Volkswagen van for $1,500 in start-up

capital. Sinyard started out importing hard-to-find "specialized" bike components, but the company was producing its own bike parts by 1976. Specialized introduced the first major production mountain bike in the world in 1980, revolutionizing the bike industry, and since then has maintained a reputation as the technological leader in the bike and bike accessory market. In fact, since the company's founding, its formal mission has been: "To Be the Best Cycling Brand in the World."

The first professional mountain bike racing team was created by Specialized in 1983. Team members often serve as design consultants. The company banks on the perception, and reality, that this race-proven technology trickles down to the entire line of Specialized bikes and products.

The company continues to innovate. It also sells road bikes and an extensive line of bike accessories, including helmets, water bottles, jerseys, and shoes. As Murphy says, "The customer is buying the ride from us, not just the bike." Sinyard believes the key to innovative product development is the synthesis of "spirit, vision, and energy." True to this belief, Specialized established the S-Works design unit. Following the motto "Innovate or Die," the unit produces designs that range from inspired to outrageous.

THE ENVIRONMENT

The bike market is driven by innovation and technology, and the market is becoming more crowded and competitive. Specialized divides the bike market into two categories: the independent retailer and the end-user consumer. While its focus in designing the product is on the end-user consumer, Specialized only sells directly to the retailer, realizing that a strong relationship with the dealers is a key factor for success. Management at Specialized refers to the retailer's on-floor salesperson as "our most important partner."

The end-user consumer is broken down into two target age groups: 18- to 25-year-old college students and 30- to 40-year-old professional "techies." To differentiate itself from the rest of the market, Specialized positions itself as the innovator in mountain bikes—its models are what the rest of the industry imitates. Mountain bikes account for approximately two-thirds of total industry bike sales, with road bikes accounting for the other third.

In addition to its mountain bikes, the company makes a full range of high-end and entry-level road bikes, commuter and city bikes, children's bikes, and of course BMX bikes.

Specialized now has an extensive global distribution network with subsidiaries in North America, Europe, and Asia, and more than 500 dealers in 35 countries.

THE ISSUES

How can Specialized stay at the forefront of an industry that now includes more than 20 manufacturers? Strategic placement in the marketplace is one way. Specialized has what it thinks is the most sophisticated website in the bike industry. With segments for specific regions of the world, the website offers international mountain bike trail and road bike trail directories, e-mail access to Specialized engineers, a trail preservation network, and a dealer directory that connects users directly to dealer home pages. Specialized believes guest appearances on TV talk shows and displays in retail shops help to keep the Specialized name in front of the end-user consumer.

Specialized is also eager to become involved in joint ventures to keep its technological edge, including one with DuPont that led to a more aerodynamic wheel. Specialized also entered into a distribution relationship with GripShift, allowing the high-end gear manufacturer access to its extensive dealer network.

Specialized creates and sponsors dozens of races, provides racer support teams, initiates mountain biking safety programs, and is involved in trail-access advocacy groups all over the world. But as it was in Specialized's early years, Sinyard sees a commitment to top quality and design as the most important factor for future success. According to Sinyard, "This company still feels like it has something to prove. I expect it will always be that way."

Questions

1 Do a SWOT situation analysis for Specialized. Use Figure 2-5 in Chapter 2 and Item 3 (part of Design of the Marketing Plan) in Appendix A as guides. In assessing internal factors (strengths and weaknesses), use the material provided in the case. In assessing external factors (opportunities and threats), augment the case material with what you see happening in the bicycle industry.

2 As part of step 2 of the planning phase, and using your SWOT situation analysis, select target markets on which you may focus for present and potential bikers.

3 As part of step 3 of the planning phase and using your answers in questions 1 and 2 above, outline Specialized's marketing programs for the target market segments you choose.

Creating a Successful Marketing Plan

In this part of *The Core*, we have looked at all of the components of a marketing plan. Now in this appendix, we look at the actual crafting of a marketing plan, including some thoughts on making the plan work for an organization. You, as a marketing student, can create useful and interesting marketing plans, a skill that will benefit you throughout your business career. We have seen plans prepared by our marketing students that are as good if not better than some of those prepared by professional marketing firms. Marketing planning is part science, part art; it requires a few key skills: research capability, analytical competence, the ability to see the "big picture" of a firm and its future potential, and interpersonal connections to assist with getting input and insights from key stakeholders.

PURPOSE OF THE PLAN

Ensuring that a company's marketing organization and execution is efficient and effective requires a detailed and specific marketing plan. Think of a marketing plan as a road map to marketing success. There are different ways the plan can be used, and several reasons to create one:

- A marketing plan may communicate company goals and directions to employees, and give them some guidelines about their role in the process.
- The company may require financing, and the plan is a way for them to present the company and its requirements to potential financial backers (banks, investors).
- Creating the plan may be the best structure for becoming aware of problems, market opportunities, and market or competitor threats.

Some marketers feel that the planning process itself is as important as the plan. In creating an effective plan, a company undertakes a substantial amount of research, and this gives them information and market savvy that is critical to how they plan to evolve their future. The planning process forces company executives and managers to make decisions and identify priorities, and to face some realities about company strengths and weaknesses.

HOW TO PLAN EFFECTIVELY

Many excellent marketing plans have been laboured over and written, only to sit on shelves. To make good use of the plan, it must be actionable, readable, and of a reasonable length. A few guidelines for effective planning include:

- Set goals and a time frame for developing the plan.
- Identify the target audience for the plan, that is, who is it intended for.
- Establish what you want to know and the time frame you have to undertake your research. Research can be a challenge, as there is so much information that you may have difficulty setting parameters about how much is enough, and when you should end your researching and go with the information you have
- Planning is *never* finished—a good marketing plan is a dynamic document, and it evolves, changes, and refocuses as the organization grows—so keep it current.
- Consider your audience and write to them. Avoid using jargon and complex explanations; some readers will not comprehend your language, and the plan will not have the desired effect on them.
- People absorb information in different ways: some like the written word, some see the message more clearly with a chart or graph, and some are pictorial learners. Craft your plan so that it has a mixture of ways of presenting information to ensure that you engage as much of your audience as possible.
- Involve different people with different perspectives, different skill sets, and different relationships to the company; solid teamwork with a variety of perspectives will result in the best plan.

BUSINESS VERSUS MARKETING PLANS

Business plans, marketing plans—what is the difference? Do we need both? Don't they overlap? The answers to these questions depend on the organization, who is doing the planning, and what the purpose of the plan is. The following chart shows the differences

COMPARING A BUSINESS PLAN TO A MARKETING PLAN

	MARKETING PLAN	BUSINESS PLAN
Executive Summary	✓	✓
Table of Contents	✓	✓
Company Overview	✓	more detailed
Strategic Plan		✓
Situation Analysis	✓	✓
Mission Statement and Goals	✓	✓
Target Markets	✓	✓
Marketing Strategy	✓	✓
Research and Development Program		✓
Budget and Financials	✓	more detailed
Organizational Structure and Staffing		✓
Implementation	✓	✓
Control and Evaluation	✓	✓
Contingency Plans	✓	✓
Appendix A: Biographies of Key Personnel		✓
Other Appendixes: Details on Other Topics	✓	✓

between the two types of plans, how they overlap, and how to determine the type of plan needed for the organization.

THE PLANNING PROCESS

It may seem like an overwhelming task to create a marketing plan, but it is actually a fairly straightforward process, if it is done properly. Appointing a plan champion is a must—establishing one person who will take ownership of the plan, make sure that it gets done on time, and bring in resources as needed. A team then needs to be assembled to ensure that all the important inputs are represented, as well as to foster consistency of thinking across all the product and organizational considerations. The plan must be realistic and thorough. A short, specific and actionable plan will be a strategic tool in executing your marketing activities. The marketing plan is just one indication of a move toward a more strategic and planned approach. This is a direction that many businesses are taking, because a finely tuned strategy is key to a company's future.

HOW TO CREATE THE PLAN

First, read over the following plan layout to get a sense of what kind of marketing directions are suggested and what work you have to do to furnish the details of the plan. Then, create a list of the information you need to prepare the various sections. Finally, put the pieces together and have your colleagues work with you to refine and improve it. The following list identifies the components of a typical plan and their role in the plan.

DESIGN OF THE MARKETING PLAN

Executive Summary:

A quick overview of the plan. If a reader had time to read only one page, it would be the Executive Summary, and it should give the highlights of the contents of the entire plan. Usually this is the last part of the plan that you write, once all the other details have been considered and documented.

1. Table of Contents

A listing of the topics covered in the plan and the order in which they will be presented. Usually, the following key topics should be covered:

Executive Summary
Table of Contents
Company Overview
Situation Analysis
Mission Statement and Goals
Target Markets
Marketing Strategy
Financial Considerations
Implementation
Control and Evaluation
Contingency Plans
Appendixes
Checklists

2. Company Overview

A brief description of the company, its history, its current direction and basic type of business it operates, product lines, and product mix. This section should also include resources (financial and personnel), financial health/situation, and market position.

3. Situation Analysis

A detailed analysis of the current market situation of the company that establishes the information base for the marketing plan and sets the scene. Before beginning the plan, you must have a clear idea of the environment in which the company is working, and how the company will proceed based on these findings. The situation analysis includes several key elements:

- Environmental scan (economic, political, international perspectives)
- Competitive environment (main competitors and their product lines, promotions, product plans, strengths and weaknesses, state of the firm's relationship with them)
- Industry environment (growth patterns and trends in the overall industry)
- Technology environment (degree of utilization of technology of the industry, currency of use of technology by major industry players, innovations that will affect the product/service)
- Consumer environment (consumer demand, characteristics, social and cultural factors, trends)
- Financial environment (availability of funds)
- Regulatory environment (legislation, taxation, rules that affect the business)
- Media environment (how the media feels about the firm and its business activities, and how they are likely to respond to the firm's plan)
- SWOT analysis (company strengths and weaknesses, i.e., internal factors; and opportunities and threats, i.e., external factors)
- The company's core competencies and market capabilities
- Keys to success, i.e., a few key factors that make the difference between success and failure (for example, quality control, customer service, unique product offering, or manufacturing resources)

4. Mission Statement and Goals

- Mission statement: the company's statement of the type of business it is in, its business philosophy, and its intended markets
- Goals: detailed financial and marketing objectives that the company wants to achieve. These goals must be SMART (**S**pecific, **M**easurable, **A**ttainable, **R**elevant, and **T**ime bound).

5. Target Markets

Description of the target markets in terms of business customers or consumers, product awareness, how they value product attributes, followed by these evaluations:

- Consumers: demographics, psychographics, lifestyles, geographics (where customers are physically located), wants, buying behaviour (preferences and frequency of purchases)
- Businesses: characteristics of the firm's North American Industry Classification System (NAICS) classification, operating practices, geographics, size, revenue levels, number of employees

- Market needs that company seeks to fill: value that company will be providing to market; benefits to customers; description of target markets in terms of size and growth, previous and forecast (rather than features of products). Figures should include market potential, sales potential, company sales forecast for the period.

6. Marketing Strategy

Alternatives for overall marketing strategy, how to successfully capture the target markets, desired market positioning, differentiation approach, and:

- Marketing mix: state each component in detail; the product, place, price, and promotion must all work together
- Marketing tactics: how the strategy will be implemented (action plans)
- Ongoing market research to be undertaken

7. Financial Considerations

Analysis of budget required, break-even calculations, profit analysis, and sales forecasts; charts and tables show this information best. Ask questions to complete this section fully: What level of sales is being projected? How fast will sales grow? What are the most important components of sales performance? Why? What risks are involved? What events may turn the sales forecast downward? What assumptions have been used in creating the sales forecast?

8. Implementation

Organize time plan and activities for each time frame, monitor new developments in internal and external environments, use planning chart to ensure that implementation is on track and responsibilities are assigned and completed.

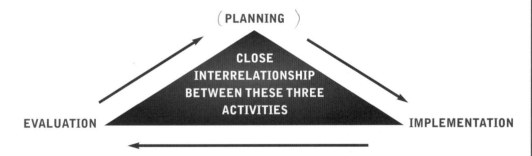

10. Control and Evaluation

Measures for tracking results, steps to take to counter competitor responses, monitoring progress in sales, comparison of budget to actual expenditures, methods of adjusting the plan if need be.

11. Contingency Plans

What will company do if things don't work out? Is there a contingency plan? What happens if things go wrong? What factors are most likely to cause trouble? What trouble could they cause? How will the company react?

SAMPLE CHECK LIST: IMPLEMENTING AND EVALUATING THE MARKETING PLAN

STRATEGIES AND TACTICS	FREQUENCY	2-YEAR TIME FRAME							
		1ST QUARTER 2005	2ND QUARTER 2005	3RD QUARTER 2005	4TH QUARTER 2005	1ST QUARTER 2006	2ND QUARTER 2006	3RD QUARTER 2006	4TH QUARTER 2006
DATABASE									
Follow-up with past clients (25 per month)	annually	X	X	X	X	X	X	X	X
Complaint tracking—summarize and evaluate all incoming complaints	quarterly	X				X			
Track cyclical effect of purchases	annually				X				X
Contact 2 weeks after purchase	event-driven								
Evaluate business coming from each market segment	annually	X				X			
RESEARCH									
Call any clients who dropped us, determine why	event-driven		X				X		
Survey suppliers to determine satisfaction with program	annually			X				X	
Track cyclical effect of purchases	annually				X				X
TRAINING									
Prepare a video/CD for office staff			X						
Prepare marketing training/seminar for clients	event-driven				X	X	X	X	
Offer training seminars in large firms	coordinate with visits to firms					X		X	
PROMOTION									
Advertising tactics:									
Have new packages designed	early 2005	X							
Advertise in industry magazines	3 times per year			X				X	
Generate media coverage	ongoing	X	X	X	X	X	X	X	X
Direct Marketing:									
Acquire list of all firms in identified target markets			X						
Mail introductory letter to 150 new clients		X				X			
Phone to follow-up on mail piece		X				X			

STRATEGIES AND TACTICS	FREQUENCY	1ST QUAR-TER 2005	2ND QUAR-TER 2005	3RD QUAR-TER 2005	4TH QUAR-TER 2005	1ST QUAR-TER 2006	2ND QUAR-TER 2006	3RD QUAR-TER 2006	4TH QUAR-TER 2006
SAMPLE CHECK LIST: IMPLEMENTING AND EVALUATING THE MARKETING PLAN									
Direct Marketing:									
Plan visits to potential clients with >50 employees	ongoing	X	X	X	X	X	X	X	X
Prepare and mail newsletter to all clients and suppliers	every 6 months	X		X		X		X	
Send a postcard-style holiday card to everyone on database					Dec,				Dec.
Contact all clients with a direct-mail initiative during quarters other than where newsletters and holiday cards are being sent			X				X		
Trade shows:									
Generate a list of trade shows with potential for display				X					
Offer speakers for conferences	event-driven				X				
Prepare information package for delegates' info kits	event-driven				X				
Website:									
Build a secure area on website where clients can view progress of their order									
Monitor and track website visits	ongoing	X	X	X	X	X	X	X	X
Respond to e-mails	ongoing	X	X	X	X	X	X	X	X
Monitor competitor and complementary organization websites	ongoing	X	X	X	X	X	X	X	X
RELATIONSHIP MANAGEMENT									
Suppliers:									
Visit once per quarter	ongoing	X	X	X	X	X	X	X	X
Call monthly	ongoing	X	X	X	X	X	X	X	X
Clients:									
Call all existing clients two times per year	ongoing	X	X	X	X	X	X	X	X
Visit large clients (>100 employees) once per year	ongoing	X	X	X	X	X	X	X	X

Scanning the Marketing Environment

AFTER READING THIS CHAPTER YOU SHOULD BE ABLE TO:

- Understand how environmental scanning provides information about social, economic, technological, competitive, and regulatory forces.

- Explain how social forces such as demographics and culture and economic forces such as macroeconomic conditions and consumer income affect marketing.

- Describe how technological changes can affect marketing.

- Understand the forms of competition that exist in a market, key components of competition, and the impact of competition on corporate strategy.

- Explain the key legislation that ensures competition and regulates the elements of the marketing mix.

HOW AN 18-YEAR-OLD CHANGED THE WORLD . . . WITH MUSIC!

Have you ever downloaded a song from the Internet? Created a collection of music hits on your computer? Burned a CD of your favourites? If you have, you may be one of the more than 50 million users of Internet-based music file-sharing services. Napster creator Shawn Fanning was just 18 when he devised the software program that allowed computer users to share music files. It changed the music industry dramatically. Suddenly, musicians, recording companies, computer companies like Apple, retail stores, and consumers like you are part of a completely different music marketplace. How did this happen? The marketing environment changed!

First, consumers changed. As one expert explains, the music industry "forces consumers to go to unpleasant stores to buy high-priced CDs, bundles bad songs along with good, encases its products in cheap plastic boxes that frequently break, then deliberately wraps the boxes in hard-to-open cellophane."[1] As a result, music buyers started searching for a more customer-friendly distribution system.

Second, changes in technology allowed the development of new products and services previously impossible to offer consumers. New computers with improved speed and storage capabilities were introduced. CD drives that could "burn" a customized CD became available. The Internet reached millions of computer users. And Fanning created a service, called Napster, that let almost anyone "share" a music file with anyone else on the Internet.

The creation of file-sharing services has led to other changes in the marketing environment. Regulatory factors, for example, are influencing the activities of the services. The Recording Industry Association of America sued Napster and several other music-swapping services for copyright violations. In response, U.S. courts ruled that Napster had to stop helping its users exchange copyrighted material, effectively shutting Napster down in mid-2001. Napster and other key file-sharing companies responded to these changes by attempting to develop new technology that would

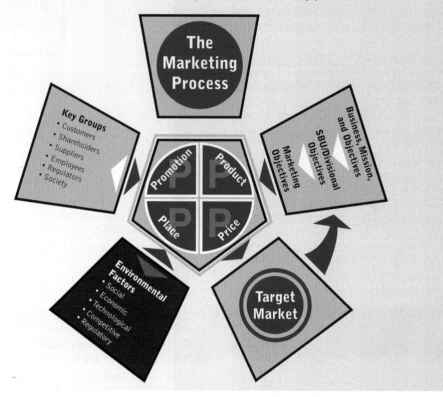

WHERE IN THE MARKETING PROCESS ARE WE GOING IN THIS CHAPTER?

In Chapter 3, we focus on the environment where marketing takes place and how the components of the environment form part of the marketing process.

recognize copyrighted songs on a network and enable the copyright owners to set a fee for anyone wishing to download them. The music labels EMI, Bertelsmann, and Warner Music created an online clearinghouse for their music called MusicNet, and Sony and Universal formed a joint venture called Pressplay. Computer suppliers such as Apple introduced its new iMac complete with iTunes software, so users can put their entire music collection on their computer or on iPod, Apple's portable digital music player, which holds as many as 10,000 songs. A small Ottawa company, Kokopelli Networks, is also entering the fray with software called BluFilter that can sniff out pirated MP3 music files and request payment for copyrighted songs before allowing downloads to proceed—if the downloader refuses, BluFilter destroys the files before they can be downloaded.[2]

Napster ran out of money and filed for bankruptcy in 2002; its assets were bought by Roxio, Inc. Roxio planned to reintroduce Napster as a legitimate fee-based service in 2004. As part of its plans, Roxio also purchased the Pressplay subscription service from Universal and Sony to use it a building block for the new Napster, which will offer pay-per-download and subscription services. Meanwhile, Apple has gone one step further and launched an online music store that allows consumers to buy songs one at a time for under US$1. "The iTunes Music Store is changing the way people buy music," Steve Jobs, Apple's chief executive says in a statement. It "has far surpassed our expectations and clearly illustrates that many customers are hungry for a legal way to acquire their music online."[3]

Will this eliminate copyright violations? That all depends! If other leading producers of file-sharing software, such as Kazaa, Morpheus, and Grokster, adopt a similar business philosophy to that proposed by Napster and Apple, it may.[4] Stay tuned!

Changes such as these are clearly changing the market environment. When firms anticipate these changes and respond to them, this often means the difference between marketing success and failure. This chapter describes how the marketing environment has changed in the past and how it is likely to change in the future.

ENVIRONMENTAL SCANNING IN THE NEW MILLENNIUM

environmental scanning
Process of acquiring information on events outside the organization to identify and interpret potential trends

Changes in the marketing environment are a source of opportunities and threats to be managed. The process of continually acquiring information on events occurring outside the organization to identify and interpret potential trends is called **environmental scanning**.

We scanned the music industry to determine its trends and current situation. Environmental trends typically arise from five sources: social, economic, technological, competitive, and regulatory forces. As shown in Figure 3–1 and described later in this chapter, these forces affect the marketing activities of a firm in numerous ways.

An Environmental Scan of Canada

What trends might affect marketing in the future? A firm conducting an environmental scan of Canada might uncover key trends such as those listed in Figure 3–2 for each of the five environmental factors. Although the list of trends is far from complete, it reveals the breadth of an environmental scan—from population shifts to urban areas, to the growth of wireless messaging, to the emergence of "network corporations." These trends affect consumers and the businesses and nonprofit organizations that serve them. Trends such as these are covered as the five environmental forces are described in the following pages.

FIGURE 3–1

Environmental forces affecting the organization, as well as its suppliers and customers

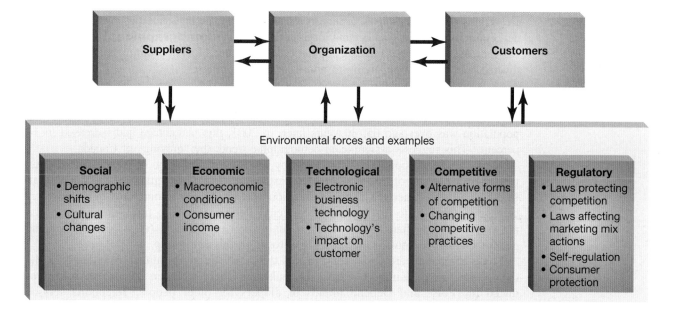

ENVIRONMENTAL FORCE	TREND IDENTIFIED BY AN ENVIRONMENTAL SCAN
Social	• Increasingly multi-ethnic and multi-cultural. • Movement toward healthful products and services. • Growing interest in life balance.
Economic	• Concern about the extent of economic integration and convergence with other countries. • Increase in income and standard of living. • Fluctuating Canadian dollar and uncertainty about economic growth.
Technological	• Increased use of wireless messaging technology. • Declining cost of computers and increasing connectivity. • Advances in biotechnology and medicine.
Competitive	• Working towards staying competitive in the knowledge-based economy. • Market Canada as having very highly skilled workforce. • Challenge to keep brightest and best professionals in Canada, and also attract others.
Regulatory	• Improving business policies and regulations to support innovation. • New legislation related to electronic copyright, intellectual property, and e-mail spam. • Increasing concern for personal privacy and information collection.

FIGURE 3–2

An environmental scan of Canada

social forces
Demographic characteristics, lifestyles, cultural values, and beliefs

demographics
Description of a population according to characteristics such as age, gender, ethnicity, income, and occupation

SOCIAL FORCES

The **social forces** of the environment include the demographic characteristics of the population, as well as consumer lifestyles, cultural values, and beliefs. Changes in these forces can have a dramatic impact on marketing strategy.

Demographics

Describing the population according to selected statistical characteristics such as age, gender, ethnicity, income, and occupation is referred to as **demographics**. The 2001 Census indicates that the Canadian population is growing older, becoming more ethnically diverse, and increasingly living in non-traditional families.[5]

Population Trends   According to the Conference Board of Canada, the Canadian population in 2003 was estimated to be 31.7 million people.[6] In 1971, only 8 percent of the population was over age 65; 30 years later, in 2001, this percentage had increased to 14 percent.[7] This suggests a significant demographic trend: the "greying" of Canada.

Marketers are responding to this trend by focusing attention on households headed by people over the age of 50, as this is the fastest-growing age segment of the population. In 2001, nearly 30 percent of the population was in this age group;[8] by 2026, this percentage is expected to rise to over 40 percent.[9] People over 50 control 75 percent of the net worth of Canadian households.[10] Usually between 55 and 60, a person's income peaks—another reason for marketers to zero in on this age group.

Some companies are responding to this trend with products aimed specifically at the over-50 age group. Kimberly-Clark, the maker of Huggies diapers for babies, has introduced the Poise and Depend brands of diapers for older people. Telephone service providers are marketing products such as emergency dialing mechanisms and amplifiers for phones. Many developers are building retirement communities offering specialized services such as clubhouses, fitness centres, computer labs, and party rooms. Financial

Which population groups are these advertisers trying to reach?

institutions such as the Royal Bank are now offering wealth management services targeted to seniors.

The Baby Boom, Generation X, and Generation Y

baby boomers
Generation of children born between 1946 and 1964

Baby boomers are the main reason for the "greying" of North America. During the baby boom generation—between 1946 and 1964—families had an average of four children; in 2001, this average had dropped to just 1.1 children. [11] The baby boom was a phenomenon that happened in only four countries in the world (United States, Australia, New Zealand, and Canada).

As Canada's nearly 9 million baby boomers have aged,[12] their earnings have increased, giving them significant economic power.[13] The size of this group—comprising 30 percent of the population—makes them a very important component of the Canadian workforce, and a major consumer market. This group accounts for nearly 60 percent of expenditures on consumer goods and services.[14] Baby boomers will continue to be a key force on the consumer landscape as they move into their senior years. Their interests include health, self-image, their children, and their retirement, and they are known to be interested in anything that makes them look and feel younger. Many marketers are targeting goods and services toward them—have you noticed the number of ads for anti-wrinkle creams and cover-the-grey hair dye?

Generation X
Members of the population born between 1965 and 1976

Generation X is the group born after the baby boomers, between 1965 and 1976. In Canada, this generation numbers some 5 million, accounting for 16.5 percent of the population.[15] As consumers, they differ substantially from the baby boomers. Marketers have called Generation X grumpy and not brand loyal! They tend to be self-reliant, entrepreneurial, and well educated. They are less prone to materialism and extravagance than the baby boomers. Their lifestyles are quite different from those of baby boomers, and they prefer different products and services. Generation Xers plan for their financial future and are becoming a key influence on the marketplace.[16]

Generation Y
Canadian born after 1976, the year that many baby boomers began having children

Generation Y members were born between 1977 and 1994.[17] Mostly children of the baby boomers, some marketers refer to them as the baby boomlet, or the echo boom. The 7.2 million of them make up 24 percent of the Canadian population.[18] Music, video-game, sports, and computer purchases are influenced by them. Later in the twenty-first century they will be as influential on the market as their baby-boom parents.

Each of these three generations has very different tastes, consumption patterns, and attitudes. For each generation, marketers develop distinct marketing programs, products, and services that "talk" differently to each group, in a way that speaks to their interests and outlooks.

MARKETING NEWSNET

FINGERS ON THE CANADIAN PULSE

Savvy companies find out what consumers want, what they need, and what they are thinking, so that they can plan their products and services accordingly. "Canadians are bombarded with more information and media than at any other time in history, causing their attitudes, values, and consumer behaviours to change rapidly and sometimes drastically" says Ipsos Canada, the fastest-growing public opinion and market research company in the world. Over 2,000 research studies were completed by the company in 2002, and these studies looked into the perspectives, attitudes, feelings, and behaviours of people in 5 continents and 23 countries. The firm's website, www.ipsos.ca, details many studies and reports; visit the site, follow the "Polls & Research" link, and check out the long list of recent research that examines many aspects of the Canadian psyche. Here are some recent polls. What companies that you know could use information from each of these reports, and how would they make marketing decisions based on the results?

- One in Three (36%) Employed Canadians Keep in Contact with Work When on Vacation
- Ipsos CASH Index: Consumers More Optimistic Than Pessimistic about Their Economic Future
- While Seven in Ten (71%) Canadians Agree Parliament, Not Courts, Should Make Laws in Canada. . .
- Same-Sex Marriage: The Debate Enjoined
- Majority (55%) of Canadians Say Pellet Guns Should Be Banned Outright
- Mail Order Becomes More Important to Prescription Purchasing
- Driving a Better Deal: The Internet Is Changing the Face of Buying Cars in Canada
- Despite the Downturn, the High-Tech Sector Is Still Regarded as a Significant Contributor to the BC Economy

Source: Ipsos Canada, www.ipsos.ca

Figure 3-3 shows the distribution of the population of Canada by age; you can clearly see the size of the baby-boom generation, as well as the relative size of Generation X and Generation Y. In contrast, the population pyramid for Mexico is radically different. Mexico did not have a baby boom, and the country's population overall is much younger than Canada's.

Population Shifts   Canada's people are on the move, and the country is growing, but not as quickly as it has grown in the past. Between 1996 and 2001, the population grew by 1.16 million people, or 4 percent,[19] and most of Canada's growth in the past few years has come from immigration. Compare this growth with other developed countries:

Mexico	8.5%
World	**7.0%**
Australia	5.9%
United States	5.4%
Canada	**4.0%**
France	1.9%
United Kingdom	1.4%
Japan	1.3%
Germany	0.4%
Italy	0.4%[20]

Canada is one of the most urbanized nations in the world. In 2001, 79.4 percent of Canadians lived in a city or town with a population of over 10,000, compared with 78.5 percent five years before—we are increasingly moving to cities! Look at this another way: the urban population of Canada has grown by 5.2 percent between 1996 and 2001, but the rural population has declined by 0.4 percent.[21]

FIGURE 3-3

Comparison of age distribution—Canada and Mexico.

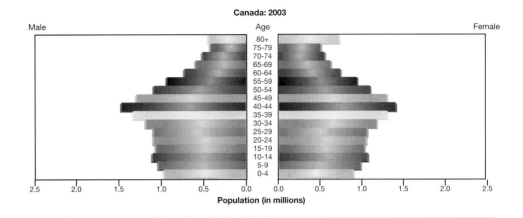

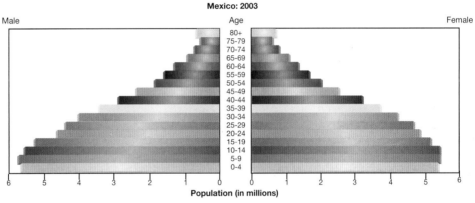

Source: US Census Bureau, International Data Base

Canadian cities are not the huge metropolises that U.S. cities are. We have just four urban areas with a population greater than 1 million people: Toronto, Montreal, Vancouver, and Ottawa-Hull. An interesting thing is happening in our biggest cities: the core municipality in the centre of the city is growing much more slowly than the suburbs around it. Among metropolitan areas with a population of at least 120,000, Calgary is the urban area with the strongest growth, at 15.8 percent over the five-year period of 1996-2001, and Oshawa, adjacent to Toronto, showed the next largest growth at 10.2 percent. Population declined in Sudbury (-6%), Thunder Bay (-3.7%), and five other cities across the country.[22] See Figure 3-4 for metropolitan area growth and decline over the five-year period.

Alberta is the fastest growing province, with an increase of 10.3 percent. Newfoundland lost 7 percent of its population, the largest decline of any province. Overall, the country is six times as large as it was 100 years ago: in 1901 Canada had 5.4 million inhabitants. And Alberta has grown by 40 times its 1901 population.[23]

Ethnic Diversity   Canada has often been called a "mosaic" because of the number of different backgrounds and ethnicities that make up the country's population. Since 1901, 13.4 million immigrants have come to the country, 2.2 million of which came between 1991 and 2001. This makes 18 percent of Canada's population foreign-born; Australia is the only country with a higher proportion of foreign-born residents, at 22 percent. Across the country, the multi-ethnic and multi-cultural picture changes from province to province and from city to city.[24]

Our history books tell us that Canada was founded by two groups, the English and the French; when they came to the country they found it inhabited by aboriginals, or First Nations people. The original ethnicities were these three: now "English" forms 20

FIGURE 3-4

Canadian cities—which ones have grown, which have lost population in the 1996–2001 period

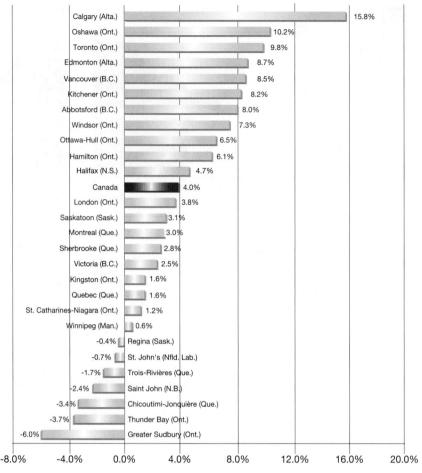

Source: Statistics Canada

percent of the population; French, 16 percent; and First Nations origins, 4.5 percent.[25]

In the early 1900s, most of the immigrants came from Europe; now most come from Asia. More than 200 ethnic groups make up the mosaic of Canada, and they are from all corners of the world. We think of the United States as welcoming immigrants, as well, but only 11 percent of its population is foreign-born.[26] Figure 3-5 shows immigration patterns in Canada between 1901 and 2000.

Where do these immigrants come from? After English and French origins, the next most popular ancestries are Scottish, Irish, German, Italian, Chinese, and Ukrainian.[27] It is difficult for statisticians to analyze ethnic origin. Until the 1996 Census, "Canadian" was not included in the list of ethnic origins respondents had to choose from; people were asked to identify their ethnic background by identifying the origin of ancestors, some of whom may have come to this country decades or centuries ago! Also, there has been a lot of cultural integration in the country—many inter-cultural marriages make identifying ethnic background very complex! If your grandparents on your father's side were from Germany and Holland, and on your mother's side, they were from Japan and China, what ethnicity does that mean you have?

There is another perspective we can take here by looking at *visible minorities*. Canada's Employment Equity Act describes visible minorities as "persons, other than Aboriginal peoples, who are non-Caucasian in race or non-white in colour." The top three visible

FIGURE 3–5

Annual number of immigrants admitted to Canada, 1901-2001

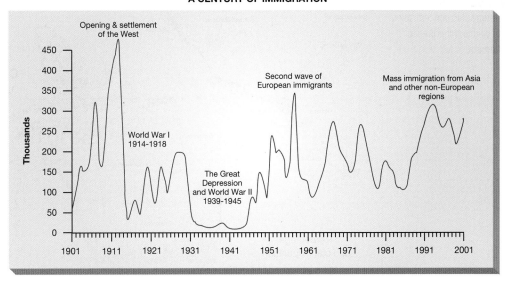

A CENTURY OF IMMIGRATION

Source: Citizenship and Immigration Canada

minority groups in Canada are Chinese, South Asian, and Black. The map in Figure 3-6 shows the concentration of visible minorities across the country.[28]

With so many different origins of people, there are obviously many different languages spoken in Canadian homes: the top five after English and French are Italian, German, Spanish, Chinese (Cantonese), and Punjabi. Have you heard of Pashto or Dogrib? A few thousand homes in this country speak these languages, too. There are over 126 languages spoken in Canada, representing many corners of the world.[29] But that number looks small beside the listing of 6,800 main languages found on www.ethnologue.com!

culture
Set of ideas and values that are learned and shared among the members of a group

Culture

Another social force, **culture**, includes the set of values, ideas, and attitudes that are learned and shared among the members of a group. Canadian culture is unique, and quite different from that of the United States, even though we consider our neighbours to the south to be similar to us in many ways. Many of the elements of culture influence consumer purchase habits, so monitoring cultural trends in Canada is very important in marketing. Culture as it applies to global marketing is discussed further in Chapter 7.

Changing Attitudes, Changing Roles
One of the most notable changes in North America in the past 30 years is the attitudes and roles of men and women in the marketplace. After the baby boomers graduated from high school beginning in the early 1960s, they entered the post-secondary education system in record numbers (some say they grew the system, and grew the suburbs of Canadian metropolitan areas). With education came increased career interest and labour force population. Starting in 1966, like in much of the rest of the developed world, fertility levels declined.[30] As more women entered the workforce and had increasingly more professional careers, they began to play a larger role in the marketplace, and began to exert a powerful voice as consumers. More women in the workforce meant more dual-income families, with increased purchasing power but an increase also in **time poverty**. In Canada, we now have a strong orientation towards gender equality, and women comprise 46 percent of the workforce.[31]

time poverty
Situation where number of tasks is expanding and time to do them is shrinking

Geographic concentration of visible minorities in Canada

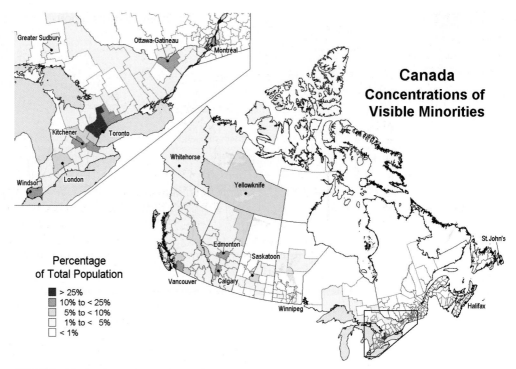

Canada
Concentrations of
Visible Minorities

Percentage
of Total Population

- ■ > 25%
- ▨ 10% to < 25%
- ▢ 5% to < 10%
- ▢ 1% to < 5%
- ▢ < 1%

SOURCE: Statistics Canada 2001 Census of Population Topic Based Tabulation catalogue number 95F0363XCB01001.

Companies have responded to this demographic shift with products designed specifically for each gender. Sporting goods companies are making female-specific products, including golf clubs, hockey skates, and workout gear, and auto manufacturers are targeting promotions towards females, in response to the knowledge that they play a major role in many auto purchase decisions. The financial services, insurance, and health industries are also developing marketing programs based on the individual interests and needs of men and women as consumers.

Canadian Values   Culture also includes values, which may vary with age and with ethnic origin, but tend not to vary by gender. Some social analysts suggest that Canadian culture and values are similar to American culture and values, but looking closer we see that there are very marked differences. Marketers who assume that they can use the same ads in Canada and the U.S. usually find that this is a very unwise idea. While both Americans and Canadians value quality of life and economic success, Americans work towards assimilation of the various peoples within their borders, and Canadians welcome diversity. People on both sides of the border are proud of their country, but Americans tend to display loud, flag-waving nationalism, in contrast to Canadians' quiet support of their country. This is likely what led Molson to create "The Rant," one of the most talked-about ads in recent Canadian history. What made this ad so popular is how different it was than most beer ads, and what a strong message it conveyed about American-Canadian differences.

If you were to describe Canadians to someone not familiar at all with North American society, what words would you use? Adjectives such as individualistic, reserved, hard-working, polite, and cynical come to mind. Think of the Canada "brand" we have created over the past few years through tourism promotion, peacekeeping missions, and international trade activities. Canada has emerged as a nation of trustworthy, worldly, organized, reliable, and conservative citizens. Marketers increasingly study the Canadian way of life and research consumers' perspectives to ensure that they are promoting products and services in a way that will appeal to the unique creature that is a Canadian!

1. Explain the term *time poverty*.

2. What are the marketing implications of ethnic diversity in Canada?

3. How are important values such as health and fitness reflected in the marketplace today?

ECONOMIC FORCES

economy
Income, expenditures, and resources that affect the cost of running a business or a household

The second component of the environmental scan, the **economy**, pertains to the income, expenditures, and resources that affect the cost of running a business or a household. We'll consider two aspects of these economic forces: a macroeconomic view of the economy as a whole, and a microeconomic perspective of consumer income.

Macroeconomic Conditions

Of particular concern at the macroeconomic level is the inflationary or recessionary state of the economy, whether actual or perceived by consumers or businesses. During an inflationary period, the cost to produce and buy products and services gets higher as prices increase. From a marketing standpoint, if prices rise faster than consumer incomes, the number of items consumers can buy decreases. This relationship is evident in the cost of university tuition fees. In 2003–04, undergraduate students in Canada paid an average of $4,025 in tuition fees—more than double the average of $1,464 in 1990–91.[32]

Whereas inflation is a period of price increases, recession is a time of slow economic activity. During recessions, businesses decrease production, unemployment rises, and many consumers have less money to spend. The way in which periods of economic growth are followed by periods of recession is called the *business cycle*. Reviewing Canada's business cycle over the last few years, economic activity slowed in 2000, dropped noticeably in 2001, and actually reported negative growth in the third quarter of that year. Activity picked up again in early 2002 only to fall again later in the year. Higher oil and gas prices led to a surge in oil and gas exploration, residential construction was steady, and both retail and wholesale trades recorded significant gains. However, that growth did not occur across the country, which suggests that Canada's economy is still in a downturn. The good news: Canada's economy still outperformed that of the United States, posting an annualized 2.4 percent increase compared to 1.9 percent for the U.S. in the first quarter of 2003.[33]

Consumer Income

The microeconomic trends in terms of consumer income are also important issues for marketers. Having a product that meets the needs of consumers may be of little value if they are unable to purchase it. A consumer's ability to buy is related to income, which can be viewed in three ways: gross, disposable, and discretionary components.

gross income
Total amount of money made in one year by a person, household, or family unit

Gross Income   The total amount of money made in one year by a person, household, or family unit is referred to as **gross income**. A typical Canadian household earned just over $7,000 in annual income in 1971; by 2000, the average household earned $58,360—an increase of over 800 percent! Prices went up too, so to look at these figures in terms of buying power, a 1970 household would have been earning $33,000, measured in the year 2000's dollars. Let's look at this another way: when gross income is adjusted for inflation, household income has grown 77 percent in the 30 years between 1971 and 2000. Figure 3-7 shows the distribution of annual income across Canadian households.[34]

FIGURE 3–7
Income distribution of
Canadian households, 2002

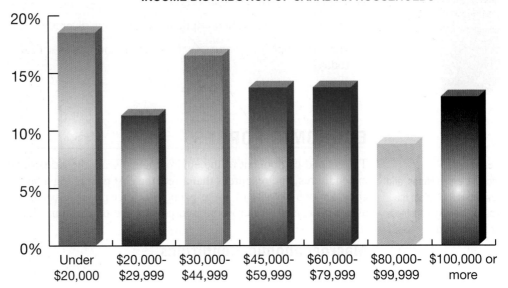

INCOME DISTRIBUTION OF CANADIAN HOUSEHOLDS

Source: Statistics Canada

disposable income
Balance of income left
after paying taxes—used
for spending and savings

Disposable Income　Another measure, **disposable income**, is the money a consumer has left after paying taxes, and is used to pay for necessities such as food, shelter, clothing, and transportation. If taxes rise at a faster rate than income, consumers will have less disposable income. In recent years, tax cuts and productivity have given Canadians more disposable income. Looked at another way, disposable income is a measure of purchasing power, the money consumers have at their disposal to purchase goods and services. When income increases faster than taxes and prices, consumers enjoy more purchasing power.

discretionary income
Money that consumers
have left after paying taxes
and paying for necessities
such as food and shelter—
used for spending on
luxuries and non-essential
items

Discretionary Income　The money that a consumer has left after paying taxes and necessities is called **discretionary income**. This is a smaller measure than disposable income (see Figure 3-8), which includes necessities such as food and shelter. It is not easy to measure discretionary income. Food, for example, is a necessity, but is all food a necessity? You need to eat, but is a 12-ounce steak a necessity? Part of your clothing, too, is a necessity, but the new outfit for Saturday's party is more likely to be a "luxury." Economists have difficulty making an accurate measurement of discretionary income, so there are few statistics in Canada that report it. What is a luxury, and what is a necessity? Often the answers depend on the individual. Discretionary income is used for luxury items such as jewellery or a vacation at a ski resort. Marketers often try to make luxury items more of a "need" than a "want" when communicating with consumers.

TECHNOLOGICAL FORCES

technology
Inventions from applied
science or engineering
research

Our society is in a period of dramatic technological change. **Technology**, a major environmental force, refers to inventions or innovations from applied science or engineering research. A new wave of technology can replace existing products and companies. Do you recognize the items pictured on the next page and what they may replace? Technologies such as satellite dishes, HDTV, and digital cameras are replacing or substituting for existing technologies such as cable, low-resolution TV, and film.[35]

FIGURE 3–8

Three levels of consumer income

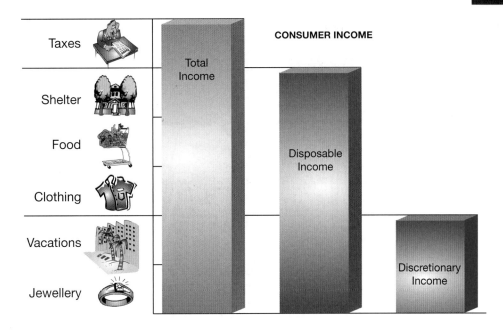

Technology's Impact on Customers

Advances in technology are having important effects on marketing. With prices for technology-based products declining, customers have begun to assess value on the basis of other dimensions such as quality, service, and relationships. When Computer Associates International introduced its software program Simply Money, it gave away the first million copies. Computer Associates reasoned that satisfied customers would later buy upgrades and related products. A similar approach is now used by many cellular telephone vendors, who charge little for the telephone if the purchase leads to a telephone service contract.[36]

Technology also provides value through the development of new products. Automakers now offer customers built-in navigation systems that use satellite signals to help the driver reach any destination. Under development are radarlike collision avoidance systems that disengage cruise control, reduce the engine speed, and even apply the brakes.[37] Other new products likely to be available soon include a "smart ski" with an embedded

Technological change leads to new products. What products might be replaced by these innovations?

Examples of recycling and precycling.

microprocessor that will adjust the flexibility of the ski to snow conditions; injectable health monitors that will send glucose and oxygen levels and other clinical information to a wristwatch-like monitor; and electronic books that will allow you to download any volume and view it on pages coated with electronic "ink" and embedded electrodes.[38]

Technology can also change existing products and the ways they are produced. Many companies are using technological developments to recycle products. Do you recycle your containers? Plastic pop bottles, as well as aluminum cans, are being recycled. According to the Canadian Plastics Industry Association, there is high demand for recycled polyethylene terephthalate (PET), the material used originally to manufacture the bottles. Recycled PET is processed into fibre for carpets, blankets, upholstery, billboard sheeting, and even under-the-hood automotive parts, all of which are growing markets for PET.[39] Recycling has become an industry in its own right. There are even trade magazines dedicated to various sectors of the industry. Another approach is precycling—efforts by manufacturers to reduce waste by decreasing the amount of packaging they use. The development of new packaging materials, for example, has allowed Du Pont to produce a collapsible pouch as an alternative to milk cartons in school lunch programs.[40]

Electronic Business Technologies

The power of technology to transform markets may be best illustrated by the rapid growth of the **marketspace**, an information- and communication-based electronic exchange environment mostly occupied by sophisticated computer and telecommunication technologies and digitized offerings. Activity that uses some form of electronic communication in the inventory, exchange, advertisement, distribution, and payment of goods and services is often called **electronic commerce**. Although e-commerce has existed through private company networks—such as those used to connect ATMs to your bank—for many years, in the mid-1990s, the World Wide Web burst onto the scene and started a new era of *electronic business*. Network technologies are now used for everything from filing expense reports, to monitoring daily sales, to sharing information with employees, to communicating instantly with suppliers.

The most widely visible application of electronic commerce exists in business-to-consumer interactive marketing, involving the Internet, the World Wide Web, and

marketspace
Information- and communication-based electronic exchange environment occupied by digitized offerings

electronic commerce
Activity that uses electronic communication in the marketing of goods or services

commercial online services. Many people view these three as being the same. They are not. The **Internet** is an integrated global network of computers that gives users access to information and documents. The **World Wide Web** is part of the Internet that supports a retrieval system—that is, some kind of browser—which formats information and documents into web pages. **Commercial online services** such as America Online (AOL) offer electronic information and marketing services to subscribers, and charge a monthly fee. The combination of these technologies caused electronic commerce activity to skyrocket to become a multi-billion-dollar industry![41]

Many companies now use Internet-based technology internally to support their electronic business strategies. An **intranet**, for example, is an Internet/Web-based network used within the boundaries of an organization. It is a private Internet that may or may not be connected to the public Internet. **Extranets**, which use Internet-based technologies, permit communication between a company and its suppliers, distributors, and other partners (such as advertising agencies).

COMPETITIVE FORCES

The fourth component of the environmental scan, **competition**, refers to alternative firms that could provide a product to satisfy a specific market's needs. There are various types of competition, and each company must consider its present and potential competitors in designing its marketing strategy. Firms also need to look at direct competitors, for example, Pizza Hut and Domino's, and indirect competitors, such as Kraft Delissio pizza. Sold in grocery stores, Delissio may not look like competition to Pizza Hut and Domino's, but it is, and Kraft is positioning it as such, with the catchy phrase, "It's not delivery. It's Delissio!"

The Four Basic Types of Competition

Figure 3-9 shows the four basic types of competition that form a continuum from perfect competition to monopolistic competition to oligopoly to monopoly.

At one end of the continuum is *perfect competition*, in which there are many sellers with nearly identical products. Companies that deal in commodities—products such as grains, vegetables, or coal—are often in a perfect competition position in which distribution (in the sense of transportation and distribution of products) is important but other elements of marketing have little impact.

At the second point on the continuum is *monopolistic competition*, where a large number of sellers compete with one another by offering customers similar or substitute products. Many of the larger firms compete on the basis of the reputation of their well-known brands, and others compete on price; the rest attempt to differentiate their products and services using some combination of the marketing mix. This is the most common form of competitive environment. The market for jeans is a good example: dominated by major brands such as Levi's and Calvin Klein, there are also dozens of smaller specialty brands (think Guess or Diesel) and lower-priced offerings.

Oligopoly occurs when just a few companies control the majority of industry sales. In Canada, this is the case with gasoline: the major oil companies such as Shell, Petro Canada, Chevron, Esso, and Mohawk dominate the market. Critics of oligopolies suggest that because there are few sellers, price competition among firms is not advisable as such competition can lead to reduced profits for all producers. Consumers tend to take an opposite view: fewer choices means less competition among firms and therefore higher prices to consumers.

The final point of the continuum, *monopoly*, occurs when only one firm sells a product. Monopolies are common for producers of goods and services considered essential to a

Internet
Integrated global network of computers that gives users access to information and documents

World Wide Web
Part of Internet that supports a retrieval system that formats information and documents into web pages

commercial online services
Companies that provide electronic information and marketing services to subscribers

intranet
Internet/Web-based network used within the boundaries of an organization

extranet
Internet-based network that permits communication between a company and its outside partners

competition
Alternative firms that could provide a product to satisfy a specific market's needs

Perfect Competition	**Monopolistic Competition**	**Oligopoly**	**Monopoly**
Many firms, identical products	Many firms, similar products	Few firms	One firm
Example: apple farmers	Example: jeans manufacturers	Example: airlines	Example: local cable service providers

community. This type of market is typically regulated by provincial or federal governments to ensure price protection for consumers in return for preventing direct competition. Common examples include utilities such as cable television and local public transit. There is a trend towards deregulation of many regulated industries, where competition is actively sought. Long distance telephone service was once a monopoly, and now it is closer to monopolistic competition: many firms are selling and reselling long distance service across Canada and internationally. Governments do not like to see unregulated monopolies and actively seek to reduce their control of the market. Microsoft's ongoing challenges from the U.S. government are a good example of this. The U.S. Court of Appeals recently ruled that Microsoft is a monopoly, claiming that its estimated 86 percent share of the PC operating system market has given the company excessive control of the computer and software industries.[42]

The New Look in Canadian Corporations

Canadian corporations are rapidly changing the way they compete. For many managers the common practices that often ensured success in the past won't work any longer. The need to expand beyond the domestic markets, a general increase in the importance of intellectual resources, and the use of Internet technologies as competitive tools have all required changes. Today's organization needs constant change rather than stability, networks rather than hierarchies, and partnerships and alliances rather than self-sufficiency. Canadian corporations are adopting a new business model that consists of small business units, empowered workers with responsibility and accountability, and managers who support rather than control. Increases in productivity come by making the most of individuals' creativity.

How will corporations bring about these changes? One approach utilizes the Web as a management tool and leads to a model called the *network organization* or the *e-corporation*. The Web gives everyone in the organization the ability to access and process information at any time and from any location. In addition, the Web allows employees to manage formal and informal networks of contractors, designers, manufacturers, and distributors. Software developer Ray Ozzie created Lotus Notes to help people quickly spread knowledge and information across organizations. It has been a huge success; more than 68 million users have purchased the product!

Concept Check

1. What is the difference between a consumer's disposable and discretionary income?

2. What is the most common form of competition?

3. What is a network organization?

REGULATORY FORCES

regulation
Restrictions municipal, provincial, and federal laws place on business

For any organization, marketing and broader business decisions are constrained, directed, and influenced by regulatory forces. **Regulation** consists of restrictions that municipal, provincial, and federal laws place on business with regard to its activities. Regulation exists to protect companies as well as consumers. For businesses, much of the regulation has been passed to ensure competition and fair business practices. For consumers, the focus of legislation is to protect them from unfair trade practices and ensure their safety. In some industries, voluntary guidelines are placed on businesses by industry itself.

Federal Regulation

Industry Canada, a department with the Government of Canada, is responsible for overseeing most business practices at the federal level. Here are some of the key organizations and regulations under Industry Canada's jurisdiction.

- *Competition Bureau.* As part of Industry Canada, the Competition Bureau is responsible for administration and enforcement of the *Competition Act*, the *Consumer Packaging and Labelling Act*, the *Textile Labelling Act*, and the *Precious Metals Marking Act*. The bureau's role is to promote and maintain fair competition so that Canadians can benefit from lower prices, product choice, and quality services. Prohibited and anti-competitive marketing practices include: abuse of dominant power, refusal to supply, exclusive dealing, tied-selling, market restriction, consignment selling, delivered pricing, price fixing, price discrimination, predatory pricing, price maintenance, bid-rigging, false or misleading advertising and labelling, and product misrepresentation. Do you know what these terms mean? If not, check them out at www.cb-bc.gc.ca.
- *Office of Consumer Affairs.* The Office of Consumer Affairs is Industry Canada's window to consumers in the marketplace. Its purpose is to ensure a fair and efficient marketplace that supports and advances the interests of Canadians as consumers and to ensure the protection of consumer interests in the event of market failure. The philosophy of the Office of Consumer Affairs is that effective and informed consumer participation in the marketplace is important to a maintaining a dynamic, competitive economy.

  For matters relating to corporations, there was a Bureau of Corporate Affairs, but that has changed. Now activities relating to corporations and how they do business in Canada are spread across various ministries and departments within the federal government. One example of a corporate regulatory body is the *Canadian Intellectual Property Office (CIPO)*, an agency associated with Industry Canada that is responsible for the administration and processing of most of the intellectual property regulation in Canada. CIPO's areas of activity include patents for new inventions (process, machine, manufacture, composition of matter), or for any new and useful improvement of an existing invention, and trademarks, words, symbols, or designs (or a combination of these) used to distinguish the wares or services of one person or organization from those of others in the marketplace. Other services for companies include financial, marketing, trade, export, and many others. Industry Canada's Strategis website (www.strategis.ic.gc.ca) has details; look for the wealth of services and information it provides.

FIGURE 3-10

Major federal legislation
designed to protect
competition and consumers

Bank Cost Borrowing Act	Hazardous Products Act
Bankruptcy Act	Income Tax Act
Bills of Exchange Act	Industrial Design Act
Board of Trade Act	Maple Products Industry Act
Broadcasting Act	Motor Vehicle Safety Act
Canada Agricultural Products	Offical Languages Act
Standards Act	Patent Act
Canada Cooperative Association Act	Personal Information and Electronic
Canada Corporations Act	Documents Act
Canada Dairy Products Act	Precious Metals Marketing Act
Canadian Human Rights Act	Privacy Act
Competition Act	Small Loans Act
Consumer Packaging and Labelling Act	Standards Council of Canada Act
Copyright Act	Textile Labelling Act
Criminal Code	The Interest Act
Department of Consumer and	Timber Marketing Act
Corporate Affairs Act	Trade-Marks Act
Electricity Inspection Act and Gas	True Labelling Act
Inspection Act	Weights and Measures Act
Fish Inspection Act	Winding-up Act
Food and Drugs Act	

The explosive growth in communications, and in particular new media and associated businesses, has created an expanded role for the *Canadian Radio-television and Telecommunications Commission (CRTC)*, another player in the legislative system. In addition to administering the Broadcast and Telecommunications acts, the CRTC has a role in more than ownership and licensing. Its mandate now covers programming content and even advertising content for commercial beverages. The CRTC is currently under the direction of the Ministry of Canadian Heritage.

Figure 3-10 lists the most significant federal regulation that protects competition and consumers in Canada.

Other Regulation

In addition to federal regulation, there is additional regulation at the provincial and municipal government levels, and it varies by jurisdiction. Every province is different in some way, and most municipalities have basic regulations covering such things as retail operating hours and outdoor advertising. For companies doing business outside of Canada, aside from regulation in Canada, they also have to contend with a myriad of international and local laws and regulations in every country in which they do business.

Self-Regulation

self-regulation
Alternative to government
control where an industry
attempts to police itself

An alternative to governmental regulation is **self-regulation**, where industries attempt to police member firms themselves. Examples of this include:

- *Advertising Standards Canada*. Representing advertisers and agencies, this organization has established a Canadian Code of Advertising Standards for its members to follow. The code addresses issues such as guidelines for comparative advertising, accuracy and clarity of price claims in advertisements, and advertising to children.

ETHICS AND SOCIAL RESPONSIBILITY ALERT
ALL IS NOT RIGHT WITH TELEMARKETING

Telemarketing does not have a good image with most consumers. In fact, survey after survey shows that the majority of consumers believe telemarketing is an invasion of privacy, an offensive way to market, and a waste of the consumer's time. Why are many Canadians turned off by telemarketers? In some cases, there are telemarketers who engage in illegal and deceptive practices as well as unethical behaviour. For example, take the case of a telemarketing company that phones consumers and tells them they have won prizes. The consumers are then asked to pay the shipping and handling costs for the prizes, the cost of which greatly exceeds the real costs of shipping and handling as well as the value of the prize.

In another case, consider telemarketing company representatives who lead consumers to believe they are volunteers requesting donations for a charity, but in fact are paid fundraisers who are working on commission. What about a telemarketer who uses a telemail program where a consumer receives a direct-mail piece and is asked to phone a toll-free number for further information? Unknown to the consumer, the telemarketer uses an automatic number identification or caller ID intrusion system that identifies the incoming caller's number without their knowledge or consent. If the consumer does not buy the product or service initially, the company now has the consumer's telephone number and begins recalling the consumer in an attempt to sell them. The telemarketer also has an opportunity to capture and sell consumers' unlisted telephone numbers.

In many cases, there are telemarketers who are simply guilty of deception, legally; in other cases they engage in unethical, but perhaps not illegal, practices. This has tarnished the image of not only reputable telemarketers but also all other professional marketers. Do you have any personal experiences with a telemarketer who has engaged in an illegal or unethical practice? What can be done about these unethical telemarketers?

- *Canadian Marketing Association (CMA).* Representing companies involved in direct marketing in Canada, it has established standards that its members must follow in matters relating to consumer privacy. Recently CMA has moved beyond simply offering guidelines on how to honour consumer "do not contact" requests, and now offers a service direct to consumers allowing them to add their names to the "do not contact" list, a list that CMA's members must respect.
- *Better Business Bureau (BBB).* The BBB is a voluntary alliance of businesses whose members are committed to be fair and honest in their dealings, to promote self-regulatory practices, and to collect and dispense information to help businesses and consumers make sound decisions. The BBB provides an extensive selection of services to its members, businesses, and the public at large, and operates at the local, provincial, and national levels, as well as through international affiliations. Have you heard of them? You can see their activities and services at www.bbb.org; there may be a local office in your area.

Is self-regulation working? Possibly, but one thing is certain—if society does not think it is effective, pressure will be exerted on governments to enact appropriate regulation. If it works, it can be more powerful than regulation, as people and companies feel a responsibility towards making it work!

Consumerism

Governments and industry are working to protect the interests of consumers. And, since the early 1960s, consumers have been taking action on their own. Back then, consumers

consumerism
A grassroots movement started in the 1960s to increase the influence, power, and rights of consumers in dealing with institutions

organized to reinforce their rights when dealing with organizations and businesses. The movement, known as **consumerism**, gained momentum and was instrumental in bringing about much of the regulation presently in effect. Today we see such organizations as the Consumers Association of Canada (CAC), the largest consumer group in Canada, working to advance the cause of consumerism. They are an important consumer voice.

Concept Check

1. What role does the Canadian Radio-television and Telecommunications Commission (CRTC) play in Canadian marketing regulation?
2. Why was the consumerism movement important?
3. Does self-regulation work? Why or why not?

SUMMARY

1 Environmental scanning involves collecting and analyzing information on the business scene to find out what opportunities and threats may affect an organization. Social forces, economic forces, technology, competition, and regulation are the most common and useful areas to scan.

2 Like the population of many industrialized nations, the population of Canada is aging. The baby boomers, a large generation with significant market power, were followed by Generation X and then Generation Y, all important target markets with different needs and interests.

3 The country is increasingly more multi-cultural and multi-ethnic, and population growth is generated more by immigration than by traditional growth. Many marketers are developing marketing initiatives with an ethnic flavour.

4 Culture incorporates values, ideas, and attitudes. Canadian culture is distinct, and global firms must be careful not to treat Canadians like their neighbours to the south. Canadian values include honesty, integrity, health, and safety.

5 Disposable income is the number of dollars left after taxes, and it has increased over the past 30 years. Discretionary income is the money that consumers have left after spending on their necessities. The average Canadian household income has increased over 75 percent in the past 30 years in terms of real income.

6 The Canadian economy has fared better than the U.S. economy in the past two years, but it is not as robust as economists and business leaders would like to see.

7 Technology has made major advances in the recent past, and customers have benefited through reduced prices, new products, and product improvements. Electronic business technologies now facilitate improved communication with customers, employees, and suppliers, a major development for marketers.

8 The Internet has had a huge impact on consumers and corporations. Some companies now use the Web as a management tool and have become "network organizations." E-commerce is changing the way people purchase goods and services.

9 Regulations and laws protect marketers, corporations, and consumers. Federal, provincial, and municipal authorities all play a role in setting regulations, depending on the nature of the marketing issue.

10 Self-regulation, where an industry sets guidelines and monitors its members' adherence to them, is an additional way in which Canadian marketers and consumers are protected.

11 Competition exists in different forms, depending on the nature of the product or service: perfect competition exists where many sellers have identical products; monopolistic competition is the most frequent form, with many sellers producing different products; oligopoly is a market with few sellers and very similar products but high barriers to entry into the industry; and monopoly occurs when there is one seller only, usually regulated by government to ensure that prices are kept fair and reasonable.

KEY TERMS AND CONCEPTS

baby boomers p. 55
commercial online services p. 65
competition p. 65
consumerism p. 70
culture p. 59
demographics p. 54
discretionary income p. 62
disposable income p. 62
economy p. 61
electronic commerce p. 64
environmental scanning p. 53
extranet p. 65

Generation X p. 55
Generation Y p. 55
gross income p. 61
Internet p. 65
intranet p. 65
marketspace p. 64
regulation p. 67
self-regulation p. 69
social forces p. 54
technology p. 62
time poverty p. 59
World Wide Web p. 65

QUESTIONS: APPLYING MARKETING CONCEPTS AND PERSPECTIVES

1 Sun-Rype Products Ltd. is Western Canada's largest producer of fruit juices. Conduct an environmental scan for them and identify three trends or factors that may significantly affect this company's future business, and then propose how Sun-Rype could respond to these changes.
2 Describe the features you would add to an automobile designed for the Generation Y market. What advertising media would you use to appeal to this target market?
3 New technologies are continuously improving and replacing existing products. Suggest how the following organizations and their products may be affected by the Internet and digital technologies: (a) Kodak cameras and film, (b) Air Canada, and (c) the National Arts Centre in Ottawa.
4 In recent years in the Canadian brewing industry, a couple of large firms that have historically had most of the beer sales

(Labatt and Molson) have faced competition from many small regional brands and microbreweries. Where would you place the brewing industry on the continuum of competition? What environmental forces and trends would help explain this increased competition?
5 When the Canadian long-distance telephone industry was deregulated, how do you think the role of marketing for those firms in the industry changed? How would each component of the marketing mix change and why?
6 One of the world's largest producers of baby and children's furniture, storkcraft baby has been in business for more than 50 years. With the recent population and age shifts in North America, how may this Canadian firm view the opportunities and threats for the future?

DISCUSSION FORUM

Do you have a digital camera? Have you thought about the impact of technology on traditional photography companies? Visit the corporate site of Polaroid (www.polaroid.com) and review its current crop of consumer and business products and services.

1 What do you think the future holds for the company? Why do you think this way?
2 If you were the chief executive officer (CEO) of Polaroid, how would you approach strategic planning for your global company?

INTERNET EXERCISE

Many sources of information, available through the Internet, could be useful in doing an environmental scan. In fact, there are often too many sources, and the trick is to find the best ones with the information you need. The Government of Canada is an excellent source of information. Strategis is a site provided by Industry Canada; its purpose is to "harness the power of the Internet to provide business and consumer information to all Canadians without the constraints of time and geography."

www.mcgrawhill.ca/college/thecore

Check out this site at www.strategis.ic.gc.ca and use it to answer these questions:

1 What is the current population of Canada?
2 What is a patent?
3 What monthly economic indicators are used to measure Canada's performance?
4 What are the key steps for starting up a business in Canada?

VIDEO CASE 3

FLYTE TYME PRODUCTIONS, INC.: THE BEST IDEA WINS!

"Terry was looking for a keyboard player to be in the band he was just starting," remembers Jimmy Jam of Flyte Tyme Productions, Inc. "I had sort of rebelled because I had first thought of myself as a drummer," says Jam. But after he listened and heard how good the drummer was, he told Terry, "I'll be the keyboard player."

The conversation took place a few weeks after Terry Lewis and Jimmy Jam met at a summer math program for gifted junior high school students, sponsored by a local university. The two came to prominence in the early 1980s as members of the funk band "The Time" that appeared as the opener on many of Prince's early tours. The pair still credit Prince for much of their tenacious work ethic and eclectic musical tastes. After leaving the band, Terry and Jimmy started a music production company—Flyte Tyme—creating the new name by adapting the old one. Now in their early 40s, the two have worked together for 20 years, most of it in Flyte Tyme Productions (www.flytetyme.com), where their clients include Mary J. Blige, Boyz II Men, Mariah Carey, Janet Jackson, Michael Jackson, Patti LaBelle, Usher, TLC, and many others.

THE MUSIC

Sunglasses, fedoras, and sharp suits are Jam and Lewis's signature image, but—curiously—they have no signature sound. Instead, their approach is to tailor tunes for each artist. Janet Jackson's steamy bedroom ballads don't sound anything like Patti LaBelle's big Diane Warren ballads. They also work in a wide variety of music genres—from gospel (Yolanda Adams) and reggae (Shaggy) to jazz (Herb Alpert) and pop (Mariah Carey).

Flyte Tyme's successes are impressive. Recently they produced Usher's No. 1 pop hit "U Remind Me," which held the top spot on the charts for four weeks. They also produced Sting's Oscar-nominated song "My Funny Friend and Me" for the film *The Emperor's New Groove*. And their work on Hikaru Utada's album helped it climb to the top of Japan's pop charts, selling 4 million copies in two weeks!

These and other hits put Flyte Tyme in extraordinary company. Having produced 16 No. 1 singles on *Billboard's* pop chart, they are second only to the producer for the Beatles (with 23) and tied with the producer for Elvis Presley. Flyte Tyme has managed to stay at the top throughout the 1980s, 1990s, and 2000s, thanks in large part to Janet Jackson, who

accounts for 10 of their 16 No. 1 songs. Recently, they wrote and produced their fifth successive album for Janet Jackson, which set an industry record when "All For You" became the first single to be played by 100 percent of the pop, R&B, and rhythm radio stations reporting to trade publication Radio & Records, in the first week after its release.

THE TEAM AND ITS FORMULA FOR SUCCESS

How have Jam and Lewis stayed at the top of the music game so long? Janet Jackson's answer: "There are no egos involved." Terry Lewis echoes this and says about his relationship with Jam: "He's the best partner a person could have. We've never had a contract—we've never had one argument in twenty-something years, not saying we don't disagree about things but our attitudes are the best idea wins. Not the right, not the wrong, but the *best*!"

"What we try to do is get everybody relaxed—check the egos at the door, that kind of thing. We find that we do it a lot more with new artists than with the older, more established artists," explains Jam. "Psychology is a big part of producing. Some artists like to work right away, others like to play pool, have lunch, talk on the phone, then they mosey in and record," he says. "If you think of Janet Jackson or Mariah Carey—the people who you would think of as superstars, you would think that they would bring a superstar ego with them. But it's almost the opposite," says Jam. "New artists often come to Flyte Tyme with a feeling they have to prove something. And what happens is, you don't really get a natural performance," says Jam.

Another of Flyte Tyme's special strengths: adapting the music and lyrics to an artist's unique talents, not the other way around. Their interest in many types of music and their experience with many artists allow them to add new ideas to the creative process. Still, Flyte Tyme may work on several different versions based on its perceptions of what radio stations or MTV will play.

Jam and Lewis work on both the music and lyrics for many of their songs, but Jam leans slightly more toward the melodies and Lewis toward the vocals and lyrics. In fact, Lewis keeps "The Book of Titles," and any time someone says something clever or in an interesting way it goes into the book. "Music is the soundtrack of life," says Lewis. "The inspiration for words I just take from watching people, and life has a lot of verses in it," he adds.

MARKETING, DISTRIBUTION, COMPETITION

Selecting the best music ideas requires an instinct to find the right blend of art and business. The elements of the art include a huge respect for and understanding of the artists, an interest in a broad palette of musical sounds, and a good ear for melodies and vocals. The business components of their formula include understanding many of the factors—such as marketing, distribution, and competition—that influence their business.

Music artists walking in the door of Flyte Tyme receive an array of services: a studio facility with Jam, Lewis, and an experienced staff providing ideas, direction, and focus—"trying to get things out of them they didn't know they had in them," says Lewis. Flyte Tyme Records, the marketing arm, develops the artist's image, the marketing plan, advertising, and distribution—everything to get the record or CD on the rack to be sold. "If you have $100,000 to spend on promotion, you can

do a nice music video and then you can spend a lot of time trying to get it played on MTV or BET or VH1 or any of the appropriate video channels," says Jam. Or sometimes the music calls for a different strategy, Flyte Tyme's "groundhog approach." For example, in the early 1990s with one of its bands, Flyte Tyme piled the band in a Winnebago and hit university campuses.

Today Flyte Tyme creates a lot of that same groundhog buzz with its website, where the music audience can learn about Flyte Tyme's artists and activities. Jam and Lewis note that Napster was a great tool in exposing music to the public. The delivery system—buying an album at a retail store, downloading music from the Internet, or burning a CD—doesn't affect the process of Flyte Tyme's making the music in its studio. But Lewis and Jam are concerned that the people who write the songs and the artists who deliver them get compensated fairly. "The record companies and everybody will eventually work it out," says Jam. "They have to because it's too valuable a commodity not to."

Questions

1 Based on the case information and what you know about today's music industry, conduct an environmental scan for Flyte Tyme to identify key trends. For each of the five environmental forces (social, economic, technological, competitive, and regulatory), identify trends likely to influence it in the near future.

2 Compared to many start-up businesses—80 percent of which fail within five years—what reasons explain Flyte Tyme's continuing success?

3 What marketing factors and actions must Jimmy Jam and Terry Lewis consider in developing music *(a)* for a new, unknown artist and *(b)* an established artist like Janet Jackson?

4 What promotional and distribution strategies should Flyte Tyme use to get its music in front of prospective buyers?

Chapter 4

Ethics and Social Responsibility in Marketing

AFTER READING THIS CHAPTER YOU SHOULD BE ABLE TO:

- Understand the nature and significance of ethics in marketing.

- Comprehend the differences between legal and ethical behaviour in marketing.

- Describe factors that influence ethical and unethical marketing decisions.

- Distinguish among the different concepts of ethics and social responsibility.

BANKING ON BEING A GOOD CORPORATE CITIZEN

In an industry where record profits are commonplace and competing against the handful of major Canadian banks is a monumental challenge, how does a credit union make its mark? For VanCity, Canada's largest credit union, the answer is social responsibility.

From its beginnings in Vancouver in 1946, values have always been a key guiding light for the organization, and they are known for operating with a strong commitment to members, staff, the community, and the environment. In 2000, VanCity created a "Statement of Values and Commitments" to communicate its values to all stakeholders, and to ensure that those values and commitments are upheld as the credit union evolves. The statement was developed by involving members, staff, advisors, and community representatives. To ensure that the values and commitments are followed, VanCity engages an outside firm to undertake a social audit, in which all of their social responsibility practices and activities are evaluated against the goals and values set out. What makes up these values? Offering products and services that are socially and environmentally responsible, investing in the well-being of the communities they serve, adopting socially and environmentally responsible business practices, and promoting social and environmental responsibility in the world around them.

When we think of social responsibility, we usually think of sponsoring events or donating money to non-profit or charitable organizations. VanCity takes this much further! The idea begins right inside the walls of their offices, striving to make the credit union a great place to work and taking responsibility toward their members very seriously. Community programs are available, including grants, student awards, disaster fund donations, the VanCity Theatre, and a staff fundraising program where the staff decides where their efforts will be focused, and they then work to raise funds for this specific organization. Community investments are another key vehicle for living out community commitments—VanCity created programs for small businesses, initiatives for entrepreneurs with disabilities, affordable housing, and financing

WHERE IN THE MARKETING PROCESS ARE WE GOING IN THIS CHAPTER?

Ethics, the topic of Chapter 4, forms part of a firm's business vision, affects key groups, and is impacted by the social environment.

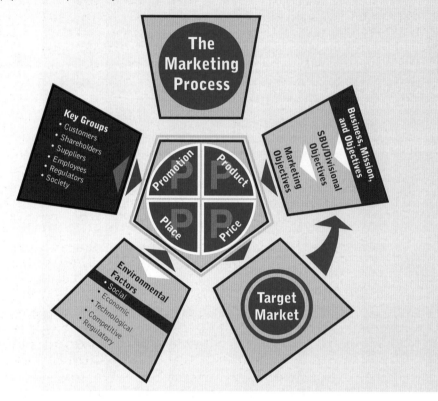

in areas that will impact the environment. Are you in the market for a hybrid car? VanCity provides a loan with 0 percent financing for a clean air car! And that's not all—socially responsible investing options allow a member to invest in companies or funds that have "socially acceptable practices."

VanCity has won a number of awards for its pioneering work in social responsibility, and the credit union has become a leader not only in Canada but also internationally. Representatives of VanCity have been invited to countries and forums around the world to talk about the credit union's social audit process and corporate social responsibility activities.

With values such as integrity, innovation, and responsibility, and a commitment to live by them and to be a positive force in their community, VanCity has set the bar high, and emerged as an ethical and moral leader.[1]

ethics
Moral principles and values that govern the actions and decisions of an individual or a group

NATURE AND SIGNIFICANCE OF MARKETING ETHICS

Ethics are the moral principles and values that govern the actions and decisions of an individual or group. They serve as guidelines on how to act rightly and justly when faced with moral dilemmas.

Ethical/Legal Judgment in Marketing

A good starting point for understanding the nature and significance of ethics is the distinction between legality and ethicality in marketing decisions. Whereas ethics deal with personal moral principles and values, **laws** are based on society's values and standards and are enforceable in the courts. This distinction can sometimes lead to the rationalization that if a behaviour is within legal limits, then it is not really unethical. When a recent survey asked the question, "Is it OK to get around the law if you don't actually break it?" 61 percent of businesspeople who took part responded yes.[2] How would you answer this question?

There are numerous situations in which judgment plays a large role in defining ethical and legal boundaries. Consider the following situations.[3]

laws
Society's standards and values that are enforceable in court

1. At Montreal's Sainte-Justine Children's Hospital, a surgeon who was HIV-positive performed over 2,000 operations between 1990 and 2003. Although the surgeon's supervisor and a committee of doctors were aware of her condition, the hospital's administration was not, nor were the parents of the children she operated on. In January of 2004, parents were contacted by the hospital and asked for the children to be tested for the virus that causes AIDS. Although the risk of a patient becoming infected in this situation is slim, many feel that the doctor's condition should have been made known to her colleagues and patients.[4]

2. The manager for new product development for a large manufacturer of packaged food products commissioned a market research firm to undertake a study to solicit consumers' opinions on three new products they were considering launching. All of the research suggested that there was no real consumer interest in the products, and consumers would not consider switching from their current product to the company's new offerings. The product manager did not circulate the results of the survey to senior management; he decided that the research was inconclusive and proceeded to develop the products further without additional consumer information or perspectives.

3. Chaperones on a trip to Europe had 24 young people aged 14 to 17 in their care. When they arrived in Germany and the students wanted to go to a pub and drink beer, they allowed them to do so and went with them. All the students were under the legal drinking age in Canada, and some of them were under the legal drinking age in Germany, although they were informed that it was not strictly illegal for them to drink beer in a pub if accompanied by an adult. The parents of the students involved had not been consulted on the topic of drinking when other trip topics were discussed.

Would you be able to determine whether these situations are clearly ethical and legal or unethical and illegal? Probably not. As you read further in this chapter, you will be asked to consider other ethical dilemmas.

Current Perceptions of Ethical Behaviour

There has been a public outcry about the ethical practices of businesspeople.[5] A recent survey undertaken by Global TV, *Maclean's*, and the *Calgary Herald* showed that 67 percent of Canadians felt that recent issues involving ethical problems within large companies created a problem in which they felt that many business executives were taking advantage of the system. Two-thirds of Canadians blame recent stock scandals on business executives, and 45 percent of the population now have a "more negative" view of business. This suggests that Canadians' faith in their business world has been seriously shaken by scandals and breaches of ethics.[6]

This feeling is not restricted to business. A poll taken in early 2002 shows that most Canadians have lost faith in government: 68 percent suggested that the federal government is "highly or somewhat corrupt," and similar sentiments were expressed for provincial and municipal levels of government.[7]

There are at least three possible reasons the state of perceived ethical business conduct is at its present level. First, there is increased pressure on businesspeople to make decisions in a society characterized by diverse value systems. Second, there is a growing tendency for business decisions to be judged publicly by groups with different values and interests. Finally, and most disturbing, ethical business conduct may have declined.

Concept Check

1. What are ethics?

2. What are three possible reasons for the present state of ethical conduct in Canada?

UNDERSTANDING ETHICAL MARKETING BEHAVIOUR

Researchers have identified numerous factors that influence ethical marketing behaviour. Figure 4–1 presents a framework that shows these factors and their relationships.

Societal Culture and Norms

Culture refers to the set of values, ideas, and attitudes that are learned and shared among the members of a group. Culture serves as a socializing force that determines what is considered by the group to be morally right and just. This means that moral standards can be different in different cultures. Sometimes differences in moral standards, particularly between societies with different cultures, can create moral dilemmas. Consider the example of a Canadian firm that manufactures heavy equipment and sells it all over the world, using agents to represent the company in every continent. The agent for South America wanted money built into his budget to enable him to pay purchasing managers a "commission" when a sale was made. The Canadian firm saw these "commissions" as bribes or under-the-table payments, but the agent felt they were necessary to secure the business in the South American countries where he was doing business. What is common practice in some countries is clearly unethical in Canada. Check out these two websites— EthicsWeb at www.ethicsweb.ca and EthicsCentre CA at www.ethicscentre.ca—for a perspective on ethical principles and issues in Canada.

Canadians are often viewed internationally as having high standards of ethics. Increasingly, it is a topic that is given more importance in companies today. Many companies have

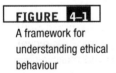

FIGURE 4–1

A framework for understanding ethical behaviour

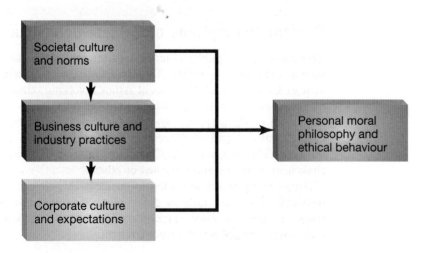

MARKETING NEWSNET

Technology & E-commerce

GLOBAL SOFTWARE PIRACY

By 2005, the Internet will link an estimated 1.17 billion Internet users worldwide. The many benefits of the Internet often overshadow its dark side: software piracy. The explosive growth of the Internet is making piracy easy, because pirated copies of software can be distributed and downloaded quickly and globally, with the click of a mouse. The Business Software Alliance (BSA), an international organization whose mandate is to "promote global policies that foster innovation, growth, and a competitive marketplace for commercial software and related technologies,"[1] reported in a 2003 study that 39 percent of the world's software is pirated. This amounts to a loss worldwide of more than US$13 billion.[2] Piracy means lost jobs, wages, tax revenues, and a potential barrier to success for software start-up companies around the globe.

Software piracy has become pandemic in many countries. According to BSA estimates, 71 percent of the software in eastern Europe is pirated, followed by a piracy rate of 60 percent in the Middle East and 59 percent in Africa and Latin America. Countries with the highest piracy rates are Vietnam (95 percent), China (92 percent), Russia (89 percent), and Indonesia (89 percent). By comparison, the piracy rate in the United States is 25 percent and Canada, 41 percent.

[1] www.bsa.org/usa/index.cfm.

[2] *Eighth Annual BSA Global Software Piracy Study: Trends in Software Piracy 1994–2002*, Business Software Alliance, June 2003.

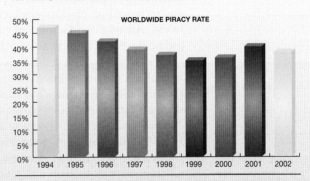

WORLDWIDE PIRACY RATE

Source: *Eighth Annual BSA Global Software Piracy Study: Trends in Software Piracy 1994-2002*, Business Software Alliance, June 2003.

---

a written code of ethics that employees are asked to read and sign. Misleading advertising, price-fixing, and deceptive practices such as telemarketing scams are considered to be wrong.

Societal values also affect ethical and legal relationships among individuals, groups, and the institutions and organizations they create. Consider the use of another's ideas, copyright, trademark, or patent. These are viewed as intellectual property, and unauthorized use is deemed unethical and illegal in Canada. However, this is not the case in some other countries.[8] In Korea, for instance, copying is partly rooted in its society's culture. According to a North American trade official, many Koreans "have the idea that the thoughts of one man should benefit all," and the Korean government rarely prosecutes infringements. One estimate suggests that the unauthorized use of intellectual property in global markets costs US$250 billion annually in lost revenue.

Copyright infringement in the global software industry is particularly widespread with the explosive growth of the Internet. Copies of software can be distributed and downloaded quickly and globally, with the click of a mouse. Read the accompanying Marketing NewsNet to find out where the unauthorized use of business software is most prevalent.[9]

Business Culture and Industry Practices

Societal culture provides a foundation for understanding moral behaviour in business activities. *Business culture* consists of "the effective rules of the game, the boundaries between competitive and unethical behaviour, [and] the codes of conduct in business dealings."[10] These may vary from industry to industry. However, consumers have seen many cases across many different industries where business culture has led to unethical and illegal practices. Recent and spectacular cases of fraudulent accounting, unfair market manipulation, and insider dealings within upper management are just some examples. Business culture affects ethical conduct both in the exchange relationship between sellers and buyers and in the competitive behaviour among sellers.

Ethics of Exchange

The exchange process is central to the marketing concept. Ethical exchanges between sellers and buyers should result in both parties being better off after a transaction.

Prior to the 1960s, most Canadian business culture believed in the legal concept of *caveat emptor*, which means "let the buyer beware." In other words, it was the responsibility of the buyer, not the seller, to ensure the quality of a purchase. As life became more complex for the Canadian consumer, and consumerism brought consumer rights and concerns to the forefront, it became clear that *caveat emptor* was no longer an acceptable way of thinking. Over the past 40 years, many new products appeared on the market; technology continued to develop at a rapid pace, becoming a factor in many products; and increased globalization meant that consumers buy products from every corner of the world. All of these factors led to the need to create laws and practices, and to consider the interests of consumers in a different light.

A wide variety of legislation has been developed to assist and protect the consumer. Both federal and provincial governments hold responsibility for consumer protection. The federal responsibility covers national standards for the marketplace and strives to ensure that fairness, efficiency. and competition are maintained. Federal legislation covers product safety, competition, labelling, and measures, and also regulates banking and telecommunications. In 1985, the Canadian government passed the federal Competition Act, which covers "misleading advertising, deceptive telemarketing, and multi-level marketing and pyramid schemes, as well as such competition issues as price discrimination and predatory pricing." The federal Hazardous Products Act provides national safety standards for many consumer products; drugs, medical supplies, cosmetics, and automobiles are also covered under special legislation.[11]

Provincial and territorial governments play a major role in consumer protection. They have legislation to cover most consumer services, transaction- and sales-of-goods issues, and unfair business practices. While each province and territory has its own laws, the protections they provide for consumers are generally very similar.

Some of the basic consumer rights that Canadian legislation covers include:

- *Right to safety.* Goods and services should not be hazardous or dangerous.
- *Right to be informed.* Consumers should have accurate and complete information about products and services.
- *Right to be heard.* There should be avenues where consumers can express viewpoints or present issues of consumer interest.
- *Right to redress.* There should be processes for consumers to remedy a situation where goods and services are unsatisfactory or do not live up to expectations.
- *Right to choose.* Consumers should have access to a variety of products and services, and not be restricted by too few competitors.
- *Right to consumer education.* Consumers should be able to access information to allow them to participate effectively in the marketplace.
- *Right to a sustainable environment.* There should be protections for resources and sur- roundings.[12]

Even the best efforts to make sure products are safe cannot foresee every possibility. Mattel's experience with its Cabbage Patch Snacktime Kids doll is a case in point.[13] The doll was designed to "eat" plastic french fries, celery, and other tidbits by drawing them into its motorized mouth. Despite exhaustive laboratory and in-home testing, Mattel executives did not consider that a child's hair might get caught in the doll's mouth and

Privacy legislation works to protect your privacy in the worlds of e-mail and the Internet.

cause harm. It did! Mattel immediately informed buyers of the safety issue, pulled the dolls from store shelves, refunded buyers, and discontinued the product.

Ethics of Competition   Business culture also affects ethical behaviour in competition with other businesses. Two kinds of unethical behaviour are most common: economic espionage and bribery.

Economic espionage involves the collection of trade secrets or proprietary information from a company's competitors. This practice is illegal and unethical and carries serious criminal penalties for the offending individual or business. Espionage activities include trespassing, theft, fraud, misrepresentation, wiretapping, the search of a competitor's trash, and violations of employment agreements with noncompete clauses. About 50 percent of large U.S. and Canadian firms have uncovered espionage in some form, costing them more than $100 billion annually in lost sales.

Economic espionage is most prevalent in high-technology industries such as electronics, specialty chemicals, industrial equipment, aerospace, and pharmaceuticals, where technical know-how and trade secrets separate industry leaders from followers. But espionage can occur anywhere—even in the ready-to-eat cookie industry! Procter & Gamble charged that competitors photographed its plants and production lines, stole a sample of its cookie dough, and infiltrated a confidential sales presentation to learn about its technology, recipe, and marketing plan. The competitors paid Procter & Gamble $120 million in damages after a lengthy dispute.[14]

Offering or accepting a bribe or kickback is also considered unethical behaviour in Canadian business culture. Bribes (where the money is paid before the exchange occurs) or kickbacks (where the money is paid afterward) are often disguised as gifts, consultant fees, and favours. This practice is more common in business-to-business and government marketing than in consumer marketing.

In general, bribery is most evident in industries experiencing intense competition and in countries in earlier stages of economic development. According to a recent United Nations' study, 15 percent of all companies in industrialized countries have to pay bribes to win or retain business. In Asia, this figure is 40 percent. In countries of the former Soviet Union, 60 percent of all companies must pay bribes to do business! A recent poll of senior executives engaged in global marketing revealed that Cameroon and Nigeria were the most likely countries to use bribery to win or retain business. Denmark and Finland were the least likely.[15]

Corporate Culture and Expectations

A third influence on ethical practices is corporate culture. Corporate culture reflects the shared values, beliefs, and purpose of employees that affect individual and group behaviour. The culture of a company demonstrates itself in the way employees dress (business casual versus business suits), how the working environment is structured (cubicles versus closed offices), and how employees are compensated (stock options versus overtime). Corporate culture is also apparent in the expectations for ethical behaviour present in formal codes of ethics and the ethical actions of top management and co-workers.

code of ethics
Formal statement of ethical principles and rules of conduct

Codes of Ethics   A **code of ethics** is a formal statement of ethical principles and rules of conduct. A study of 1,000 Canadian companies determined that over 86 percent of corporations have some form of written document that describes their values and principles, and 73 percent have a program or initiative to promote ethics. Having a "champion" or senior officer responsible for ethics programs and promotion raises the profile of ethics and enhances the likelihood that the programs are successfully integrated into the company's culture. Senior-level managers responsible for implementing and maintaining ethics initiatives exist in 42 percent of companies, and 39 percent of companies have some kind of formal training in the topic.[16]

At ZENON Environmental Inc., identified by a recent study as the most ethical company in Canada, CEO Andrew Benedek said, "From my visits to other companies, I saw that it was difficult to maintain a positive work environment; I resolved that ZENON would be different." The company, dedicated to technologies that produce safe drinking water, focuses on personal as well as professional development, and provides its employees with an environment where their well-being is clearly a major consideration. Although ZENON considers itself a small company, its employees have access to a fitness coordinator, a gym with massage and chiropractic services, and numerous outdoor recreational facilities and areas that range from hiking trails to basketball courts. The corporate headquarters in Oakville, Ontario, is are surrounded by nature and trees, and the firm is committed to making its negative impact on their environment minimal.[17] Ethics officers and codes of ethics typically address contributions to government officials and political parties, relations with customers and suppliers, conflicts of interest, and accurate recordkeeping.

The lack of specificity is one of the major reasons for the violation of ethics codes. Employees must often judge whether a specific behaviour is really unethical. The American Marketing Association has addressed this issue by providing a detailed code of ethics, which all members agree to follow. This code can be found at the American Marketing Association website (www.marketingpower.com).

Ethical Behaviour of Top Management and Co-Workers

Workers sometimes violate ethics codes because of how they perceive the behaviour of top management and co-workers. How an employee evaluates the company's response to unethical behaviour plays an important role in his or her actions. A recent study of business executives reported that 40 percent had been implicitly or explicitly rewarded for engaging in ethically troubling behaviour. Moreover, 31 percent of those who refused to engage in unethical behaviour were penalized, either through outright punishment or a diminished status in the company.[18] Clearly, ethical dilemmas often bring personal and professional conflict. For this reason, many jurisdictions have laws protecting **whistle-blowers**, employees who report unethical or illegal actions of their employers. Some firms have appointed ethics officers responsible for safeguarding these individuals from recrimination, and 21 percent of Canadian firms report having a mechanism where employees can report problems confidentially and without fear of reprisal.[19]

whistle-blowers
Employees who report unethical or illegal actions of their employers

Corporate Knights is a Canadian firm that promotes business ethics and identifies businesses that stand out as being good corporate citizens. Check out www.corporateknights.ca to find out how the firm evaluates companies that have good ethical practices. Figure 4-2 shows the firm's 2004 list of the top 10 Canadian corporate citizens.[20]

Personal Moral Philosophy and Ethical Behaviour

Business consultant Jerry Lemmon of Razorquest Inc. in Calgary contends that ethics are learned at a very early age, and cannot to a great extent be taught later in life. "The place to learn ethics is in the sandbox when we're three years old. That's when we learn our values and principles. The question is how to maintain them as we go along."[21]

Ultimately, ethical choices are based on the personal moral philosophy of the decision maker. Moral philosophy is learned through the process of socialization with friends and family and by formal education. It is also influenced by the societal, business, and

FIGURE 4-2
Top corporate citizens in
Canada

THE 2004 BEST 10 CORPORATE CITIZENS

Rank	Company Name	Type of Business
1	ZENON Environmental Inc.	Industrials
2	MDS Inc.	Health Care
3	Alcan Inc.	Materials
4	Dofasco Inc.	Materials
5	Tembec Inc.	Materials
6	Bank of Montreal	Financials
7	Royal Bank of Canada	Financials
8	TransAlta Corporation	Utilities
9	Great-West Lifeco Inc.	Financials
10	Suncor Energy Inc.	Energy

corporate culture in which a person finds him- or herself. Two prominent personal moral philosophies have direct bearing on marketing practice: moral idealism and utilitarianism.

moral idealism
Moral philosophy that considers that certain individual rights or duties apply to everyone, regardless of the outcome

Moral Idealism   **Moral idealism** is a moral philosophy that considers that certain individual rights or duties apply to everyone, regardless of the outcome. This philosophy is favoured by moral philosophers and consumer interest groups. For example, the right to know applies to probable defects in an automobile that relate to safety.

This philosophy also applies to ethical duties. A fundamental ethical duty is to do no harm. Companies that voluntarily inform consumers about the potential safety hazard of a product, or that undertake a large-scale recall of a product because of a potential problem, are likely following this philosophy.

utilitarianism
Moral philosophy that focuses on the "greatest good for the greatest number"

Utilitarianism   An alternative perspective on moral philosophy is **utilitarianism**, which is a moral philosophy that focuses on "the greatest good for the greatest number," by assessing the costs and benefits of the consequences of ethical behaviour. If the benefits exceed the costs, then the behaviour is ethical. If not, then the behaviour is unethical. This philosophy underlies the economic principles of capitalism and, not surprisingly, is embraced by many business executives and students.

Utilitarianism is apparent in the labelling of many food products. The presence of even a trace amount of peanuts in food is a serious concern for a small number of Canadians who suffer from a severe peanut allergy. Manufacturers are required to indicate on food labels the ingredients that the product contains. In some cases, a product does not contain peanuts, but has been manufactured in a factory where peanuts are used in other products. Utilitarian thinking suggests that this need not be indicated on the label because a small percentage of the population is affected and peanuts are not an ingredient. However, after some protests from affected consumers, manufacturers now tend to indicate that such a product is manufactured in a facility where peanuts are present, as there is a possibility, however remote, of the product having come in contact with peanuts.

An appreciation for the nature of ethics, coupled with a basic understanding of why unethical behaviour arises, alerts a person to when and how ethical issues exist in marketing decisions. Ultimately, ethical behaviour rests with the individual, but the consequences affect many.

Concept Check

1. Why do consumers have responsibilities as well as rights in the marketplace?

2. What is meant by moral idealism?

UNDERSTANDING SOCIAL RESPONSIBILITY IN MARKETING

social responsibility
Idea that organizations are part of a larger society and are accountable to that society for their actions

As we saw in Chapter 1, the societal marketing concept stresses marketing's social responsibility not only by satisfying the needs of consumers but also by providing for society's welfare. **Social responsibility** means that organizations are part of a larger society and are accountable to that society for their actions. As with ethics, agreement on the nature and scope of social responsibility is often difficult to come by, given the diversity of values present in different societal, business, and corporate cultures.

Three Concepts of Social Responsibility

Figure 4–3 shows three concepts of social responsibility: profit responsibility, stakeholder responsibility, and societal responsibility.

Profit Responsibility *Profit responsibility* holds that companies have a simple duty—to maximize profits for their owners or stockholders. This view is expressed by Nobel Prize–winning economist Milton Friedman, who said, "There is one and only one social responsibility of business—to use its resources and engage in activities designed to increase its profits so long as it stays within the rules of the game, which is to say, engages in open and free competition without deception or fraud."[22] Nonetheless, there are concerns about *profiteering*. Profiteering occurs when a company makes excessive profits, usually by taking advantage of a shortage of supply to charge extremely high prices.

But where should companies draw the line? Genzyme is a U.S. firm that manufactures Ceredase, a drug that treats a genetic illness called Gaucher's disease that affects 20,000 people worldwide. The company was criticized for apparently adopting the view of profit responsibility in its pricing practices. Genzyme charged up to $200,000 for a year's worth of Ceredase. Critics claimed this practice took advantage of the American federal "orphan drug" law, which grants companies a seven-year monopoly on drugs for rare diseases. A Genzyme spokesperson responded by saying that Ceredase profits were below industry standards and that the company freely gives the drug to patients without insurance.[23]

Stakeholder Responsibility Frequent criticism of the profit view has led to a broader concept of social responsibility. *Stakeholder responsibility* focuses on the obligations an organization has to those who can affect achievement of its objectives. These constituencies include customers, employees, suppliers, and distributors. Source Perrier S.A., the supplier of Perrier bottled water, exercised this responsibility when it recalled 160 million bottles of water in 120 countries after traces of a toxic chemical were found in 13 bottles. The recall cost the company $35 million, and $40 million more was lost in sales. Even though the chemical level was not harmful to humans, Source Perrier's president believed he acted in the best interests of the firm's consumers, distributors, and employees by removing "the least doubt, as minimal as it might be, to weigh on the image of the quality and purity of our product"—which it did.[24]

Failure to consider a company's broader constituencies can have negative consequences. For example, Bridgestone/Firestone, Inc., executives were widely criticized for how they

FIGURE 4-3
Three concepts of social responsibility

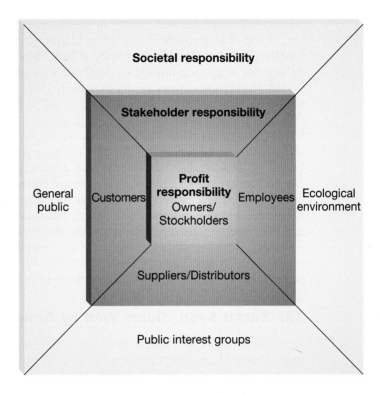

responded to complaints about the safety of selected Firestone-brand tires. These tires had been linked to crashes that killed more than 200 people and injured over 700 in the United States alone. In 2000, the company recalled 6.5 million tires—but only after getting pressure from the U.S. National Highway Traffic Administration. After the recall, Firestone tire sales fell by nearly one-half, which affected Firestone employees, suppliers, and distributors as well.

Societal Responsibility   An even broader concept of social responsibility has emerged in recent years. *Societal responsibility* refers to obligations that organizations have to preserve the ecological environment and serve the general public. Concerns about the environment and public welfare are represented by interest and advocacy groups such as Greenpeace, an international environmental organization.

Chapter 3 detailed the growing importance of ecological issues in marketing. Companies have responded to this concern through what is known as **green marketing**—marketing efforts to produce, promote, and reclaim environmentally sensitive products.

Green marketing takes many forms.[25] At 3M, product development opportunities come both from consumer research and its "Pollution Prevention Pays" program. This program solicits employee suggestions on how to reduce pollution and recycle materials. Since 1974, this program has generated over 4,000 ideas that eliminated more than 1.6 billion pounds of air, water, and solid-waste pollutants from the environment. Xerox's "Design for the Environment" program focuses on ways to make its equipment recyclable and remanufacturable. Today, 90 percent of Xerox-designed products are remanufacturable. Home Depot, the home-and-garden-centre chain, discontinued the sale of wood products from endangered forests in 2002. The aluminum industry recycles two-thirds of aluminum cans for reuse and pays consumers more than $1 billion annually for used cans. These voluntary responses to environmental issues have been implemented with little or no additional cost to consumers.

Socially responsible efforts on behalf of the general public are becoming more common. A formal practice is **cause-related marketing**, which occurs when the charitable con-

green marketing
Marketing efforts to produce, promote, and reclaim environmentally sensitive products

cause-related marketing
Tying the charitable contributions of a firm directly to sales produced through the promotion of one of its products

tributions of a firm are tied directly to the customer revenues produced through the promotion of one of its products.[26] Just Cause Marketing in Vancouver secured the support of the Grizzlies Foundation and Wood Gundy at Park Place for the "Spinoza for Kids" program—an initiative to provide funding to distribute Spinoza talking bears to children and families in challenging circumstances. In BC, over 3,000 bears have been donated to the BC Children's Hospital and other organizations, and in New York City, to children of the firefighters and rescue workers who lost their lives in the tragic events of September 11, 2001. CIBC (Canadian Imperial Bank of Commerce) is dedicated to fundraising for breast cancer, and it has made the annual Run for the Cure its largest fundraising event. One of our largest cross-Canada fundraising events, the Run takes place in 39 communities across Canada. Suncor Energy Inc., a Calgary-based company ranked as one of Canada's 50 best corporate citizens, fosters relationships with organizations such as the Science Alberta Foundation, the Odyssium, and several universities. Suncor has supported science festivals, science camps, and other science-related programs, and has also brought some of these programs to remote communities in Ontario and Alberta.[27] Cause-related marketing programs address public concerns and satisfy customer needs. They can also enhance corporate sales and profits as described in the Marketing NewsNet on the opposite page.[28]

The Social Audit: Doing Well by Doing Good

social audit
Systematic assessment of a firm's objectives, strategies, and performance in the domain of social responsibility

Converting socially responsible ideas into actions involves careful planning and monitoring of programs. Many companies develop, implement, and evaluate their social responsibility efforts by means of a **social audit**, which is a systematic assessment of a firm's objectives, strategies, and performance in terms of social responsibility. Frequently, marketing and social responsibility programs are integrated, as is the case with McDonald's. The company's concern for the needs of families with children who are chronically or terminally ill was translated into some 200 Ronald McDonald Houses around the world. These facilities, located near treatment centres, enable families to stay together during the child's care. In this case, McDonald's is contributing to the welfare of a portion of its target market.

A social audit consists of five steps:[29]

1. Recognition of a firm's social expectations and the rationale for engaging in social responsibility endeavours.
2. Identification of social responsibility causes or programs consistent with the company's mission.
3. Determination of organizational objectives and priorities for programs and activities it will undertake.
4. Specification of the type and amount of resources necessary to achieve social responsibility objectives.
5. Evaluation of social responsibility programs and activities undertaken and assessment of future involvement.

Corporate attention to social audits will increase as companies seek to achieve sustainable development and improve the quality of life in a global economy. *Sustainable development* involves conducting business in a way that protects the natural environment while making economic progress. Ecologically responsible programs such as green marketing represent one such initiative. Other programs focus on working conditions at overseas manufacturing sites that produce goods for Canadian companies. Public opinion surveys show that many North Americans are concerned about working conditions under which products are made in Asia and Latin America. Companies such as Reebok, Nike, Liz Claiborne, Levi Strauss, and Mattel have responded by imposing codes of conduct to reduce harsh or abusive working conditions at overseas manufacturing facilities.[30] Reebok, for example, now monitors production of its sporting apparel and equipment to ensure that no child labour is used in making its products.

MARKETING NEWSNET

WILL CUSTOMERS SWITCH BRANDS FOR A CAUSE? YES, IF...

American Express is credited with being the pioneer of cause-related marketing. Nearly 20 years ago, the company sponsored the renovation of the Statue of Liberty in New York in preparation for the landmark's 100th birthday celebration in 1986. The company still supports this monument and considers the work part of the firm's heritage. Its first campaign raised US$1.7 million for the renovations; the campaign benefited American Express by increasing credit card usage among existing customers as well as attracting new cardholders. The result? Good promotion of the image of American Express and solid funding for an American landmark. Since that time, many companies have adopted the idea.[1]

Sponsorship is a popular trend in marketing; many marketing specialists feel that sponsorship is the world's fastest-growing form of marketing. Analysts estimate that overall sponsorship spending in North America totalled $14.2 billion for 2003. Corporations around the world spend billions annually sponsoring a wide range of sports, arts, entertainment, causes, and events. Cause marketing is just one aspect of sponsorship. In 2003, spending in North America on cause marketing was

estimated to be $1.24 billion; however, sports sponsorship is much larger, with spending of $8.2 billion in 2003.[2]

Cause-related marketing benefits companies as well as causes. With the growing importance that society places on corporate responsibility, cause marketing can be very effective in enhancing the image of a company, providing increased media coverage, and generating additional brand exposure. And Canadians respond: 68 percent of consumers say that a news item about a company with a positive story about their social responsibility activities gets their attention, and 55 percent will choose the products of a good corporate citizen over another company.[3]

The Royal Bank has an extensive sponsorship program that extends from sports to arts and culture. Check out the website at www.rbc.com/sponsorship to find out see how the company's contributions and partnerships stretch across the country.

[1] American Express news release, November 25, 2003.

[2] "Cause marketing spends are ballooning," *Marketing Magazine*, October 6-13, 2003, vol. 108, issue 34, p. 24.

[3] "Poll rates corporate Canada on CSR," *Marketing Magazine*, October 6-13, 2003, vol. 108, issue 34, p. 26.

Companies that show societal responsibility have been rewarded for their efforts. Research has shown that these companies benefit from favourable word-of-mouth among consumers and typically outperform less responsible companies on financial performance.[31] Ipsos-Reid, the prominent Canadian pollster, surveyed Canadians about how Canadian companies are doing in the area of social responsibility: the companies scored a "B." According to 76 percent of Canadians, Canadian companies are operating in a socially responsible manner, but the other 24 percent of respondents gave them a failing grade. Over half of the respondents made a conscious decision to purchase a product based on their outlook that the company behaves as a good corporate citizen.[32]

Turning the Table: Consumer Ethics and Social Responsibility

Consumers also have an obligation to act ethically and responsibly in the exchange process and in the use of products. Unfortunately, consumer behaviour is somewhat spotty. An efficient and fair marketplace requires all of the participants to play a role in making it so.

Key consumer responsibilities include:

- Responsibility to be ethical by not engaging in unfair activities that negatively affect other consumers and businesses.
- Responsibility to protect the environment by reducing waste and pollution and participating in recycling.
- Responsibility to be vigilant and aware by gathering information, evaluating goods and services, and protecting against unfair and dishonest practices.
- Responsibility to communicate by informing other consumers, businesses, and governments about problems or issues of concern.[33]

Unethical practices of consumers are a serious concern to marketers. These practices include filing warranty claims after the claim period, misredeeming coupons, making fraudulent returns of merchandise, providing inaccurate information on credit applications, tampering with utility meters, tapping cable TV lines, recording copyrighted music and videocassettes, and submitting phony insurance claims. The cost to marketers in lost sales and prevention expenses is huge.[34] For example, consumers who redeem coupons for unpurchased products or use coupons destined for other products cost manufacturers $1 billion each year. The record industry alone loses $1 billion annually as a result of illegal recording, and about 12 percent of VCR owners make illegal copies of videotapes, costing producers millions of dollars in lost sales. Electrical utilities lose between 1 percent and 3 percent of yearly sales because of meter tampering.

Consumer purchase and use of environmentally sensitive products relate to consumer social responsibility. Research indicates that consumers are sensitive to ecological issues.[35] However, research also shows that consumers may be unwilling to sacrifice convenience and pay potentially higher prices to protect the environment. They often lack the knowledge to make informed decisions related to dealing with the purchase and use of products.[36]

Consumer confusion over which products are environmentally safe is also apparent, given marketers' rush to produce "green products." For example, few consumers realize that non-aerosol pump hairsprays are the second-largest cause of air pollution, after drying paint. And

Marketing and social responsibility programs are often integrated, as is the case with McDonald's. Its concern for ill children is apparent in the opening of another Ronald McDonald House for children and their families.

biodegradable claims on a variety of products, including garbage bags, have not proven to be accurate. All of the major auto makers are developing "green" vehicles, although calling an emissions-generating car "green" is quite a stretch of the imagination. While more fuel-efficient vehicles are catching on quickly in Europe and in China, they are much slower to be accepted in Canada and the U.S. Toyota is considered to be the greenest automobile manufacturer, and it has several models and technologies on the market. In contrast, the three major North American car manufacturers—Ford, General Motors, and DaimlerChrysler—are not as far advanced in this area, and are not putting as much emphasis on fuel-efficient and environmentally conscious vehicles.[37]

Ultimately, marketers and consumers are accountable for ethical and socially responsible behaviour. The twenty-first century will prove to be a testing period for both.

Concept Check

1. Marketing efforts to produce, promote, and reclaim environmentally sensitive products are called _____.

2. What is a social audit?

3. What is a social responsibility?

SUMMARY

1 Ethics are the moral principles and values that govern the actions and decisions of an individual or group. Laws are society's values and standards that are enforceable in the courts. Operating according to the law does not necessarily mean that a practice is ethical.

2 Ethical behaviour of businesspeople has come under severe criticism by the public. There are three possible reasons for this criticism: increased pressure on businesspeople to make decisions in a society characterized by diverse value systems, a growing tendency to have business decisions judged publicly by groups with different values and interests, and a possible decline in business ethics.

3 Numerous external factors influence ethical behaviour of businesspeople. These include the following: societal culture and norms, business culture and industry practices, and corporate culture and expectations. Each factor influences the opportunity to engage in ethical or unethical behaviour.

4 Ultimately, ethical choices are based on the personal moral philosophy of the decision maker. Two moral philosophies are most prominent: moral idealism and utilitarianism.

5 Social responsibility means that organizations are part of a larger society and are accountable to that society for their actions.

6 There are three key concepts of social responsibility: profit responsibility, stakeholder responsibility, and societal responsibility.

7 Growing interest in societal responsibility has resulted in systematic efforts to assess a firm's objectives, strategies, and performance in the domain of social responsibility. This practice is called a social audit.

8 Consumer ethics and social responsibility are as important as business ethics and social responsibility.

KEY TERMS AND CONCEPTS

cause-related marketing p. 85
code of ethics p. 81
ethics p. 76
green marketing p. 85
laws p. 77

moral idealism p. 83
social audit p. 86
social responsibility p. 84
utilitarianism p. 83
whistle-blowers p. 82

QUESTIONS: APPLYING MARKETING CONCEPTS AND PERSPECTIVES

1 What concepts of moral philosophy and social responsibility are applicable to the practices of VanCity, described in the introduction to this chapter? Why?

2 Compare and contrast moral idealism and utilitarianism as alternative personal moral philosophies. Which do you think sounds more like you?

3 How would you evaluate Milton Friedman's view of the social responsibility of a firm?

4 Cause-related marketing programs have become popular. Do you know of companies that use this technique? Why do you think the companies that you named have chosen the cause or causes they have?

5 Check out the corporate site for Sales and Marketing Executives International (www.smei.org), an organization committed to establishing standards for sales and marketing professionals around the world. Look for the organization's mission statement, its founding principles, and its published code of ethics. Research to find at least five other professional associations in other fields of business (e.g., accountants, engineers) and compare their approaches to ethics and standards.

6 In the section earlier in this chapter entitled "Corporate Culture and Expectations," we refer to the top 10 best Canadian corporate citizens. Three of these are financial institutions, and most of the others are manufacturing firms. Why do you think financial institutions are so focused on ethics and social responsibility? Compare and contrast the approach taken by manufacturing organizations to that of financial institutions. Which do you find more convincing and why?

7 Suppose you are a Canadian importer of spices and beans from southeast Asian countries. Develop a statement of ethics and a code of conduct for the company. How would you make sure that this is put into practice in your company?

DISCUSSION FORUM

Visit the Nike corporate website (www.nikebiz.com) and find the section called "Responsibility." Review the section on "Workers & Factories." There has been a lot of media attention in the past few years on Nike's treatment of and compensation to factory workers in foreign countries, and dealing with this is an ongoing challenge. Nike comments in its January 2004 report, "It is not a perfect record, and it never will be, but we're committed to the process." Discuss Nike's position, and then develop some counter arguments critiquing Nike's viewpoint and actions. What other companies with global manufacturing operations can you think of? How are they responding to similar challenges?

INTERNET EXERCISE

Bribery as a means to win and retain business varies widely by country. Transparency International, based in Germany, periodically polls employees of multinational firms and institutions and political analysts and ranks countries on the basis of their perceived level of bribery to win or retain business. To obtain the most recent ranking, visit the Transparency International website at www.transparency.org and click Info Center.

Scroll the Corruption Perceptions Index to find out where Canada stands in the worldwide rankings as well as its neighbours, the United States and Mexico. Any

surprises? Which country listed in the most recent ranking has the highest ranking and which has the lowest ranking?

VIDEO CASE 4

PRICING IN THE PHARMACEUTICAL INDUSTRY

Canadians spend billions of dollars annually for prescription drugs to treat acute and chronic ailments. The pharmaceutical industry in Canada has often been criticized for its pricing practices. Many public health officials, government departments or agencies, and consumer advocacy groups argue that, in many cases, the industry is simply charging too much money for its products. Pharmaceutical company executives have responded to such criticism by citing large research and development costs, extensive testing requirements to obtain government approval to market the products, and marketplace uncertainties as valid reasons for the prices they charge for their drugs.

FAIR AND REASONABLE PRICING

A central issue in the debate concerning prescription drug pricing relates to what is a "fair and reasonable price." Critics of drug pricing spotlight instances where they believe the prices charged are excessive. For instance, drugs to treat ulcers sell in the range of $1,300 to $1,400 annually per patient. Drugs that control cholesterol cost $1,015 to $1,265 per year per patient. Persons suffering from high blood pressure pay almost $850 annually to treat this condition. People over the age of 65, many with fixed incomes, bear a significant percentage of these costs. For example, 49 percent of the sales of high-blood-pressure medication are accounted for by the elderly.

Pharmaceutical firms counter critics' charges of excessive pricing using a variety of arguments. They note that the research and development cost of a new medication can be more than $150 million and span a decade of development and testing. Moreover, the risk is very high since most new drugs are never successfully commercialized. In addition, the pharmaceutical industry spends billions annually for marketing the newest drugs to doctors and consumers.

Debate over what is a "fair and reasonable" price for drugs typically focuses on economic versus societal factors, and the relative importance of a firm's stakeholders in setting prices. Often the final pricing decision depends on the individual judgment and moral sensitivity of the managers making the decision.

PROLIFE: PRICING ADL

Issues in the pricing of ADL, a treatment for Alzheimer's disease, which affects the elderly, were recently faced by Prolife, a small pharmaceutical company. A task force of company executives was considering the pricing strategy for ADL. Two points of view were expressed: pursuing a high-price strategy designed to recoup the costs of the drug quickly and to get a jump on the competition, and pursuing a lower-price strategy to increase the drug's availability to victims of the disease.

Steve Vaughn, an assistant product manager at Prolife, was the principal proponent of a lower-price strategy. He argued that a less aggressive price strategy made sense even though it would take slightly longer to recoup the initial investment in ADL. Having a family member afflicted with Alzheimer's disease, Vaughn believed that the ability of victims and their families to pay for the drug should be considered when setting the price for ADL. He was overruled, however, by the task force members. Believing that his views deserved attention and action, and that "bottom-line" considerations did not negate his position, he lobbied other task force members and has considered expressing his opinion to senior executives at Prolife. He was cautioned by Bill Compton, a Prolife senior product manager and Vaughn's mentor, to reconsider his position, noting that Prolife is a business and that "rocking the boat" might not be an advantage to his career at Prolife.

Questions

1 Who are the primary stakeholders who must be considered when setting prices for prescription drugs?

2 How might the personal moral philosophies of moral idealism and utilitarianism be applied to prescription drug pricing in general and in the specific case of ADL?

3 How might the three concepts of social responsibility described in Chapter 4 be applied to prescription pricing in general and in the specific case of ADL?

4 If you were Steve Vaughn, what would you do in this situation?

Understanding Buyers and Markets

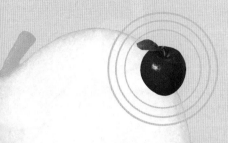

CHAPTER 5
Consumer Behaviour

CHAPTER 6
Organizational Markets and Buyer Behaviour

CHAPTER 7
Reaching Global Markets

People—whether they are individual consumers or representatives of companies that are organizational buyers—are the focus of intelligent marketing. In Part 2, we look at utilizing local and global perspectives to understand people. Chapter 5 examines the actions buyers take in purchasing and using products, and explains how and why one product or brand is chosen over another. In Chapter 6, TIR's specialty lighting systems are purchased by a variety of business consumers, helping to illustrate the industrial purchasing process, its nature, and its characteristics. Chapter 7 describes the nature and scope of world trade and examines the global marketing activities of companies such as Breathe Right Strips maker CNS, Inc., Coca-Cola, Ericsson, IBM, IKEA, and Nestlé. Together these chapters help marketing students understand individual, family, and organizational purchases in a variety of cultural environments.

Consumer Behaviour

CHICK CARS

AFTER READING THIS CHAPTER YOU SHOULD BE ABLE TO:

- Describe the stages in the consumer decision process.

- Distinguish among three variations of the consumer decision process: routine, limited, and extended problem solving.

- Explain how psychological influences affect consumer behaviour, particularly purchase decision processes.

- Identify major sociocultural influences on consumer behaviour and their effects on purchase decisions.

- Understand how marketers can use knowledge of consumer behaviour to better understand and influence individual and family purchases.

SAVVY AUTOMAKERS: KNOW YOUR CUSTOMER!

Who purchases about 55 percent of all the new cars in Canada? Who influences at least 80 percent of all other purchases? Women![1]

Women are a driving force in the automotive industry. Enlightened automakers have hired women design engineers and marketing executives to help them understand this valuable customer. What have they learned? Automakers are very aware of the market power of women in this industry. Although some of them may deny it, automakers are designing cars with women in mind—so-called "chick cars." What do women look for in a "chick car"? Size and shape, colour, styling, reliability, driveability, and value for money are key factors, as well as something that's fun to drive. Price is not always a major factor, as many women can afford any vehicle they want.[2]

Women approach car buying, usage, and maintenance in a deliberate manner. They often visit auto-buying websites and scan car advertisements to gather information, but recommendations of friends and relatives matter most. Women shop an average of three dealerships before making a purchase decision—one more than men. Although men and women look for the same car features, their priorities differ. Both sexes value dependability, but more women consider it a higher priority. Women also rank low price, ease of maintenance, and safety higher than men. Men view horsepower and acceleration as being more important than women. Automakers have learned that 78 percent of women dislike the car-buying process.

This better understanding of women as purchasers and influencers in car and truck buying has also altered the behaviour of dealers.

Industry research indicates that 68 percent of new-car buyers dread the price negotiation process involved in buying a car, and some women often refuse to do it at all.[3] Many dealers now use a one-price policy and have stopped negotiating a vehicle's price.

WHERE IN THE MARKETING PROCESS ARE WE GOING IN THIS CHAPTER?

This chapter's focus is on consumer behaviour. Effective marketers keep an eye on their target market, and work to understand them and satisfy consumers' wants and needs.

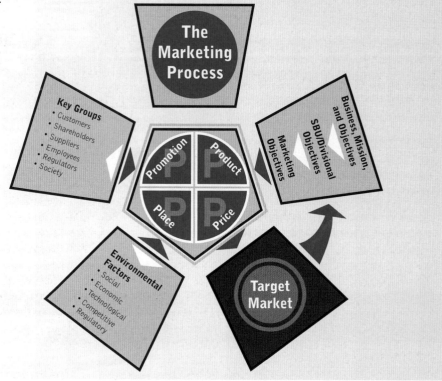

consumer behaviour
Actions a person takes in purchasing and using products and services

This chapter examines **consumer behaviour**, the actions a person takes in purchasing and using products and services, including the mental and social processes that come before and after these actions. This chapter shows how the behavioural sciences help answer questions such as why people choose one product or brand over another, how they make these choices, and how companies use this knowledge to provide value to consumers.

CONSUMER PURCHASE DECISION PROCESS

Behind the visible act of making a purchase lies an important decision process. The stages a buyer passes through in making choices about which products and services to buy is the **purchase decision process**. This process has the five stages shown in Figure 5–1: problem recognition, information search, alternative evaluation, purchase decision, and postpurchase behaviour.

purchase decision process
Stages a buyer passes through in making choices about which products or services to buy

Problem Recognition: Perceiving a Need

Problem recognition, the initial step in the purchase decision, occurs when a person realizes that the difference between what he or she has and what he or she would like to have is big enough to actually do something about it.[4] The process may be triggered by a situation as simple as finding an empty milk carton in the refrigerator; noting, as a first-year university student, that your high school clothes are not in the style that other students are wearing; or realizing that your laptop computer may not be working properly.

FIGURE 5-1

Purchase decision process

In marketing, advertisements or salespeople can activate a consumer's decision process by showing the shortcomings of competing (or currently owned) products. For instance, an advertisement for an MP3 player could stimulate problem recognition by emphasizing the features, versatility, and storage capacity of new MP3 players over the CD player you may now own.

Information Search: Seeking Value

After recognizing a problem, consumers begin to search for information about what product or service might satisfy the newly discovered need. First, they may scan their memory for knowledge of or previous experiences with products or brands.[5] This action is called *internal search*. For frequently purchased products such as shampoo and conditioner, this may be enough. Or a consumer may undertake an *external search* for information.[6] This is especially needed when one does not have much past experience or knowledge, the risk of making a bad decision is high, and the cost of gathering information is low. The primary sources of external information are: *personal sources*, such as relatives and friends who the consumer trusts; *public sources*, including various product-rating organizations such as Consumer Reports or government agencies; and *marketer-dominated* sources, such as information from sellers that include advertising, company websites, salespeople, and point-of-purchase displays in stores.

Suppose you consider buying your first MP3 player. You will probably tap several of these information sources: friends and relatives, MP3-player advertisements, brand and company websites, and stores carrying MP3 players (for demonstrations).

Alternative Evaluation: Assessing Value

The information search stage clarifies the problem for the consumer by suggesting criteria, or points to consider, for the purchase; providing brand names that might meet the criteria; and developing consumer value perceptions. What selection criteria would you use in buying a portable MP3 player? Would you use price, ease of using the controls, or some other combination?

Consider all the factors you may consider when evaluating portable MP3 players. These factors are a consumer's *evaluative criteria*, which represent both the objective attributes of a brand (such as sound quality) and the subjective ones (such as prestige) you use to compare different products and brands.[7] Firms try to identify and make the most of both types of evaluative criteria to create the best value for consumers. These criteria are often emphasized in advertisements.

For a product like a portable MP3 player, the information search process would probably involve visiting retail stores, seeing different brands in magazines, viewing promotions on a home shopping television channel, or visiting a seller's website. Consumers often have several criteria for comparing products. For example, among the evaluative criteria you might think of, suppose that you use three in considering brands of portable MP3 players: a list price under $400, a battery life of more than 20 hours, and ease of use. These criteria establish the brands in your *evoked set*—the group of brands that a consumer would consider acceptable from among all the brands in the product class of which he or she is aware.[8] Your three evaluative criteria may result in four models and three brands (Sony, Panasonic, and SonicBlue) in your evoked set. If these alternatives don't satisfy you, you can change your evaluative criteria to create a different evoked set of models and brands.

Purchase Decision: Buying Value

Having examined the alternatives in the evoked set, you are almost ready to make a purchase decision. Two choices remain: from whom to buy and when to buy. The choice of which seller to buy from will depend on such considerations as the seller's location, your past experience buying from the seller, and the return policy.

Deciding when to buy is frequently determined by a number of factors. For instance, you might buy sooner if one of your preferred brands is on sale or its manufacturer offers a rebate. Other factors such as the store atmosphere, pleasantness of the shopping experience, salesperson persuasiveness, time pressure, and financial circumstances could also affect whether a purchase decision is made or postponed.

Use of the Internet to gather information, evaluate alternatives, and make buying decisions adds a technological dimension to the consumer purchase decision process. Consumer benefits and costs associated with this technology and its marketing implications are detailed in Chapter 15.

Postpurchase Behaviour: Value in Consumption or Use

After buying a product, the consumer compares it with his or her expectations and is either satisfied or dissatisfied. A company's sensitivity to a customer's consumption experience strongly affects the value a customer perceives after the purchase. Studies show that satisfaction or dissatisfaction affects consumer communications and repeat-purchase behaviour. Satisfied buyers tell three other people about their experience. Dissatisfied buyers complain to nine people![9] Satisfied buyers also tend to buy from the same seller each time a purchase occasion arises. The financial impact of repeat-purchase behaviour is significant.[10] Accordingly, firms such as General Electric (GE), Johnson & Johnson, Coca-Cola, and British Airways focus attention on postpurchase behaviour to maximize customer satisfaction and retention.[11] These firms, among many others, now provide toll-free telephone numbers, offer liberalized return and refund policies, and engage in staff training to handle complaints, answer questions, and record suggestions. Lands' End has a particularly interesting way of maximizing customer satisfaction: with its guarantee. Instead of having pages and paragraphs of legal-sounding explanations of the limitations of the guarantee, Lands' End makes it simple: "Guaranteed. Period."[12] This simplicity gives consumers peace of mind and a feeling that Lands' End is a consumer-friendly place to shop.

Involvement and Problem-Solving Variations

involvement
Personal, social, and economic significance of a purchase to the consumer

Sometimes consumers don't engage in the five-step purchase decision process. Instead, they skip or minimize one or more steps depending on the level of involvement. The level of **involvement** that a consumer has in a particular purchase depends on the personal, social, and economic consequences of that purchase to the consumer.[13] Items such as soft drinks or toothpaste may have such a low level of involvement for consumers that they may skip or minimize one or more steps in the process. But they may do just the opposite for a high-involvement purchase like a computer or an automobile.

High-involvement purchase occasions typically have at least one of three characteristics: the item to be purchased is expensive, it can have serious personal consequences, or it could reflect on one's social image. For these occasions, consumers engage in extensive information search, consider many product attributes and brands, form attitudes, and participate in word-of-mouth communication. Researchers have identified three general variations in the consumer purchase process based on consumer involvement and product knowledge. Figure 5–2 summarizes some of the important differences between the three problem-solving variations.[14]

Routine Problem Solving   For products such as table salt and milk, consumers recognize a problem, make a decision, and spend little effort seeking external information and evaluating alternatives. The purchase process for such items is virtually a habit and typifies low-involvement decision making. Routine problem solving is typically the case for low-priced, frequently purchased products.

Limited Problem Solving   In limited problem solving, consumers typically seek some information or rely on a friend to help them evaluate alternatives. In general, several brands might be evaluated using a moderate number of different attributes. You might use limited problem solving in choosing a pair of jeans, a restaurant for dinner, and other purchase situations in which you have little time or effort to spend researching options.

Extended Problem Solving   In extended problem solving, each of the five stages of the consumer purchase decision process is used in the purchase, including considerable time and effort on external information search and in identifying and evaluating alternatives. Several brands are in the evoked set, and these are evaluated on many attributes. Extended problem solving exists in high-involvement purchase situations for items such as automobiles, houses, and financial investments.

Figure 5–3 shows the many influences that affect the consumer purchase decision process. The decision to buy a product also involves important situational, psychological, and sociocultural influences, the topics discussed during the remainder of this chapter. Marketing mix influences are described later in Part 4 of the book.

FIGURE 5-2

Comparison of problem-solving variations

	LOW ◄ CONSUMER INVOLVEMENT ► HIGH		
CHARACTERISTICS OF PURCHASE DECISION PROCESS	**ROUTINE PROBLEM SOLVING**	**LIMITED PROBLEM SOLVING**	**EXTENDED PROBLEM SOLVING**
Number of brands examined	One	Several	Many
Number of sellers considered	Few	Several	Many
Number of product attributes evaluated	One	Moderate	Many
Number of external information sources used	None	Few	Many
Time spent searching	Minimal	Little	Considerable

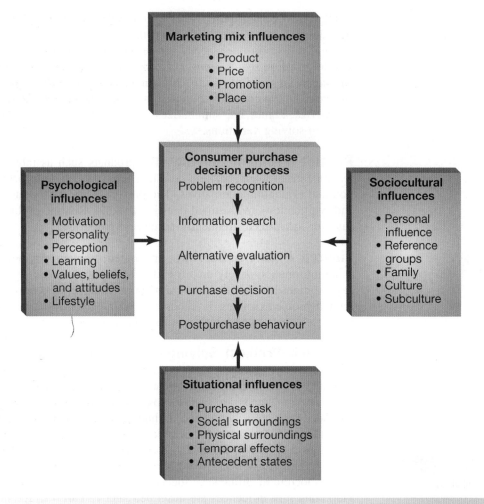

FIGURE 5–3
Influences on the consumer purchase decision process

Concept Check

1. What is the first step in the consumer purchase decision process?

2. The brand a consumer considers buying is called the _____.

SITUATIONAL INFLUENCES

Often the purchase situation will affect the purchase decision process. Five *situational influences* have an impact on your purchase decision process: the purchase task, social surroundings, physical surroundings, temporal effects, and antecedent states.[15] The purchase task is the reason for engaging in the decision in the first place. Information searching and evaluating alternatives may differ depending on whether the purchase is a gift, which often involves social visibility, or for the buyer's own use. Social surroundings, including the other people present when a purchase decision is made, may also affect what is purchased. Physical surroundings such as decor, music, and crowding in retail stores may alter how purchase decisions are made. Temporal effects such as time of day or the amount of time available will influence where consumers have breakfast and lunch and what is ordered. Finally, antecedent states, which include the consumer's mood or the amount of cash on hand, can influence purchase behaviour and choice.

group $\bar{x}$

PSYCHOLOGICAL INFLUENCES ON CONSUMER BEHAVIOUR

Psychology helps marketers understand why and how consumers behave as they do. In particular, concepts such as motivation and personality; perception; learning; values, beliefs, and attitudes; and lifestyle are useful for interpreting buying processes and directing marketing efforts.

Motivation and Personality

Motivation and personality are two familiar psychological concepts that have specific meanings and marketing implications. They are both used frequently to describe why people do some things and not others.

motivation

Energizing force that stimulates behaviour to satisfy a need

Motivation   **Motivation** is the energizing force that stimulates behaviour to satisfy a need. Because consumer needs are the focus of the marketing concept, marketers try to arouse these needs.

An individual's needs are boundless. People have physiological needs for basics such as water, food, and shelter. They also have learned needs, including esteem, achievement, and affection. Psychologists point out that these needs are hierarchical; that is, once physiological needs are met, people seek to satisfy their learned needs. Figure 5–4 shows one need hierarchy and classification scheme that contains five need classes.[16] *Physiological needs* are basic to survival and must be satisfied first. A Burger King advertisement featuring a juicy hamburger attempts to activate the need for food. *Safety needs* involve self-preservation and physical well-being. Smoke detector and burglar alarm manufacturers focus on these needs. *Social needs* are concerned with love and friendship. Dating services and fragrance companies try to arouse these needs. *Personal needs* are represented by the need for achievement, status, prestige, and self-respect. The American Express Gold Card and Holt Renfrew appeal to these needs. Sometimes firms try to arouse multiple needs to stimulate problem recognition. Michelin combined security with parental love to

great

FIGURE 5–4

Hierarchy of needs

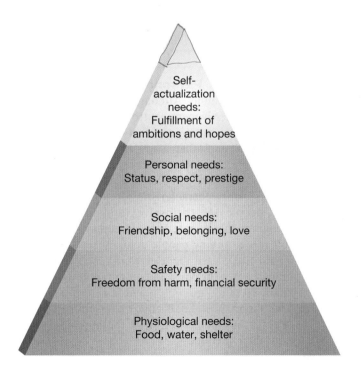

Self-actualization needs:
Fulfillment of ambitions and hopes

Personal needs:
Status, respect, prestige

Social needs:
Friendship, belonging, love

Safety needs:
Freedom from harm, financial security

Physiological needs:
Food, water, shelter

ETHICS AND SOCIAL RESPONSIBILITY ALERT

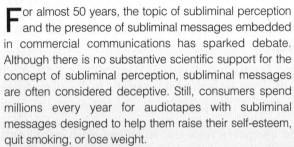

THE ETHICS OF SUBLIMINAL MESSAGES

For almost 50 years, the topic of subliminal perception and the presence of subliminal messages embedded in commercial communications has sparked debate. Although there is no substantive scientific support for the concept of subliminal perception, subliminal messages are often considered deceptive. Still, consumers spend millions every year for audiotapes with subliminal messages designed to help them raise their self-esteem, quit smoking, or lose weight.

Subliminal messages are not illegal and marketers occasionally pursue opportunities to create these messages. For example, Time Warner Interactive's Endorfun, a CD-ROM puzzle game, has a music soundtrack with more than 100 subliminal messages meant to make players feel good about themselves, even if they can't solve the puzzle. One message says, "I am a winner." Puzzle players are informed that subliminal messages exist and instructions on how to turn off the soundtrack are provided.

Do you believe that attempts to implant subliminal messages are a deceptive practice and unethical, regardless of their intent?

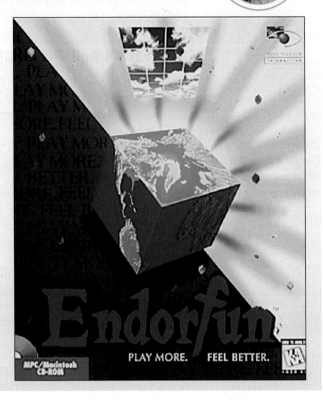

promote tire replacement for automobiles. *Self-actualization needs* involve personal fulfillment. For example, Volkswagen uses the phrase, "Every girl's dream," in marketing the Cabrio.

personality
A person's consistent behaviours or responses to recurring situations

Personality **Personality** refers to a person's consistent behaviours or responses to recurring situations. Although numerous personality theories exist, most identify key traits such as assertiveness, extroversion, compliance, dominance, and aggression, among others. Research suggests that compliant people prefer known brand names and use more mouthwash and toilet soaps. In contrast, aggressive types use razors, not electric shavers, apply more cologne and after-shave lotions, and purchase signature goods such as Gucci, Yves St. Laurent, and Donna Karan as an indicator of status.[17]

Personality characteristics are often revealed in a person's *self-concept*, which is the way people see themselves and the way they believe others see them. Marketers recognize that people have an actual self-concept and an ideal self-concept. The actual self refers to how people actually see themselves. The ideal self describes how people would like to see themselves. These two self-images are reflected in the products and brands a person buys, including automobiles, home appliances and furnishings, magazines, clothing, grooming and leisure products, and in the stores where a person shops. The importance of self-concept is summed up by a senior executive at Barnes & Noble: "People buy books for what the purchase says about them—their taste, their cultivation, their trendiness."[18]

Perception

perception
Process by which someone selects, organizes, and interprets information to create a meaningful picture of the world

One person sees a BMW as a mark of achievement; another sees it as showing off. This is the result of **perception**—the process by which an individual selects, organizes, and interprets information to create a meaningful picture of the world.

Selective Perception   The average consumer operates in a complex, information-rich environment. The human brain organizes and interprets all this information with a process called *selective perception*, which filters the information so that only some of it is understood or remembered or even available to the conscious mind. *Selective exposure* occurs when people pay attention to messages that are consistent with their attitudes and beliefs and ignore messages that are inconsistent. Selective exposure often occurs in the postpurchase stage of the consumer decision process, when consumers read advertisements for the brand they just bought. It also occurs when a need exists—you are more likely to "see" a McDonald's advertisement when you are hungry rather than after you have eaten a pizza.

Selective comprehension involves interpreting information so that it is consistent with your attitudes and beliefs. A marketer's failure to understand this can have disastrous results. For example, Toro introduced a small, lightweight snowblower called the Snow Pup. Even though the product worked, sales failed to meet expectations. Why? Toro later found out that consumers perceived the name to mean that Snow Pup was a toy or too light to do any serious snow removal. When the product was renamed Snow Master, sales increased sharply.[19]

Selective retention means that consumers do not remember all the information they see, read, or hear, even minutes after exposure to it. This affects the internal and external information search stage of the purchase decision process. This is why furniture and automobile retailers often give consumers product brochures to take home after they leave the showroom.

Why does the Good Housekeeping seal for Clorox's new Fresh Step Crystals cat litter appear in the ad and why does Mary Kay, Inc., offer a free sample of its new Velocity brand fragrance through its mkvelocity.com website? The answer appears in the text.

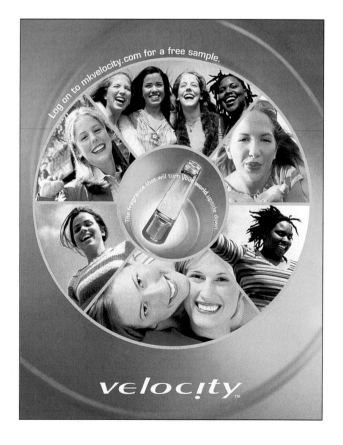

Perceived Risk   Consumers' beliefs about the potential negative consequences of a product or service strongly affect their purchasing decisions. **Perceived risk** represents the anxieties felt because the consumer cannot anticipate the outcomes of a purchase but believes that there may be negative consequences. Examples of possible negative consequences are the price of the product (Can I afford $300 for those skis?), the risk of physical harm (Is bungee jumping safe?), and the performance of the product (Will the hair colouring work?). Sometimes the consequence is psychosocial (What will my friends say if I wear that fur coat?). Perceived risk affects the information search stage: the greater the perceived risk, the more extensive the external search is likely to be.

Recognizing the importance of perceived risk, companies develop strategies to make consumers feel more at ease about their purchases. Strategies and examples of firms using them include the following:

- Obtaining seals of approval: the Good Housekeeping seal for Fresh Step Crystals cat litter.
- Securing endorsements from influential people: The National Fluid Milk Processor Promotion Board's "Got Milk" advertising campaign.
- Providing free trials of the product: samples of Mary Kay's Velocity fragrance.
- Giving extensive usage instructions: Clairol hair colouring.
- Providing warranties and guarantees: BMW's two-year, unlimited-mileage warranty on all of their automobiles.[20]

Learning

Why do consumers behave in the marketplace as they do? Over consumers' lifetimes, they learn behaviours, and they also learn responses to those behaviours—this learning is a continual process. Consumers learn which sources to use for information about products and services, which evaluative criteria to use when assessing alternatives, and how to make purchase decisions. **Learning** refers to those behaviours that result from repeated experience and reasoning.

Behavioural Learning   *Behavioural learning* is the process of developing automatic responses to a type of situation built up through repeated exposure to it. Four variables are central to how one learns from repeated experience: drive, cue, response, and reinforcement. A *drive* is a need, such as hunger, that moves an individual to action. A *cue* is a stimulus or symbol that one perceives. A *response* is the action taken to satisfy the drive, and a *reinforcement* is the reward. Being hungry (a drive), a consumer sees a cue (a billboard), takes action (buys a hamburger), and receives a reward (it tastes great!). If what the consumer experiences upon responding to a stimulus is not pleasant (I feel sick now!), then *negative reinforcement* has occurred. Behavioural learning plays a major role in consumer decision making—in this case, causing the consumer to avoid the behavioural response rather than repeat it.

Marketers use two concepts from behavioural learning theory. *Stimulus generalization* occurs when a response brought about by one stimulus (cue) is generalized to another stimulus. Using the same brand name to launch new products is one common application of this concept, as when the makers of Tylenol followed up their original pain reliever with Tylenol Cold, Tylenol Flu, Tylenol Sinus, and others. Consumers familiar with one product will often transfer their feelings to others that seem similar—whether the similarity is in a brand name or in the shape and colour of the packaging. Are you familiar with President's Choice Cola or Costco's Simply Soda? They use red cans, similar in colour to Coca-Cola cans—this is stimulus generalization in action!

Stimulus discrimination refers to one's ability to perceive differences among similar products. Consumers may do this easily with some groups of products, such as auto-

perceived risk
Anxiety felt when a consumer cannot anticipate possible negative outcomes of a purchase

learning
Behaviours that result from repeated experience or reasoning

mobiles. But in many cases, often low-involvement purchases, advertisers work to point out the differences. For example, consumers' tendency to perceive all light beers as being alike led to Budweiser Light commercials that distinguished between many types of lights and Bud Light.

Cognitive Learning   Consumers also learn without direct experience—through thinking, reasoning, and mental problem solving. This type of learning, called *cognitive learning*, involves making connections between two or more ideas or simply observing the outcomes of others' behaviours and adjusting your own accordingly. Firms also influence this type of learning. Through repetition in advertising, messages such as "Advil is a headache remedy" attempt to link a brand (Advil) and an idea (headache remedy) by showing someone using the brand and finding relief.

Brand Loyalty   Learning is also important to marketers because it relates to habit formation. Developing habits means that a consumer is solving problems (such as what to do when she's hungry) routinely and consistently, without much thought. Not surprisingly, there is a close link between habits and **brand loyalty**, which is a favourable attitude toward and consistent purchase of a single brand over time. Brand loyalty results from positive reinforcement. If a consumer is satisfied with a product, he reduces his risk and saves time by consistently purchasing that same brand.

Values, Beliefs, and Attitudes

Values, beliefs, and attitudes play a central role in consumer decision making.

Attitude Formation   An **attitude** is a "learned predisposition to respond to an object or class of objects in a consistently favourable or unfavourable way."[21] Attitudes are shaped by our values and beliefs, which we develop in the process of growing up.

brand loyalty
Favourable attitude toward and consistent purchase of a single brand over time

attitude
Tendency to respond to something in a consistently favourable or unfavourable way

Attitudes toward Colgate toothpaste and Extra Strength Bayer aspirin were successfully changed by these ads. How? Read the text to find out how marketers can change consumer attitudes toward products and brands.

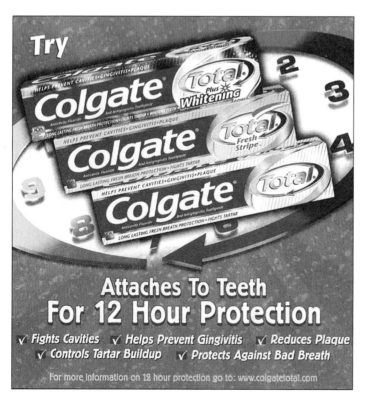

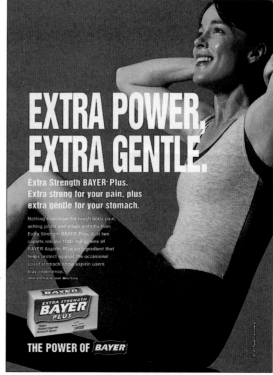

For example, we speak of core values, including material well-being and humanitarianism. We also have personal values, such as thriftiness and ambition. Marketers are concerned with both, but focus mostly on personal values. Personal values affect attitudes by influencing the importance assigned to specific product attributes, or features. Suppose thriftiness is one of your personal values. When you evaluate cars, fuel economy (a product attribute) becomes important. If you believe a specific car has this attribute, you are likely to have a favourable attitude toward it.

Beliefs also play a part in attitude formation. In consumer terms, **beliefs** are one's perception of how a product or brand performs on different attributes. Beliefs are based on personal experience, advertising, and discussions with other people. Beliefs about product attributes are important because, along with personal values, they create the favourable or unfavourable attitude the consumer has toward certain products and services.

beliefs
Consumer's perceptions of how a product or brand performs

Attitude Change Marketers use three approaches to try to change consumer attitudes toward products and brands, as shown in the following examples.[22]

1. *Changing beliefs about the extent to which a brand has certain attributes.* To reduce consumer concern that aspirin use causes an upset stomach, Bayer Corporation successfully promoted the gentleness of its Extra Strength Bayer Plus aspirin.
2. *Changing the perceived importance of attributes.* Pepsi-Cola made freshness an important product attribute when it stamped freshness dates on its cans. Prior to doing so, few consumers considered cola freshness an issue. After Pepsi spent about $25 million on advertising and promotion, a consumer survey found that 61 percent of cola drinkers believed freshness dating was an important attribute.
3. *Adding new attributes to the product.* Colgate-Palmolive included a new antibacterial ingredient, tricloson, in its Colgate Total toothpaste and spent $100 million marketing the brand. The result? Colgate replaced Crest as the market leader for the first time in 25 years.

FIGURE 5–5

Goldfarb psychographic market segments for Canada

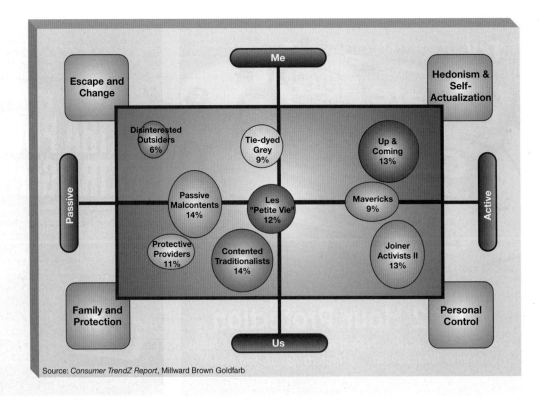

Source: *Consumer TrendZ Report*, Millward Brown Goldfarb

FIGURE 5–6 Goldfarb psychographic market segments for Canada

SEGMENT	PERCENTAGE OF CANADIAN POPULATION	DESCRIPTION	MARKETING IMPLICATIONS
Disinterested Outsiders	6%	Materialistic, price conscious, willing to bend rules, younger, fewer married, lower education, lack respect for authority, not intellectually curious, less into technology, dislike change	Materialistic yet price conscious, low income (offer financing, incentives, and discounts), need to know immediate benefits, like irreverent tone of communications, want non-mainstream items, TV is a good way to reach them
Tie-Dyed Grey	9%	Older, lower income, more unmarried (single, divorced), urban dwellers, few with children, open minded, environmentally conscious, slightly uncomfortable with technology, like cultural events, independent	Do not respond well to family focus or romantic appeals, big readers (like newspapers, TV, magazines, current affairs shows), natural market for travel/holiday packages, marketing should have little jargon and technospeak, like personal touch in services
Passive Malcontents	14%	Older, maybe ethnic, patriotic, lack self-confidence, trusting, not too health conscious, participate in on-line chat	Unhappy (may respond well to products that improve), full-service offerings, health concerns, stress "made in Canada," respectful of authority figures, enjoy reading (magazine & newspaper ads appeal to them), very loyal
Protective Providers	11%	Hard-working, personal initiative, committed to family, financial pressures, distrustful, dislike change, enjoy outdoor activities, married with children, patriotic and proud, not highly educated	Very price conscious, looking for best value and incentives, home improvement and children's products appeal to them, brand names important, respond to respectful promotion, reinforce ideas of safety and security for family to attract them, use TV
Contented Traditionalists	12%	Older, married, religious focus, family oriented, conservative, ethical, respectful of authority, organized, brand loyal, not materialistic	Products/brands with a clean image, tone not irreverent or disrespectful, appreciate products that promote healthy living and family togetherness, like full service offerings, like to take care of future, need reassurance
Up & Comers	12%	Younger, many visible minorities or foreign-born, materialistic, outgoing, looking for quick gratification, optimistic, value friendships	Latest trends and gadgets, entertainment and sports-related products, brand names important, conservative advertising tastes, reach through TV and cinema ads, not newspapers/magazines
Mavericks	9%	Higher household income, solid employment, natural leaders, enjoy challenge, seek wealth, conservative views on family issues	Early adopters, voracious consumers, willing to pay, time poor, like to see benefits emphasized, technology is important to them and high-tech items, make them feel in control and empowered
Joiner Activists II	13%	Married, younger, higher income, optimistic, financially sound, non-religious, environmentalists, health conscious, like cultural activities, comfortable with online purchases	Crave information, like details, interested in new experiences/products, good quality and unique, upscale products, expect intelligent and sophisticated promotions, socially responsible companies attract them, early adopters
Les "Petite Vie"	12%	Friends and family very important, relaxed life, not leaders, respect business leaders, support government, open-minded, many French-speaking, low university attendance	Watch lots of TV, do not trust outsiders, not materialistic, believe spokespeople or experts, brand names are important, do not respond well to "new and improved" (instead they like tried and true)

Source: *Consumer TrendZ Report*, Millward Brown Goldfarb

Lifestyle

Lifestyle is a way of living that is identified by how people spend their time and resources (activities), what they consider important in their environment (interests), and what they think of themselves and the world around them (opinions). The analysis of consumer lifestyles, called *psychographics*, has produced many insights into consumer behaviour. For example, lifestyle analysis has proven useful in segmenting and targeting consumers for new and existing products.

One of the most popular examples of psychographic analysis is the VALS™ Program developed by SRI International.[23] The VALS Program identifies eight interconnected categories of adult lifestyles based on a person's self-orientation and resources. Self-orientation describes the patterns of attitudes and activities that help a person reinforce his or her social self-image. Three patterns have been uncovered; they are oriented toward principles, status, and action. A person's resources range from minimal to abundant and include income, education, self-confidence, health, eagerness to buy, intelligence, and energy level. Each of these categories exhibits different buying behaviour and media preferences.

VALS is an American-based system, and the psychographics of Americans differ significantly from those of Canadians. When some market researchers have tried to use American values and lifestyles to describe Canadians, they have not succeeded. The firm Millward Brown Goldfarb created psychographic groups based on an extensive survey of Canadian values, ethics, opinions and interests over a three-year period. Figure 5-5 shows their nine segments and the percentage of the Canadian adult population that matches the characteristics of each group. The axes of the chart show orientations towards key traits: for example, a "Tie-dyed Grey" is more oriented towards themselves as individuals, while a "Contended Traditionalist" considers family or other close group as more important.

Figure 5-6 summarizes the nine lifestyle types and highlights selected behavioural characteristics of each and their implications for marketers, who can use this information in a variety of ways.

Concept Check

1. The problem with the Toro Snow Pup was an example of selective _____.

2. What three attitude-change approaches are most common?

3. What does the concept of *lifestyle* mean?

SOCIOCULTURAL INFLUENCES ON CONSUMER BEHAVIOUR

Sociocultural influences, which evolve from a consumer's formal and informal relationships with other people, also have an impact on consumer behaviour. These include personal influence, reference groups, family, culture, and subculture.

Personal Influence

A consumer's purchases are often influenced by the views, opinions, or behaviours of others. Two aspects of personal influence are important to marketing: opinion leadership and word-of-mouth activity.

opinion leaders
Individuals who have social influence over others

Opinion Leadership Individuals who have social influence over others are called **opinion leaders**. Opinion leaders are more likely to be important for products that

Firms use actors or athletes as spokespersons to represent their products, such as hockey icon Wayne Gretzky for Ford and gold medal figure skaters Jamie Salé and David Pelletier for Crest, in the hope that they are opinion leaders.

provide a form of self-expression. Automobiles, clothing, and club memberships are products affected by opinion leaders, but appliances usually are not.[24]

A small percentage of adults—from influential community leaders and business executives to movie stars—are opinion leaders.[25] Identifying, reaching, and influencing opinion leaders is a major challenge for companies. Some firms use sports figures or celebrities as spokespersons to represent their products, such as hockey icon Wayne Gretzky for Ford and gold medal figure skaters Jamie Salé and David Pelletier for Crest, in the hope that they are opinion leaders. Others promote their products in media believed to reach opinion leaders.

word of mouth
People influencing each other in personal conversations

Word of Mouth   People influencing each other during conversations is called **word of mouth**. Word of mouth is perhaps the most powerful information source for consumers, because it typically involves friends or family who are viewed as trustworthy.

The power of personal influence has prompted firms to make efforts to increase positive and decrease negative word of mouth.[26] For instance, "teaser" advertising campaigns are run in advance of new-product introductions to stimulate conversations. Other techniques such as advertising slogans, music, and humour also heighten positive word of mouth. On the other hand, rumours about McDonald's (worms in hamburgers) and Corona Extra beer (contaminated beer) have resulted in negative word of mouth, none of which was based on fact. Overcoming negative word of mouth is difficult and costly. Firms have found that supplying factual information, providing toll-free numbers for consumers to call the company, and giving appropriate product demonstrations also have been helpful.

The power of word of mouth has been magnified by the Internet and e-mail. Chapter 15 describes how marketers initiate and manage word of mouth in this setting.

Reference Groups

reference groups
People to whom an individual looks as a basis for self-appraisal or as a source of personal standards

Reference groups are people to whom an individual looks as a basis for self-appraisal or as a source of personal standards. For example, you might consider the other students in your school, or your family, as a reference group. Reference groups affect consumer purchases because they influence the information, attitudes, and aspiration levels that help set a consumer's standards. Reference groups have an important influence on the purchase of luxury products but not of necessities— reference groups exert a strong influence on the brand chosen when its use or consumption is highly visible to others.[27]

Consumers have many reference groups, but three groups have clear marketing implications. A *membership group* is one to which a person actually belongs, including fraternities and sororities, social clubs, and the family. Such groups are easily identifiable and are targeted by firms selling insurance, insignia products, and vacation packages. An *aspiration group* is one that a person wishes to be a member of or wishes to be identified with, such as a professional society. Firms frequently rely on spokespeople or settings associated with their target market's aspiration group in their advertising. A *dissociative group* is one that a person wishes to maintain a distance from because of differences in values or behaviours.

Family Influence

Family influences on consumer behaviour result from three sources: consumer socialization, passage through the family life cycle, and decision making within the family or household.

Consumer Socialization   The process by which people acquire the skills, knowledge, and attitudes necessary to function as consumers is *consumer socialization*.[28] Children learn how to purchase by interacting with adults in purchase situations and through their own purchasing and product usage experiences. Research demonstrates that children show signs of brand preferences as early as age two, and these preferences often last a lifetime. This knowledge has prompted Sony to introduce My First Sony, a line of portable audio equipment for children; Time, Inc., to launch *Sports Illustrated for Kids*; and Polaroid to develop the Cool Cam camcorder for children between ages 9 and 14. The brand of toothpaste, laundry detergent, or soft drink used in your home will very likely influence your brand choice when you purchase these items for yourself.

family life cycle
A family's progression from formation through to retirement, with each phase bringing distinct needs and purchasing behaviours

Family Life Cycle   Consumers act and purchase differently as they go through life. The **family life cycle** concept describes the distinct phases that a family progresses through from formation to retirement, each phase bringing with it identifiable purchasing behaviours.[29] Today, the traditional family—married couples with children younger than 25 years—constitute just over 30 percent of all Canadian households. Nearly 26 percent are single-person households, and another 28 percent are couples without children (or with older children over the age of 25). Multiple-family households, single-parent households, and other groupings account for 16 percent.[30]

Young singles' buying preferences are for nondurable items, including prepared foods, clothing, personal care products, and entertainment. They represent a significant target market for recreational travel, automobile, and consumer electronics firms. Young married couples without children are typically more affluent than young singles because usually both spouses are employed. These couples exhibit preferences for furniture, housewares, and gift items for each other. Young marrieds with children are driven by the needs of their children. These families make up a sizable market for life insurance, various children's products, and home furnishings. Single parents with children are the least financially secure type of households. Their buying preferences are usually affected by a limited economic status and tend toward convenience foods, child care services, and personal care items.

Middle-aged married couples with children are typically better off financially than their younger counterparts. They are a significant market for leisure products and home improvement items. Middle-aged couples without children typically have a large amount of discretionary income. These couples buy better home furnishings, status automobiles, and financial services. Persons in the last two phases—older married and older unmarried—make up a sizable market for prescription drugs, medical services, vacation trips, and gifts for younger relatives.

The Haggar Clothing Co. recognizes the important role women play in the choice of men's clothing. The company directs a large portion of its advertising toward women because they influence and purchase men's clothing.

In the female the ability to match colors comes at an early age.

In the male it comes when he marries a female.

The City Casuals three-button, crepe jacket, 100% cotton, French-yarn shirt, Bedford cord pants, and a touch of color.

HAGGAR
Stuff you can work with

Family Decision Making   A third family-based influence on consumer decision making occurs in the context of the relationship dynamics of the household. Two decision-making styles exist: spouse-dominant and joint decision making. With a joint decision-making style, most decisions are made by both husband and wife. Spouse-dominant decisions are those for which either the husband or the wife is responsible. Research indicates that wives tend to have the most say when purchasing groceries, children's toys, clothing, and medicines. Husbands tend to be more influential in home and car maintenance purchases. Joint decision making is common for cars, vacations, houses, home appliances and electronics, medical care, and long-distance telephone services. As a rule, joint decision making increases with the education of the spouses.[31]

Roles of individual family members in the purchase process are another element of family decision making. Five roles exist: information gatherer, influencer, decision maker, purchaser, and user. Family members assume different roles for different products and services.[32] For example, 89 percent of wives either influence or make outright purchases of men's clothing. Knowing this, Haggar Clothing, a menswear marketer, now advertises in women's magazines such as *Vanity Fair* and *Redbook*. Even though women are often the grocery decision maker, they are not necessarily the purchaser. More than 40 percent of all food-shopping dollars are spent by male customers. Increasingly, preteens and teenagers are the information gatherers, influencers, decision makers, and purchasers of products and services items for the family, given the prevalence of working parents and single-parent households. Children and teenagers directly influence billions of dollars in annual family purchases. These figures help explain why, for example, Johnson & Johnson, Apple Computer, Kellogg, P&G, Sony, and Oscar Mayer, among countless other companies, spend more than $32 billion annually in media that reach preteens and teens.[33]

Culture and Subculture

As described in Chapter 3, culture refers to the set of values, ideas, and attitudes that are learned and shared among the members of a group. Thus we often refer to Canadian culture, American culture, or Japanese culture.

Chinese New Year celebrations take place in Vancouver each year and have become an integral part of the city's cultural fabric.

subcultures
Subgroups within a larger culture that have unique values, ideas, and attitudes

main.

Subgroups within the larger, or national, culture with unique values, ideas, and attitudes are referred to as **subcultures**. Subcultures can be defined by regions, by demographic groups, or by values. The most prominent types of subcultures are racial and ethnic, and many of these exist within the Canadian mosaic of people. French, German, Italian, Chinese, and Ukrainian subcultures are the ones we see most in Canada, and they make up nearly 40 percent of the Canadian population. Each one exhibits unique buying patterns and social/cultural behaviours.

Canada's outlook on ethnicity is that cultural and ethnic groups are welcome to continue with their traditions, languages, and values. We are a nation of many faces, and people have been immigrating to Canada continually over many decades. A person may regard themselves as Italian, yet never have been to Italy—their grandparents may have immigrated here many years ago. If Italian customs have been maintained by the family, this person may behave much like a recently arrived Italian. Some countries encourage immigrants to join the mainstream national culture, while in Canada we encourage diversity.

Our ethnic composition, and the philosophy that we take towards it, has led to the creation of many ethnic neighbourhoods in our cities. As our population becomes more diverse, people immigrating here bring foods from their native lands. Canadians do not have a lot of native food and preparation styles, so the country has been particularly welcoming of cuisine from around the world. Immigration has had a major influence on the food market, both in the many restaurants and in the food items available from all corners of the globe. Not only food consumption is affected by immigration: many cultural events have become mainstream, and many local happenings are the result of a tradition or celebration brought here by some new Canadians.

French-Canadian Subculture   There are more than 9 million French-speaking Canadians in this country, about 30 percent of the population.[34] By far the largest majority of them live in the province of Quebec. Research shows that French-speaking Quebecers do exhibit different consumption behaviour from the rest of Canada.[35] French Quebecers link price to perceived value but will decide against buying rather than buy on credit. They are more willing to pay higher prices for convenience and premium brands, and they believe advertising more than the average Canadian.

French Quebecers are cautious about new products and often postpone trying something new until they see that the product has proven itself. They exhibit brand loyalty, but they will switch brands if offered a special. They also prefer convenience and health food stores over food warehouses and local grocery stores. French Quebecers are less likely to buy grocery items on impulse, and are increasingly calculating in their food purchases. Some grocery chains have responded to this characteristic by offering more discount coupons, weekly specials, and money-saving tips. Personal grooming and fashion are more important to French Quebecers than to the average Canadian, and they are more likely to shop in specialty clothing boutiques.

French Quebec has a higher percentage of wine and beer drinkers and more smokers; while Quebecers enjoy their beer, Molson says its research indicates that French Quebecers prefer a stronger beer, so it launched the O'Keefe 6.2 brand (which contains 6.2% alcohol) exclusively for the Quebec market. There are fewer golfers, joggers, and gardeners in Quebec, and the proportion of people who entertain at home or go to movies is also lower. By contrast, Quebec has more cyclists, skiers, and live theatre fans.

French Quebecers are big buyers of lottery tickets and more likely to subscribe to book clubs, but they make fewer long-distance phone calls. They travel less, whether for business or pleasure. More French Quebec adults hold life insurance policies, but they are less likely to have a credit card. They also tend to use the services of credit unions (*caisses populaires*) rather than banks.

Some people feel that French Quebec can be characterized by a set of values that are traditional, consistent, and relatively static, but changes are evident. While values are still strong regarding family life, having children in a marriage, and about giving the children religious training, the use of birth control is rising, and the marriage rate is below the national average.

Marketers must realize that certain products and other elements of the marketing mix may have to be modified in order to be successful in French Quebec. In addition to cultural differences, there are other issues that marketers must address. Commercial advertising to children is prohibited and greater restrictions exist for alcohol advertising. Provincial regulations also require that labels and packages must be both English and French, while storefront signage must be in French, not English. Good investigation and analysis of this market is a requirement for all companies wishing to do business in this province.

Chinese-Canadian Subculture   The Chinese comprise the largest visible minority group in Canada, and more than a million people (3.5% of the population) represent this ethnic group. There were restrictions on immigration from China up until the 1960s, but since then the Chinese have become one of Canada's fastest-growing ethnic populations. Many of them reside in Vancouver, which has the largest proportion of Chinese of any Canadian metropolitan area at 343,000 (17% of the metropolitan area's population). Another 409,000 Chinese residents live in Toronto, to comprise 9 percent of the population.[36]

Chinese-Canadians have unique characteristics and values. While most Canadians value straight-line thinking (logic), the Chinese value circular thinking (what goes around, comes around). They value work, family, and education. Their purchasing patterns are quite different from those of the average Canadian, and they often perceive products differently. Many prefer to be communicated with in their own language, and this has caused many companies to produce ads in Mandarin or Cantonese and run them in specialty Chinese newspapers, such as Toronto's *Sing Tao* or Vancouver's *Ming Pao*. The average Chinese Canadian has a higher income, is better educated, and is less likely to be unemployed than the general Canadian population.

Chinese-Canadians have a preference for luxury vehicles, and many car dealerships see them as good potential customers for new cars. In general, they tend to eat out at restaurants more than the average Canadian, and there has been significant growth in the number of Chinese restaurants in Canada, and particularly in Vancouver and Toronto, over the past 10 years. For these, and a number of other factors, many marketers cater to the Chinese market as they see them as being good prospective customers.

Concept Check

1. What are the two primary forms of personal influence?
2. What two challenges must marketers overcome when marketing to ethnic subcultural groups?

SUMMARY

1   When a consumer buys a product, it is not an act but a process. There are five steps in the purchase decision process: problem recognition, information search, alternative evaluation, purchase decision, and postpurchase behaviour.

2   Consumers evaluate alternatives on the basis of attributes. Identifying which attributes are most important to consumers, along with understanding consumer beliefs about how a brand performs on those attributes, can make the difference between successful and unsuccessful products.

3   Consumer involvement with what is bought affects whether the purchase decision process involves routine, limited, or extended problem solving. Situational influences also affect the process.

4   Perception is important to marketers because of the selectivity of what a consumer sees or hears, comprehends, and retains.

5   Much of the behaviour that consumers exhibit is learned. Consumers learn from repeated experience and reasoning. Brand loyalty is a result of learning.

6   Attitudes are learned predispositions to respond to an object or class of objects in a consistently favourable or unfavourable way. Attitudes are based on a person's values and beliefs concerning the attributes of products or services.

7   Personal influence takes two forms: opinion leadership and word-of-mouth activity. A specific type of personal influence exists in the form of reference groups.

8   Family influences on consumer behaviour result from two sources: family life cycle and decision making within the household.

9   Within Canada there are subcultures that affect consumer values and behaviour. Marketers must be sensitive to these influences when developing a marketing mix.

KEY TERMS AND CONCEPTS

attitude p. 105
beliefs p. 106
brand loyalty p. 105
consumer behaviour p. 96
family life cycle p. 110
involvement p. 98
learning p. 104
motivation p. 101

opinion leaders p. 108
perceived risk p. 104
perception p. 103
personality p. 102
purchase decision process p. 96
reference groups p. 109
subcultures p. 112
word of mouth p. 109

QUESTIONS: APPLYING MARKETING CONCEPTS AND PERSPECTIVES

1   Assume that you are going to purchase a candy bar, a pair of shoes, and a new computer. Identify the steps in the purchase decision process you would use to purchase each one, and determine how the process differs for the three items.

2   Suppose research at Panasonic reveals that prospective buyers are anxious about buying high-definition television sets. What strategies might you recommend to the company to reduce consumer anxiety?

3   Assign one or more levels of the hierarchy of needs and the motives described in Figure 5–4 to the following products: (a) life insurance, (b) cosmetics, (c) *Maclean's* magazine, and (d) hamburgers.

4   With which stage in the family life cycle would the purchase of the following products and services be most closely identified: (a) bedroom furniture, (b) life insurance, (c) a Caribbean cruise, (d) a house mortgage, and (e) children's toys?

DISCUSSION FORUM

Assume that you are the marketing manager for one of the major automobile manufacturers. You want to develop a clear picture of consumers, and the decision process that consumers go through in making a vehicle purchase decision. Using Figure 5-3, create a picture of consumers, including the influences on them, and the decision process they go through in purchasing a brand new car for the first time. Identify how the automobile manufacturer will use this information in their marketing.

INTERNET EXERCISE

Visit the SRI Consulting Business Intelligence (SRIC-BI) website at www.sric-bi.com/VALS, and then click on "VALS™ Survey." First, look at "The VALS™ Types" and their descriptions. Which segment do you think you fall into? Take the survey to find out whether you guessed correctly. Does the description of your segment describe you in some ways? (Note that this is a very simple and stripped-down version of the firm's psychographic test; the long version contains some 200 questions.) This questionnaire will give you a flavour for the type of questions asked to determine psychographic characteristics.

Review the description of the segment that you are in and then click on the other segments on the site to find out how your segment relates to others.

In this chapter, we looked in some detail at the Millward Brown Goldfarb segments, but at present they do not have an online test you can take. How do you think their segments relate to the VALS segments? Compare them, and then take on a marketing analyst's role:

1 What companies that you are familiar with do you think could best use this type of segmentation?
2 If you were the marketing manager for Zellers, what segments would you choose and why?
3 Visit the Environics Research Group site (http://erg.environics.net/), click on "Connect Here to Your Tribe," and look at the Canadian market segments this company has crafted. Compare them with the VALS segments, and also with the Goldfarb segments discussed earlier in this chapter.
4 On the VALS site, check out "Japan-VALS™." What differences do you see between the Japanese and the other VALS segments? Between the Japanese segments and the Environics and Goldfarb segments?

VIDEO CASE 5

CBC

THE CONSUMER ON THE COUCH

To retailers, there is no more important question than "why do consumers buy?" Understanding the influences that affect purchasing behaviour can spell the difference between commercial success and failure.

Paco Underhill is a New York City–based "retail anthropologist" who has been retained by dozens of top-flight companies, including the Canadian Imperial Bank of Commerce, Burger King, and Calvin Klein, to determine what attracts customers to their locations, what makes them linger, and what makes them spend. His empirical findings, many of which are documented in his *Why We Buy: The Science of Shopping*, are based mainly on analysis of tens of thousands of hours of clandestine videotaping of shoppers in action. Underhill's studies have significantly expanded our understanding of the purchase decision process while raising important questions about the privacy rights of consumers.

SHAPE UP OR SHIP OUT

At last count, the retail sector recorded sales of $277 billion and provided 12 percent of all jobs (about 1.75 million positions) in Canada. But while the sector has 100 percent more stores than it did 15 years ago, it has only 15 percent more customers. As participants in a key economic sector that is subject to tremendous domestic competition, Canadian retailers must do everything they can to understand consumer needs and motivations.

Their need for greater insight into consumer behaviour became critical in the mid-1990s, when international retailers began to vie for market share in Canada. Global competitors with deep pockets, such as Wal-Mart, Pottery Barn, and Payless ShoeSource, threatened the viability of many domestic firms. According to Underhill, Canada can expect even more competition from foreign retailers in the years ahead. Part of the problem, as he sees it, is that most Canadian outlets are "frumpy." By this, he means more than unattractive; he means that most are not designed with shoppers in mind. As he says in the *Venture* video, "If the 20th century was about marketers being leaders, the 21st century is about marketers being followers." Satisfying consumer expectations is the key to success at the cash register.

At the same time, Underhill is a stalwart fan of firms like Canadian Tire, which completely redesigned its hardware stores to curb the market penetration of big-box competitors such as Home Depot and Wal-Mart. Examples like this show clearly that domestic firms can compete successfully for the attention of increasingly fickle shoppers. And Underhill believes they must. "In the Canadian marketplace," he says, "retailers must shape up or go out of business."

READING THE RETAIL LANDSCAPE

Traditional market research on consumer behaviour has been done through analysis of barcodes scanned at the cash register and from direct surveys of shoppers conducted via telephone, one-on-one interviews, or focus groups. While the resulting data are valuable, rarely do they shed light on the discrepancy between what customers say about the process of making purchasing choices and what they actually do at the store. Consequently, Underhill and like-minded students of shopping are less concerned with what people buy than why they so often fail to buy.

To gain more understanding of shoppers, some retailers have turned to in-store customer surveillance. Using hidden cameras that videotape consumers as they approach, enter, and exit a store, and supplementing that evidence with surreptitious observations by in-store "trackers" who add a more qualitative dimension, retail anthropologists provide micro-level documentation of consumer behaviour. Nothing escapes their scrutiny. The result, when time-series data are compiled, is a telling view of a single store's failings as a shopping environment from the perspective of the customer. Retailers who have implemented changes based on such evidence attest that catering directly to the needs of their existing customer base has significantly improved their bottom line.

FOUR KEY OBSERVATIONS
A sharp turn to the right

Eighty percent of buying decisions are made on the shop floor, so the layout of the shop floor and the manner in which customers are lured onto it are crucial to raising sales volumes and profit levels. The fact that people will not read more than three or four words in a shop window, for example, implies that window displays must be primarily visual in content. And contrary to popular belief, the entry to a store is not the ideal location for a retailer's most desirable goods; rather, it is a commercially dead zone where customers orient themselves but almost never buy. Reserving the entry for a display that appeals to the senses and pulls uncommitted shoppers into the bowels of the store where they will spend is the best tactic.

But the real key to effective layout, says Underhill, is the tendency of almost all customers to enter a store and turn, immediately, to the right. That is the prime spot for snagging a customer's attention. In fact, Underhill has determined that sales can be increased as much as 15 percent merely by shifting the cash register from the right side of a store to the left. Once they have made that initial right turn, customers navigate the store in a counter-clockwise

orbit. Articles placed strategically along that path are much more likely to be purchased.

Appealing to the senses

Underhill has found a strong, direct correlation between sensory stimulation and sales volume. The idea is akin to creating a bazaar-like atmosphere within the store: fill the air with a seductive scent, let customers sample some delicious food, place clothing so that it can be touched, and watch sales increase. Have a salesperson talk to the customer while they taste or touch the merchandise, and the odds of them buying increase by half again. Let them try on an article of clothing, and the odds get even better. In short, involving them directly with the product pays big dividends.

Women are a retailer's best friends

Seventy percent of shoppers are women, and women are believed to influence as much as 85 percent of all retail purchasing decisions. And if two women shop together, they will spend almost twice as much time in the store as a male–female couple. All of this is important in view of the strong relationship between the time spent shopping and the amount spent.

After observing shoppers for some 20 years, Underhill is adamant that women care much more than men about the shopping experience. Enhance a store's atmosphere according to the interests and concerns of the female shopper and the typical customer will stay longer and spend more. Generous, well-lit display spaces rank high on the list of vital enhancements, but pristine washrooms and garbage cans in fitting rooms matter too. Provide amenities for male companions and children, and the sales volume climbs even further. The Chapters-Indigo book chain, with its wide aisles, consistent lighting, clear signs, comfortable chairs, and aromatic coffee-house corner has been a particularly apt pupil when it comes to designing what Underhill defines as "female-friendly" retail space.

Butt-brushing

Culturally and socially, Western women are averse to anything that touches their posteriors. Video after video in the Underhill archives shows that females who inadvertently back into awkwardly placed display racks or narrowly spaced rows of shelving will leave a store immediately. And with them goes the potential sale. This is what he calls the "butt-brush factor," and it exemplifies the respect for unspoken customer sensitivities that every retailer must possess if they wish to succeed in business.

MEETING FUTURE CONSUMER NEEDS

Underhill says that change is good, but that constant change is better. He is referring not only to modifying today's retailing methods, but also to the importance of anticipating and addressing the needs of traditionally neglected customers and emerging markets. The first kind of change deals with tactical options, while the second is about choosing a long-term, strategic marketing direction. To assist companies in this, he has identified a number of key opportunities that lie ahead:

* the high-income seniors' market
* marketing to ethnic and minority groups
* addressing the needs of women who are buying non-traditional products (e.g., technology, automobiles, hardware)
* addressing the needs of men who are doing the family shopping and buying clothing

If retailers have what Underhill calls the "good manners" to identify and satisfy the different needs and expectations of these diverse groups, he is convinced they will profit.

Questions

1 Identify specific examples of Canadian retailers whose sales have been affected by international competitors. What behavioural factors can you cite to account for their success or failure?

2 If a single store offers a range of merchandise that appeals to various demographic groups, how can it hope to satisfy all their needs?

3 Corporate collection of customer data without permission has been controversial in the online retail world. How does that situation differ, if at all, from the methods typically employed by retail anthropologists like Paco Underhill?

4 What are the principal behavioural factors that need to be considered in addressing the rapidly growing seniors market? Discuss how a retailer selling goods or services via the Internet might use this information.

Chapter 6

Organizational Markets and Buyer Behaviour

AFTER READING THIS CHAPTER YOU SHOULD BE ABLE TO:

- Identify the distinguishing characteristics of industrial, reseller, government, and not-for-profit markets.

- Recognize the key characteristics of organizational buying that make the process different from consumer buying.

- Understand how buying centres and buying situations influence organizational purchasing.

- Understand the growing importance of and the approaches in online buying for industrial, reseller, and government markets.

LED LIGHTING-NEW LIGHT IDEAS FOR THE WORLD

Does "Corporate Identity" sound like the name for a line of products? It really is! At TIR Systems Ltd., light and colour are used to communicate an identity that will attract potential customers to a retail location, be it a gas station, a store, or a cinema complex. The Famous Players Colossus theatre, shown above, uses products developed by TIR Systems to project its name to the public. For TIR, this is the market known as Corporate Identity, and there are many, many potential buyers.

A fast-growing Canadian company, TIR is a world leader in specialty lighting systems for businesses. It has developed-high efficiency power supplies, full-range digital control, advanced optical films, thin coatings, and next-generation communications protocols to enable compound semi-conductor technology in the form of light emitting diodes (LEDs) for use as lighting. Sounds complicated, and it is. Solid state lighting technology is poised "to change the way we light the world," according to Caren Holtby of TIR.[1]

TIR suggests that this change is equivalent to the change from the horse and buggy to the automobile, or the change from oil lamps to electric light bulbs.[2] This quote from TIR's website gives an interesting capsule of the potential: "In the next few decades, general illumination technology will undergo a remarkable transformation. Just as transistors replaced vacuum tubes 50 years ago, and just as flat panel displays are now replacing CRT monitors and televisions, solid state lighting will likely take the place of incandescent and fluorescent lamps used for applications in general illumination. . . . Many believe that solid state technology has similar potential to radically change the future of general lighting. . . . "[3]

TIR understands the needs of companies who must balance the requirements of maintaining a consistent image with keeping operational costs low. Its products are energy-efficient, low-maintenance, and effective lighting solutions designed to decrease the world's rising energy consumption and cost. The company

THE MARKETING PROCESS

Just as Chapter 5 focuses on consumer behaviour, Chapter 6 focuses on the organizational consumer. Marketers identify, analyze, and seek to satisfy their organizational target markets.

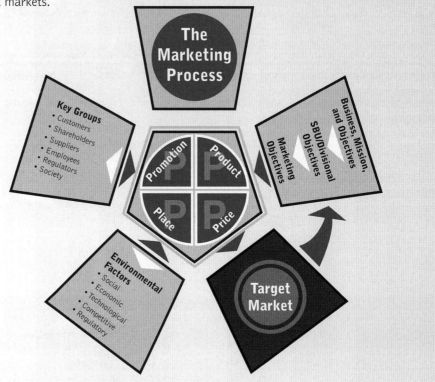

concentrates on industrial and commercial markets, and its products are used for lighting tunnels, bridges, and other traffic applications; specialty lighting arrangements in buildings; and in the Corporate Identity market.

Canada's Petro-Canada has installed products containing TIR's solid state lighting technology to replace neon contour lights on gas station canopies in Australia, New Zealand, and the U.S. With an expected life of 15 to 20 years, these products will be around for a long time. The next time you go by a well-lit building, gas station, or store, your attention may just be drawn to its state-of-the-art lighting designed by TIR. For now, the company is co centrating on the business market, but who knows? Did you see those new strings of LED lights that were so popular last Christmas? They use this type of technology. Have you changed a light bulb and wondered why you need to do so often? With TIR's products, all of that may change!

Petro-Cananda's purchase of lighting products is one example of organizational buying. This chapter examines the types of organizational buyers, key characteristics of organizational buying including online buying, and some typical buying decisions in organizational markets.

THE NATURE AND SIZE OF ORGANIZATIONAL MARKETS

business marketing
Marketing to firms, governments, or not-for-profit organizations

Understanding organizational markets and buying behaviour is necessary for effective business marketing. **Business marketing** is the marketing of products to companies, governments, or not-for-profit organizations for use in the creation of goods and services that they then produce and market to others.[4] It is also referred to as business-to-business (B2B) marketing. So many firms engage in business marketing that it is important to understand the characteristics of organizational buyers and their buying behaviour, as they differ from consumer buying behaviour.

organizational buyers
Manufacturers, wholesalers, retailers, and government agencies that buy goods and services for their own use or for resale

Organizational buyers are those manufacturers, wholesalers, retailers, and government agencies that buy goods and services for their own use or for resale. For example, these organizations buy computers and telephone services for their own use. Manufacturers buy raw materials and parts that they reprocess into the finished goods they sell, and wholesalers and retailers resell the goods they buy without reprocessing them. Organizational buyers include all buyers in a nation except ultimate consumers. These organizational buyers purchase and lease large volumes of equipment, raw materials, manufactured parts, supplies, and business services. They often buy raw materials and parts, process them, and sell them. This upgraded product may pass through several different organizations (as it is bought and resold by different levels of manufacturers, distributors, wholesalers, and retailers) before it is purchased by the final organizational buyer or final consumer. So the total purchases of organizational buyers in a year are far greater than those of ultimate consumers.

Organizational buyers are divided into three different markets: industrial, reseller, and government markets (Figure 6–1).[5]

Industrial Markets

There are over 1.6 million firms in the industrial, or business, market. These *industrial firms* in some way reprocess a product or service they buy before selling it again to the next buyer. This is certainly true of Nortel Networks Limited, a prominent Canadian producer of telecommunications equipment, which assembles optical network systems from parts they manufacture themselves, as well as some they source from other companies. More than 75 percent of all North American backbone Internet traffic travels on Nortel Network optical systems.[6] It is also true (if you stretch your imagination) of a firm

FIGURE 6–1

Type and number of organizational customers, as reported by Statistics Canada

BUSINESS MARKETS IN CANADA

KIND OF BUSINESS MARKET	TYPE OF ORGANIZATION	NUMBER OF FIRMS IN CANADA
All industries		2,024,508
Industrial markets: 1,641,170	Primary industries (agriculture, fishing, mining, forestry)	209,657
	Utilities	4,926
	Manufacturers	105,256
	Construction	225,837
	Services	691,779
	Transportation, storage, and communications	102,168
	Finance, insurance, and real estate	301,547
Reseller markets: 375,538	Wholesale trade	132,666
	Retail trade	242,872
Government markets: 7,800	Public administration (federal, provincial, municipal, regional)	7,800

Source: Statistics Canada (www.statcan.ca/english/Pgdb/econ18.htm)

selling services, such as a bank that takes money from its depositors, "stores" it, and "sells" it as loans to borrowers.

The importance of services in Canada today is emphasized by the composition of the industrial markets shown in Figure 6–1. Primary industries (agriculture, fishing, mining, and forestry), utilities, manufacturers, and construction sell physical products and represent 27 percent of all of the industrial firms, or about 546,000. The service market sells diverse services such as legal advice, auto repair, and dry cleaning. Along with finance, insurance, and real estate businesses; transportation, communication, and public utility firms; and not-for-profit associations, these service firms represent about 54 percent of all industrial firms, or about 1.1 million.

Reseller Markets

Wholesalers and retailers that buy physical products and resell them again without any reprocessing are *resellers*. In Canada there are almost 243,000 retailers and 133,000 wholesalers. In this chapter we look at these resellers mainly as organizational buyers in terms of how they make their own buying decisions and which products they choose to carry.

Government Markets

Government units are the federal, provincial, regional, and municipal agencies that buy goods and services for the constituents that they serve. With a spending budget of close to $180 billion annually, the federal government is a major customer, possibly the largest in Canada.[7] In addition to specialized purchases for the military, government agencies also buy almost everything that regular consumers buy, from toilet paper to chewing gum to cars for federal prisons, hospitals, and schools. At the federal government level, the bulk of the purchasing is done by Public Works and Government Services Canada. Provincial and municipal governments typically have government departments that do the buying for them. In addition, hundreds of government departments, agencies, and Crown Corporations (owned by the government on behalf of the people of Canada) such as CBC, VIA Rail, and the Royal Canadian Mint purchase supplies and services to operate.

Not-for-Profit Organizations

Organizations that operate without having financial profit as a goal, and which seek to provide goods and services for the good of society, are called *not-for-profit organizations*. They are also known as charitable organizations, and some 80,000 of them are registered with Canada Revenue Agency.[8] Tax advantages make it beneficial for this type of organization to register with the federal government.

You are probably familiar with many not-for-profit organizations. Were you a member of the Boy Scouts or Girl Guides? Have you participated in a Canadian Cancer Society run or marathon? Have you been asked for a donation to the United Way? Hospitals, arts organizations, cultural groups, and some research institutes can be classified as not-for-profit organizations. In your school, you may have a foundation office that raises money for student awards and aid; this too is a not-for-profit organization. In the past, marketing in these organizations has been limited, but increasingly they are adopting the same types of marketing techniques that other business firms employ, and with good success. As purchasers, this sector of business buys a wide array of goods and services to conduct their operations.

MEASURING INDUSTRIAL, RESELLER, GOVERNMENT, AND NOT-FOR-PROFIT MARKETS

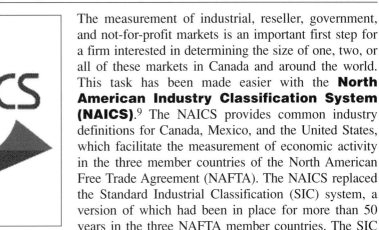

North American Industry Classification System (NAICS)
Provides common industry definitions for Canada, Mexico, and the United States

The measurement of industrial, reseller, government, and not-for-profit markets is an important first step for a firm interested in determining the size of one, two, or all of these markets in Canada and around the world. This task has been made easier with the **North American Industry Classification System (NAICS)**.[9] The NAICS provides common industry definitions for Canada, Mexico, and the United States, which facilitate the measurement of economic activity in the three member countries of the North American Free Trade Agreement (NAFTA). The NAICS replaced the Standard Industrial Classification (SIC) system, a version of which had been in place for more than 50 years in the three NAFTA member countries. The SIC neither permitted comparability across countries nor accurately measured new or emerging industries. Furthermore, the NAICS is consistent with the International Standard Industrial Classification of All Economic Activities, published by the United Nations, to help measure global economic activity.

The NAICS groups economic activity to permit studies of market share, demand for goods and services, competition from imports in domestic markets, and similar studies. The NAICS designates industries with a numerical code in a defined structure. A six-digit coding system is used. The first two digits designate a sector of the economy, the third digit designates a subsector, and the fourth digit represents an industry group. The fifth digit designates a specific industry and is the most detailed level at which comparable data is available for Canada, Mexico, and the United States. The sixth digit designates individual country-level national industries. Figure 6-2 presents an abbreviated breakdown within the Arts, Entertainment, and Recreation Sector (code 71) to illustrate the classification scheme.

FIGURE 6-2

NAICS breakdown for the Arts, Entertainment, and Recreation Sector: NAICS code 71 (abbreviated)

The NAICS permits a firm to find the NAICS codes of its present customers and then obtain NAICS-coded lists of similar firms. Also, it is possible to monitor NAICS categories to determine the growth in various sectors and industries to identify promising marketing opportunities. However, NAICS codes, like the earlier SIC codes, have important limitations. The NAICS assigns only one code to each organization based on its major economic activity, but large firms that engage in many different activities are

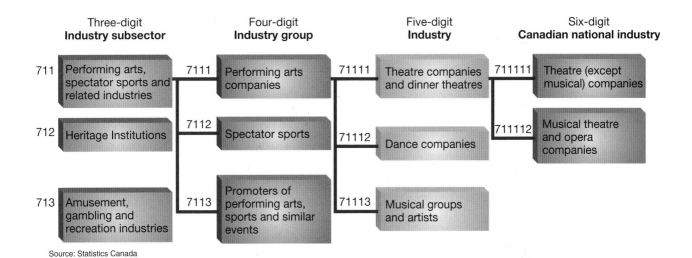

Source: Statistics Canada

still given only one NAICS code. A second limitation is that five-digit national industry codes are not available for all three countries because the respective governments will not reveal data when too few organizations exist in a category. Despite these limitations, the NAICS represents yet another effort toward economic integration in North America and the world.

Concept Check

1. What are the three main types of organizational buyers?
2. What is the North American Industry Classification System (NAICS)?

CHARACTERISTICS OF ORGANIZATIONAL BUYING

Organizations are different from individuals in the way they purchase goods and services, so buying for an organization is different from buying for yourself and your family. In both cases the objective in making the purchase is to solve the buyer's problem—to satisfy a need or want. Unique objectives and policies of an organization put special constraints on how it makes buying decisions. Understanding the characteristics of organizational buying is essential in designing effective marketing programs to reach these buyers. Key characteristics of organizational buying are listed in Figure 6–3 and discussed next.[10]

FIGURE 6–3

Key characteristics of organizational buying behaviour

CHARACTERISTICS	DIMENSIONS
Market characteristics	• Demand for industrial products and services is derived. • The number of business customers is typically small, and their purchase orders are typically large.
Product or service characteristics	• Products or services are technical in nature and purchased on the basis of specifications. • Many goods purchased are raw or semifinished. • Heavy emphasis is placed on delivery time, technical assistance, and postsale service.
Buying process characteristics	• Technically qualified and professional buyers follow established purchasing policies and procedures. • Buying objectives and criteria are typically spelled out, as are procedures for evaluating sellers and their products or services. • There are multiple buying influences, and multiple parties participate in purchase decisions. • There are reciprocal arrangements, and negotiation between buyers and sellers is commonplace. • Online buying over the Internet is widespread.
Marketing mix characteristics	• Personal selling to organizational buyers is used extensively, and distribution is very important. • Advertising and other forms of promotion are technical in nature. • Price is often negotiated, evaluated as part of broader seller and product or service qualities, and frequently affected by quantity discounts.

Demand Characteristics

derived demand
Demand for industrial products and services driven by demand for consumer products and services

Consumer demand for products and services is affected by their price and availability and by consumers' personal tastes and discretionary income. By comparison, industrial demand is derived. **Derived demand** means that the demand for industrial products and services is driven by, or derived from, demand for consumer products and services, as demonstrated in Figure 6-4. For example, the demand for Weyerhaeuser's pulp and paper products is based on consumer demand for newspapers, Domino's "keep warm" pizza-to-go boxes, FedEx packages, and disposable diapers. Derived demand is often based on expectations of future consumer demand. For instance, Whirlpool purchases parts for its washers and dryers in anticipation of consumer demand, which is affected by the replacement cycle for these products and by consumer income.

Size of the Order or Purchase

The size of the purchase involved in organizational buying is typically much larger than that in consumer buying. The dollar value of a single purchase made by an organization often runs into the thousands or millions of dollars. For example, Nortel Networks, Canada's largest phone equipment supplier, recently won a $500 million contract to upgrade the wireless network of Cingular Wireless in the U.S. and Puerto Rico.[11] With so much money at stake, most organizations place constraints on their buyers in the form of purchasing policies or procedures. Buyers must often get competitive bids from at least three prospective suppliers when the order is above a specific amount, such as $5,000. When the order is above an even higher amount, such as $50,000, it may require the review and approval of a vice president or even the president of the company. Knowing how the size of the order affects buying practices is important in determining who participates in the purchase decision and makes the final decision and also the length of time required to arrive at a purchase agreement.

FIGURE 6–4
Direct versus derived demand

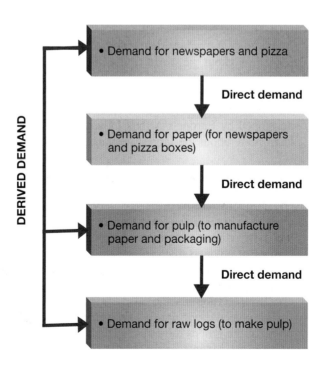

Number of Potential Buyers

Firms selling consumer products or services often try to reach thousands or millions of individuals or households. For example, your local supermarket or bank probably serves thousands of people, and Kellogg tries to reach millions of Canadian households with its breakfast cereals and probably succeeds in selling to a third or half of these in any given year. In contrast, firms selling to organizations are often restricted to far fewer buyers. Bombardier Aerospace can sell its Challenger business jets to a few thousand organizations throughout the world, and B. F. Goodrich sells its original equipment tires to fewer than 10 car manufacturers.

Derived demand, the size of the purchase order, and the number of potential buyers will play a part in the commercial success of the new A380 superjumbo jet being developed by Europe's Airbus Industrie. Read the accompanying Marketing NewsNet to learn more about the largest airplane ever built.[12]

Organizational Buying Objectives

Organizations buy products and services for one main reason: to help them achieve their objectives. For business firms the buying objective is usually to increase profits through reducing costs or increasing sales. 7-Eleven buys automated inventory systems to increase the number of products that can be sold through its convenience stores and to keep them fresh. Nissan Motor Company switched its advertising agency because it expects the new agency to devise a more effective ad campaign to help it sell more cars and increase sales. To improve executive decision making, many firms buy advanced computer systems to process data.

The objectives of not-for-profit firms and government agencies are usually to meet the needs of the groups they serve. Thus, a hospital buys a high-technology diagnostic device to serve its patients better. Understanding buying objectives is a necessary first step in marketing to organizations.

Organizational Buying Criteria

In Chapter 5, we talked about the criteria consumers use when purchasing a product. Businesses also use criteria in their purchasing: they specify *organizational buying criteria*, which are detailed specifications for the products and services they want to buy and the characteristics of the suppliers that will supply them. When suppliers are selected, their products and their firm's characteristics are evaluated using these criteria. Some of the most commonly used criteria are:

- Price,
- Ability to meet the quality specifications required,
- Ability to meet the required delivery schedules,
- Technical capability,
- Warranties and claim policies,
- Past performance on previous contracts, and
- Production facilities and capacity.

Suppliers that meet or exceed the criteria create customer value for the business doing the purchasing.

Many organizational buyers today are transforming their buying criteria into specific requirements that are communicated to suppliers. This practice, called *reverse marketing*, means that organizational buyers are attempting to work with suppliers to make their products, services, and capabilities fit the buyer's needs. Working closely and collaboratively like this with suppliers also helps build buyer-seller relationships and leads to supply partnerships.

Buyer–Seller Relationships and Supply Partnerships

Another distinction between organizational and consumer buying behaviour lies in the nature of the relationship between organizational buyers and suppliers. Specifically, organizational buying is more likely to involve complex and lengthy negotiations concerning delivery schedules, price, technical specifications, warranties, and claim policies. These negotiations can last for more than a year. In the Marketing NewsNet box about the Airbus A380, we are told that FedEx has 10 of the superjumbo jets on order. But the planes are not scheduled to be in service until 2006, suggesting a long negotiating, processing, and manufacturing time.

Reciprocal arrangements also exist in organizational buying. Reciprocity is an industrial buying practice in which two organizations agree to purchase each other's products and services. Governments frown on reciprocal buying because it restricts the normal operation of the free market. However, the practice exists and can limit the flexibility of organizational buyers in choosing alternative suppliers.

In some cases, buyer–seller relationships develop into supply partnerships.[13] A **supply partnership** exists when a buyer and its supplier adopt mutually beneficial objectives, policies, and procedures for the purpose of lowering the cost or increasing the value of products and services delivered to the ultimate consumer. Intel, the world's largest manufacturer of microprocessors and famous for the "intel inside" sticker on most personal computers, is a case in point. Intel supports its suppliers by offering them quality management programs and by investing in supplier equipment that produces fewer product defects and boosts supplier productivity. Suppliers, in turn, provide Intel with consistent high-quality products at a lower cost for its customers, the makers of personal computers, and finally you, the ultimate customer. Retailers, too, are developing partnerships with their suppliers. Wal-Mart has such a relationship with Procter & Gamble for ordering and replenishing P&G's products in their stores. By using computerized cash register scanning equipment and direct electronic linkages to P&G, Wal-Mart can tell P&G what

supply partnership
Relationship between a buyer and supplier that adopt mutually beneficial objectives, policies, and procedures

merchandise is needed, along with how much, when, and to which store to deliver it on a daily basis.

1. What is derived demand?

2. A supply partnership exists when _____.

THE ORGANIZATIONAL BUYING PROCESS AND THE BUYING CENTRE

organizational buying behaviour
Process by which organizations determine the need for goods and then choose among alternative suppliers

Organizational buyers, like consumers, engage in a decision process when selecting products and services. **Organizational buying behaviour** is the decision-making process that organizations use to establish the need for products and services and identify, evaluate, and choose among alternative brands and suppliers. There are important similarities and differences between the two decision-making processes. To better understand the nature of organizational buying behaviour, we first compare it with consumer buying behaviour. We then describe a unique feature of organizational buying—the buying centre.

Stages in the Organizational Buying Process

As shown in Figure 6–5, the five stages a student might use in buying a portable MP3 player also apply to organizational purchases. However, comparing the two right-hand columns in Figure 6–5 reveals some key differences. For example, when a portable MP3 player manufacturer buys earphones for its units from a supplier, more individuals are involved, supplier capability becomes more important, and the postpurchase evaluation behaviour is more formal. The earphone-buying decision process is typical of the steps made by organizational buyers.

The Buying Centre: A Cross-Functional Group

buying centre
Group of people in an organization who participate in the buying process

For routine purchases with a small dollar value, a single buyer or purchasing manager often makes the purchase decision alone. In many instances, however, several people in the organization participate in the buying process. The individuals in this group, called a **buying centre**, share common goals, risks, and knowledge important to purchase decisions. For most large multistore chain resellers, such as Sears, 7-Eleven convenience stores, or Safeway, the buying centre is very formal and is called a *buying committee*. However, most industrial firms or government units use informal groups of people or call meetings to arrive at buying decisions.

A firm marketing to industrial firms and government units must understand the structure, technical and business functions represented, and the behaviour of the buying centre. One researcher has suggested four questions to provide guidance in understanding the buying centre in these organizations:[14]

- Which individuals are in the buying centre for the product or service?
- What is the relative influence of each member of the group?
- What are the buying criteria of each member?
- How does each member of the group perceive the potential supplier, its products and services, and its salespeople?

STAGE IN THE BUYING DECISION PROCESS	CONSUMER PURCHASE: PORTABLE MP3 PLAYER FOR A STUDENT	ORGANIZATIONAL PURCHASE: EARPHONES FOR A PORTABLE MP3 PLAYER
Problem recognition	Student doesn't like the features of the portable MP3 player now owned and desires a new portable MP3 player.	Marketing research and sales departments observe that competitors are improving the earphones on their portable MP3 models. The firm decides to improve the earphones on their own new models, which will be purchased from an outside supplier.
Information search	Student uses past experience, that of friends, ads, the Internet, and magazines to collect information and uncover alternatives.	Design and production engineers draft specifications for earphones. The purchasing department identifies suppliers of portable MP3 player earphones.
Alternative evaluation	Alternative portable MP3 players are evaluated on the basis of important attributes desired in a portable MP3 player, and several stores are visited.	Purchasing and engineering personnel visit with suppliers and assess facilities, capacity, quality control, and financial status. They drop any suppliers not satisfactory on these factors.
Purchase decision	A specific brand of portable MP3 player is selected, the price is paid, and the student leaves the store.	They use quality, price, delivery, and technical capability as key buying criteria to select a supplier. Then they negotiate terms and award a contract.
Postpurchase behaviour	Student reevaluates the purchase decision, may return the portable MP3 player to the store if it is unsatisfactory.	They evaluate the supplier using a formal vendor rating system and notify the supplier if earphones do not meet their quality standard. If the problem is not corrected, they drop the firm as a future supplier.

FIGURE 6-5

Comparing the stages in consumer and organizational purchases

People in the Buying Centre Who makes up the buying centre in a given organization depends on the specific item being bought. Although a buyer or purchasing manager is almost always a member of the buying centre, individuals from other functional areas are included, depending on what is to be purchased. In buying a million-dollar machine tool, the president (because of the size of the purchase) and the production vice president would probably be members. For key components to be included in a final manufactured product, a cross-functional group of individuals from research and development (R&D), engineering, and quality control are likely to be added. For new word-processing software, experienced office staff who will use the equipment would be members. Still, a major question in understanding the buying centre is finding and reaching the people who will initiate, influence, and actually make the buying decision.

Roles in the Buying Centre   Researchers have identified five specific roles that an individual in a buying centre can play.[15] In some purchases the same person may perform two or more of these roles.

- *Users* are the people in the organization who actually use the product or service, such as office staff who will use new word-processing software.
- *Influencers* affect the buying decision, usually by helping define the specifications for what is bought. They usually have specialized knowledge. The information systems manager would be a key influencer in the purchase of a new computer network.

- *Buyers* have formal authority and responsibility to select the supplier and negotiate the terms of the contract. The purchasing manager probably would perform this role in the purchase of a computer network.
- *Deciders* have the formal or informal power to select or approve the supplier that receives the contract. Whereas in routine orders the decider is usually the buyer or purchasing manager, in important technical purchases it is more likely to be someone from R&D, engineering, or quality control. The decider for a key component being included in a final manufactured product might be any of these three people.
- *Gatekeepers* control the flow of information in the buying centre. Purchasing personnel, technical experts, and office staff can all help or prevent salespeople (or information) from reaching people performing the other four roles.

buy classes
Three types of organizational buying situations: straight rebuy, modified rebuy, or new buy

Buying Situations and the Buying Centre   The number of people in the buying centre largely depends on the specific buying situation. Researchers who have studied organizational buying identify three types of buying situations, called **buy classes**. These buy classes vary from the routine reorder, or *straight rebuy*, to the completely new purchase, termed *new buy*. In between these extremes is the *modified rebuy*. Some examples will clarify the differences.[16]

FIGURE 6–6
How the buying situation affects buying centre behaviour

- *Straight rebuy*. Here the buyer or purchasing manager reorders an existing product or service from the list of acceptable suppliers, probably without even checking with users or influencers from the engineering, production, or quality control departments. Office supplies and maintenance services are usually obtained as straight rebuys.

| | BUY-CLASS SITUATION | | |
BUYING CENTRE DIMENSION	STRAIGHT REBUY	MODIFIED REBUY	NEW BUY
People involved	1	2–3	Many
Decision time	Short	Short	Long
Problem definition	Well-defined	Minor modifications	Uncertain
Buying objective	Low-priced supplier	Low-priced supplier	Good solution
Suppliers considered	Present	Present	New/present
Buying influence	Purchasing agent	Purchasing agent and others	Technical/operating personnel

- *Modified rebuy*. In this buying situation, the company is purchasing a product that it has experience purchasing, such as new laptops for salespeople, but it wants to change the product specifications, price, delivery schedule, or supplier. The changes usually mean involving users, influencers, and/or deciders in the buying decision—more input than would be necessary for a straight rebuy.
- *New buy*. In this situation, the company is buying the product or service for the first time. This purchase involves greater potential risk and is more complex than other buying situations. The buying centre is larger, comprised of people representing those parts of the organization having a stake in the new buy. Procter & Gamble's recent purchase of a multimillion-dollar fiber-optic network from Corning, Inc., linking its corporate offices, represented a new buy.[17]

Figure 6–6 summarizes how buy classes affect buying centre tendencies in different ways.[18]

Concept Check

1. What one department is almost always represented by a person in the buying centre?
2. What are the three types of buying situations or buy classes?

ONLINE BUYING IN ORGANIZATIONAL MARKETS

Organizational buying behaviour and business marketing continue to change with the use of the Internet and e-commerce. Organizations vastly outnumber consumers both in terms of online transactions made and purchase volume.[19] In fact, organizational buyers account for about 80 percent of the total worldwide dollar value of all online transactions. It is projected that online organizational buyers around the world will purchase between $6 and $7.5 trillion worth of products and services by 2005. Organizational buyers in North America will account for about 60 percent of these purchases.

Prominence of Online Buying in Organizational Markets

Online buying in organizational markets is prominent for three major reasons.[20] First, organizational buyers depend heavily on timely supplier information that describes product availability, technical specifications, application uses, price, and delivery schedules. This information can be conveyed quickly online. Second, web-based technology has been shown to substantially reduce buyer order processing costs. At General Electric, online buying has cut the cost of a transaction from $50 to $100 per purchase to about $5. Third, business marketers have found that web-based technology can reduce marketing costs, particularly sales and advertising expense, and broaden their potential customer base for many types of products and services. For these reasons, online buying is popular in all three kinds of organizational markets. For example, airlines order over $400 million in spare parts from the Boeing Company website each year. Customers of Provigo, a large Canadian food wholesaler, can buy online; provincial and municipal governments across Canada also engage in online purchasing.

E-Marketplaces: Virtual Organizational Markets

e-marketplaces
Online trading communities that bring together buyers and supplier organizations

A significant development in organizational buying has been the creation and growth of online trading communities, called **e-marketplaces**, that bring together buyers and supplier organizations.[21] These online communities go by a variety of names, including

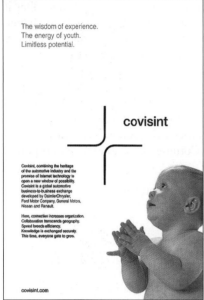

The wisdom of experience.
The energy of youth.
Limitless potential.

covisint

Covisint, combining the heritage
of the automotive industry and the
promise of Internet technology to
open a new window of possibility.
Covisint is a global automotive
business-to-business exchange
developed by DaimlerChrysler,
Ford Motor Company, General Motors,
Nissan and Renault.

Here, connection increases organization.
Collaboration transcends geography.
Speed breeds efficiency.
Knowledge is exchanged securely.
This time, everyone gets to grow.

covisint.com

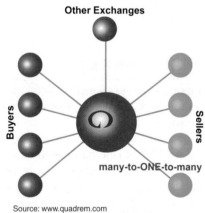

Other Exchanges

Buyers

Sellers

many-to-ONE-to-many

Source: www.quadrem.com

FIGURE 6-7

This diagram from
Quadrem's website shows
the efficiency of
e-marketplaces

portals, exchanges and e-hubs, and make possible the real-time exchange of information, money, products, and services. E-marketplaces will account for almost one-half of all online organizational purchases in 2005.

E-marketplaces can be independent trading communities or private exchanges. Independent e-marketplaces typically focus on a specific product or service, or serve a particular industry. They act as a neutral third-party and provide an online trading platform and a centralized market that enable exchanges between buyers and sellers. Independent e-marketplaces charge a fee for their service and exist in settings that have one or more of the following features:

- Thousands of geographically dispersed buyers and sellers,
- Frequently changing prices caused by demand and supply fluctuations,
- Time sensitivity due to perishable offerings and changing technologies, and
- Easily comparable offerings between a variety of suppliers.

Well-known independent e-marketplaces include PaperExchange (paper products), PlasticNet (plastics), Altra Energy (electricity, natural gas, and crude oil), and MRO.com (maintenance, repair, and operating supplies). Small business buyers and sellers, in particular, benefit from independent e-marketplaces. These e-marketplaces offer suppliers an economical way to expand their customer base and reduce the cost of purchased products and services.

Large companies tend to favour private exchanges that link them with their network of qualified suppliers and customers. Private exchanges focus on streamlining a company's purchase transactions with its suppliers and customers. Like independent e-marketplaces, they provide a technology trading platform and central market for buyer–seller interactions. They are not a neutral third party, however, but represent the interests of their owners.

Quadrem is an e-marketplace for the mining industry that now accounts for over $1.3 billion. It was set up by 14 of the world's most prominent mining, minerals, and metals companies "as a one-stop solution to specifically meet the e-procurement needs of the natural resource industry. Taking this vision and turning it into a reality, we have developed into a fully functional global eMarketplace, with 19 shareholders, thousands of sellers and hundreds of buying locations, located across the globe. . . . We are available 24x7x365 to address our customers' needs."[22] Figure 6-7 diagrams how Quadrem facilitates its e-marketplace.

The most ambitious e-marketplace yet devised is Covisint, which is expected to revolutionize the worldwide automotive industry. Owned principally by General Motors, Ford, and DaimlerChrysler, Covisint will be the world's largest exchange when it is fully operational and will process $750 billion in transactions annually.

Online Auctions in Organizational Markets

Online auctions have grown in popularity among organizational buyers and business marketers. Many e-marketplaces offer this service. Two general types of auctions are common: a traditional auction and a reverse auction.[23] Figure 6–8 shows how buyer and seller participants and price behaviour differ by type of auction. Let's look at each auction type more closely to understand the implications of each for buyers and sellers.

In a **traditional auction** a seller puts an item up for sale and would-be buyers are invited to bid in competition with each other. As more would-be buyers become involved, there is an upward pressure on bid prices. Why? Bidding is sequential—that is, bidders bid in order, one at a time. Prospective buyers observe the bids of others and decide

traditional auction

Occurs when a seller puts
an item up for sale and
would-be buyers bid in
competition with each other

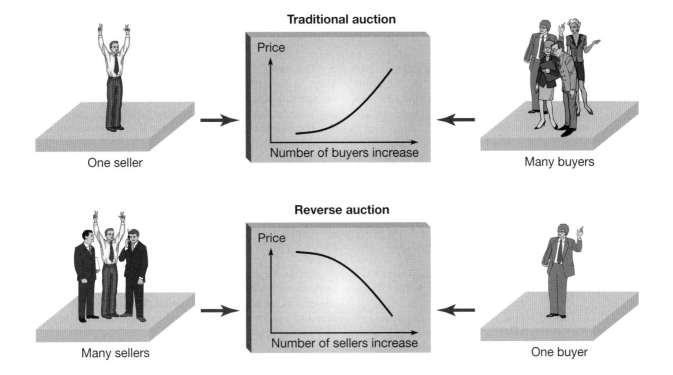

Traditional auction

Price

Number of buyers increase

One seller

Many buyers

Reverse auction

Price

Number of sellers increase

Many sellers

One buyer

FIGURE 6–8

How buyer and seller participants and price behaviour differ by type of online auction

reverse auction

Occurs when a buyer communicates a need for something and would-be suppliers bid in competition with each other

whether or not to increase the bid price. The auction ends when a single bidder remains and "wins" the item with its highest price. Traditional auctions are frequently used to dispose of excess merchandise. For example, Dell Computer sells surplus, refurbished, or closeout computer merchandise at its dellauction.com website.

A reverse auction works in the opposite direction from a traditional auction. In a **reverse auction**, a buyer communicates a need for a product or service and would-be suppliers are invited to bid in competition with each other. As more would-be suppliers become involved, there is a downward pressure on bid prices for the buyer's business. Why? Like traditional auctions, bidding is sequential and prospective suppliers observe the bids of others and decide whether or not to decrease the bid price. The auction ends when a single bidder remains and "wins" the business with its lowest price. Reverse auctions benefit organizational buyers by reducing the cost of their purchases. As an example, General Electric, one of the world's largest companies, has its own Global eXchange Services unit, which runs online reverse auctions for the company. It claims that it recently saved US$780 million on the purchase of US$6 billion worth of products and services.[24]

Clearly, buyers welcome the lower prices generated by reverse auctions. Some suppliers also favour the reverse auction process because it gives them a chance to capture business that they might not have otherwise had because of a long-standing purchase relationship between the buyer and another supplier. On the other hand, suppliers argue that reverse auctions put too much emphasis on prices, discourage consideration of other important buying criteria, and threaten supply partnership opportunities.[25]

Concept Check

1. What are e-marketplaces?

2. How do traditional auctions and reverse auctions affect bid prices?

SUMMARY

1 Organizational buyers are divided into four different markets: industrial, reseller, government, and not-for-profit. There are about 1.6 million industrial firms, 376,000 resellers, 7,800 government units, and 80,000 not-for-profit (charitable) organizations in Canada.

2 Measuring industrial, reseller, government, and not-for-profit markets is an important first step for firms interested in determining the size of markets. The North American Industry Classification System (NAICS) is a convenient starting point to begin this process.

3 Many aspects of organizational buying behaviour are different from consumer buying behaviour. Some key differences between the two include demand characteristics, number of potential buyers, buying objectives, buying criteria, size of the order or purchase, buyer – seller relationships and partnerships, and multiple buying influences within companies.

4 The three types of buying situations, or buy classes, are the straight rebuy, the modified rebuy, and the new buy. These range from a routine reorder to a totally new purchase.

5 The stages in an organizational buying decision are the same as those for consumer buying decisions: problem recognition, information search, alternative evaluation, purchase decision, and postpurchase behaviour.

6 The buying centre concept is central to understanding organizational buying behaviour. Knowing who makes up the buying centre and the roles they play in making purchase decisions is important in marketing to organizations. The buying centre usually includes a person from the purchasing department and possibly representatives from R&D, engineering, and production, depending on what is being purchased. These people can play one or more of five roles in a purchase decision: user, influencer, buyer, decider, or gatekeeper.

7 Online buying is prevalent in industrial, reseller, and government markets. E-marketplaces will account for almost one-half of all online organizational purchases in 2005. Online auctions are commonly used by organizational buyers and business marketers.

KEY TERMS AND CONCEPTS

business marketing p. 120
buy classes p. 130
buying centre p. 128
derived demand p. 125
e-marketplaces p. 131
North American Industry Classification System (NAICS) p. 123

organizational buyers p. 121
organizational buying behaviour p. 128
reverse auction p. 133
supply partnership p. 127
traditional auction p. 132

QUESTIONS: APPLYING MARKETING CONCEPTS AND PERSPECTIVES

1 Describe the major differences among industrial firms, resellers, government units, and not-for-profit organizations in Canada.

2 Explain how the North American Industry Classification System (NAICS) might be helpful in understanding industrial, reseller, government, and not-for-profit markets, and discuss the limitations inherent in this system.

3 List and discuss the key characteristics of organizational buying that make it different from consumer buying.

4 What is a buying centre? Describe the roles assumed by people in a buying centre and what useful questions a supplier should ask about the participants in a buying centre.

5 Assume you are a food manufacturer and you are trying to sell your line of imported jams and jellies to a major grocery store chain. Who in the chain's buying centre would you expect to attend a meeting with you, and what would each member's concerns be?

6 Think about all of the materials and parts that go into the manufacturing of an automobile. How does derived demand play a role in this?

DISCUSSION FORUM

Suppose you and your classmates are a committee in charge of a new Business School building on your campus. You have been assigned the challenge of taking the project from the idea stage to the completion of the building to the stage where it is ready for classes to be held in it, and you have been given a budget and a time frame.

1 You decide first of all to assemble a buying centre. What departments will you involve, and what do you expect each of the representatives of the various departments to contribute to your project?

2 Draw a flowchart with the purchase process you will undertake, and identify what you will do at each stage of the process

3 Identify five items you will have to purchase, and determine the type of purchase that each represents. Make sure that you choose items from all of the buying situations.

4 How can you use e-procurement in your work? (Hint: you may have to do some research here.)

INTERNET EXERCISE

The North American Industrial Classification System structures industrial sectors into their component industries. The NAICS can be accessed at www.statcan.ca/english/concepts/industry.htm by clicking NAICS 2002 (under "Classifications, Canada"), Industry information can be obtained by navigating through the codes.

You have been hired as a market analyst by a textile company that is looking for opportunities outside its normal business. The vice president of marketing has asked you to

www.mcgrawhill.ca/college/thecore

look into the upholstered wood furniture manufacturing industry to determine its size. She suggests that a good place to start is the NAICS, beginning with the two-digit manufacturing sectors (codes 31–33).

1 What is the three-digit industry subsector code for furniture and related products manufacturing?

2 What is the six-digit Canadian code for upholstered household furniture manufacturing?

VIDEO CASE 6

CBC

LANDS' END: NO END IN SIGHT TO SUCCESS!

Hard to imagine that a company that began with a spelling mistake in its name—that to this day has not corrected the error—has gone on to become one of the world's largest direct marketers. Perhaps by fate, it had help from an executive who used to run the Sears mail-order operation. Today, Lands' End is owned by Sears, which purchased it for close to US$2 billion in 2002. Better known for its retail operations, Lands' End also has a sizeable B2B sales operation via its Lands' End Business Outfitters. Its success in part is due to its suppliers and the relationships with them. According to the company's founder Gary Comer, "We have learned to cherish those suppliers who share our obsession with quality, wherever they call home." He finished by saying, "Frankly, we think the world of them, one and all!" The other side of the supplier relationship is the buyers at Lands' End, and they are guided by published business principles and quality standards.

LAND OF THE BUYERS

Organizational buying is a part of the marketing effort that influences every aspect of business at Lands' End. As senior vice president of operations Phil Schaecher explains, "When we talk about purchasing at Lands' End, most people think of the purchase of merchandise for resale, but we buy many other things aside from merchandise, everything from the simplest office supply to the most sophisticated piece of material-handling equipment." As a result, Lands' End has developed a sophisticated approach to organizational buying, which is one of the keys to its incredible success.

COMPANY HISTORY

The company started by selling sailboat equipment, duffle bags, rain suits, and sweaters from a basement location in Chicago's old tannery district. In its first catalogue, the company name was printed with a typing error—the apostrophe in the wrong place—but the fledgling company couldn't afford to correct and reprint it. So ever since, the company name has been Lands' End, with the misplaced apostrophe.

When the company outgrew its Chicago location, founder Gary Comer relocated it to Dodgeville, Wisconsin, where he had fallen in love with the rolling hills and changing seasons. The original business ideas were simple: "Sell only things we believe in, ship every order the day it arrives, and unconditionally guarantee everything." Over time, the company developed eight principles of doing business:

1. Do everything possible to make products better. Never reduce the quality of a product to make it cheaper.
2. Price products fairly and honestly.
3. Accept any return for any reason.
4. Have a goal to ship items in stock the day after the order is received.
5. Customer service—what is best for the customer is best for Lands' End.
6. Place contracts with manufacturers who are cost-conscious and efficient.
7. Operate efficiently.
8. Make it possible for customers to shop for Lands' End products in whatever way they find most convenient.

These principles became the guidelines for the company's dedicated local employees and helped create extraordinary expectations from Lands' End customers. These principles exemplify excellence in marketing. Today, Lands' End is one of the world's largest direct marketers, with annual sales of traditionally styled clothing, luggage, and home products exceeding US$1.4 billion. The products are offered through catalogues, the Internet, and retail stores to customers in North America, Europe, and Asia. Lands' End distributes close to 270 million catalogues annually worldwide, some of which are designed for specific segments, including *The Lands' End Catalog, Lands' End Men, Lands' End Women, Lands' End Kids, Lands' End for School, Lands' End Home,* and *Lands' End Corporate.* In a typical day, catalogue shoppers place 40,000 to 50,000 telephone calls to the company. The Lands' End website (www.landsend.com) also offers every Lands' End product and a wide variety of Internet shopping innovations such as a 3-D model customized to each customer (called My Virtual Model); a "personal shopper," to suggest products that match the consumer's preferences; and a feature that allows customers to "chat" online directly with a customer service representative. Lands' End also operates 20 stores in the United States, the United Kingdom, and Japan. It has separate websites for various countries, including a bilingual section on its main website just for Canadians. The

company's goal is to please customers with the highest levels of quality and service in the industry.

Lands' End maintains the high quality of its products through several important activities. For example, the company works directly with mills and manufacturers to retain control of quality and design. "The biggest difference between Lands' End and some other retailers or catalogue businesses is that we actually design all the product here and we do all the specifications. Therefore, the manufacturer is building that product directly to our specs; we are not buying off of somebody else's line," explains Joan Mudget, vice president of quality assurance. In addition, Lands' End tests its products for comfort and fit by paying real people (local residents and children) to "wear-test" and "fit-test" all types of garments. Service has also become an important part of the Lands' End reputation. Customers expect prompt, professional service at every step—initiating the order, making selections, shipping, and follow-up (if necessary). One way Lands' End meets these expectations is by offering the simplest guarantee in the industry: "Guaranteed. Period." The company also offers toll-free telephone lines open 24 hours a day, 364 days a year, continuous product training for telephone representatives, and 2-day shipping. The company answers the phone more than 15 millions times a year. Lands' End operators even send personal responses to all e-mail messages—approximately 230,000 per year.

ORGANIZATONAL BUYING AT LANDS' END

The sixth Lands' End business principle (described above) is accomplished through the company's organizational buying process. First, its buyers specify fabric quality, construction, and sizing standards, which typically exceed industry standards, for current and potential Lands' End products. Then the buyers literally search around the world for the best possible source of fabrics and products. Once a potential supplier is identified, one of the company's 150 quality assurance personnel makes an information-gathering visit. The purpose of the visit is to understand the supplier's values, to assess four criteria (economic, quality, service, and vendor), and to determine if the Lands' End standards can be achieved.

Lands' End's evaluations of potential suppliers lead to the selection of what the company hopes will become long-term partners. As Mudget explains, "When we're looking for new manufacturers we are looking for the long term. I think one of the most interesting things is we're not out there looking for new vendors every year to fill the same products." In fact, Lands' End believes that the term *supplier* does not adequately describe the importance the company places on the relationships. Lands' End suppliers are viewed as allies, supporters, associates, colleagues, and stakeholders in the future of the company. Once an alliance is formed, the product specifications and the performance on those specifications are regularly evaluated.

Lands' End buyers face a variety of buying situations. Straight rebuys involve reordering an existing product—such as shipping boxes—without evaluating or changing specifications. Modified rebuys involve changing some aspect of a previously ordered product—such as the collar of a knit shirt—based on input from consumers, retailers, or other people involved in the purchase decision. Finally, new buys involve first-time purchases—such as Lands' End's addition of men's suits to its product line. The complexity of the process can vary with the type of purchase. Schaecher explains, "As you get more complicated in the purchase there are more things you look at to decide on a vendor."

FUTURE CHALLENGES FOR LANDS' END

Lands' End faces several challenges as it pursues improvements in its organizational buying process. First, new technologies offer opportunities for fast, efficient, and accurate communication with suppliers. Ed Smidebush, general inventory manager, describes a new system at Lands' End: "Our quick response system is a computerized system where we transmit electronically to our vendors each Sunday night, forecast information as well as stock positions and purchase order information so that on Monday morning this information will be incorporated directly into their manufacturing reports so that they can prioritize their production." Occasionally, Lands' End must work with its suppliers to improve their technology and information system capabilities.

Another challenge for Lands' End is to anticipate changes in consumer interests. While it has many years of experience with retail consumers, preferences for colours, fabrics, and styles change frequently, requiring buyers to constantly monitor the marketplace. In addition, Lands' End's more recent offerings to corporate customers require constant attention "because business customers' wants and incentives, and the environment in which they're shopping, are very different from consumers at home," explains marketing manager Hilary Kleese.

Finally, Lands' End must anticipate the quantities of each of its products consumers are likely to order. To do this, historical information is used to develop forecasts. One of the best tests of their forecast accuracy is the holiday season, when Lands' End receives more than 100,000 calls each day. Having the right products available is important because, as every employee knows, from principle four above, every order must be shipped the day after it is received.

Questions

1 Who is likely to make up the buying centre in the decision to select a new supplier for Lands' End? Which of the buying centre members are likely to play the roles of users, influencers, buyers, deciders, and gatekeepers?

2 Which stages of the organizational buying decision process is Lands' End following when it selects a new supplier? What selection criteria does the company use in the process?

3 Describe products Lands' End buyers typically buy in each of the three buying situations: straight rebuy, modified rebuy, and new buy.

Reaching Global
Markets

AFTER READING THIS CHAPTER YOU SHOULD BE ABLE TO:

- Understand the importance and dynamics of global marketing.

- Explain the effects of economic protectionism and the implications of economic integration for global marketing practices.

- Understand the importance of environmental factors (cultural, economic, and political) in shaping global marketing efforts.

- Describe different approaches firms use to enter and compete in global markets.

- Identify specific challenges marketers face when crafting worldwide marketing programs.

RIDING AROUND THE WORLD

Canadians are prominent participants in the world-renowned Tour de France cycling race—but it is Canadian bicycles, not riders, that take part! Cervélo Cycles Inc. is internationally known as one of the most innovative bicycle designers and manufacturers. Cyclists in many countries, and professional cyclists in particular, love these bikes, and they are used in pro cycling events in many countries.

In 1995, two engineers started designing a leading-edge bike that would combine time trialing and aerodynamics with the "need for speed." Today, Cervélo produces nine different models of bicycles; in late 2003, the firm launched a line of cycling apparel for athletes. From its base in Toronto, Cervélo sells through dealers around North America, as well as in Europe, Singapore, Korea, Australia, and New Zealand. And Cervélo is on the move: its next expansion plans includes Italy, among other countries.

Going into international markets is a decision largely based on cycling populations and competitive situations.

Cervélo sells a lot of bikes in Australia; cyclists there welcome a variety of brands and are open to purchasing North American brands. In contrast, Italy has more of a cyclist population, but also many local brands and manufacturers, so gaining a brand following there is much more difficult. While the basic bike designs are used around the world, there are adaptations to local markets; reflectors, for example, are required safety equipment in Canada, but not in the United States, Cervélo's largest market.

Promotion is simple, clear, and obviously effective: Cervélo won the bike industry's BRAINY award in late 2003 for the best advertising campaign. The firm has utilized its partnership with Team CSC, a European high-profile professional cycling team, as the focus of some of its promotional messages. And this initiative has worked, putting Cervélo on the radar screen of the media and the cycling world.

Cervélo's main focus is on pursuing the design and engineering of more innovative and better bikes, relying

WHERE IN THE MARKETING PROCESS ARE WE GOING IN THIS CHAPTER?

Chapter 7 introduces us to global marketing. Firms consider their goals, as well as the factors, benefits, challenges, and adaptations in the marketing mix needed to satisfy the needs of target markets in other parts of the world.

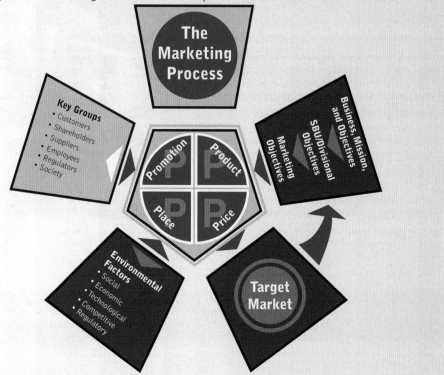

heavily on their customers for feedback, ideas for improvement, and word-of-mouth promotion. Cervélo's target market is cyclists, wherever on the globe they may be found.[1]

Canadian marketers cannot ignore the vast potential of global markets. Canada has less than one-half of one percent of the world's population—at 31 million people, we are a relatively small market.[2] Although we rank twelfth in terms of world purchasing power, our US$923 billion is just 1.9 percent of the world's US$48 trillion, compared with 21 percent for the U.S. or 12.5 percent for China.[3] For Canadian companies to expand, they frequently have to look beyond our borders to the lucrative markets in other countries.

Pursuit of global markets by Canadian and foreign marketers ultimately has resulted in world trade. This chapter describes the nature and scope of world trade and highlights challenges firms such as Cervélo face when they undertake global marketing.

DYNAMICS OF WORLD TRADE

The dollar value of world trade has more than doubled in the past decade and will exceed US$11.5 trillion in 2006. Manufactured goods and commodities account for 75 percent of world trade. Service industries, including telecommunications, transportation, insurance, education, banking, and tourism, represent the other 25 percent of world trade.

Four trends in the past decade have significantly affected world trade:

Trend 1: Gradual decline of economic protectionism by individual countries.
Trend 2: Formal economic integration and free trade among nations.
Trend 3: Global competition among global companies for global customers.
Trend 4: Development of networked global marketspace.

Decline of Economic Protectionism

protectionism

Practice of shielding one or more industries of a country's economy from foreign competition through the use of tariffs or quotas

Protectionism is the practice of shielding one or more industries within a country's economy from foreign competition, usually through the use of tariffs or quotas. The economic argument for protectionism is that it preserves jobs, protects a nation's political security, discourages economic dependency on other countries, and encourages the development of domestic industries.

tariffs

Government tax on goods or services entering a country, primarily serving to raise prices on imports

A **tariff** is a tax on goods or services entering a country. Because a tariff raises the price of an imported product, tariffs give a price advantage to domestic products competing in the same market. The effect of tariffs on world trade and consumer prices is substantial.[4] For over 20 years, the softwood lumber dispute between Canada and the U.S. has been a problem in an otherwise significant and positive trading relationship. In May 2001, the U.S. government imposed tariffs averaging 27 percent on softwood lumber coming from Canada. The rationale is that they wanted to protect U.S. lumber producers, raise the cost of lumber, and generate increased sales and profits for them. However, there is another issue involved: the Americans feel that the Canadian softwood lumber industry is unfairly subsidized. After this latest round of tariffs were imposed, Canadian producers lowered their costs, produced more lumber than previous production levels, and still provided lower cost competition to the U.S. producers. U.S. lumber prices have been driven down, and the protectionism has not yielded the expected benefits. There have been bitter disputes, political involvement, and hardship caused to lumber manufacturers on both sides of the border.

Since the imposition of the U.S. tariffs, Canada launched several appeals under the auspices of the North American Free Trade Agreement (NAFTA) and the World Trade Organization (WTO), and the U.S. counter-challenged. As of June 2004, Canada appears to have won a partial victory and will see at least a reduction, if not the elimination, of most of the U.S. tariffs on Canadian lumber. But with so much at stake on both sides of the border, this dispute may drag on for years.[5]

quota

Restriction placed on the amount of a product allowed to enter or leave a country

A **quota** is a restriction placed on the amount of a product allowed to enter or leave a country. By limiting supply of foreign products, an import quota helps domestic industries retain a certain percentage of the domestic market. For consumers, however, the limited supply may mean higher prices for domestic products. The best-known quota concerns the limits of foreign automobile sales in many countries. Quotas imposed by European

FIGURE 7-1

How protectionism affects world trade

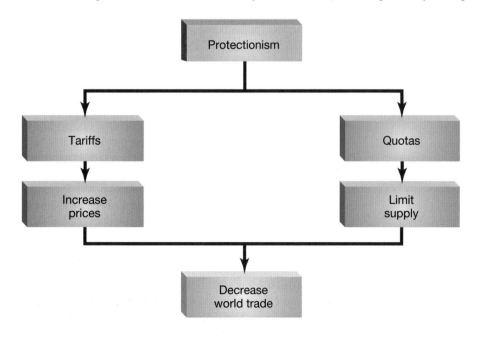

countries make imported cars 25 percent more expensive than similar models in the United States or Japan, costing European customers US$40 billion per year. In Canada, import controls are imposed in four key product types: textiles and clothing, agricultural products, steel products, and weapons and munitions. If we look more specifically at the quotas for agricultural products, they exist for turkey, chicken and egg products, a variety of dairy products, and wheat and barley.[6]

Both tariffs and quotas discourage world trade (Figure 7–1). As a result, the major industrialized nations of the world formed the **World Trade Organization** (WTO) in 1995 to address a broad array of world trade issues.[7] The 145 member countries of the WTO, which include Canada, account for more than 90 percent of world trade. The WTO sets rules governing trade between its members through panels of trade experts who decide on trade disputes between members and issue binding decisions. The WTO reviews more than 200 disputes annually. For instance, the WTO has been involved in the U.S.–Canada softwood lumber dispute on several occasions.[8]

There are other barriers to trade that do not involve tariffs or quotas. Some of these include import licensing, customs barriers, product standards, requirements for testing, labelling and certification laws, environmental measures, and lack of protection for intellectual property. In Canada, we have requirements for product labelling in both French and English, and this is seen by some importers to be a barrier to doing business here.

Rise of Economic Integration

In recent years, a number of countries with similar economic goals have formed transnational trade groups or signed trade agreements for the purpose of promoting free trade among member nations and enhancing their individual economies. Four of the best-known examples are the European Union (or simply EU), the North American Free Trade Agreement (NAFTA), the Association of Southeast Asian Nations (ASEAN), and the Southern Common Market (MERCOSUR).

European Union   In 1993, 12 European countries effectively removed most of the barriers to the free flow of goods, services, capital, and labour across their borders. This event, after decades of negotiation, formed a single market composed of more than 375 million consumers with a combined gross domestic product larger than that of the United States. Original members of the European Union were Great Britain, Ireland, Denmark, Belgium, the Netherlands, Luxembourg, Germany, France, Italy, Greece, Portugal, and Spain. Austria, Finland, and Sweden joined the European Union in 1995, and as of June 2004, ten more countries joined: Cyprus, Czech Republic, Estonia, Hungary, Latvia, Lithuania, Malta, Poland, Slovakia, and Slovenia (see Figure 7–2). The Swiss have elected not to join.

The European Union creates vast marketing opportunities because firms no longer need to market their products and services on a nation-by-nation basis. Rather, European-wide marketing strategies are possible due to greater uniformity in product and packaging standards; fewer regulatory restriction on transportation, advertising, and promotion imposed by countries; and removal of most tariffs that affect pricing practices. For example, Colgate-Palmolive Company now markets its Colgate toothpaste with one formula and package across EU countries at one price. This practice was impossible before because of different government regulations and tariffs. Pan-European marketing opportunities will benefit further from the issuance of a common currency called the *euro*, which replaced national currencies in 2002 in 12 EU countries. Great Britain, Denmark, and Sweden have so far retained their own currencies.

North American Free Trade Agreement   The North American Free Trade Agreement became effective in 1994 and lifted many trade barriers between Canada, the United States, and Mexico. This agreement, when coupled with the 1988 U.S. – Canada Fair Trade

FIGURE 7–2

The 25 countries of the European Union in 2004

Agreement, established a North American trade arrangement similar to that of the European Union. The reduction of tariffs and other provisions of NAFTA promoted relatively free trade among the United States, Canada, and Mexico and created a marketplace with over 400 million consumers. Negotiations are under way to expand NAFTA to create a 34-country Free Trade Area of the Americas. This agreement would include the United States, Canada, Mexico, plus Latin American and Caribbean countries.

NAFTA has increased trade among member nations as well as cross-border manufacturing and investment. For example, Whirlpool Corporation shifted the production of household trash compactors, kitchen ranges, and compact dryers to Canada. Ford invested US$60 million in its Mexico City manufacturing plant to produce smaller cars and light trucks for global sales.

Asian Free Trade Agreements   ASEAN is an agreement between 10 Southeast Asian countries—Brunei Darussalam, Burma/Myanmar, Cambodia, Indonesia, Laos, Malaysia, Philippines, Singapore, Thailand, and Vietnam—representing a market of over 503 million people. Peace and stability in that region of the world are two key driving principles. Their goals include accelerating economic growth among member countries, fostering social progress and cultural development, and shared prosperity.[9]

Efforts to increase trade in East Asia—from Japan and the four "Little Dragons" (Hong Kong, Singapore, South Korea, and Taiwan) through Thailand, Malaysia, and Indonesia—are also growing. Although the trade agreements are less formal than those

underlying the European Union and NAFTA, they have reduced tariffs among countries and promoted trade.

MERCOSUR has six member countries in South America: Argentina, Bolivia, Brazil, Chile, Paraguay, and Uruguay. They formulated their agreement patterned somewhat after the European Union agreement, and their goals are the creation of a common market and customer union, and to establish various forms of economic cooperation.[10]

In order for trade to function smoothly, some form of international agreement is necessary. GATT, the General Agreement on Tariffs and Trade, was first signed in 1947 and now has 110 member countries worldwide. Its key functions are to provide an international forum that fosters free trade by regulating and lowering tariffs on traded products, and to work with members to resolve trade disputes.[11]

A New Reality: Global Competition among Global Companies for Global Consumers

Today, world trade is driven by global competition among global companies for global consumers. Communications, technology, trade agreements, economic development, and travel have brought countries of the world closer and created a new reality for marketers.

The Canadian government recognizes both the complexity and the opportunity and encourages Canadian firms to become involved in global expansion as a way to offset global competition. One of the ways it does this is by sponsoring firms to participate in what it calls "Team Canada" trade missions to various regions of the world. The companies, accompanied by high-ranking government officials, showcase their products and services on these trips.

global competition
Occurs when firms originate, produce, and market their products and services worldwide

Global Competition   **Global competition** exists when firms originate, produce, and market their products and services worldwide. The automobile, pharmaceutical, clothing, electronics, aerospace, and telecommunication fields represent well-known industries with sellers and buyers on every continent. Other industries that are increasingly global in scope include soft drinks, cosmetics, ready-to-eat cereals, snack foods, and retailing.

Global competition broadens the competitive landscape for marketers. The familiar "cola war" waged by Pepsi-Cola and Coca-Cola in the United States has been repeated around the world, including India, China, and Argentina. Procter & Gamble's Pampers and Kimberly-Clark's Huggies have taken their disposable diaper rivalry from the United States to Western Europe. Boeing and Bombardier vie for lucrative aircraft contracts on virtually every continent.

Global Companies   Three types of companies compete in the global marketplace: international firms, multinational firms, and transnational firms.[12] All three employ people in different countries, and many have administrative, marketing, and manufacturing operations (often called *divisions* or *subsidiaries*) around the world. However, a firm's strategy for global markets and marketing defines the type of company it is.

MARKETING NEWSNET

Global

THE GLOBAL TEENAGER: A MARKET OF 500 MILLION CONSUMERS WITH $100 BILLION TO SPEND

The "global teenager" market consists of 500 million 13- to 19-year-olds. These teens live in Europe, North and South America, and industrialized nations of Asia and the Pacific Rim, and they've experienced intense exposure to television, movies, travel, the Internet, and global advertising by companies such as Benetton, Sony, Nike, and Coca-Cola. The similarities among teens across these countries are greater than their differences. For example, a global study of middle-class teenagers' rooms in 25 industrialized countries indicated it was difficult, if not impossible, to tell whether the rooms were in Los Angeles, Mexico City, Tokyo, Rio de Janeiro, Sidney, or Paris. Why? Teens spend $100 billion annually for a common gallery of products: Sony video games, Tommy Hilfiger apparel, Levi's blue jeans, Nike athletic shoes, Procter & Gamble Cover Girl makeup, and Clearasil facial medicine.

Teenagers around the world appreciate fashion and music and desire novelty and trendier designs and images. A study of 6,500 teens in 26 countries has shown that they also acknowledge an Americanization of fashion and culture. When asked what country had the most influence on their attitudes and purchase behaviour, the United States was named by 54 percent of teens from the United States, 87 percent of those from Latin America, 80 percent of the Europeans, and 80 percent of those from the Far East. This phenomenon has not gone unnoticed by parents. As one parent in India said, "Now the youngsters dress, talk, and eat like Americans."

An *international firm* markets its existing products and services in other countries the same way it does at home. Avon, for example, successfully distributes its product line through direct selling in Asia, Europe, and South America, employing nearly the same marketing strategy used in Canada.

A *multinational firm* views the world as consisting of unique parts and markets to each part differently. Multinationals use a **multidomestic marketing strategy**, which means that they have as many different product variations, brand names, and advertising programs as countries in which they do business. For example, Lever Europe—a division of Unilever—markets its fabric softener known as Snuggle in Canada in ten different European countries under seven brand names, including Kuschelweich in Germany, Coccolino in Italy, and Mimosin in France. These products have different packages, different advertising programs, and occasionally different formulas.[13]

A *transnational firm* views the world as one market and emphasizes universal consumer needs and wants more than differences among cultures. Transnational marketers employ a **global marketing strategy**—the practice of standardizing marketing activities when there are cultural similarities and adapting them when cultures differ.

Global marketing strategies are popular among many business-to-business marketers such as Caterpillar and Komatsu (heavy construction equipment) and Texas Instruments, Intel, Hitachi, and Motorola (semiconductors). Consumer goods marketers such as Timex, Seiko, and Citizen (watches), Coca-Cola and Pepsi-Cola (cola soft drinks), Gillette (personal care products), L'Oréal and Shiseido (cosmetics), and McDonald's (fast foods) successfully execute this strategy.

Global Consumers   Global competition among global companies often focuses on the identification and pursuit of global consumers as described in the accompanying Marketing NewsNet.[14] **Global consumers** consist of customer groups living in many different countries who have similar needs or seek similar features and benefits from products or services. Evidence suggests the emergence of a global middle-income class, a global youth market, and a global elite segment. Each consumes a common assortment of products and services regardless of geographic location. A variety of companies have capitalized on the global consumer. Whirlpool, Sony, and IKEA have benefited from the growing global middle-income class desire for kitchen appliances, consumer electronics, and home furnishings, respectively. Levi's, Nike, Coca-Cola, and Benetton have tapped the global youth market. DeBeers, Chanel, Gucci, and Rolls Royce cater to the elite segment for luxury goods worldwide.

Emergence of a Networked Global Marketspace

The use of Internet/Web-based technology as a tool for exchanging goods, services, and information on a global scale is the fourth trend affecting world trade.[15] The broad reach of this technology suggests that its potential for promoting world trade is huge. In fact, sales arising from electronic commerce are projected to represent 9 percent of world trade in 2005, up from about 1 percent in 2001.

The promise of a networked global marketspace is that it enables the exchange of goods, services, and information from companies anywhere to customers anywhere at any time and at a lower cost. This promise has become a reality for buyers and sellers in industrialized countries that possess the telecommunications infrastructure necessary to support Internet/Web-based technology. In particular, companies engaged in business-to-business marketing have spurred the growth of global electronic commerce. Ninety percent of global electronic commerce revenue arises from business-to-business transactions among a dozen countries in North America, Western Europe, and the Asia/Pacific Rim region. Industries that have benefited from this technology include industrial chemicals

---

multidomestic marketing strategy
A multinational firm's offering as many different product variations, brand names, and advertising programs as countries in which it does business

global marketing strategy
Practice of standardizing marketing activities when there are cultural similarities and adapting them when cultures differ

global consumers
Customers living around the world who have similar needs or seek similar benefits from products or services

Bienvenidos
Nestlé, Colombia ◀
Productos y marcas ◀
Servicio al consumidor ◀
Menú del mes ◀
Un fantástico viaje ◀
al mundo de la nutrición
Novedades ◀
Recetas Lácteos ◀
Trabajar con Nestle ◀

Disfrute nuestro
menú de...

Nestle

Nestlé
Calidad y Confianza para ti

C   o   l   o   m   b   i   a

El principal objetivo de Nestlé es ofrecer productos de la más
alta calidad y valor nutricional, para satisfacer las necesidades
alimentarias del ser humano durante todos los momentos del
día y a lo largo de toda la vida.

Es por ello que en Nestlé trabajamos constante y
comprometidamente para cumplir con este propósito que busca
llenar las expectativas de nuestros consumidores.

Friskies

Nuevas
Recetas

Nestlé features multiple country and language websites that customize content and communicate with consumers in their native tongue. The website for Colombia shown here is an example.

and controls, maintenance, repair, and operating supplies, computer and electronic equipment and components, aerospace parts, and agricultural and energy products. The United States, Canada, United Kingdom, Germany, Sweden, Japan, and Taiwan are among the most active participants in worldwide business-to-business electronic commerce.

Marketers recognize that the networked global marketspace offers unheard of access to prospective buyers on every continent. Companies that have successfully taken advantage of this access manage multiple country and language websites that customize content and communicate with consumers in their native tongue. Nestlé, the world's largest packaged food manufacturer, coffee roaster, and chocolate maker is a case in point. The company operates 31 individual country websites in 16 languages that span 5 continents. Amazon.com has Spanish, Japanese, French, and German language websites.

Concept Check

1. What is protectionism?
2. What is the difference between a multidomestic marketing strategy and a global marketing strategy?

A GLOBAL ENVIRONMENTAL SCAN

Global companies conduct continuing environmental scans of the five sets of environmental factors described earlier in Chapter 3, Figure 3–1 (social, economic, technological, competitive, and regulatory forces). Here in this section we will focus on three kinds of uncontrollable environmental variables—cultural, economic, and political–regulatory variables—that affect global marketing practices in strikingly different ways than those in domestic markets.

Cultural Diversity

Canada has become increasingly multi-ethnic and multi-cultural, making it one of the most diverse countries in the world. Different countries take different approaches to admitting immigrants and integrating them into society. Canada's approach is often referred to as a mosaic, meaning that people who come to the country from another are welcome to maintain their cultural identities and customs—the belief is that this will create a situation where all Canadians can learn from the rich variety of over 200 cultures that make up the citizenry of the country. This environment works to increase Canadian companies' sensitivity and orientation towards other cultures, so the transition to global activities and relationships is facilitated.

Marketers must be sensitive to the cultures of different societies if they are to develop successful exchange relationships with global consumers. A necessary step in this process is **cross-cultural analysis**, which involves the study of similarities and differences among consumers in two or more nations or societies.[16] A thorough cross-cultural analysis involves an understanding of and an appreciation for the values, customs, symbols, and language of other societies.

cross-cultural analysis
Study of similarities and differences among consumers in two or more societies

values
Socially preferable modes of conduct or states of existence that tend to persist over time

Values   A society's **values** represent socially preferable modes of conduct or states of existence that tend to persist over time. Understanding and working with these aspects of a society are important factors in global marketing. For example,[17]

- McDonald's does not sell hamburgers in its restaurants in India because the cow is considered sacred by almost 85 percent of the population. Instead, McDonald's sells the McMaharajah: two all-mutton patties, special sauce, lettuce, cheese, pickles, onions on a sesame-seed bun.
- Germans have not responded to the promotion of credit cards such as Visa or MasterCard, nor to the idea of borrowing to purchase goods and services. The German word for "debt," *schuld*, is the same as the German word for "guilt."

customs
Norms and expectations about the way people do things in a specific country or culture

Customs   **Customs** are what is considered normal and expected about the way people do things in a specific country or culture. Clearly, customs can vary significantly from country to country. Some customs may seem unusual to Canadians. Consider, for example, that in France men wear more than twice the number of cosmetics that women do, and that the Japanese consider slurping their food to be a sign of approval and appreciation to the chef.

The custom of giving token business gifts is popular in many countries where they are expected and accepted. However, bribes, kickbacks, and payoffs offered to entice someone to commit an illegal or improper act on behalf of the giver for economic gain is considered corrupt in most cultures. The widespread use of bribery in global marketing has led to an agreement among the world's major exporting nations to make bribery of foreign government officials a criminal offence.

The Organization for Economic Cooperation and Development (OECD) is an international body whose goal is to foster democratic government and a market-driven economy. With its global reach, it addresses issues of general interest to its members and affiliates. Corruption has become an issue of major importance in the past decade, and the OECD has taken action to set guidelines and procedures for preventing international bribery and corruption. Canada has adopted the OECD's anti-corruption convention and has made bribery of foreign public officials a criminal offence.[18]

Bribery paid to foreign companies is another matter. In France and Greece, bribes paid to foreign companies are a tax-deductible expense!

cultural symbols
Objects, ideas, or processes that represent a particular group of people or society

Cultural Symbols   **Cultural symbols** are objects, ideas, or processes that represent a particular group of people or society. Symbols and symbolism play an important

What cultural lesson did Coca-Cola executives learn when they used the Eiffel Tower and the Parthenon in a recent global advertising campaign?

role in cross-cultural analysis because different cultures attach different meanings to things. By cleverly using cultural symbols, global marketers can tie positive symbolism to their products and services to enhance their attractiveness to consumers. However, improper use of symbols can spell disaster. A culturally sensitive global marketer will know that[19]

- North Americans are superstitious about the number 13, and Japanese feel the same way about the number 4. *Shi*, the Japanese word for "four," is also the word for "death." Knowing this, Tiffany & Company sells its fine glassware and china in sets of five, not four, in Japan.
- "Thumbs-up" is a positive sign in Canada. However, in Russia and Poland, this gesture has an offensive meaning when the palm of the hand is shown, as AT&T learned. The company reversed the gesture depicted in ads, showing the back of the hand, not the palm.

Cultural symbols stir up deep feelings. Consider how executives at Coca-Cola Company's Italian office learned this lesson. In a series of advertisements directed at Italian vacationers, the Eiffel Tower, Empire State Building, and the Tower of Pisa were turned into the familiar Coca-Cola bottle. However, when the white marble columns in the Parthenon that crowns Athens's Acropolis were turned into Coca-Cola bottles, the Greeks were outraged. Greeks refer to the Acropolis as the "holy rock," and a government official said the Parthenon is an "international symbol of excellence" and that "whoever insults the Parthenon insults international culture." Coca-Cola apologized for the ad.[20]

Language   Global marketers should know not only the basics of the native tongues of countries in which they market their products and services but also the subtleties and unique expressions of the language. About 100 official languages exist in the world, but anthropologists estimate that at least 3,000 different languages are actually spoken. There are 11 official languages spoken in the European Union, and Canada has two official languages (English and French). Seventeen major languages are spoken in India alone.

English, French, and Spanish are the principal languages used in global diplomacy and commerce. However, the best language with which to communicate with consumers is their own, as any seasoned global marketer will agree. Language usage and translation can present challenges. Unintended meanings of brand names and messages have ranged from the absurd to the obscene:

- When the advertising agency responsible for launching Procter & Gamble's successful Pert shampoo in Canada realized that the name means "lost" in French, it substituted the brand name Pret, which means "ready."

- The Vicks brand name common in North America is German slang for sexual intimacy; therefore, Vicks is called Wicks in Germany.

back translation
Retranslating a word or phrase back into the original language by a different interpreter to catch errors

Experienced global marketers use **back translation**, where a translated word or phrase is retranslated back into the original language by a different interpreter to catch errors.[21] IBM's first Japanese translation of its "Solution for a small planet" advertising message yielded "Answers that make people smaller." The error was caught by back translation and corrected.

Economic Considerations

Global marketing is also affected by economic considerations. Therefore, a scan of the global marketplace should include an assessment of the economic infrastructure in different countries, measurement of consumer income in different countries, and recognition of a country's currency exchange rates.

Economic Infrastructure   The *economic infrastructure*—a country's communications, transportation, financial, and distribution systems—is a critical consideration in determining whether to try to market to a country's consumers and organizations. Parts of the infrastructure that North Americans or Western Europeans take for granted can be huge problems elsewhere. This is true not only in developing nations but even in countries of the former Soviet Union, Eastern Europe, the Indian subcontinent, and China where such an infrastructure is assumed to be in place.

The communication infrastructures in these countries also differ. Their telecommunication systems and networks in use—such as telephones, cable television, broadcast radio and television, computers and the Internet, satellite, and wireless telephone—are often limited or outdated compared with that of developed countries.

Even the financial and legal systems can cause problems. Formal operating procedures among financial institutions and private companies did not exist under communism and are still limited.[22] As a consequence, it is estimated that two-thirds of the commercial transactions in Russia involve nonmonetary forms of payment. The legal red tape involved in obtaining titles to buildings and land for manufacturing, wholesaling, and retailing operations also has been a huge problem. Nevertheless, the Coca-Cola Company invested US$750 million from 1991 through 1998 to build bottling and distribution facilities in Russia. Allied Lyons spent US$30 million to build a plant to make Baskin-Robbins ice cream. And Mars recently opened a US$200 million candy factory outside Moscow.

Consumer Income and Purchasing Power   A global marketer selling consumer goods must also consider the average per capita income or the average household income in a country and how the income is distributed to determine a nation's purchasing power. Per capita income varies greatly between nations. Average yearly per capita income in Canada is $21,800[23] and is less than $200 in some developing countries such as Vietnam. A country's income distribution is important because it gives a more reliable picture of a country's purchasing power. Generally speaking, the greater the number of middle-income households in a country, the greater a nation's purchasing power tends to be.

Seasoned global marketers recognize that people in developing countries often have government subsidies for food, housing, and health care that supplement their income. Accordingly, people with seemingly low incomes are actually promising customers for a variety of products. For example, a consumer in South Asia earning the equivalent of $250 per year can afford Gillette razors. When that consumer's income rises to $1,000, a Sony television becomes affordable, and a new Volkswagen or Nissan can be bought with an annual income of $10,000. In developing countries of Eastern Europe, a $1,000 annual income makes a refrigerator affordable, and $2,000 brings an automatic washer within reach.[24]

The Coca-Cola Company has made a huge financial investment in bottling and distribution facilities in Russia.

currency exchange rate

Price of one country's currency expressed in terms of another country's currency

Currency Exchange Rates A **currency exchange rate** is the price of one country's currency expressed in terms of another country's currency. As economic conditions change, so can the exchange rate between countries. On any one day, 10 Canadian dollars may be worth 7.60 U.S. dollars, 5.90 euros, 62.6 Chinese yuan, or 4.00 British pounds. As currencies fluctuate, these values can change significantly from one day to another. Check out this currency converter website (www.xe.com/ucc) to find out what the Canadian exchange is for these four currencies today.

Fluctuations in exchange rates among the world's currencies can affect everyone from international tourists to global companies.[25] For example, when the Canadian dollar is "strong" against the euro, it takes fewer dollars to purchase goods in the EU. As a result, more Canadian tourists will travel to Europe—good news for Europe's travel industry, but not so good for European consumers who want to buy Canadian goods, as they will have to pay more for them. And they may choose not to buy. Mattel learned this lesson the hard way. The company was recently unable to sell its popular Holiday Barbie doll and accessories in many international markets because they were too expensive. Why? Barbie prices were set without regard for how they would translate into other currencies and were too high for many foreign buyers.

Political–Regulatory Climate

Assessing the political and regulatory climate for marketing in a country or region of the world means not only identifying the current climate but determining how long a favourable or unfavourable climate will last. An assessment of a country or regional political–regulatory climate includes an analysis of political stability and trade regulations.

Political Stability Trade among nations or regions depends on political stability. Billions of dollars have been lost in the Middle East, the former Federal Republic of Yugoslavia, and Africa as a result of internal political strife, government philosophy and actions, terrorism, and war. Losses encourage more careful selection of politically stable countries and regions of the world for trade.

Political stability in a country is affected by numerous factors, including a government's ideas about foreign companies and trade with other countries. These factors combine to create a political climate that is favourable or unfavourable for foreign marketing and financial investment.

Trade Regulations   Countries have a variety of rules that govern business practices within their borders. These rules often serve as trade barriers.[26] For example, Japan has some 11,000 trade regulations. Japanese car safety rules effectively require all automobile replacement parts to be Japanese and not American or European; public health rules make it illegal to sell aspirin or cold medicine without a pharmacist present. The Malaysian government has advertising regulations stating that "advertisements must not project or promote an excessively aspirational lifestyle," Greece bans toy advertising, and Sweden outlaws all advertisements to children.

Concept Check

1. Cross-cultural analysis involves the study of _____.

2. When foreign currencies can buy more Canadian dollars, are Canadian products more or less expensive for a foreign consumer?

GLOBAL MARKET-ENTRY STRATEGIES

Once a company has decided to enter the global marketplace, it must select a means of market entry. A company can consider four basic options:

- Exporting,
- Licensing,
- Joint venture, and
- Direct investment.[27]

As Figure 7–3 demonstrates, the amount of financial commitment, risk, marketing control, and profit potential increases as the firm moves from exporting to direct investment.

Exporting

exporting
Producing goods in one country and selling them in another country

Exporting is producing goods in one country and selling them in another country. This entry option allows a company to make the least number of changes in terms of its product, its organization, and even its corporate goals.

Indirect exporting is when a firm sells its domestically produced goods in a foreign country through an intermediary. This kind of exporting is ideal for the company that has no overseas contacts but wants to market abroad. The intermediary is often a distributor that has the marketing know-how and the resources necessary for the effort to succeed. Terrapin Communications of Ottawa sells its safety alarm system in many countries; a distributor in France handles distribution to all of Western Europe. This is an indirect exporting approach that works very well for the company, as it does not have offices or contacts in the European countries that are its target markets. Read the upcoming Marketing NewsNet to learn about the export strategies this innovative marketer uses to get its product around the world.[28]

Direct exporting is when a firm sells its domestically produced goods in a foreign country without intermediaries. Companies decide to use direct exporting when they believe that selling internationally can be more efficiently and effectively done without intermediaries. There are several reasons why a company may make this decision; the volume of sales may be large, selling the product or service may require a lot of negotiation or customization, or specialized knowledge of the industry is key to reaching the target customers. Direct

FIGURE 7-3

Alternative global market-entry strategies

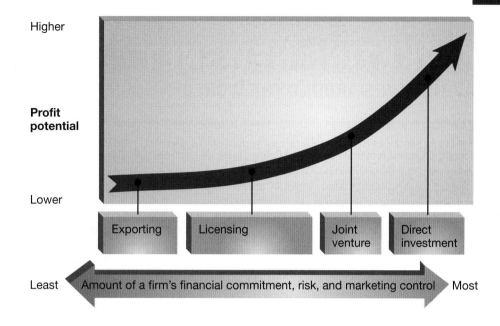

exporting involves more risk for the company than indirect exporting does, but it also may be the route to increased profits. Bombardier, Canada's world-class manufacturer of innovative transportation solutions, utilizes some agents, but it also relies on a direct exporting approach in marketing its aircraft and rail transportation solutions. With 90 percent of its revenues coming from markets outside of Canada, it is important to have a strong competence in approaching global markets with the right strategy.[29]

Even though exporting is commonly employed by large firms, it is the prominent global market-entry strategy among small- and medium-sized companies.

Licensing

Under licensing, a company offers the right to a trademark, patent, trade secret, or other similarly valued items of intellectual property in return for a royalty or a fee. The advantages to the company granting the licence, the licensor, are low risk and the chance to enter a foreign market at virtually no cost. The licensee gains information that allows it to start with a competitive advantage, and the foreign country gains employment by having the product manufactured locally. Yoplait yogourt is licensed from Sodima, a French cooperative, by General Mills for sales in North America.

There are some serious drawbacks to this mode of entry, however. The licensor gives up control of its product. In addition, some licensees are able to modify the product somehow and enter the market with product and marketing knowledge gained at the expense of the company that got them started. To offset this disadvantage to the licensor, many companies strive to keep the licensee dependent on them for improvements and successful operation. Finally, should the licensee prove to be a poor choice, the name or reputation of the company may be harmed.

A variation of licensing is *franchising*. Franchising, in which a company contracts with an individual to set up an operation to provide products or services under the company's established brand name, is one of the fastest-growing market-entry strategies. There are thousands of franchises in many countries. We often think of fast food companies when we think of franchises, but there are also automotive, business service, retail, lodging (hotels), restaurant and maintenance franchises as well. McDonald's has always relied on franchising to grow its worldwide business—it currently operates more than 30,000 restaurants in 119 countries, and some 70 percent of these operations are franchises.[30]

MARKETING NEWSNET

SAVING LIVES AROUND THE WORLD

How does a small Canadian innovator make a presence in the world market? Ask Terrapin Communications, the Ottawa firm that developed Safety Turtle, an alarm system that detects immersion in water and sends out a loud warning signal. Many children drown every year in residential swimming pools, and the Safety Turtle helps to reduce that number. The original target market was pool and spa owners, but Safety Turtle is now seeing that resorts, marinas, and waterfront property owners are also good prospects, and that pets as well as children can benefit from the noisy little reptile!

Terrapin is gaining momentum around the world—75 percent of sales are in the U.S., where Terrapin has an office. The 15 percent of sales that come from Europe are largely handled out of the office of a Paris distributor; Protection Piscine Enfants sells to 13 countries, including Belgium, Luxembourg, Italy, Spain, and Germany, as well as France. Safety Turtles are also sold through arrangements with pool and spa retailers from Singapore to South Africa, which has one of the highest drowning rates in the world. And Terrapin is on the move:

new products that leverage the Safety Turtle's technology are in the works, and new markets are sought—with, of course, the right exporting strategy. Check out their website at www.safetyturtle.com to find out where this product is taking them.[1]

[1] www.safetyturtle.com; and "The Turtle that Hollers for Help," International Trade Canada (www.itcan-cican.gc.ca), Stories of the Week, August 11, 2003.

Joint Venture

joint venture

Occurs when a foreign company and a local firm invest together to create a local business, sharing ownership, control, and profits of the new company

When a foreign company and a local firm invest together to create a local business, it is called a **joint venture**. These two companies share ownership, control, and profits of the new company. Investment may be made by having either of the companies buy shares in the other or by creating a third and separate entity. This was done by Caterpillar, Inc., the world's largest manufacturer of earthmoving and construction equipment. It created NEVAMASH with its joint venture partner, Kirovsky Zvod, a large Russian manufacturer of heavy equipment.

The advantages of this option are twofold. First, one company may not have the necessary financial, physical, or managerial resources to enter a foreign market alone. The joint venture between Ericsson, a Swedish telecommunications firm, and CGCT, a French switch maker, enabled them together to beat out AT&T for a US$100 million French contract. Ericsson's money and technology combined with CGCT's knowledge of the French market helped them to win the contract that neither of them could have won alone. Similarly, Ford and Volkswagen formed a joint venture to make four-wheel-drive vehicles in Portugal. Second, a government may require or strongly encourage a joint venture before it allows a foreign company to enter its market. This is the case in China. Today, more than 75,000 Chinese–foreign joint ventures operate in China.

The disadvantages arise when the two companies disagree about policies or courses of action for their joint venture or when government bureaucracy bogs down the effort. For example, Canadian firms often prefer to reinvest earnings gained, whereas some foreign companies may want to spend those earnings. Or a Canadian firm may want to return profits earned to Canada, while the local firm or its government may oppose this—the

McDonald's uses franchising as a market-entry strategy, and over 70 percent of the company's fast food outlets are franchises.

direct investment
Occurs when a domestic firm actually invests in and owns a foreign subsidiary or division

problem now faced by many potential joint ventures in Eastern Europe, Russia, Latin America, and South Asia.

Direct Investment

The biggest commitment a company can make when entering the global market is **direct investment**, which entails a domestic firm actually investing in and owning a foreign subsidiary or division. Examples of direct investment are Toyota's manufacturing location in Vancouver, where aluminum wheels are made for the Canadian market as well as the U.S. and Japanese markets.[31] Honda is very involved in direct investment, with more than 100 factories in 33 countries; on January 12, 2004, its Alliston, Ontario, plant produced its 3-millionth vehicle—a silver Acura.[32] Many global companies use this mode of entry. Reebok entered Russia by creating a subsidiary known as Reebok Russia, Motorola established a Chinese subsidiary that manufactures mobile phones and other telecommunication equipment, and Ford built a $1.9 billion automobile plant in Brazil.

For many firms, direct investment often follows one of the other three market-entry strategies. For example, Ernst & Young, an international accounting and management consulting firm, entered Hungary first by establishing a joint venture with a local company. Ernst & Young later acquired the company, making it a subsidiary with headquarters in Budapest. Following on the success of its European and Asian exporting strategy, Harley-Davidson now operates marketing and sales subsidiaries in Germany, Italy, the United Kingdom, and Japan, among other countries.

The advantages to direct investment include cost savings, better understanding of local market conditions, and fewer local restrictions. Firms entering foreign markets using direct investment believe that these advantages outweigh the financial commitments and risks involved.

Concept Check

1. What mode of entry could a company follow if it has no previous experience in global marketing?

2. How does licensing differ from a joint venture?

CRAFTING A WORLDWIDE MARKETING EFFORT

The choice of a market-entry strategy is a necessary first step for a marketer when joining the community of global companies. The next step involves the challenging task of designing, implementing, and controlling marketing programs worldwide. Below we discuss the marketing mix factors—product, promotion, place, and price—as they apply to global markets.

Product and Promotion Strategies

Global companies have five strategies for matching products and their promotion efforts to global markets. As Figure 7–4 shows, the strategies focus on whether a company extends or adapts its product and whether it must adapt its promotion message for consumers in different countries.

A product may be sold globally in one of three ways: in the same form as in its home market, with some adaptations, or as a totally new product:[33]

1. *Product extension.* Selling virtually the same product in other countries is a product extension strategy. This works well for products such as Coca-Cola, Gillette razors, Wrigley's gum, Levi's jeans, and Cervélo bicycles.
2. *Product adaptation.* Changing a product in some way to make it more appropriate for a country's climate or consumer preferences is a product adaptation strategy. Gerber baby food comes in different varieties in different countries. Vegetable and Rabbit Meat is a favourite food in Poland. Freeze-Dried Sardines and Rice is popular in Japan. Maybelline's makeup is formulaically adapted in labs to local skin types and weather across the globe, including an Asia-specific mascara that doesn't run during the rainy season.
3. *Product invention.* Alternatively, companies can invent totally new products designed to satisfy common needs across countries. Black & Decker did this with its Snake Light Flexible Flashlight. Created to address a global need for portable lighting, the product became a best-seller in North America, Europe, Latin America, and Australia and is the most successful new product developed by Black & Decker.

An identical promotion message can be used for the product extension and product adaptation strategies around the world. Gillette uses the same global message for its men's toiletries: "Gillette, the Best a Man Can Get." In September 2003, McDonald's launched its first-ever global marketing campaign with the tagline, "I'm lovin' it." McDonald's wants to generate worldwide brand appeal to their millions of consumers.[34]

FIGURE 7–4

Five product and promotion strategies for global marketing

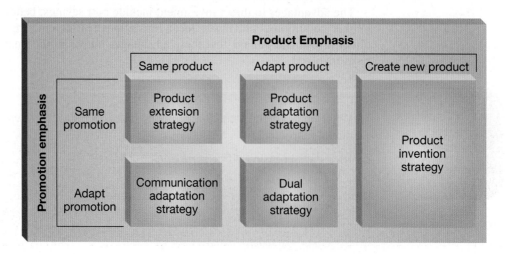

Global companies may also adapt their promotion message. For instance, the same product may be sold in many countries but advertised differently. As an example, L'Oréal, a French health and beauty products marketer, introduced its Golden Beauty brand of sun care products through its Helena Rubenstein subsidiary in Western Europe with a communication adaptation strategy. L'Oréal recognized that cultural and buying motives related to skin care and tanning are different in different places. Golden Beauty advertising features dark tanning for northern Europeans, skin protection to avoid wrinkles among Latin Europeans, and beautiful skin for Europeans living along the Mediterranean Sea, even though the products are the same. Other companies use a dual adaptation strategy by modifying both their products and promotion messages. Nestlé does this with Nescafé coffee. Nescafé is marketed using different coffee blends and promotional campaigns to match consumer preferences in different countries.

These examples illustrate a simple rule applied by global companies today: Standardize product and promotion strategies whenever possible and adapt them wherever necessary. This is the art of global marketing.[35]

Distribution (Place) Strategy

Distribution is of critical importance in global marketing. The availability and quality of retailers and wholesalers as well as transportation, communication, and warehousing facilities are often determined by a country's economic infrastructure. Figure 7–5 outlines the channel through which a product manufactured in one country must travel to reach its destination in another country. The first step involves the seller; its headquarters is responsible for the successful distribution to the ultimate consumer.

The next step is the channel between two nations, moving the product from one country to another. Intermediaries that can handle this responsibility include resident buyers in a foreign country, independent merchant wholesalers who buy and sell the product, or agents who bring buyers and sellers together.

Gillette delivers the same global message whenever possible, as shown in the Gillette for Women Venus ads from Greece, Germany, and Canada.

Once the product is in the foreign nation, that country's distribution channels take over. These channels can be very long or surprisingly short, depending on the product line. In Japan, fresh fish go through three intermediaries before getting to a retail outlet. Conversely, shoes go through only one intermediary. The sophistication of a country's distribution channels increases as its economic infrastructure develops. Supermarkets are helpful in selling products in many nations, but they are not popular or available in many

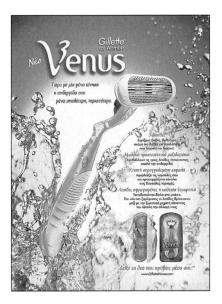
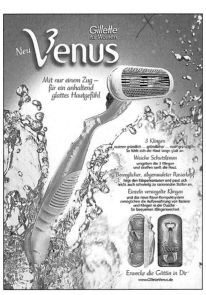
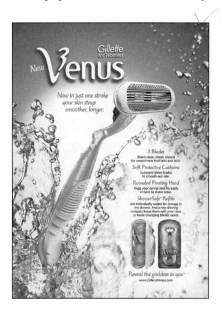

FIGURE **7–5**

FIGURE **7–5**

Channels of distribution in global marketing

others where culture and lack of refrigeration dictate shopping on a daily rather than a weekly basis. For example, when Coke and Pepsi entered China, both had to create direct-distribution channels, investing in refrigerator units for small retailers.

Pricing Strategy

Global companies face many challenges in determining a pricing strategy as part of their worldwide marketing effort. Individual countries, even those with free trade agreements, may place considerable competitive, political, and legal constraints on the pricing flexibility of global companies. For example, Wal-Mart was told by German antitrust authorities that the prices in its stores were too low, relative to competitors, and faced a fine for violating the country's trade if the prices weren't raised![36]

Pricing too low or too high can have dire consequences. When prices appear too low in one country, companies can be charged with "dumping," a practice subject to severe penalties and fines. **Dumping** is when a firm sells a product in a foreign country below its domestic price or below its actual cost. A recent trade dispute involving U.S. apple growers and Mexico is a case in point. Mexican trade officials claimed that U.S. growers were selling their red and golden delicious apples in Mexico below the actual cost of production. They imposed a 101 percent tariff on U.S. apples, and a severe drop in U.S. apple exports to Mexico resulted. Later negotiations set a price floor on the price of U.S. apples sold to Mexico.[37]

When companies price their products very high in some countries but competitively in others, they face a grey market problem. A **grey market**, also called *parallel importing*, is a situation where products are sold through unauthorized channels of distribution. A grey market comes about when individuals buy products in a lower-priced country from a manufacturer's authorized retailer, ship them to higher-priced countries, and then sell them below the manufacturer's suggested retail price through unauthorized retailers. Many well-known products have been sold through grey markets, including Olympus cameras, Seiko watches, IBM personal computers, and Mercedes-Benz cars. Parallel channels are not strictly illegal in Canada, but there are mounting legal challenges to them. Parallel importing is legal in the United States. It is illegal in the European Union.[38]

dumping

Occurs when a firm sells a product in a foreign country below its domestic prices or below its actual cost

grey market

Situations where products are sold through unauthorized channels of distribution

Concept Check

1. Products may be sold globally in three ways. What are they?
2. What is dumping?

SUMMARY

1 The dollar value of world trade has more than doubled in the past decade and will exceed US$11.5 trillion in 2006. Manufactured goods and commodities account for 75 percent of world trade, while services account for 25 percent.

2 Four recent trends have significantly affected world trade: a gradual decline of economic protectionism, an increase in formal economic integration and free trade among nations, global competition among global companies for global consumers, and the emergence of a networked global marketspace.

3 Although global and domestic marketing are based on the same marketing principles, many underlying assumptions must be reevaluated when a firm pursues global opportuni-

ties. A global environmental scan typically considers three kinds of uncontrollable environmental variables. These include cultural diversity, economic conditions, and political–regulatory climate.

4 Four global market-entry strategies are exporting, licensing, joint venture, and direct investment. The relative difficulty of global marketing, as well as the amount of financial commitment, risk, marketing control, and profit potential, increase in moving from exporting to direct investment.

5 Crafting a worldwide marketing effort involves designing, implementing, and controlling a marketing program that standardizes marketing mix elements when there are cultural similarities and adapts them when cultures differ.

KEY TERMS AND CONCEPTS

back translation p. 150
cross-cultural analysis p. 148
cultural symbols p. 148
currency exchange rate p. 151
customs p. 148
direct investment p. 155
dumping p. 158
exporting p. 152
global competition p. 144
global consumers p. 146

global marketing strategy p. 146
grey market p. 158
joint venture p. 154
multidomestic marketing strategy p. 146
protectionism p. 141
quota p. 141
tariffs p. 141
values p. 148
World Trade Organization p. 142

QUESTIONS: APPLYING MARKETING CONCEPTS AND PERSPECTIVES

1 Coca-Cola is sold all over the world. In many countries, Coca-Cola owns the bottling facilities; in others, it has signed contracts with licensees or relies on joint ventures. Canada, Cuba, and Panama had the first bottling plants outside of the U.S., and they opened in 1906. What factors should Coca-Cola consider when selecting a licensee in Australia, Brazil, Nigeria, and France? Give specific factors it should consider for each of these countries.

2 If you were recommending global marketing strategies to a small Canadian manufacturer of rain boots, and the firm wanted some advice on the market entry strategies to consider, what strategy would you recommend to start with? Why? What other alternatives are there to consider, and why did you not select them?

3 Because English is the official language in Australia, New Zealand, and Britain, some global Canadian companies may think that it is easier to market their products there than in countries where the language is different. What aspects may make it easier to market in these countries? How may it be harder?

4 In this chapter we talked about regional trade agreements between countries, such as NAFTA and ASEAN. How do you think these trade agreements affect a company's marketing strategy?

5 Some Canadian global marketers feel that they can treat the U.S. market similarly to the way they deal with the Canadian market. Comment on whether or not you think that this is wise, and give your reasons. How does the U.S. market differ from the Canadian market, from a marketing perspective?

6 Successful marketers identify their competitive advantage and use it to promote their products. When companies enter global markets, how may they have to change or rethink their competitive advantage to compete in other countries?

7 When a Canadian company expands into the global market, how does this benefit the firm? How does it benefit Canada?

DISCUSSION FORUM

You are the president of a mid-sized Canadian company that produces award-winning ice wine. You have decided to expand into international markets in the next two years, and you know that you have to make some significant changes in your marketing plan to do so. Discuss:

1 How you would change your marketing objectives,
2 How you would adjust your target market, and
3 Implications for each element of your marketing mix.

INTERNET EXERCISE

The World Trade Organization is the only international organization dealing with the global rules of trade between nations. Its intended function is to ensure that trade flows as smoothly, predictably, and freely as possible. Understanding how the WTO operates is a necessary prerequisite for global marketing.

Visit the WTO website at www.wto.org to learn more about how this organization functions and the issues it faces. A useful starting point for familiarizing yourself with the WTO is to find answers to the following questions:

www.mcgrawhill.ca/college/thecore

1   Countries are constantly seeking WTO membership. How many countries are now members of this organization? Which country is the newest member?
2   What are the 10 most common misunderstandings about the WTO identified by this organization?

VIDEO CASE 7

CNS BREATHE RIGHT® STRIPS: REACHING THE WORLD'S NOSES

"When we first began marketing this product, what was so gratifying, particularly as a physician, were the literally thousands of letters and phone calls we would receive talking about how much better people slept at night. Almost all the letters began with 'thank you, thank you, thank you!' And not just three thank you's. It was, 'I haven't gotten a good night's sleep like this in 10 years.'"

What is Dr. Dan Cohen, CEO of CNS, Inc., talking about? It's Breathe Right® nasal strips, the innovative adhesive pad with a small spring inside that, when attached to the nose, pulls the nasal passages open and makes it easier to breathe. Since their introduction, Breathe Right strips have been coveted by athletes hoping to improve their performance through increased oxygen flow, snorers (and, more often, snorers' spouses) hoping for a sound night's sleep, and allergy and cold sufferers looking for relief for their stuffed noses.

HOW THIS WEIRD-LOOKING STRIP CAME ABOUT

The Breathe Right strip was invented by Bruce Johnson, who suffered from chronic nasal congestion. At times he would put straws or paper clips up his nose at night to keep his nasal passages open. After tinkering in his workshop for years, he came up with a prototype design for the Breathe Right strip.

He brought the prototype to CNS, which was in the sleep disorders diagnostic equipment business at the time. Dr. Cohen knew instantly the market for the strips would be huge. After the products received Food and Drug Administration (FDA) approval in the U.S. and became successful in the market, CNS divested its other interests and went to work marketing the strips full time.

Being a small company, CNS did not have the budget to launch a large-scale marketing campaign. But it got the break it needed when Jerry Rice, the wide receiver for the San Francisco 49ers, wore one of the strips on national TV when the 49ers won the 1995 Super Bowl. The entire nation became aware of the product overnight, and demand for the strips increased dramatically. An indication of this national awareness was discussion on TV talk shows and even appearances of the strip in cartoons.

EVERYBODY HAS A NOSE: THE DECISION TO GO INTERNATIONAL

The problems that the Breathe Right strips solve—snoring, congestion—are not unique to the U.S. population. Also, with the media being so global today, people around the world were seeing U.S. athletes wearing the strip and wondering how they could get their noses on some. CNS decided to take Breathe Right international. But because it was still a relatively small company and had no experience in the global marketplace, it opted to take on a distribution partner that had extensive global outlets already in place as well as the ability to market the product abroad. 3M, makers of such products as Post-It notes and the leader in stick-to-skin products around the world, became the international distributor for Breathe Right strips.

David Reynolds-Gooch, the manager of International Business at 3M, explains that the strips fit in well with 3M's existing adhesive line of first-aid products and are sold in channels with which 3M has extensive leverage: pharmacies, hypermarkets, and food markets. 3M agreed to take control of all the marketing and communication responsibilities in addition to the distribution in return for a percentage of the sales of the strips. The strips are co-branded in the international markets: The packages say both Breathe Right and 3M.

BREATHING RIGHT AROUND THE WORLD

3M introduced the Breathe Right strip in Japan, then it was rolled out in Europe, and now can be found in more than 40 countries from Australia to South America. 3M used a similar approach to that used by CNS in the United States: Create awareness during the introduction phase through public relations—sports-related and otherwise. "The first year we had incredible PR success," remembers Reynolds-Gooch. "We believe we got about $14 million worth of free TV, radio, and print time around the world." This was done through such tactics as having the South African rugby team wear the strips while it won the World Cup of rugby and having pulmonologists and breathing experts describe the benefits of the product on talk shows in Japan, Australia, Europe, and Latin America.

CNS quickly discovered some major differences in marketing the product here and abroad. For instance, as Gary Tschautscher, vice president of International Marketing at CNS explains, "In the United States, we positioned and distributed the strips as part of the cough/cold category of products. As we rolled it out internationally, suddenly we realized in some countries that section in the store doesn't even exist. So where do you position your product?" Additionally, says Reynolds-Gooch, "There really aren't many large drug chains

or pharmacy chains. By law, the stores are independent in most countries. So what that means is you have to go through multiple layers of distribution, and ultimately we were able to influence the pharmacists because of the other products 3M distributes in the stores." Finally, there is no couponing in most countries in the world. That vehicle for inducing trial of a new product is not available, and hence a lot more in-store sampling is needed.

BREATHE RIGHT IN THE TWENTY-FIRST CENTURY

Both CNS and 3M face some issues for the future as Breathe Right strips gain in popularity around the globe. While the athletic segment of the market gets most of the publicity, the snorers are the bulk of the market for the strips internationally. Reynolds-Gooch has identified creating heavy users—those who use the strip every night—as the most important marketing point for the future, ahead of people with seasonal colds or allergies.

Also, many of the markets that have been identified as hot new markets throughout the business community may not be appropriate for the Breathe Right strips. For example, Latin America and Asia, especially China, are emerging markets with steadily increasing income levels and large populations, but the average age in these countries is under 30, and people under 30 typically do not have snoring problems with the frequency that older people do.

Questions

1   What are the advantages and disadvantages of CNS taking its Breathe Right strip into international markets?

2   What advantages does CNS gain by having 3M as its international licensing partner? What are the advantages for 3M?

3   What criteria might CNS and 3M use in selecting countries to enter? Using these criteria, which five or six countries would you enter?

4   Which market segment would you target in entering the international markets—snorers, athletes, people with chronic congestion and allergies, or a new segment?

5   Which marketing mix variables do you think CNS should concentrate on the most to succeed in a global arena? Why?

Targeting Marketing Opportunities

CHAPTER 8
Turning Marketing Information into Action

CHAPTER 9
Identifying Market Segments and Targets

P art 3 focuses on identifying marketing opportunities by collecting data about segments of consumers and reaching these segments with marketing programs. Chapter 8 describes how people with similar wants and needs become the target of marketing opportunities. This chapter details how information about prospective consumers is linked to marketing strategy and decisive actions, and how information technology improves the process. Chapter 9 describes how shoe manufacturing giants like Reebok and Nike, and upstarts like Heelys and Customatix, design shoes to satisfy different customers. In addition, this chapter covers the steps a firm uses in segmenting and targeting a market and then positioning its offering in the marketplace. The application of segmentation, targeting, and positioning are illustrated with Apple Computer's strategy for its hardware and software.

Turning Marketing Information into Action

AFTER READING THIS CHAPTER YOU SHOULD BE ABLE TO:

- Understand the importance of market information to companies, and the challenges and issues with acquiring and implementing a well-functioning information system.

- Comprehend the use and benefits of a marketing information system and market intelligence.

- Describe a step-by-step approach to conducting market research.

- Explain how secondary and primary data are used in marketing.

- Explain the uses of market research instruments such as questionnaires, observations, experiments, and panels.

- Comprehend alternative methods to forecast sales and use basic methods to generate a simple forecast.

THE LORD OF THE RINGS
THE TWO TOWERS

TEST SCREENINGS: LISTENING TO CONSUMERS TO REDUCE MOVIE RISKS

"Blockbuster" movies are essential for today's fiercely competitive world of filmmaking — examples being *The Lord of the Rings* trilogy, *Shoeless Joe*, *Teenie Weenies*, and *3000*.

What's in a Movie Name?

Can't remember those last three movies, even after scratching your head? Well, test screenings by the studio—a form of marketing research—found that moviegoers had problems with those titles, too. Here's what happened:

- *Shoeless Joe* became *Field of Dreams* because audiences thought Kevin Costner might be playing a homeless person.
- *Teenie Weenies* became *Honey, I Shrunk the Kids* when moviegoers couldn't relate the original title to what they saw in the movie.
- *3000* became *Pretty Woman* when audiences didn't have a clue what the number meant. (Hint: It was the number of dollars to spend an evening with Julia Roberts.)[1]

Filmmakers want movie titles that are concise, attention-getting, capture the essence of the film, and have no legal restrictions—basically the same factors that make a good brand name.

How Filmmakers Try to Reduce Risk

Is research on movie titles expensive? Very! But the greater expense is selecting a bad title that can kill a movie and cost the studio millions of dollars, not to mention the careers of producers and directors. So with today's films averaging over $80 million to produce and market,[2] movie studios use market research to reduce their risk of losses by tracking—and adapting to—the ever-changing tastes of moviegoers. This includes conducting test screenings.

For test screenings, 300 to 400 prospective viewers are recruited to attend a "sneak preview" of a film before its release. After viewing the movie, the audience fills out an exhaustive survey to critique the title, plot, characters, music, and ending as well as the

THE MARKETING PROCESS

WHERE IN THE MARKETING PROCESS ARE WE GOING IN THIS CHAPTER?

Chapter 8 discusses the information marketers need and how they acquire that information—with tools, techniques, and sources.

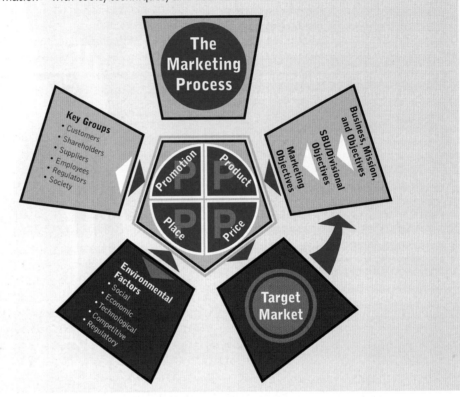

marketing program (posters, trailers, etc.) to identify improvements to make in the final edit of the movie.

Virtually every major movie produced today uses test screenings to obtain the key reactions of consumers likely to be in the target audience. Test screenings resulted in *Fatal Attraction* having probably the most commercially successful "ending-switch" of all time. In its sneak previews, audiences liked everything but the ending, which had Alex (Glenn Close) committing suicide and managing to frame Dan (Michael Douglas) as her murderer by leaving his fingerprints on the knife she used. The studio shot US$1.3 million of new scenes for the ending that audiences eventually saw.[3]

New Line Cinema was able to continue its success with its *Lord of the Rings* trilogy, which has cost the studio over US$310 million to produce and an additional US$150 million to market. The first two films, *Fellowship of the Ring* and *The Two Towers*, were huge commercial and critical successes—Academy Award® nominees. The third film, *The Return of the King*, continued the trilogy's commercial success acclaim and capped its critical acclaim with an Academy Award for best picture in 2003. Though episodes were planned for release over a long period of time, New Line overcame the huge risks associated with that timetable to maintain audience interest in J. R. R. Tolkien's classic epic.

These examples show how marketing information is the link between marketing strategy and decisive actions, the main topic of this chapter. Also, marketing research is often used to help a firm develop sales forecasts, the final topic in the chapter.

MARKETING INFORMATION REQUIREMENTS AND SYSTEMS

Companies are constantly in need of information. They need to know the state of the economy; the moves their competitors are planning; their customers' wants, needs, and preferences; and more! Information can be an important competitive advantage for firms, as well as a key marketing tool and a strategic benefit. There are many forms, sources, and uses of information, and there are also many challenges for the information user. We are in an information-rich era, so there is no shortage of information, but there is a problem: how to find the right information that will assist in making good marketing decisions, and how to wade through the wide range of available information to sort out the nice-to-know and irrelevant from the important.

Most managers receive too much information. Today's technologies facilitate collecting and accessing facts, figures, and data from a wealth of sources. So the manager's task is not to find enough information, but to find good-quality, current material that will assist in marketing decision making. Risk is a key consideration—information itself does not provide strategic help, but using the information to make informed decisions and to minimize the risk of making a poor decision makes it very powerful.

Companies answer their need for information in two basic ways. They establish systems that generate a flow of information on an ongoing basis—marketing intelligence—and they also undertake specific projects to assist with specific decisions—marketing research. Most of this chapter deals with the process, tools, and techniques of marketing research, which is the most utilized and recognized part of the information picture.

Before we delve into marketing research, however, we will talk briefly about marketing intelligence systems. Many companies have established a *marketing information system (MIS)*, which is a set of procedures and processes for collecting, sorting, analyzing, and summarizing information to be accessible to decision makers on an ongoing and regular basis. The MIS may, for example, collect information on market conditions, currency exchange rates, and competitor marketing actions and then analyze them to provide current market environment assessments.

The growing area of marketing intelligence comes from publicly available sources. Companies are keenly interested in knowing what their competitors are doing, and this is a part of marketing intelligence called *competitive intelligence*. By keeping a close watch on competitors' product developments, promotional strategies, market share, and other factors, a company can better decide what actions to take to secure the best market position that it can.

THE ROLE OF MARKETING RESEARCH

To place marketing research in perspective, we will look at what it is, some of the difficulties in conducting it, and the six key steps marketing executives can use in conducting marketing research.

What Is Marketing Research?

marketing research
Process of collecting and analyzing information in order to recommend actions to improve marketing activities

Marketing research is the process of defining a marketing problem or opportunity, systematically collecting and analyzing information, and recommending actions to improve an organization's marketing activities.[4] Although marketing research isn't perfect at predicting consumer reaction, it can reduce risk and uncertainty and help marketing managers take more effective marketing actions. It is important to realize what marketing research is and what it is not: it does not make decisions; it simply provides the knowledge for managers to be more informed in the decisions they make.

How can the Insurance Corporation of British Columbia (ICBC) do research to determine what makes people behave in a way that gets them into accidents?

The scope of marketing research is very broad. The benefits to the company are significant. Good marketing decisions come from a combination of the results of research together with the knowledge, experience, and intuition of managers.

Challenges in Marketing Research

Ask a moviegoer if she liked the title for a film she just saw and you'll probably get a straightforward answer. But often marketing researchers face difficulties in asking consumers questions about new, unknown products. For example,

- Suppose your company is developing a brand new product, never before seen by consumers. Would consumers really know whether they are likely to buy a particular product that they probably have never thought about before?
- Imagine if you, as a consumer, were asked about your personal hygiene habits. Even though you knew the answer, would you reveal it? When personal or status questions are involved, will people give honest answers?
- Will consumers' actual purchase behaviour be the same as their stated interest or intentions? Will they buy the same brand they say they will?
- If your company wants to determine the play value of a children's toy, how could they find that out? Asking a 3-year-old is not likely to give an answer that is very useful.

A task of marketing research is to overcome these challenges and obtain as much information as needed to make reasonable estimates about how consumers will behave and react in the marketplace. We often say that information is power, and when companies equip themselves with good, solid, relevant research information, the likelihood increases that they will use it to make informed decisions and to understand the market better.

Researchers work hard to ensure that they undertake their research using scientific methods, in which they collect information in an organized and systematic fashion, with two important considerations to achieve: reliability and validity. Reliability means that if the same research methods were used over and over again, they would produce similar results, so we can conclude that the methods are reliable. Validity means that the research measured what it intended to measure—in other words, it gave the researchers the type of information they wanted.

Let's look at the types of information market researchers may use and how they go about collecting this storehouse of information.

Types of Research Information

There are three basic types of information available to the market researcher. Each is collected with specific techniques and serves different functions.

Exploratory Research Exploratory research is preliminary research conducted to clarify the scope and nature of the marketing problem. It is generally carried out to provide the researcher with a better understanding of the dimensions of the problem. Exploratory research is often conducted with the expectation that subsequent and more conclusive research will follow. For example, the Dairy Farmers of Canada, an association representing dairy producers in the country, wanted to discover why milk consumption was declining in Canada.

They conducted a search of existing literature on milk consumption, talked to experts in the field, and even conducted preliminary interviews with consumers to get ideas about why consumers were drinking less milk. This exploratory research helped the association to crystallize the problem, and identify issues for more detailed follow-up research. We examine exploratory research as an integral component of the basic marketing research process later in the chapter.

Descriptive Research Descriptive research is research designed to describe basic characteristics of a given population or to profile particular marketing situations. Unlike exploratory research, with descriptive research the researcher has a general understanding of the marketing problem and is seeking conclusive data that answer the questions necessary to determine a particular course of action.

Examples of descriptive research include profiling product purchasers (e.g., the Canadian health food store shopper), describing the size and characteristics of markets (e.g., the Canadian pizza restaurant market), detailing product usage patterns (e.g., ABM usage by Canadian bank consumers), or outlining consumer attitudes toward particular brands (e.g., Canadian attitudes toward national, private, and generic brands). Magazines, radio stations, and television stations almost always do descriptive research to identify the characteristics of their audiences in order to present it to prospective advertisers.

As a follow-up to its exploratory research, the Dairy Farmers of Canada conducted descriptive research to determine the demographic characteristics of milk consumers, current usage patterns, and consumer attitudes toward milk consumption.

Causal Research Causal research is research designed to identify cause-and-effect relationships among variables. In general, exploratory and descriptive research normally precede causal research. With causal research there is typically an expectation about the relationship to be explained, such as predicting the influence of a price change on product demand. Researchers usually attempt to establish that one event (e.g., a price change) will produce another event (e.g., a change in demand).

Typical causal research studies examine the effect of advertising on sales, the relationship between price and perceived quality of a product, and the impact of a new package on product sales. When the Dairy Farmers of Canada conducted its descriptive research on milk consumers, it discovered that many believed milk was too fattening and too high in cholesterol. The association felt that these beliefs might be related to the overall decline in milk consumption in Canada. To test this assumption, the association ran a television advertising campaign to demonstrate that milk was a healthful product and essential to a person's diet. In its tracking studies, it found that the ad campaign did change consumer attitudes toward milk which, in turn, was causally related to a subsequent increase in milk consumption. We refer to causal research later in this chapter when we deal with experiments as a basic research technique.

Steps in the Marketing Research Approach

Effective marketing research is done with a plan. A systematic approach ensures that the research is done thoroughly and with consideration to all of the important elements. Here are six key steps that researchers use:

1. Define problem/issue
2. Design the research plan
3. Conduct exploratory research
4. Collect primary research information
5. Compile, analyze, and interpret data
6. Generate report and recommendations

Figure 8-1 shows this sequence of steps, and in the next few pages we will discuss these steps in detail.

Marketing research is useful in many different areas in a company. We have talked about it assisting with identifying consumer habits or intentions, but it can also be used in assessing opportunities, testing out advertising campaigns, evaluating new ideas, understanding behaviours, analyzing competitor and market situations, and troubleshooting problems. It is important that we think of marketing research as a tool that not only assists with problems and opportunities but also provides information for other key marketing decisions.

Concept Check

1. What is marketing research?
2. What is the process that market researchers use in undertaking their research?

STEP 1: DEFINE PROBLEM/ISSUE

At the Insurance Corporation of British Columbia (ICBC), the Crown corporation responsible for providing auto insurance and administering driver licensing and vehicle registration for BC drivers, they are committed to reducing injuries and fatalities, and they have spent millions of dollars advertising to try to get British Columbians to drive more safely. Here's an example of how they utilized research, and the process involved.

Looking at the large amount of money spent on advertising, ICBC realized that one thing they needed to know was whether anti-speeding ads had an effect on speeders—would they change the speeders' behaviour? This was their definition of the problem!

Establish Research Objectives

objectives
Specific, measurable goals to achieve in solving a problem

Objectives are specific, measurable goals the decision maker—in this case, the executives at ICBC—seeks to achieve in solving a problem. The most common marketing objectives are increased sales and profits, discovering consumer needs and wants, and finding out why a product is not selling well. For ICBC, the immediate research objectives were to determine whether their ads were working, which ones were working, and why.

FIGURE 8-1

The basic marketing
research process

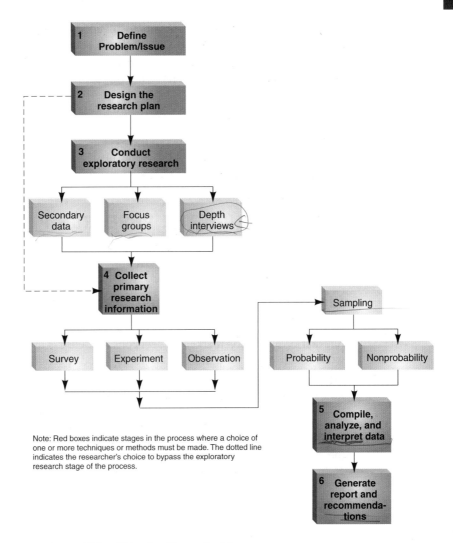

Note: Red boxes indicate stages in the process where a choice of
one or more techniques or methods must be made. The dotted line
indicates the researcher's choice to bypass the exploratory
research stage of the process.

Identify Possible Marketing Actions

measures of success
Criteria or standards used
in evaluating proposed
solutions to a problem

Effective decision makers develop specific **measures of success**, which are criteria used in evaluating proposed solutions to the problem. Different research outcomes—based on the measure of success—lead to different marketing actions. For the ICBC situation, if a measure of success were reduction of the total number of accidents caused by speeding, the results of researching effects of ads on speeder behaviour may lead to decisive actions like these:

Measure of Success	Possible marketing action
Accident reduction	Continue with anti-speeding ads
No reduction of accidents	Stop anti-speeding campaign and rethink ads

One test of whether marketing research should be done is to determine whether different outcomes for the research will lead to different marketing actions. For example, if ICBC intends to continue the anti-speeding ads regardless of whether the research suggests that they are not working to reduce accidents, there is no point in doing the research—it is a waste of time and money. Here's what happened: ICBC did the research and found out that those people who like speeding resist the ads. The research told them that they had been wasting money running them, so ICBC did a 180-degree change, altering their approach.[5]

Accident reduction and the factors involved is the subject of research around the world. Here in Canada, the Transport Canada Road Safety directorate researches and reports on a wide range of motor vehicle issues, and its goal is "for Canada to have the safest roads in the world."[6] Check out their research at www.tc.gc.ca/roadsafety.

Most marketing researchers would agree with the saying that "a problem well-defined is half-solved," but they know that defining a problem is an incredibly difficult task. For example, if the objectives are too broad, the problem may not be researchable. If they are too narrow, the value of the research results may be seriously lessened. This is why marketing researchers spend so much time in defining a marketing problem precisely and writing a formal proposal that describes the research to be done.[7]

STEP 2: DESIGN THE RESEARCH PLAN

The second step in the marketing research process involves identifying the data required, and the sources of the data, and designing methods of collecting the data.

Identify Data Required and Sources of Data

Often marketing research studies end up collecting data that are interesting, but are not relevant or useful for marketing decisions. In ICBC's situation, it might be nice to know what colour of cars are more likely to be found speeding, or what makes and models are driven by speeders. Knowing the answers to these questions could help in future with determining what cars to show in the ads of crashed cars, and it could lead to research in collaboration with manufacturers. For now, however, the challenge is to determine whether or not the ads work on speeders, so the research must focus on collecting information that will allow the corporation executives to determine whether to continue with the speeders ad campaign.

In ICBC's case, they need to determine where best to get the information they need. Obviously speeders can tell them what they need to know, but what exactly is a speeder—a driver who has received a speeding ticket in the past year? A driver with three or more speeding tickets in the past year? Drivers who have not necessarily received a speeding ticket, but who admit to consistently driving 30 or more kilometres per hour over the speed limit? ICBC has to define who can provide the information they need in order to meet their research challenge effectively.

Design Methods of Collection

In order to collect data in an organized way, it is important to have a data collection plan. There are scientific considerations that the researcher must make, and there are operational issues. A research plan lays out the types of data to be collected (primary, secondary), the types of research to be undertaken (exploratory, descriptive, causal), and the tools and techniques to be employed. In the upcoming section related to Step 3 of the marketing research process, we go into depth about all of these types and tools.

Determining *how* to collect useful marketing research data is often as important as actually collecting the data. Two key elements in deciding how to collect the data are concepts and methods.

Concepts   In the world of marketing, *concepts* are ideas about products or services. To find out about consumer reaction to a potential new product, market researchers must frequently rely on a concept—that is, a picture or verbal description of the item—to convey to consumers what they're planning to develop.

One valuable type of concept, a *hypothesis*, is an idea about the relationship between two or more factors or about what might happen in the future. Hypotheses that lead to marketing actions can come from many sources:

- Technical breakthroughs (if wireless technology can deliver web content to cellular phones, consumers will be willing to buy new phones with colour imaging).
- Marketing studies (if consumers are driving more with young children, autos with built-in DVD players will become more popular).
- Customer suggestions (if consumers have complained about getting around websites for online purchases, sales will go up if the site is made easier to use).

Methods   *Methods* are the approaches that can be used to collect data. For example, if you are the marketing researcher at ICBC responsible for the advertising program, you may be faced with some methods questions like these:

- Will drivers actually tell us about their speeding habits?
- Will drivers be able to determine the extent to which advertising may affect their road behaviour?
- How do we locate speeders who have not gotten tickets in order to get their views on the ad campaign?

Millions of people have asked questions about millions of products and services. How can you find and use the methodologies that other marketing researchers have found successful? Information on useful methods is available in tradebooks, textbooks, and handbooks that relate to marketing and marketing research. Some periodicals and technical journals, such as the *Journal of Marketing* and the *Journal of Marketing Research* published by the American Marketing Association, summarize methods and techniques valuable in addressing marketing problems.

The Professional Marketing Research Society is a Canadian organization for marketing research professionals, and they offer resources and training in research techniques to members. Their monthly publication, "***imprints***," is also a good source of Canadian market research information. Check out their website at www.pmrs-aprm.com.

1. How do research objectives relate to marketing actions?
2. What is the difference between concepts and methods?

STEP 3: CONDUCT EXPLORATORY RESEARCH

Often a company has an idea about a challenge or issue that needs research, but additional information is needed to further define the situation. This is where exploratory research comes in. The most popular techniques are focus groups, depth interviews, and collecting secondary data.

Suppose for a minute that you are the marketing manager for cranberry juice at Ocean Spray. You want to know whether Asian consumers would buy cranberry juice when they have never heard of cranberries. And you have another problem: because cranberries are native to North America and not found in other countries, there is no translation of the word "cranberry" into other languages. If you are going to try to market the product in Asia, you have to find a way to encourage consumers there to try the new product. You have to make a decision early on in the marketing research process as to whether exploratory research should be conducted in an attempt to help answer the question: Is there a market opportunity in Asia for cranberry juice?

As we saw earlier in the chapter, exploratory research is preliminary research conducted to clarify the scope and nature of a marketing problem. In general, it is designed to provide the researcher with a better understanding of the dimensions of the problem and is often conducted with the expectation that subsequent and more conclusive research may follow.

Most researchers will usually conduct some basic exploratory research during the early stage of the research process. The extent of the exploratory research will depend on the magnitude of the problem as well as its complexity. If the researcher decides to conduct exploratory research, he or she has three basic techniques to choose from: focus groups, depth interviews, and secondary data analysis.

Focus Groups

focus group
A research technique where a small group of people (usually six to ten) meet for a few hours (two to three) with a trained moderator to discuss important issues related to a product, service, or image of a company or some other marketing challenge

A popular exploratory research technique designed to obtain primary data is the use of focus groups. A **focus group** is an informal interview session in which six to ten persons, relevant to the research project, are brought together in a room with a moderator to discuss topics surrounding the marketing research problem. The moderator poses questions and encourages the individuals to answer in their own words and to discuss the issues with each other. Often, the focus-group sessions are watched by observers through one-way mirrors and/or the sessions are videotaped. Of course, participants should be informed they are being observed and/or taped. Focus-group sessions often provide the marketer with valuable information for decision making or can uncover other issues that should be researched in a more quantitative fashion.

Britain's Lewis Woolf Griptight, a manufacturer of infant and toddler products, conducted focus groups about possible brand names for their products before bringing a new product line to market. U.K. consumers turned thumbs down on using "Griptight" as a brand name for kids' products because they thought it sounded like "a carpet glue, a denture fixative, a kind of tire." So the firm called its product line by the name Kiddiwinks, a British word for children.

Depth Interviews

Another exploratory research technique used to obtain primary data involves the use of depth interviews. Depth interviews are detailed individual interviews with people relevant to the research project. The researcher questions the individual at length in a free-flowing conversational style in order to discover information that may help solve the marketing problem being investigated. Sometimes these interviews can take a few hours, and they are often recorded on audio or videotape.

Hamburger Helper didn't fare too well with consumers when General Mills first introduced it. Initial instructions called for cooking a half-pound of hamburger separately from the noodles, which were later mixed with the hamburger. Depth interviews revealed that consumers didn't think the recipe called for enough meat and that they didn't want the hassle of cooking in two different pots. So the Hamburger Helper product manager changed the recipe to call for a full pound of meat and to allow users to prepare it in one dish; this converted a potential failure into a success.[8]

Researchers have also become creative in devising other exploratory research techniques. For example, finding "the next big thing" for consumers has become the obsession in many industries.[9] In order to unearth the next big thing, marketing researchers have developed some unusual techniques sometimes referred to as "fuzzy front-end" methods. These techniques are designed to identify elusive consumer tastes or trends far before typical consumers have recognized them themselves. For example, having consumers take

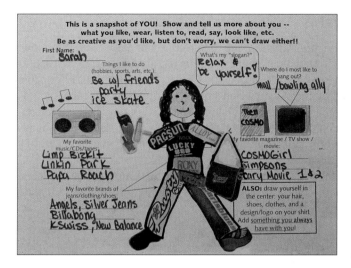

a photo of themselves every time they snack resulted in General Mills' Homestyle "Pop Secret" popcorn, which delivers the real butter and bursts of salt in microwave popcorn consumers thought they could only get from the stovetop variety.[10]

Other unusual techniques are also being used to try to spot trends early. For example, Teenage Research Unlimited had teenagers complete a drawing to help discover what teenagers like, wear, listen to, and read.[11] Other companies hire "cool hunters," people with tastes far ahead of the curve, to identify the "next big things" likely to sweep popular culture. Wet Seal and Skechers use this method to anticipate teenage girls' fashion picks and footwear trends.[12]

Figure 8–2 shows how the different kinds of marketing information fit together. **Data**, the facts and figures related to the problem, are divided into two main parts: secondary data and primary data. **Secondary data** are facts and figures that have already been recorded before the project at hand, whereas **primary data** are facts and figures that are newly collected for the project.

data
Facts and figures related to a problem

secondary data
Facts and figures that have already been recorded before the project at hand

primary data
Facts or figures that are newly collected for a project

Secondary Data: Internal

Secondary data divide into two parts—internal and external secondary data—depending on whether the data come from inside or outside the organization needing the research.

Data that have already been collected and exist inside the business firm or other organization are internal secondary data. There are many types of internal secondary data and many places in an organization where they may be stored—including on managers' desks! Some of the internal data most commonly used include product sales data and sales reports.

FIGURE 8–2

Types of marketing information

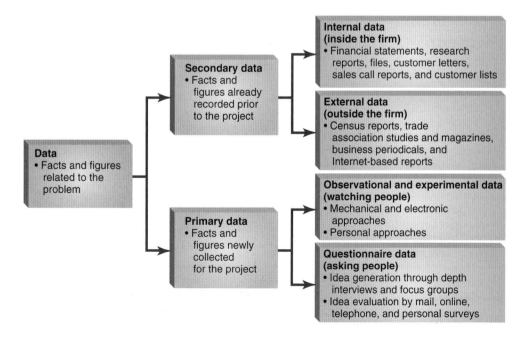

Secondary Data: External

Published data from outside the organization are external secondary data. Statistics Canada, the federal government's statistical agency, publishes a wide variety of useful reports. One very important data set they produce is the Census of Population. Every five years they count the population of the country and collect information on other demographic characteristics. The resulting Census data include information on Canadian households, such as the number of people per household and their age, sex, race/ethnic background, income, occupation, and education. Marketers use these data to identify characteristics and trends of ultimate consumers.

Statistics Canada also publishes a wide range of other statistical reports that are used extensively by businesses across the country. These reports include information on:

- Economic indicators
- International trade
- Agriculture
- Manufacturing
- Environment
- Health

- Education
- Culture and leisure
- Tourism and travel
- Government
- Justice and crime

FIGURE 8-3

Selected sources of
secondary data

SELECTED GUIDES, INDEXES, AND DIRECTORIES

Business Periodical Index
Canadian Almanac and Directory
Canadian Business Index
Canadian News Index
Canadian Periodical Index
Canadian Statistics Index
Canadian Trade Index
Directory of Associations in Canada
Fraser's Canadian Trade Directory
Predicasts Index
Scott's Directories
Standards Periodical Directory
Ulrich's International Periodicals Directory

SELECTED PERIODICALS AND NEWSPAPERS

Advertising Age
Adweek
American Demographics
Business Horizons
Canadian Business
Canadian Consumer
Forbes
Fortune
Harvard Business Review
Journal of Advertising
Journal of Advertising Research
Journal of Consumer Research
Journal of Marketing
Journal of Marketing Management
Journal of Marketing Research
Journal of Personal Selling and Sales Management
Journal of Retailing

Journal of Small Business
Marketing Magazine
Marketing & Media Decisions
Marketing News
Progressive Grocer
Sales and Marketing Management
The Globe and Mail
The Financial Post
The Financial Post Magazine
The Wall Street Journal

SELECTED STATISTICS CANADA PUBLICATIONS

Annual Retail Trade
Canadian Economic Observer
Canada Yearbook
Family Expenditure Guide
Market Research Handbook
Statistics Canada Catalogue

SELECTED TRADE SOURCES

ACNielsen
Conference Board of Canada
Dun & Bradstreet Canada
Financial Post Publishing
Find/SVP
Gale Research
MacLean Hunter Research Bureau
MapInfo Canada
Predicasts International
R. L. Polk

MARKETING NEWSNET

ONLINE DATABASE AND INTERNET RESOURCES USEFUL FOR MARKETERS

In recent years the wealth of information available via the Internet has grown exponentially. For marketing research, this is a gold mine! Databases, company websites, and other resources are plentiful, but finding the right information and doing it in an efficient way requires understanding the data sources and methods of sourcing the information. Here are some guidelines for using online sources.

Online databases are basically of two types:

- Periodical databases that index publications such as journals, magazines and newspapers, and provide abstracts (summaries) of articles and the full text content of articles, and
- Reference databases that provide statistical, financial, or directory data on businesses, organizations, products, or markets.

Periodical and reference databases are available by subscription. Users can access them via the Internet through public, academic or corporate libraries that have paid the subscription fees. Users should log on to library websites and look for headings such as "Electronic Resources," "Databases," "Journals," "Article Indexes," or "Find Articles."

Periodical databases that users can expect to find include the following:

- *ABI/Inform.* Business, management, marketing, company, product, and industry publications;
- *Business & Industry.* A database of 1,000 trade and business publications, covering business events, companies, industries, products, and markets in over 190 countries worldwide;
- *Business Source Premier.* Full text for nearly 3,300 business journals;
- *Canadian Newsstand.* Canadian newspapers;
- *CBCA (Canadian Business and Current Affairs).* Canadian publications;
- *CPI.Q.* Canadian periodicals; and
- LexisNexis. International newspapers, journals, market reports, legal cases, law reports, and patents.

Reference databases include the following:

- *Canadian Trade Index.* Directory of manufacturers, exporters, and distributors in Canada;

- *CanCorp Financials.* Financial and management information on Canadian corporations;
- *CBR: Canadian Business Resource.* Detailed profiles of top Canadian companies, includes biographical information on senior executives;
- *Export Market Insight.* International marketing, political, and economic reports;
- *FP (Financial Post) Corporate Reports*. Historical, investor, and industry reports on Canada's top public companies;
- *Gartner Group.* Research and analysis of IT trends and developments;
- *Hoover's Online.* Comprehensive company, industry, and market intelligence;
- *Investext Plus.* Investment, company and, industry analyst reports from North America, Europe, Asia/Pacific, Latin America, Africa, and the Middle East;
- *Mergent Online.* Canadian and international (non-U.S.) company information; and
- *Reuters Business Insight.* Global industry reports on technology, consumer goods, health care, energy, and financial services.

Internet portals and search engines are free to all users. Useful sites include the following:

- *Edgar Online* (www.edgar-online.com). Regulatory reporting by U.S. public companies;
- *Google* (www.google.ca). Enter a company name to find a corporate website;
- *Government of Canada* (www.canada.gc.ca/depts/major/depind_e.html);
- *Statistics Canada* (www.statcan.ca);
- *Strategis* (http://strategis.ic.gc.ca). Industry Canada portal provides company profiles, business information by sector, economic analysis, and statistics;
- SEDAR (www.sedar.com). Canadian securities filings including public company profiles and annual reports;
- *U.S. Census Bureau* (www.census.gov/econ/www/index.html); and
- *Statistical Abstract of the United States* (www.census.gov/statab/www).

Check out these sources and note the wealth of information they can provide for you.

Also, Statistics Canada provides classifications of businesses and other organizations on the basis of the North American Industry Classification System (NAICS).

There are many sources of information in print. Figure 8-3 shows some of those most popular with market researchers.

Trade associations, universities, and business periodicals provide detailed data of value to market researchers and planners. Many of these data are now available online via the Internet, and located using a search engine such as Google. The Marketing NewsNet box provides examples.

Advantages and Disadvantages of Secondary Data

A general rule among marketing people is to obtain secondary data first and then collect primary data. Two important advantages of secondary data are the tremendous time savings if the data have already been collected and published or exist internally and the low cost, such as free or inexpensive census reports. Furthermore, a greater level of detail is often available through secondary data, especially Census data.

However, these advantages must be weighed against some significant disadvantages. First, the secondary data may be out of date, especially if they are Census data collected only every five years. Second, the definitions or categories might not be quite right for your project. For example, the age groupings might be wrong for your project. Finally, because the data are collected for another purpose, they may not be specific enough for your project. In such cases it may be necessary to collect primary data.

Performing a Situation Analysis

In Chapter 2 we talked about performing a situation analysis to determine where a firm is in terms of its market position and performance, and to guide the firm in generating a strategic plan that reflects the current situation. Some of the information collected for a situation analysis is actually a marketing research activity. Customer research is done using the concepts and techniques of marketing research. In many firms this is an ongoing activity, with a variety of techniques involved. At ICBC, for example, they held focus groups to show the participants the ads and collect their responses. They then determined the personality profile of the speeders, allowing them to suggest the linkage between personality and speeding. This was their exploratory research stage, and it was followed by research on a larger group of people with more quantitative data being collected to confirm the personality/speeding linkage.

Concept Check

1. What are data?
2. What is the difference between secondary and primary data?
3. What are some advantages and disadvantages of secondary data?

STEP 4: COLLECT PRIMARY RESEARCH INFORMATION

Primary Data: Observing Behaviour

The two principal ways to collect new or primary data for a marketing study are by observing people and asking them questions. Both can be accomplished in a variety of ways.

Mechanical and Electronic Observation

Facts and figures obtained by watching, either mechanically or in person, how people actually behave is the way marketing researchers collect **observational data**. National TV ratings, such as those of Nielsen Media Research shown in Figure 8–4, are an example of electronic observational data collected by a "people meter." The people meter is a box that is attached to TV sets, VCRs, cable boxes, and satellite dishes in 5,100 homes across the country. It has a remote that operates the meter when a viewer begins and finishes watching a TV program. Finally, it stores and then transmits the viewing information each night to Nielsen Media Research.[13]

observational data
Facts and figures obtained by watching, either mechanically or in person, how people behave

On the basis of all this observational data, Nielsen Media Research then calculates the "rating" and "share" of each TV program. With 12.5 million Canadian households, nearly all of which have a television, a single ratings point equals 1 percent, or 125,000 TV households.[14] A share point is the percentage of TV sets in use tuned to a particular program. Because network and local broadcast stations, cable systems, and other TV programmers use this information to set advertising rates and make programming decisions, the Nielsen data have a significant effect. For example, a change of 1 percentage point in a rating can mean gaining or losing up to $50 million in advertising revenue because advertisers pay rates on the basis of the size of the audience for a TV program. Nielsen//NetRatings also record Internet user behaviour by using an electronic meter attached to a personal computer.

Personal Observation

Watching consumers in person or by videotaping them are other observational approaches. For example, Aurora Foods observes how consumers bake cakes in its test kitchens to see if baking instructions on the cake box are understood and followed correctly. Gillette marketing researchers actually videotaped consumers brushing their teeth in their own bathrooms to see how they really brush—not just how they say they brush. The new-product result: Gillette's Oral-B CrossAction toothbrush.[15]

Personal observation is both useful and flexible, but it can be costly and unreliable when different observers report different conclusions in watching the same event. Also, although observation can reveal what people do, it cannot easily determine why they do it, such as why they are buying or not buying a product. This is the principal reason for using questionnaires.

Nielsen ratings of the top 10 national television programs from January 27, 2003, through February 2, 2003

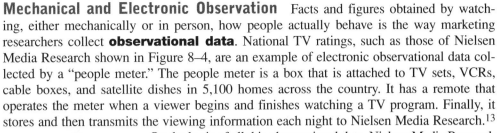

RANK	PROGRAM	RATING	SHARE
1	CSI	16.6	24.0
2	Friends	16.3	25.0
3	American Idol—Wednesday	14.3	21.0
4	E.R.	14.3	23.0
5	American Idol—Tuesday	13.7	20.0
6	Joe Millionaire	12.1	17.0
7	CSI: Miami	11.2	18.0
8	Everybody Loves Raymond	11.1	16.0
9	Scrubs	11.1	17.0
10	Without a Trace	10.8	17.0

SOURCE: Nielsen Media Research. Used by permission.

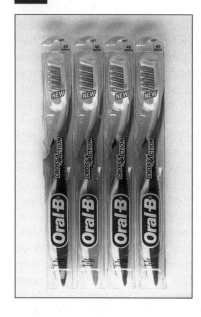

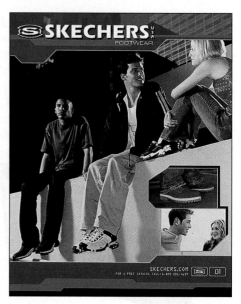

How do you do marketing research on things as diverse as toothbrushes, soap pads, and fashion products for teenagers?

Primary Data: Questioning Consumers

The second principal way of gathering information from consumers is by asking them questions. Questions can be standardized and asked to a large number of people, as in a survey, or questions can be posed less formally to a smaller number of people, as in a focus group. Personal interviews allow a researcher to follow up standard questions to get in-depth answers, while panels can be used to track a group of the same consumers over a period of time. Questions can be asked "live," face-to-face or over the phone, or through e-mail, regular mail, or "comment cards." How many times have you filled out a questionnaire?

questionnaire data
Facts or figures obtained by asking people about their attitudes, awareness, intentions, characteristics, and behaviours

Questionnaire data are facts and figures obtained by asking people about their attitudes, awareness, intentions, characteristics, and behaviours. Because so many questions might be asked in questionnaires, it is essential that the researcher concentrate on those directly related to the marketing problem at hand. Many marketing researchers divide questionnaire data used for hypothesis generation from those used for hypothesis evaluation.

The marketing researcher tests ideas discovered in the exploratory research stage to help the marketing manager recommend marketing actions. This test usually is a mail, telephone, personal, e-mail, fax, or Internet survey of a large sample of past, present, or prospective consumers.

In choosing between these alternatives, the marketing researcher has to make important trade-offs to balance cost against the expected quality of information obtained. Personal interview surveys have a major advantage of enabling the interviewer to be flexible in asking probing questions or getting reactions to visual materials, but are very costly to conduct. Mail surveys are usually biased because those most likely to respond have had especially positive or negative experiences with the product or brand. And response to mail surveys is typically very low. While telephone interviews allow flexibility, they are increasingly difficult to complete because respondents may hang up on the interviewer. Voice mail, caller ID, and call screening all work against successful telephone interviewing. Fax and Internet surveys are restricted to respondents having the technologies but are expanding rapidly.[16]

Figure 8–5 shows typical problems to guard against in wording questions to obtain meaningful answers from respondents. For example, in a question of whether you eat at fast-food restaurants regularly, the word *regularly* is ambiguous. Two people might answer yes to the question, but one might mean "once a day" while the other means "once or twice a month." Both answers appear as yes to the researcher who tabulates them, but they suggest that dramatically different marketing actions be directed to each of these two prospective consumers. It is essential that marketing research questions be worded precisely so that all respondents interpret the same question similarly.

Primary Data: Panels and Experiments

Two special ways that observations and questionnaires are sometimes used are panels and experiments.

Marketing researchers often want to know if consumers change their behaviour over time, and so they take successive measurements of the same people. A *panel* is a sample of consumers or stores from which researchers take a series of measurements. For example, The NPD Group collects data about consumer purchases such as apparel, food, and electronics from its Online Panel, which consists of over 600,000 individuals worldwide. With this information, a firm like General Mills can measure a consumer's switching behaviour from one brand of its breakfast cereal (Wheaties) to another (Cheerios) or to a competitor's (Kellogg's Special K).

A marketing *experiment* involves changing a variable factor involved in a customer purchase and seeing what happens as a result. Ideally, the researcher changes just one element—usually, one of the factors in the marketing mix—and keeps all the other variables constant. The example may be as simple as an independent bookstore or pet store owner suggesting to her clerks, "Let's try to learn the first names of our good customers"—a strategy that has been incredibly successful for independents competing with large chains such as Starbucks or PetSmart.

Large companies often use *test markets*, a kind of marketing experiment discussed in Chapter 10, to determine if consumers will buy a new product, brand, or store concept. In 1988, Wal-Mart opened three experimental stand-alone supercenters to gauge consumer acceptance before deciding to open others. Today, Wal-Mart operates over 1,250 supercenters internationally.[17]

FIGURE 8-5

Typical problems in wording

PROBLEM	SAMPLE QUESTION	EXPLANATION OF PROBLEM
Leading question	Why do you like Wendy's fresh meat hamburgers better than those of competitors?	Consumer is led to make statement favouring Wendy's hamburgers.
Ambiguous question	Do you eat at fast-food restaurants regularly? ☐ Yes ☐ No	What is meant by word *regularly*—once a day, once a month, or what?
Unanswerable question	What was the occasion for eating your first hamburger?	Who can remember the answer? Does it matter?
Two questions in one	Do you eat Wendy's hamburgers and chili? ☐ Yes ☐ No	How do you answer if you eat Wendy's hamburgers but not chili?
Nonmutually exclusive answers	What is your age? ☐ Under 20 ☐ 20–40 ☐ 40 and over	What answer does a 40-year-old check?

How might Wal-Mart have done early marketing research to help develop its supercenters, which have achieved international success?

Advantages and Disadvantages of Primary Data

FIGURE **8–6**

Primary data—how do the techniques compare?

Compared with secondary data, primary data have the advantage of being more specific to the problem being studied. The main disadvantages are that primary data are usually far more costly and time consuming to collect than secondary data. See Figure 8-6 for more detail about the advantages and disadvantages of primary data.

TECHNIQUE	ADVANTAGES	DISADVANTAGES
Observation	• Flexible • May indicate things a consumer cannot articulate clearly	• Does not indicate why consumers behave as they do • Different researchers may interpret behaviours differently
Questioning consumers (interviews/surveys)	• Large number of people can be asked a standard set of questions • Interviewers can probe to get in-depth answers • Questions can be administered via e-mail, mail, telephone, or in-person interviews	• Interviewers can bias results for in-person or telephone interviews • Mail or e-mail surveys may be done mainly by those with a strong positive or negative bias • Can be very expensive and take a long time to analyze data
Panels	• Provides identified control group • Can tracks changes in consumer behaviour over time	• Can be difficult to keep consumers in the panel over a time period of several months • Original participants needed for consistency
Experiments	• Researchers able to change some key factors and measure the results	• Can be expensive • Takes time • Controlling factors that are not changed can be a problem
Test markets	• Allows company to launch product or promotional campaign in a controlled area • Can monitor and make adjustments • Can avoid the costly failures of products launched nationally with testing	• Tells competitors what company is doing • Requires as much effort as a major roll-out and in some cases is costly and time consuming

Concept Check

1. A mail questionnaire asks: "Do you regularly eat pizza?" What is the difficulty with this question?

2. Which survey provides the greatest flexibility for asking probing questions: mail, telephone, or personal interview?

3. What is the difference between a panel and an experiment?

STEP 5: COMPILE, ANALYZE, AND INTERPRET DATA

After data has been collected, it has to be compiled, analyzed, and summarized in order to turn it into information. The researcher must know how to analyze the data and what tools to use. There are many statistical packages and functions that can make the task easier.

The level of analysis conducted on the data depends on the nature of the research and the information needed to provide a solution to the marketing problem. For survey data, frequency analysis is done—calculating the number of responses to each question for each category of response. For example, if a question asked, "Have you seen the movie *The Lord of the Rings: The Two Towers*, and the respondents could answer "yes" or "no," a frequency count would simply be a tally of the number of "yes" responses and the number of no responses. After that, the researcher may wish to identify patterns in the data, or examine how data pertaining to some questions may relate to data obtained from asking other questions.

STEP 6: GENERATE REPORT AND RECOMMENDATIONS

After the data have been analyzed, the researcher will usually consult marketing managers and discuss the results. A key question to ask is, "What does this information tell us?" One of the most important aspects of the marketing researcher's job is to interpret the information and make conclusions that will assist with decision making. The researcher will usually prepare a report to communicate the research findings, and the report will include recommendations for action to solve the marketing challenge.

Many researchers have generated lengthy and highly technical reports that contain a wealth of valuable information but are not used. Managers generally prefer clear and concise reports with the key findings highlighted. Including charts, graphs, and tables of data will assist the reader to understand the information.

The best results from a research project happen when the researcher and managers work together to interpret the findings of the research and make conclusions as to how to convert them into marketing action. Management must be committed to acting on the research—to implement the recommendations. When managers do not act on their marketing research, the market research activity is of little or no value. In addition to a commitment to acting on the results of the research, good management monitors their progress to ensure that the intended results do take place.

Marketing data and information have little value unless they are translated into findings and recommendations that lead to marketing actions for the marketing managers. How do we prepare the work so that managers can use it to support actions? Step 6 in the marketing research approach involves delivering a useful report to marketing managers by presenting the findings, and making recommendations.[18]

OTHER CONSIDERATIONS IN MARKETING RESEARCH

Marketing research is part science, part art. There are many tools to use, and many techniques to be employed. Two considerations that are very important are sampling and information technology issues.

Sampling

Although sampling is an inherent component of the research design stage, it is a distinctive aspect of the research process. The researcher's sampling plan indicates who is to be sampled, how large a sample is needed, and how sampling units will be selected. Rarely does a research project involve a complete census of every person in the research population, because of its time and cost. So sampling is used. Sampling is the process of gathering data from a subset of the total population rather than from all members (census) of that particular population. A sample, then, is a subset from a larger population.

If proper statistical procedures are followed, a researcher does not need to select every member in a population, because a properly selected sample should be representative of the population as a whole. However, errors can and do occur in sampling, and thus the reliability of the data obtained through sampling can sometimes become an issue. Savvy researchers know that the first and most critical sampling question for researchers to ask is: Who is to be sampled?

Another key question concerns the sample size: How big should the sample be? As mentioned, it is usually unrealistic to expect a census of the research population to be conducted. In general, larger samples are more precise than smaller ones, but proper sampling can allow a smaller subset of the total population to provide a reliable measure of the whole.

The final question of the sampling plan concerns how to select the sampling units. There are two basic sampling techniques: probability and nonprobability sampling. *Probability sampling* involves precise rules to select the sample such that each element of the population has a specific known chance of being selected. For example, if your university wants to know how last year's 1,000 graduates are doing, it can put their names into a bowl and randomly select 100 names of graduates to contact. The chance of being selected—100 out of 1,000, or one in 10—is known in advance, and all graduates have an equal chance of being contacted. This procedure helps to select a sample (100 graduates) that should be representative of the entire population (the 1,000 graduates) and allows conclusions to be drawn about the entire population.

Nonprobability sampling involves the use of arbitrary judgment by the marketing researcher to select the sample so that the chance of selecting a particular element of the population is either unknown or zero. If your university decided to talk to 100 of last year's graduates, but only those who lived closest to the institution, many class members would be arbitrarily eliminated. This has introduced a bias, or possible lack of representativeness, which likely means that conclusions cannot be accurately drawn about the entire graduating class. Nonprobability samples are often used when time and budgets are limited, and are most often used for exploratory research purposes. In general, marketing researchers use data from such samples with caution. They can furnish valuable information, but the results should not be assumed to represent the overall population.

The Internet as a Research Tool

There is a small but rapidly growing orientation towards using the Internet as a research medium. Online research is quick, easy, and much less expensive than traditional methods, and it is convenient for respondents. Some hard-to-reach segments of the market can be contacted and surveyed online effectively. Not just surveys can be done in this way; focus groups can be conducted virtually as well. Participants can sign in from anywhere in the world, and the logistics of the focus group setup are much easier than getting six to ten people in a room together. Of course, the interpersonal interaction and the body language that are usually a part of focus groups are lost, but there are the advantages of being able to include participants who would not otherwise attend and the speed and availability of the recorded dialogue that takes place in the online discussion.

Some researchers are predicting that a large percentage of research will eventually take place on the Internet. Time will tell!

Making the Most of Information Technology

The Internet and the PC provide a gateway to extensive sources of information on the competition, the market, and the consumer. Information sources for these databases range from internal data about sales and customers to external data from marketing research services such as TV ratings. Today's marketing managers, who are responsible for increasing the sales of their product or brand, can be swamped in an ocean of marketing data like those shown in Figure 8–7. So they need to adopt strategies for dealing with it all. The marketer's task is to convert this data ocean into useful analyses on which to base informed decisions.

Information technology involves designing and managing computer and communication networks that can store and process data. Such systems make data accessible to managers who can query a system to analyze information in various ways and with the results make effective marketing decisions. Generally speaking, time is scarce and the available information is incredibly complex. Professionals must organize and interpret data clearly, quickly, and simply—and information technology can make the job much easier.

Today, information technology is used to extract hidden information from large databases. Marketing research services now offer the ability to track household demographics and lifestyles *and* combine this information with those households' product purchases, TV viewing behaviour, and responses to coupon or free-sample promotions. Firms such as Information Resources' InfoScan and AC Nielsen's ScanTrack collect this information from the checkout counters at supermarket, drug, convenience, and mass merchandise retailers around the world.[19] Campbell Soup, maker of Swanson frozen dinners, used the information from one of these services to shift a TV ad campaign from a serious to a light theme, which increased sales of Swanson dinners by 14 percent.[20]

Retail stores also use a technique called *data mining* to find statistical links that suggest marketing opportunities. You may not need a computer analysis to tell you that peanut butter and grape jelly purchases are linked. But would you have expected that men buying diapers in the evening sometimes buy a six-pack of beer as well?

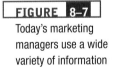

FIGURE 8–7

Today's marketing managers use a wide variety of information

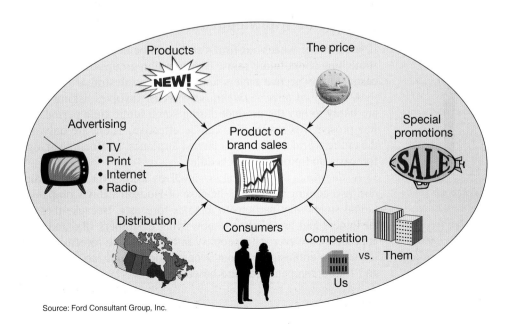

Source: Ford Consultant Group, Inc.

SALES FORECASTING TECHNIQUES

sales forecast
Total sales of a product that a firm expects to sell during a specified time period under specified conditions

Forecasting or estimating potential sales is often a key goal in a marketing research study. Good sales forecasts are important for a firm as it schedules production.[21] The term **sales forecast** refers to the total sales of a product that a firm expects to sell during a specified time period under specified environmental conditions and its own marketing efforts. For example, Hudson's Bay Company might develop a sales forecast of $8.6 billion across its The Bay, Zellers, and Home Outfitters stores for 2005, assuming customers remain loyal to shopping at their stores.

Three main sales forecasting techniques are often used: judgments of the decision maker, surveys of knowledgeable groups, and statistical methods.

Judgments of the Decision Maker

Probably 99 percent of all sales forecasts are simply the judgment of the person who must act on the results of the forecast—the individual decision maker. A direct forecast involves estimating the value to be forecast without any intervening steps. Examples appear daily: How many litres of milk should I buy? How much money should I get out of the ABM?

You probably get the same cash withdrawal most times you use the ABM. But if you need to withdraw more than the usual amount, you would probably make some intervening steps (such as counting the cash in your pocket or estimating what you'll need for special events this week) to obtain your direct estimate.

A *lost-horse forecast* involves starting with the last known value of the item being forecast, listing the factors that could affect the forecast, assessing whether they have a positive or negative impact, and making the final forecast. The technique gets its name from how you'd find a lost horse: go to where it was last seen, put yourself in its shoes, consider those factors that could affect where you might go (to the pond if you're thirsty, the hayfield if you're hungry, and so on), and go there. For example, a product manager for Wilson's tennis rackets in 2003 who needed to make a sales forecast through 2006 would start with the known value of 2003 sales and list the positive factors (more tennis courts, more TV publicity) and the negative ones (competition from other sports, high prices of graphite and ceramic rackets) to arrive at the final series of annual sales forecasts.

Surveys of Knowledgeable Groups

If you wonder what your firm's sales will be next year, ask people who are likely to know something about future sales. Two common groups that are surveyed to develop sales forecasts are prospective buyers and the firm's salesforce.

A *survey of buyers' intentions forecast* involves asking prospective customers if they are likely to buy the product during some future time period. For industrial products with few prospective buyers, this can be effective. There are only a few hundred customers in the entire world for Boeing's largest airplanes, so Boeing surveys them to develop its sales forecasts and production schedules.

A *salesforce survey forecast* involves asking the firm's salespeople to estimate sales during a coming period. In the case of Hudson's Bay Company, the managers of the individual stores may participate in sales forecasts. Because these people are in contact with customers and are likely to know what customers like and dislike, there is logic to this approach. However, salespeople can be unreliable forecasters—painting too rosy a picture if they are enthusiastic about a new product and too grim a forecast if their sales quota and future compensation are based on it.

How might a marketing manager for Wilson tennis rackets forecast sales through 2006? Use a lost-horse forecast, as described in the text.

FIGURE 8–8

Linear trend extrapolation of sales revenues of Xerox, made at the start of 1999

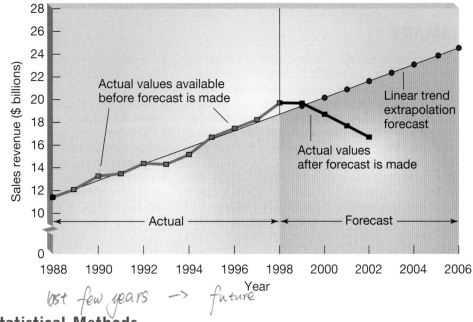

FIGURE 8–8

Statistical Methods

The best-known statistical method of forecasting is trend extrapolation, which involves extending a pattern observed in past data into the future. When the pattern is described with a straight line, it is called linear trend extrapolation. Suppose that in early 1999 you were a sales forecaster for the Xerox Corporation and had actual sales running from 1988 to 1998 (Figure 8–8). Using linear trend extrapolation, you draw a line to fit the past data and project it into the future to give the forecast values shown for 1999 to 2006.[22]

If in 2002 you want to compare your forecasts with actual results, you are in for a surprise—illustrating the strength and weakness of trend extrapolation. Trend extrapolation assumes that the underlying relationships in the past will continue into the future, which is the basis of the method's key strength: simplicity. If this assumption proves correct, you have an accurate forecast. However, if this proves wrong, the forecast is likely to be wrong. In this case your forecasts from 2000 through 2002 were too high, as shown in Figure 8–8, largely because of fierce competition in the photocopying industry.

1. What are three kinds of sales forecasting techniques?

2. How do you make a lost-horse forecast?

3. What is linear trend extrapolation?

SUMMARY

1 Marketing research is the process of defining a marketing problem or opportunity, systematically collecting and analyzing information, and recommending actions to improve an organization's marketing activities. The chapter uses a six-step marketing research sequence that can lead to better decisions.

2 The first step in the process is describing the problem or issue and establishing the research objectives that will guide the process.

3 Next, the research plan is designed, which involves identifying the information that is needed and where it can be found, and designing methods of gathering information.

4 Exploratory research comes next: defining the problem more specifically, collecting secondary data, and performing a situation analysis.

5 Primary information is collected in the fourth step, and usually this involves sample design and survey administration.

6 Analyzing and interpreting the data, in light of the objectives of the research, converts it into information.

7 The final step is generating the report and the recommendations for how decisions should use the results of the research in marketing activities.

8 Sales forecasting is another marketing research activity, and three methods are the most common: judgment of individuals, surveys of knowledgeable groups, and statistical methods.

KEY TERMS AND CONCEPTS

data p. 175
focus group p. 174
marketing research p. 167
measures of success p. 171

objectives p. 170
observational data p. 179
primary data p. 175
questionnaire data p. 180

sales forecast p. 186
secondary data p. 175

QUESTIONS: APPLYING MARKETING CONCEPTS AND PERSPECTIVES

1 Nielsen Media Research obtains ratings of local TV stations by having households fill out diary questionnaires. These give information on *(a)* who is watching TV and *(b)* what program. What are the limitations of this questionnaire method?

2 A rich aunt has decided to set you up in a business of your own choosing. To her delight, you decide on a service business—giving flying lessons in ultralight planes to your fellow college students. Some questions from the first draft of a mail questionnaire you plan to use are shown below. In terms of Figure 8–5, *(a)* identify the problem with each question and *(b)* correct it. Note: Some questions may have more than one problem.

a. Have you ever flown in commercial airliners and in ultralight planes? ☐ Yes ☐ No

b. Why do you think ultralights are so much safer than hang gliders? _____

c. At what age did you first know you like to fly?
☐ Under 10 ☐ 10 to 20 ☐ 21 to 30 ☐ Over 30

d. How much did you spend on recreational activities last year?
☐ $100 or less ☐ $801 to $1,201
☐ $101 to $400 ☐ $1,201 to $1,600
☐ $401 to $800 ☐ $1,600 or more

e. How much would you pay for ultralight flying lessons?
_____

f. Would you sign up for a class that met regularly?
☐ Yes ☐ No

3 The format in which information is presented to a harried marketing manager is often vital. *(a)* If you were a marketing manager and queried your information system, would you rather see the results in tables or charts and graphs? *(b)* What are one or two strengths and weaknesses of each format?

4 Aim Toothpaste puts a cents-off coupon in the Saturday paper across the entire country (freestanding insert, or FSI). In addition, Aim provides retailers with additional incentives to set up an in-store display and advertise the toothpaste in their local market newspapers. Using retail sales data for Aim, an analysis of sales performance is made contrasting the retailers without displays and local ads, to the retailers with these added promotions. Assume that the retailers who promoted Aim with displays and ads received a special payment in the form of product discounts of 25 percent. *(a)* What measures of success are appropriate? *(b)* Depending on the answer to *(a)*, what recommendations might be made?

5 Scott Jamieson is the sales manager for a real estate company in the Ottawa area. He notes the sales for the previous five years:

- Year 1 - $10,260,000
- Year 2 - $11,390,000
- Year 3 - $11,875,000
- Year 4 - $12,530,000
- Year 5 - $14,115,000

He wants to prepare a sales forecast for the next two years for the company. What methods of forecasting could he use?

Which one is the best for this situation? Develop a quick forecast for Scott for the next two years. Identify which forecasting method you used, and justify your choice.

6 Food for the World is a national non-profit organization that works to raise money for third-world countries where starvation is a problem. They are conducting some focus groups to determine people's perceptions of their organization. Suggest some questions they might ask and justify your suggestions.

DISCUSSION FORUM

You are the manager of a marketing research firm, and you are reviewing five projects on your desk. Here are the project descriptions:

- A retail chain with 15 outlets wants to know what their customers think of their new loyalty program.
- A food products manufacturer wants to launch their new line of frozen bread dough, and they would like to see how the product launch and advertising program will work out.
- A provincial political party wants to determine the characteristics of the population of each electoral district in the province.
- An advertising agency has generated a new logo and ad campaign for a well-known soft drink, and they need consumer feedback on their ideas before launching the campaign in the media.
- The owner of a shopping centre management firm wants to analyze the flow of people traffic through each of their centres to help them decide on the extent of renovations they will do.

Suggest what type of research you would recommend for each and generate a brief description of the information you would collect and any problems or challenges you foresee for each of these situations.

INTERNET EXERCISE

WorldOpinion calls its website "The World's Market Research Web Site." To check out the latest marketing research news, job opportunities, and directories of more than 8,500 research locations in 99 countries, go to www.worldopinion.com and do the following:

www.mcgrawhill.ca/college/thecore

1 Click on the "News" link on WorldOpinion's home page to read about the current news and issues facing the market research industry.

2 Click on the "Current Issue" link for The Frame, a set of online articles published by Survey Sampling, International.

VIDEO CASE 8

SUGAR—HOW CAN WE CUT BACK TO 10 PERCENT?

How many ways can you say "sugar"—5? 10? Check the labels of that can of pop on your desk, or the cereal you had for breakfast. If you see dextrose, fructose, sucrose, maple syrup, molasses, turbinado, amazake, sorbitol, carob powder, corn syrup, maltose, or honey, you are seeing a form of sugar. And it's becoming a problem. Obesity, diabetes, heart disease, and some cancers are directly linked to an excessive sweet tooth.

The World Health Organization's report—"Diet, Nutrition and the Prevention of Chronic Diseases"—cites high sugar consumption as a worldwide concern. Health experts generated recommendations that they want to see governments implement, after analyzing the latest research available from countries around the world. They also suggest banning advertising sugar-laden foods to children, eliminating sugary foods at schools, and possibly imposing a sugar tax.

Just what does the research tell us about our almost-addiction to sugar in its many forms? Statistics Canada reports that we in Canada eat some 23 teaspoons of sugar every day—in our refined sugars, honey, and maple syrup. Corn sweeteners, the main ingredient in pop, and the sugars in fruit juices are not even included in this total—so the average consumption is more than 23 teaspoons. Sugar lurks in foods we think of as healthy—often fruit juices contain as much sugar as pop. A label announcing a "fruit drink" is usually just a non-carbonated soft drink. What about the lowly hot dog? It, too, contains sugar: the bun has some, and that blob of ketchup on the side is 1/3 sugar. Peanut butter, granola bars, and fruit snacks—many of which are labelled "low fat"—list sugar in some form as ingredients. No wonder the health watch is growing!

This all adds up to a shocking statistic—some people are eating more than half of their body weight in sugars every year. Sugar means calories, and excess calories mean obesity, diabetes, and other conditions.

What accounts for this growing problem? The World Health Organization's report suggests that we are seeing worldwide changes in diet and lifestyles, mainly attributable to changes in the world food economy. People are changing their eating patterns, and many are consuming more saturated fats and unrefined carbohydrates. Although exercise and physical activity is a major topic of news and conversation, many people are becoming more sedentary. Ready-made foods, less labour-intensive jobs, and more use of motorized transportation all keep us less active and, maybe, less inclined to prepare our own meals.

Nutrition is a key factor in disease prevention. Research shows that a good, balanced diet is a recipe for health throughout one's life. Almost half of Canadian adults are overweight, and 15 percent are considered obese. These numbers are growing at a disturbing rate. Does this suggest sugar addiction? What is happening to the balanced diet?

Marion Nestle, a New York University nutrition professor, wrote *Food Politics*, in which she reveals some surprising facts about sugar. She indicates that food manufacturers are keen to incorporate more sugar, as it is a very inexpensive ingredient. In order for food to be cheap, manufacturers use corn sweeteners—and they are sugar! Nestle concedes that the research does not prove scientifically that sugar is the only culprit in the calorie overload, but it does play a role.

To be fair, sugar is not all bad. We could not function without some sugar—but natural sugars from fruits and vegetables are much better for us.

Why aren't they telling us what sugar we are getting? Health Canada's new labelling guidelines require all foods to be detailed by ingredients and nutrients. The total amount of sugar per serving, along with the percentage of sugar in the food, will appear on the label. The list of ingredients must include all of the forms of sugar present in the food. If the label reads "sugar free," it has less than 0.5 grams of sugar per serving, and "reduced" or "less" sugar means 25 percent less sugar per serving than a normal serving of the food. While this information is helpful, not everyone reads it, not everyone heeds it, and it is not mandatory until 2006. The new food labelling requirements will make it easier to determine how much sugar every food contains, if we pay attention to them. Check the label the next time you choose a fruit drink or pop —the information may surprise you.

Researchers and government organizations around the world have amassed quantities of information about sugar and its effects on our health. Based on this secondary data, most of it quantitative, and international forums to discuss the problem, the World Health Organization recommends that sugar consumption be cut back to 10 percent of our diet. This would be a major adjustment in eating habits for many people. The sugar industry is worried. The Canadian Sugar Institute does not agree that sugar is the culprit in our obesity problem or the increasing rate of diabetes. This organization's own study found no change in sugar consumption in the past 20 or 30 years. Government research contradicts this, and there are enough studies to suggest that the government side of the story is correct.

If governments take the World Health Organization's recommendations seriously, they will take steps to educate the public and change their behaviour, and they will seek the cooperation of food manufacturers. This is a mammoth task. Health Canada, the federal government department responsible for this type of initiative, must embark on a nation-wide project to accomplish it.

Let's suppose that you are given responsibility for this project. Your goal is to launch a program that will result in people lowering their sugar intake from the current 23 teaspoons per day to nearly half of that—12 teaspoons. First, you need to do some primary research with Canadians to complement the wealth of secondary research available. You will need to assess how people feel about this, and to determine their willingness to change. How would you, as a market researcher, go about this?

Questions

1 Define the problem or challenge that is the focus of your research.

2 What information do you need to collect? List the data you require.

3 Draft a market research plan for you and your team. In it, identify the research techniques you will use to conduct your research (hint: you should use at least three research techniques to do a thorough job), and describe the methods you will use for deciding on the people from whom you will collect the information—that is, your sampling plan.

4 Generate five sample questions you could use to collect the key information.

5 Suggest how you will present the information to your colleagues at Health Canada.

Identifying Market Segments and Targets

walk.

freedom is a wheel in your sole.

HEELYS
THE ONLY SHOE WITH A REMOVABLE WHEEL IN THE HEEL.

freedom is a wheel in your sole.

SNEAKERS MARKETING WARS: HEELYS, AIR PUMPS, AND THREE BILLION TRILLION CHOICES

Late for a flight out of the Dallas/Ft. Worth airport, Roger Adams rushed to the gate . . . by "heeling"! Adams, a former psychologist and skateboarder, had just invented Heelys, the latest craze in sneakers.

Heelys combine the thrill of in-line skating, skateboarding, and scooting—along with running and walking—in one set of shoes. The sneakers come with an imbedded, detachable wheel located in the heel of each shoe. To "heel," you lift up the foot at the heel on one shoe, push off on the other foot, and glide (carefully).

Heeling Sports Ltd. sold over $25 million worth of Heelys sneakers in 2001, its first full year of operations.[1] In 2002, Heelys, which average $80 to $110 per pair, were so hot that retailers couldn't keep them on their shelves.

Since then Heeling Sports Ltd. has purchased Soap Shoes, a product with replaceable plastic in their soles that allows the wearer to slide along street curbs, rails, or other edges, an activity called "soaping" or "grinding."[2] It also sells a line of skateboard shoes and has its own line of clothing targeted to its very unique customer base.[3]

Consumers are faced with hundreds of athletic shoe choices, often on sneaker "walls," like those that you see when you enter sporting goods and specialty shoe stores. What do you need in the sneaker business to stand out from the pack? This is the multibillion-dollar question for manufacturers. Today, the North American athletic footwear or "sneakers" market exceeds US$15 billion. But Adams and Heeling Sports believe they've found a unique niche, or market segment, of buyers.

All sneaker manufacturers continue to search for new market segments of consumers and ways to differentiate their products from the competition. This challenge applies from the giants such as Reebok and Nike to upstarts such as Heelys and Customatix.

Changing consumer tastes and global competition have forced sneaker manufacturers to come up with new product technologies, advertising campaigns, and endorsements to develop and position their new and

WHERE IN THE MARKETING PROCESS ARE WE GOING IN THIS CHAPTER?

Chapter 9 talks about identifying and marketing to the best customers for the firm. This is done through segmenting markets and then by targeting the most appropriate groups of customers. Companies can't be all things to all people!

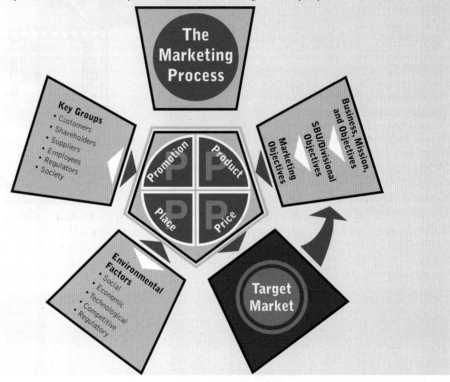

existing products for their target market segments. Here are several North American trends to consider in planning for the sneaker wars for 2005 and beyond:[4]

- *Age segments.* Teenagers, at 31 percent of total sales, are the largest segment, and are willing to spend more for sneakers than older consumers.
- *Gender segments.* Both women and men are important segments. However, men still buy more sneakers in total at higher average prices.
- *Price.* Over 60 percent of sneakers purchased in 2001 cost less than US$50 per pair.
- *Kinds of sports.* In 2001 running shoes were number 1 (US$4.5 billion); basketball shoes, number 2 (US$2.8 billion); and cross-training, number 3 (US$2.2 billion). Running and basketball sales were up and cross-training was down slightly.

The strategies sneaker manufacturers use to satisfy needs of different customers illustrate successful market segmentation, the main topic of this chapter. After discussing why markets need to be segmented, this chapter covers the steps a firm uses in segmenting and targeting a market and then positioning its offering to the marketplace.

SEGMENTING MARKETS?

A business firm segments its markets so it can respond more effectively to the wants of groups of potential buyers and thus increase its sales and profits. Not-for-profit organizations also segment the clients they serve to satisfy client needs more effectively while achieving the organization's goals. Let's use the dilemma of sneaker buyers finding their

ideal Reebok shoes to describe what market segmentation is and when it is necessary to segment markets.

What Market Segmentation Means

market segmentation
Sorting potential buyers into groups that have common needs and will respond similarly to a marketing action

People have different needs and wants. **Market segmentation** involves aggregating prospective buyers into groups that have common needs and will respond similarly to a marketing action. The groups that result from this process are **market segments**, relatively homogeneous groups of prospective buyers. Each market segment consists of people who are relatively similar to each other in terms of their consumption behaviour.

market segments
Groups that result from market segmentation

There is normally more than one firm vying for the attention of prospective buyers in the various market segments, and this has caused firms to use a marketing strategy of **product differentiation**. This strategy involves a firm's using different marketing mix activities, such as product features and advertising, to help consumers perceive the product as being different and better than competing products. The perceived differences may involve physical features or nonphysical ones, such as image or price. The Reebok example discussed on the next page shows how the company is using both market segmentation and product differentiation strategies.

product differentiation
Strategy of using different marketing mix activities, such as product features or advertising, to help consumers perceive a product as being different and better than competing products

Segmentation: Linking Needs to Actions

For market segmentation to work for both buyers and the firm, two things have to happen:

- An organization's products have to appeal to and benefit the buyers by meeting the buyers' needs, and
- The organization itself must be able reach the buyers with appropriate communications and persuade them to buy one product over another.

The organization achieves this by taking specific marketing actions. These actions may involve separate products or other aspects of the marketing mix such as price, advertising or personal selling activities, or distribution strategies.

The process of segmenting a market and selecting specific segments as targets can be viewed as the way to link the various buyers' needs and the organization's marketing program (see Figure 9-1). Market segmentation is only a means to an end: to lead to tangible marketing actions that can increase sales and profitability. The Marketing NewsNet box[5] on the next page describes how Reebok, Nike, Vans, and Customatix have succeeded in using market segmentation and product differentiation strategies to reach special groups of customers.

FIGURE 9-1

Market segmentation links market needs to an organization's marketing program

Identify market needs Benefits in terms of • Product features • Expense • Quality • Savings in time and convenience	**Process of segmenting and targeting markets**	**Execute marketing program** A marketing mix in terms of • Product • Price • Promotion • Place

MARKETING NEWSNET

SNEAKER STRATEGIES: WHO'S DOING WHAT

Torsion bars, shock absorbers, and cushions. Off-the-shelf versus design-your-own-shoe with trillions of design combinations. These are some of the innovative technologies and strategies used by sneaker manufacturers to attract new consumers and differentiate their products from those offered by their competitors.

Reebok

For 2003, Reebok introduced two new lines of sneakers. Its Premier Series of shoes targets the specific needs of runners and features the new DMX Foam cushioning and Playdry™ moisture management technologies. Because one style does not fit all, Reebok has designed the Premier Control for runners whose feet tend to turn outward; and the Premier Road with extra cushioning for pavement runners; among others. Its Gravity SCS (Suspension Control System) cross-training shoe was inspired by the performance features of a luxury automobile. The technology includes a "torsion bar" that holds the foot in place and "shock absorbers" that distribute pressure in the heel and forefoot.

Nike

Originally launched in 1985, the 2003 "Michael-inspired" Air Jordan XVIII all-suede basketball shoe incorporated the latest Zoom-Air cushioning that "MJ" wore during his final season. Because 2002 sales were disappointing, the 2003 Air Jordan XVIII was priced lower and comes in a silver paper box instead of a metal shoebox.

Vans

Vans has targeted the rising wave of skateboard, snowboard, biking, and outdoor enthusiasts. To reach its targeted skateboard shoe market, Vans relies heavily on its endorsing athletes to design and market its signature lines and promote its skateboard events. Vans had a breakthrough when Foot Locker carried its shoes in more than 1,500 retail outlets.

How Reebok's Segmentation Strategy Developed   In 1979, Paul Fireman, who had dropped out of college to run his family's business, wandered through an international trade fair and saw Reebok's custom track shoes. He bought the U.S. licence from the British manufacturer.

In a brilliant marketing decision, Fireman introduced soft-leather aerobic dance shoes in flamboyant colours—the Reebok Freestyle—in 1982. Figure 9–2 shows that Reebok has introduced a variety of shoes since 1982—from tennis and basketball shoes in 1984 to high-technology kids and adult shoes in 2003. For simplicity, Figure 9–2 covers only shoes and does not show nonshoe lines, such as NBA/NFL apparel (2002).

A US$3 billion-a-year sneaker business has a huge need to generate sales from new opportunities. As a result, Reebok has expanded both the markets it targets and the products it develops to satisfy this need, as detailed in Figure 9–2.

What segmentation strategy will Reebok use to take it further into the twenty-first century? Only Reebok knows, but it will certainly involve trying to differentiate its products more clearly from its global competitors and perhaps target new or retarget existing global consumers.

Using Market-Product Grids   A **market-product grid** is a framework to relate the segments of a market to products offered or potential marketing actions by the firm. The grid in Figure 9–2 shows different market segments of sneaker users as rows in the grid, whereas the columns show the different shoe product lines chosen by Reebok. In a complete market-product grid analysis, each cell in the grid can show the estimated market size of a given product sold to a specific market segment.

market-product grid
Framework relating the segments of a market to products or marketing actions of the firm

The cells with red boxes in Figure 9–2, labeled P, represent Reebok's primary target market segment when it introduced each type of shoe. The blue boxes, labeled S, represent the secondary target market segments that also bought these products. In some cases,

MARKET SEGMENT		PRODUCT									
GENERAL	GROUP WITH NEED	RUNNING SHOES	AEROBIC SHOES	TENNIS SHOES	BASKETBALL SHOES	KIDS SHOES	WALKING SHOES	CROSS-TRAINING SHOES	GOLF SHOES	KIDS TRAXTAR SHOES	ADULT PRECISION DMX SHOES
		(1981)	(1982)	(1984)	(1984)	(1984)	(1986)	(1988)	(1997)	(2001)	(2003)
Performance-oriented 30%	Runners	P						P			P
	Aerobic/fitness exercisers		P					P			
	Tennis players			P				P			
	Basketball players				P			P			
	Golfers								P		
	Adventure seekers							P			
Nonathletic-oriented 70%	Walkers	S	S	S	S		P	P			S
	Children					P				P	
	Comfort/Style-conscious	S	S	S	S		S	S			S

Key: P = Primary market   S = Secondary market

FIGURE 9–2

Market-product grid showing how different Reebok shoes reach segments of customers with different needs

Reebok discovered that large numbers of people in a segment not originally targeted for a particular shoe style bought it anyway. Thus, Reebok products are purchased by two types of segments: "performance-oriented" consumers (30 percent), who buy sneakers and apparel for athletic purposes; and "nonathletic-oriented" consumers (70 percent), who buy sneakers and apparel for comfort, style, price, or other nonathletic reasons. But as Figure 9–2 depicts, two segments of consumers in the nonathletic-oriented category, "comfort/style conscious" and "walker," bought running, aerobic, and cross-trainer shoes not initially targeted at their respective segments. When this trend became apparent to Reebok, it introduced its walking shoe line directly at the walker segment.

When to Segment Markets

A business firm goes to the trouble and expense of segmenting its markets when it expects that this will ultimately increase its sales, profit, and return on investment. When expenses are greater than the potentially increased sales from segmentation, a firm should not attempt to segment its market. The specific situations that illustrate this point are the cases of one product and multiple market segments, multiple products and multiple market segments, and "segments of one," or mass customization.

Does Harry Potter appeal only to the kids' segment?

One Product and Multiple Market Segments   Firms producing a single product and marketing it to two or more segments avoid the extra costs of developing and producing additional versions of the product and associated research, engineering, and manufacturing expenses, which can run very high. There are some extra costs involved in taking the same product into another market, but these typically only involve separate promotional campaigns or those associated with establishing a new channel of distribution. Movies, magazines, and books are single products frequently directed to two or more distinct market segments. Movie companies often run different TV commercials or magazine ads featuring different aspects of a newly released film (love, or drama, or spectacular scenery) that are targeted to different market segments. *Time* magazine now publishes more than 200 different U.S.

editions and more than 100 international editions, each targeted at unique geographic and demographic segments using a special mix of advertisements.

Harry Potter's phenomenal success is based both on author J. K. Rowling's fiction-writing wizardry and her publisher's creativity in marketing to preteen, teen, and adult segments of readers. By 2002, more than 100 million Harry Potter books had been sold worldwide, and the books were often at the top of the *New York Times* fiction best-seller list—for *adults*.[6] Although multiple TV commercials for movies and separate covers or advertisements for magazines or books are expensive, they are minor compared with the costs of producing an entirely new movie, magazine, or book for another market segment.

Multiple Products and Multiple Market Segments

Reebok's different styles of shoes, each targeted at a different type of user, are an example of multiple products aimed at multiple markets. Designing and manufacturing these different styles of shoes is clearly more expensive than producing only a single style but seems worthwhile if it serves customers' needs better, doesn't reduce quality or increase price, and adds to the sales revenues and profits.

Segments of One: Mass Customization

Marketers are rediscovering today what their ancestors running the corner general store knew a century ago: Every customer is unique, has unique wants and needs, and desires special tender loving care from the seller—the components of one-to-one marketing. Efficiencies in manufacturing and marketing during the past century made mass-produced goods so affordable that most customers were willing to compromise their individual tastes and settle for standardized products. Today's Internet ordering and flexible manufacturing and marketing processes have made *mass customization* possible, tailoring goods or services to the tastes of individual customers on a high-volume scale. The Marketing NewsNet shows how mass customization lets you design your own personalized running shoe or hiking boot.

Mass customization is the next step beyond *build-to-order* (BTO), manufacturing a product only when there is an order from a customer. Dell Computer uses BTO systems that trim work-in-progress inventories and shorten delivery times to customers. Dell's three-day deliveries are made possible by restricting its computer line to only a few basic models and stocking a variety of each. This gives customers a good choice with quick delivery. Dell PCs can be assembled in four minutes. Most Dell customization comes from spending 90 minutes loading the unique software each customers selects. But even this system falls a bit short of total mass customization with virtually unlimited specification of features by customers.[7]

The Segmentation Trade-Off

The key to successful product differentiation and market segmentation strategies is finding the ideal balance between satisfying a customer's individual wants and being able to do this profitably. The "increased customer value" can take many forms: more products, improved quality of existing products, lower prices, easier access to product through improved distribution, and so on. So the ultimate criterion for an organization's marketing success is that customers should be better off as a result of the increased synergies.

Concept Check

1. Market segmentation involves aggregating prospective buyers into groups that have two key characteristics. What are they?

2. What is product differentiation?

3. What is the benefit of mass customization to a manufacturer?

STEPS IN SEGMENTING AND TARGETING MARKETS

The process of segmenting a market and then selecting and reaching the target segments is divided into the five steps discussed in this section, as shown in Figure 9–3. Segmenting a market is not a science — it requires large doses of common sense and managerial judgment.

Put on your entrepreneur's hat to use the market segmentation process to choose target markets and take useful marketing actions. Imagine that you own a Tim Hortons franchise, located next to a large urban campus of a community college that runs classes year-round, day, weekend, and evening. As Canada's largest coffee and baked goods chain, your restaurant offers donuts, soups, chili, sandwiches, and, of course, coffee. Even though you are part of a chain and have some restrictions on menu and decor, you are free to set your hours of business and to undertake local advertising. How can market segmentation help?

Step 1: Form Potential Buyers into Segments

Grouping potential buyers into meaningful segments involves meeting some specific criteria that answer the question, "Would segmentation be worth doing and is it possible?" If so, the next step is to find specific variables that can be used to create the various segments.

Criteria to Use in Forming the Segments
A marketing manager should develop segments for a market that meet five main criteria:

- *Potential for increased profit.* The best segmentation approach is the one that maximizes the opportunity for future profit and ROI. If this potential can be maximized without segmentation, don't segment. For not-for-profit organizations, the criterion as opposed to profits or revenues might be the potential for serving client users more effectively.
- *Similarity of needs of potential buyers within a segment.* Potential buyers within a segment should be similar in terms of a marketing activity, such as product features sought or advertising media used.
- *Difference of needs of buyers among segments.* If the needs of the various segments aren't significantly different, combine them into fewer segments. A different segment usually requires a different marketing action that, in turn, means greater costs. If increased sales don't offset extra costs, combine segments and reduce the number of marketing actions.
- *Feasibility of a marketing action to reach a segment.* Reaching a segment requires a simple but effective marketing action. If no such action exists, don't segment.
- *Simplicity and cost of assigning potential buyers to segments.* A marketing manager must be able to put a market segmentation plan into effect. This means being able to recognize the characteristics of potential buyers and then assigning them to a segment without encountering excessive costs.

FIGURE 9–3
The process of segmenting and targeting markets involves five key steps

Steps in segmenting and targeting markets

Identify market needs

1 Form prospective buyers into segments
2 Form products to be sold into groups
3 Develop a market-product grid and estimate size of markets
4 Select target markets
5 Take marketing actions to reach target markets

Execute marketing program

Ways to Segment Consumer Markets Figure 9–4 shows the main dimensions used to segment Canadian consumer markets. These include geographic, demographic, psychographic, and behavioural segmentation.[8] By examining Figure 9–4, you can also see that a number of variables can be used within each dimension for segmentation purposes. What you should remember is that segmenting markets is not a pure science—it requires large doses of common sense and managerial judgment. A marketer may have to use several dimensions and multiple variables within each dimension to form proper market segments. Let's take a look at how some marketers might segment consumer markets using the information in Figure 9–4.

FIGURE 9–4

Segmentation variables and breakdowns for Canadian consumer markets

- *Geographic segmentation.* Using geographic segmentation, a marketer segments based on where consumers live. Geographic variables such as countries, regions, provinces, counties, cities, or even neighbourhoods could be used. Marketers often find that Canadians differ in terms of needs or preferences based on the region in which they live. This is a form of geographic segmentation. For example, Colgate-Palmolive markets Arctic Power, its cold-water detergent, on an energy-cost-saving dimension in Quebec, but as a clothes saver (cold-water washing is easier on clothes) in Western Canada.

MAIN DIMENSIONS	VARIABLES	TYPICAL BREAKDOWNS
Geographic segmentation	Region	Atlantic; Quebec; Ontario; Prairies; British Columbia
	City or census metropolitan area (CMA) size	Under 5,000; 5,000–19,999; 20,000–49,000; 50,000–99,999; 100,000–249,000; 250,000–499,999; 500,000–999,000; 1,000,000–3,999,999; 4,000,000+
	Density	Urban; suburban; rural
	Climate	Cold; warm
Demographic segmentation	Age	Infant; under 6; 6–11; 12–17; 18–24; 25–34; 35–49; 50–64; 65+
	Gender	Male; female
	Family size	1–2; 3–4; 5+
	Stage of family life cycle	Young single; young married, no children; young married, youngest child under 6; young married, youngest child 6 or older; older married, with children; older married, no children under 18; older single; other older married
	Income	Under $10,000; $10,000–19,999; $20,000–29,999; $30,000–39,999; $40,000–54,999; $55,000–74,999; $75,000+
	Occupation	Professional; managerial; clerical; sales; labourers; students; retired; housewives; unemployed
	Education	Grade school or less; some high school; high school graduate; some college; college graduate
	Race	White; Black; Asian; Native; other
	Home ownership	Own home; rent home
Psychographic segmentation	Personality	Gregarious; compulsive; extroverted; introverted
	Lifestyle (Goldfarb Segments)	Structured; discontented; fearful; assured; resentful; caring
Behavioural segmentation	Benefits sought	Quality; service; low price
	Usage rate	Light user; medium user; heavy user
	User status	Non-user; ex-user; prospect; first-time user; regular user
	Loyalty status	None; medium; strong

- *Demographic segmentation.* One of the most common ways to segment consumer markets is to use demographic segmentation, or segmenting a market based on population characteristics. This approach segments consumers according to variables such as age, gender, income, education, occupation, and so forth. Cyanamid Canada Inc. uses age as a segmentation variable, producing and marketing its vitamins to various age groups including children, young adults, and older Canadians. Centrum Select, for instance, is specifically designed for adults over 50. Trimark Investments of Ontario segments the financial services market by gender, targeting males and females with different products and different advertising campaigns. General Electric uses family size as a segmentation variable, targeting smaller families with compact microwaves and larger families with extra-large refrigerators. You should note, however, that a single demographic variable may not be sufficient in understanding and segmenting a given market. Thus, many marketers combine a number of demographic variables that might clearly distinguish one segment from another. For example, cosmetics companies such as Clinique combine gender, income, and occupation in order to examine market segments for different lines of cosmetic products.
- *Psychographic segmentation.* Marketers use psychographic segmentation when they segment markets according to personality or lifestyle. It has been found that people who share the same demographic characteristics can have very different psychographic profiles. As we saw in Chapter 5, personality traits have been linked to product preferences and brand choice. In addition, a person's lifestyle (his or her activities, interests, and opinions) also affects the types of products, and the particular brands of products that may be purchased. Remember the Goldfarb segments from Chapter 5? Members of the discontented segment like package deals when they buy because they do not want to make decisions.[9] On the other hand, those in the resentful segment like expensive brands and they don't worry about price.[10]
- *Behavioural segmentation.* When marketers use consumers' behaviour with or toward a product to segment the market, they are using behavioural segmentation. A powerful form of behavioural segmentation is to divide the market according to the benefits consumers seek from a product category. Using benefits sought, the marketer examines the major benefits consumers look for in the product category, the kinds of consumers who look for each benefit, and the major brands that deliver each benefit. For example, Telus Mobility and Bell Mobility both market their wireless communications products and services to young adults under 24 years of age who want text messaging "rather than talk" in order to ensure privacy. On the other hand, Rogers AT&T targets CEOs of large businesses who want to improve employee productivity through the use of wireless technology.[11]

usage rate
Quantity consumed or patronage—store visits—during a specific period; varies significantly among different customer groups.

80/20 rule
A concept that suggests 80 percent of a firm's sales are obtained from 20 percent of its customers.

Another behavioural segmentation variable often used by marketers is **usage rate**—quantity consumed or patronage during a specific period, which varies significantly among different customer groups. Air Canada, for example, focuses on usage rate for its frequent-flyer program, which is designed to encourage passengers to use its airline repeatedly. Usage rate is sometimes referred to in terms of the **80/20** rule, a concept that suggests that 80 percent of a firm's sales are obtained from 20 percent of its customers. The percentages in the 80/20 rule are not really fixed; rather, the rule suggests that a small fraction of customers provide a large percentage of sales. For example, Air Canada pays special attention to the business travel segment that comprises only 20 percent of the airline seats but 40 percent of overall revenues.[12]

Research shows that the fast-food market can also be segmented into light, medium, or heavy users. For every $1.00 spent by a light user in a fast-food restaurant, each heavy user spends over $5.00.[13] This is the reason for the emphasis in almost all marketing strategies on effective ways to reach heavy users of products and services. Thus, as a Tim Hortons restaurant owner you want to keep the heavy-user segment constantly in mind. With advances in information technology, marketers are now able to conduct detailed

What variables might Xerox use to segment the organizational markets for its answer to colour copying problems? For the possible answer and related marketing actions, see the text.

segmentation studies. Some Canadian telecommunications companies, for example, can now segment based on more than 100 criteria, from calling patterns to promotional response.

Variables to Use in Forming Segments

In determining one or two variables to segment the market for your Tim Hortons restaurant, very broadly we find two main markets: students and nonstudents. To segment the students, we could try a variety of demographic variables, such as age, sex, year in school, or college major, or psychographic variables, such as personality characteristics, attitudes, or interests. But none of these variables really meets the five criteria listed previously—particularly the fourth criterion about leading to a doable marketing action to reach the various segments. Four student segments that *do* meet these criteria include the following:

- Students living in dormitories (college residence halls, sororities, fraternities).
- Students living near the college in apartments.
- Day commuter students living outside the area.
- Night commuter students living outside the area.

These segmentation variables are really a combination of where the student lives and the time he or she is on campus (and near your restaurant). For nonstudents who might be customers, similar variables might be used:

- Faculty and staff members at the college.
- People who live in the area but aren't connected with the college.
- People who work in the area but aren't connected with the college.

People in each of these segments aren't quite as similar as those in the student segments, which makes them harder to reach with a marketing program or action. Think about whether the needs of all these segments are different, and how various advertising media can be used to reach these groups effectively.

Ways to Segment Organizational Markets

There are also a number of variables that might be used to segment organizational markets. For example, a product manager at Xerox responsible for its new network colour printer might use several of these segmentation variables, as follows:

- *Geographic.* Firms located in major cities might receive a personal sales call, but those outside in remote areas (for example, oil exploration companies in northern Alberta) might be contacted by telephone or e-mail.
- *NAICS code.* Firms categorized by the North American Industry Classification System (NAICS) code as manufacturers that deal with customers throughout the world might have different document printing needs than do retailers or lawyers serving local customers.
- *Number of employees.* The size of the firm is related to the volume of digital documents produced for a given industry or NAICS, so firms with varying numbers of employees might be specific target markets for different Xerox systems.
- *Benefits sought.* Xerox can target organizations needing different benefits from its new network colour printer, such as speed for high-volume print production or precise colour for corporate communications such as annual reports.

DILBERT   by Scott Adams

Step 2: Form Products to Be Sold into Groups

As important as grouping customers into segments is finding a means of grouping the products you're selling into meaningful categories. If the firm has only one product or service, this isn't a problem, but when it has dozens or hundreds, these must be grouped in some way so buyers can relate to them. This is why department stores and supermarkets are organized into product groups, with the departments or aisles containing related merchandise. Likewise, manufacturers have product lines that are the groupings they use in the catalogues sent to customers.

What are the groupings for your restaurant? It could be the item purchased, such as, chili, sandwiches, and donuts. This is where judgment—the qualitative aspect of marketing—comes in. Students really buy an eating experience, or a meal that satisfies a need at a particular time of day, so alternatively the product grouping can be defined by meal or time of day as breakfast, lunch, between-meal snack, dinner, and after-dinner snack. These groupings are more closely related to the way purchases are actually made and permit you to market the entire meal, not just your donuts or coffee.

Step 3: Develop a Market-Product Grid and Estimate Size of Markets

Developing a market-product grid means labelling the markets (or horizontal rows) and products (or vertical columns), as shown in Figure 9–5. In addition, the size of the market in each cell (the market-product combination) must be estimated. For your restaurant, this involves estimating the sales of each kind of meal that can reasonably be expected to be sold to each market segment. This is a form of the usage rate analysis discussed earlier in the chapter.

The market sizes in Figure 9–5 may be simple "guesstimates" if you don't have time for formal marketing research (as discussed in Chapter 8). But even such crude estimates of the size of specific markets using a market-product grid are far better than simply using estimates of the entire market.

Step 4: Select Target Markets

A firm must take care to choose its target market segments carefully. If it picks too narrow a group of segments, it may fail to reach the volume of sales and profits it needs. If it selects too broad a group of segments, it may spread its marketing efforts so thin that the extra expenses to reach and serve them are more than the increased sales and profits.

FIGURE 9-5

Selecting a target market for your Tim Hortons restaurant next to an urban campus of a community college

MARKETS	PRODUCTS: MEALS				
	BREAK-FAST	LUNCH	BETWEEN-MEAL SNACK	DINNER	AFTER-DINNER SNACK
STUDENT					
Dormitory	1	2	2	2	2
Apartment	3	2	2	3	1
Day commuter	3	3	3	1	0
Night commuter	2	0	0	2	1
NONSTUDENT					
Faculty or staff	3	3	2	1	0
Live in area	1	1	0	2	0
Work in area	2	2	1	0	0

Key: 3 = Large market; 2 = Medium market; 1 = Small market; 0 = No market.

Criteria to Use in Picking the Target Segments

There are two different kinds of criteria in the market segmentation process: those to use in dividing the market into segments (discussed earlier), and those to use in actually picking the target segments. Even experienced marketing executives often confuse these two different sets of criteria. The five criteria to use in actually selecting the target segments apply to your Tim Hortons restaurant this way:

- *Market size.* The estimated size of the market in the segment is an important factor in deciding whether it's worth going after. There is very little market for after-dinner snacks among commuter students (see Figure 9-5), so why devote any marketing effort towards reaching a small or non-existent market?
- *Expected growth.* Although the size of the market in the segment may be small now, perhaps it is growing significantly or is expected to grow in the future. Between now and 2007, sales of fast-food meals eaten outside the restaurants are projected to grow three times as fast as those eaten inside. And Wendy's, which in Canada often co-locates with Tim Hortons, is the fast-food leader in average time to serve a drive-thru order—for example, 150.3 seconds per order, 16.7 seconds faster than McDonald's. This speed and convenience is potentially very important to night commuters in adult education programs.[14]
- *Competitive position.* Is there a lot of competition in the segment now or is there likely to be in the future? The less the competition, the more attractive the segment is. For example, if the college dormitories announce a new policy of "no meals on weekends," this segment is suddenly more promising for your restaurant. With McDonald's recent introduction of pay-by-credit-card processing at its restaurants, will Tim Hortons have to offer the same option to its customers?
- *Cost of reaching the segment.* A segment that is inaccessible to a firm's marketing actions should not be pursued. For example, the few nonstudents who live in the area may not be reachable with ads in newspapers or other media. As a result, do not waste money trying to advertise to them.
- *Compatibility with the organization's objectives and resources.* If the company doesn't have the cooking equipment to make eggs and sausages, and has a policy against spending more money on restaurant equipment, then you should not seek the target market that wants a full breakfast, but instead focus on the coffee, donut, and muffin market.

As is often the case in marketing decisions, a particular segment may appear attractive according to some criteria and very unattractive according to others.

Choose the Segments   Ultimately, a marketing executive has to use these criteria to decide which segments to target with special marketing efforts. As shown in Figure 9–5, let's assume you've written off the after-dinner market for two reasons: too small of a market size and incompatibility with your objectives and resources. In terms of competitive position and cost of reaching the segment, you choose to focus on the four student segments and one nonstudent segment (although you're certainly not going to turn away business from the other nonstudent segments—you just don't want to spend any money or effort trying to reach them). This combination of market-product segments—your target market—is shaded in Figure 9–5.

Step 5: Take Marketing Actions to Reach Target Markets

The purpose of developing a market-product grid is to trigger marketing actions to increase sales and profits. This means that someone must develop and execute an action plan.

How can Tim Hortons target different market segments such as drive-thru customers with different advertising programs? Have you noticed the variety of different types of locations they have?

Your Tim Hortons Segmentation Strategy   With your Tim Hortons restaurant, you have already reached one significant decision: the market for breakfast is a very specific one that focuses on coffee and donuts, and breakfast begins early, so you will need to open by 5:30 A.M. The market for after-dinner snacks is small by comparison. Tim Hortons evaluates possible new menu items continuously, to compete not only with McDonald's and Burger King but also with a complex array of supermarkets, convenience stores, and gas stations that sell coffee, donuts, and other on-the-go breakfast items and snacks.

Another essential decision is where and what meals to advertise to reach specific market segments. An ad in the student newspaper could reach all the student segments, but you might consider this approach too expensive and want a more focused effort to reach smaller segments. If you choose three segments for special actions (Figure 9–), advertising actions to reach them might include

Ho
Who is Tim Horton
What target
market .

- *Day commuters (an entire market segment).* Run ads inside transit trains and buses and put flyers under the windshield wipers of cars in parking lots used by day commuters. These ads and flyers promote all the meals at your restaurant to a single segment of students—a horizontal cut through the market-product grid.
- *Between-meals snacks* (directed to all four student markets and one nonstudent market). To promote eating during this downtime for your restaurant, offer "Ten percent off all purchases between 2:00 and 4:30 P.M. during this semester." This ad promotes a single meal to five market segments—a vertical cut through the market-product grid.
- *Dinners to night commuters.* The most focused of all three campaigns, this ad promotes a single meal to two student segments. The campaign might consist of a windshield flyer offering a free coffee with the coupon when the person buys a drive-thru meal between 5:00 and 7:00 P.M.

Depending on how your advertising actions work, you can repeat, modify, or drop them and design new campaigns for other segments you feel are worth the effort. This example of advertising your restaurant is just a small piece of a complete marketing program using all the elements of the marketing mix.

FIGURE 9–6
Promotional actions to
reach specific target
markets

MARKETS	BREAK-FAST	LUNCH	BETWEEN-MEAL SNACK	DINNER
PRODUCTS: MEALS				
STUDENT				
Dormitory	1	2	2	2
Apartment	3	2	2	3
Day commuter	3	3	3	1
Night commuter	2	0	0	2
NONSTUDENT				
Faculty or staff	3	3	2	1

Transit ads, flyers under windshield wipers of cars in parking lots

Ad campaign: 10% off all purchases between 2:00 – 4:30pm during this semester

Flyers on windshields of cars in night parking lots, coupons for free coffee with meal purchase between 5:00 – 7:00pm

Key: 3 = Large market; 2 = Medium market; 1 = Small market; 0 = No market.

Apple's Ever-Changing Segmentation Strategy Steve Jobs and Steve Wozniak didn't realize they were developing today's multibillion-dollar PC industry when they invented the Apple I in a garage on April Fool's Day, 1976. Hobbyists, the initial target market, were not interested in the product. However, when the Apple II was displayed at a computer trade show in 1977, consumers loved it and Apple Computer was born. Typical of young companies, Apple focused on its products and had little concern for its markets. When IBM—"Big Blue"—entered the PC market in 1981, Apple was forced to become a "real company," much to the disappoint-ment of its creative young engineers who were likened to "Boy Scouts without adult supervision."

Original Apple II

Fast-forward to the twenty-first century. Jobs believes that the personal computer entered the Age of the Digital Lifestyle in 2001. In a keynote address, Jobs said that "the proliferation of digital devices—CD players, MP3 players, cellphones, handheld organizers, digital cameras, digital camcorders, and more — will never have enough processing power and memory to stand alone." Jobs enthusiastically proclaimed, "the Mac can become the digital hub of this new digital lifestyle." By repositioning Apple as the "digital hub" with "killer apps," such as iTunes, iMovie, iDVD, and iPhoto—now bundled as iLife—Jobs believes consumers can take full advantage of the new digital lifestyle era.[15]

In most segmentation situations, a single product does not fit into an exclusive market niche. Rather, there is overlap among products in the product line and also among the markets to which they are directed. But a market segmentation strategy enables Apple to offer different products to meet the needs of different market segments, as shown in the accompanying Marketing NewsNet. Stay tuned to see if Steve Jobs and these market-product strategies for his vision of the digital lifestyle era are on target. He's betting the company on it!

MARKETING NEWSNET

Customer Value

APPLE'S SEGMENTATION STRATEGY: CAMP RUNAMOK NO LONGER

Camp Runamok was the nickname given to Apple Computer in the early 1980s because the innovative company had no coherent series of product lines directed at identifiable market segments.

Today, Apple has targeted its various lines of Macintosh computers at specific market segments, as shown in the market-product grid below. Because the market-product grid shifts as a firm's strategy changes, the one below is based on Apple's product lines in mid-2003. This market-product grid is a simplification because each product grouping consists of a line of Macintosh computers. Nevertheless, the grid suggests the market segmentation strategy Steve Jobs is using to compete in what he sees as the Age of the Digital Lifestyle, as described in the text.

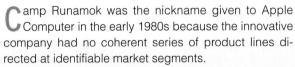

MARKETS		HARDWARE PRODUCTS					
SECTOR	SEGMENT	Power Macintosh G4	PowerBook G4	iMac	iBook	eMac	iPod
CONSUMER	Individuals			✓	✓	✓	✓
	Small/home office	✓	✓	✓	✓	✓	
	Students			✓	✓	✓	✓
	Teachers	✓	✓	✓		✓	
PROFESSIONAL	Medium/large business	✓	✓	✓			
	Creative	✓	✓	✓			✓
	College faculty	✓	✓	✓		✓	
	College staff			✓	✓	✓	

Concept Check

1. What are some of the variables used to segment consumer markets?

2. What are some criteria used to decide which segments to choose for targets?

3. Why is usage rate important in segmentation studies?

synergy
Increased effectiveness achieved through planned interaction of two or more marketing actions, where results exceed the sum of the effects of the individual actions

Market-Product Synergies: A Balancing Act

Recognizing opportunities for **synergy**—that is, increased effectiveness and efficiencies —is vital to success in selecting target market segments and making marketing decisions. Market-product grids illustrate where such synergies can be found. How? Let's consider Apple's market-product grid (in the Marketing NewsNet above) and examine the difference between marketing synergies and product synergies shown there.

- *Marketing synergies*. Running horizontally across the grid, each row represents an opportunity for efficiency in terms of a market segment. Were Apple to focus on just one group of consumers, such as the Medium/Large Business segment, its marketing efforts could be streamlined. Time would not have to be spent learning about the buying habits of students or college faculty. So Apple could probably do a single ad piece to reach the Medium/Large Business target segment (the yellow row), highlighting the only products they'd need to worry about developing: Power Mac G5, the iBook G4, and the iMac. Although clearly this is not Apple's strategy today, focusing on a single consumer segment is a common marketing strategy for new companies.
- *Product synergies*. Running vertically down the market-product grid, each column represents an opportunity for efficiency in research and development (R&D) and production. If Apple wanted to simplify its product line, reduce R&D and production expenses, and manufacture only one computer, which might it choose? Based on the market-product grid, Apple might do well to focus on the iMac (the brown column), since the iMac is purchased by the most consumer segments—in this case, every segment.

A choice to take advantage of marketing synergies can often come at the expense of production ones because a single consumer segment will likely require a variety of products—each of which will have to be designed and manufactured. The company saves money on marketing, but spends more in production. Conversely, if product synergies are emphasized, marketing will have to address the concerns of a wide variety of consumers, which costs more time and money. Marketing managers responsible for developing a company's product line must balance both product and marketing synergies as they try to increase the company's profits.

product positioning
The space a product occupies in consumers' minds on important features relative to competing products

---
FIGURE 9-7

Your challenge as a marketing manager: Try to position chocolate milk to make it more appealing to adults

POSITIONING THE PRODUCT

When a company offers a product for sale, a decision critical to its long-term success is how to position it in the market upon introduction. **Product positioning** refers to the place an offering occupies in consumers' minds on important attributes relative to competitive offerings.

Chocolate Milk . . . for Adults?

Finding the right way to position a product or service in the minds of potential customers is hard, creative work for a marketing manager.

But what about chocolate milk? What can dairies do to give some zip to chocolate milk sales? The answer: Target sales at a new market—adults! But how? Think about this for a minute in the way these marketing managers approached the problem. These managers had to figure out a way to change the image—or position—of chocolate milk in the minds of adults. So they asked themselves these questions:

1. On a scale from "low nutrition" to "high nutrition," where do adults place chocolate milk?
2. On a scale from "children's drink" to "adult drink," where do adults place chocolate milk?
3. Where would we like to position chocolate milk in the minds of adults to increase its sales?

Tough questions? Yes, but very practical ones. To compare your ideas with those of the marketing managers, see the text and Figure 9–8.

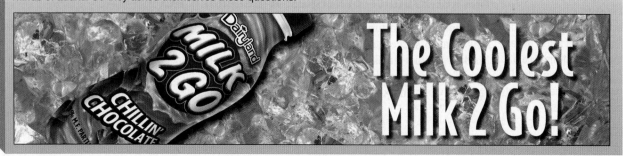

Before the company can begin to position a product in the mind of the consumer, other marketing actions must be undertaken. Through research, the company can determine the needs and perceptions of consumers, as well as the way they look at the different products (and brands) offered to them in the marketplace. These factors become one basis for segmenting the market. The company then decides which segments are the most appropriate for them to pursue, and these become the target markets. All of the consumer characteristics and factors make up the description of the target market that the company uses in building the marketing mix.

Positioning affects each of the four Ps, and it is often a thread that ensures that they work together. If a product is destined to be viewed as a prestige item (the product P), the price must reflect this. Promotion for a prestige item will be placed, for example, in higher-end magazines than promotion for a low-end item. A prestige item may be sold at a retailer of similar items (the place P), such as Holt Renfrew or Harry Rosen, while a more economical item may be retailed at Zellers or Wal-Mart.

Positioning Using Perceptual Maps

A key to positioning a product or brand effectively is the perceptions of customers. In determining its position and the preferences of customers, companies obtain three types of data from consumers:

perceptual map
Means of displaying the position of products or brands in the consumers' minds

1. The important attributes for a type of product.
2. Judgments of where existing products or brands are located on these attributes.
3. The location of the firm's own product or brand on these attributes.

The firm can then develop market strategies to establish or move its product or brand to any "ideal" position.

From these data, it is possible to develop a **perceptual map**, a means of displaying or graphing, in two dimensions, the location of products or brands in the minds of consumers to enable a marketer to see how consumers perceive competing products or brands and then take marketing actions. Look at Figure 9–7 and develop a positioning strategy to make chocolate milk more appealing to adults.

FIGURE 9–8

A perceptual map to suggest a strategy for positioning chocolate milk to reach adults

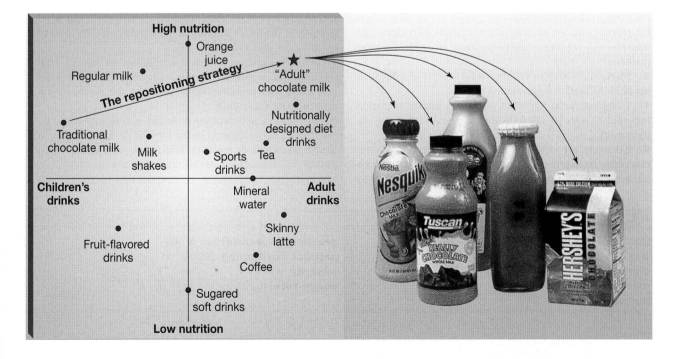

www.beavercanada.(Positioning

Positioning Chocolate Milk for Adults   Figure 9–8 shows the positions that consumer beverages might occupy in the minds of adults. Note that even these positions vary from one consumer to another. But for simplicity, let's assume these are the typical positions on the beverage perceptual map of adults.

Dairies, struggling to increase milk sales, hit on a wild idea: Try to target adults by repositioning chocolate milk to the location of the star shown in the perceptual map in Figure 9–8. Their arguments are nutritionally powerful. For women chocolate milk provides calcium, critically important in female diets. And dieters can get a more filling, nutritious beverage than with a soft drink for about the same calories. The result: Chocolate milk sales increased dramatically, much of it because of adult consumption.[16]

Concept Check

1. What is product positioning?

2. Why do marketers use perceptual maps in product positioning decisions?

SUMMARY

1   Market segmentation is sorting potential buyers into groups that have common needs and will respond similarly to a marketing action.

2   A straightforward approach to segmenting, targeting, and reaching a market involves five steps: (a) form potential buyers into segments by characteristics such as their needs, (b) form products to be sold into groups, (c) develop a market-product grid and estimate size of markets, (d) select target markets, and (e) take marketing actions to reach the target markets.

3   Marketing variables are often used to represent customer needs in the market segmentation process.

4   Usage rate is an important factor in a market segmentation study. Users are often divided into heavy, medium, and light users.

5   Nonusers are often divided into prospects and nonprospects. Nonusers of a firm's brand may be important because they are prospects—users of some other brand in the product type who may be convinced to change brands.

6   Criteria used (a) to segment markets and (b) to choose target segments are related but different. The former includes potential to increase profits, similarity of needs of buyers within a segment, difference of needs among segments, and whether or not a resulting marketing action is possible. The latter includes market size, expected growth, the competitive position of the firm's offering in the segment, and the cost of reaching the segment.

7   A market-product grid is a useful way to display what products can be directed at which market segments, but the grid must lead to marketing actions for the segmentation process to be worthwhile.

8   In positioning a product or brand, a company can consider consumer judgments in the form of perceptual maps to locate its brand or product relative to competing ones, through its management of the marketing mix.

KEY TERMS AND CONCEPTS

80/20 rule p. 201
market-product grid p. 196
market segmentation p. 195
market segments p. 195
perceptual map p. 210

product differentiation p. 195
product positioning p. 209
synergy p. 208
usage rate p. 201

QUESTIONS: APPLYING MARKETING CONCEPTS AND PERSPECTIVES

1 What variables might be used to segment these consumer markets? *(a)* lawnmowers, *(b)* frozen dinners, and *(c)* dry breakfast cereals.

2 What variables might be used to segment these industrial markets? *(a)* industrial vacuums, *(b)* photocopiers, and *(c)* car rental agencies.

3 In Figure 9–6, the dormitory market segment includes students living in college-owned residences. What market needs are common to these students that justify combining them into a single segment in studying the market for your Tim Hortons restaurant?

4 Suppose you want to increase revenues for your fastfood restaurant shown in Figure 9–5 even further. What advertising actions might you take to increase revenues from *(a)* dormitory students, *(b)* dinners, and *(c)* snacks from commuters?

5 Choose a product class with which you are familiar—such as automobiles, snack foods, or apparel—and create a perceptual map, positioning several products within it. Be sure to consider all aspects of the marketing mix, not just product.

6 When do you segment a market: When you are launching a new product? When you are launching a new promotional campaign? When you do your annual marketing planning? Justify your answer.

DISCUSSION FORUM

You have just landed your dream job: a marketing analyst for a sports marketing firm. However, it is full of challenges! Your first assignment is to analyze the market for professional hockey, and your client is the National Hockey League (NHL). Attendance at games is low, and fans are fickle. Here are the tasks that you and your fellow analysts must do—sketch out your ideas for them:

- Design a basic segmentation strategy.
- Describe the market segments you feel apply to the NHL products and services, explaining your criteria.

- Develop a market-product grid.
- Suggest how to estimate the size of your markets.
- Select target markets.
- Identify some market actions to reach your targets.

Hint: Both consumer and business markets may be NHL customers!

INTERNET EXERCISE

In its 25-year history, Apple Computer has initiated a series of creative market segmentation strategies. In fact, by the time you read this, Apple will probably have launched new product lines targeted at specific market segments. For the latest updates of Apple's market-product strategies, go to www.apple-history.com and click on the "Intro" and "His-

www.mcgrawhill.ca/college/thecore

tory" menu options. As you read the narrative, identify the new and remaining markets Apple has targeted with new and existing products compared to those described in the text and the Marketing NewsNet. Can Apple survive as a niche PC marketer like BMW has with autos? Why or why not?

VIDEO CASE 9

NOKIA: A PHONE FOR EVERY SEGMENT

"While practically everybody today is a potential mobile phone customer, everybody is simultaneously different in terms of usage, needs, lifestyles, and individual preferences," explains Nokia's media relations manager, Keith Nowak. Understanding those differences requires that Nokia conduct ongoing research among different consumer groups throughout the world. The approach is reflected in the company's business strategy:

We intend to exploit our leadership role by continuing to target and enter segments of the communications market that we believe will experience rapid growth or grow faster than the industry as a whole.

In fact, Nowak believes that "to be successful in the mobile phone business of today and tomorrow, Nokia has to fully understand the fundamental nature and rationale of segmentation."

THE COMPANY

Nokia started in 1865, when a mining engineer built a wood-pulp mill in southern Finland to manufacture paper. Over the next century, the company diversified into industries ranging from paper to chemicals and rubber. In the 1960s, Nokia ventured into telecommunications by developing a digital telephone exchange switch. In the 1980s, Nokia developed the first "transportable" car mobile phone and the first "handportable" one. During the early 1990s, Nokia divested all of its nontelecommunications operations to focus on its telecommunications and mobile handset businesses.

Today, Nokia is the world leader in mobile communications. The company generates sales of more than US$31 billion and employs more than 56,000 people. Its simple mission: "connecting people."

The mission is accomplished by understanding consumer needs and providing offerings that meet or exceed those needs. Nokia believes that excellence in three areas—product design; services such as mobile Internet, messaging, and network security; and state-of-the-art technology—is the most important aspect of its offerings.

THE MOBILE PHONE MARKET

In the 1980s, first generation (1G) mobile phones consisted of voice-only analog devices with limited range and features that were sold mainly in North America. In the 1990s, second generation (2G) devices consisted of voice/data digital mobile phones with higher data transfer rates, expanded range, and more features. Sales of these devices expanded to Europe and Asia. In the twenty-first century, Nokia and other companies are combining several digital technologies into third-generation (3G) communication devices that reach globally and feature the convergence of the mobile phone, personal digital assistant (PDA), Internet services, and multimedia applications.

The global demand for cellphones has increased significantly over the years—from 284 million in 1999 to 423 million units in 2002, up 6 percent from 2001. By 2006, mobile phone handset sales could reach 606 million units. The total number of worldwide wireless subscribers reached 1 billion in 2001 and is expected to grow to 1.5 billion by 2005. By 2003, global penetration of mobile phones reached 18 percent.

Producers of first- and second-generation mobile phones used a geographic segmentation strategy as global wireless communication networks were developed. Most started with the United States and then proceeded to Western Europe and Asia. However, by 2003, these markets were at or very close to saturation—in a number of European countries, penetration has exceeded 80 percent while reaching 50 percent in the United States. In terms of market share, Nokia led all producers with 32 percent in 2000 and has increased its share to 36 percent in 2002. Motorola (15 percent) and Samsung (10 percent) are the second and third share leaders respectively.

Future demand for mobile phones should increase due to the growing demand by teens for high-speed handsets that will provide Internet and multimedia applications and replacement sales as current users upgrade their handsets to include these and other new features. For 2003, Nokia estimates that 28 percent of current users replaced their phones.

HOW NOKIA SEGMENTS ITS MARKETS

According to Debra Kennedy, director of America's Brand Marketing at Nokia, "Different people have different usage needs. Some people want and need all of the latest and most advanced data-related features and functions, while others are happy with basic voice connectivity. Even people with similar usage needs often have differing lifestyles representing various value sets. For example, some people have an active lifestyle in which sports and fitness play an important role, while for others arts, fashion and trends may be very important."

Based on its information about consumer usage, lifestyles, and price, Nokia currently defines six segments: "Basic" consumers who need voice connectivity and a durable style; "Expression" consumers who want to customize and personalize features; "Classic" consumers who prefer a traditional appearance and web browser function; "Fashion" consumers who want a very small phone as a fashion item; "Premium" consumers who are interested in all technological and service features; and "Communicator" consumers who want to combine all of their communication devices (e.g., telephone, pager, PDA).

NOKIA'S PRODUCT LINE

To target the Basic segment, Nokia provides very easy-to-use, low-priced phones that are likely to be used primarily for voice communication. They are designed for consumers who are buying their first mobile phone. "We want it to be a very easy choice for the consumer," explains Kennedy.

Products designed for the Expression segment are still in the low price range but allow young adults to have fun while communicating with friends. Nokia recently introduced the 5210, a mobile phone that offers a youthful and vibrant style with improved durability, for this group. Features include a removable shell, a built-in stopwatch, a thermometer, downloadable game packs, a personalized logo, and a personal information manager.

Nokia's 6340 phone allows Classic consumers to roam between various global networks; has a new wallet feature that stores the user's credit and debit card information for quick wireless Internet e-commerce transactions; supports voice-activated dialing, control of the user interface, and three minutes of voice memo recording; and includes a personal information manager (phone book and calendar).

Nokia also designs phones for the Fashion segment—people who want a phone to "show off." The Nokia 8260 and 8390 products are in this category. They provide basic communication and other features but are not designed for heavy use. One of Nokia's television commercials for fashion phones showed two people sitting on a couch trying to talk to each other at a loud party—so they call each other on their phones!

In addition, Nokia offers phones for the Premium segment—people who also want a distinctive and elegant design, but as a fine item to appreciate rather than to show off. The Nokia 8890, a phone with a chrome case and blue back light, was designed for this group. Nokia also recently introduced the all-in-one 5510, which features an MP3 player that can store up to two hours of music, an FM radio, a messaging machine with full keyboard, a game platform with game controls for two hands and keys located on either side of the screen, and of course, the mobile phone.

To meet the needs of these segments, Nokia has recently introduced several innovative products. For example, for the Communicator segment, Nokia's 7650 mobile phone features a built-in digital camera, an enhanced user interface, large colour display, and multimedia messaging (MMS) functionality that allows users to combine audio, graphic, text, and imaging content in one message. Once the user has selected a picture, written text, and included an audio clip, a multimedia message can be sent directly to another multimedia messaging-capable terminal as well as to the recipient's e-mail address.

THE FUTURE FOR NOKIA

To target existing and new market segments, Nokia has recently introduced several new and exciting products. The Nokia 3650 is a smart imaging mobile phone that has video recording and video streaming capability through a RealOne video player. Users can take or receive motion or still pictures with a built-in, higher resolution digital camera. It also sports a large colour display and a unique round keypad instead of the typical phone keys to select phone numbers or special functions. Finally, the phone can function as a voice recorder, allowing the user to send a voice e-mail message.

In 2003, Nokia also introduced two new products designed to target two new and different markets. First, Nokia entered the video-game market with its N-Gage mobile game deck. The device is shaped like a fan and has a large colour screen and game controls. Several games are available for this new device. Second, Nokia introduced the Nokia 3300 music device that is capable of playing MP3 files.

Another fast-growing segment for wireless mobile phones is the automobile. According to the ARC Group, the number of cars with "telematic" systems will increase from 1 million units to 56 million units by 2005. Ford, Nissan, and other automobile manufacturers have recently introduced systems in selected models. One reason for the expected popularity of these devices is their "hands-free, voice-activated" operation, which is designed to reduce mobile phone-related automobile accidents. The CTIA has recently developed a public service announcement (PSA) to curb this dangerous behaviour and forestall legislation designed to eliminate mobile phone use in the car entirely.

Nokia Executive Vice President Olli-Pekka Kallasvuo is so optimistic he recently commented that "our ambition should be extremely high," as the company has set its sights on capturing 40 percent of the worldwide mobile-phone market.

Questions

1   Why has segmentation been a successful marketing strategy for Nokia?

2   What customer characteristics were used by cellular phone manufacturers during the industry's early stages of growth? Which customer characteristics and segmentation variables are used by Nokia today?

3   Create a market-product grid for Nokia today. What potential new markets could you add to the grid?

Satisfying Marketing Opportunities

Part 4 covers the development of the marketing mix—the unique combination of product, price, place, and promotion that results in an offering for potential customers. How products and services are developed and managed is the focus of Chapters 10 and 11. Pricing is covered in Chapter 12. Chapters 13 and 14 address the place (distribution) element with examples such as Avon's use of multiple marketing channels, Dell's responsive supply chain, and the introduction of "smart cards" and other retailing innovations. Three promotion chapters cover topics ranging from Disney's integrated marketing communications program, to "virtual advertisements" that don't really exist, to Xerox CEO Anne Mulcahy's efforts to increase market share by "selling the way customers want to buy."

Developing New Products and Services

"I see. And how long have you had these feelings of inferiority to tape?"

With all the advantages of 3M™ VHB™ Tape, no wonder traditional fasteners are feeling insecure. For 20 years, VHB tape has helped engineers make their products look better, sound quieter, weigh less and last longer. For information and samples, call 1-800-567-1639, ext. 1410. Or visit **www.3M.com/bonding**.

3M *Innovation*

3M: CONTINUOUS IMPROVEMENTS + GENUINE BENEFITS = SATISFIED CUSTOMERS

Ken Hart, Ph.D., 3M™ Business Development Manager for its VHB™ tape, knows that "having a better mousetrap"—or in his case a new 3M industrial adhesive—isn't enough!

Before potential customers will buy and use it, he must help them learn about the adhesive and its benefits and get them to think about ways to actually use it in their designs.[1] Here's a quick take on the marketing issues he faced recently:

- *The product?* A revolutionary 3M VHB (for "very high bond") tape made with high-strength, pressure-sensitive adhesives that can make a continuous metal bond stronger than spot welds or rivets on cargo trailers and highway signs.
- *The target market?* Mechanical engineers responsible for the designs of everything from trucks, airplanes, and cars to ceilings in buildings.
- *The special marketing task?* To get mechanical engineers, who normally specify welds, screws, or rivets

in their designs, to seriously consider the 3M VHB tape adhesive and actually use it in applications.

Ken Hart and his marketing staff developed the tongue-in-cheek ad shown above—it runs in design engineering magazines and its goal is to change engineers' traditional design solutions. The team's continuing challenge is to do marketing research on customer needs to develop an integrated marketing communications (IMC) strategy (Chapter 15) with advertising, public relations, and direct marketing that explains VHB's benefits to design engineers. Although 3M received the original adhesive patent two decades ago, continuous innovation improved the formula and mechanical delivery system for new applications and market opportunities.[2]

A brief look at two other 3M products provides insights into how its new-product research has enabled the company to become a global leader in adhesive technology:

THE MARKETING PROCESS

WHERE IN THE MARKETING PROCESS ARE WE GOING IN THIS CHAPTER?

Chapter 10's topic is developing new products and services. Clearly, this is one of the 4 Ps, and it is central to a firm's marketing activities.

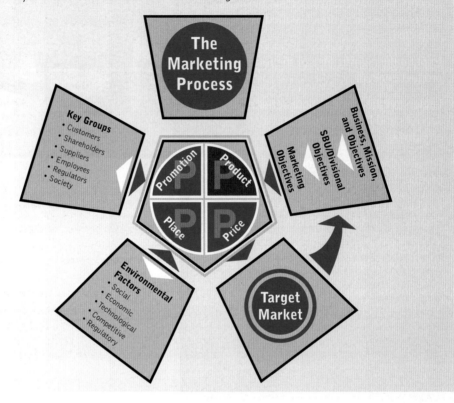

- Post-it® Notes. The adhesive enables you to stick and unstick a note anywhere.
- Nexcare™ Tattoo™ Waterproof Bandages for kids. The bandage combines superior waterproof wound protection with fun designs.

product

Good, service, or idea consisting of tangible and intangible features that satisfy consumers and is received in exchange for money or some other unit of value

The essence of marketing is in developing products such as a new, technologically advanced adhesive to meet buyer needs. A **product** is a good, service, or idea consisting of a bundle of tangible and intangible attributes that satisfies consumers and is received in exchange for money or some other unit of value. Tangible attributes include physical characteristics such as colour or sweetness, and intangible attributes include those aspects of a product that can't be "touched," such as the way driving a Porsche may make you feel or how a product makes you healthier or makes you feel relaxed. Products include the breakfast cereal you eat, the public transportation you take, and the fundraising campaign by the Breast Cancer Society of Canada.

The ongoing success of a company often depends on how it conceives, produces, and markets new products. This is the exact reason that 3M encourages its researchers to spend up to 15 percent of their time on new technologies and product ideas of their own choosing—"scouting time," they call it. This strategy contributes to more than 500 3M patents a year, routinely placing 3M among the top 10 U.S. corporations each year in patents received.[3]

This chapter covers decisions involved in developing and marketing new products and services. Chapter 11 discusses the process of managing existing products, services, and brands.

THE PRODUCT: TOTAL PRODUCT CONCEPT

THE TOTAL PRODUCT CONCEPT

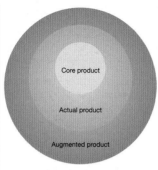

Layer	Description	Example
Core (generic) product	What the product does for the customer—the benefits derived from using the product	Provides transportation and leisure activity
Actual product	What is the physical good the consumer receives	A metal frame with two wheels and a seat attached
Augmented product	Additional features or benefits that accompany the product	Warranty, repair service

You purchase a product, and what do you get? Not just a physical item, but much more! Marketers think of products as having three different layers: the core product, the actual product, and the augmented product. These layers provide ideas and possibilities to marketers—ways they can satisfy customers' needs and can differentiate their product from those of competitors.

Figure 10-1 shows how these layers work together. The centre, or the *core product*, shows the benefits a consumer derives from having the product. In the case of a bicycle, for example, consumers can benefit from the transportation it provides, or they may cycle for leisure or for sport. A sturdy mountain bike may provide excitement or involvement with friends.

The *actual product* is the physical good that the consumer takes possession of when making a purchase. With a bicycle, the consumer leaves the bike store with a piece of equipment with two wheels and a seat attached to a frame, along with a few other components. Part of the actual product is what makes each bicycle brand and model unique—their styling, features, and details.

Finally, the *augmented product* is the additional features and attributes, such as a warranty, a service contract, and a website with repair information for owners. Often, the augmented-product layer offers marketers the most opportunity to differentiate their product from those of competitors. With a comprehensive understanding of their consumers' needs and wants, marketers can also use the augmented-product layer to help them position the product in consumers' minds.

FIGURE 10–1

The total product concept applied to a bicycle

product line
Group of products that are closely related because they satisfy a class of needs, are used together, are sold to the same customer group, are distributed through the same outlets, or fall within a given price range

THE VARIATIONS OF PRODUCTS

For most organizations, the product decision—that is, the choice of what products to offer—is made after taking into consideration the range of products already offered by the company. Products differ in terms of whether they are intended for consumers or businesses. To better appreciate the product decision, let's first define some terms pertaining to products.

FIGURE 10–2

Some of Nike's products explained as product lines and product mix

Product Line and Product Mix

A **product line** is a group of products—goods or services—that are closely related because they satisfy a class of needs, are used together, are sold to the same customer group, are distributed through the same type of outlets, or fall within a given price range.[4] Nike's product lines are sports-related shoes, clothing, and equipment, as shown in Figure 10-2, whereas the Toronto Hospital for Sick Children's product lines consist of inpatient hospital care, outpatient physician services, and medical research. Each product line has its own marketing strategy.

Within each product line is the *product item*, a specific product as noted by a unique brand, size, or price. For example, Downy softener for clothes comes in 20-ounce and 40-ounce sizes; each size is considered a separate item,

PRODUCT LINES AND PRODUCT MIX AT NIKE

← Width of product mix →

Product line: shoes	Product line: clothing	Product line: equipment
Running	T-shirts	Sunglasses
Basketball	Shorts	Golf gear
Training	Socks	Bags, backpacks
Sandals	Hoodies	Basketball
Tennis	Sweatshirts	Watches
Lifestyle	Yoga wear	Sport monitoring items
Soccer	Track pants	Sport audio equipment
Walking	Jackets	
Baseball		

(PRODUCT MIX — Depth of product mix; product item)

Out here you're nobody. Perfect.

HUMMER® like nothing else.™

Sometimes you find yourself in the middle of nowhere. And sometimes in the middle of nowhere you find yourself. The legendary H1.

Hummer's striking ads gain attention for its product line of unique, upscale vehicles.

product mix
All the product lines offered by a company

consumer goods
Products purchased by the ultimate consumer

business goods
Products that are purchased by organizations, and that are used for resale, as inputs for further production or in the operation of the organization

or *stock keeping unit* (SKU), which is a unique identification number that defines an item for ordering or inventory purposes.

The third way to look at products is by the **product mix**, or the number of product lines offered by a company. Cray, Inc., has a single product line consisting of supercomputers, which are sold mostly to governments and large businesses. In contrast, Pillsbury Canada (now owned by General Mills, a worldwide marketer of consumer foods) has many product lines including Green Giant canned and frozen vegetables, Pillsbury refrigerated baked goods, Prima Pasta, Old El Paso Mexican foods, and Häagen-Dazs ice creams.[5]

Classifying Products

Both the federal government and companies classify products, but for different purposes. The government's classification method—the NAICS (see Chapter 6)—helps it collect information on industrial activity. Companies classify products to help develop marketing strategies for the wide range of products offered. Two major ways companies classify products are by type of user and degree of product tangibility.

Type of User   The first major type of product classification is according to the user. **Consumer goods** are products purchased by the ultimate consumer, whereas **business goods** (also called *industrial goods* or *organizational goods*) are products that are purchased by organizations, and that are used for resale, as inputs for further production or in the operation of the organization. In many instances the differences are distinct: Oil of Olay face moisturizer and Bass shoes are clearly consumer products, whereas Cray computers and high-tension steel springs are industrial goods used in producing other products or services. Services also differ by the type of user. H&R Block's tax preparation services are used by consumers, while IBM's consulting services are used by other businesses.

FIGURE 10-3

Importance of services in the Canadian gross domestic product (GDP)

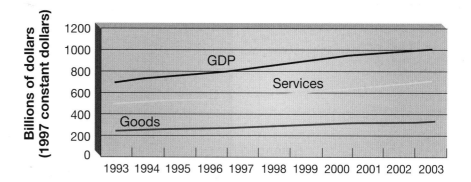

There are limitations, however, with this classification because some products can be considered both consumer and business items. A Dell computer can be sold to consumers as a final product or to business firms for office use. Each classification results in different marketing actions. Viewed as a consumer product, the Dell computer would be sold directly from the company website. As a business product, the Dell computer might be sold by a salesperson offering discounts for multiple or volume purchases.

Degree of Tangibility   Classification by degree of tangibility divides products into one of three categories. First is a *nondurable* good, an item consumed in one or a few uses, such as food products and fuel. By comparison, a *durable* good is an item that usually lasts over an extended number of uses, such as appliances, automobiles, and stereo equipment. *Services* are defined as intangible activities, benefits, or satisfactions offered for sale, such as marketing research, health care, and education. Recent government data indicate that Canada has a strong and growing service-based economy (see Figure 10-3); in fact, services comprise close to 70 percent of Canada's gross domestic product (GDP).[6] Because of the increasing importance of services, intangibility and several other unique elements of services are discussed separately in an upcoming section.

This classification method (tangibility versus intangibility) also provides direction for marketing actions. For nondurable products such as Wrigley's chewing gum, which is inexpensive and frequently purchased, consumer advertising and wide distribution in retail outlets is essential. Durable products such as cars, however, generally cost more than nondurable goods and last longer, so personal selling becomes an important marketing activity in answering consumer questions and concerns. The marketing of services requires a very different approach to that of goods, as we will explain later.

The Service Continuum

Most products sold cannot be defined as "pure goods" or "pure services." For example, does IBM Canada sell goods or services? While the company sells computers and software, a major component of its business is information technology services including consulting and training. Does Rogers Communications provide only goods when it publishes *Marketing magazine*, or does it consider itself a service because it presents up-to-date Canadian business information? As companies look at what they bring to the market, there is a range from the tangible to the intangible, or goods-dominant to service-dominant offerings referred to as the **service continuum** (see Figure 10-4). Teaching, nursing, and the theatre are very much intangible, service-dominant activities. Salt, neckties, and dog food are definitely tangible goods.

In today's marketplace, firms are combining goods and services; many goods are augmented with intangible service elements such as warranties. Services also use goods to ensure more complete satisfaction of customer needs and wants; your university, for example, gives

service continuum
A range from tangible to the intangible or goods-dominant to service-dominant offerings available in the marketplace

FIGURE 10-4

Service continuum

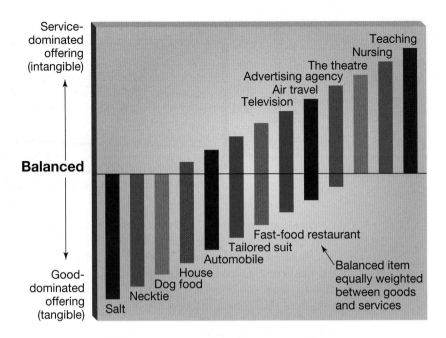

you educational services, but it also provides you with a hard-copy diploma to show that you have completed the required courses. Combining the two—goods and services—is the way many firms elect to differentiate their product offering.

The products of some businesses require a mix of intangible-service and tangible-good factors. A clothing tailor provides a service but also a good—the finished suit. How pleasant, courteous, and attentive the tailor is to the customer is an important component of the service, and how well the clothes fit is an important part of the product. As shown in Figure 10-4, a fast-food restaurant is about half tangible goods (the food) and half intangible services (courtesy, cleanliness, speed, convenience).

For many businesses today, it is useful to distinguish between their core service and their supplementary services. A core service offering such as a bank account, for example, also has supplementary services such as deposit assistance, parking or drive-through availability, ABMs, and monthly statements. Supplementary services often allow service providers to differentiate their offering from competitors while adding value for consumers. Key categories of supplementary services include information delivery, consultation, order taking, billing and payment options.[7]

The Uniqueness of Services

There are four unique elements to services: intangibility, inconsistency, inseparability, and inventory. These four elements are referred to as the *four Is of services.*

Intangibility   Services are intangible; that is, for the most part, they can't be held, touched, or seen before the purchase decision. In contrast, before purchasing a physical good, a consumer can touch a box of laundry detergent, kick the tire of an automobile, or sample a new breakfast cereal. Because services tend to be a performance rather than an object, they are much more difficult for consumers to evaluate. To help consumers assess and compare services marketers try to make them appear somewhat tangible or show the benefits of using the service.

Inconsistency   Developing, pricing, promoting, and delivering services is challenging because the quality of a service is often inconsistent. Because services depend on the people who provide them, their quality varies with each person's capabilities and day-to-day job performance. Inconsistency is much more of a problem in services than it is with tangible goods. Tangible products can be good or bad in terms of quality, but with modern production lines the quality will at least be consistent. On the other hand, one day the Toronto Blue Jays baseball team may have great hitting and pitching and look like a pennant winner and the next day lose by 10 runs.

Inseparability   A third difference between services and goods, and related to problems of consistency, is inseparability. In most cases, the consumer cannot (and does not) separate the deliverer of the service from the service itself. For example, to receive an education, a person may attend a university. The quality of the education may be high, but if the student has difficulty interacting with instructors, finds counseling services poor, or does not receive adequate library or computer assistance, he or she may not be satisfied with the educational experience. Students' evaluations of their education will be influenced primarily by their perceptions of instructors, counselors, librarians, and other people at the university.

Inventory   Inventory of services is different from that of goods. Inventory problems exist with goods because many items are perishable and because there are costs associated with handling inventory. With services, inventory carrying costs are more subjective and are related to **idle production capacity**, which is when the service provider is available but there is no demand. The inventory cost of a service is the cost of paying the person used to provide the service along with any needed equipment. If a medical doctor is paid to see patients but no one schedules an appointment, the fixed cost of the idle doctor's salary is a high inventory carrying cost. In some service businesses, however, the provider of the service is on commission (the Re-Max real estate agent) or is a part-time employee (a clerk at Sears Canada). In these businesses, inventory carrying costs can be significantly lower or nonexistent because the idle production capacity can be cut back by reducing hours or having no salary to pay because of the commission compensation system.

idle production capacity
When the supply of the service exceeds demand for it

Specialty goods like Rolex watches require distinct marketing programs to reach narrow target markets.

CLASSIFYING GOODS AND SERVICES

Because marketing focuses on the buyer—that is, the product user—let's look a bit more closely at the two types of users and the way in which goods and services are classified as consumer or business products.

Classification of Consumer Goods

Convenience, shopping, specialty, and unsought products are the four types of consumer goods. They differ in terms of effort the consumer spends on the decision, attributes used in purchase, and frequency of purchase.

Convenience goods are items, such as toothpaste, that the consumer purchases frequently and with a minimum of shopping effort. *Shopping goods*, such as everyday clothing, are items for which the consumer compares several alternatives on criteria, such as price, quality, or style. *Specialty goods* are items, such as Rolex watches, that a consumer makes a special effort to search out and buy. *Unsought goods* are items that the consumer either does not know about or knows about but does not initially want or think is needed. Figure 10–5

TYPE OF CONSUMER GOOD

BASIS OF COMPARISON	CONVENIENCE	SHOPPING	SPECIALTY	UNSOUGHT
Purchase behaviour of consumers	Frequent purchases; little time and effort spent shopping	Occasional purchases; needs much comparison shopping time	Infrequent purchases; needs extensive search and decision time	Very infrequent purchases; some comparison shopping
Brand loyalty of consumers	Aware of brand, but will accept substitutes	Prefer specific brands, but will accept substitutes	Very brand loyal; will not accept substitutes	Will accept substitutes
Product	Toothpaste, chocolate bars, soft drinks, laundry detergent	Cameras, TVs, briefcases, clothing	Wedding dresses, luxury items such as Rolex watches	Insurance products, such as life and disability insurance
Price	Relatively inexpensive	Fairly expensive	Usually very expensive	Varies
Place (distribution)	Widespread; many outlets	Large number of selected outlets	Very limited	Often limited
Promotion	Price, availability, and awareness stressed	Differentiation from competitors stressed	Uniqueness of brand and status stressed	Awareness is essential

FIGURE 10–5

Classification of consumer goods

shows how the classification of a consumer product into one of these four types results in different aspects of the marketing mix being stressed. Consumers display different degrees of brand loyalty and amounts of shopping effort for products in each of the four classes.

The manner in which a consumer good is classified depends on the individual. One person may view a camera as a shopping good and visit several stores before deciding on a brand, whereas a friend may view cameras as a specialty good and will only buy a high-end Nikon camera.

Classification of Business Goods

A major characteristic of business goods is that their sales are often the result of *derived demand*; that is, sales of industrial products frequently result, or are derived, from the sale of consumer goods. For example, if consumer demand for Ford cars (a consumer product) increases, the company may increase its demand for industrial-grade paint-spraying equipment (a business product). Business goods may be classified as production or support goods.

Production Goods Items used in the manufacturing process that become part of the final product are *production goods*. These include raw materials, such as grain or lumber, or component parts, such as door hinges used by Ford in its car doors.

Support Goods The second class of business goods is support goods, which are items used to assist in producing other goods and services. Support goods include installations, accessory equipment, supplies, and services.

- *Installations* consist of buildings and fixed equipment. Industrial buyers purchase these assets through sales representatives, who often submit competitive bids.
- *Accessory equipment* includes tools and office equipment and is usually purchased in small-order sizes by buyers. As a result, sellers of industrial accessories use distributors to contact and deal directly with a large number of buyers.
- *Supplies* are the business equivalent of consumer convenience goods and consist of products that are used continually such as stationery, paper clips, and brooms. These are purchased with little effort, using the straight rebuy decision sequence discussed in Chapter 6. Price and delivery are key factors considered by the buyers of supplies.
- *Services* are intangible activities to assist the business in its operations and in producing its goods and services. This category can include transportation services, maintenance and repair services, and advisory services such as tax or legal counsel.

Classification of Services

Services can be classified according to whether they are delivered by people or equipment.

Delivery by People Increasingly, consumers and business customers are turning to businesses to provide them with services that they previously looked after themselves or hired their own staff to perform. They benefit by having the services performed when they need them and, at the same time, saving the time it would take to do it themselves. They also avoid the investment in personnel, machinery, and facilities required to perform the services. Depending on the nature of the service and the level of complexity, many companies employ people to deliver all or part of their services. For example, a small consulting firm could prepare their own tax returns, but may decide to have an accountant do so.

Delivery by Equipment Inconsistency is less of a concern for equipment-based services, because the provision of these services relies more on the equipment and less on people. Electrical utilities, for example, can provide service without frequent personal contact with customers. Motion picture theatres have projection systems that most consumers never see. And a growing number of customers use online banking services such as checking account balances, paying bills, and transferring funds from one account to another.

Concept Check

1. Explain the difference between product mix and product line.
2. What are the four main types of consumer goods?
3. What are the ways to classify services?

THE NEW-PRODUCT PROCESS

new-product process
Sequence of activities a firm uses to identify business opportunities and convert them into salable goods or services

Companies such as General Electric, Sony, and Procter & Gamble follow a sequence of steps before their products are ready for market. The **new-product process,** shown in Figure 10-6, consists of seven stages a firm goes through to identify business opportunities and convert them to a salable good or service. This sequence begins with new-product strategy development and ends with commercialization.

FIGURE 10–6

Stages in the new-product process

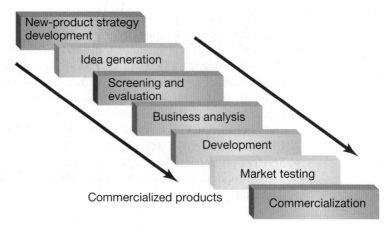

New-product strategy development

Idea generation

Screening and evaluation

Business analysis

Development

Market testing

Commercialized products

Commercialization

New-Product Strategy Development

For companies, *new-product strategy development* involves defining the role for a new product in terms of the firm's overall corporate objectives. When Alan G. Lafley became CEO of Procter & Gamble (P&G) in 2000, he refocused its new-product strategy from looking for new-to-the-world products to more modest improvements of P&G's existing core brands such as Crest, Tide, and Pampers. For example, Crest's Whitestrips for tooth whitening and its SpinBrush for better dental care helped Crest global sales grow 50 percent in two years, a rare event for a mature brand like Crest.[8] This step in the new-product process has been added by many companies recently to provide a needed focus for ideas and concepts developed in later stages.

Identifying Markets and Strategic Roles   During this new-product strategy development stage, the company uses the environmental scanning process described in Chapter 3 to identify trends that pose either opportunities or threats. Relevant company strengths and weaknesses are also identified. The outcome of new-product strategy development is not only new-product ideas but also identifying markets for which new products will be developed and strategic roles new products might serve—this is the vital protocol activity we explain later in this chapter.

Cross-Functional Teams and New-Product Development   Key to success in new-product development at Hewlett-Packard (HP) is its use of *cross-functional teams* groups made up of a small number of people from different departments in an organization who are mutually accountable to a common set of performance goals. Today in HP, teams are especially important in new-product development so that individuals from R&D, marketing, sales, manufacturing, and finance can simultaneously work together to improve both the new products and the process to develop and produce them. In the past, HP and other firms often utilized these department people in sequence—possibly resulting in R&D designing new products that the manufacturing department couldn't produce economically and that the marketing department couldn't sell.

Effective cross-functional teams at Hewlett-Packard have reduced new-product development times significantly.

Idea Generation

Idea generation, where a pool of concepts is developed as possible new products, must build on the previous stage's results. New-product ideas are generated by consumers, suppliers, employees, R&D, and competitors.

The i-Zone Pocket Camera is popular with teens for its portability and for the cool instant mini-photos that it produces. What fun.

Customer and Supplier Suggestions Companies often analyze consumer complaints or supplier ideas to identify new-product opportunities. Listening to growing concerns about cholesterol and fat in its food, McDonald's reformulated its shakes with a low-fat mixture and introduced a low-fat hamburger. Whirlpool, trying to reduce costs by cutting the number of different product platforms in half, got ideas from suppliers on ways to standardize components.[9]

Employee Suggestions Employees may be encouraged to suggest new-product ideas through suggestion boxes or contests. The idea for Nature Valley Granola Bars from General Mills came when one of its marketing managers observed co-workers bringing granola to work in plastic bags.

In 1997, a Polaroid employee in Tokyo saw a group of teenage girls crammed into a photo booth that took instant minipictures. Over objections from many company scientists, this idea became the $25 Polaroid I-Zone Instant Pocket camera, a number one selling camera in early 2000, only four months after introduction.[10]

Research and Development Breakthroughs Another source of new products is a firm's basic research, but the costs can be huge. Sony is the global leader in new-product development in electronics. Its R&D scientists and engineers produce an average of four new products each business day, which have led to innovative products such as the VCR, the Walkman, and—coming into your future?—flat-panel organic electroluminescence (OEL) monitors about the thickness of a credit card providing brighter images on large, 30-inch screens.

Professional R&D laboratories also provide new-product ideas. Labs at Arthur D. Little helped put the crunch in Cap'n Crunch cereal and the flavor in Carnation Instant Breakfast. IDEO is a world-class new-product development firm, having designed more than 4,000 of them. These range from the Handspring Treo Communicator and Heartstream portable defibrillator to Crest's neat-squeeze toothpaste dispenser and Nike's all-terrain sunglasses.

Competitive Products New-product ideas can also be found by analyzing the competition. A six-person intelligence team from the Marriott Corporation spent six months traveling around the country staying at economy hotels. The team measured the competition's strengths and weaknesses on everything from the soundproof qualities of the rooms to the softness of the towels. Marriott then budgeted $500 million for a new economy hotel chain, Fairfield Inns.

Screening and Evaluation

The third stage of the new product process is *screening and evaluation*, which involves internal and external evaluations of the new-product ideas to eliminate those that should not be developed further.

Internal Approach Internally, the firm evaluates the technical difficulty of the product and whether the idea meets the objectives defined in the new-product strategy development step. In the 1990s, Penn Racquet Sports, the largest U.S. producer of tennis balls, faced flat sales because of a decade-long lull in recreational tennis. What to do? Penn Racquet employees observed that many used tennis balls were given as a toy to the family

A year's worth of consumer interviews went into the development of Sun Chips.

dog. So in 1998 the company designed and introduced R.P. Fetchem—a dye-free "natural felt fetch toy" that looks remarkably like . . . a tennis ball![11]

External Approach   *Concept tests* are external evaluations that consist of preliminary testing of the new-product idea, rather than the actual product, with consumers. Concept tests usually rely on written descriptions of the product but may be augmented with sketches, mockups, or promotional literature. Several key questions are asked during concept testing: How does the customer perceive the product? Who would use it? How would it be used?

Frito-Lay spent a year interviewing 10,000 consumers about the concept of a multi-grain snack chip. The company experimented with 50 different shapes before settling on a thin, rectangular chip with ridges and a slightly salty, nutty flavor. The product, Sun Chips, is highly successful.

Concept Check

1. What step in the new-product process has been added in recent years?
2. What are four sources of new-product ideas?

Business Analysis

Business analysis involves specifying the features of the product and the marketing strategy needed to commercialize it—that is, bring it to market—and making necessary financial projections. This is the last checkpoint before significant resources are invested in creating a *prototype*—usually, a full-scale operating model of the product.

Assessing the "Business Fit" of the New Product   The business analysis stage of new product development really involves assessing the total "business fit" of the proposed new product with the company's mission and objectives—from whether the product can be developed and manufactured economically to the marketing strategy needed to have it succeed in the marketplace. This process requires not only detailed financial analyses and projections but also assessments of the marketing and product synergies related to the company's existing operations and products. Will the product require a lot of new machinery to produce it or can we utilize unused capacity of existing machines? Will adding the new product cannibalize sales of our existing products or increase revenues by reaching new market segments? Financial projections of expected profits require estimates of the number of units to be sold and expected prices per unit, as well as detailed estimates of the costs of R&D, production, and marketing.

The proposed new product is also studied to determine whether it can and should be protected with a patent or copyright. An attractive new-product proposal is one in which the technology, product, or brand cannot easily be copied by competitors.

Important aspects of the "Business Fit" are the synergies that result and the ease of access to new market segments. For example, in 2001 General Mills and Pillsbury merged, resulting in a firm with US$13 billion in annual sales. The merger is expected to generate major synergies in new product development, distribution, and supply-chain operations.

Steve Sanger, CEO of the merged firm, gets very excited when he talks about carrying his consumer convenience and "one-handedness" synergies into the Pillsbury product line.

He looks at what he calls "Pillsbury's marvelous dough technology" and points out that "if you think of hand-held foods, most of them are dough wrapped around something." So, on the drawing boards may be a Pillsbury biscuit or the cookie dough "wrapped around something," a new product you might be able to buy soon. But the competition is tough: Kraft Foods' barbequed chicken on a stick covered in dough and 7-Eleven's macaroni and cheese on a push-up stick.[12]

As shown in the Marketing NewsNet box, General Mills has cereal brands targeted at many segments, some large and others only niche segments. With Big G's Milk 'n Cereal

MARKETING NEWSNET

Customer Value

BUSINESS ANALYSIS AT BIG G: "ONE HANDED" CONVENIENCE PLUS COVER ALL THE BASES

What do you do when you're chief executive officer of a firm in the low-growth food industry? This is the problem facing Steve Sanger, CEO of General Mills — or "Big G" from its cereal logo. His remarkable answers: one-handedness and covering all the bases. Both focus on today's consumers and keeping the business analysis stage of new product planning simple and clear.

One-Handedness

When Steve Sanger gets proposals for a new food product or a way to reposition an old one, he asks one question, "Can we make it 'one-handed'?" This doesn't mean build it one-handed but being able to eat it one-handed!

With today's consumers, Sanger says, "You have to make everything more convenient" — like letting people have a free hand while eating and typing or driving. Go-Gurt (for kids) and Yoplait Exprèsse (for adults) yogourts, Chex Morning Mix, and Big G Milk 'n Cereal Bars are examples of Sanger's one-handed strategy.

Cover-All-the-Bases

Big G also faces the challenge of finding growth in its cereal business when over half its profits come from cereal sales. So it monitors consumers' changing tastes and implements new-product and diversification strategies like those shown below:

PRODUCTS

Markets	Current	New
Current	**Market Penetration** Finding ways to make current products appeal to current customers: Cheerios, with games or CDs included in or on the package	**Product Development** Reaching current customers with a new product: Harmony, a nutritiously fortified cereal for women wanting a healthier breakfast
New	**Market Development** Reaching new customers with basically a current product: Wheaties Energy Crunch, for those needing "all-day energy"	**Diversification** Reaching new customers with a new product: Sunrise Organic, for those wanting a cereal grown without pesticides that receives formal organic certification

Bars, commuters on the way to work can try "dashboard dining"—eating a cereal break-fast without a bowl or spoon. The basic components: General Mills' traditional cereals, now bought in a box. Its Cereal Partners Worldwide (CPW), a joint venture with Nestlé, now holds 20 percent market share across 75 countries. This enables General Mills' traditional strengths in food product brands to reach new segments of international consumers.[13]

Development

Product ideas that survive the business analysis proceed to actual *development*, turning the idea on paper into a prototype. This results in a demonstrable, producible product in hand.

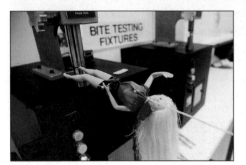

Outsiders seldom understand the technical complexities of the development stage, which involves not only manufacturing the product but also performing laboratory and consumer tests to ensure that it meets standards. Design of the product becomes an important element.

Some new products can be so important and costly that the company is literally betting its very existence on success. And creative, out-of-the-box thinking can be critical. In the pharmaceutical industry, no more than one out of every 5,000 to 10,000 new compounds developed in the labs emerges as an approved drug.[14]

Exhaustive laboratory and safety tests are used to verify that the product meets required consumer safety standards and is also safe even if used improperly. A case in point: To make sure young children can't bite Barbie's head off and choke, Mattel clamps her foot in steel jaws in a test stand and then pulls on her head with a wire. Similarly, car manufacturers crash test cars into each other because consumer groups are increasingly concerned about what happens when a pickup truck or sport utility vehicle hits a small car when their bumpers don't line up. Such tests can identify some feasible, but costly, solutions.[15] Check out the Ethics and Social Responsibility Alert box nearby, entitled "Sports Utilities versus Cars: Godzilla Meets a Chimp."

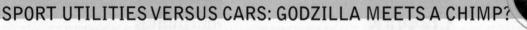

ETHICS AND SOCIAL RESPONSIBILITY ALERT
SPORT UTILITIES VERSUS CARS: GODZILLA MEETS A CHIMP?

Make car wrecks safer. This sounds sort of stupid. But . . . the problem is death! The high and heavy pickups, vans, and sport utility vehicles (SUVs) are now involved in an increasing number of highway deaths. When one huge vehicle meets a bitty little car, the larger, higher one smashes the smaller one's passenger compartment, instead of going head-to-head at bumper level. The people in the cars, unfortunately, are more likely to be killed in such accidents.

The problem is also money. These mega-vehicles now account for a large percentage of Canadian automakers' sales and profits. Improving the smaller cars—with side air bags and steel supports—is cheaper than lowering the frame or adding a crumple zone for the frame of the bigger vehicle. Nothing is easy. And consumers love the power of these hefty vehicles that are about 1,000 kilograms heavier than a compact car.

But changes are on the way. Mercedes Benz has completely redesigned its M-class SUV. Mercedes engineers addressed the compatibility of their SUV with smaller cars so the Mercedes SUV frame and bumper is as much as 20 centimetres lower than its competitor's SUV models. This makes the bumpers of Mercedes SUVs and those of small cars more likely to meet in a crash, dramatically increasing the safety for small-car passengers.

Who should address the problem here? The federal government? The insurance companies? The vehicle manufacturers? Consumers?

Market Testing

The *market testing* stage of the new-product process involves exposing perspective consumers to actual products under realistic purchase conditions to see if they will buy. Often a product is developed, tested, refined, and then tested again to get consumer reactions through test marketing.

Test Marketing

Test marketing involves offering a product for sale on a limited basis in a defined geographic area. This test is done to determine whether consumers will actually buy the product, and to try different ways of marketing it. Only about a third of the products test marketed do well enough to go on to the next phase. These market tests are usually conducted in cities that are viewed as being representative of Canadians. Typical Canadian cities used for market tests include Peterborough and London in Central Canada, Edmonton and Kelowna in Western Canada, and Moncton in the Maritimes. All of these are selected because their population is considered to be a representative cross-section of the Canadian population, and they have their own newspapers, radio, and television stations. The media in those cities is essentially isolated, not overlapping with a nearby major metropolitan area. This means that firms can deliver advertising and test special promotions and measure the responses of consumers, reasonably confident that the results are related to those marketing actions in a specific time frame and not overly impacted by events outside the area. Using tracking systems by firms such as AC Nielsen, they can correlate local advertising campaigns to in-store purchases using data from the scanners at the store check-out counters.

This gives marketers an indication of potential sales volume and market share in the test area. Market tests are also used to check other elements of the marketing mix besides the product itself such as price and distribution. Market tests are time consuming and expensive because production lines as well as promotion and sales programs must be set up. Costs can run several million dollars. There are also risks associated with using market tests. Market tests reveal plans to competitors, sometimes enabling them to get a product into national distribution first. Competitors can also try to sabotage test markets. With such problems, some firms skip test markets completely.

When Test Markets Don't Work

Test marketing is a valuable step in the new-product process, but not all products can use it. Testing a service beyond the concept level is very difficult because the service is intangible and consumers can't see what they are buying. Similarly, test markets for expensive consumer products such as cars or costly industrial products such as jet engines are impractical. For these products, consumer reactions to mockup designs or one-of-a-kind prototypes are all that is possible. Carmakers test new style designs on "early adopters" (discussed in Chapter 11), who are more willing than the average customer to buy new designs or products.[16]

An emerging trend is the use of virtual reality testing. This can work well for high-ticket products, as well as those products that require hands-on demonstration. One company, Elumens Corporation, has developed VisionDome, which can accommodate up to 45 people at a time and provide them with a 3-D immersion experience and even allow for interactivity. Used extensively for business products, it is an approach being used more and more for consumer marketing—anything from a simulated in-store experience to actually "using" the product.[17]

Commercialization

Finally, the product is brought to the point of *commercialization*—positioning and launching a new product in full-scale production and sales. Companies proceed very carefully at the commercialization stage because this is the most expensive stage for most new

Commercializing a new french fry: How did Burger King improve its french fries?

FIGURE 10–7

Marketing information and methods used in the new-product process

products, especially consumer products. To minimize the risk of financial failure, some companies use regional rollouts, introducing the product sequentially into geographical areas of the country to allow production levels and marketing activities to build up gradually. Grocery product manufacturers and some telephone service providers are two examples of firms that use this strategy.

Figure 10–7 identifies the purpose of each stage of the new-product process and the kinds of marketing information and methods used. The third column of the figure also suggests information that might help avoid some new-product failures. Although using the new-product process does not guarantee successful products, it does increase a firm's success rate.

Burger King's French Fries: The Complexities of Commercialization

Burger King's "improved french fries" are an example of what can go wrong at the commercialization stage. In the fast-food industry, McDonald's french fries are the gold standard against which all other fries are measured. In 1996, Burger King decided to take on McDonald's fries and spent millions of R&D dollars developing a starch-coated fry designed to retain heat longer and add crunch.

A 100-person team set to work and developed the starch-coated fry that beat McDonald's fries in taste tests, 57 percent to 35 percent, with 8 percent no opinion. After "certifrying" 300,000 managers and employees on the new frying procedures, the fries were launched in early 1998 with a US$70 million marketing budget. The launch turned to disaster. The reason: The new fry proved too complicated to get right day after day in Burger King restaurants, except under ideal conditions.[18]

STAGE OF PROCESS	PURPOSE OF STAGE	MARKETING INFORMATION AND METHODS USED
New-product strategy development	Identify new-product niches to reach in light of company objectives	Company objectives; assessment of firm's current strengths and weaknesses in terms that include market and product
Idea generation	Develop concepts for possible products	Ideas from employees and co-workers, consumers, R&D, and competitors; brainstorming and focus groups
Screening and evaluation	Separate good product ideas from bad ones inexpensively	Internal evaluation of technical requirements, concept tests
Business analysis	Identify the product's features and its marketing strategy, and make financial projections	Product's key features, anticipated marketing mix strategy; economic, marketing, production, legal, and profitability analyses
Development	Create the prototype product, and test it in the laboratory and on consumers	Laboratory and consumer tests on product prototypes
Market testing	Test product and marketing strategy in the marketplace on a limited scale	Test marketing in defined areas
Commercialization	Position and offer product in the marketplace	Perceptual maps, product positioning, regional rollouts

By summer 2000, Burger King realized something had to be done. Solution: Launch a "new," coated fry in early 2001 — not requiring "seven audible crunches." A commercialization stage success? Have you tasted them? If you have, you be the judge.

The Risks and Uncertainties of the Commercialization Stage   As the Burger King french fries show, the job is far from over when the new product gets to the commercialization stage. If the firm moves quickly, sometimes a potential commercialization stage disaster can be avoided, as with Coca-Cola's decision to reintroduce old Coke as Coca-Cola Classic three months after New Coke was launched in 1985. The hundreds of dot-com failures in 2000 and 2001 show the difficulty of launching successful new products and services in spite of brilliant technologies.

Speed as a Factor in New-Product Success   In recent years, companies have discovered that speed, or time to market (TtM), is often vital in introducing a new product. Recent studies have shown that high-tech products coming to market on time are far more profitable than those arriving late. So some companies—such as Sony, Honda, AT&T, and Hewlett-Packard—have overlapped the sequence of stages described in this chapter. With this approach, termed parallel development, cross-functional team members who carry out the simultaneous development of both the product and the production process stay with the product from conception to production. This has allowed Hewlett-Packard to reduce the development time for computer printers from 54 months to 22.

Concept Check

1. Describe the business analysis stage of the new-product process.

2. What is a test market?

3. What is commercialization of a new product?

NEW PRODUCTS AND WHY THEY SUCCEED OR FAIL

New products are the lifeblood of a company and keep it growing, but the financial risks can be large. Before discussing how new products reach the market, we'll begin by looking at *what* a new product is.

What Is a New Product?

The term *new* is difficult to define. Is Sony's PlayStation 2 new when there was a PlayStation 1? Is Microsoft's Xbox *new* when Microsoft wasn't previously a video-console manufacturer? What does *new* mean for new-product marketing?

The answer is, it depends. New can refer to a product being *functionally* different from existing products. Industry Canada, the federal government's department that regulates business practices, has determined that a product can be called "new" for up to 12 months. Overlapping with these views is the company idea that a new product is simply anything different. That difference could be as little as modifying the Gillette Mach3 Turbo razor to become the Gillette Venus Razor for Women or as significant as introducing a truly revolutionary product like the first Apple computer in 1976.

Once again, marketing's focus is on the customer: Newness from the point of view of consumers is what counts most. Marketers often classify new products according to the degree of learning required by a consumer in order to use the product properly. Figure 10–8 summarizes the three categories described below.

*As you read the discussion about what **new** means in new-product development, think about how it affects the marketing strategies of Sony and Microsoft in their **new** video-game console launches.*

With *continuous innovation*, no new behaviours must be learned to use these products. In marketing its latest wireless phone, Samsung communicates the message that its stylish cellphone with several functions is easy to use. Clearly, Samsung is marketing a user-friendly cellphone, but it is a continuous innovation *not* requiring new learned behaviours. Under these conditions, the beauty of this innovation is that effective marketing simply depends on generating awareness and having strong distribution in appropriate outlets, not completely reeducating customers.

With *dynamically continuous innovation*, only minor changes in behaviour are required to use these new products. An example is built-in, fold-down child seats such as those available in Chrysler minivans. Built-in car seats for children require only minor education and changes in behaviour, so the marketing strategy is to educate prospective buyers on their benefits, advantages, and proper use.

A *discontinuous innovation* involves making the consumer learn entirely new behaviours or consumption patterns in order to use the product. Handheld personal digital assistants (PDAs), such as those marketed by 3Com® under the Palm brand, require the user to learn

FIGURE 10-8

Product "newness," as defined by the degree of consumer learning needed to use the product

	LOW Degree of New Consumer Learning Needed HIGH		
BASIS OF COMPARISON	**CONTINUOUS INNOVATION**	**DYNAMICALLY CONTINUOUS INNOVATION**	**DISCONTINUOUS INNOVATION**
Definition	Requires no new learning by consumers	Changes consumer's normal routine but does not require totally new learning	Requires new learning and consumption patterns by consumers
Examples	New improved shaver or detergent	Electric toothbrush, compact disc player, and digital cameras	Personal digital assistants (PDAs), voice recognition software
Marketing emphasis	Gain consumer awareness and wide distribution	Advertise points of difference and benefits to consumers	Educate consumers through product trial and personal selling

a special Graffiti alphabet to enter text when using a stylus—a new experience and skill set for most people. After decades of research, IBM introduced its ViaVoice speech recognition software. To use ViaVoice, you speak into a microphone connected to your computer to open programs such as Microsoft Word and watch your words appear on the screen. The risk that IBM faced in introducing this discontinuous innovation was that consumers had to learn new behaviours in producing their word-processed memos and reports. Marketing efforts for discontinuous innovations involve not only gaining initial consumer awareness but also educating consumers on both the benefits and proper use of the innovative product, activities that can cost millions of dollars.

Why Products Succeed or Fail

We all know giant product successes—such as Microsoft's Hotmail service, Swatch watches, or Disney World. Yet the thousands of failures every year that slide quietly into oblivion cost Canadian businesses billions of dollars. Recent research suggests that it takes about 3,000 raw unwritten ideas to produce a single commercially successful new product.[19] To learn marketing lessons and convert potential failures to successes, we can analyze why new products fail and then study several failures in detail. As we go through the new-product process later in the chapter, we can identify ways such failures might have been avoided—admitting that hindsight is clearer than foresight.

Marketing Reasons for New-Product Failures   Both marketing and nonmarketing factors contribute to new-product failures. Using the research results from several studies[20] on new-product success and failure and also those described in the Marketing NewsNet on the next page, we can identify critical marketing factors that often spell failure for new-product launches:

1. *Insignificant point of difference.* Shown as the most important factor in the Marketing NewsNet, a distinctive point of difference is essential for a new product to defeat competitive ones—through having superior characteristics that deliver unique benefits to the user. In the mid-1990s, General Mills introduced Fingos, a sweetened cereal flake about the size of a corn chip. Consumers were supposed to snack on them dry, but they didn't.[21] The point of difference was not important enough to get consumers to give up eating competing snacks such as popcorn, potato chips, or Cheerios from the box late at night.

2. *Incomplete market and product definition before product development starts.* Ideally, a new product needs a precise protocol, a statement that, before product development begins, identifies a well-defined target market; specific customers' needs, wants, and preferences; and what the product will be and do. Without this protocol, a lot of money can be used up as research and development (R&D) tries to design a vague product for a phantom market. Apple Computer's hand-sized Newton MessagePad personal digital assistant (PDA) that intended to help keep the user organized fizzled badly because no clear protocol existed and users found it too complicated to use. As described in the Marketing NewsNet "When Less Is More" on page 237, sometimes large markets can be served by taking features out of a product and actually making it simpler.

3. *Too little market attractiveness.* Market attractiveness refers to the ideal situation every new-product manager looks for: a large target market with high growth and real buyer need. But often, when looking for ideal market niches, the target market is too small and competitive to warrant the R&D, production, and marketing expenses necessary to reach it. In the early 1990s, Kodak discontinued its Ultralife lithium battery with its 10-year shelf life, although the battery was designed to last twice as long as an alkaline battery. The problem was the product was only available in the 9-volt size, which accounted for less than 10 percent of the batteries sold in North America.

4. *Poor execution of the marketing mix: name and package (product), price, promotion, distribution (place).* Coca-Cola thought its Minute Maid Squeeze-Fresh frozen orange juice concentrate in a squeeze bottle was a hit. The idea was that consumers could make one glass of juice at a time, and the concentrate stayed fresh in the refrigerator for over a month. After two test markets, the product was finished. Consumers loved the idea, but the product was messy to use, and the advertising and packaging didn't educate them effectively on how much concentrate to mix.

5. *Poor product quality or insensitivity to customer needs on critical factors.* Overlapping somewhat with point 1, this factor stresses that problems on one or two critical factors can kill a product, even though the general quality is high. For example, the Japanese, like the British, drive on the left side of the road. Until 1996, North American carmakers sent Japan few right-drive cars—unlike German carmakers who exported right-drive models in a number of their brands.[22]

6. *Bad timing.* The product is introduced too soon, too late, or at a time when consumer tastes are shifting dramatically. Bad timing gives new-product managers nightmares. In March 2001, Boeing announced it would start multibillion-dollar development of its Sonic Cruiser, designed to cross oceans at almost the speed of sound and seat over 400 passengers. But the tragic attacks of September 11, 2001, caused such declines in air

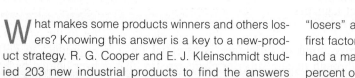

MARKETING NEWSNET
WHAT SEPARATES NEW-PRODUCT WINNERS FROM LOSERS

What makes some products winners and others losers? Knowing this answer is a key to a new-product strategy. R. G. Cooper and E. J. Kleinschmidt studied 203 new industrial products to find the answers shown below.

The researchers defined the "product success rate" of new products as the percentage of products that reached the company's own profitability criteria. Product "winners" are the best 20 percent of performers and

"losers" are the worst 20 percent. For example, for the first factor in the table below, 98 percent of the winners had a major point of difference compared with only 18 percent of the losers.

The table below includes mainly the marketing factors identified by the researchers. Most of these marketing factors tie directly to the reasons cited in the text for new-product failures that are taken from a number of research studies.

FACTOR AFFECTING PRODUCT SUCCESS RATE	PRODUCT "WINNERS" (BEST 20%)		PRODUCT "LOSERS" (WORST 20%)		% DIFFERENCE (WINNERS – LOSERS)
• Point of difference, or uniquely superior product	98%	–	18%	=	80%
• Well-defined product before actual development starts	85	–	26	=	59
• Synergy, or fit, with marketing mix activities	71	–	31	=	40
• Quality of execution of marketing mix activities	71	–	32	=	39
• Market attractiveness, ones with large markets, high growth	74	–	43	=	31

travel that airlines were no longer able to afford new, expensive aircraft. By late 2002, the Sonic Cruiser was shelved, unlikely to emerge for years to come.[23]

7. *No economical access to buyers.* Grocery products provide an example. Today's mega-supermarkets carry 30,000 different SKUs. With about 34 new food products introduced each day, the fight for exposure is tremendous in terms of costs for advertising, distribution, and shelf space.[24] Because shelf space is judged in terms of sales per square foot, Thirsty Dog! (a zesty beef-flavoured, vitamin-enriched, mineral-loaded, lightly carbonated bottled water for your dog) must displace an existing product on the supermarket shelves, a difficult task with the exact measures of sales per square foot these stores use.

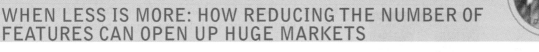

MARKETING NEWSNET

WHEN LESS IS MORE: HOW REDUCING THE NUMBER OF FEATURES CAN OPEN UP HUGE MARKETS

New products! To invent them, the natural thing is to add more features, new technologies, more glitz. Many new-product successes do just that.

But huge new markets can open up by doing the reverse: Taking features away and simplifying the product. Here are some less-is-more new-product breakthroughs that revolutionized national or global markets:

1. Canon's tabletop copiers. Canon found it couldn't sell its little copiers to big companies, which were happy with their large Xerox machines. So Canon sold its little machines by the zillions to little companies with limited copying needs.

2. Palm Computing's PalmPilot PDA. and Apple Computer's Newton MessagePad personal digital assistant (PDA) seemed like a great idea, but users found them too complicated. Enter: PalmPilot inventors Donna Dubinsky and Jeff Hawkins who deleted features to achieve the market breakthrough.

3. Intuit's QuickBooks accounting software. Competitors offered complex accounting software containing every feature professional accountants might possibly want. Intuit introduced QuickBooks, a smaller, cheaper program with less functionality that won 70 percent of the huge market for small-business accounting software within two years.

4. Swatch watches. In 1983, a slim plastic watch with only 51 components appeared on the global market. That simplicity—plus top quality, affordable price, and creative designs—is the reason that by today more than 250 million Swatch watches have been sold.

Sometimes much less is much, much more!

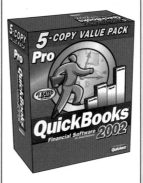

FIGURE 10-9
Why did these two new
products fail?

New products often fail because of one or a combination of seven reasons. Look at the two products described below, and try to identify which reason explains why they failed in the marketplace.

- Kimberly Clark's Avert Virucidal tissues that contained vitamin C derivatives scientifically designed to kill cold and flu germs when users used them.
- OUT! International's Hey! There's A Monster In My Room spray that was designed to rid scary creatures from kids' rooms and had a bubble-gum fragrance.

Compare your insights with those in the text.

A Look at Some Failures

Before reading further and trying to remember a lesson from Chapter 1, study the two product failures described in Figure 10–9. Then try to identify which of the seven reasons listed earlier in the text is the most likely explanation for their failure.

Kimberly Clark's Avert Virucidal tissues lasted 10 months in test market in upstate New York before being pulled from the shelves. People didn't believe the claims and were frightened by the "-cidal" in the name—which they connected to terms like *suicidal* and *homicidal*. So the tissue probably failed because of a bad name and not having a clear point of difference and hence, bad marketing mix execution—probably reasons 1 and 4 in the list in the text.

OUT! International's Hey! There's A Monster In My Room spray was creative and cute when introduced in 1993. But the name probably kept the kids awake at night more than their fear of the monsters because it suggested the monster was still hiding in the room. Question: Wouldn't calling it the Monster-Buster Spray—the secondary name shown at the bottom of the package—have licked the name problem? It looks like the spray was never really defined well in a protocol (reason 2) and definitely had poor name execution (reason 4). Another problem: It could be that there was insufficient market demand or need for the product (reason 3).

OUT! International changed the name to Monster B-Gone!, then discontinued the product and sold their stock to Family Times. The name then changed to Boo Buster, and it is still listed on the website (www.familytimestore.com/monstersspray.cfm).[25]

Simple marketing research should have revealed the problems. Developing successful new products involves having a product that really meets a need and has significant points of difference over competitive products. The likelihood of success is improved by paying attention to the early steps of the new-product process described earlier in this chapter.

Concept
Check

1. Describe the three categories of innovations that marketers use to classify new products.

2. Explain how "insignificant point of difference" can be a reason for new-product failure.

SUMMARY

1 A product is a good, service, or idea consisting of a bundle of tangible and intangible features that satisfies consumers and is received in exchange for money or some other unit of value. A company's product decisions involve the product item, product line, and range of its product mix.

2 Products have three distinct layers—core, actual, and augmented—and they are important for creating a competitive advantage, as well as for positioning the product in consumers' minds. This is known as the total product concept.

3 Products can be classified by user and tangibility. By user, the major distinctions are consumer or business goods or services. By degree of tangibility, products divide into nondurable goods, durable goods, and services. Services have four unique elements: intangibility, inconsistency, inseparability, and inventory.

4 Consumer goods consist of convenience, shopping, specialty, and unsought products. Business goods are products purchased by organizations, that are used for resale, as inputs for further production or in the operation of the organization. Services can be classified according to whether they are provided by people or equipment.

5 In terms of its effect on a consumer's use of a product, a discontinuous innovation represents the greatest change and a continuous innovation the least. A dynamically continuous innovation is disruptive but not totally new.

6 The failure of a new product is usually attributable to one of seven marketing reasons: insignificant point of difference, incomplete market and product definition before product development begins, too little market attractiveness, poor execution of the marketing mix, poor product quality on critical factors, bad timing, and no economical access to buyers.

7 The new-product process consists of seven stages. Objectives for new products are determined in the first stage, new-product strategy development; this is followed by idea generation, screening and evaluation, business analysis, development, market testing, and commercialization.

8 Ideas for new products come from several sources, including consumers, suppliers, employees, R&D laboratories, and competitors.

9 Screening and evaluation can be done internally or externally.

10 Business analysis involves defining the features of the new product, a marketing strategy to introduce it, and a financial forecast.

11 Development involves not only producing a prototype product but also testing it in the lab and on consumers to see that it meets the standards set for it.

12 In market testing new products, companies often rely on market tests to see that consumers will actually buy the product when it's offered for sale and that other marketing mix factors are working. Products surviving this stage are commercialized—taken to market.

KEY TERMS AND CONCEPTS

business goods p. 220
consumer goods p. 220
idle production capacity p. 223
new-product process p. 225
product p. 218
product line p. 219
product mix p. 220
service continuum p.222

QUESTIONS: APPLYING MARKETING CONCEPTS AND PERSPECTIVES

1 Products can be classified as either consumer or business goods. How would you classify the following products: *(a)* Johnson's baby shampoo, *(b)* a Black & Decker cordless drill, and *(c)* an airplane?

2 Are products such as Nature Valley Granola bars and Eddie Bauer hiking boots convenience, shopping, specialty, or unsought goods?

3 Based on your answer to problem 2, how would the marketing actions differ for each product and the classification to which you assigned it?

4 In terms of the behavioural effect on consumers, how would a portable PC, such as a Macintosh PowerBook or an IBM ThinkPad, be classified? In light of this classification, what actions would you suggest to the manufacturers of these products to increase their sales in the market?

5 What methods would you suggest to assess the potential commercial success for the following new products: *(a)* a new flavour of barbeque sauce, *(b)* a high-definition television system, and *(c)* a new children's toy on which the company holds a patent?

6 Concept testing is an important step in the new-product process. Outline the concept tests for *(a)* an electrically powered car and *(b)* e-ticketing and e-check-in at airports. What are the differences in developing concept tests for products as opposed to services?

DISCUSSION FORUM

You and your group of fellow marketing students have been assigned the task of working with a consumer packaged-goods company that continuously generates new household cleaning and maintenance products, although the firm is only able to successfully launch a few new products into the commercial market each year. The firm's challenge is to identify how to produce more winners from its inventions and how to waste less money in research and development. You decide to give the executives a seminar on product strategy to help them understand their challenges and improve their situation. Design the outline of what you will say to them, using these topic headings:

- Existing product mix and product lines
- Classifying products
- Consumer products
- Business products
- Why products succeed or fail
- A step-by-step process for developing successful new products
- Importance of market research and test marketing

Suggest what visuals and charts you will use in your explanations to them, and make sure that your message is very targeted toward their company.

INTERNET EXERCISE

Jalapeño soda? Aerosol mustard? Fingos? These are just three of the more than 70,000 products (both successes and failures) on the shelves of the NewProductWorks Showcase in Ann Arbor, Michigan. Visit its new website (www.newproductworks.com). Study the "Hits & Misses" categories such as "We Expect Them to Be Successes," which are those that probably will be commercial successes; "Jury Is Out," products whose future is in doubt; "Failures," which are recent products that have failed miserably; and "Favorite Failures," which are those that cause people to ask "What were they thinking?" Pick two of the

www.mcgrawhill.ca/college/thecore

failed products and try to identify the reasons discussed earlier in the chapter that may have led to their failure. Contrast these failed products with those that are deemed successes to learn why they became "sure-fire winners."

VIDEO CASE 10

PALM INC.: DEVELOPING COMPETITIVE NEW PRODUCTS

Developing new products often requires a complicated and challenging sequence of activities. "It's not as simple as taking what the customer wants and creating a product," says Joe Sipher, director of wireless products at Palm Inc. "If we did that, we would have ended up with something like Apple Computer's Newton, which was a failure because it incorporated too many features into the product." While this perspective may have seemed counterintuitive, it proved highly successful for Palm Inc., the pioneer in the development of the handheld computers often called personal digital assistants (PDAs). With advances in technology and the convergence of computing and communication devices, Palm's new products, like those in its Tungsten series, have much more capability than their predecessors. We are now seeing the development of a whole new generation of

software aimed at making PDAs compatible with commonly used business software.

The Treo line of smartphones (combined cellphone and PDA) now offers wireless phone service, e-mail, web and digital camera, electronic organizer capability, and more—surpassing the capability of the visionary Apple device—enough to make Joe Sipher's earlier comments seem way off track.

THE HISTORY

Jeff Hawkins and Donna Dubinsky, the inventors of the first Palm products, started out developing software for other PDA manufacturers in the spring of 1994. Dubinsky recalls, "Most people thought a PDA should be a smaller version of a laptop computer." But industry sales were too low to keep the company running. "The reasons why early handheld computers failed were because they had too many features, making them too big, too slow, too heavy, and too expensive," explains Andrea Butter, vice president of marketing. Palm managers saw a dismal future in being the leading software applications provider for a nonexistent market. They were still optimistic, though, as Butter states, "We felt we knew what customers wanted to do in handheld computing and one day an investor challenged us and said, 'If you know how to do it, why don't you do it?'" So Palm accepted the challenge and became the leader in handheld computers. Now the market is exploding. Can Palm maintain its status as the leader? Time, technology, competition, and the marketplace's acceptance of Palm's new products and Palm's marketing efforts will determine that.

THE POSITIONING DILEMMA

How do you define this type of product? This has always been a challenge. These products have been referred to as information appliances, handheld computers, personal information managers, and personal digital assistants. They typically include a pen or stylus and handwriting recognition software to allow users to store addresses and telephone numbers, enter appointments on a calendar, make notes and to-do lists, and interface with personal computers to transfer e-mail and other data. Now with competition from multifunctional devices such as competitor Research In Motion's Blackberry handheld devices (shown here), which began life as sophisticated pagers, the challenge is not getting any easier. Most handheld devices today are accompanied by a full line of accessories including such things as tiny keyboards. This is a long way from Hawkins's and Dubinsky's view of PDAs as just digital replacements for paper-based systems such as DayTimers and other agenda planners.

PALM INC.'S NEW PRODUCT PROCESS

Hawkins's research and development consisted of carrying a rectangular block of wood in his shirt pocket with "function buttons" glued to it. When people asked him if he was free for lunch, he would take out his "connected organizer," tap on a button, and observe their reactions. Hawkins tried several

variations before settling on a final design: the PalmPilot had only four function buttons (calendar, addresses and phone numbers, to-do lists, and memos) because those were the most frequently used applications. Marketing research showed that 90 percent of PDA users also used personal computers, sparking the idea to build PC-connectivity into the PalmPilot; the PDA was sold only in computer and office supply stores, because Palm Inc. felt that the salespeople there had greater skills in selling technology-based products.

The original PalmPilot was launched in 1996 at Demo '96, a trade show attended by technology opinion leaders. The PalmPilot was the media darling of the show, and sales skyrocketed. Now, as new Palm models are introduced, each continues with the design philosophy of the original PalmPilot: They must be simple, small, and connected. Obviously "simple" is a concept in itself that is evolving; "simple" in 1996 has a different meaning from "simple" today.

COMPETITION AND THE PDA MARKET

By 1997, hardware manufacturers such as Hewlett-Packard, Casio, and Philips had partnered with Microsoft to create products that had functions similar to Palm and offered simplified versions of Microsoft's popular Word and Excel programs, the familiar Windows-like interface, and Internet searching and paging via a PC-card interface. However, these products were pricey, sluggish, and consumed more power than the Palm products.

Palm also faced competition from Web-based personal information managers (PIMs), which performed identical functions to the PalmPilot. These organizers were stored at the user's Internet service provider and accessed via browsers such as Netscape or Internet Explorer or portals such as Yahoo! or America Online (AOL).

PDA technology has converged with other digital technologies and now offers such things as a wireless modem, a digital camera, and a mobile telephone. This trend has created many new competitors including Research In Motion and mobile telephone manufacturer Nokia; no doubt more are to come in the future.

PALM'S RESPONSE

Palm is responding to changes in the market by developing new products to meet consumers' needs and to compete in a very hot market. Some of their wins have come from making relatively simple product modifications offering easy and inexpensive personalization, including changeable faceplates; sleek, ultra-slim industrial designs; recessed buttons; and rechargeable batteries.

The Palm VII revolutionized the PDA marketplace by targeting the rapidly growing wireless and mobile market, which had an estimated potential of 20 million subscribers in 2002. The unit offered wireless Internet access through the proprietary Palm.Net "web clipping" technology. Ticketmaster, the Weather Channel, USA Today, Yahoo!, and other content partners provided information tailored for the PDA's small screen.

Palm has more than 175,000 third-party software developers. Another strategy Palm is using is to work with these developers to get them to extend the Palm operating system functionality by developing new applications to make its products even more versatile and marketable.

BEHIND THE SCENES

Palm is a very progressive and dynamic company. It was founded in 1992 as Palm Computing Inc., specializing in software for handheld devices produced by other companies. In 1995, it was acquired by US Robotics, a leading computer modem producer. The success of both its software and hardware units attracted a lot of industry attention. 3Com Corporation acquired US Robotics in 1997, and so Palm became a subsidiary of 3Com. 3Com was, and still is, a major player in the enterprise data and voice network market. This combination provided Palm with tremendous resources in research and development, manufacturing, software development, finances, and marketing skills—hard to go wrong with these in place! In 2000, Palm became an independent, publicly traded company called Palm Inc.

GETTING IT RIGHT

In 2002, the number of units worldwide powered by Palm software hit 20 million, prompting another change. The software side of the business had grown to a point that the decision was made to spin it off as an independent company. Later that year, Palm reported that sales of its own handheld units had surpassed 20 million units. In early 2003, Palm acquired a competitor, Handspring, Inc., and the combined company is now called palmOne. So far, palmOne's new products, marketed under its sub-brands ZireTM, TungstenTM, and TreoTM, are meeting with huge success. palmOne will never have the luxury of being able to stay with the same products for long, so new product development is vital to its future. Check out the company website (www.palmone.com) for details on the company's latest product offerings.

Questions

1 Which of the steps in the new product process discussed in Chapter 10 did Palm Computing use to develop the PalmPilot? What activities did Palm Computing undertake in each step?

2 What are the characteristics of the target market for PDAs?

3 What kinds of learning or behavioural changes were required by consumers who purchased PDAs?

4 What are the key points of difference of the Palm devices when compared to substitute products (check websites for current information)?

5 Choose a new unit from palmOne and rate its reason for success on the following aspects: (1) significant points of difference, (2) size of market, (3) product quality, (4) market timing, and (5) access to consumer.

Managing Products, Services, and Brands

AFTER READING THIS CHAPTER YOU SHOULD BE ABLE TO:

- Explain the product life cycle and how to manage it, and how to relate a marketing strategy to each of its stages.

- Recognize how the product life cycle is different for different products, and understand the implications of this for marketing decisions.

- Comprehend the process consumers go through in adopting products.

- Understand the different approaches required for managing services.

- Explain the purpose of branding, and why different branding strategies are employed by companies.

- Describe elements of brand personality and brand equity and the criteria for a good brand name.

- Understand the role of packaging and labelling in the marketing of a product.

"RUN WITH THE LITTLE GUY ... CREATE SOME CHANGE."[1]

In the fiercely competitive world of consumer beverages, how can a line of soft drinks succeed when it is not sold in major supermarkets and venues? Well, Jones Soda does just that, and does it very well; just ask Peter van Stolk, the founder and president. He has gone from being a beverage distributor—selling fresh juices in Western Canada—to being the CEO of a $20-million-plus company with a huge following.

Unconventional, cultish, fresh—and distinctly different from traditional beverages such as Coke and Pepsi—are some reasons Jones Soda is a key player in the alternative beverages market. They knew that, to succeed, they had to be different, and different they are! Their beverages have personality, and they get the consumer involved. Having a party? Order your favourite Jones flavour with your picture on the label. Going shopping for Jones? Skip the big grocery stores and head for a skate and snowboard shop or a tattoo parlour.

When van Stolk first charged into the beverage world, his psychiatrist father wanted him to go to university, but Peter decided to prove that he could do his own thing, so he began selling Just Pik't orange juice in Calgary. He then distributed drinks such as Arizona Iced Tea and Thomas Kemper Root Beer. In 1995, he decided he did not want to sell other peoples' beverages, he wanted to create his own. His first brand, WAZU Natural Spring Water, was born in 1995, and Jones was launched with six flavours in 1996. Some of his other milestones include bringing out an energy drink—WhoopAss—in 2000, and creating Jones Juice, with six flavours, in 2001. He originally located the company in Vancouver, but the financial climate in the U.S. seemed more friendly to him, and in May 2000 the company relocated to Seattle.

What keeps Jones so popular? Different strategies, distinctive marketing, and a growing collection of loyal customers; van Stolk knew from the beginning that, to

WHERE IN THE MARKETING PROCESS ARE WE GOING IN THIS CHAPTER?

Chapter 11 builds on the product concepts introduced in Chapter 10 and discusses managing products, services, and brands. This is again focusing on the product P of the 4Ps that make up the marketing mix.

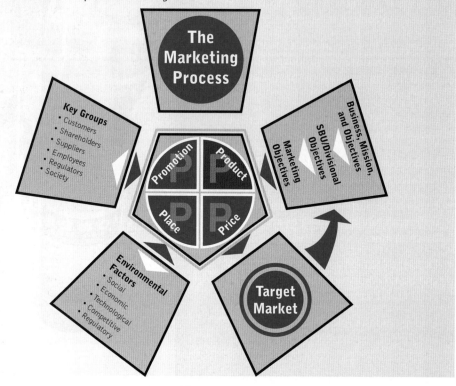

succeed, he had to have a premium product with a twist. He researched the beverage world, with all of its product successes and failures, and determined that he could carve out a niche for Jones. That niche is creating unique flavours and colours of beverages, and marketing them in a way that the large beverage companies would not. Turkey & Gravy soda for Thanksgiving was a risk, but one that paid off well as bottles nearly flew off the shelves. Chocolate Fudge, FuFu Berry, and Bada Bing! may not sound like soft drink names, but for Jones, they are winners.

The distribution process has been termed an "alternative distribution strategy." Jones has its own coolers, placing them in a number of small stores and other places where they find their customers are. They attacked the marketplace by going "up and down the street," locating appropriate stores and creating interest. More recently, they have placed their

Innovative marketing techniques at Jones Soda.

beverages in larger chain stores, such as Starbucks, Safeway, 7-Eleven, and, in the U.S., Barnes and Noble cafes.

Some interesting marketing initiatives have seen Jones in the news. They have two brightly coloured, orange-flame decor RVs that travel across North America, giving out product samples, attending concerts and sports events, and communicating with customers. Their presence at some extreme sports events, such as skateboard championships, and their sponsorship of surfers and skateboarders has given them an image of hip and cool with their target market, 12- to 24-year-olds. At the firm's website, www.jonessoda.com, these aficionados can review movies, rate products, download videos, and send in their picture to try to make the cut on a soda label.

If van Stolk realizes his goal—to reach $100 million in revenues by about 2006—he will still be a little guy in the $12 billion alternative beverage market, but he is a strong and vibrant player, still trendy and appealing to the ever-changing teen market, still edgy and innovative.[2]

THE PRODUCT LIFE CYCLE

product life cycle
Stages a new product goes through in the marketplace: introduction, growth, maturity, and decline

Products, like people, are thought of as having a *life cycle*. The concept of the **product life cycle** describes the stages a new product goes through in the marketplace: introduction, growth, maturity, and decline (see Figure 11-1). There are two curves shown in this figure, total industry sales dollars (total revenues) and total industry profit. By the phrase "total industry," we mean the total dollars for all brands by all firms manufacturing that particular product. One brand or one firm normally cannot alter the shape of the industry curve because it represents the accumulation or trend, over time, of industry sales and profits. In other words, it is the sum of individual life cycles for the various brands. It is quite common at a specific point in time to see different brands at different stages of the overall product life cycle.

The shape of the product life cycle is influenced primarily by things such as consumer demand, competition (size, strength, and number of firms marketing similar products), and other aspects of the external business environment such as economic, legislative and technological factors. Individual firms, however, can and do alter the shape of the life cycle for their brands by adjusting their marketing strategies at each stage of the life cycle.

In Figure 11-2, Part 1 shows the life cycles for several brands of CD players produced by different firms and brought to market at different times using different marketing strategies. Brand A, for example, was the first to market with the first CD player—a new, innovative, and premium-priced product—and there were no competitors initially. Brand B, produced by a competitor, was soon introduced at a lower price and slightly lower quality. Other competitors, seeing the huge demand for CD players, quickly brought their own CD players to market: some (Brands C and D) were look-alikes; some were low-priced, stripped-down economy versions; and others (Brands E and F) were premium-priced, technologically advanced versions.

Part 2 of Figure 11-2 shows the cumulative totals of all brands—in other words, the industry total—in the product life cycle. Because CD players are still being marketed by all of the firms we surveyed, it is likely that no brand has yet reached the decline stage, although demand is starting to slow and level off, as competition from DVD and MP3 players gets stronger and new technologies begin to appear in the marketplace.

So as you read through the following explanations of how the curve changes over the life of the product—and the marketing decisions typically made at each stage—remember that the marketing manager will look at the overall industry curve and take this into consideration when developing marketing strategies for the individual brands.

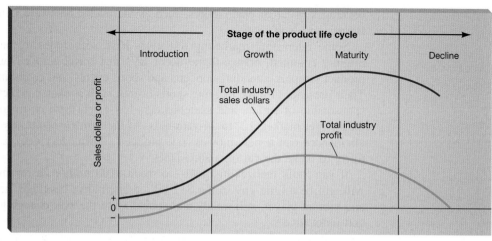

RELATING MARKETING ACTIONS TO THE PRODUCT LIFE CYCLE

GENERAL MARKETING OBJECTIVE	INCREASE AWARENESS	DIFFERENTIATION	BRAND LOYALTY	PRODUCT RATIONALIZATION

MARKETING STRATEGIES

Product	Focus on one product only	Introduce more versions	Ensure full product line	Retain only best sellers
Price	Use skimming or penetration	Build market share	Defend market share	Work with profitable products only
Promotion	Inform, educate	Stress points of difference from competition	Reminder orientation	Use only minimal promotion
Place (distribution)	Use limited distribution	Increase number of outlets	Maximize number of outlets	Reduce outlets

OTHER LIFE CYCLE CONSIDERATIONS

Profit	Minimal, if any	Increasing, reaches maximum	Maximized, levels off	Decreasing
Competition	Few competitors	More enter the market	Many competitors	Reduced—some competitors leave market

Introduction Stage

The introduction stage of the product life cycle occurs when a product is first introduced to its intended target market. During this period, sales grow slowly, and profit is minimal. The lack of profit is often the result of large investment costs in product development, such as the US$1 billion spent by Gillette to develop and launch the MACH3 razor shaving system.[3] The marketing objective for a company at this stage is to create consumer awareness and stimulate trial—that first purchase of a product by a consumer.

Companies often spend heavily on advertising and other promotion tools to build awareness among consumers in the introduction stage. These expenditures are often made to stimulate *primary demand*, or desire for the product class rather than for a specific brand since there are few competitors with the same product.

Other marketing mix variables also are important at this stage. Gaining distribution

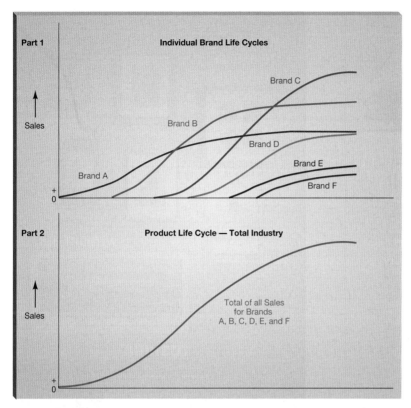

Part 1

Individual Brand Life Cycles

Sales

Brand C

Brand B

Brand D

Brand E

Brand A

Brand F

+
0

Part 2

Product Life Cycle — Total Industry

Sales

Total of all Sales
for Brands
A, B, C, D, E, and F

+
0

can be a challenge because channel members may be hesitant to carry a new product. In this stage a company often restricts the number of variations of the product to ensure control of product quality. For example, Jones Soda began with only six flavours, expanding over time to more than 40 flavours in several different bottle styles. Gillette initially offered only a single version of the MACH3 razor, expanding to several models for both men and women.

During introduction, pricing can be either high or low. A high initial price may be used as part of a *skimming strategy* to help the company recover the costs of development as well as take advantage of the price insensitivity of early buyers. High prices tend to attract competitors eager to enter the market because they see the opportunity for profit. To discourage competitive entry, a company can price low, referred to as *penetration pricing*. This pricing strat-egy helps build unit volume, but a company must closely monitor costs. These and other pricing techniques are covered in Chapter 12.

Several product classes are now in the introductory stage of the product life cycle. These include high-definition television (HDTV) and hybrid (gasoline- and electric-powered) automobiles.

Growth Stage

The second stage of the product life cycle, growth, is characterized by rapid increases in sales. It is in this stage that competitors appear. As more competitors introduce their own products and the product progresses along its life cycle, company attention is focused on creating selective demand, or demand for a specific brand.

The result of more competitors and more aggressive pricing is that profit usually peaks during the growth stage. At this point the emphasis of advertising shifts to stimulating selec-tive demand, in which product benefits are compared with those of competitors' offerings.

Product sales in the growth stage grow at an increasing rate because of new people try-ing or using the product and a growing proportion of *repeat purchasers*—people who tried the product, were satisfied, and bought again. As a product moves through the life cycle, the ratio of repeat to trial purchasers grows. Failure to obtain repeat purchasers usually means an early death for a product. Profits steadily increase and are usually maximized towards the end of this stage.

Changes start to appear in the product during the growth stage. To help differentiate a company's brand from its competitors, an improved version or new features are added to the original design, and product proliferation occurs. For Jones Soda, new flavours and package sizes were added during the growth stage.

In the growth stage it is important to gain as much distribution for the product as possible.

Numerous product classes or industries are in the growth stage of the product life cycle. Examples include DVD players and personal digital assistants (PDAs).

Hybrid automobiles made by Honda are in the introductory stage of the product life cycle. DVD players produced by Toshiba are in the growth stage. Each product and company faces unique challenges based on its product life cycle stage.

Maturity Stage

The third stage, maturity, is generally the longest stage in the product life cycle. Many very well-known products are quite successful at this stage, with high market share and significant sales. For some products, maturity brings a slowing of total industry sales for the product class and a decrease in profitability. Also, weaker competitors begin to leave the market. Most consumers who would buy the product are either repeat purchasers of the item or have tried and abandoned it. Sales increase at a decreasing rate in the maturity stage as fewer new buyers enter the market. Profit declines because there is fierce price competition among many sellers.

Marketing attention in the maturity stage is often directed toward holding market share through further product differentiation and finding new buyers. Gillette, for example, differentiated its MACH3 razor through new product features specifically designed for women and then launched the Gillette Venus Razor for Women just as the MACH3 razor entered its maturity stage. Jones Soda created Jones Juice and WhoopAss, an energy drink, in addition to the firm's continual introduction of new flavours and colours of beverages and use of alternative packaging formats.

Numerous product classes and industries are in the maturity stage of their product life cycle. These include carbonated soft drinks, automobiles, and TVs.

Decline Stage

The decline stage occurs when sales begin to drop. Frequently, a product enters this stage not because of any wrong strategy on the part of the company but because of environmental changes. Technological innovation often comes before the decline stage as newer technologies replace older ones. The word-processing capability of personal computers pushed typewriters into decline. Compact discs did the same to cassette tapes in the pre-recorded music industry. Will Internet technology and e-mail spell doom for fax machines? The accompanying Marketing NewsNet offers one perspective on this question.[4]

A company will follow one of two strategies to handle a declining product: deletion or harvesting.

Deletion   Product *deletion*, or dropping the product from the company's product line, is the most drastic strategy. Because a residual core of consumers still consume or use a product even in the decline stage, product elimination decisions are not taken lightly. For example, Jones Soda's website shows a number of "retired" products—flavours that are no longer in production. Check out their website at www.jonessoda.com and review the current line of flavours; look for the "retired" flavours and suggest why they were discontinued. Gillette sold its stationery products division, which included the Liquid Paper product line and Waterman writing instruments, to Newall Rubbermaid; for Gillette, these represented a declining market and no longer part of its primary market thrust.

Harvesting   A second strategy, *harvesting*, is when a company keeps the product but reduces marketing costs. The product continues to be offered, but salespeople do not spend time in selling nor are advertising dollars spent. The purpose of harvesting is to maintain the ability to meet customer requests. Coca-Cola, for instance, still sells TaB, its first diet cola, to a small group of die-hard fans. According to Coke's CEO, "It shows you care. We want to make sure those who want TaB, get TaB."[5]

Some Dimensions of the Product Life Cycle

Two important aspects of product life cycles are their length and the shape of their curves.

MARKETING NEWSNET

WILL E-MAIL SPELL DOOM FOR THE FAMILIAR FAX?

Technological substitution often causes the decline stage in the product life cycle. Will the Internet and e-mail replace fax machines?

This question has caused heated debates. Even though sales of computers with Internet access are in the growth stage of the product life cycle, fax machine sales continue to grow as well. Industry analysts estimate that there are one billion e-mail mailboxes worldwide. However, the growth of e-mail has not affected faxing because the two technologies do not directly compete for the same messaging applications.

E-mail is used for text messages and faxing is predominately used for communicating formatted documents by business users. Fax usage is expected to increase through 2005, and sales of stand-alone fax machines are expected to increase as well. Internet technology may eventually replace facsimile technology, but not in the immediate future. Are the experts right? Time will tell.

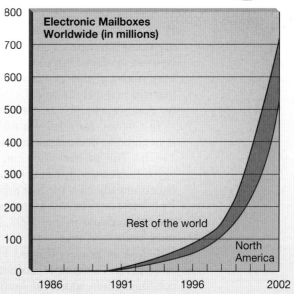

FIGURE 11–3
Different product life cycles

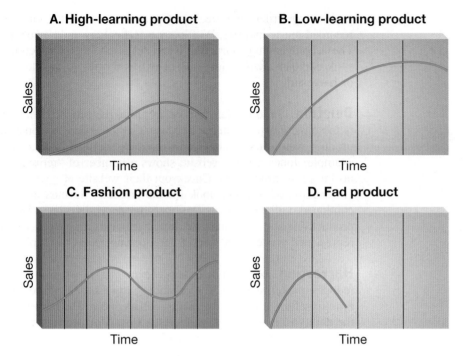

A. High-learning product

B. Low-learning product

C. Fashion product

D. Fad product

Length of the Product Life Cycle There is no exact time that a product takes to move through its life cycle. As a rule, consumer products have shorter life cycles than business products. For example, many new consumer food products such as Frito-Lay's WOW brand potato chips move from the introduction stage to maturity in 18 months. The availability of mass communication vehicles—such as television and the Internet—informs consumers faster and shortens life cycles. Also, technological change tends to shorten product life cycles as new product innovation replaces existing products. Video game consoles and software move from the introduction stage to the maturity stage in five years.

Shape of the Product Life Cycle The product life-cycle curve shown in Figure 11–1 is the *generalized life cycle*, but not all products have the same shape to their curve. In fact, there are several different life-cycle curves, each type suggesting different marketing strategies. Figure 11–3 shows the shape of life-cycle curves for four different types of products: high-learning, low-learning, fashion, and fad products.

A *high-learning product* is one for which significant education of the customer is required and there is an extended introductory period (Figure 11–3A). Convection ovens, for example, required a consumer to learn a new way of cooking and alter familiar recipes.

In contrast, for a *low-learning product* sales begin immediately because little learning is required by the consumer, and the benefits of purchase are readily understood (Figure 11–3B). This product often can be easily imitated by competitors, so the marketing strategy is to broaden distribution quickly. In this way, as competitors rapidly enter, most retail outlets already have the first product. It is also important to have the manufacturing capacity to meet demand. An example of a successful low-learning product is Gillette's MACH3 razor. Introduced in mid-1998, MACH3 recorded $1 billion in sales in the brief span of three years.[6]

A *fashion product* (Figure 11–3C), such as hemline lengths on skirts or lapel widths on jackets, is introduced, declines, and then seems to return. Life cycles for fashion products most often appear in women's and men's clothing styles. The length of the cycles may be years or decades.

A *fad* experiences rapid sales on introduction and then an equally rapid decline (Figure 11–3D). These products are novelties and have a short life cycle. They include car tattoos—described as the first removable and reusable graphics for automobiles—vinyl dresses, fleece bikinis, and an AstroTurf miniskirt made by Thump, Inc., a U.S. clothing company.[7]

The Life Cycle and Consumers   The life cycle of a product depends on sales to consumers. Not all consumers rush to buy a product in the introductory stage, and the shapes of the life-cycle curves indicate that most sales occur after the product has been on the market for some time. In essence, a product diffuses, or spreads, through the population, a concept called the *diffusion of innovation*.[8]

Some people are attracted to a product early, whereas others buy it only after they see their friends with the item. Figure 11–4 shows the consumer population divided into five categories of product adopters based on when they adopt, or choose to buy, a new product. Brief profiles accompany each category. For any product to be successful, it must be purchased by innovators and early adopters. This is why manufacturers of new pharmaceuticals try to gain adoption by leading hospitals, clinics, and physicians that are widely respected in the medical field. Once accepted by innovators and early adopters, the adoption of new products moves on to the early majority, late majority, and laggard categories.

Several factors affect whether a consumer will adopt a new product or not. Common reasons for resisting a product in the introduction stage are usage barriers (the product is not compatible with existing habits), value barriers (the product provides no incentive to change), risk barriers (physical, financial, economic, or social), and psychological barriers (cultural differences or image).[9]

Companies attempt to overcome these barriers in numerous ways. They provide warranties, money-back guarantees, extensive usage instructions, demonstrations, and free samples to stimulate initial trial of new products. For example, software developers offer demonstrations downloaded from the Internet. Procter & Gamble's Cover Girl cosmetic line allows consumers to get a beauty consultation online and to create a new look for

FIGURE 11–4

Five categories and profiles
of product adopters

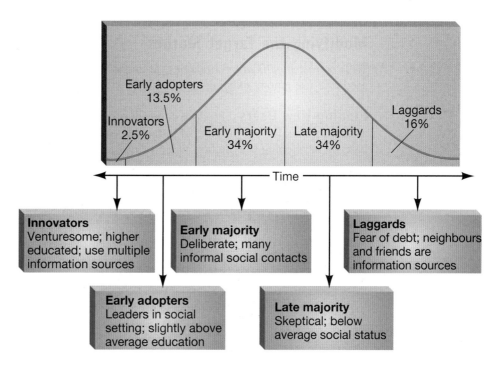

each season with the latest products—check them out at www.covergirl.com.[10] Free samples are one of the most popular means to gain consumer trial. In fact, 71 percent of consumers consider a sample to be the best way to evaluate a new product.[11]

1. Advertising plays a major role in the _____ stage of the product life cycle, and _____ plays a major role in maturity.

2. How do high-learning and low-learning products differ?

MANAGING THE PRODUCT LIFE CYCLE

An important task for a firm is to manage its products through the successive stages of their life cycles. Marketers rely on three ways to manage a product through its life cycle: modifying the product, modifying the target market, and repositioning the product.

Modifying the Product

Product modification involves altering a product's characteristic, such as its quality, performance, or appearance, to try to increase and extend the product's sales. Wrinkle-free cotton slacks sold by Levi Strauss and Haggar revitalized sales of men's casual pants and now account for 60 percent of the men's cotton pants product class sales.[12]

New features or packages can be used to change a product's characteristics and give the sense of a revised product. Procter & Gamble revamped Pantene shampoo and conditioner with a new vitamin formula and relaunched the brand with a multimillion-dollar advertising and promotion campaign. The result? Pantene, a brand first introduced in the 1940s, became the top-selling shampoo and conditioner in North America in an industry with more than 1,000 competitors.[13]

Modifying the Target Market

With *market modification* strategies, a company tries to find new customers, increase a product's use among existing customers, or create new use situations.

Finding New Users Produce companies have begun marketing and packaging prunes as dried plums for the purpose of attracting younger buyers. Sony has expanded its user base by developing PlayStation video games for children under 13 years old.

Increasing Use Promoting more frequent usage has been a strategy of Campbell Soup Company. Because soup consumption rises in the winter and declines during the summer, the company now advertises more heavily in warm months to encourage consumers to think of soup as more than a cold-weather food. Similarly, orange juice producers advocate drinking orange juice throughout the day rather than for breakfast only.

Creating New Use Situations Finding new uses for an existing product has been the strategy behind Woolite, a laundry soap. Originally intended for the hand washing of woollen material, Woolite now promotes itself for use with all fine clothing items. Arm & Hammer Baking Soda is a 155-year-old brand that continues to find new uses,

Arm & Hammer uses different packaging to highlight the variety of uses for its baking soda.

from household and personal care to environmental clean-up. It is recommended for use in swimming pools, to disinfect and to keep the water clear; at laundry time, it is suggested for freshening sheets and towels. Arm & Hammer has developed many new uses for an old product, and not just for consumer use—the product is used extensively in businesses. And it is still used for baking![14]

Repositioning the Product

Often a company decides to reposition its product or product line in an attempt to increase sales. *Product repositioning* is changing the place a product occupies in a consumer's mind relative to competitive products. A firm can reposition a product by changing one or more of the four marketing mix elements. Four factors that trigger a repositioning action are discussed next.

Reacting to a Competitor's Position   One reason to reposition a product is because a competitor's entrenched position is negatively affecting sales and market share. Procter & Gamble repositioned its Ivory soap bar in response to the success of Lever 2000, sold by Lever Brothers. Lever 2000, a bar soap that moisturizes, deodorizes, and kills bacteria, became a threat to P&G's dominance of the bar soap market. P&G responded with its own triple-threat soap called New Ivory Ultra Safe Skin Care Soap.

Reaching a New Market   When Unilever introduced iced tea in Britain in the mid-1990s, sales were disappointing. British consumers viewed it as leftover hot tea, not suitable for drinking. The company made its tea carbonated and repositioned it as a cold soft drink to compete as a carbonated beverage and sales improved. New Balance, Inc., has repositioned its athletic shoes for aging baby boomers. Instead of competing head-on against Nike, Reebok, and Fila, the company offers an expansive range of widths tailored for older consumers and networks with podiatrists who use the wide models to insert foot-support devices.

ETHICS AND SOCIAL RESPONSIBILITY ALERT

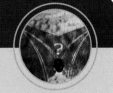

CONSUMER ECONOMICS OF DOWNSIZING: GET LESS, PAY MORE

For more than 30 years, Starkist put 185 grams of tuna into its regular-sized can. Today, Starkist puts 175 grams of tuna into its can, but charges the same price. Frito-Lay (Doritos and Lay's snack chips), Procter & Gamble (Pampers disposable diapers), Nestlé (bottled water distributor) have whittled away at package contents 5 to 10 percent while maintaining their products' package size, dimensions, and prices. Kimberly-Clark cut its retail price on its jumbo pack of Huggies diapers but also reduced the number of diapers per pack from 48 to 42.

Consumer advocates charge that downsizing the content of packages while maintaining prices is a subtle and unannounced way of taking advantage of consumer buying habits. They also say downsizing is a price increase in disguise and deceptive, but legal. Manufacturers argue that this practice is a way of keeping prices from rising beyond psychological barriers for their products.

Is downsizing an unethical practice if manufacturers do not inform consumers that the package contents are less than they were previously?

Catching a Rising Trend Changing consumer trends can also lead to repositioning. Consumer interest in "functional foods" is an example. These foods offer health and dietary benefits beyond nutrition. A number of products have taken advantage of this trend. Quaker Oats now makes a government-approved claim that oatmeal, as part of a low saturated fat, low cholesterol diet, may reduce the risk of heart disease. Calcium-enriched products, such as Nutri-Grain bars and Uncle Ben's Calcium Plus rice, emphasize healthy bone structure for children and adults. Marketers of juices, such as V-8 and Tropicana, focus on the natural health benefits of their product.

Changing the Value Offered In repositioning a product, a company can decide to change the value it offers buyers and trade up or down. *Trading up* involves adding value to the product (or line) through additional features or higher-quality materials. Michelin and Goodyear have done this with a "run-flat" tire that can travel up to 70 kilometres after suffering total air loss.

Trading down involves reducing the number of features, quality, or price. For example, airlines have added more seats, thus reducing leg room, and some, like WestJet, have eliminated extras, such as meal service and in-flight entertainment. Trading down often exists when companies engage in *downsizing*—reducing the content of packages without changing package size and maintaining or increasing the package price. Firms have been criticized for this practice, as described in the accompanying Ethics and Social Responsibility Alert.

Concept Check

1. What does "creating new use situations" mean in managing a product's life cycle?
2. Explain the difference between trading up and trading down in repositioning.

MANAGING THE MARKETING OF SERVICES

Let's use the four Ps framework of the text for discussing the marketing mix for services.

Product (Service)

To a large extent, the concepts of the product component of the marketing mix apply equally well to Cheerios (a good) and to MasterCard (a service). Yet there are three aspects of the product/service element of the mix that warrant special attention when dealing with services: exclusivity, brand name, and capacity management.

Exclusivity Chapter 10 pointed out that one favourable dimension in a new product is its ability to be patented. Remember that a patent gives the manufacturer of a product exclusive rights to its production for 17 years. A major difference between products and services is that services cannot be patented. Hence the creator of a successful fast-food hamburger chain could quickly discover the concept being copied by others. Domino's Pizza, for example, has seen competitors copy the quick-delivery advantage that propelled the company to success. Many businesses today try to distinguish their core product with new or improved supplementary services.[15]

Branding   An important aspect in marketing goods is the branding strategy used. However, because services are intangible and, therefore, more difficult to describe, the brand name or identifying logo of the service organization is particularly important in consumer decisions.[16] The financial services industry, for example, has failed to use branding to distinguish what consumers perceive to be similar offerings by banks, mutual fund companies, brokerage firms, and insurance companies. FedEx, however, is a strong service brand name because it suggests the possibility that it is government sanctioned, and it describes the nature and benefit (speed) of the service.[17]

Capacity Management   Most services have a limited capacity due to the inseparability of the service from the service provider and the perishable nature of the service. For example, a patient must be in the hospital at the same time as the surgeon to "buy" an appendectomy, and only one patient can be helped at that time. Similarly, no additional surgery can be conducted tomorrow because of an unused operating room or an available surgeon today—the service capacity is lost if it is not used. So the service component of the mix must be integrated with efforts to influence consumer demand.[18] This is referred to as **capacity management**.

capacity management
Integrating the service component of the marketing mix with efforts to influence consumer demand

Pricing

In the service industries, *price* is referred to in various ways. Hospitals refer to charges; consultants, lawyers, physicians, and accountants to fees; airlines to fares; and hotels to rates. Regardless of the term used, price plays two essential roles: to affect consumer perceptions and to be used in capacity management. Because of the intangible nature of services, price can indicate the quality of the service. Would you wonder about the quality of a $100 surgery? Studies have shown that when there are few well-known cues by which to judge a product or service quality, consumers use price.[19]

The capacity management role of price is also important to movie theatres, airlines, restaurants, and hotels. Many service businesses use **off-peak pricing**, which consists of charging different prices during different times of the day or days of the week to reflect variations in demand for the service. Airlines offer discounts for off-peak time travel, and movie theatres offer matinee prices.

off-peak pricing
Charging different prices during different times of the day or days of the week to reflect variations in demand for the service

Place (Distribution)

Place or distribution is a major factor in developing a service marketing strategy because of the inseparability of services from the producer. Historically in services marketing, little attention has been paid to distribution. But as competition grows, the value of convenient distribution is being recognized. Hairstyling chains such as Great Clips for Hair, tax preparation offices such as H & R Block, and accounting firms such as Deloitte and Touche all use multiple locations for the distribution of services. In the banking industry, customers of participating banks using the Interac system can access any one of thousands of automatic teller systems throughout Canada. The availability of electronic distribution through the World Wide Web now provides global coverage for travel services, banking, entertainment, and many other information-based services.

Promotion

The value of promotion, specifically advertising, for many services is to show the benefits of purchasing the service. It is valuable to stress availability, location, consistent quality, and efficient, courteous service.[20] In addition, services must be concerned with their image. Promotional efforts, such as Merrill Lynch's use of the bull in its ads, contribute to image and positioning strategies.[21] In most cases promotional concerns of services are similar to those of products.

In the past, advertising has been viewed negatively by many nonprofit and professional service organizations. In fact, professional groups such as law, dentistry, and medicine had previously used their respective professional codes of conduct to prevent their members from advertising. Although opposition to advertising remains strong in some professional groups, the barriers to promotion are gradually disappearing. In recent years, advertising has been used by religious groups; legal, medical, and dental services; educational institutions; and many other service organizations.[22]

Another form of promotion, publicity, has played a major role in the promotional strategy of nonprofit services and some professional organizations. Nonprofit organizations such as public school districts, religious organizations, and hospitals have used publicity to disseminate their messages. Because of the heavy reliance on publicity, many services use public service announcements (PSAs), ads that are run by the media (television, radio) at no cost to the advertiser; however, the ads are run when the media can fit them in. Because PSAs are free, nonprofit groups have tended to rely on them as the foundation of their media plan.[23] However, the timing and location of a PSA are under the control of the medium, not the organization. So the nonprofit service group cannot control who sees the message or when the message is given.

Concept Check

1. How do service businesses use off-peak pricing?
2. Explain the role of packaging in terms of perception.

BRANDING AND BRAND MANAGEMENT

branding
Organization's use of a name, phrase, design, symbol, or combination of these to identify and distinguish its products

A basic decision in marketing products is **branding**, in which an organization uses a name, phrase, design, symbol, or combination of these to identify its products and distinguish them from those of competitors. A **brand name** is any word, "device" (design, sound, shape, or colour), or combination of these used to distinguish a seller's goods or services. Some brand names can be spoken, such as a Jones Soda or Rollerblade. Other brand names cannot be spoken, such as the rainbow-coloured apple (the *logotype* or *logo*) that Apple Computer originally put on its machines and in its ads.

Consumers may benefit most from branding. Recognizing competing products by brand names allows them to be more efficient shoppers. Consumers can recognize and avoid products with which they are dissatisfied, while becoming loyal to other, more satisfying brands.

brand name
Any word, "device" (design, shape, sound, or colour), or combination of these used to distinguish a seller's goods or services

Brand Loyalty

brand loyalty
The extent of consumer connection with a brand of product or service

Just how much do consumers like a particular brand? Will they choose another, if their first choice is not available, or will they insist on "their brand"? These are considerations about brand loyalty. The degree of attachment a consumer has to a particular brand tells the marketer how brand loyal they are. Consumers can have a fairly weak connection to a brand of beverage or cosmetics; they will usually choose it if it is readily available, but an offer or promotion may lure them to a competing brand. With a stronger brand attachment, consumers may prefer a brand, but if it is not available, they may be prepared to accept another brand, though usually infrequently. The brand's most loyal consumers will insist on purchasing their brand of choice and will not even consider competing products.

They will search extensively for their brand, and they may postpone the purchase if it is not found. If a manufacturer decides to discontinue the brand, they may lobby the manufacturer to reconsider. This level of brand loyalty is a marketer's dream, and some, but not all, consumers feel this way. As we discuss in Chapter 5, brand loyalty often eases consumers' decision making by eliminating the need for an external search.

Consider the products you purchase: Are there some—a soft drink, toothpaste, headache remedy—that you are loyal to? When a consumer is convinced that a brand lives up to its promises, delivers the quality and value they expect, and is superior for them to others, that's loyalty!

Brand Personality and Brand Equity

brand personality
Set of human characteristics associated with a brand name

Product managers recognize that brands offer more than product identification and a means to distinguish their products from competitors. Successful and established brands take on a **brand personality**, a set of human characteristics associated with a brand name.[24] Research shows that consumers often assign personality traits to products—traditional, romantic, rugged, sophisticated, rebellious—and choose brands that are consistent with their own or desired self-image. Marketers can and do provide a brand with a personality through advertising that depicts a certain user or usage situation and conveys certain emotions or feelings to be associated with the brand. For example, the personality traits associated with Coca-Cola are real and cool; with Pepsi, young, exciting, and hip; and with Dr Pepper, nonconforming, unique, and fun.

brand equity
Added value a given brand name gives to a product beyond the functional benefits provided

Brand name importance to a company has led to a concept called **brand equity**, the added value a given brand name gives to a product beyond the functional benefits provided.[25] This value has two distinct advantages. First, brand equity provides a competitive advantage, such as the Sunkist label that implies quality fruit and the Disney name that defines children's entertainment. A second advantage is that consumers are often willing to pay a higher price for a product with brand equity. Brand equity, in this instance, is represented by the premium a consumer will pay for one brand over another when the functional benefits provided are identical. Intel microchips, Alpine audio systems, Duracell batteries,

Can you describe the brand personality traits for these two brands?

Microsoft computer software, and Burton snowboards all enjoy a price premium arising from brand equity.

Creating Brand Equity   Brand equity doesn't just happen. It is carefully crafted and nurtured by marketing programs that create strong, favourable and unique consumer associations and experiences with a brand. Brand equity resides in the minds of consumers and results from what they have learned, felt, experienced, seen, and heard about a brand over time. Marketers recognize that brand equity is not easily or quickly achieved. Rather, it arises from a sequential building process consisting of four steps (Figure 11–5).[26]

1. The first step is to develop positive brand awareness and an association of the brand in consumers' minds with a product class or need to give the brand an identity. Gatorade and Kleenex have done this in the sports drink and facial tissue product classes, respectively.
2. Next, a marketer must establish a brand's meaning the minds of consumers. Meaning arises from what a brand stands for and has two dimensions—a functional, performance-related dimension and an abstract, image-related dimension. Nike has done this through continuous product development and improvement and its links to peak athletic performance in its integrated marketing communications program.
3. The third step is to get consumers to develop proper responses to a brand's identity and meaning. Here attention is placed on how consumers think and feel about a brand. Thinking focuses on a brand's perceived quality, credibility, and superiority relative to other brands. Feeling relates to the consumer's emotional reaction to a brand. Michelin elicits both responses for its tires. Not only is Michelin thought of as a credible and superior-quality brand, but consumers also experience a warm and secure feeling of safety, comfort, and self-assurance without worry or concern about the brand.
4. The final, and most difficult, step results in an intense, active loyalty relationship between consumers and the brand. A deep psychological bond characterizes consumer-brand connection and the personal identification consumers have with the brand. Examples of brands that have achieved this status include Harley-Davidson, Apple, and eBay.

FIGURE 11-5

Customer-based brand equity pyramid

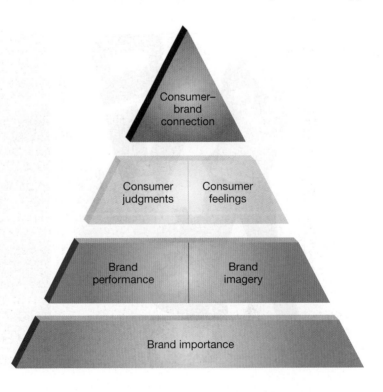

Example of a Harley-Davison product—one the best known global brands for motorcycles

Valuing Brand Equity

Brand equity also provides a financial advantage for the brand owner.[27] We can all think of well-known brands that have been around for many years. Successful brands have an economic value, just as a building or a warehouse full of inventory has. What dimensions are used to determine how much a brand is worth? The consulting firm Interbrand has a 30-year worldwide history in all aspects of branding—research, valuation, strategy, naming, management, and the list goes on. In 2001 Interbrand started producing a ranking of the world's most valuable brands. The criteria: the brands had to be global (about a third of their sales coming from outside their home country), they had to have a value of more than US$1 billion, and there had to be marketing and financial information on them publicly available. These criteria eliminate companies such as Visa and Wal-Mart. Also, brands are ranked, not parent companies, so a firm such as Procter & Gamble does not show up in the rankings.

A complex process of considering brand revenues, tangible and intangible assets, and brand strength results in a dollar value being estimated for each of the major world brands. Factors such as whether the brand is a market leader, how stable the brand is expected to be over time, how global it is, and what risks there are to its future success are assessed. The results might surprise you. Figure 11-6 shows the top 10 ranked brands in Interbrand's 2004 brand scoreboard. Check out www.interbrand.com to find the others in the top 100.[28]

FIGURE 11-6

Interbrand ranks the top brands in the world.

RANK 2004/2003			2004 BRAND VALUE $MILLIONS	2003 BRAND VALUE $MILLIONS	PERCENT CHANGE	COUNTRY OF OWNERSHIP	DESCRIPTION
1	1	Coca-Cola	67,394	70,453	-4%	U.S.	Little innovation beyond its flagship brand and poor management has caught up with Coke as consumers' thirst for cola has diminished.
2	2	Microsoft	61,372	63,174	-6%	U.S.	Its logo pops up on 400 million computer screens worldwide. But virus plagues and rival Linux took some luster off Gates & Co.
3	3	IBM	53,791	51,767	4%	U.S.	A leader in defining e-business, with services making up more than half of Big Blue's sales.
4	4	GE	44,111	42,340	4%	U.S.	With acquisitions in areas from bioscience to bomb detection, it's easier to buy GE's new theme of "imagination at work."
5	5	Intel	33,499	31,112	8%	U.S.	No longer just inside PCs, Intel is using its muscle to set the agenda for everything from wireless standards to the digital home.
6	7	Disney	27,113	28,036	-3%	U.S.	Long the gold seal in family entertainment, but newcomers like Nickelodeon and Pixar are siphoning off some of its brand equity.
7	8	McDonald's	25,001	24,699	1%	U.S.	Big Mac has pulled out of a two-year slump but still has to battle its reputation for supersizing the world's kids.
8	6	Nokia	24,041	29,440	-18%	Finland	Tough times for the mobile-phone giant as its market share has slipped and younger buyers turn to rivals such as Samsung.
9	11	Toyota	22,673	20,784	9%	Japan	With rock-solid quality and the edge in hybrid cars, the Japanese auto maker is on track to overtake Ford in worldwide sales.
10	9	Marlboro	22,128	22,183	0%	U.S.	The No. 1 name in cigarettes has cut prices and upped marketing to beat back the challenges of higher taxes and fewer smokers.

Source: *Business Week*, August 2, 2004.

FIGURE 11–7

Canada's best- and worst-managed brands

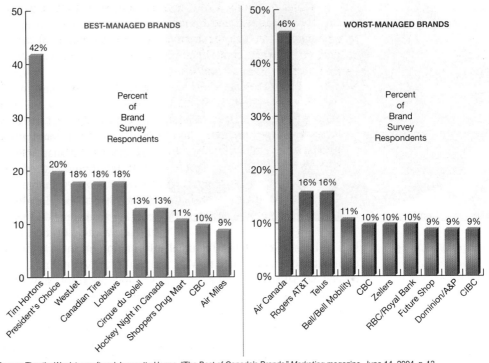

Source: Timothy Woolstencroft and Jeannette Hanna, "The Best of Canada's Brands," *Marketing* magazine, June 14, 2004, p. 13

In terms of Canadian brands, Tim Hortons tops the list of Canada's best-managed brands. It got there by offering "strong customer service, extremely popular products, and community involvement," according to a recent survey conducted by the research firm Strategic Counsel and design and branding firm Spencer Francey Peters.[29] The charts shown in Figure 11-7 summarize the results of the survey and list the top 10 best- and worst-managed Canadian brands. How does your experience and impressions of the brands shown compare with the listing? Obviously, some really well-known household brands are in trouble and in danger of eroding their brand equity, equity that was once high and was earned over a long time. Missing on the best-managed list are brands such as Molson and Labatt, beer brands that are literally Canadian icons. Canadian banks also did not fare well. A relative newcomer on the best-managed list is WestJet, one of Canada's newest and rapidly expanding airlines. What does that suggest to the management and marketing staff at Air Canada, which fared the worst of all brands, not just among airlines?

Picking a Good Brand Name

When we say Sony, Porsche, Pepsi, or Adidas, we probably do not think about how the companies arrived at these choices for names. It is often a long, difficult, and expensive process to pick a winning brand name. Companies sometimes spend many thousands of dollars developing and testing a new brand name. As an example, Intel spent some US$60,000 for the Pentium name it gave its family of microchips.

Here are some of the key considerations made when selecting a good brand name:[30]

- The name should suggest the product benefits. For example, Accutron (watches), Easy Off (oven cleaner), Glass Plus (glass cleaner), Cling-Free (antistatic cloth for drying clothes), PowerBook (laptop computer), and Tidy Bowl (toilet bowl cleaner) all clearly describe the benefits of purchasing the product.
- The name should be memorable, distinctive, and positive. In the auto industry, when a competitor has a memorable name, others quickly imitate. When Ford named a car

the Mustang, Pintos, Colts, and Broncos soon followed. The Thunderbird name led to the use of Sunbird and Firebird by General Motors.

- The name should fit the company or product image. Sharp is a suitable name for audio and video equipment. Excedrin, Anacin, and Nuprin are scientific-sounding names, good for a pain-relieving drug.

- The name should have no legal or regulatory restrictions. Companies that attempt to use others' trademarked material may face lawsuits. Regulatory restrictions arise through improper use of words. Increasingly, brand names need a corresponding address on the Internet. This further complicates name selection because millions of domain names are already registered. For example, a teenager in Victoria, BC, named Mike Rowe set up a website—www.MikeRoweSoft.com—to promote his web-design business. The software giant Microsoft sent him a 25-page letter demanding that Mike give up the domain name, because of its similarity to its corporate name and the firm's lawyers' perception that his site name violated the Microsoft trademark. Mike told his story to the media, which generated a lot of negative publicity for Microsoft, which backed down and admitted that it had acted improperly. A settlement was reached with Mike Rowe, and his site now has a new name: www.MikeRoweForums.com.[31]

- Finally, the name should be simple (such as Bold laundry detergent, Sure deodorant, and Bic pens) and should be expressive (such as Joy and Obsession perfumes). In the development of names for international use, in some cases having a brand name that does not describe the product can be considered a benefit. The name Exxon, a created word which has no meaning in any language, can be used globally because it does not have any prior impressions or undesirable images among a diverse world population of different languages and cultures. The 7Up name is another matter. In the local dialect in Shanghai, China, 7Up translates roughly into "death through drinking," and the beverage's sales have suffered as a result.[32]

Branding Strategies

Branding requires companies to make complex decisions. Manufacturers make brand decisions, and so do resellers (retailers and wholesalers). Figure 11-8 shows the main branding alternatives.

Manufacturers produce one or more products, and they are faced with the decisions of how to brand them. For their brands—known as manufacturer brands—they may choose one of four strategies: family branding, individual branding, a combination of family and individual, or private-label branding. Resellers have the same branding strategies available to them, but the choices are different. Retailers, for example, must decide whether to carry manufacturers' brands, their own private-label brands, or both. Most retailers do not manufacture their own products, so if they want to have their own private-label brand, they usually contract with manufacturers to produce products for them. This can be beneficial for both parties; manufacturers produce private-label brands but do not have to incur the expense of promoting them or securing shelf space for them, and retailers often reap higher profits from their own brands than from more expensive manufacturer brands.

family branding
Manufacturer's branding strategy that uses one name for all products

With **family branding**, a manufacturer uses one name for all of its products. This could be the name of the company, such as Sony or Kodak. This strategy can be very advantageous when new products are launched, because the brand name is already known, so consumers may feel favourable towards the new product because it is related to others with which they are familiar. Advertising and promotional costs may be lower, as brand awareness is already established.

individual branding
Manufacturer's branding strategy that gives each product a distinct name

Procter & Gamble's Tide, Cheer, and Ivory brands are examples of **individual branding**. Each product is given a distinct name. These three products are from Procter & Gamble's laundry product line; each of these is destined for a different target market, and each has a separate identity. With this type of branding decision, advertising and

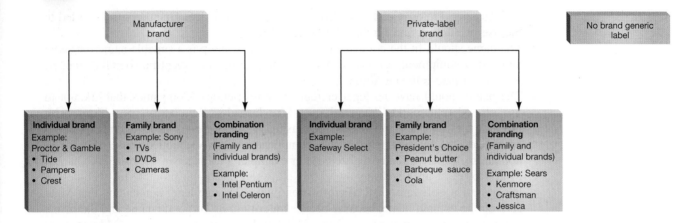

Manufacturer brand			Private-label brand			No brand generic label

Individual brand	Family brand	Combination branding	Individual brand	Family brand	Combination branding
Example: Proctor & Gamble • Tide • Pampers • Crest	Example: Sony • TVs • DVDs • Cameras	(Family and individual brands) Example: • Intel Pentium • Intel Celeron	Example: Safeway Select	Example: President's Choice • Peanut butter • Barbeque sauce • Cola	(Family and individual brands) Example: Sears • Kenmore • Craftsman • Jessica

FIGURE 11–8

Examples of branding strategies

promotion are done individually for each brand, so costs tend to be higher. However, if one brand is struggling, others are not affected in this scenario. This can be a complex and costly strategy, but it obviously works for some companies.

Most branding is a combination of family and individual branding. The beverages sold by the Coca-Cola Company include Coca-Cola, which follows a family branding strategy, as well as Sprite, TaB, Fruitopia, Barq's, Mad River, and Minute Maid, which are individually branded.

A strong brand equity also allows for *brand extension*, the practice of using a current brand name to enter a completely different product class. For instance, the equity in the Tylenol name as a trusted pain reliever allowed Johnson & Johnson to successfully extend this name to Tylenol Cold & Flu and Tylenol PM, a sleep aid. Fisher-Price, an established name in children's toys, was able to extend this name to children's shampoo and conditioners and baby bath and lotion products.

However, there is a risk with brand extensions. Too many uses for one brand name can dilute the meaning of a brand for consumers. Marketing experts claim this has happened to the Arm & Hammer brand, given its use for toothpaste, laundry detergent, gum, cat litter, air freshener, carpet deodorizer, and antiperspirant.[33]

Black & Decker's combination branding strategy allows it to reach do-it-yourselfers with the Black & Decker name and professionals with the DeWalt name.

MARKETING NEWSNET

CREATING CUSTOMER VALUE THROUGH PACKAGING: PEZ HEADS DISPENSE MORE THAN CANDY

Customer Value

Customer value can assume numerous forms. For Pez Candy, Inc. (www.pez.com), customer value manifests itself in some 250 Pez character candy dispensers. Each refillable dispenser ejects tasty candy tablets in a variety of flavours that delight preteens and teens alike.

Pez was formulated in 1927 by Austrian food mogul Edward Haas III and successfully sold in Europe as an adult breath mint. Pez, which comes from the German word for peppermint, pfefferminz, was originally packaged in a hygienic, headless plastic dispenser. Pez first appeared in North America in 1953 with a headless dispenser, marketed to adults. After conducting extensive marketing research, Pez was repositioned with fruit flavours, repackaged with licensed character heads on top of the dispenser, and remarketed as a children's product in the mid-1950s. Since then, most top-level licensed characters and hundreds of other characters have become Pez heads. Consumers eat more than 3 billion Pez tablets annually, and company sales growth exceeds that of the candy industry as a whole.

The unique Pez package dispenses a "use experience" for its customers beyond the candy itself: namely, fun. And fun translates into a 98 percent awareness level for Pez among teenagers and 89 percent among mothers with children. Pez has not advertised its product for years. With that kind of awareness, who needs advertising?

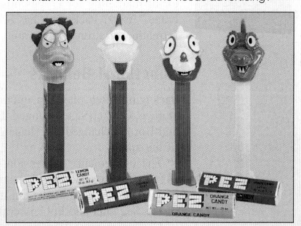

Most of the leading brands in the world are manufacturer brands; this is true not only for consumable goods such as food and personal care products but also for vehicles, computers, and other durable items.

Firms also may decide to have unbranded or generic products—products with no names and no frills that are sold at a low cost. They use basic packaging with the product and plain labelling—for example, "Sugar"—to describe the package contents. These products are most commonly found in supermarkets. You will find them in inferior shelf positions (such as on a lower shelf), and you rarely see any advertising or promotional specials for them. To retailers, they can be as profitable as manufacturer or private-label brands.

CREATING CUSTOMER VALUE THROUGH PACKAGING AND LABELLING

packaging

Part of a product that refers to any container in which it is offered for sale and on which label information is displayed

The **packaging** component of a product refers to any container in which it is offered for sale and on which label information is conveyed. A label is an integral part of the package and typically identifies the product or brand, who made it, where and when it was made, how it is to be used, and product contents and ingredients. To a great extent, the customer's first exposure to a product is the package and label and both are an expensive and important part of marketing strategy. For Pez Candy, Inc., the character head-on-a-stick plastic container that dispenses a miniature brick candy is the central element of its marketing strategy as described in the accompanying Marketing NewsNet.[34]

Packaging and labelling cost companies billions of dollars annually and account for about 15 cents of every dollar spent by consumers for products.[35] Despite the cost, packaging and labelling are essential because both provide important benefits for the manufacturer, retailer, and ultimate consumer.

Communication Benefits

A major benefit of packaging is the information conveyed to the consumer via labelling such as directions on how to use the product and what the product is made of, needed to satisfy legal requirements of product disclosure. Other information consists of seals and symbols, either government-required or commercial seals of approval (such as the Good Housekeeping seal).

Packaging also can have brand equity benefits for a company. According to the director of marketing for L'eggs hosiery, "Packaging is important to the equity of the L'eggs brand." Why? Packaging has been shown to enhance brand recognition and facilitate the formation of strong, favourable, and unique brand associations.[36]

Functional Benefits

Packaging often plays an important functional role, such as convenience, protection, or storage. Quaker State changed its oil containers to eliminate the need for a separate spout, and Borden changed the shape of its Elmer's Wonder Bond adhesive to prevent clogging of the spout.

The convenience dimension of packaging is becoming increasingly important. Kraft Miracle Whip salad dressing and Heinz ketchup are sold in squeeze bottles, microwave popcorn that can be cooked in its package has been a major market success, and Chicken of the Sea tuna and Folgers coffee are packaged in single-serving portions.

Consumer protection has become an important function of packaging, including the development of tamper-resistant containers. Today, companies commonly use safety seals or pop-tops that reveal previous opening. Nevertheless, no package is truly tamper-proof. Laws now provide stiff penalties for package tampering. Labelling also protects consumers through "open dating," which states the expected shelf life of the product.

Perceptual Benefits

A third benefit of packaging and labelling is the perception created in the consumer's mind. Just Born Inc., a candy manufacturer of such brands as Jolly Joes and Mike and Ike Treats, discovered the importance of this component of packaging. For many years the brands were sold in old-fashioned black and white packages, but when the packaging was changed to full-colour, with animated grape and cherry characters, sales increased 25 percent.

A package can give the idea of status, economy, and product quality. Procter & Gamble's Original Pringles, with its unique cylindrical packaging, offers uniform chips, minimal breakage, freshness, and better value for the money than flex-bag packages for chips.

In the past, the colour of packages was selected subjectively. For example, the famous Campbell's soup can was the inspiration of a company executive who liked Cornell University's red and white football uniforms. Today, there is greater recognition that colour affects consumers' perceptions. When the colour of the can of Barrelhead Sugar-Free Root Beer changed to beige from blue, consumers said it tasted more like old-fashioned root beer.

SUMMARY

1 Products have a finite life cycle consisting of four stages: introduction, growth, maturity, and decline. The marketing objectives for each stage differ.

2 In the introductory stage the need is to establish primary demand, whereas the growth stage requires selective demand strategies. In the maturity stage the need is to maintain market share; the decline stage requires a deletion or harvesting strategy.

3 There are various shapes to the product life cycle. High-learning products have a long introductory period, and low-learning products rapidly enter the growth stage. There are also different curves for fashions and fads.

4 In managing a product's life cycle, changes can be made in the product itself or in the target market. Product modification approaches include changes in quality, performance, or appearance. Target market modification approaches involve increasing a product's use among existing customers, creating new use situations, or finding new users.

5 Product repositioning can come about by reacting to a competitor's position, reaching a new market, taking advantage of a rising trend, or changing the value offered in a product.

6 The four Ps framework also applies to services with some adaptations. Because services cannot be patented, unique offerings are difficult to protect. In addition, because services are intangible, brands and logos (which can be protected) are particularly important. The inseparability of production and consumption of services means that capacity management is important to services. The intangible nature of services makes price an important indication of service quality. Distribution has become an important marketing tool for services, and electronic distribution allows some services to provide global coverage. In recent years, service organizations have increased their promotional activities.

7 Branding enables a firm to distinguish its product in the marketplace from those of its competitors. Successful and established brands take on a brand personality, a set of human characteristics associated with a brand name. A good brand name should suggest the product benefits, be memorable, fit the company or product image, be free of legal restrictions, and be simple and emotional. A good brand name is of such importance that it has led to a concept of brand equity, the added value a given brand name gives to a product beyond the functional benefits provided.

8 Manufacturers can follow one of three branding strategies: a manufacturer brand, a reseller brand, or a mixed brand approach. With a manufacturer branding approach, the company can use the same brand name for all products in the line (family branding) or can give products different brands (individual branding).

9 A reseller, or private, brand is used when a firm manufactures a product but sells it under the brand name of a wholesaler or retailer.

10 Packaging and labelling provide communication, functional, and perceptual benefits.

KEY TERMS AND CONCEPTS

brand equity p. 259
brand loyalty p. 258
brand name p. 258
brand personality p. 259

branding p. 258
capacity management p. 257
family branding p. 263
individual branding p. 263

off-peak pricing p. 257
packaging p. 265
product life cycle p. 247

QUESTIONS: APPLYING MARKETING CONCEPTS AND PERSPECTIVES

1 Here are three different products in various stages of the product life cycle. What marketing strategies would you suggest to these companies? *(a)* cellular telephone company—growth stage, *(b)* tap-water purifying system—introductory stage, and *(c)* handheld manual can openers—decline stage.

2 It has often been suggested that products are intentionally made to break down or wear out. Is this strategy a planned product modification approach?

3 A product manager is reviewing the market penetration of garbage compactors in North American homes. After being available in the marketplace for more than two decades, this product is in relatively few homes. What problems can account for this? What is the shape of the garbage compactor life cycle?

4 For several years Ferrari has been known as the manufacturer of expensive luxury automobiles. Now the company plans to attract the major segment of the car-buying market who purchase medium-priced automobiles. As Ferrari considers this trading-down strategy, what branding strategy would you recommend? What are the trade-offs to consider with your strategy?

5   Prefabricated houses have been produced and sold in Canada for decades. There are emerging markets for factory-manufactured homes in Japan and other parts of Asia. What kinds of changes would Canadian producers have to make to their products to adapt them to these new markets?

6   What are the roles of packaging today from the following standpoints: *(a)* environmental, *(b)* legislative, *(c)* technological, and *(d)* consumer?

DISCUSSION FORUM

The Body Shop, the international skin and body care retailer, uses an environmentally friendly approach to packaging as a statement of social responsibility. Then they utilize this strategy to position its brand in the minds of consumers, and to differentiate its products from those of the competition.

1   Discuss the merits of this orientation towards packaging.
2   Discuss the ethics of this strategy.

3   If such an approach to packaging actually costs the company more money than conventional packaging, does that change your position on these issues?
4   The Body Shop rarely advertises; how do you think this impacts the other aspects of the marketing mix?

INTERNET EXERCISE

Hot Product News provides a central Internet location on the latest new products. It provides a forum for companies to present their most recent new products. Hot Product News is updated daily with company press releases from the entire world. Some 30 product categories with one or more new products are typically listed by Hot Product News each day. A unique feature of Hot Product News is that a company website address that can be accessed immediately follows each new product description.

Visit the Hot Product News website at www.hotproduct news.com and go to "new items this week." Your assignment is outlined below:

www.mcgrawhill.ca/college/thecore

1   Identify and describe how a new product listed promotes more frequent usage, creates a new use situation, reaches a new market or new users, or changes the value offered to consumers.
2   Identify and describe a new product that is branded using a family branding strategy, an individual branding strategy, or a brand extension strategy.

VIDEO CASE 11

BMW: "NEWNESS" AND THE PRODUCT LIFE CYCLE

"We're fortunate right now at BMW in that all of our products are new and competitive," says Jim McDowell, vice president of marketing at BMW, as he explains BMW's product life cycle. "Now, how do you do that? You have to introduce new models over time. You have to logically plan out the introductions over time, so you're not changing a whole model range at the same time you're changing another model range."

BMW's strategy is to keep its products in the introduction and growth stages by periodically introducing new models in each of its product lines. In fact, BMW does not like to have any products in the maturity or decline stage of the product life cycle. Explains McDowell, "If a product is declining, we would prefer to withdraw it from the market, as opposed to

having a strategy for dealing with the declining product. We're kind of a progressive, go get 'em company, and we don't think it does our brand image any good to have any declining products out there. So that's why we work so hard at managing the growth aspect."

BMW—THE COMPANY AND ITS PRODUCTS

BMW is one of the best-known luxury car manufacturers in Europe, North America, and the world today. BMW produces several lines of cars, including the 3 series, the 5 series, the 7 series, the Z line (driven by Pierce Brosnan as James Bond in *Goldeneye*), and the new X line, BMW's "sport activity" vehicle line. In addition, BMW is now selling its Mini line, a re-engineered version of another well-known version of an old British car, and began selling Rolls Royce vehicles in 2003. Sales of all the BMW and Mini vehicles have been on the rise globally. High-profile image campaigns (such as the James Bond promotion) and the award-winning BMW website (where users can design their own car) continue to increase the popularity of BMW's products.

PRODUCT LIFE CYCLE

BMW cars typically have a product life cycle of seven years. To keep products in the introductory and growth stages, BMW regularly introduces new models for each of its series to keep the entire series "new." For instance, with the 3 series, it will introduce the new sedan model one year, the new coupe the next year, then the convertible, then the station wagon, and then the sport hatchback. That's a new product introduction for five of the seven years of the product life cycle. McDowell explains, "So, even though we have seven-year life cycles, we constantly try and make the cars meaningfully different and new about every three years. And that involves adding features and other capabilities to the cars as well." How well does this strategy work? BMW often sees its best sales numbers in either the sixth or seventh year after the product introduction.

As global sales have increased, BMW has become aware of some international product life-cycle differences. For example, it has discovered that some competitive products have life cycles that are shorter or longer than seven years. In Sweden and Britain automotive product life cycles are eight years, while in Japan they are typically only four years long.

BRANDING

"BMW is fortunate—we don't have too much of a dilemma as to what we're going to call our cars." McDowell is referring to BMW's trademark naming system that consists of the product line number and the motor type. For example, the designation "328" tells you the car is in the 3 series and the engine is 2.8 liters in size. BMW has found this naming system to be clear and logical and can be easily understood around the world. The Z and X series don't quite fit in with this system. BMW had a tradition of building experimental, open-air cars and calling them Zs, and hence when the prototype for the Z3 was built, BMW decided to continue with the Z name. For the sport activity vehicle, BMW also used a

letter name—the X series—since the four-wheel drive vehicle didn't fit with the sedan-oriented 3, 5, and 7 series. Other than the Z3 (the third in the Z series) and the X5 (named 5 to symbolize its mid-sized status within that series), the BMW branding strategy is quite simple, unlike the evocative names many car manufacturers choose to garner excitement for their new models.

MANAGING THE PRODUCT THROUGH THE WEB — THE WAVE OF THE FUTURE

One of the ways BMW is improving its product offer-ings even further is through its innovative website (www.bmw.ca). At the site, customers can learn about the particular models, e-mail questions, and request literature or test-drives from their local BMW dealership. What really sets BMW's website apart from other car manufacturers, though, is the ability for customers to configure a car to their own specifications (interior choices, exterior choices, engine, packages, and options) and then transfer that information to their local dealer. As Carol Burrows, product communications manager for BMW, explains, "The BMW website is an integrated part of the overall marketing strategy for BMW. The full range of products can be seen and interacted with online. We offer pricing options online. Customers can go to their local dealership via the website to further discuss costs for purchase of a car. And it is a distribution channel for information that allows people access to the information 24 hours a day at their convenience."

Questions

1 Compare the product life cycle described by BMW for its cars to the product life cycle shown in Figure 11–1. How are they *(a)* similar and *(b)* dissimilar?

2 Based on BMW's typical product life cycle, what marketing strategies are appropriate for the 3 series? The X5?

3 Which of the three ways to manage the product life cycle does BMW utilize with its products—modifying the product, modifying the market, or repositioning the product?

4 How would you describe BMW's branding strategy (manufacturer branding, private branding, or combination branding)? Why?

5 Go to the BMW website (www.bmw.ca) and design a car to your own specifications. How does this enable you as a customer to evaluate the product differently than would be otherwise possible?

Pricing Products and Services

AFTER READING THIS CHAPTER YOU SHOULD BE ABLE TO:

- Identify the elements that make up a price.

- Understand the approaches to pricing and the major factors considered in arriving at a final price.

- Explain what a demand curve is and what price elasticity of demand means.

- Explain the role of revenues (sales) and costs in pricing decisions.

- Understand the value of break-even analysis and be able to perform break-even calculations.

- Recognize the price objectives a firm may have, and the constraints under which they operate.

- Explain the adjustments made to price because of factors such as geography, discounts, and allowances.

GOING ONLINE FOR THE BEST DEAL!

Need a break? Dreaming of that beach in Mexico or the surf "down under"? Head for your computer. According to a recent Ipsos-Reid survey, more and more Canadians are using the Internet to make and book their travel plans. More than half of those with Internet access currently use it for travel plans, and 86 percent indicate they plan to use it in the future for that purpose. Expedia was found to be the favourite online travel website. Why, you may ask? Convenience, speed, selection, ability to compare prices, or best prices are all possible reasons—likely a combination of all of these.[1]

The prospect of lower prices might have been the original motivation for trying the online approach, but if you were to factor in the cost of your own time, would the result be cheaper for you? Obviously, most consumers feel that they are getting what they want at a good price. For those firms supplying the actual travel services, they too must feel that they are getting a good price for what they offer.

It would be wrong to evaluate everything in terms of the actual price paid by the consumers or the price received by the service providers. There is a misconception that consumers always want to pay the lowest price, while companies want to be able to sell at the highest price—conflicting objectives!

Most consumers look at the value they are receiving for the dollars they are spending. Value to them is a mix of things like quality and availability. For the service providers, they look at the dollars they receive as being enough to offset their costs and contribute to their profits and enough to meet their business objectives.

Welcome to the fascinating—and complex—world of pricing, where many forces come together in the price potential buyers are asked to pay. This chapter covers important factors used in setting prices.

WHERE IN THE MARKETING PROCESS ARE WE GOING IN THIS CHAPTER?

Chapter 12 introduces the all-important question of pricing, and its many implications for marketing. This topic focuses on the price P of the 4Ps that make up the marketing mix.

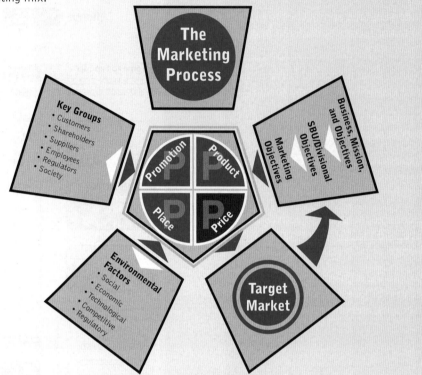

NATURE AND IMPORTANCE OF PRICE

The price paid for goods and services goes by many names. You pay *tuition* for your education, *rent* for an apartment, *interest* on a bank credit card, and a *premium* for car insurance. Your dentist or physician charges you a *fee*, a professional or social organization charges *dues*, and airlines charge a *fare*. And what you pay for clothes or a haircut is termed a *price*.

What Is a Price?

price

Money or other considerations exchanged for the ownership or use of a good or service

These examples highlight the many and varied ways that price plays a part in our daily lives. From a marketing viewpoint, **price** is the money or other considerations, including other goods and services, exchanged for the ownership or use of a product. Recently, Wilkinson Sword exchanged some of its knives for advertising used to promote its razor blades. This practice of exchanging goods and services for other goods and services rather than for money is called *barter*. These transactions account for billions of dollars annually in domestic and international trade.

For most products, money is exchanged. However, the amount paid is not always the same as the list, or quoted, price because of discounts, allowances, and extra fees. While discounts, allowances, and rebates make the effective price lower, other marketing tactics raise the real price. One new pricing tactic is to use "special fees" and "surcharges."

Lamborghini Murciélago

PRICE EQUATION

ITEM PURCHASED	PRICE	= LIST PRICE	INCENTIVES AND − ALLOWANCES	+ EXTRA FEES
New car bought by an individual	Final price	= List price	− Rebate Cash discount Old car trade-in	+ Financing charges Special accessories Destination charges
Term in college bought by a student	Tuition	= Published tuition	− Scholarship Other financial aid	+ Special activity fees
Merchandise bought from a wholesaler by a retailer	Invoice price	= List price	− Quantity discount Cash discount Seasonal discount Functional or trade discount	+ Penalty for late payment

FIGURE 12–1

The price of three different purchases

This practice is driven by consumers' zeal for low prices combined with the ease of making price comparisons on the Internet. Buyers are more willing to pay extra fees than a higher list price, so sellers use add-on charges as a way of having the consumer pay more without raising the list price. Examples of such special fees include a Telus Mobility "system licensing charge" and "911 emergency service access charge" that increase the monthly cellphone bill, or an environmental surcharge on new tires and batteries for cars in some provinces.

All these different factors that increase or decrease the price are put together in a "price equation," which is shown for several different products in Figure 12–1.

Suppose you decide you want to buy a Lamborghini Murciélago ("bat" in Spanish) because its 6.2 liter, 571-horsepower V-12 engine moves you from 0 to 100 kmph in 3.8 seconds at a top speed of 325 kmph. The list price is $300,000. As a rebate for buying the current year's model, you receive $20,000 off the list price. You agree to pay half down ($140,000) and the other half when the car is delivered in six months, which results in a financing fee of $3,285. To ship the car from Italy, you will pay a $5,000 destination charge. For your 1996 Honda Civic DX 4-door sedan that has 100,000 kilometres and is in fair condition, you are given a trade-in allowance of $6,000, which is the appraised trade-in value of your car.[2]

Applying the price equation (as shown in Figure 12–1) to your purchase, your final price is:

$$\text{Final price} = \text{List price} - (\text{Incentives} + \text{Allowances}) + \text{Extra fees}$$
$$= \$300,000 - (\$20,000 + \$6,000) + (\$3,285 + \$5,000)$$
$$= \$284,285$$

Your monthly payment for the six-month loan of $140,000 is $23,880.79. Are you still interested?

Price as an Indicator of Value

For some products, price influences consumers' perception of overall quality. In a survey of home furnishing buyers, 84 percent agreed with the statement: "The higher the price, the higher the quality."[3] For example, Kohler introduced a walk-in bathtub that is safer for children and the elderly. Although priced higher than conventional step-in bathtubs, it has proven very successful because buyers are willing to pay more for what they perceive as the value of the extra safety.

From a consumer's standpoint, price is often used to indicate value when price is compared with benefits of the product. At a given price, as perceived benefits increase, value increases. If you are used to paying $60 for a haircut, and your friend tells you she pays $15.99, wouldn't you assume that she had an inferior stylist or went to a less fashionable salon with fewer services?

Creative marketers, aware that consumers often compare value between competing products, engage in *value pricing*. Value pricing is the practice of increasing a product's benefits while maintaining or decreasing price. "Super-sizing" at fast-food restaurants is one example. Here value comes from getting "more bang for your buck."

Price in the Marketing Mix

profit equation
Profit = Total revenue − Total cost

Pricing is a critical decision made by a marketing executive because price has a direct effect on a firm's profits. This is apparent from a firm's **profit equation**:

$$\text{Profit} = \text{Total revenue} - \text{Total cost}$$
$$= (\text{Unit price} \times \text{Quantity sold}) - \text{Total cost}$$

What makes this relationship even more complicated is that price affects the quantity sold, as illustrated with demand curves later in this chapter, since the quantity sold sometimes affects a firm's costs because of efficiency of production, price also indirectly affects costs. Thus, pricing decisions influence both total revenue (sales) and total cost, which makes pricing one of the most important decisions marketing executives face.

GENERAL PRICING APPROACHES

A key to a marketing manager's setting a final price for a product is to find an "approximate price level" to use as a reasonable starting point. Four common approaches to helping find this approximate price level are demand-oriented, cost-oriented, profit-oriented, and competition-oriented approaches (Figure 12–2). Although these approaches are discussed separately below, some of them overlap, and an effective marketing manager will consider several in searching for an approximate price level.

Demand-Oriented Approaches

Flatscreen TVs: Probably using skimming pricing to enter the market!

Demand-oriented approaches emphasize factors underlying expected customer tastes and preferences more than such factors as cost, profit, and competition when selecting a price level.

Skimming Pricing   A firm introducing a new product can use *skimming pricing*, setting the highest initial price that those customers really desiring the product are willing to pay. These customers are not very price sensitive because they weigh the new product's price, quality, and ability to satisfy their needs against the same characteristics of substitutes. As the demand of these customers is satisfied, the firm lowers the price to attract another, more price-sensitive segment. Thus, skimming pricing gets its name from skimming successive layers of "cream," or customer segments, as prices are lowered in a series of steps.

In early 2003, many manufacturers of flatscreen TVs were pricing them at about $5,000 and using skimming pricing because many prospective customers were willing to buy the product immediately at the high price. But by the time you read this, flatscreen TVs will probably be far less expensive.

Penetration Pricing   Setting a low initial price on a new product to appeal immediately to the mass market is *penetration pricing*, the exact opposite of skimming pricing. Nintendo consciously chose a penetration strategy when it introduced its GameCube video game console first in Japan and later in the United States in 2001. GameCube was launched with an introductory price of $199.95—$100.00 less than the list price for Microsoft's Xbox and Sony's PlayStation 2 consoles because many buyers were price sensitive.[4]

In some situations, penetration pricing may follow skimming pricing. A company might price a product high at first to attract price-insensitive consumers. Once the company has earned back the money spent on research and development and introductory promotions, it uses penetration pricing to appeal to a broader segment of the population and increase market share.[5]

Prestige Pricing   Although consumers tend to buy more of a product when the price is lower, sometimes the reverse is true. If consumers are using price as a measure of the quality of an item, a company runs the risk of appearing to offer a low-quality product if it sets the price below a certain point. *Prestige pricing* involves setting a high price so that quality- or status-conscious consumers will be attracted to the product and buy it. Rolls-Royce cars, Chanel perfume, and Cartier jewellery have an element of prestige pricing in them and may not sell as well at lower prices than at higher ones.[6] As described in the Marketing NewsNet, this is the pricing strategy Energizer used with its very successful e[2] high-performance AA batteries.

Odd-Even Pricing   Suppose Sears offers a Craftsman radial saw for $599.99, the suggested retail price for a MACH3 razor set (razor and two blades) is $11.99, and Zellers sells Windex glass cleaner on sale for 99 cents. Why not simply price these items at $600, $12, and $1, respectively? These firms are using *odd-even pricing*, which involves setting prices a few dollars or cents under an even number. The presumption is that consumers see the Sears radial saw as priced at "something over $500" rather than "about $600." The effect this strategy has is psychological: $599.99 *feels* significantly lower than $600— even though there is only one cent difference. There is some evidence to suggest this does work. However, research suggests that overuse of odd-ending prices tends to mute its effect on demand.[7]

Target Pricing   Manufacturers will sometimes estimate the price that the ultimate consumer would be willing to pay for a product. They then work backward through markups taken by retailers and wholesalers to determine what price they can charge for the product. This practice, called *target pricing*, results in the manufacturer deliberately adjusting the composition and features of a product to achieve the target price to consumers. Canon uses this practice for pricing its cameras, as does Heinz for its complete line of pet foods.[8]

FIGURE 12–2

Four approaches for selecting an approximate price level

Demand-oriented approaches	**Cost-oriented approaches**	**Profit-oriented approaches**	**Competition-oriented approaches**
• Skimming • Penetration • Prestige • Odd-even • Target • Bundle • Yield management	• Standard markup • Cost-plus	• Target profit • Target return on sales • Target return on investment	• Customary • Above, at, or below market • Loss leader

MARKETING NEWSNET

ENERGIZER'S LESSON IN PRESTIGE PRICING: A HIGHER PRICE CAN INCREASE SALES AND PROFITS

Battery manufacturers are as tireless as a certain drum-thumping bunny in their efforts to create products that perform better, last longer, and, not incidentally, outsell the competition. Pricing a new product is not always obvious or easy. Just ask the marketing executives at Energizer about their experience with pricing Energizer Advanced Formula and Energizer e² alkaline AA batteries.

When Duracell launched its high-performance Ultra brand AA alkaline battery with a 25 percent price premium over standard Duracell batteries, Energizer quickly countered with its own high-performance battery—Energizer Advanced Formula. Believing that consumers would not pay the premium price, Energizer priced its new Advanced Formula brand at the same price as its standard AA alkaline battery, expecting to gain market share from Duracell. It did not happen. Why? According to industry analysts, consumers associated Energizer's low price with inferior quality in the high-performance segment. So, surprise! Energizer lost market share to competitors Duracell and Rayovac.

Having learned its lesson, Energizer subsequently released its e² high-performance AA battery, this time priced 4 percent higher than Duracell Ultra and about 50 percent higher than its own Advanced Formula. The result? Energizer recovered lost sales and market share. The lesson learned? When consumers believe a higher price means higher quality, prestige pricing can increase sales and profits.

Bundle Pricing   A frequently used demand-oriented pricing practice is *bundle pricing* —the marketing of two or more products in a single "package" price. For example, Air Canada offers vacation packages that include airfare, car rental, and hotel. Bundle pricing is based on the idea that consumers value the package more than the individual items. This is due to benefits received from not having to make separate purchases as well as increased satisfaction from one item in the presence of another. Bundle pricing often provides a lower total cost to buyers and lower marketing costs to sellers.[9]

Yield Management Pricing   Have you ever been on an airplane and discovered the person next to you paid a lower price for her ticket than you paid? Annoying, isn't it? But what you observed is *yield management pricing*—the charging of different prices to maximize revenue for a set amount of capacity at any given time.[10] Airlines, hotels, and car rental firms engage in capacity management by varying prices based on time, day, week, or season to match demand and supply.

Concept Check

1. What is the profit equation?
2. What is the difference between skimming and penetration pricing?
3. What is odd-even pricing?

Cost-Oriented Approaches

With cost-oriented approaches, a price is more affected by the cost side of the pricing problem than the demand side. Price is set by looking at the production and marketing costs and then adding enough to cover direct expenses, overhead, and profit.

markup
The difference between selling price and cost

Standard Markup Pricing   In order to make a profit, firms sell their products at a price that exceeds their costs of producing or sourcing the items and the costs of marketing them. Conventionally, the difference between the selling price of an item and its cost is referred to as the markup and this is normally expressed as a percentage.

Manufacturers commonly express markup as a percentage of cost, which is the difference between selling price and cost, divided by cost. This is also referred to as *standard markup*. Manufacturers use this approach because they are concerned most of the time with costs.

Parties who buy and resell products, for example wholesalers and retailers, are nearly always dealing with selling prices. They often express markup as a percentage of price, which is the difference between selling price and cost, divided by the selling price. Using the same markup percentage for both of the above approaches will result in a different selling price (see the example in Figure 12-3).

Consider the example of a product that is produced by a manufacturer and sold to a wholesaler, who in turn sells it to a retailer, who then sells it to a consumer. The product will be subjected to a series of markups as shown below.

Manufacturer's cost:	**$50.00**
Markup % (based on cost):	40%
Markup $:	$20.00
Selling price to wholesaler:	**$70.00**
Wholesaler cost:	**$70.00**
Markup% (based on price):	15%
Markup $:	$10.50
Selling price to retailer:	**$80.50**
Retailer cost:	**$80.50**
Markup % (based on price):	35%
Markup $:	$28.18
Retailer selling price:	**$108.68**

This may surprise you to find out that a product costing $50 to produce can end up costing a consumer nearly two-and-a-half times that when bought at a retailer, but this is not unusual. It is important to remember that markup is necessary at each stage so that companies involved can cover their costs of purchasing the item, can pay to market it to the next stage in the distribution channel, and can generate some profit. The markups shown would be representative of some items such as designer furniture.

FIGURE 12-3
Markup examples

MARKUP TABLE BASED ON SELLING PRICE	$	%
Selling price	$75.00	100%*
– (minus) Cost	$60.00	80%
= (equals) Markup	$15.00	20%

* Price is always 100% when markup is relative to price.

MARKUP TABLE BASED ON COST	$	%
Selling price	$72.00	120%
– (minus) Cost	$60.00	100%**
= (equals) Markup	$12.00	20%

** Cost is always 100% when markup is relative to cost.

This percentage markup varies depending on the type of retail store (such as furniture, clothing, or grocery) and on the product involved. High-volume products usually have smaller markups than do low-volume products. Supermarkets such as Loblaws and Safeway mark up staple items like sugar, flour, and dairy products 10 to 25 percent, whereas they mark up discretionary items like snack foods and candy 25 to 47 percent. These markups must cover all expenses of the store, pay for overhead costs, and contribute something to profits. For supermarkets, these markups, which may appear very large, can result in only a 1 percent profit on sales revenue.

Cost-Plus Pricing   Many manufacturing, professional services, and construction firms use a variation of standard markup pricing. *Cost-plus pricing* involves summing the total unit cost of providing a product or service and adding a specific amount to the cost to arrive at a price. Cost-plus pricing is the most commonly used method to set prices for business products.[11] Increasingly, however, this method is finding favour among business-to-business marketers in the service sector. For example, the rising cost of legal fees has prompted some law firms to adopt a cost-plus pricing approach. Rather than billing business clients on an hourly basis, lawyers and their clients agree on a fixed fee based on expected costs plus a profit for the law firm. Many advertising agencies now use this approach. Here, the client agrees to pay the agency a fee based on the cost of its work plus some agreed-on profit.[12]

Profit-Oriented Approaches

A company may choose to balance both revenues and costs to set price using profit-oriented approaches. These might either involve setting a target of a specific dollar volume of profit or expressing this target profit as a percentage of sales or investment.

Target Profit Pricing   When a firm sets an annual target of a specific dollar amount of profit, this is called *target profit pricing*. For example, if you owned a picture frame store and wanted to achieve a target profit of $7,000 in the coming year, how much would you need to charge for each frame? Since profit depends on revenues and costs, you would have to know your costs and then estimate how many frames you would sell. Let's assume, based on sales in previous years, you expect to frame 1,000 pictures next year. The cost of your time and materials to frame an average picture is $22, while your overhead expenses (rent, manager salaries, etc.) are $26,000. Finally, your goal is to achieve a profit of $7,000. How do you calculate your price per picture?

$$\text{Profit} = \text{Total revenue} - \text{Total costs}$$
$$= (\text{Pictures sold} \times \text{Price/picture}) -$$
$$[(\text{Cost/picture} \times \text{Pictures sold}) + \text{overhead cost}]$$

Solving for Price/picture, the equation becomes,

$$\text{Price/picture} = \frac{\text{Profit} + [(\text{Cost/picture} \times \text{Pictures sold}) + \text{overhead cost}]}{\text{Pictures sold}}$$

$$= \frac{\$7,000 + [(\$22 \times 1,000) + \$26,000]}{1,000}$$

$$= \frac{\$7,000 + \$48,000}{1,000}$$

$$= \$55 \text{ per picture}$$

Clearly, this pricing method depends on an accurate estimate of demand. Because demand is often difficult to predict, this method has the potential for disaster if the estimate is too high. Generally, a target profit pricing strategy is best for firms offering new or unique products, without a lot of competition. What if other frame stores in your area were charging $40 per framed picture? As a marketing manager, you'd have to offer increased customer value with your more expensive frames, lower your costs, or settle for less profit.

Target Return-on-Sales Pricing   Firms such as supermarkets often use *target return-on-sales pricing* to set prices that will give them a profit that is a specified percentage—say, 1 percent—of the sales volume. This pricing method is often used because of the difficulty in establishing a benchmark of sales or investment to show how much of a firm's effort is needed to achieve the target.

Target Return-on-Investment Pricing   Firms such as General Motors and many public utilities use *target return-on-investment pricing* to set prices to achieve a return-on-investment (ROI) target such as a percentage that is mandated by its board of directors or regulators. For example, an electric utility may decide to seek 10 percent ROI. If its investment in plant and equipment is $50 million, it would need to set the price of electricity to its customers at a level that results in $5 million a year in profits.

Competition-Oriented Approaches

Rather than emphasize demand, cost, or profit factors, a company's approach may be based on an analysis of what competitors are doing.

Customary Pricing   For some products where tradition, a standardized channel of distribution, or other competitive factors dictate the price, *customary pricing* is used. Candy bars offered through standard vending machines have a customary price of a dollar, and a significant departure from this price may result in a loss of sales for the manufacturer. Hershey typically has changed the amount of chocolate in its candy bars depending on the price of raw chocolate rather than vary its customary retail price so that it can continue selling through vending machines.

Above-, At-, or Below-Market Pricing   The "market price" of a product is what customers are generally willing to pay, not necessarily the price that the firm sets. For most products it is difficult to identify a specific market price for a product or product class. Still, marketing managers often have a subjective feel for the competitors' price or the market price. Using this benchmark, they then may deliberately choose a strategy of *above-, at-,* or *below-market pricing*.

Among watch manufacturers, Rolex takes pride in emphasizing that it makes one of the most expensive watches you can buy—a clear example of above-market pricing. Manufacturers of national brands of clothing such as Christian Dior and retailers such as Holt Renfrew deliberately set higher prices for their products than those seen at Sears.

Large mass-merchandise chains such as Sears and The Bay generally use at-market pricing. These chains often are seen as establishing the going market price in the minds of their competitors. They also provide a reference price for competitors that use above- and below-market pricing.

In contrast, a number of firms use below-market pricing. Zellers is one retailer that positions itself this way. Manufacturers of generic products and retailers that offer their own private brands of products ranging from peanut butter to shampoo deliberately set prices for these products about 8 percent to 10 percent below the prices of nationally branded competitive products such as Skippy peanut butter or Herbal Essences shampoo.

Loss-Leader Pricing   For a special promotion, retail stores deliberately sell a product below its regular price to attract attention. The purpose of this *loss-leader pricing* is not to increase sales but to attract customers in hopes they will buy other products as well, particularly the discretionary items with large markups. Mass merchandisers have sold home videos at half their regular price to attract customers to their stores. According to an industry observer, "Video is one of the mass merchandisers' favourite traffic-building devices."[13]

ESTIMATING DEMAND AND REVENUE

Basic to setting a product's price is the extent of customer demand for it. Marketing executives must also translate this estimate of customer demand into estimates of revenues the firm expects to receive.

Fundamentals of Estimating Demand

How much money would you pay for your favourite magazine? If the price kept going up, at some point you would probably quit buying it. Conversely, if the price kept going down, you might eventually decide not only to keep buying your magazine but also to get your friend a subscription, too. The lower the price, the higher the demand. The publisher wants to sell more magazines, but will it sell enough additional copies to make up for the lower price per copy? That is an important question for marketing managers. Here's how one firm decided to find out.

Newsweek decided to conduct a pricing experiment at newsstands in 11 cities. In one city, newsstand buyers paid $2.25. In five other cities, newsstand buyers paid the regular $2.00 price. In another city, the price was $1.50, and in the remaining four cities it was only $1.00. By comparison, the regular newsstand price for a competing magazine, *Time*, was $1.95. Why did *Newsweek* conduct the experiment? According to a *Newsweek* executive, "We wanted to figure out what the demand curve for our magazine at the newsstand is."[14]

demand curve

Graph relating quantity sold and price, which shows how many units will be sold at a given price

The Demand Curve   A **demand curve** shows the number of products that will be sold at a given price. Demand curve D1 in Figure 12–4A shows the newsstand demand for *Newsweek* under the existing conditions. Note that as price falls, more people decide to buy and unit sales increase. But price is not the complete story in estimating demand. Economists emphasize three other key factors:

1. *Consumer tastes.* As we saw in Chapter 3, these depend on many factors such as demographics, culture, and technology. Because consumer tastes can change quickly, up-to-date marketing research is essential.
2. *Price and availability of similar products.* The laws of demand work for one's competitors, too. If the price of *Time* magazine falls, more people will buy it. That then means fewer people will buy *Newsweek. Time* is considered by economists to be a substitute for *Newsweek.* Online magazines are also a substitute—one whose availability has increased tremendously in recent years. The point to remember is, as the price of substitutes falls or their availability increases, the demand for a product (*Newsweek,* in this case) will fall.
3. *Consumer income.* In general, as real consumer income (allowing for inflation) increases, demand for a product also increases.

The first of these two factors influences what consumers *want* to buy, and the third affects what they *can* buy. Along with price, these are often called *demand factors*, or factors that determine consumers' willingness and ability to pay for goods and services.

As discussed earlier in Chapters 8 and 10, it is often very difficult to estimate demand for new products, especially because consumer likes and dislikes are often so difficult to read clearly.

Movement along versus Shift of a Demand Curve   Demand curve D_1 in Figure 12–4A shows that as the price is lowered from $2.00 to $1.50, the quantity demanded increases from 3 million (Q_1) to 4.5 million (Q_2) units per year. This is an example of a *movement along a demand curve* and assumes that other factors (consumer tastes, price and availability of substitutes, and consumer income) remain unchanged.

What if some of these factors change? For example, if advertising causes more people to want *Newsweek*, newsstand distribution is increased, or if consumer incomes rise, then the demand increases. Now the original curve, D_1 (the blue line in Figure 12–4B), no longer represents the demand; a new curve must be drawn (D_2). Economists call this a *shift in the demand curve*—in this case, a shift to the right, from D_1 to D_2. This increased demand means that more *Newsweek* magazines are wanted for a given price: At a price of $2, the demand is 6 million units per year (Q_3) on D_2 rather than 3 million units per year (Q_1) on D_1.

What price did *Newsweek* select after conducting its experiment? It kept the price at $2.00. However, through expanded newsstand distribution and more aggressive advertising, Newsweek was later able to shift its demand curve to the right and charge a price of $2.50 without affecting its newsstand volume.

Price Elasticity of Demand   Marketing managers must also pay attention to *price elasticity*—a key consideration related to the product's demand curve. Price elasticity refers to how sensitive consumer demand and the firm's revenues are to changes in the product's price.

A product with *elastic demand* is one in which a slight decrease in price results in a relatively large increase in demand, or units sold. The reverse is also true: With elastic demand, a slight increase in price results in a relatively large decrease in demand. Marketing experiments on cola, coffee, and snack foods show them often to have elastic demand. So marketing managers may cut price to increase the demand, the units sold, and total revenue for one of these products, depending on what competitors' prices are.

FIGURE 12–4

Illustrative demand curves for *Newsweek*

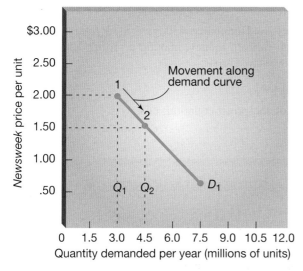

A   Demand curve under initial conditions

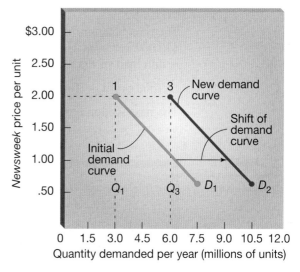

B   Shift in the demand curve with different conditions

The demand for many consumer products is elastic—think jeans, DVDs, and car stereos.

In contrast, a product with *inelastic demand* means that slight increases or decreases in price will not significantly affect the demand, or units sold, for the product. Products and services considered as necessities, such as electricity, usually have inelastic demand. What about gasoline for your car or SUV? Will an increase of a few cents per litre cause you to drive fewer kilometres and buy less gasoline? No? Then you're like millions of other consumers, which is why gasoline has inelastic demand. This means that an increase of a few cents per litre may have a relatively minor impact on the number of litres sold, and may actually increase the total revenue of the gasoline producer. Inelastic demand is usually a relatively short-term phenomenon. Consumers, when they are faced with high prices for something they have to have, will seek out an alternative, and/or producers will see an opportunity to develop a new product. A hybrid car is, in some ways, a producer's response to high gas prices. Or maybe you could learn to love the bus!

Concept Check

1. What is loss-leader pricing?

2. What are four demand factors that determine consumers' willingness and ability to pay for goods and services?

3. What is the difference between movement along a demand curve and a shift in a demand curve?

Fundamentals of Estimating Revenue

total revenue
Total money received from the sale of a product

While economists may talk about "demand curves," marketing executives are more likely to speak in terms of "revenues generated." Demand curves lead directly to an essential revenue concept critical to pricing decisions: **total revenue**. As summarized in Figure 12–5, total revenue (TR) equals the unit price (P) times the quantity sold (Q). Using this equation, let's recall our picture frame shop and assume our annual demand has improved so we can set a price of $100 per picture and sell 400 pictures per year. So,

$$TR = P \times Q$$
$$= \$100 \times 400$$
$$= \$40,000$$

This combination of price and quantity sold annually will give us a total revenue of $40,000 per year. Is that good? Are you making money, making a profit? Total revenue is only part of the profit equation that we saw earlier:

Total profit = Total revenue − Total cost

The next section covers the other part of the profit equation: cost.

FIGURE 12–5
Total revenue concept

Total revenue (TR) is the total money received from the sale of a product. If
TR = Total revenue
P = Unit price of the product
Q = Quantity of the product sold
Then
TR = P × Q

DETERMINING COST, VOLUME, AND PROFIT RELATIONSHIPS

While revenues are the monies received by the firm from selling its products or services to customers, costs or expenses are the monies the firm pays out to its employees and suppliers. Marketing managers often use break-even analysis to relate revenues and costs, topics covered in this section.

The Importance of Controlling Costs

Understanding the role and behaviour of costs is critical for all marketing decisions, particularly pricing decisions. Many firms go bankrupt because their costs get out of control, causing their total costs to exceed their total revenues over an extended period of time. This is why sophisticated marketing managers make pricing decisions that balance both their revenues and costs. Three cost concepts are important in pricing decisions: **total cost**, **fixed cost**, and **variable cost** (Figure 12–6).

total cost
Total expenses incurred by a firm in producing and marketing a product; total cost is the sum of fixed cost and variable costs

Break-Even Analysis

fixed cost
Firm's expenses that are stable and do not change with the quantity of product that is produced and sold

Marketing managers often employ an approach that considers cost, volume, and profit relationships, based on the profit equation. **Break-even analysis** is a technique that analyzes the relationship between total revenue and total cost to determine profitability at various levels of output. The *break-even point* (BEP) is the quantity at which total revenue and total cost are equal. Profit comes from any units sold after the BEP has been reached. In terms of the definitions in Figure 12–6,

$$BEP_{Quantity} = \frac{Fixed\ cost}{Unit\ price - Unit\ variable\ cost}$$

variable cost
Sum of the expenses of the firm that vary directly with the quantity of products that is produced and sold

Calculating a Break-Even Point   Consider again your picture frame store. Suppose you wish to identify how many pictures you must sell to cover your fixed cost at a given price. Let's assume demand for your framed pictures has increased so the average price customers are willing to pay for each picture is $100. Also, suppose your fixed cost (FC) has grown to $28,000 (for real estate taxes, interest on a bank loan, and other fixed expenses) and unit variable cost (UVC) for a picture is now $30 (for labour, glass, frame, and matting). Your break-even quantity ($BEP^{Quantity}$) is 400 pictures, as follows:

break-even analysis
Examines the relationship between total revenue and total cost to determine profitability at different levels of output

$$BEP_{Quantity} = \frac{Fixed\ cost}{Unit\ price - Unit\ variable\ cost}$$

$$= \frac{\$28,000}{\$100 - \$30}$$

$$= 400\ pictures$$

FIGURE 12–6
Total cost concept

Fixed cost (FC) is the sum of the expenses of the firm that are stable and do not change with the quantity of product that is produced and sold. Examples of fixed costs are rent on the building, executive salaries, and insurance.

Variable cost (VC) is the sum of the expenses of the firm that vary directly with the quantity of product that is produced and sold. Examples are the direct labour and direct materials used in producing the product. Variable cost expressed on a per unit basis is called unit variable cost (UVC).

TC = FC + VC

Total cost (TC) is the total expense incurred by a firm in producing and marketing the product. Total cost is the sum of fixed cost and variable cost.

QUANTITY OF PICTURES SOLD (Q)	PRICE PER PICTURE (P)	TOTAL REVENUE (TR) = (P x Q)	UNIT VARIABLE COST (UVC)	TOTAL VARIABLE COST (TVC) = (UVC x Q)	FIXED COST (FC)	TOTAL COST (TC) = (FC + TVC)	PROFIT = (TR – TC)
0	$100	$0	$30	$0	$28,000	$28,000	2$28,000
200	100	20,000	30	6,000	28,000	34,000	214,000
400	100	40,000	30	12,000	28,000	40,000	0
600	100	60,000	30	18,000	28,000	46,000	14,000
800	100	80,000	30	24,000	28,000	52,000	28,000
1,000	100	100,000	30	30,000	28,000	58,000	42,000
1,200	100	120,000	30	36,000	28,000	64,000	56,000

FIGURE 12–7

Calculating a break-even point for a picture frame store

The row shaded in blue in Figure 12–7 shows that your break-even quantity at a price of $100 per picture is 400 pictures. At less than 400 pictures your picture frame store incurs a loss, and at more than 400 pictures it makes a profit. Figure 12–7 also shows that if you could double your annual picture sales to 800, your store would make a profit of $28,000—the row shaded in brown in the figure.

Figure 12–8 shows a graphic presentation of the break-even analysis, called a *break-even chart*. It shows that total revenue and total cost intersect and are equal at a quantity of 400 pictures sold, which is the break-even point at which profit is exactly $0. You want to do better? If your frame store could double the quantity sold annually to 800 pictures, the graph in Figure 12–8 shows you can earn an annual profit of $28,000, as shown by the row shaded in brown in Figure 12–7.

Applications of Break-Even Analysis Because of its simplicity, break-even analysis is used extensively in marketing, most frequently to study the impact on profit of changes in price, fixed cost, and variable cost. The mechanics of break-even analysis are the basis of the widely used electronic spreadsheets offered by computer programs

FIGURE 12–8

Break-even analysis graph for a picture frame store

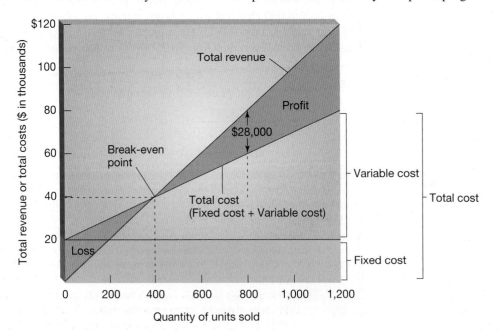

such as Microsoft Excel that permit managers to answer hypothetical "what if" questions about the effect of changes in price and cost on their profit.

PRICING OBJECTIVES AND CONSTRAINTS

With such a variety of alternative pricing strategies available, marketing managers must consider the pricing objectives and constraints that will impact their decisions. While pricing objectives frequently reflect corporate goals, pricing constraints often relate to conditions existing in the marketplace.

Identifying Pricing Objectives

pricing objectives
Expectations that specify the role of price in an organization's marketing and strategic plans

Pricing objectives specify the role of price in an organization's marketing and strategic plans. To the extent possible, these pricing objectives are carried to lower levels in the organization, such as in setting objectives for marketing managers responsible for an individual brand. These objectives may change, depending on the financial position of the company as a whole, the success of its products, or the segments in which it is doing business. H. J. Heinz, for example, has specific pricing objectives for its Heinz ketchup brand that vary by country.

Profit   Three different objectives relate to a firm's profit, which is often measured in terms of return on investment (ROI). These objectives have different implications for pricing strategy. One objective is *managing for long-run profits*, in which a company—such as many Japanese car or TV set manufacturers—gives up immediate profit in exchange for achieving a higher market share. Products are priced relatively low compared to their cost to develop, but the firm expects to make greater profits later because of its high market share.

A *maximizing current profit* objective, such as for a quarter or year, is common in many firms because the targets can be set and performance measured quickly. North American firms are sometimes criticized for this short-run orientation. As noted earlier, a *target return* objective occurs when a firm sets a profit goal (such as 20 percent for return on investment), usually determined by its board of directors. These three profit objectives have different implications for a firm's pricing objectives.

Another profit consideration for firms such as movie studios and manufacturers is to ensure that those firms in their channels of distribution make adequate profits. For example, Figure 12–9 shows where each dollar of your movie ticket goes. The 51 cents the movie studio gets must cover its profit plus the cost of making and marketing the movie, which averaged an all-time high of $81 million in 2000.[15] Although the studio would like more than 51 cents of your dollar, it settles for this amount to make sure theatres and distributors are satisfied and willing to handle its movies.

Theatre
19¢

Distributor
30¢

Movie
studio
51¢

10¢ = Theatre expenses

9¢ = Left for theatre

6¢ = Misc. expenses

24¢ = Left for distributor

20¢ = Advertising and publicity expenses

8¢ = Actors' share of gross

23¢ = Left for movie studio

FIGURE 12–9
Where each dollar of your movie ticket goes

This collector's item jersey sells for around $200 and is a replica of the last jersey that Wayne Gretzky will ever wear on ice—the one he wore for an NHL alumni game in 2003. Imagine what an original Gretzky Oilers jersey would cost, especially if it was signed by the Great One.

Sales   As long as a firm's profit is high enough for it to remain in business, an objective may be to increase sales revenue, which will in turn lead to increases in market share and profit. Cutting price on one product in a firm's line may increase its sales revenue but reduce those of related products. Objectives related to sales revenue or unit sales have the advantage of being translated easily into meaningful targets for marketing managers responsible for a product line or brand.

Market Share   Market share is the ratio of the firm's sales to those of the industry (competitors plus the firm itself). Companies often pursue a market share objective when industry sales are relatively flat or declining. In the late 1990s, Boeing, one of the world's leading aircraft manufacturers, cut prices drastically to try to maintain its 60 percent market share and encountered huge losses. Although increased market share is a primary goal of some firms, others see it as a means to increasing sales and profits.

Volume   Many firms use volume, the quantity produced or sold, as a pricing objective. These firms often sell the same product at several different prices, at different times, or in different places in an attempt to match customer demand with the company's production capacity. Using volume as an objective can sometimes be misleading from a profit standpoint. Volume can be increased by using sales incentives (lowering prices, giving rebates, or offering lower interest rates). By doing this, the company chooses to lower profits in the short run to sell its product quickly.

Survival   In some instances, profits, sales, and market share are less important objectives of the firm than mere survival. Air Canada has struggled to attract passengers with low fares and aggressive promotions to improve the firm's cash flow. This pricing objective has helped Air Canada to stay alive in the competitive airline industry.

Social Responsibility   A firm may forgo higher profit on sales and follow a pricing objective that recognizes its obligations to customers and society in general. Medtronics followed this pricing policy when it introduced the world's first heart pacemaker (see Chapter 1). Gerber supplies a specially formulated product free of charge to children who cannot tolerate foods based on cow's milk.

Identifying Pricing Constraints

pricing constraints
Factors that limit the range of price a firm may set

Factors that limit the range of price a firm may set are **pricing constraints**. Consumer demand for the product clearly affects the price that can be charged. Other constraints on price vary from factors within the organization to competitive factors outside it.

Demand for the Product Class, Product, and Brand   The number of potential buyers for a product class (cars), product (sports cars), and brand (Lamborghini Murciélago) clearly affects the price a seller can charge. So does whether the item is a luxury, like a Murciélago, or a necessity, like bread and a roof over your head.

Newness of the Product: Stage in the Product Life Cycle   The newer the product and the earlier it is in its life cycle, the higher the price that can usually be charged. The high initial price is possible because of limited competition in the early stage. Sometimes, such as when nostalgia or fad factors are present, prices may rise later in the product's life cycle. Collectibles such as a Wayne Gretzky hockey jersey can experience skyrocketing prices. One of Gretzky's jerseys, from a 1980s Edmonton Oilers game, was sold for $45,000.[16] The jersey pictured above is a replica and sells for $200 at the NHL online store; however, the original of this jersey, signed by Gretzky, sold in an online auction for $26,000. Publishing competitive prices on the Internet has revolutionized access to price comparisons for both collectors and buyers and has also created a very competitive marketplace.

Cost of Producing and Marketing the Product
In the long run, a firm's price must cover all the costs of producing and marketing a product. If the price doesn't cover these costs, the firm will fail; so in the long run, a firm's costs set a floor under its price.

Competitors' Prices
When a firm sets its prices, an important consideration is the prices being charged by the competition. As we talked about previously, a firm has three choices: it can charge a higher price, the same price, or a lower price than its competitors. Each choice conveys a message to customers.

A high price signifies that the firm believes its offering represents a higher value in comparison to competing products—value being quality, brand image, benefits and unique features offering extra benefits, or something as simple as instant availability. Sony is known as a firm that typically prices higher than most of its competitors. Consumers wanting quality will pay a higher price.

Charging the same price as the competition means that the firm is relying on some aspect other than price to position and differentiate its products in the minds of customers—that differentiation may be a unique attribute, widespread availability, or an intensive marketing campaign. Thinking again of consumer electronics, Panasonic, JVC, and Sharp are examples of manufacturers whose prices are close for similar products. Consumers typically buy these brands on the basis of some unique attribute of the product, or because they prefer to deal with a specific retailer.

Lower prices can be a challenge, but many firms rely on this strategy. From the company standpoint, lower prices can mean lower profits on each sale, which may need to be offset by larger volume sales. In addition, larger volumes can result in production efficiencies and lower costs. Less well-known brands and some of the larger manufacturers such as RCA use this strategy. For consumers, the lower prices often mean forgoing some aspect such as quality or brand image.

The decision to charge a certain price is impacted by marketing and pricing objectives. If winning market share is an objective, lower prices may be the solution. If being perceived as the "best brand" is an objective, higher prices may be part of the answer. Being known as a *market leader* based on pricing is a title that could be ascribed to firms using either strategy.

Charging prices in line with the competition earns firms the title of *market follower*. This is a conscious choice of many smaller firms manufacturing and selling similar or often the same products. Emphasis is shifted away from price to some other aspect of the marketing mix.

There are occasions where other objectives override any consideration of competitor pricing, such as selling off discontinued models or time-sensitive items (summer-vacation packages, for example).

Legal and Ethical Considerations

Deciding on a final price is a complex process. In addition to the considerations we have just presented, there are laws and regulations that also play a role in the price decision. We will look at four of the most prominent considerations.

Price Fixing
When competitors collaborate and conspire to set prices, they agree to increase, decrease, or stabilize a price for the benefit of some competitors. This is called *price fixing*, and it is illegal—the Competition Act prohibits this practice. Price fixing usually occurs where price is the most important factor in the marketing mix. Some drug companies and gas companies have been found to be involved in this practice.

FIGURE 12-10

Most common deceptive pricing practices

DECEPTIVE PRACTICE	DESCRIPTION
Bait and switch	A firm offers a very low price for a product (the bait), and when consumers come to purchase it, they are persuaded to buy a more expensive product (the switch). Uses techniques such as downgrading the advertised item or not having it in stock.
Bargains conditional on other purchases	A firm advertises "buy one, get one free" or "get two for the price of one." If the first items are sold at the regular price, this is legal. If the price for the first items is inflated for the offer, it is not.
Price comparisons	Advertising "retail value $100—our price $85" is deceptive if a substantial number of stores in the area are not using the $100 price—in other words, if it is not the "going price." Advertising "below manufacturer's suggested list price" is deceptive if no sales occur at the manufacturer's list price. Advertising that the price is reduced 50% is deceptive if the item was not offered for sale at the higher price for a substantial previous period of time.
Double ticketing	When more than one price tag is placed on an item, it must be sold at the lower price; this practice is not illegal, but the law requires that the lower price be charged.

Price Discrimination If different prices are charged to different customers for the same or very similar goods and the same terms, *price discrimination* has occurred. The Competition Act prohibits this, but in order for a firm to be charged with the offence, there has to be evidence of a "practice" of price discrimination—that is, that it is not just a one time or occasional event.

Deceptive Pricing Price offers that mislead the consumer are considered *deceptive pricing*, and this is prohibited under the Competition Act. Figure 12-10 shows the most common deceptive pricing practices. Many companies across the country have been accused of deceptive pricing, but it can be difficult to police and the laws are hard to enforce. Often regulators rely on the ethical standards of those making and publicizing pricing decisions. The Canadian Code of Advertising Standards provides guidelines for various aspects of promotion, and pricing is one of these; advertising industry members are expected to follow this Code and to self-regulate (ensure that they and their colleagues adhere to the Code).

Predatory Pricing Charging a very low price for a product with the intent of undercutting competitors and possibly driving them out of the market is called *predatory pricing*. Once the competitors have been driven out, the offending firm raises its prices. If a company can genuinely operate more efficiently than others, and this lets them offer its products at a lower price, should this be classified as predatory pricing? No! Proving that the intent of the lower price is to eliminate a competitor, and that the prices set are unreasonably and artificially low, is not easy, so there are many more charges of predatory pricing than there are convictions.

Concept Check

1. What is the difference between pricing objectives and pricing constraints?

2. Explain what bait and switch is and why it is an example of deceptive pricing.

SETTING A FINAL PRICE

The final price set by the marketing manager serves many functions. It must be high enough to cover the cost of providing the product *and* meet the objectives of the company. Yet it must be low enough that customers are willing to pay it. But not too low, or customers may think they're purchasing an inferior product. Confused? Setting price is one of the most difficult tasks the marketing manager faces, but four generalized steps are useful to follow.

Step 1: Select an Approximate Price Level

Before setting a final price, the marketing manager must understand the market environment, the features and customer benefits of the particular product, and the goals of the firm. A balance must be struck between factors that might drive a price higher (such as a profit-oriented approach) and other forces (such as increased competition from substitutes) that may drive a price down.

Marketing managers consider pricing objectives and constraints first, then choose among the general pricing approaches—demand-, cost-, profit-, or competition-oriented—to arrive at an approximate price level. This price is then analyzed in terms of cost, volume, and profit relationships. Break-even analyses may be run at this point, and finally, if this approximate price level "works," it is time to take the next step: setting a specific list or quoted price.

Step 2: Set the List or Quoted Price

A seller must decide whether to follow a one-price or flexible-price policy.

One-Price Policy   A *one-price policy* involves setting one price for all buyers of a product or service. For example, Saturn Corporation uses this approach in its dealerships and features a "no haggle, one price" price for its cars. Some retailers such as Dollar Valley have married this policy with a below-market approach and sell everything in their stores for $1 or less!

Flexible-Price Policy   In contrast, a *flexible-price policy* involves setting different prices for products and services depending on individual buyers and purchase situations in light of demand, cost, and competitive factors. Dell Computer adopted flexible pricing as it continually adjusts prices in response to changes in its own costs, competitive pressures, and demand from its various personal computer segments (home, small business, corporate, etc.). "Our flexibility allows us to be [priced] different even within a day," says a Dell spokesperson.[17] This practice is becoming more popular due to improvements in pricing software, as described in the upcoming Ethics and Social Responsibility Alert.

Step 3: Make Special Adjustments to the List or Quoted Price

When you pay $1.00 for a bag of M&Ms in a vending machine or receive a quoted price of $10,000 from a contractor to renovate a kitchen, the pricing sequence ends with the last step just described: setting the list or quoted price. But when you are a manufacturer of M&M candies and sell your product to dozens or hundreds of wholesalers and retailers in your channel of distribution, you may need to make a variety of special adjustments to the list or quoted price. Wholesalers also must adjust list or quoted prices they set for retailers. Three special adjustments to the list or quoted price are discounts, allowances, and geographical adjustments.

ETHICS AND SOCIAL RESPONSIBILITY ALERT

HOW TO BEAT THE PRICING SOFTWARE AT RETAILERS: VISIT THE GAP ON WEDNESDAY, J. CREW ON...?

Remember when you lucked out to buy that sweater at the once-a-year sale at your local retailer? No more! Times have changed. In 2002, 63 percent of all clothing was sold on some kind of sale, and the trend is rising.

Behind all the sales and discounting — on items from clothing and furniture to digital cameras and DVDs — is new sophisticated retail pricing software, sometimes called *price optimization technology*. This retail secret weapon is patterned after the pricing software airlines use for yield management pricing intended to fill airline seats at the best price possible.

The average markdown for retailers has increased from 8 percent of total sales in 1971 to more than 33 percent currently. The goal of this new pricing software is to increase margins and profitability and reduce average inventory by deciding when to put merchandise on sale to clear the shelves.[1]

How can consumers beat the pricing software code? One secret is to recognize that big discounts vary among products. Some examples:

- *Clothing at chain apparel stores.* Chains use the beginning of the week to discover what isn't selling well to make plans for the high-traffic weekends. So the best deals come Wednesdays through Fridays, right before the weekend. Some apparel chains have specific days for nationwide price markdowns: Wednesdays for The Gap and Thursdays for J. Crew and Eddie Bauer.

- *Digital cameras and DVD players.* Deals start before Christmas in November with greatest discounts coming in March or April, when retailers try to clear their shelves for new models.

- *CDs and DVDs.* In direct contrast to digital cameras and DVD players, buy these early while they're hot — within five days of their typical Tuesday release. Prices typically stay low until Saturday night.

Even high-end department stores are starting to use retail pricing software, but probably not for items like designer lines of women's dresses. Is it ethical for stores to use price optimization technology? Is it right for consumers to try to beat the system by shopping on certain days? Remember, there's another method for getting a lower price: Just ask!

[1] Jane Spencer, "Cracking the Code: How Not to Pay Retail," *The Wall Street Journal*, November 27, 2002, pp. D1, D2; Bob Tedeschi, "Specifically Priced Retail Goods," *New York Times*, September 2, 2002, pp. F1.8; and www.spotlightsolutions.com.

Discounts *Discounts* are reductions from list price that a seller gives a buyer as a reward for some activity of the buyer that is favourable to the seller. Four kinds of discounts are especially important in marketing strategy: quantity, seasonal, trade (functional), and cash.[18]

- *Quantity discounts.* To encourage customers to buy larger quantities of a product, firms at all levels in the channel of distribution offer quantity discounts, which are reductions in unit costs for a larger order. For example, an instant photocopying service might set a price of 10 cents a copy for 1 to 24 copies, 9 cents a copy for 25 to 99, and 8 cents a copy for 100 or more. Because the photocopying service gets more of the buyer's business and has longer production runs that reduce its order-handling costs, it is willing to pass on some of the cost savings in the form of quantity discounts to the buyer.

Toro uses seasonal discounts to stimulate consumer demand and smooth out seasonal manufacturing peaks and troughs.

- *Seasonal discounts.* To encourage buyers to stock inventory earlier than their normal demand would require, manufacturers often use seasonal discounts. A firm such as Toro that manufactures lawn mowers and snow blowers offers seasonal discounts to encourage wholesalers and retailers to stock up on lawn mowers in January and February and on snow blowers in July and August—months before the seasonal demand by ultimate consumers. This enables Toro to smooth out seasonal manufacturing peaks and troughs, thereby contributing to more efficient production. It also rewards wholesalers and retailers for the risk they accept in assuming increased inventory carrying costs and gives them the benefit of having supplies in stock at the time they are wanted by customers.
- *Trade (functional) discounts.* To reward wholesalers and retailers for marketing functions they will perform in the future, a manufacturer often gives trade, or functional, discounts. These reductions off the list or base price are offered to resellers in the channel of distribution on the basis of where they are in the channel and the marketing activities they are expected to perform in the future.

Traditional trade discounts have been established in various product lines such as hardware, food, and pharmaceutical items. Although the manufacturer may suggest trade discounts, the sellers are free to alter the discount schedule depending on their competitive situation. Suppose that a manufacturer quotes prices in the following form:

List price—$100, less 30/10/5

The first number in the percentage sequence (in this example, 30/10/5) always refers to the retail end of the channel, and the last number always refers to the wholesaler or jobber closest to the manufacturer in the channel. The trade discounts are simply subtracted one at a time. This price quote shows that $100 is the manufacturer's suggested retail price:

- For the retailer, 30 percent of the suggested retail price ($100 × 0.3 = $30) is available to cover costs and provide a profit;
- Wholesalers closest to the retailer in the channel get 10 percent of their selling price ($70 × 0.1 = $7); and
- The final group of wholesalers in the channel (probably jobbers) that are closest to the manufacturer get 5 percent of their selling price ($63 × 0.05 = $3.15).

Thus, starting with the manufacturer's retail price and subtracting the three trade discounts shows that the manufacturer's selling price to the wholesaler or jobber closest to the manufacturer is $59.85 (see Figure 12-11).

- *Cash discounts.* To encourage retailers to pay their bills quickly, manufacturers offer them cash discounts. Suppose a retailer receives a bill quoted at $1,000, 2/10 net 30. This means that the bill for the product is $1,000, but the retailer can take a 2 percent discount ($1,000 × 0.02 = $20) if payment is made within 10 days and send a cheque for $980. If the payment cannot be made within 10 days, the total amount of $1,000 is due within 30 days. It is usually understood by the buyer that an interest charge will be added after the first 30 days of free credit.

Retailers provide cash discounts to consumers as well, to eliminate the cost of credit granted to consumers. These discounts take the form of discount-for-cash policies.

Allowances   Allowances—like discounts—are reductions from list or quoted prices to buyers for performing some activity.

FIGURE 12–11
How trade discounts work

- *Trade-in allowances.* A new car dealer can offset the list price of that new Toyota Camry by offering you a trade-in allowance of $500 for your old Honda. A trade-in allowance is a price reduction given when a used product is part of the payment on a new product. Trade-ins are an effective way to lower the price a buyer has to pay without formally reducing the list price.
- *Promotional allowances.* Sellers in the channel of distribution can qualify for promotional allowances for undertaking certain advertising or selling activities to promote a product. Various types of allowances include an actual cash payment or an extra amount of "free goods" (as with a free case of pizzas to a retailer for every dozen cases purchased). Frequently, a portion of these savings is passed on to the consumer by retailers.

Geographical Adjustments   Geographical adjustments are made by manufacturers or even wholesalers to list or quoted prices to reflect the cost of transportation of the products from seller to buyer. The two general methods for quoting prices related to transportation costs are FOB origin pricing and uniform delivered pricing.

- *FOB origin pricing.* FOB means "free on board" some vehicle at some location, which means the seller pays the cost of loading the product onto the vehicle that is used (such as a barge, railroad car, or truck). FOB origin pricing usually involves the seller's naming the location of this loading as the seller's factory or warehouse (such as "FOB Montreal" or "FOB factory"). The title and ownership to the goods passes to the buyer at the point of loading, so the buyer becomes responsible for picking the specific mode of transportation, for all the transportation costs, and for subsequent handling of the product. Buyers farthest from the seller face the big disadvantage of paying the higher transportation costs.
- *Uniform delivered pricing.* When a uniform delivered pricing method is used, the price the seller quotes includes all transportation costs. It is quoted in a contract as "FOB buyer's location," and the seller selects the mode of transportation, pays the freight charges, and is responsible for any damage that may occur because the seller retains title to the goods until delivered to the buyer.

Step 4: Monitor and Adjust Prices

Rarely can a firm set a price and leave it at that. As you have learned, there are many constraints that affect setting prices, and the firm has objectives that it also takes into account. Things change both in the external business environment and within the firm itself; as a result, prices need to be reviewed and revised if necessary. A key activity is the monitoring of competitor activity, legislative changes, economic conditions, and—the ultimate measure—consumer demand! These factors, and their potential impact on the firm's ability to achieve its marketing goals, have to be examined and action taken when necessary.

1. Why would a seller choose a flexible-price policy over a one-price policy?

2. What is the purpose of (a) quantity discounts and (b) promotional allowances?

SUMMARY

1 Price is the money or other considerations exchanged for the ownership or use of a product or service. Although price typically involves money, the amount exchanged is often different from the list or quoted price because of allowances and extra fees.

2 Consumers use price as an indicator of value when it is paired with the perceived benefits of a good or service. Sometimes price influences consumer perceptions of quality itself and at other times consumers make value assessments by comparing the costs and benefits of substitute items.

3 Four general approaches for finding an approximate price level for a product or service are demand-oriented, cost-oriented, profit-oriented, and competition-oriented pricing.

4 Demand-oriented pricing approaches stress consumer demand and revenue implications of pricing and include seven types: skimming, penetration, prestige, odd-even, target, bundle, and yield management.

5 Cost-oriented pricing approaches emphasize the cost aspects of pricing and include two types: standard and cost-plus pricing.

6 Profit-oriented pricing approaches focus on a balance between revenues and costs to set a price and include three types: target profit, target return-on-sales, and target return-on-investment pricing.

7 Competition-oriented pricing approaches emphasize what competitors or the marketplace are doing and include three types: customary; above-, at-, or below-market; and loss-leader pricing.

8 A demand curve shows the maximum number of products consumers will buy at a given price and for a given set of (a) consumer tastes, (b) price and availability of other products, and (c) consumer income. When any of these change, there is a shift in the demand curve.

9 It is necessary to consider cost behaviour when making pricing decisions. Important cost concepts include total cost, variable cost, and fixed cost. An essential revenue concept is total revenue.

10 Break-even analysis shows the relationship between total revenue and total cost at various quantities of output for given conditions of price, fixed cost, and variable cost. The break-even point is where total revenue and total cost are equal.

11 Pricing objectives, which specify the role of price in a firm's marketing strategy, may include pricing for profit, sales revenue, market share, unit sales, survival, or some socially responsible price level.

12 Pricing constraints such as demand, product newness, costs, competitors, other products sold by the firm, and the type of competitive market restrict a firm's pricing range.

13 Given an approximate price level for a product, a manager must set a list or quoted price by considering factors such as one-price versus a flexible-price policy.

14 List or quoted price is often modified through discounts, allowances, and geographical adjustments. The pricing environment needs to be monitored continually.

KEY TERMS AND CONCEPTS

break-even analysis p. 283
demand curve p. 280
fixed cost p. 283
markup p. 277
price p. 272
pricing constraints p. 286

pricing objectives p. 285
profit equation p. 274
total cost p. 283
total revenue p. 282
variable cost p. 283

QUESTIONS: APPLYING MARKETING CONCEPTS AND PERSPECTIVES

1 How would the price equation apply to the purchase price of (a) gasoline, (b) an airline reservation, and (c) a chequing account?

2 What would be your response to the statement, "Profit maximization is the only legitimate pricing objective for the firm"?

3 Touché Toiletries, Inc., has developed an addition to its Lizardman Cologne line tentatively branded Ode d'Toade Cologne. Unit variable costs are 45 cents for a 3-ounce bottle, and heavy advertising expenditures in the first year would result in total fixed costs of $900,000. Ode d'Toade Cologne is priced at $7.50 for a 3-ounce bottle. How many bottles of Ode d'Toade must be sold to break even?

4 Suppose that marketing executives for Touché Toiletries reduced the price to $6.50 for a 3-ounce bottle of Ode d'-Toade and the fixed costs were $1,100,000. Suppose further that the unit variable cost remained at 45 cents for a 3-ounce

bottle. (a) How many bottles must be sold to break even? (b) What dollar profit level would Ode d'Toade achieve if 200,000 bottles were sold?

5 Under what conditions would a camera manufacturer adopt a skimming price approach for a new product? A penetration approach?

6 What are some similarities and differences between skimming pricing, prestige pricing, and above-market pricing?

7 A manufacturer of exercise equipment sets a suggested price to the consumer of $395 for a particular piece of equipment in line with other equipment on the market. The manufacturer sells its equipment to a sporting goods wholesaler who receives a 25 percent markup, who then sells it to a retailer who receives a 50 percent markup. What demand-oriented pricing approach is being used, and at what price will the manufacturer sell the equipment to the wholesaler?

DISCUSSION FORUM

Pharmaceutical companies are continually involved in research and development of new products. They face huge costs and time frames when bringing new drugs to market. It can take several years and upwards of $100 million for a new drug to be successfully launched. Not only do they have to fund research and development, but field trials and marketing costs are also very high. Winning government approval is a time-consuming and expensive task. They need to convince the medical community to try out, adopt, and prescribe the drug for patients and they also need to create awareness at the consumer level so that patients will ask their doctors for the drug by name.

Once in the marketplace, companies often face costly legal challenges over the safety of the drug, and while registered patents offer some protection for limited periods of time, the likelihood of a competitor launching a potentially superior product into the marketplace first is very real. The result? Very high prices to consumers. Yes, some people have medical plans that cover part, and in some cases all, of the drug costs, but many simply cannot afford the drugs even though

they would benefit health-wise from them.

Profit margins on prescription drugs are reportedly large, but sales volumes are not necessarily high. Conversely, over-the-counter drugs, available without a doctor's prescription, have lower profit margins and typically very high sales volumes.

Discuss these aspects of drug pricing with your group and sketch out your answers:

1 Recognizing that access to effective and quality medication is a real need for all consumers, should government regulate pricing and place controls on the profits that drug companies make?

2 What do you think would be the effect on the drug industry and on consumers if the government moved towards such controls?

3 How would you, as the senior marketing executive in a pharmaceutical company, react to these issues? What impact would this have on your overall marketing strategy and your pricing strategy in particular?

4 Who or what do you feel should set drug pricing and why?

INTERNET EXERCISE

It's Wednesday and you just completed your midterm exams. As a reward for your hard work, a friend sent you a pair of free tickets to a popular Broadway show in New York City for 7:00 P.M. Saturday night. Check out the following online

travel services to book a round-trip ticket, leaving from Toronto's Pearson (YYZ) airport around 4:00 P.M. on Friday to New York City's La Guardia (LGA) airport. On Sunday, you'll leave La Guardia around 5:00 P.M. and return to

Toronto. Which of the following online travel services provides the cheapest fare and fewest restrictions? See what prices you can get for your airfare! And don't forget to eat at the Carnegie Deli while you're in New York!

- Cheap Tickets (www.cheaptickets.ca).

- Flight Centre (www.flightcentre.ca).
- Travelocity (www.travelocity.ca).

(*Note*: You were not asked to search Expedia.ca or Priceline.com because you may accidentally order a ticket without meaning to do so.)

VIDEO CASE 12

WASHBURN INTERNATIONAL: GUITARS AND BREAK-EVEN POINTS

"The relationship between musicians and their guitars is something really extraordinary — and is a fairly strange one," says Brady Breen in a carefully understated tone of voice. Breen has the experience to know. He's production manager of Washburn International, one of the most prestigious guitar manufacturers in the world. Washburn's instruments range from one-of-a-kind, custom-made acoustic and electric guitars and basses to less-expensive, mass-produced ones.

THE COMPANY

The modern Washburn International started in 1977 when a small Chicago firm bought the century-old Washburn brand name and a small inventory of guitars, parts, and promotional supplies. At that time, annual revenues of the company were $300,000 for the sale of about 2,500 guitars. Washburn's first catalogue, appearing in 1978, told a frightening truth:

> "Our designs are translated by Japan's most experienced craftsmen, assuring the consistent quality and craftmanship for which they are known."

At that time, the American guitar-making craft was at an all-time low. Guitars made by Japanese firms such as Ibane and Yamaha were in use by an increasing number of professionals.

Times have changed for Washburn. Today the company sells about 250,000 guitars a year. Annual sales exceed $50 million. All this resulted from Washburn's aggressive marketing strategies to develop product lines with different price points targeted at musicians in distinctly different market segments.

THE PRODUCTS AND MARKET SEGMENTS

Arguably the most trendsetting guitar developed by the modern Washburn company appeared in 1980. This was the Festival Series of cutaway, thin-bodied flattops, with built-in bridge pickups and controls, which went on to become the virtual standard for live performances. John Lodge of the Moody Blues endorsed the 12-string version—his gleaming white guitar appearing in both concerts and ads for years. In the time since the Festival Series appeared, countless rock and country stars have used these instruments including Bob Dylan, Dolly Parton, Greg Allman, John Jorgenson, and George Harrison.

Until 1991 all Washburn guitars were manufactured in Asia. That year Washburn started building its high-end guitars in the United States. Today Washburn marketing executives divide its product line into four levels. From high end to low end these are,

- One-of-a-kind, custom units.
- Batch-custom units.
- Mass-customized units.
- Mass-produced units.

The one-of-a-kind custom units are for the many stars that use Washburn instruments. The mass-produced units targeted at first-time buyers are still manufactured in Asian factories.

PRICING ISSUES

Setting prices for its various lines presents a continuing challenge for Washburn. Not only do the prices have to reflect the changing tastes of its various segments of musicians, but the prices must also be competitive with the prices set for guitars manufactured and marketed globally. In fact, Washburn and other well-known guitar manufacturers have a prestige-niche strategy. For Washburn this involves endorsements by internationally known musicians who play its instruments and lend their names to lines of Washburn signature guitars. This has the effect of reducing the price elasticity or price sensitivity for these guitars. Stars playing Washburn guitars such as David Gilmour of Pink Floyd, Joe Perry of Aerosmith, and Darryl Jones of the Rolling Stones have their own lines of signature guitars—the "batch-custom" units mentioned earlier.

Joe Baksha, Washburn's executive vice president, is responsible for reviewing and approving prices for the company's lines of guitars. Setting a sales target of 2,000 units for a new line of guitars, he is considering a suggested retail price of $329 per unit for customers at one of the hundreds of retail outlets carrying the Washburn line. For planning purposes, Baksha estimates that half of the final retail price will be the price Washburn nets when it sells its guitar to the wholesalers and dealers in its channel of distribution.

Looking at Washburn's financial data for its present Chicago plant, Baksha estimates that this line of guitars must bear these fixed costs:

Rent and taxes	= $12,000
Depreciation of equipment	= $ 4,000
Management and quality control program	= $20,000

In addition, he estimates the variable costs for each unit to be:

Direct materials	= $25/unit
Direct labour	= 8 hours/unit @ $14/hour

Carefully kept production records at Washburn's Chicago plant make Baksha believe that these are reasonable estimates. He explains, "Before we begin a production run, we have a good feel for what our costs will be. The U.S.-built N-4, for example, simply costs more than one of our foreign-produced Mercury or Wing series electrics."

Caught in the global competition for guitar sales, Washburn searches for ways to reduce and control costs. After much agonizing, the company decided to move to Nashville, Tennessee. In this home of country music, Washburn expects to lower its manufacturing costs because there are many skilled workers in the region, and its fixed costs will be reduced by avoiding some of the expenses of having a big city location. Specifically, Washburn projects that it will reduce its rent and taxes expenses by 40 percent and the wage rate it pays by 15 percent in relocating from Chicago to Nashville.

Questions

1 What factors are most likely to affect the demand for the lines of Washburn guitars *(a)* bought by a first-time guitar buyer and *(b)* bought by a sophisticated musician who wants a signature model signed by David Gilmour or Joe Perry?

2 For Washburn what are examples of *(a)* shifting the demand curve to the right to get a higher price for a guitar line (movement *of* the demand curve) and *(b)* pricing decisions involving moving *along* a demand curve?

3 In Washburn's Chicago plant what is the break-even point for the new line of guitars if the retail price is *(a)* $329, *(b)* $359, and *(c)* $299? Also, *(d)* if Washburn achieves the sales target of 2,000 units at the $329 retail price, what will its profit be?

4 Assume that Washburn moves its production to Nashville and that the costs are reduced as projected in the case. Then, what will be the *(a)* new break-even point at a $329 retail price for this line of guitars and *(b)* the new profit if it sells 2,000 units?

5 If for competitive reasons Washburn eventually has to move all its production back to Asia, *(a)* which specific costs might be lowered and *(b)* what additional costs might it expect to incur?

Marketing Channels and Channel Logistics

AFTER READING THIS CHAPTER YOU SHOULD BE ABLE TO:

- Explain what is meant by a channel of distribution and the differences between distribution channels for consumer products and for business-to-business products.

- Explain why intermediaries are necessary in distribution and the functions they perform.

- Describe the factors considered by marketing executives when selecting and managing a channel of distribution.

- Understand the use of multichannel marketing.

- Differentiate between types of vertical marketing systems.

- Discuss supply chain and logistics management and how they relate to marketing strategy.

AVON'S MAKEOVER IS MORE THAN COSMETIC

Avon Products, Inc. is in the midst of its own makeover. As the world's leading direct seller of beauty and related items to women in 139 countries, Avon has begun calling on new customers, in new ways, with new products.

Avon's makeover represents a noticeable expansion beyond its traditional manner of doing business. For more than 115 years, the company successfully marketed its products through an extensive network of independent representatives, which today number 3.4 million worldwide. However, Avon's marketing research indicated that 59 percent of women who don't buy Avon products would if they were more accessible. The message to Avon's senior management was clear: Give busy women a choice in how they do their buying—through an Avon representative, in a store, or online. According to Andrea Jung, Avon's chief executive officer, "While direct selling will always be our principal sales channel, expanding access to new customers will help accelerate top-line [sales] growth."

The goal of expanded access to new customers has materialized in new ways. Avon set aside US$60 million to build a website (www.avon.ca www.avon.com) focused around the company's representatives and brochures. Avon experimented with a shop-within-a-store format in selected JCPenney stores in the United States. The stores are "not without risk, but with great opportunity," Ms. Jung says. "It's a giant step."

Is Avon's makeover achieving its goal? Yes. "We've learned that at retail, we attract new customers, not the same people that our representatives are serving directly," said Debora Coffey, an Avon spokeswoman.[1]

This chapter focuses on marketing channels (also called distribution channels) and their role as part of the marketing mix.

WHERE IN THE MARKETING PROCESS ARE WE GOING IN THIS CHAPTER?

Chapter 13 focuses on the concept of distribution—getting the product to the customer—the place P of the 4Ps that make up the marketing mix.

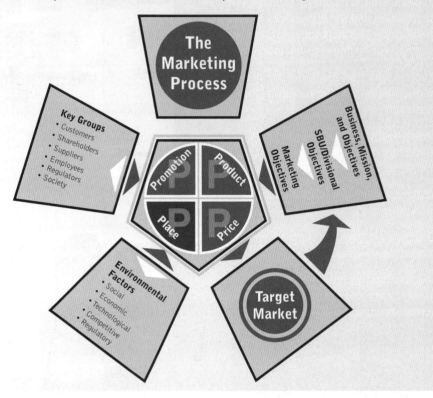

NATURE AND IMPORTANCE OF MARKETING CHANNELS

Reaching potential buyers is obviously a critical part of successful marketing. Buyers benefit from well-structured and efficient distribution systems. The route to do this is direct in some cases and indirect in others.

What Is a Marketing Channel?

You see the results of distribution every day. You may have purchased Lay's Potato Chips at the 7-Eleven store, a book through chapters.indigo.ca, or Levi's jeans at Sears. Each of these items was brought to you by a marketing channel of distribution, or simply a **marketing channel**, which consists of individuals and firms involved in the process of making a product or service available.

    Marketing channels can be compared with a pipeline through which water flows from a source to an endpoint. Marketing channels make possible the flow of goods from a producer, through **intermediaries**, to a buyer. There are several types of intermediaries—and specific names or terms for each type—and, as shown in Figure 13-1, they perform various functions.[2] Some intermediaries actually purchase items from the producer, store them, and resell them to buyers. For example, Krave's Candy Company produces Clodhoppers candy and sells it to wholesalers. The wholesalers then sell the candy to supermarkets and retailers, which in turn sell it to consumers. Other intermediaries such as brokers and agents represent sellers but do not actually ever own the products—their role is to bring a seller and buyer together. Real estate agents are examples of this type of intermediary.

marketing channel
The set of individuals or firms involved in the process of making a product available

intermediaries ɪnˈtəˈmiˈdjə
Individuals or firms performing a role in the marketing channel, involved in making a product available

TERM	DESCRIPTION
Middleman	Another name for intermediary *(individuals or firms)*
Agent or broker	Any intermediary with legal authority to act on behalf of another channel member (for example, a manufacturer)
Wholesaler	Any intermediary who sells to other intermediaries, usually to retailers—this term usually applies to intermediaries who deal in consumer goods
Retailer	An intermediary who sells to consumers
Distributor	A general term used to describe intermediaries who perform a variety of functions, including selling, maintaining inventories, extending credit, and others—usually used for those in business markets
Dealer	A general term that can mean the same as a distributor, a retailer, or a wholesaler

FIGURE 13–1

Terms used for marketing intermediaries

Value Created by Intermediaries

The importance of intermediaries is made clear when we consider the functions they perform and the value they create for buyers.

Functions Performed by Intermediaries Intermediaries make possible the flow of products from producers to ultimate consumers by performing three basic functions (Figure 13–2). Intermediaries perform a transactional function when they buy and sell goods or services. But an intermediary such as a wholesaler also performs the function of sharing risk with the producer when it stocks merchandise in anticipation of sales. If the stock is unsold for any reason, the intermediary—not the producer—suffers the loss.

The logistics of a transaction (described at length later in this chapter) involve the details of preparing and getting a product to buyers. Gathering, sorting, and dispersing products are some of the logistical functions of the intermediary—imagine the various fruits and vegetables displayed at your local grocery store! Finally, intermediaries perform facilitating functions that, by definition, make a transaction *easier* for buyers. For example, Sears issues credit cards to consumers so they can buy now and pay later.

All three groups of functions must be performed in a marketing channel, even though each channel member may not participate in all three. Channel members often negotiate about which specific functions they will perform. Sometimes disagreements result, and a breakdown in relationships among channel members occurs. This happened when PepsiCo's bottler in Venezuela switched to Coca-Cola. Given the intermediary's logistical role—storing and transporting Pepsi to Venezuelan customers in this case—PepsiCo either had to set up its own bottling operation to perform these marketing channel functions, or find another bottler, which it did.[3]

Consumer Benefits from Intermediaries Consumers also benefit from the actions of intermediaries. Having the goods and services you want, when you want them, where you want them, and in the form you want them is the ideal result of marketing channels. In more specific terms, marketing channels help create value for consumers through

TYPE OF FUNCTION	ACTIVITIES RELATED TO FUNCTION
Transactional function	• *Buying*: Purchasing products for resale • *Selling*: Contacting potential customers, promoting products, and seeking orders • *Risk taking*: Assuming business risks in the ownership of inventory
Logistical function	• *Selection:* Putting together a selection of products from several different sources • *Storing*: Assembling and protecting products at a convenient location • *Sorting*: Purchasing in large quantities and dividing into smaller amounts • *Transporting*: Physically moving a product to customers
Facilitating function	• *Financing*: Extending credit to customers • *Marketing information and research*: Providing information to customers and suppliers, including competitive conditions and trends

FIGURE 13–2

Marketing channel functions performed by intermediaries

the five utilities described in Chapter 1: time, place, form, information, and possession. Time utility refers to having a product or service when you want it. For example, FedEx provides next-morning delivery. Place utility means having a product or service available where consumers want it, such as having a Petro Canada gas station located on a long stretch of a provincial highway. Form utility involves enhancing a product or service to make it more appealing to buyers. For example, Compaq Computer delivers unfinished PCs to dealers, which then add memory, chips, modems, and other parts, based on consumer specifications. Information utility means providing consumers with the information they need to make an informed choice; information-packed websites and user manuals provide this type of utility. Possession utility involves efforts by intermediaries to help buyers take possession of a product or service, such as providing various ways for payment to be made for a product—by credit card, debit card, cash, or cheque.

Concept Check

1. What is meant by a marketing channel?

2. What are the three basic functions performed by intermediaries?

CHANNEL STRUCTURE AND ORGANIZATION

A product can take many routes on its journey from a producer to buyers, and marketers search for the most efficient route from the many alternatives available. As you'll see, there are some important differences between the marketing channels for consumer goods and those for business goods.

Marketing Channels for Consumer Goods and Services

Figure 13–3 shows the four most common marketing channel configurations for consumer goods and services. It also shows the number of levels in each marketing channel, that is, the number of intermediaries between a producer and ultimate buyers. As the number of intermediaries between a producer and buyer increases, the channel is viewed as increasing in length. The producer → wholesaler → retailer → consumer channel is longer than the producer → consumer channel.

FIGURE 13-3

Common marketing
channels for consumer
goods and services

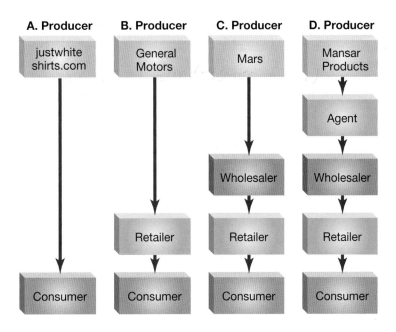

Channel A in Figure 13–3 represents a *direct channel* because a producer and ultimate consumers deal directly with each other. Many products and services are distributed this way. A number of insurance companies sell their financial services using a direct channel and branch sales offices. The online store justwhiteshirts.com designs and produces high-quality men's shirts that are sold online and by catalogue to consumers around the world. Because there are no intermediaries with a direct channel, the producer must perform all channel functions.

The remaining three channel forms are *indirect channels* because intermediaries are inserted between the producer and consumers and perform numerous channel functions. Channel B, with a retailer added, is most common when the retailer is large and can buy in large quantities from a producer or when the cost of inventory makes it too expensive to use a wholesaler. Automobile manufacturers use this channel, with a local car dealer acting as a retailer. Why is there no wholesaler? So many variations exist in the product that it would be impossible for a wholesaler to stock all the models required to satisfy buyers; in addition, the cost of maintaining an inventory would be too high. Large retailers such as Sears, 7-Eleven, and Safeway buy in sufficient quantities to make it cost effective for a producer to deal with only a retail intermediary.

Adding a wholesaler in channel C is most common for low-cost, low-unit value items that are frequently purchased by consumers, such as candy, confectionary items, and magazines. For example, Mars sells its line of candies to wholesalers in case quantities; then wholesalers can break down (sort) the cases so that individual retailers can order in boxes or much smaller quantities.

Channel D, the most indirect channel, is employed when there are many small manufacturers and many small retailers and an agent is used to help coordinate a large supply of the product. Mansar Products, Ltd., is a Belgian producer of specialty jewellery that uses agents to sell to wholesalers, which then sell to many small retailers.

Marketing Channels for Business Goods and Services

The four most common channels for business goods and services are shown in Figure 13–4. In contrast with channels for consumer products, business channels typically are shorter and rely on one intermediary or none at all because business users are fewer in number, tend to be more concentrated geographically, and buy in larger quantities. For

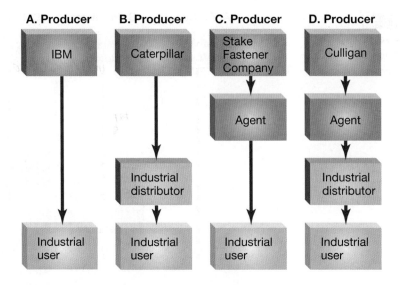

these reasons, business channels can be served directly or by a limited number of inter-mediaries.

Channel A, represented by IBM's large, mainframe computer business, is a direct chan-nel. Firms using this kind of channel maintain their own sales force and perform all chan-nel functions. This channel is employed when buyers are large and well defined, the sales effort requires extensive negotiations, and the products are of high unit value and require hands-on expertise in terms of installation or use. Bombardier and Airbus Industries would be other examples.

Channels B, C, and D are indirect channels with one or more intermediaries to reach industrial users. In channel B an *industrial distributor* performs a variety of marketing channel functions, including selling, stocking, and delivering a full product assortment and financing. In many ways, industrial distributors are like wholesalers in consumer channels. Caterpillar relies on industrial distributors to sell and service its construction and mining equipment in almost 200 countries.

Channel C introduces another intermediary, an agent, who serves primarily as the inde-pendent selling arm of producers and represents a producer to industrial users. For exam-ple, Stake Fastener Company, a producer of industrial fasteners, has an agent call on industrial users rather than employing its own sales force.

Channel D is the longest channel and includes both agents and distributors. For instance, Culligan, a small producer of water treatment equipment, uses agents to call on distributors who sell to industrial users.

Electronic Marketing Channels

The marketing channels that we have just discussed for consumer and business goods and services are not the only routes to the marketplace. Advances in electronic commerce have opened new avenues for reaching buyers and creating customer value.

Interactive electronic technology has made possible *electronic marketing channels*, which employ the Internet to make goods and services available to consumers or busi-ness buyers. A unique feature of these channels is that they can combine electronic and traditional intermediaries to create time, place, form, and possession utility for buyers.[4]

Figure 13–5 shows the electronic marketing channels for books (Amazon.ca), reserva-tion services (Travelocity.ca), and personal computers (Dell.ca). Are you surprised that they look a lot like common marketing channels? An important reason for the similarity resides in channel functions detailed in Figure 13–2. Electronic intermediaries can and do

FIGURE 13-5

Examples of electronic marketing channels

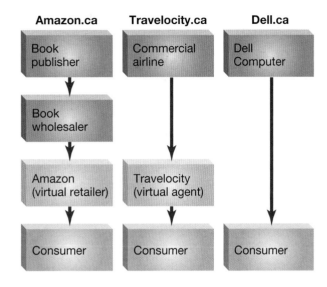

perform transactional and facilitating functions effectively and at a relatively lower cost than traditional intermediaries because of efficiencies made possible by information technology. However, electronic intermediaries are incapable of performing elements of the logistical function, particularly for products such as books and automobiles. This function remains with traditional intermediaries or with the producer, as seen with Dell Computer Corporation with its direct channel.

Many services are distributed through electronic marketing channels, such as travel reservations marketed by Travelocity.ca, financial securities by Royal Bank, and insurance by Metropolitan Life. Software, too, can be marketed this way. However, many other services such as health care and auto repair still involve traditional intermediaries.

Multiple Channels and Strategic Alliances

dual distribution
Arrangement whereby a firm reaches buyers by using two or more different types of channels for the same basic product

In some situations producers use **dual distribution**, an arrangement whereby a firm reaches different buyers by employing two or more different types of channels for the same basic product. For instance, GE sells its large appliances directly to home and apartment builders but uses retail stores, including Wal-Mart, to sell to consumers. In some instances, firms pair multiple channels with a multibrand strategy. This is done to minimize cannibalization of the firm's family brand and to differentiate the channels. For example, Hallmark sells its Hallmark greeting cards through Hallmark stores and select department stores, and its Ambassador brand of cards through discount and drugstore chains.

A recent development in marketing channels is the use of *strategic channel alliances*, whereby one firm's marketing channel is used to sell another firm's products.[5] An alliance between Kraft Foods and Starbucks is a case in point. Kraft distributes Starbucks coffee in North American supermarkets and internationally. Strategic alliances are popular in global marketing, where the creation of marketing channel relationships is expensive and time consuming. For example, General Mills and Nestlé have an extensive alliance that spans 70 international markets from Brazil to Poland to Thailand. Read the accompanying Marketing NewsNet so you won't be surprised when you are served Nestlé (not General Mills) Cheerios in Europe, South America, and parts of Asia.[6]

Multichannel Marketing to the Online Consumer

Consumers and companies populate two market environments today. One is the traditional marketplace, where buyers and sellers engage in face-to-face exchange relation-

MARKETING NEWSNET

NESTLÉ AND GENERAL MILLS: CEREAL PARTNERS WORLDWIDE

Can you say Nestlé Cheerios *miel amandes*? Millions of French start their day with this European equivalent of General Mills' Honey Nut Cheerios, made possible by Cereal Partners Worldwide (CPW). CPW is the food industry's first strategic alliance designed to be a global business; it joined the cereal manufacturing and marketing capability of General Mills with the worldwide distribution clout of Nestlé.

From its headquarters near Lake Geneva, Switzerland, CPW first launched General Mills cereals under the Nestlé label in France, the United Kingdom, Spain, and Portugal in 1991. Today, CPW competes in 70 markets worldwide and soon expects to achieve its goal of US$1 billion in profitable sales.

The General Mills–Nestlé strategic alliance is also likely to increase the worldwide ready-to-eat-cereal market share of these companies, which are already rated as the two best-managed firms in the world. CPW is on track to reach its goal of a 20 percent worldwide share.

ships in an environment characterized by physical facilities (stores and offices) and mostly tangible objects. The other is the marketspace, an Internet/Web-enabled digital environment characterized by "face-to-screen" exchange relationships and electronic images and offerings.

The existence of two market environments has benefited consumers tremendously. Today, consumers can shop for and purchase a wide variety of products and services in either market environment. Many consumers now browse and buy in both market environments, and more are expected to do so in the future. Online retail sales are predicted to reach US$24 billion by 2006. Perhaps just as significant is the forecast that the Internet will influence another US$59 billion of purchases in that same time period, as consumers use the web to seek out and research products and suppliers.[7] With so many consumers browsing and buying in two market environments, few companies limit their marketing programs exclusively to the traditional marketplace or to the online marketspace. Today, it is commonplace for companies to maintain a presence in both market environments. This dual presence is called *multichannel marketing*.

Integrating Multiple Channels with Multichannel Marketing Companies often employ multiple marketing channels for their products and services. Multichannel marketing bears some resemblance to dual distribution. For example, different communication and delivery channels are used, such as catalogues, kiosks, retail stores, and websites. However, the resemblance ends at this point. **Multichannel marketing** is the *blending* of different communication and delivery channels that are *mutually reinforcing* in attracting, retaining, and building relationships with consumers who shop and buy in the traditional marketplace and in the online marketspace. Multichannel marketing seeks to integrate a firm's communication and delivery channels, not differentiate them. In doing so, consumers can browse and buy anytime, anywhere, any way, expecting that the experience will be similar regardless of channel. At Eddie Bauer, for example, every effort is made to make the apparel shopping and purchase process for its customers the same in its retail stores, through its catalogues, and at its website. According to an Eddie Bauer

multichannel marketing
Blending of different communication and delivery channels that are mutually reinforcing in attracting, retaining, and building relationships with customers

marketing manager, "We don't distinguish between channels because it's all Eddie Bauer to our customers."[8] We will discuss the retail slant on this practice further in Chapter 14.

Implementing Multichannel Marketing It should not be surprising to you that not all companies use websites for multichannel marketing the same way. Different companies apply the value-creation capabilities of Internet/Web technology differently depending on their overall marketing program. Websites can play multiple roles in multichannel marketing because they can serve as either a communication or delivery channel, or as both. There are two general types of websites, classified based on their intended purpose: transactional websites and promotional websites.

Transactional websites are essentially electronic storefronts. They focus mainly on converting an online browser into an online, catalogue, or in-store buyer using website design elements. Transactional websites are most common among store and catalogue retailers and direct-selling companies, such as Tupperware. The Gap, for instance, generates more sales volume from its website than from any one of its stores, except for one.[9]

Retailers and direct-selling firms have found that their websites, while cannibalizing sales volume from stores, catalogues, and sales representatives, attract new customers and influence sales. Consider Victoria's Secret, specialty retailer of intimate apparel for women aged 18 to 45. Almost 60 percent of its website customers are men, most of whom generate new sales volume for the company.[10] Sears' website is estimated to account for millions of dollars worth of Sears in-store appliance sales. Why? Sears customers first research appliances online before visiting a store.[11]

Transactional websites are used less frequently by manufacturers of consumer products. A recurring issue for manufacturers is the threat of *channel conflict* and the potential harm to trade relationships with their retailing intermediaries. Still, manufacturers do use transactional websites, often cooperating with retailers. For example, Ethan Allen, the furniture manufacturer, markets its product line at www.ethanallen.com whenever feasible. Ethan Allen retailers fill online orders and receive 25 percent of the sales price. For items shipped directly from the Ethan Allen factory, the store nearest the customer receives 10 percent of the sales price.[12]

In addition, Ethan Allen, like other manufacturers, typically lists stores on its website where consumers can shop for and buy its merchandise. More often than not, however, manufacturers employ multichannel channels, using websites as advertising and promotional vehicles.

Promotional websites have a different purpose than transactional sites: no actual selling takes place on them, but they showcase products and services and provide information. We will discuss them in detail in Chapter 15.

Vertical Marketing Systems

The traditional marketing channels described so far represent a network of independent producers and intermediaries brought together to distribute goods and services. However, channel arrangements have emerged for the purpose of improving efficiency in performing channel functions and achieving greater marketing effectiveness. These arrangements are called vertical marketing systems. **Vertical marketing systems** are professionally managed and centrally coordinated marketing channels designed to achieve channel economies and maximum marketing impact.[13] Figure 13–6 depicts the major types of vertical marketing systems: corporate, contractual, and administered.

Corporate Systems The combination of successive stages of production and distribution under a single ownership is a *corporate vertical marketing system*. For example, a producer might own the intermediary at the next level down in the channel. This practice,

vertical marketing systems
Professionally managed and centrally coordinated marketing channels designed to achieve channel economies and maximum marketing impact

Sherwin Williams and Home Hardware represent two different types of vertical marketing systems. Read the text to find out how they differ.

called forward integration, is exemplified by Polo/Ralph Lauren, which manufactures clothing and also owns apparel shops. Other examples of *forward integration* include Goodyear and Sherwin Williams. Alternatively, a retailer might own a manufacturing operation, a practice called *backward integration*. For example, Safeway supermarkets operate their own bakeries and have a subsidiary company, Lucerne Foods, that produces a wide variety of food products for their stores. Some of these products are sold as Safeway brand, and some under the Lucerne name.

Companies seeking to reduce distribution costs and gain greater control over supply sources or resale of their products pursue forward and backward integration. Many companies favour contractual vertical marketing systems to achieve channel efficiencies and marketing effectiveness.

Contractual Systems   Under a *contractual vertical marketing system*, independent production and distribution firms combine their efforts on a contractual basis to obtain greater functional economies and marketing impact than they could achieve alone. Contractual systems are the most popular among the three types of vertical marketing systems. They account for about 40 percent of all retail sales.

Three variations of contractual systems exist. *Wholesaler-sponsored voluntary chains* involve a wholesaler that develops a contractual relationship with small, independent retailers to standardize and coordinate buying practices, merchandising programs, and inventory management efforts. With the organization of a large number of independent retailers, economies of scale and volume discounts can be achieved to compete with chain stores. IGA is an example of a wholesaler-sponsored voluntary chain.

Retailer-sponsored cooperatives exist when small, independent retailers form an organization that operates a wholesale facility cooperatively. Member retailers then concentrate their buying power through the wholesaler and plan collaborative promotional and pricing activities. Home Hardware is an example of a retailer-sponsored cooperative.

The most visible variation of contractual systems is **franchising**, a contractual arrangement between a parent company (a franchiser) and an individual or firm (a franchisee) that allows the franchisee to operate a certain type of business under an established name and according to specific rules.

Four types of franchise arrangements are most popular. *Manufacturer-sponsored retail franchise systems* are prominent in the automobile industry, where a manufacturer such as Ford licenses dealers to sell its cars subject to various sales and service conditions. *Manufacturer-sponsored wholesale franchise systems* appear in the soft-drink industry, where Pepsi-Cola licenses wholesalers (bottlers) that purchase concentrate from Pepsi-Cola and then carbonate, bottle, promote, and distribute its products to

franchising
Contractual arrangement in which a parent company (the franchiser) allows an individual or firm (the franchisee) to operate a certain type of business under an established name and according to specific rules

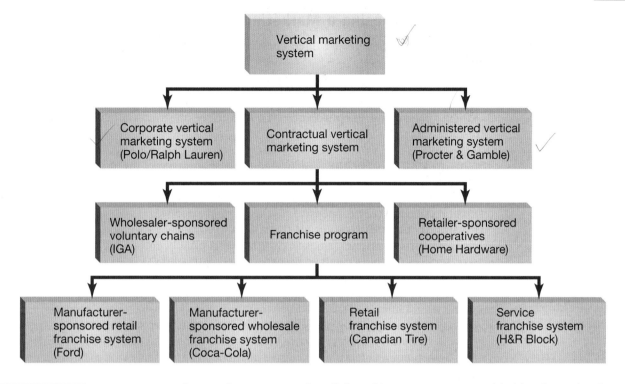

Types of vertical marketing systems

supermarkets and restaurants. *Retail franchise systems* are provided by firms that have designed a unique approach for selling merchandise to consumers. Canadian Tire and McDonald's represent this franchising approach. *Service franchise systems* exist when franchisers license individuals or firms to dispense a service under a trade name and specific guidelines. An example is H&R Block tax services. Service franchise arrangements are the fastest-growing type of franchise.

Administered Systems   By comparison, *administered vertical marketing systems* achieve coordination at successive stages of production and distribution by the size and influence of one channel member rather than through ownership. Procter & Gamble, given its broad product assortment ranging from disposable diapers to detergents, is able to obtain cooperation from supermarkets in displaying, promoting, and pricing its products. Wal-Mart can obtain cooperation from manufacturers in terms of product specifications, price levels, and promotional support, given its position as the world's largest retailer.

Concept Check

1. What is the difference between a direct and an indirect channel?
2. What is the major distinction between a corporate vertical marketing system and an administered vertical marketing system?

CHANNEL CHOICE AND MANAGEMENT

Marketing channels not only link a producer to its buyers but also provide the means through which a firm executes various elements of its marketing strategy. Therefore, choosing a marketing channel is a critical decision.

Factors in Choosing a Marketing Channel

Marketing executives consider three questions when choosing a marketing channel and intermediaries:

1. Which channel and intermediaries will best reach the target market?
2. Which channel and intermediaries will best serve the needs of the target market?
3. Which channel and intermediaries will lead to the most cost-efficient and profitable results?

intensive distribution
A firm tries to place its products or services in as many outlets as possible

exclusive distribution
Only one retail outlet in a specific geographical area carries the firm's products

selective distribution
A firm selects a few retail outlets in a specific geographical area to carry its products

Target Market Coverage   Achieving the best coverage of the target market requires attention to the density—that is, the number of stores in a given geographical area—and type of intermediaries to be used at the retail level of distribution. Three degrees of distribution intensity exist: intensive, exclusive, and selective.

Intensive distribution means that a firm tries to place its products and services in as many outlets as possible. Intensive distribution is usually chosen for convenience products or services, such as candy, newspapers, and soft drinks. For example, Coca-Cola's retail distribution objective is to place its products "within an arm's reach of desire."

Exclusive distribution is the extreme opposite of intensive distribution because only one retail outlet in a specified geographical area carries the firm's products. Exclusive distribution is typically chosen for specialty products or services such as specialty automobiles, some women's fragrances, men's and women's apparel and accessories, and yachts. Sometimes retailers sign exclusive distribution agreements with manufacturers and suppliers.

Selective distribution lies between these two extremes and means that a firm selects a few retail outlets in a specific geographical area to carry its products. Selective distribution combines some of the market coverage benefits of intensive distribution with the control measures possible with exclusive distribution. For this reason, selective distribution is the most common form of distribution intensity. It is usually associated with shopping goods or services such as Swatch watches, Wilson tennis racquets, and Ping golf clubs.

Satisfying Buyer Requirements   A second objective in channel design is gaining access to channels and intermediaries that satisfy at least some of the interests buyers might have when they purchase a firm's products or services. These requirements fall into four categories: information, convenience, variety, and pre- or postsale services.

Information is an important requirement when buyers have limited knowledge or desire specific data about a product or service. Properly chosen intermediaries communicate with buyers through in-store displays, demonstrations, and personal selling. Electronics manufacturers such as Apple Computer and Sony have opened their own retail outlets, with highly trained personnel to inform buyers about their products and how they can meet the buyers' needs.

Convenience has multiple meanings for buyers, such as proximity or driving time to a retail outlet or hours of operation. For example, 7-Eleven stores with outlets nationwide, many of which are open 24 hours a day, satisfy this interest for buyers. Candy and snack food firms benefit by gaining display space in these stores. For other consumers, convenience means a minimum of time and hassle. Jiffy Lube and Mr. Lube, which promise to change engine oil and filters quickly, appeal to this aspect of convenience.

Variety reflects buyers' interest in having numerous competing and complementary items from which to choose. Variety is seen in both the breadth and depth of products carried by intermediaries, which enhances their attractiveness to buyers. Thus, manufacturers of pet food and supplies seek distribution through Canada's largest pet store, Petcetera, which offers over 10,000 pet products.[14]

MARKETING NEWSNET

APPLE COMPUTER INC.: ATTENTION SWITCHERS—DO IT DIFFERENT; SHOP DIFFERENT!

Apple Computer followed up its earlier catchy "think different" advertising campaign with a new one targeted at "switchers," getting computer users to jump from PCs to Apple's Macs. The notion of doing things differently is part of Apple's mantra. Apple ignited the personal computer revolution in the 1970s with the Apple II, reinvented the Apple computer in the 1980s with the Macintosh, and captured the imagination of personal computer buyers worldwide with the introduction of the iMac™ in 1998—a design and technological breakthrough. Apple has since done this over and over, with technological breakthroughs in both software and hardware. The Mac™ OS X software and devices such as the iPod TM and high-resolution Apple Cinema high-definition displays continue to make waves in the industry.

It has not stopped there! Not relying on traditional channels to sell its products and services, Apple is making waves on the retailing scene by adding new direct channels.

Now Apple invites buyers to *shop different* at its new Apple stores that seek to satisfy the buying requirements of today's PC purchaser. At each Apple store, knowledgeable salespeople demonstrate Macs® running exciting new applications such as iTunes for burning custom CDs and iMovie™ for making home videos, as well as Mac OS x, Apple's new operating system. All of the Macs are connected to the Internet. Several Macs are connected to digital lifestyle products that complement the Mac experience, such as digital cameras, digital camcorders, MP3 players, and handheld organizers. The stores carry over 300 third-party software titles for creative professionals, students, educators, and consumers. And they maintain inventory for every Apple and third-party product to ensure immediate fulfillment of buyer requests. If a buyer has a question about specific applications, he or she can visit the "Genius Bar," staffed by Apple-trained personnel, for the answer.

Between 2001 and 2003, Apple opened an extensive network of more than 80 stores across the U.S., and one in Tokyo, Japan—none so far in Canada. By December 2002, its stores had greeted a million customers.

Also, Apple has extended its reach with new online stores for both music and computer products. As of May 2003, iTunes™ had already sold more than 70 million songs to consumers around the world, and is now selling more than 3 million songs per week. The Apple Store™, Apple's online store, sells direct to buyers globally in some 20 countries and provides service in 8 languages. With a simple mouse click, the Canadian site offers service in both of Canada's official languages.

Interested in looking at what Apple has to offer? Log on to www.apple.ca and click on "Store" to visit the Apple Store.

Services provided by intermediaries are an important buying requirement for products such as large household appliances that require delivery, installation, and credit. Therefore, Whirlpool seeks dealers that provide such services.

Steven P. Jobs, Apple Computer's CEO, is one person who believes that computer retailers have failed to satisfy the buying requirements of today's consumer. Believing that "Buying a car is no longer the worst purchasing experience. Buying a computer is no. 1," he launched Apple stores. Read the accompanying Marketing NewsNet to see how Apple stores intend to satisfy the information, convenience, variety, and service interests of consumers.[15]

Profitability   The third consideration in designing a channel is profitability, which is determined by the revenues earned minus cost for each channel member and for the channel as a whole. Cost is the critical factor of channel profitability. These costs include distribution, advertising, and selling expenses. The extent to which channel members share these costs determines the profitability of each member and of the channel as a whole.

Channel Relationships: Conflict and Cooperation

Unfortunately, because channels consist of independent individuals and firms, there is always potential for disagreements concerning who performs which channel functions, how profits are distributed, which products and services will be provided by whom, and who makes critical channel-related decisions. These channel conflicts necessitate measures for dealing with them.

channel conflict
Arises when one channel member believes another channel member is engaged in behaviour that prevents it from achieving its goals

disintermediation
Channel conflict that arises when a channel member bypasses another member and sells or buys products direct

Conflict in Marketing Channels   **Channel conflict** arises when one channel member believes another channel member is engaged in behaviour that prevents it from achieving its goals. Two types of conflict occur in marketing channels: vertical conflict and horizontal conflict.[16]

Vertical conflict occurs between different levels in a marketing channel; for example, between a manufacturer and a wholesaler or between a wholesaler and a retailer. Three sources of vertical conflict are most common. First, conflict arises when a channel member bypasses another member and sells or buys products direct, a practice called **disintermediation**. Such a conflict emerged when Jenn-Air, a producer of kitchen appliances, decided to terminate its distributors and sell direct to retailers. Second, disagreements over how profits are distributed among channel members produce conflict. This happened when Compaq Computer Corporation and one of its dealers disagreed over how price discounts were applied in the sale of Compaq's products. A third conflict situation arises when manufacturers believe wholesalers or retailers are not giving their products adequate attention. For example, H. J. Heinz Company found itself in a conflict situation with supermarkets in Great Britain when the supermarkets promoted and displayed private brands at the expense of Heinz brands.

Horizontal conflict occurs between intermediaries at the same level in a marketing channel, such as between two or more retailers or two or more wholesalers that handle the same manufacturer's brands. For instance, the launch of Elizabeth Taylor's Black Pearls fragrance by Elizabeth Arden was put on hold when some upscale department store chains refused to stock the item once they learned that mass merchants would also carry the brand. Elizabeth Arden subsequently introduced the brand only through department stores.[17]

Cooperation in Marketing Channels   Conflict can have disruptive effects on the workings of a marketing channel, so it is necessary to secure cooperation among channel members. One means is through a *channel captain*, a channel member that coordinates, directs, and supports other channel members. Channel captains can be producers, wholesalers, or retailers. Procter & Gamble assumes this role because it has a strong consumer following in brands such as Crest, Tide, and Pampers. Therefore, it can set policies or terms that supermarkets will follow. Wal-Mart and Home Depot are retail channel captains because of their strong consumer image, number of outlets, and purchasing volume.

A firm becomes a channel captain because it is the channel member with the ability to influence the behaviour of other members.[18] Influence can take four forms. First, economic influence arises from the ability of a firm to reward other members because of its strong financial position. Microsoft Corporation and Toys "Я" Us have such influence. Expertise is a second source of influence. Third, identification with a particular channel member creates influence for that channel member. For instance, retailers may compete to carry the Anne Klein line, or clothing manufacturers may compete to be carried by The Bay or Holt Renfrew. In both instances the desire to be associated with a channel member gives that firm influence over others. Finally, influence can arise from the legitimate right of one channel member to direct the behaviour of other members. This situation occurs under contractual vertical marketing systems where a franchiser can legitimately direct how a franchisee behaves.

Concept Check

1. What are the three degrees of distribution density?
2. What are the three questions marketing executives consider when choosing a marketing channel and intermediaries?

LOGISTICS AND SUPPLY CHAIN MANAGEMENT

logistics

Activities that focus on getting the right amount of the right products to the right place at the right time at the lowest possible cost

A marketing channel relies on logistics to make products available to consumers and industrial users. **Logistics** involves those activities that focus on getting the right amount of the right products to the right place at the right time at the lowest possible cost. The performance of these activities is *logistics management,* the practice of organizing the cost-effective flow of raw materials, in-process inventory, finished goods, and related information from point of origin to point of consumption to satisfy *customer requirements.*[19]

Three elements of this definition deserve emphasis. First, logistics deals with decisions from the source of raw materials to consumption of the final product—that is, the *flow* of the product. Second, those decisions have to be *cost-effective.* While it is important to drive down logistics costs, there is a limit: a firm needs to drive down logistics costs as long as it can deliver expected *customer service*, while satisfying customer requirements. The role of management is to see that customer needs are satisfied in the most cost-effective manner. When properly done, the results can be spectacular. Procter & Gamble is a case in point. Beginning in the 1990s, the company set out to meet the needs of consumers more effectively by collaborating and partnering with its suppliers and retailers to ensure that the right products reached store shelves at the right time and at a lower cost. The effort was judged a success when, during an 18-month period, P&G's retailers recorded a US$65 million savings in logistics costs while customer service increased.[20]

The Procter & Gamble experience is not an isolated incident. Today, logistics management is a more effective and broader view of physical distribution. Companies now recognize that getting the right items needed for consumption or production to the right place at the right time in the right condition at the right cost is often beyond their individual capabilities and control. Instead, collaboration, coordination, and information sharing among manufacturers, suppliers, and distributors are necessary to create a seamless flow of goods and services to customers. This perspective is represented in the concept of a supply chain and the practice of supply chain management.

Supply Chains versus Marketing Channels

supply chain

Sequence of firms that perform activities required to create and deliver a product to consumers or industrial users

A **supply chain** is a series of firms that perform activities required to create and deliver a good or service to consumers or industrial users. It differs from a marketing channel in terms of the firms involved. A supply chain is longer and includes suppliers who provide raw material inputs to a manufacturer as well as the wholesalers and retailers who deliver finished goods to you. The management process is also different. *Supply chain* *management* is the integration and organization of information and logistics activities *across firms* in a supply chain for the purpose of creating and delivering goods and services that provide value to consumers. The relation among marketing channels, logistics management, and supply chain management is shown in Figure 13–7. An important feature of supply chain management is its use of sophisticated information technology that allows companies to share and operate systems for order processing, transportation scheduling, and inventory and facility management.

Sourcing, Assembling, and Delivering a New Car: The Automotive Supply Chain

All companies are members of one or more supply chains. A supply chain is essentially a series of linked suppliers and customers in which every customer is, in turn, a supplier to another customer until a finished product reaches the ultimate consumer. Even a simplified supply chain diagram for carmakers shown in Figure 13–8 illustrates how complex a supply chain can be.[21] A carmaker's supplier network includes thousands of firms that provide the 5,000 or so parts in a typical automobile. They provide items ranging from raw materials such as steel and rubber to components, including transmissions, tires, brakes, and seats, to complex subassemblies and assemblies such as in chassis and suspension systems that make for a smooth, stable ride. Coordinating and scheduling material and component flows for their assembly into actual automobiles by carmakers is heavily dependent on logistical activities, including transportation, order processing, inventory control, materials handling, and information technology. A central link is the carmaker supply chain manager, who is responsible for translating customer requirements into actual orders and arranging for delivery dates and financial arrangements for automobile dealers.

Logistical aspects of the automobile marketing channel are also an important part of the supply chain. Major responsibilities include transportation (which involves the selection and management of external carriers—trucking, airline, railroad, and shipping companies—for

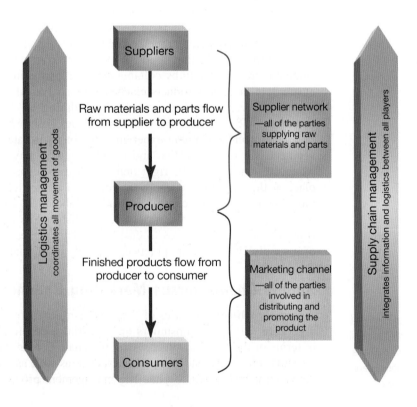

FIGURE 13-7

How distribution channels work: the relationships between supplier networks, marketing channels, logistics management, and supply chain management

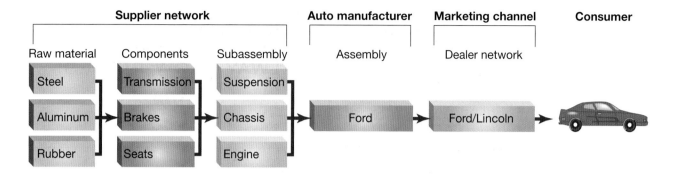

| Supplier network | | | Auto manufacturer | Marketing channel | Consumer |

| Raw material | Components | Subassembly | Assembly | Dealer network | |

Steel, Aluminum, Rubber → Transmission, Brakes, Seats → Suspension, Chassis, Engine → Ford → Ford/Lincoln →

FIGURE 13-8

The automotive supply chain

cars and parts to dealers), the operation of distribution centres, the management of finished goods inventories, and order processing for sales. Supply chain managers also play an important role in the marketing channel. They work with extensive car dealer networks to ensure that the right mix of automobiles is delivered to each location. In addition, they make sure that spare and service parts are available so that dealers can meet the car maintenance and repair needs of consumers. All of this is done with the help of information technology that links the entire automotive supply chain. What does all of this cost? It is estimated that logistics costs represent 25 percent to 30 percent of the retail price of a typical new car.

Supply Chain Management and Marketing Strategy

The automotive supply chain illustration shows how logistics activities are interrelated and organized across firms to create and deliver a car for you. What's missing from this illustration is the linkage between a specific company's supply chain and its marketing strategy. Just as companies have different marketing strategies, they also manage supply chains differently. The goals to be achieved by a firm's marketing strategy determine whether its supply chain needs to focus on being more responsive or more efficient in meeting customer requirements.

Aligning a Supply Chain with Marketing Strategy   There are a variety of supply chain configurations, each of which is designed to perform different tasks well. Marketers today recognize that the choice of a supply chain follows from a clearly defined marketing strategy and involves three steps:[22]

1. *Understand the customer.* To understand the customer, a company must identify the needs of the customer segment being served. These needs, such as a desire for a low price or convenience of purchase, help a company define the relative importance of efficiency and responsiveness in meeting customer requirements.
2. *Understand the supply chain.* Second, a company must understand what a supply chain is designed to do well. Supply chains range from those that emphasize being responsive to customer requirements and demand to those that emphasize efficiency with a goal of supplying products at the lowest possible delivered cost.
3. *Harmonize the supply chain with the marketing strategy.* Finally, a company needs to ensure that what the supply chain is capable of doing well is consistent with the targeted customer's needs and its marketing strategy. If a mismatch exists between what the supply chain does particularly well and a company's marketing strategy, the company will either need to redesign the supply chain to support the marketing strategy or change the marketing strategy. The bottom line is that a poorly designed supply chain can do serious damage to an otherwise brilliant marketing strategy.

How are these steps applied and how are efficiency and response considerations built into a supply chain? Let's briefly look at how two market leaders—Dell

World-class marketers Dell Computer and Wal-Mart emphasize responsiveness and efficiency in their supply chains, respectively.

Computer Corporation and Wal-Mart, Inc.—have harmonized their supply chain and marketing strategy.

Dell Computer Corporation: A Responsive Supply Chain

The Dell marketing strategy targets customers who want to have the most up-to-date personal computer equipment customized to their needs. These customers are also willing to wait to have their customized personal computer delivered in a few days, rather than picking out a prepackaged model at a retail store; and pay a reasonable, though not the lowest, price in the marketplace. Given Dell's market segments, the company has the option of choosing either an efficient or a responsive supply chain. An efficient supply chain may use inexpensive but slower modes of transportation, emphasize economies of scale in its production process by reducing the variety of PC configurations offered, and limit its assembly and inventory storage facilities to a single location, say Austin, Texas, where the company is headquartered. If Dell opted only for efficiency in its supply chain, it would be difficult if not impossible to satisfy its target customer's desire for rapid delivery and a wide variety of customizable products. Dell instead has opted for a responsive supply chain. It relies on more expensive express transportation for receipt of components from suppliers and delivery of finished products to customers. The company achieves product variety and manufacturing efficiency by designing common platforms across several products and using common components. Dell operates manufacturing facilities in the U.S., Brazil, Ireland, Malaysia, and China to assure rapid delivery. Dell also has invested heavily in information technology to link itself with suppliers and customers.

Wal-Mart, Inc.: An Efficient Supply Chain

Now let's consider Wal-Mart. Wal-Mart's marketing strategy is to be a reliable, lower-price retailer for a wide variety of mass consumption consumer goods. This strategy favours an efficient supply chain designed to deliver products to consumers at the lowest possible cost. Efficiency is achieved in a variety of ways. For instance, Wal-Mart keeps relatively low inventory levels, and most inventory is stocked in stores available for sale, not in warehouses gathering dust. The low inventory arises from Wal-Mart's use of *cross-docking*—a practice that involves unloading products from suppliers, sorting products for individual stores, and quickly reloading products onto its trucks for a particular store. No warehousing or storing of products occurs, except for a few hours or, at most, a day. Cross-docking allows Wal-Mart to operate only a small number of distribution centers to service its vast network of Wal-Mart Stores, Supercentres, and SAM'S CLUB warehouse stores, which contributes to efficiency. On the other hand, the company runs its own fleet of trucks to service its stores. This does increase cost and investment, but the benefits in terms of responsiveness justify the cost in Wal-Mart's case. Wal-Mart has invested significantly more than its competitors in information technology to operate its supply chain. The company feeds information about customer requirements and demand from its stores back to its suppliers, which manufacture only what is being demanded. This large investment has improved the efficiency of Wal-Mart's supply chain and made it responsive to customer needs.

Three lessons can be learned from these two examples. First, there is no one best supply chain for every company. Second, the best supply chain is the one that is consistent with the needs of the customer segment being served and complements a company's marketing strategy. And finally, supply chain managers are often called upon to make trade-offs between efficiency and responsiveness on various elements of a company's supply chain.

Concept Check

1. What is the principal difference between a marketing channel and a supply chain?
2. The choice of a supply chain involves what three steps?

TWO CONCEPTS OF LOGISTICS MANAGEMENT IN A SUPPLY CHAIN

The objective of logistics management in a supply chain is to minimize total logistics costs while delivering the appropriate level of customer service.

Total Logistics Cost Concept

total logistics cost
Expenses associated with transportation, materials handling and warehousing, inventory, stockouts, order processing, and return goods handling

For our purposes **total logistics cost** includes expenses associated with transportation, materials handling and warehousing, inventory, stockouts (being out of inventory), order processing, and return goods handling.[23] Note that many of these costs are interrelated so that changes in one will impact the others. For example, as the firm attempts to minimize its transportation costs by shipping in larger quantities, it will also experience an increase in inventory levels. Larger inventory levels will not only increase inventory costs but should also reduce stockouts. It is important, therefore, to study the impact on all of the logistics decision areas when considering a change.

Customer Service Concept

customer service
Ability of logistics management to satisfy users in terms of time, dependability, communication, and convenience

Because a supply chain is a *flow*, the end of it—or *output*—is the service delivered to customers. Within the context of a supply chain, **customer service** is the ability of logistics management to satisfy users in terms of time, dependability, communication, and convenience. As suggested by Figure 13–9, a supply chain manager's key task is to balance these four customer service factors against total logistics cost factors.

Time   In a supply chain setting, time refers to *order cycle* or *replenishment* time for an item, which means the time between the ordering of an item and when it is received and ready for use or sale. The various elements that make up the typical order cycle include recognition of the need to order, order transmittal, order processing, documentation, and transportation. A current emphasis in supply chain management is to reduce order cycle time so that the inventory levels of customers may be minimized. Another emphasis is to make the process of reordering and receiving products as simple as possible, often through inventory systems called *quick response* and *efficient consumer response* delivery systems. For example, at Wal-Mart stores, point-of-sale scanner technology records each day's sales. When stock falls below a minimum level, a replenishment order is automatically produced. Vendors receive the order, which is processed and delivered promptly.[24]

FIGURE 13-9

FIGURE 13-9

Supply chain managers balance total logistics cost factors against customer service factors

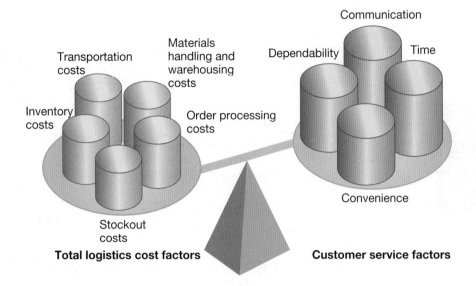

Transportation costs

Materials handling and warehousing costs

Inventory costs

Order processing costs

Communication

Dependability

Time

Convenience

Stockout costs

Total logistics cost factors

Customer service factors

Dependability
Dependability is the consistency of replenishment. This is important to all firms in a supply chain—and to consumers. How often do you return to a store if it fails to have in stock the item you want to purchase? Dependability can be broken into three elements: consistent lead time, safe delivery, and complete delivery. Consistent service allows planning (such as appropriate inventory levels), whereas inconsistencies create surprises. Intermediaries may be willing to accept longer lead times if they know about them in advance and can thus make plans.

Communication
Communication is a two-way link between buyer and seller that helps in monitoring service and anticipating future needs. Status reports on orders are a typical example of communication between buyer and seller.

Convenience
The concept of convenience for a supply chain manager means that there should be a minimum of effort on the part of the buyer in doing business with the seller. Is it easy for the customer to order? Are the products available from many outlets? Will the seller arrange all necessary details, such as transportation? This customer service factor has promoted the use of **vendor-managed inventory (VMI)**, whereby the *supplier* determines the product amount and assortment a customer (such as a retailer) needs and automatically delivers the appropriate items.

Campbell Soup's system illustrates how VMI works.[25] Every morning, retailers electronically inform the company of their demand for all Campbell products and the inventory levels in their distribution centres. Campbell uses that information to forecast future demand and determine which products need replenishment based on upper and lower inventory limits established with each retailer. Trucks leave the Campbell shipping plant that afternoon and arrive at the retailer's distribution centres with the required replenishments the same day.

vendor-managed inventory
Inventory management system whereby the supplier determines the product amount and assortment a customer (such as a retailer) needs and automatically delivers the appropriate items

Concept Check

1. What is the logistics management objective in a supply chain?

2. A manager's key task is to balance which customer service factors against which logistics cost factors?

SUMMARY

1 A marketing channel consists of individuals and firms involved in the process of making a product or service available for use by consumers or business users.

2 Intermediaries make possible the flow of products and services from producers to buyers by performing transactional, logistical, and facilitating functions. At the same time, intermediaries create time, place, form, and possession utility.

3 In general, marketing channels for consumer products and services contain more intermediaries than do channels for business products and services. In some situations, producers use Internet, multiple channels and strategic channel alliances to reach buyers.

4 The prevalence of consumer shopping online, as well as buying in retail stores, has made multichannel marketing popular. Multichannel marketing is the blending of different communication and delivery channels that are mutually reinforcing in attracting, retaining, and building relationships with consumers who shop and buy in the traditional marketplace as well as in the online marketspace.

5 Not all companies approach multichannel marketing the same way. A major difference in approach is the use of transactional websites and promotional websites.

6 Vertical marketing systems are channels designed to achieve channel function economies and marketing impact. A vertical marketing system may be one of three types: corporate, administered, or contractual.

7 Channel design considerations are based on the target market coverage sought by producers, the buyer requirements to be satisfied, and the profitability of the channel. Target market coverage comes about through one of three levels of distribution density: intensive, exclusive, and selective distribution. Buyer requirements are evident in the amount of information, convenience, variety, and service sought by con-

sumers. Profitability—of each channel member and the channel as a whole—is largely affected by costs and whether or not costs can be shared by members.

8 Conflicts in marketing channels are inevitable. Vertical conflict occurs between different levels in a channel. Horizontal conflict occurs between intermediaries at the same level in the channel.

9 Logistics involves those activities that focus on getting the right amount of the right products to the right place at the right time at the lowest possible cost. Logistics management includes the coordination of the flows of both inbound and outbound goods, an emphasis on making these flows cost effective, and customer service.

10 A supply chain is a sequence of firms that perform activities required to create and deliver a good or service to consumers or industrial users. Supply chain management is the integration and organization of information and logistics across firms for the purpose of creating value for consumers.

11 The goals to be achieved by a firm's marketing strategy determine whether its supply chain needs to be more responsive or efficient in meeting customer requirements. Marketers today recognize that the choice of a supply chain involves three steps: (a) understand the customer, (b) understand the supply chain, and (c) harmonize the supply chain with the marketing strategy.

12 The objective of logistics management in a supply chain is to minimize logistics costs while delivering maximum customer service. Minimizing total logistics cost must be weighed against specifying an acceptable customer service level that must be maintained. Although key customer service factors depend on the situation, important elements of the customer service program are likely to be time-related dependability, communications, and convenience.

KEY TERMS AND CONCEPTS

channel conflict p. 312
customer service p. 317
disintermediation p. 312
dual distribution p. 305
exclusive distribution p. 310
franchising p. 308
intensive distribution p. 310
intermediaries p. 300

logistics p. 313
marketing channel p. 300
multichannel marketing p. 306
selective distribution p. 310
supply chain p. 313
total logistics cost p. 317
vendor-managed inventory p. 318
vertical marketing systems p. 307

QUESTIONS: APPLYING MARKETING CONCEPTS AND PERSPECTIVES

1 A distributor for Celanese Chemical Company stores large quantities of chemicals, blends these chemicals to satisfy requests of customers, and delivers the blends to a customer's warehouse within 24 hours of receiving an order. What utilities does this distributor provide?

2 Suppose the president of a carpet manufacturing firm has asked you to look into the possibility of bypassing the firm's wholesalers (who sell to carpet, department, and furniture stores) and selling direct to these stores. What caution would you voice on this matter, and what type of information would you gather before making this decision?

3 How does the channel captain idea differ among corporate, administered, and contractual vertical marketing systems?

4 List the customer service factors that would be vital to buyers in the following types of companies: *(a)* manufacturing, *(b)* retailing, *(c)* hospitals, and *(d)* construction.

5 A digital camera manufacturer tells you that the firm has been selling its cameras through large camera and electronics retailers for the past 10 years, but now wants to expand distribution. The manufacturer plans to work with a distributor who will provide access to many smaller retailers, as well as sell cameras direct to the consumer through an online store.

What type of channel conflict is likely to be caused by this dual distribution? How can conflict be reduced? What would you advise the manufacturer?

6 At a telecommunications conference, you hear some service providers talking about the need for them to set up online stores so that consumers can purchase directly from their websites, but they are concerned about this dual distribution and what it may do to their business. How would you respond to their concerns?

DISCUSSION FORUM

You are a distribution consultant in a large strategic marketing firm serving clients from all over the world. Here are the projects on your desk for this week. Using a flowchart similar to Figure 13-7, outline a distribution strategy for each of these projects and determine the players and the activities to take place at each step.

1 A flower grower in Ecuador who ships her flowers all over North and South America

2 A medical supplies firm that manufactures heart pacemakers, and sells them to the European, Asian, and North American medical market

3 A mining equipment producer that makes machinery to be used in copper and silver mines around the world

4 A Taiwanese shoe manufacturer that produces women's high-fashion shoes for the Canadian and Australian markets

INTERNET EXERCISE

Franchising is a large and growing industry. For many individuals, franchising offers an opportunity to operate one's own business.

The Internet provides a number of websites that feature franchising opportunities. The International Franchise Association (www.franchise.org) features extensive information, including answers to questions about franchising. The Canadian Franchise Association website (www.cfa.ca)

www.mcgrawhill.ca/college/thecore

shows franchise opportunities for the aspiring franchisee.

1 Visit www.cfa.ca. What are some of the more interesting franchise opportunities available to Canadians?

2 Visit the International Franchise Association website, and go to Frequently Asked Questions about Franchising. What are the current trends in franchising?

VIDEO CASE 13

CRESTON VINEYARDS: FACING CHANNEL CHALLENGES

Larry Rosenbloom's customers include individuals, retail stores, restaurants, hotels, and even the White House! Because of the many types and large numbers of customers, distribution is as important as production at Creston Vineyards. As Larry explains, "We need distributors in our business . . . as most other [businesses] do, to get the product to the end user, to the consumer."

THE COMPANY

In 1772, Franciscan Padres introduced wine to the La Panza Mountains of California when they founded Mission San Luis Obispo south of what is now San Francisco. The potential of the region for growing grapes remained a secret, however, until 1980, when Stephanie and Larry Rosenbloom purchased an abandoned ranch and started Creston Vineyards.

Because it takes several years for vines to grow and produce grapes, Creston did not sell its first wine until 1982. Today, the 569-acre ranch has 155 acres of planted vineyards and produces more than 55,000 cases of eight varieties of wines. The production facilities include a 15,000-square-foot winery and 2,000 square feet of laboratory and office space. Since 1982, Creston wines have won more than 500 awards in wine-tasting events and competitions.

THE INDUSTRY AND DISTRIBUTION CHANNELS

The wine industry is undergoing several very interesting changes. First, sales have increased in recent years after a general decline since 1984. At least some of the recent interest in wine is related to press reports suggesting the possible health benefits of red wine. A second change is the significant increase in the price of wine due to a low supply of good international wines and changing exchange rates, and an infestation of vine-eating insects (phylloxera) on over 20 percent of California's vineyards. Finally, many wine producers are trying to change the image of wine from a beverage only for special occasions and gourmet foods to a beverage for any occasion.

The industry also faces several distribution challenges. The large number of wine producers and the variety of consumers requires a sophisticated system of distribution channels. By combining different types of intermediaries, the industry is able to meet the requirements of many customers. In addition, because the sale of wine is regulated, the use of multiple distribution channels facilitates the sale of wine in many locations.

One of the most common channels of distribution involves a distributor buying wine directly from the vineyard and reselling it to retail stores and restaurants within a geographic area. Some distributors, however, may not need quantities large enough to warrant purchasing directly from the vineyard. They usually purchase several brands at the same time from a warehouse. A broker may facilitate sales by providing information to distributors, training the distributor's sales force, and even assisting in sales calls to retailers. John Drady, 1 of 12 brokers for Creston Vineyards, explains: "It's very important that we translate our knowledge and our selling skills to the distributor's salespeople so they can, in turn, go out and [sell] more readily on their own."

Other channels are also used by Creston. In California, for example, Creston can sell directly to some large retailers. Another channel of distribution is through wine clubs, which provide club members with information about wines and an average of six wines per year. The popularity of wine clubs has been increasing and they now account for 15 percent of Creston's sales. The newest type of distribution channel is through online services. Creston now has a site on the Web (www.wines.com) that provides information about its wines and allows orders to be shipped directly to consumers. Customers will also find greetings from Alex Trebek, the Canadian-born game-show host, who is the owner of Creston Vineyards.

THE ISSUES

In an industry with thousands of products and hundreds of producers, Creston is relatively new and small. Selecting and managing its distribution channels to best meet the needs of many constituents is a key task. Providing marketing assistance, product information, and appropriate assortment, transportation, storage, and credit are just a few of the functions the warehouse, brokers, distributors, and retailers may provide as the product moves from the vineyard to the end user.

Creston also faces a situation where new, and possibly more efficient, channels are becoming available. Direct sales, wine clubs, and online services have generated substantial sales for Creston. Other channels, or new variations of existing channels, may also be available in the future. Overall, Creston must continue to utilize distribution channels to provide value to customers ranging from large retailers, to hotels and restaurants, to individuals.

Questions

1 What functions must be performed by intermediaries in the wine industry?

2 What intermediaries and distribution channels are currently used by Creston Vineyards?

3 Are there any market segments Creston does not reach with its current channels?

Retailing
and Wholesaling

AFTER READING THIS CHAPTER YOU SHOULD BE ABLE TO:

- Understand the benefits that retailing provides for the consumer.

- Explain different ways to classify retail outlets.

- Understand nonstore retailing and its role in the retail world.

- Describe why consumers shop and buy online, what they purchase, and how marketers influence online purchasing behaviour.

- Explain how the retail mix is modified over the life cycle of the retail store.

- Describe the types of wholesalers and the functions they perform.

TRULY "CANADIAN"—AND MORE THAN TIRES!

Canada's largest hard-goods retailer, Canadian Tire, reaches every corner of the country with its network of unique stores. The statistics are impressive and tell an interesting story about how Canadians are involved with the store's retail concept: 450 stores are located so that they can serve 91 percent of the population; 40 percent of the population shops at Canadian Tire each week, more than half of Canadians shop there monthly, and almost 80 percent have visited one of the stores in the past six months; one in every two Canadians has gone to a Canadian Tire for automotive service in the past two years. That's a truly national retailer with enviable loyalty.

In an era when retail is a challenging industry, Canadian Tire has built a reputation and an interesting and unique retail offering. When the first store opened in 1922 in Toronto, cars were just becoming recognized as a form of transportation, and Canadian Tire sold a very narrow range of repair parts for only the two most popular cars on the road. Today, shelves feature auto-motive products and services, sports and leisure goods, home products, and more. Best-selling items include bicycles and bike equipment, hockey equipment, gardening items, outdoor barbeques, basketball gear, camping and fishing equipment, and, of course, tires!

What makes Canadian Tire special? The store's competitors—Wal-Mart, Zellers, and even some of the supermarket chains—have tried to determine this. It is a combination of things: consistent advertising, an integrated shopping experience, continual improvement of retail operations, and a well-oiled marketing and strategic planning process. And what does each of these things bring to the customers?

Canadian Tire is one of the country's largest advertisers: Do you remember some of these advertising messages: "Let's Get Started," "Still the Right Place," and the Bike Story?

Check your wallet—did you find any Canadian Tire money in there? Many of us have a few of those little bills picturing Sandy McTire grinning his Scottish best

THE MARKETING PROCESS

WHERE IN THE MARKETING PROCESS ARE WE GOING IN THIS CHAPTER?

Chapter 14 continues with the concept of distribution—creating a place where the customer can access the product—the place P of the 4Ps that make up the marketing mix.

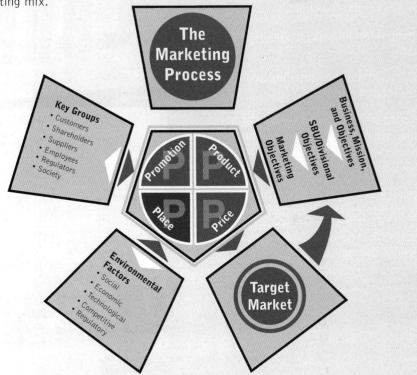

and promising to be the best. The store launched this idea in 1958 as a coupon at Canadian Tire gas bars in Toronto. Now, millions of these are in circulation, and they are given out with every cash purchase at a Canadian Tire store. Customers love this loyalty program, and it has become the oldest, most-popular and best-known retail-reward concept in the country.

How many ways can you shop at Canadian Tire? At www.canadiantire.ca, the firm's online store; through its regular print catalogue; by phone; and, of course, by cruising the aisles at stores. You can use your Canadian Tire credit card to complete the transaction. Giving customers many different options increases both satisfaction and the amount they purchase, and Canadian Tire is one of the few retailers in the country that uses all of these shopping channels. A new concept for the stores was developed recently; design, product offerings, and value-added services are all being updated and enhanced. These include everything from equipment rentals, to home delivery and assembly, to gift registries.

Over 80 years old, but still very modern and unique, Canadian Tire is proud to be designated as Canada's most shopped retailer. "Let's Get Started" is their new slogan, and they are doing just that![1]

What types of products will consumers buy directly through catalogues, television, or the Web, or by telephone? In what type of store will consumers look for products they don't buy directly? How important is the location of the store? Will customers expect services such as alterations, delivery, installation, or repair? What price should be charged for each product? These are difficult and important questions that are an essential part of retailing. In the channel of distribution, retailing is where the customer

retailing
All activities involved in selling, renting, and providing goods and services to ultimate consumers for personal, family, or household use

meets the product. It is through retailing that exchange (a central aspect of marketing) occurs. **Retailing** includes all activities involved in selling, renting, and providing goods and services to ultimate customers for personal, family, or household use.

THE VALUE OF RETAILING

Retailing is an important marketing activity. Retailing engages the consumer; it provides a place for showcasing products and creates interest and excitement. Shopping is not only a way to acquire necessities but also a social activity and often an adventure—retailing makes this possible. Producers and consumers are brought together through retailing actions, and retailing also creates customer value and has a significant impact on the economy. To consumers, the value of retailing is in the form of utilities provided, which were discussed in Chapter 1. Retailing's economic value is represented by the number of people employed in retailing as well as by the total amount of money exchanged in retail sales.

Consumer Utilities Offered by Retailing

The utilities provided by retailers create value for consumers. Time, place, possession, information, and form utilities are offered by most retailers in varying degrees, but one utility is often emphasized more than others. Look at Figure 14–1 to see how well you can match the retailer with the utility being emphasized in the description.

Providing minibanks in supermarkets, as BMO does[2], puts the bank's products and services close to the consumer, providing place utility. By providing financing or leasing and taking used cars as trade-ins, Saturn makes the purchase easier and provides possession utility. Form utility—production or alteration of a product—is offered by Levi Strauss &

FIGURE 14–1
Which company best represents which utilities?

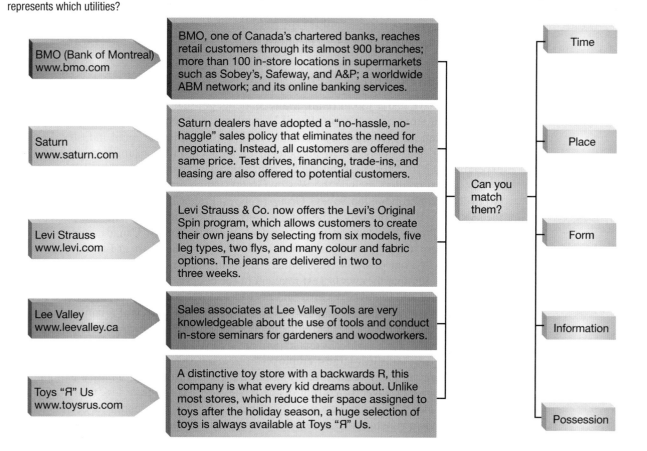

BMO (Bank of Montreal)
www.bmo.com

BMO, one of Canada's chartered banks, reaches retail customers through its almost 900 branches; more than 100 in-store locations in supermarkets such as Sobey's, Safeway, and A&P; a worldwide ABM network; and its online banking services.

Saturn
www.saturn.com

Saturn dealers have adopted a "no-hassle, no-haggle" sales policy that eliminates the need for negotiating. Instead, all customers are offered the same price. Test drives, financing, trade-ins, and leasing are also offered to potential customers.

Levi Strauss
www.levi.com

Levi Strauss & Co. now offers the Levi's Original Spin program, which allows customers to create their own jeans by selecting from six models, five leg types, two flys, and many colour and fabric options. The jeans are delivered in two to three weeks.

Lee Valley
www.leevalley.ca

Sales associates at Lee Valley Tools are very knowledgeable about the use of tools and conduct in-store seminars for gardeners and woodworkers.

Toys "Я" Us
www.toysrus.com

A distinctive toy store with a backwards R, this company is what every kid dreams about. Unlike most stores, which reduce their space assigned to toys after the holiday season, a huge selection of toys is always available at Toys "Я" Us.

Can you match them?

Time

Place

Form

Information

Possession

FIGURE 14–2

Retail sales ($billions) by type of retail business

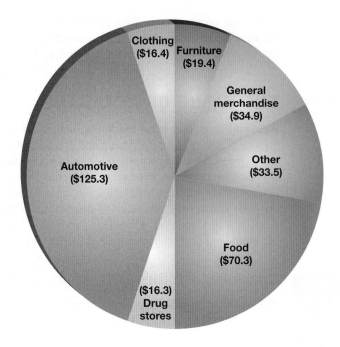

Source: Statistics Canada, Catalogue No. 63 005, Retail Trade, December 2003.

Co. as it creates Original Spin jeans to meet each customer's specifications. Finding toy shelves well stocked all year round is the time utility dreamed about by every child (and many parents) who enters Toys "Я" Us. Many retailers offer a combination of the four basic utilities. Some supermarkets, for example, offer convenient locations (place utility) and are open 24 hours (time utility). In addition, consumers may seek additional utilities such as entertainment, recreation, or information.[3]

The Canadian Retail Scene

Maybe you have had a job in retail. Many students get their first taste of employment by working in a store or restaurant. Retail is a vibrant and important part of the Canadian economy; some 6 percent of our nation's GDP comes from the retail industry. Looking at individual households, 50 to 55 percent of their current consumption goes to retail expenditures.[4] In 2003, $316 billion in retail sales were recorded in Canada.[5]

Our largest retailers include the Weston Group (which operates stores such as Loblaws, No Frills, and Fortinos), the Sobeys Group (Sobeys, Price Chopper, Lawtons Drug Stores), the Hudson's Bay Company (The Bay, Zellers, Home Outfitters), Wal-Mart stores, and Costco. Together they account for 17 percent of retail sales in Canada, and their combined numbers of stores total more than 3,760.[6] Look at the chart in Figure 14-2, which tells us that two out of every three dollars spent in retail go to food or automobiles.[7] It follows logically that the two largest retailers in the country are predominantly in the food business. In the top five list, we also find the oldest corporation in Canada—the Hudson's Bay Company, now Canada's largest non-food retailer. Not only is it a national icon, but The Bay is one of the oldest and still-functioning companies in the world. Founded in 1670, it began as a fur-trading company and has evolved into the country's largest department store chain and fifth-largest employer.[8]

While there are many retail chains that dot the country, the retail industry is dominated by small businesses. Over 50 percent of the retailers in Canada have less than 10 employees.[9] It is an industry that operates with tight margins, it is very susceptible to economic fluctuation, and the competition is fierce. Visit your local mall and notice the turnover in stores!

FIGURE 14-3
Where do we find the top retailers in the world? Who are they?

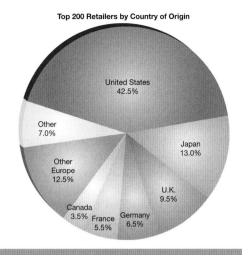

Top 200 Retailers by Country of Origin

United States 42.5%

Other 7.0%

Other Europe 12.5%

Canada 3.5%

France 5.5%

Germany 6.5%

U.K. 9.5%

Japan 13.0%

RANK	COUNTRY OF ORIGIN	NAME OF COMPANY	2002 SALES (US$ millions)	COUNTRIES OF OPERATION
1	U.S.	Wal-Mart	$229,617	Argentina, Brazil, Canada, China, Germany, Japan, South Korea, Mexico, Puerto Rico, U.K., U.S.
2	France	Carrefour	$65,011	Argentina, Belgium, Brazil, Chile, China, Colombia, Czech Republic, Dominican Republic, Egypt, France, Greece, Indonesia, Italy, Japan, Malaysia, Mexico, Oman, Poland, Portugal, Qatar, Romania, Singapore, Slovakia, Spain, South Korea, Switzerland, Taiwan, Thailand, Tunisia, Turkey, UAE
3	U.S.	Home Depot	$58,247	Canada, Mexico, Puerto Rico, U.S.
4	U.S.	Kroger	$51,760	U.S.
5	Germany	Metro	$48,349	Austria, Belgium, Bulgaria, China, Croatia, Czech Republic, Denmark, France, Germany, Greece, Hungary, Italy, Japan, Luxembourg, Morocco, Netherlands, Poland, Portugal, Romania, Russia, Slovakia, Spain, Switzerland, Turkey, U.K., Viet Nam
6	U.S.	Target	$42,722	U.S.
7	Netherlands	Ahold	$40,755	Argentina, Brazil, Chile, Costa Rica, Czech Republic, Denmark, Ecuador, El Salvador, Estonia, Guatemala, Honduras, Indonesia, Latvia, Lithuania, Malaysia, Netherlands, Nicaragua, Norway, Paraguay, Peru, Poland, Portugal, Slovakia, Spain, Sweden, Thailand, U.S.
8	U.K.	Tesco	$40,071	Czech Republic, Hungary, Republic of Ireland, Malaysia, Poland, South Korea, Slovakia, Taiwan, Thailand, U.K.
9	U.S.	Costco	$37,993	Canada, Japan, South Korea, Mexico, Puerto Rico, Taiwan, U.K., U.S.
10	U.S.	Sears	$35,698	Canada, Puerto Rico, U.S.

Source: "2004 Global Powers of Retailing," *Stores*, January 2004, www.stores.org

The Global Retail Picture

Retailing is also a very important factor in the global economy, and it is a difficult retail climate for store owners. In the past few years, the worldwide economy has been challenged by issues such as terrorism, economic downturn, reduced tourism, political crises, and low consumer confidence. All of these issues translate into lower sales for retail. At the same time, consumers are more savvy and empowered, and it is more difficult to gain and maintain their loyalty. Profits have to be worked at very diligently. Technology is making the industry more sophisticated and streamlined, and consolidation makes some competitors large and very powerful. It is a demanding and thorny business.

Not all countries have experienced the soft demand and market challenges that have characterized the major industrialized nations. Some of the developing countries or emerging markets in Asia and Eastern Europe are experiencing solid growth and are developing modern types of retailing. China, India, and Russia are seen as some of the biggest growth opportunities for retail in the next few years.

On a global scale, who is biggest? Wal-Mart! In 2002, the Wal-Mart Group recorded sales of US$230 billion, and the next largest retailer trails at US$65 billion. A study of the top 200 global retailers by the firm Deloitte Touche Tohmatsu ranks the world's biggest in the retail industry. Of the top 200 firms, 85 are American, and 68 are located in Europe (see Figure 14-2). There are seven Canadian retailers in the world's top 200 (Loblaws, Sobeys, Hudson's Bay Company, Métro-Richelieu, Canadian Tire, Jean Coutu, and Shoppers Drug Mart).[10] The chart in Figure 14-3 tells an interesting story: most of the large U.S. companies operate in their home country but in few, if any, other countries. In contrast, the large European retailers have a presence in many countries in many parts of the globe.

Concept Check

1. When Levi Strauss makes jeans cut to a customer's exact preferences and measurements, what utility is provided?
2. Two measures of the importance of retailing in the economy are _____ and _____.

RETAILING STRATEGY

Retailing involves many decisions and considerations, for example, deciding what type and format of retail presence to launch, determining who the target market will be, and deciding on a marketing mix to suit the particular retail concept. In this section we look at the issues in selecting a target market, the different types or classifications of retail to consider, the factors and components of the retail marketing mix, and the growing phenomenon of nonstore retailing.

Selecting a Target Market

The first task in developing a retail strategy is to define a target market, describing it in detail. In Chapter 9 we discussed in detail how to segment a market and then how to choose the targets to focus on. Without customers, even the best-conceived retail concept is nothing, so focusing on customers is the guiding principle of successful retail businesses. This focus involves understanding wants and needs, knowing customer preferences, analyzing behaviour, and deciding how to craft all of the dimensions of the retail concept to appeal to the targeted customer. Look at any mall or shopping district, and you will see the varied selection of retail offerings the customer has to choose from. This provides a challenge to retailers. It is no longer enough to appeal to customers; now the retailer has to interest, delight, and wow customers so that they will become loyal customers.

How do we define target markets? The most common descriptors are demographics, psychographics, geographics, and behaviour. Retailers study these factors and adjust their retail mix accordingly. McDonald's and Subway look at demographics—population, family, and age characteristics—to determine where new restaurants should be located and what formats to offer. Retailers such as Zellers and Canadian Tire look at consumers' trends and tastes and adjust their product offerings and store composition to match customer preferences. Office Depot and Shoppers Drug Mart have adjusted their store hours to respond to the behaviour of consumers; many now prefer to shop and do errands in the evening after working during the day.

Classifying Retail Outlets

For manufacturers, consumers, and the economy, retailing is an important component of marketing that has several variations. Because of the large number of alternative forms of retailing, it is easier to understand the differences among retail institutions by recognizing that outlets can be classified in several ways. First, **form of ownership** distinguishes retail outlets on the basis of whether individuals, corporate chains, or contractual systems own or control the outlet. Second, **level of service** is used to describe the degree of service provided to the customer. Three levels of service include self-, limited-, and full-service retailers. Finally, the type of **merchandise mix** describes how many different types of products a store carries and in what assortment. The alternative types of outlets are discussed in greater detail in the following pages.

Form of Ownership

Independent Retailer   One of the most common forms of retail ownership is the independent business, owned by an individual. Small independent retailers account for more than 60 percent of the total retail trade in Canada. They tend to be retailers such as bakeries, sporting goods stores, jewellery stores, or gift stores. Other types of small independent retailers include restaurants, automotive supply stores, bookstores, paint stores, flower shops, and women's accessories outlets. The advantage of this form of ownership for the owner is that he or she can be his or her own boss. For customers, the independent store can offer convenience, quality personal service, and lifestyle compatibility.[11]

Corporate Chain   A second form of ownership, the corporate chain, involves multiple outlets under common ownership. If you've ever shopped at The Bay, Sears, or Loblaws, you've shopped at a chain outlet.

In a chain operation, centralization of decision making and purchasing is common. Chain stores have advantages in dealing with manufacturers, particularly as the size of the chain grows. A large chain can bargain with a manufacturer to obtain good service or volume discounts on orders. Loblaws' large volume makes it a strong negotiator with manufacturers of most products. The buying power of chains is obvious to consumers who compare chain store prices with other types of stores. Consumers also benefit in dealing with chains because there are multiple outlets with similar merchandise and consistent management policies.

Contractual System   Contractual systems involve independently owned stores that band together to act like a chain. The three kinds described in Chapter 13 are retailer-sponsored cooperatives, wholesaler-sponsored voluntary chains, and franchises. One retailer-sponsored cooperative is Home Hardware, which is a collection of independent hardware and home-renovation stores across Canada. Home Hardware actually created its

---

form of ownership
Distinguishes retail outlets on the basis of whether individuals, corporate chains, or contractual systems own the outlet

level of service
The degree of service provided to the customer by self-, limited-, and full-service retailers

merchandise mix
How many different types of products a store carries and in what assortment

FRANCHISE	TYPE OF BUSINESS	TOTAL # OF UNITS	# OF UNITS FRANCHISED	% OF UNITS FRANCHISED	# OF UNITS IN CANADA	INVESTMENT REQUIRED (IN US$)
McDonald's	Fast food outlet	30,189	22,179	73%	1,320	$506,000–$1,630,000
Sylvan Learning Centres	Educational services provider	1,015	875	86%	75	$121,000–$219,000
Century 21	Real estate	6,585	6,585	100%	323	$12,000–$522,000
Church's Chicken	Chicken restaurant	1,229	761	62%	80	$194,000–$750,000
Second Cup	Coffee retailer	399	391	98%	399	$90,000–$335,000

FIGURE 14-4

Selected franchises and key issues

own wholesale operation to take full advantage of dealings with manufacturers and suppliers. As a cooperative, members can take advantage of volume discounts commonly available to chains and also give the impression of being a large chain, which may be viewed more favourably by some consumers. Wholesaler-sponsored voluntary chains such as Independent Grocers' Association (IGA) try to achieve similar benefits.

As noted in Chapter 13, in a franchise system an individual or firm (the franchisee) contracts with a parent company (the franchiser) to set up a business or retail outlet. McDonald's, Holiday Inn, Radio Shack, and Blockbuster Video all offer franchising opportunities. The franchiser usually assists in selecting the store location, setting up the store, advertising, and training personnel. In addition, the franchiser provides step-by-step procedures for

the major aspects of the business and guidelines for the most likely decisions a franchisee will confront. The franchisee pays a one-time franchise fee and an annual royalty, usually tied to the store's sales.

Franchise fees paid to the franchiser can range from $10,000 for a Church's Chicken to $45,000 for a McDonald's restaurant franchise. When these fees are combined with other costs, such as building and equipment, the total investment becomes much higher. Figure 14-2 shows five franchises that operate across Canada, and indicates the range of investment required and the number of units operating. By selling franchises, an organization reduces the cost of expansion, although they lose some control. A good franchiser concentrates on enhancing the image and reputation of the franchise name.[12]

Level of Service

Most customers perceive little variation in retail outlets by form of ownership. Rather, differences among retailers are more obvious in terms of level of service. In some department stores, such as Zellers, very few services are provided. Some grocery stores, such as Superstore, have customers bag the food themselves. Other outlets, such as Holt Renfrew, provide a wide range of customer services from gift wrapping to wardrobe consultation.

Self-Service   Self-service is at the extreme end of the level-of-service continuum because the customer performs many functions and little is provided by the outlet. Home building supply outlets and gas stations are often self-service. Warehouse stores such as Costco, usually in buildings several times larger than a conventional store, are self-service with all nonessential customer services eliminated. Several new forms of self-service include FedEx's placement of self-service package shipping stations in retail stores and office buildings, and self-service scanning systems currently being installed in supermarkets such as Loblaws.

Limited Service   Limited-service outlets provide some services, such as credit, and merchandise return, but not others, such as alterations to clothes. General merchandise stores such as Zellers, Shoppers Drug Mart, and Ikea are usually considered limited-service outlets. Customers are responsible for most shopping activities, although salespeople are available in departments such as cosmetics, home office, and consumer electronics.

Full Service   Full-service retailers, which include most specialty stores and department stores, provide many services to their customers. Holt Renfrew, a Canadian specialty fashion retailer with nine stores across the country, is very committed to exemplary customer service. Its stores feature more salespeople on the floor than other similarly sized stores, and Holt Renfrew offers a national concierge service, as well as personal shopping in each store. Employees are trained in customer follow-up, and many call their clients to advise them of new merchandise and send thank-you notes after purchase. With an eye kept fixed on customers and their evolving needs, Holt Renfrew is a leader in merchandise assortments and in innovations in customer services.[13]

Merchandise Mix

depth of product line
The size of the assortment of each item a store carries

breadth of product line
The variety of different items a store carries

Retail outlets also vary by their merchandise mix, the key distinction being the breadth and depth of the items offered to customers (Figure 14–5). **Depth of product line** means that the store carries a large assortment of each item, such as a shoe store that offers running shoes, dress shoes, and children's shoes. **Breadth of product line** refers to the variety of different items a store carries, such as women's clothing, men's clothing, children's clothing, cosmetics, and housewares.

Depth of Line   Stores that carry a large assortment (depth) of a related line of items are limited-line stores. SportChek sporting goods stores carry considerable depth in sports equipment ranging from golf accessories to running shoes. Stores that carry tremendous depth in one primary line of merchandise are single-line stores. La Senza, a nationwide chain, carries great depth in women's lingerie. Both limited- and single-line stores are often referred to as *specialty outlets*.

Specialty outlets focus on one type of product, such as electronics (Future Shop), office supplies (Office Depot), or books (Chapters-Indigo) at very competitive prices. These outlets are referred to in the trade as *category killers* because they often dominate the market. Chapters-Indigo, for example, controls a large percentage of the retail book market in Canada.

scrambled merchandising
Offering several unrelated products lines in a single retail store

Breadth of Line   Stores that carry a broad product line, with limited depth, are referred to as *general merchandise stores*. For example, large department stores such as The Bay, Sears, and Zellers carry a wide range of different types of products but not unusual sizes. The breadth and depth of merchandise lines are important decisions for a retailer. Traditionally, outlets carried related lines of goods. Today, however, **scrambled merchandising**, offering several unrelated product lines in a single store, is common. The modern drugstore

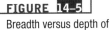

FIGURE 14–5
Breadth versus depth of merchandise lines

Breadth: Number of different product lines

| | Shoes | Appliances | CDs | Men's clothing |

Depth:
Number of items within each product line

| Nike running shoes
Florsheim dress shoes
Top Sider deck shoes
Adidas tennis shoes | Sony TV sets
JVC DVD players
General Electric
  dishwashers
Sharp microwave
  ovens | Classical
Rock
Jazz
Country western | Suits
Ties
Jackets
Overcoats
Socks
Shirts |

carries food, camera equipment, magazines, paper products, toys, small hardware items, and pharmaceuticals. Supermarkets rent carpet-cleaning equipment, operate pharmacy departments, and sell flowers.

Scrambled merchandising is convenient for consumers because it eliminates the number of stops required in a shopping trip. However, for the retailer this merchandising policy means there is competition between very dissimilar types of retail outlets, or **intertype competition**. A local bakery may compete with a department store, discount outlet, or even a local gas station. Scrambled merchandising and intertype competition make retailing more challenging.

intertype competition
Competition between very dissimilar types of retail outlets

1. Centralized decision making and purchasing are an advantage of _____ ownership.

2. What are some examples of stores with scrambled merchandising?

3. Would a shop for big men's clothes carrying pants in sizes 40 to 60 have a broad or deep product line?

Retailing Mix

retailing mix
The goods and services, physical distribution, and communications tactics chosen by a store

The marketing mix, or the 4 Ps (product, price, place, and promotion), are used in retail just as they are in other businesses, but with some unique considerations. In this section we look at the retail marketing mix, which includes product and service considerations, retail pricing, physical location factors, and communications, as shown in Figure 14-6. All of these components of the mix focus on the consumer. In retail it is often said that the consumer is king, and treating them that way is a winning idea for successful retailing.

Products and Services

One of the first decisions retailers make is what they are going to sell. Usually both services and products are offered. A department store such as The Bay sells many products—from clothing to housewares—and also provide services such as bridal registries. Great Clips provides services such as hair cuts, colouring, and styling, but also sells hair care products. The balance between products and services involves a trade-off between costs and customer satisfaction. Retailers decide where their concentration will be—on convenience, goods, or service offerings—and what their target customers will most value.

In the previous section we talked about decisions to be made regarding the breadth and depth of the product assortment. Merchandise selection is one of the major attracting factors for customers, so choices and combinations must be made carefully and continually updated to reflect current trends and tastes. This involves finding sources of supply of the products, or having them manufactured, as well as managing inventory and warehousing.

Product and service strategy evolves over time. In retail stores in Canada, we have products available to us from all over the world. This makes a wide selection of choices for the consumer, but a significant challenge for the retailer. Think about food stores for a minute: in your shopping basket, you may have a mango from Mexico, cookies from England, spices from India, and rice from China. Imagine the task of the merchandiser to decide on, order, store, and shelve all of these products from every corner of the globe!

Retail Pricing

In setting prices for merchandise, retailers must decide on the markup, markdown, and timing for markdowns. The *markup* refers to how much should be added to the cost the retailer paid for a product to reach the final selling price. We discussed the calculation of

FIGURE 14-6
The retailing mix

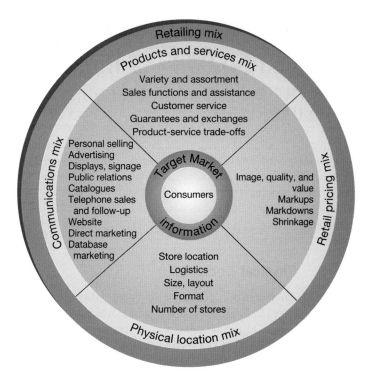

markup in Chapter 12. The difference between the final selling price and retailer cost is called the *gross margin*.

Discounting a product, or taking a *markdown*, occurs when the product does not sell at the original price and an adjustment is necessary. Often new models or styles force the price of existing models to be marked down. Discounts may also be used to increase demand for related products.[14] For example, retailers might take a markdown on stereos to increase sales of CDs or reduce the price of cake mix to generate frosting purchases. The *timing* of a markdown can be important. Many retailers take a markdown as soon as sales fall off, to free up valuable selling space and obtain cash. However, other stores delay markdowns to discourage bargain hunters and maintain an image of quality. There is no clear answer, but retailers must consider how the timing might affect future sales.

Although most retailers plan markdowns, many retailers use price discounts as a part of their regular merchandising policy. Wal-Mart and Home Depot, for example, emphasize consistently low prices and eliminate most markdowns with a strategy often called *everyday low pricing*.[15] Consumers often use price as an indicator of product quality; however, the brand name of the product and the image of the store become important decision factors in these situations.[16]

A special issue for retailers trying to keep prices low is **shrinkage**, or breakage and theft of merchandise by customers and employees. Who do you think steals more? For the answer, see the accompanying Ethics and Social Responsibility Alert.[17]

Off-price retailing is a retail pricing practice that is used by retailers such as Winners. **Off-price retailing** involves selling brand-name merchandise at lower than regular prices. The difference between the off-price retailer and a discount store is that off-price merchandise is bought by the retailer from manufacturers with excess inventory at prices below wholesale prices, whereas the discounter buys at full wholesale price but takes less of a markup than do traditional department stores. Because of this difference in the way merchandise is purchased by the retailer, selection at an off-price retailer is unpredictable, and searching for bargains has become a popular activity for many consumers. Savings to the consumer at off-price retailers are reported as high as 70 percent off the prices of a traditional department store.

shrinkage
Breakage and theft of merchandise by customers and employees

off-price retailing
Selling brand-name merchandise at lower than regular prices

ETHICS AND SOCIAL RESPONSIBILITY ALERT

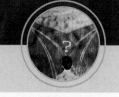

WHO TAKES THE FIVE-FINGER DISCOUNT? YOU'LL BE SURPRISED

Retailers lose almost 2 percent of their sales to theft each year. To combat the problem, many stores attempt to discourage consumers from shoplifting with magnetic detectors, locked cases, and other deterrents. What you may find surprising, though, is that more than 50 percent of the thefts are not made by consumers but by employees. The most popular items to steal are candy from convenience stores, shirts from department stores, and batteries from discount stores. When does this happen? The most popular time is between 3 and 6 p.m. Why do you think shoplifting is such a large problem? What recommendations would you make to retailers?

Physical Location

Another aspect of the retailing mix involves deciding where to locate the store and how many stores to have. Department stores, which started downtown in most cities, have followed customers to the suburbs, and in recent years more stores have been opened in large regional malls. Most stores today are near several others in one of five settings: the central business district, the regional centre, the community shopping centre, the strip, or the power centre.

The **central business district** is the oldest retail setting, the community's downtown area. Until the regional outflow to suburbs, it was the major shopping area, but the suburban population has grown at the expense of the downtown shopping area.

Regional shopping centres consist of 50 to 150 stores that typically attract customers who live or work within a 5- to 15-kilometre range. These large shopping areas often contain two or three *anchor stores*, which are well-known national or regional stores such as Sears and The Bay. The largest variation of a regional centre is the West Edmonton Mall in Alberta. The shopping centre is a conglomerate of 800 stores, seven amusement centres, 110 restaurants, and a 355-room Fantasyland hotel.[18]

A more limited approach to retail location is the **community shopping centre**, which typically has one primary store (usually a department store branch) and often about 20 to 40 smaller outlets. Generally, these centres serve a population of consumers who are within a 2- to 5-kilometre drive.

Not every suburban store is located in a shopping mall. Many neighbourhoods have clusters of stores, referred to as a **strip location**, to serve people who are within a 5- to 10-minute drive. Gas station, hardware, laundry, grocery, and pharmacy outlets are commonly found in a strip location. Unlike the larger shopping centres, the composition of these stores is usually unplanned. A variation of the strip shopping location is called the **power centre**, which is a large shopping strip with multiple national stores. Power centres are seen as having the convenient location found in many strip centres and the additional power of national stores. These large strips often have two to five anchor stores plus a supermarket, which brings the shopper to the power centre on a weekly basis.[19]

Several new types of retail locations include carts, kiosks, and wall units. These forms of retailing have been popular in airports and mall common areas because they provide consumers with easy access and rental income for the property owner. Retailers benefit from the relatively low cost compared with a regular store.

Communications

The elements of the retailing communication mix described in Figure 14–6 represent an exciting menu of choices for creating customer value in the marketplace. Each format allows

Margin glossary

central business district
The oldest retail setting, the community's downtown area

regional shopping centres
Consist of 50 to 150 stores that typically attract customers who live within a 5- to 15-kilometre range; often containing two or three anchor stores

community shopping centre
Retail location that typically has one primary store and 20 to 40 smaller outlets, serving a population of consumers within a 2- to 5-kilometre drive

strip location
A cluster of stores serving people who live within a 5- to 10-minute drive

power centre
Large shopping strip with multiple anchor stores, a convenient location, and a supermarket

retailers to offer unique benefits and meet particular needs of various customer groups. Today, retailers combine many of the formats to offer a broader spectrum of benefits and experiences. These **multichannel retailers** utilize and integrate a combination of traditional store and nonstore formats such as catalogues, television, and online retailing. Chapters-Indigo, for example, created chapters.indigo.ca to compete with Amazon.com. Similarly, Office Depot has integrated its store, catalogue, and Internet operations.

multichannel retailers
Use a combination of traditional store formats and nonstore formats such as catalogues, television, and online retailing

Integrated channels can make shopping simpler and more convenient. A consumer can research choices online or in a catalogue and then make a purchase online, over the telephone, or at the closest store. In addition, the use of multiple channels allows retailers to reach a broader profile of customers. While online retailing may cannibalize catalogue business to some degree, a Web transaction costs about half as much to process as a catalogue order. Multichannel retailers also benefit from the synergy of sharing information among the different channel operations. Online retailers, for example, have recognized that the Internet is more of a transactional medium than a relationship-building medium and are working to find ways to complement traditional customer interactions.[20]

Concept Check

1. How does original markup differ from maintained markup?
2. A large shopping strip with multiple anchor stores is a _____ centre.
3. How do multichannel retailers make shopping simpler and more convenient?

Nonstore Retailing

Most of the retailing examples discussed earlier in the chapter, such as corporate chains, department stores, and limited- and single-line specialty stores, involve store retailing. Many retailing activities today, however, are not limited to sales in a store. Nonstore retailing occurs outside a retail outlet through activities that involve varying levels of customer and retailer involvement. Forms of nonstore retailing include automatic vending, television home shopping, and direct marketing (direct mail and catalogue retailing, telemarketing, and direct selling). Many traditional "brick and mortar" stores are involved in nonstore retailing, making them "click and mortar" concepts; for example, Chapters-Indigo has developed chapters.indigo.ca, its online store. Dell Computers, in contrast, has no stores and relies totally on nonstore retailing for its consumer sales.

Automatic Vending

Nonstore retailing includes vending machines, which make it possible to serve customers when and where stores cannot. Maintaining and operating vending machines is expensive, so product prices in vending machines tend to be higher than those in stores. Typically, small convenience products are available in vending machines. In North America, some 60 percent of vending machines are soft-drink machines. In Japan, however, products available in vending machines include dried squid, hair tonic, boxers, green tea, beer, CDs, books, clothing, and even music downloaded from a satellite transmission system. Sanyo Electric recently introduced a fully automated convenience store![21]

Improved technology will soon make vending machines easier to use by reducing the need for cash. In Europe, for example, Marconi Online Systems has installed 6,000 vending machines that allow consumers to pay for products using a cellphone. Similarly, the world's largest vending machine company, Canteen Vending Services, is testing a cashless system called FreedomPay, which allows consumers to wave a small wand in front of a sensor to make a purchase.

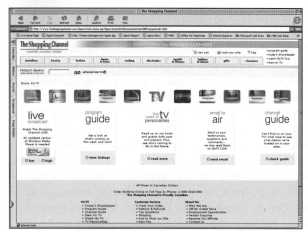

Another improvement in vending machines—the use of wireless technology to notify retailers when their machines are empty—is one reason automatic merchandising sales are expected to increase in the future.[22]

Television Home Shopping

Television home shopping is possible when consumers watch a shopping channel on which products are displayed; orders are then placed over the telephone or the Internet. One popular program is The Shopping Channel, which has 24-hour programming and calls itself a broadcast retailer. A limitation of TV shopping has been the lack of buyer–seller interaction. New Internet technologies, however, now allow consumers to simultaneously shop, chat, and interact with their favourite show host while watching TV.[23]

Direct Marketing from a Retailing Perspective

We talk in detail about direct marketing in Chapter 15; here we introduce the idea, as it is an important form of retailing. In its simplest terms, direct marketing is an interactive process of marketing that uses advertising media or direct consumer contact to offer products or services. When a direct communication to a consumer or a business market is intended to generate a response from the recipient, direct marketing is the tactic being used.

Direct Mail and Catalogues Direct-mail and catalogue retailing is attractive because it eliminates the cost of a store and clerks. It costs a traditional retail store more than twice the amount to acquire a new customer than it costs a catalogue retailer. Why? Because catalogues improve marketing efficiency through segmentation and targeting. In addition, they create customer value by providing a fast and convenient means of making a purchase. In Canada, the amount spent on direct-mail catalogue merchandise continues to increase; internationally, spending is also increasing. Direct marketers offer rural Japanese farmers outdoor gear at discount prices through direct-mail campaigns—and deliver within 72 hours![24]

One reason for the growth in catalogue sales is that traditional retailers such as Office Depot are adding catalogue operations. Another reason is that many Internet retailers such as Amazon.com have also added catalogues. As consumers' direct-mail purchases have increased, the number of catalogues and the number of products sold through catalogues have increased. A typical Canadian household now receives dozens of catalogues every year, and there are billions circulated around the world. The competition, combined with recent increases in postal rates, however, have caused catalogue retailers to focus on proven customers rather than "prospects." Another successful new approach used by many catalogue retailers is to send specialty catalogues to market niches identified in their databases. L. L. Bean, a longstanding catalogue retailer, has developed an individual catalogue for fly-fishing enthusiasts. Lee Valley sends out specialized catalogues for hardware, woodworking, gardening, and Christmas.[25]

telemarketing

Using the telephone to interact with and sell directly to consumers

Telemarketing Another form of nonstore retailing, called **telemarketing**, involves using the telephone to interact with and sell directly to consumers. Compared with direct mail, telemarketing is often viewed as a more efficient means of targeting consumers, although the two techniques are often used together. Sears Canada utilizes telemarketing to increase sales of extended warranty programs and other services. Communications companies such as Sprint and Bell Mobility telemarket new potential customers, and financial institutions such as HSBC and MBNA use telemarketing for customer follow-up and cross-selling. (Just in case you have not heard of these financial companies, here's a glimpse at who they are. HSBC, or the HSBC Group, is one of the largest banking and financial services organizations in the world, and over 100 years old, named from The Hongkong and Shanghai Banking Corporation Limited. MBNA is the largest independent credit-card issuer in the world; you may think that the letters MBNA should stand for some longer name, but apparently it does not.) Telemarketing has grown in popularity as companies search for ways to cut costs but still provide convenient access to their customers. According to the American Teleservices Association, annual telemarketing sales exceed US$500 billion.[26]

As the use of telemarketing grows, consumer privacy has become a topic of discussion among consumers, governments, and businesses. Issues such as industry standards, ethical guidelines, and new privacy laws are evolving to provide a balance between the varying perspectives. The federal government introduced privacy legislation in January 2001 that set out regulations about how companies can collect and use information about individuals for marketing purposes, and also set some restrictions on telemarketers. Visit the Canadian Marketing Association's website (www.the-cma.org) for the privacy information they present for the industry.[27]

Direct Selling Direct selling, sometimes called door-to-door retailing, involves direct sales of goods and services to consumers through personal interactions and demonstrations in their home or office. A variety of companies, including familiar names such as Avon, Tupperware, and Mary Kay Cosmetics, have created an industry with billions in sales by providing consumers with personalized service and convenience. However, sales have been declining as retail chains begin to carry similar products at discount prices and as the increasing number of dual-career households reduces the number of potential buyers who can be found at home.

In response to change, many direct-selling retailers are expanding into other markets. Avon, for example, already has 3 million sales representatives in 137 countries including Mexico, Poland, Argentina, and China.[28] Similarly, other retailers such as Amway, Herbalife, and Electrolux are rapidly expanding. More than 70 percent of Amway's US$7 billion in sales now comes from outside North America, and sales in Japan alone exceed sales in North America.[29] Direct selling is likely to continue to grow in markets where the lack of effective distribution channels increases the importance of door-to-door convenience and where the lack of consumer knowledge about products and brands will increase the need for a person-to-person approach.[30]

1. Why are catalogue sales growing?

2. Where are direct-selling retail sales growing? Why?

Online Retailing

Online retailing allows customers to search for, evaluate, and order products through the Internet. For many consumers, the advantages of this form of retailing are the 24-hour access, the ability to comparison shop, the in-home privacy, and the variety. Studies of online shoppers indicated that men were initially more likely than women to buy something online. As the number of online households increased to more than 50 percent, however, the profile of online

shoppers changed to include all shoppers. In addition, the number of online retailers grew rapidly for several years but then declined as many stand-alone, Internet-only businesses failed or consolidated. Today, there has been a melding of traditional and online retailers—"bricks and clicks"—that are using experiences from both approaches to create better value and experiences for customers. At WalMart.com, for example, CEO Jeanne Jackson has advocated a streamlined and intuitive website layout and new services such as real-time inventories in individual stores in the U.S. that allow customers to decide whether to go to the store or to buy online. Experts predict that online sales will exceed US$100 billion in 2004.[31]

Consumers can make online retail purchases in several different ways.

- They can pay dues and become members of an online discount service.
- They can use a shopping "bot" such as www.mysimon.com.
- They can go directly to online malls or online shopping directories (portals) such as www.retailcanada.com, which features more than 5,000 Canadian online stores.
- They can simply go to a specific online retailer's website.
- A final, and quickly growing, approach to online retailing is the online auction, such as www.ebay.ca, where consumers bid on more than 1,000 categories of products.

One of the biggest problems online retailers face is that nearly two-thirds of online shoppers make it to "checkout" and then leave the website to compare shipping costs and prices on other sites. Of the shoppers who leave, 70 percent do not return. One way online retailers are addressing this issue is to offer consumers a comparison of competitors' offerings. Online retailers are also trying to improve the online retailing experience by adding experiential, or interactive, activities to their websites, such as apparel stores' use of "virtual models" to involve consumers in the purchase process and help with product selection.[32] Other changes on the horizon include the merger of television home shopping and online retailing through TV-based Web platforms such as WebTV, AOLTV, and UltimateTV, which use an "Internet appliance" attached to a television to connect to the Internet.[33]

Why Consumers Shop and Buy Online   Consumers typically offer six reasons why they shop and buy online: convenience, choice, customization, communication, cost, and control (see Figure 14-7).

- *Convenience*. Online shopping and buying is *convenient*, so websites must be easy to locate and navigate, and image downloads must be fast.
- *Choice*. There are two dimensions to choice: *selection*—numerous websites for almost anything consumers want—and *assistance*—interactive capabilities of Internet/Web-enabled technologies assist customers to make informed choices.
- *Customization*. Internet/Web-enabled capabilities make possible a highly interactive and individualized information and exchange environment for shoppers and buyers. Consumers get what they want and feel good about the experience.

FIGURE 14-7

Why consumers shop and
buy online

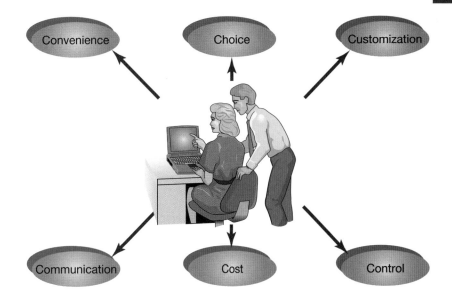

- *Communication.* Communication can take three forms: marketer-to-consumer e-mail notification, consumer-to-marketer buying and service requests, and consumer-to-consumer chat rooms and instant messaging.[34]
- *Cost.* Many popular items bought online can be purchased at the same price or cheaper than in retail stores. Lower prices also result from Internet/Web-enabled software that permits *dynamic pricing*, the practice of changing prices for products and services in real time in response to supply and demand conditions.
- *Control.* Online shoppers and buyers are empowered consumers. They readily use Internet/Web-enabled technology to seek information, evaluate alternatives, and make purchase decisions on their own time, terms, and conditions.

When and Where Online Consumers Shop and Buy Shopping and buying also happen at different times in the online marketspace than in the traditional marketplace.[35] About 80 percent of online retail sales occur Monday through Friday. The busiest shopping day is Wednesday. By comparison, 35 percent of retail store sales are registered on the weekend. Saturday is the most popular shopping day. Monday through Friday online shopping and buying often occurs during normal work hours—some 40 percent of online consumers say they visit websites from their place of work, which partially accounts for the sales level during the workweek. Favourite websites for workday shopping and buying include those featuring event tickets, online periodical subscriptions, flowers and gifts, consumer electronics, and travel. Websites offering health and beauty items, apparel and accessories, and music and video tend to be browsed and bought at home. Consumers are more likely to browse than buy online. Although 9 in 10 online consumers regularly shop in the marketspace of websites, over half (51 percent) confine their purchases to the traditional retail store marketplace.[36]

Describing the Online Consumer Who are online consumers, and what do they buy? Why do they choose to shop and purchase products and services in the new marketspace rather than or in addition to the traditional marketplace? Cybershoppers, Netizens, and e-shoppers—whatever name you use for them—they do differ demographically from the general population, although over time they will likely become one and the same. Online consumers own or have access to a computer or an Internet/Web-enabled device, such as a wireless cellular telephone. Nearly two out of every three Canadians accessed the Internet at least once a month, according to a Leger Marketing poll taken in July 2003. This access may

FIGURE 14–8
Product and service
categories for online
shopping

**TYPE OF PRODUCT
OR SERVICE BOUGHT
ONLINE**   **EXAMPLES**

TYPE OF PRODUCT OR SERVICE BOUGHT ONLINE	EXAMPLES	
1. Product information important, prepurchase trial not critical	Computers, computer accessories, books	
2. Audio or video demonstration important	CDs, videos	
3. Items that can be delivered digitally	Software, travel reservations, financial brokerage services	
4. Unique items	Collectibles, gifts	
5. Regularly purchased items where convenience is important	Consumer packaged goods, grocery items	
6. Highly standardized products, price very important	Insurance (auto, home), home improvement products, toys, some casual clothing	

be via a computer at home with Internet/Web access, although access is often possible at work or school.

Online consumers are the sub-segment of all Internet/Web users who use this technology to research products and services and make purchases. Research indicates that about 80 percent of all adult Internet/Web users have sought online product or service information at one time or another.[37] For example, some 70 percent of prospective travellers have researched travel information online, even though fewer than 25 percent have actually made online travel reservations. Over 40 percent have researched automobiles before making a purchase, but only 8 percent of users actually bought a vehicle online. About two-thirds of adult Internet/Web users have actually purchased a product or service online at one time or another.

As a group, online consumers, like Internet/Web users, are evenly split between men and women and tend to be better educated, younger, and more affluent than the general population, which makes them an attractive market. Even though online shopping and buying is growing in popularity, a small percentage of online consumers still account for a disproportionate share of online retail sales in North America. It is estimated that 20 percent of online consumers who spend $1,000-plus per year online account for 87 percent of total consumer online sales.[38]

What Online Consumers Buy There is a lot marketers have to learn about online consumer purchase behaviour. Although research has documented the most frequently purchased products and services bought online, marketers also need to know why these items are popular. There are six general product and service categories that dominate online consumer buying today and for the foreseeable future, as shown in Figure 14-8.[39]

THE CHANGING NATURE OF RETAILING: THE RETAIL LIFE CYCLE

Retailing is the most dynamic aspect of a channel of distribution. New retailers are always entering the market, searching for a new position that will attract customers. The reason for this continual change is explained by the retail life cycle.

The Retail Life Cycle

The process of growth and decline that retail outlets, like products, experience is described by the **retail life cycle**.[40] Figure 14–9 shows the retail life cycle and the position of various current forms of retail outlets on it. Early growth is the stage when a retail outlet first appears, with a major difference from existing competition. Market share rises gradually, although profits may be low because of start-up costs. In the next stage, accelerated development, both market share and profit achieve their greatest growth rates. Usually multiple outlets are established as companies focus on the distribution element of the retailing mix. In this stage some later competitors may enter. Wendy's, for example, appeared on the hamburger chain scene almost 20 years after McDonald's had begun operation. The key goal for the retailer in this stage is to establish a dominant position in the fight for market share.

The battle for market share is usually fought before the maturity phase, and some competitors drop out of the market. New retail forms enter in the maturity phase, stores try to maintain their market share, and price discounting occurs. For example, when McDonald's

retail life cycle
The process of growth and decline that retail outlets, like products, experience over time

FIGURE 14–9
The retail life cycle

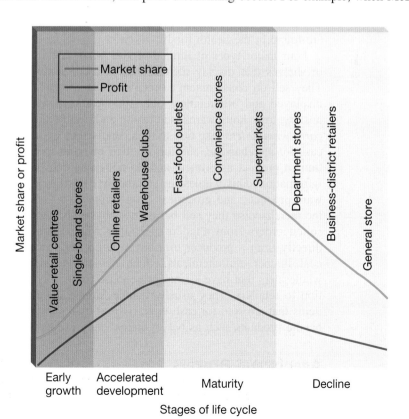

introduced its Extra Value Meal, a discounted package of burger, fries, and drink, Wendy's followed with a kid's Value Menu.

WHOLESALING

Many retailers rely on intermediaries to provide them with selection and availability of the products sold in their retail operations. Many other businesses also use intermediaries to provide them with selection and availability plus value-added services for products that they need to operate their businesses. Those intermediaries are commonly called wholesalers and agents (described briefly in Chapter 13), according to the functions that they fulfill in the distribution process. In addition, there are manufacturers' sales offices operated by the original manufacturers of the products. All of these wholesaling intermediaries play an important role in the retailing process and in helping other businesses get the products they need.

Merchant Wholesalers

merchant wholesalers
Independently owned firms that take title to the merchandise they handle

Merchant wholesalers are independently owned firms that take title to—that is, they buy—the merchandise they handle. They go by various names, described in detail below. About 83 percent of the firms engaged in wholesaling activities are merchant wholesalers.

Merchant wholesalers are classified as either full-service or limited-service wholesalers, depending on the number of functions performed. Two major types of full-service wholesalers exist. *General merchandise* (or *full-line*) *wholesalers* carry a broad assortment of merchandise and perform all channel functions. This type of wholesaler is most prevalent in the hardware, drug, and clothing industries. However, these wholesalers do not maintain much depth of assortment within specific product lines. *Specialty merchandise* (or *limited-line*) *wholesalers* offer a relatively narrow range of products but have an extensive assortment within the product lines carried. They perform all channel functions and are found in the health foods, automotive parts, and seafood industries.

Four major types of limited-service wholesalers exist. *Rack jobbers* furnish the racks or shelves that display merchandise in retail stores and perform all channel functions. They sell on consignment to retailers, which means they retain the title to the products displayed and bill retailers only for the merchandise sold. Familiar products such as hosiery, toys, housewares, and health and beauty aids are sold by rack jobbers. *Cash and carry wholesalers* take title to merchandise but sell only to buyers who call on them, pay cash for merchandise, and furnish their own transportation for merchandise. They carry a limited product assortment and do not make deliveries, extend credit, or supply market information. This wholesaler commonly deals in electric supplies, office supplies, hardware products, and groceries. *Drop shippers*, or *desk jobbers*, are wholesalers that own the merchandise they sell but do not physically handle, stock, or deliver it. They simply solicit orders from retailers and other wholesalers and have the merchandise shipped directly from a producer to a buyer. Drop shippers are used for bulky products such as coal, lumber, and chemicals, which are sold in large quantities. *Truck jobbers* are small wholesalers that have a small warehouse from which they stock their trucks for distribution to retailers. They usually handle limited assortments of fast-moving or perishable items that are sold for cash directly from trucks in their original packages. Truck jobbers handle products such as bakery items, dairy products, and meat.

Agents and Brokers

Unlike merchant wholesalers, agents and brokers do not take title to merchandise and typically provide fewer channel functions. They make their profit from commissions or fees paid for their services, whereas merchant wholesalers make their profit from the sale of the merchandise they have bought and resold.

Manufacturers' agents and selling agents are the two major types of agents used by producers. **Manufacturers' agents**, or *manufacturers' representatives*, work for several producers and carry noncompetitive, complementary merchandise in an exclusive territory. Manufacturers' agents act as a producer's sales arm in a territory and are principally responsible for the transactional channel functions, primarily selling. They are used extensively in the automotive supply, footwear, and fabricated steel industries. By comparison, **selling agents** represent a single producer and are responsible for the entire marketing function of that producer. They design promotional plans, set prices, determine distribution policies, and make recommendations on product strategy. Selling agents are used by small producers in the textile, apparel, food, and home furnishing industries.

Brokers are independent firms or individuals whose main function is to bring buyers and sellers together to make sales. Brokers, unlike agents, usually have no continuous relationship with the buyer or seller but negotiate a contract between two parties and then move on to another task. Brokers are used extensively in the real estate industry.

A unique broker that acts in many ways like a manufacturer's agent is a food broker, representing buyers and sellers in the grocery industry. Food brokers differ from conventional brokers because they act on behalf of producers on a permanent basis and receive a commission for their services. For example, food giant Nabisco uses food brokers to sell its candies, margarine, and Planters peanuts, but it sells its line of cookies and crackers directly to retail stores.

Manufacturer's Branches and Offices

Unlike merchant wholesalers, agents, and brokers, manufacturer's branches and sales offices are wholly owned extensions of the producer that perform wholesaling activities. Producers assume wholesaling functions when there are no intermediaries to perform these activities, customers are few in number and geographically concentrated, orders are large or require significant attention, or they want to control the distribution of their products. A *manufacturer's branch office* carries a producer's inventory and performs the functions of a full-service wholesaler. A *manufacturer's sales office* does not carry inventory, typically performs only a sales function, and serves as an alternative to agents and brokers.

manufacturers' agents
Work for several producers and carry noncompetitive, complementary merchandise in an exclusive territory

selling agents
Represent a single producer and are responsible for the entire marketing function of that producer

brokers
Independent firms or individuals whose main function is to bring buyers and sellers together to make sales

Concept Check

1. Where in the retail life cycle is market share usually fought between competitors?
2. What is the difference between merchant wholesalers and agents?

SUMMARY

1 Retailing provides customer value in the form of various utilities: time, place, possession, information, and form. Economically, retailing is important in terms of the people employed and money exchanged in retail sales.

2 Retailing outlets can be classified along several dimensions: the form of ownership, level of service, or merchandise mix.

3 There are several forms of ownership: independent, chain, retailer-sponsored cooperative, wholesaler-sponsored chain or franchise.

4 Stores vary in the level of service they provide. Three levels are self-service, limited service, or full service.

5 Retail outlets vary in terms of the breadth and depth of their merchandise lines. Breadth refers to the number of different items carried, and depth refers to the assortment of each item offered.

6 Nonstore retailing includes automatic vending, television home shopping, online retailing, and direct marketing (direct mail and catalogue retailing, telemarketing, and direct selling).

7 Retailing strategy is based on the retailing mix, consisting of goods and services, retail pricing, physical location, and communications.

8 In retail pricing, retailers must decide on the markup, markdown, and timing for the markdown. Off-price retailers offer brand-name merchandise at lower than regular prices.

9 Online consumers represent a segment of all Internet/Web users and differ demographically from the general population. Six general product and service categories are bought by online consumers. However, travel reservations, computer hardware and consumer electronics, media, and clothing and accessories account for the majority of consumer purchases. The increasing sales and number of people purchasing online suggest that the profile of the online consumer is becoming more and more like the profile of the consumer of the traditional marketplace.

10 Consumers refer to six reasons they shop and buy online: convenience, choice, customization, communication, cost, and control. Marketers capitalize on these reasons using a variety of approaches, including electronic shopping agents (bots), web communities, viral marketing, and dynamic pricing.

11 Retail store location is an important retail mix decision. The common alternatives are the central business district, a regional shopping centre, a community shopping centre, or a strip location. A variation of the strip location is the power centre, which is a strip location with multiple national anchor stores and a supermarket.

12 Multichannel retailers use a combination of store and nonstore formats.

13 Like products, retail outlets have a life cycle consisting of four stages: early growth, accelerated development, maturity, and decline.

14 Many retailers depend on the numerous types of intermediaries that engage in wholesaling activities.

15 The main difference between the various types of wholesalers lies in whether or not they take title to the items they sell.

KEY TERMS AND CONCEPTS

breadth of product line p. 331
brokers p. 343
central business district p. 334
community shopping centre p. 334
depth of product line p. 331
form of ownership p. 329
intertype competition p. 332
level of service p. 329

manufacturers' agents p. 342
merchandise mix p. 329
merchant wholesalers p. 342
multichannel retailers p. 335
off-price retailing p. 333
power centre p. 334
regional shopping centres p. 334
retailing p. 325

retailing mix p. 332
retail life cycle p. 341
scrambled merchandising p. 331
selling agents p. 343
shrinkage p. 333
strip location p. 334
telemarketing p. 336

QUESTIONS: APPLYING MARKETING CONCEPTS AND PERSPECTIVES

1 Discuss the impact of the growing number of dual-income households on *(a)* nonstore retailing and *(b)* the retail mix.

2 What are the similarities and differences between the product and retail life cycles?

3 Develop a chart to highlight the role of each of the three main elements of the retailing mix across the four stages of the retail life cycle.

4 Breadth and depth are two important components in distinguishing among types of retailers. Discuss breadth and depth implications for the following retailers discussed in this chapter: *(a)* The Bay, *(b)* Costco, *(c)* Dell, and *(d)* SportChek.

5 According to the retail life cycle, what will happen to warehouse clubs?

6 The text discusses the development of online retailing. How does the development of this retailing form agree with the implications of the retail life cycle?

7 Comment on this statement: The only distinction among merchant wholesalers and agents and brokers is that merchant wholesalers take title to the products they sell.

8 Online retailing is popular, but it has not taken off nearly as fast as predicted. Why do you think online retailing has been slower to diffuse through society than originally anticipated? What are consumers' reasons for not shopping online? What can retailers do to deal with customer concerns?

DISCUSSION FORUM

Imagine that a wealthy uncle leaves you a large inheritance, and you decide that you will use it to start a retail chain of stores selling environmentally friendly products. First, you develop a retail plan. Suggest what information will go into each of these sections of your plan:

- Type of retail outlet, and ownership
- Level of service to be provided
- Merchandise mix, merchandise lines, breadth and depth
- In-store versus nonstore retailing
- Pricing considerations
- Store locations
- Target market

What other considerations will you need to make in planning your retail stores?

INTERNET EXERCISE

For many consumers, comparison shopping is not appealing because of the inconvenience of traveling to multiple locations. Even on the Internet, finding and searching multiple websites can be tedious. One solution is a form of software called an "intelligent agent," or "bot" (derived from robot), which automatically searches for the best price. Try each of the following shopping bots—www.mysimon.com and www.dealtime.com—to find the best price for one of the following products:

www.mcgrawhill.ca/college/thecore

1 Wilson tennis racket

2 Sony TV

3 Guess jeans

How did the agents differ? What range of prices did you obtain? What shipping and handling charges would apply to each purchase? Why are different recommendations made by the agents?

VIDEO CASE 14

KRISPY KREME: A LOVE STORY WITH A HOLE IN IT

To Canadians this is something new, but to our neighbours south of the border, Krispy Kreme donuts date back to 1937. Well, it goes further than that—it's what you could call a "cult brand." The company has come a long way since its humble beginnings. As of September 2004, more than 390 stores serve up donuts in 5 countries spanning 3 continents, producing 7.5 million donuts daily and approaching 3 billion donuts annually. Some people obviously love them!

The first store in Canada opened in December 2001 in Mississauga, Ontario, and it broke company records for the most donuts sold both on an opening day and in the first week of operation. Maybe this not surprising as Canada is often re-ferred to as a nation of donut lovers, a title earned partially through our loyal following for Tim Hortons, Canada's most famous home-grown franchise. Some regions of Canada reportedly boast a "Tim's" on every corner, no doubt contributing to Canadians' reputation as the world's most voracious consumers of donuts.

How does one company enter a new country and take on an established leader or, more specifically, a tradition? Krispy Kreme did it by being different and making donut buying a retail experience. If you walk into one of the green-and-white stores that exude nostalgia and home-grown hospitality, you experience the aura of mystery and excitement the company has created around the production of donuts. Outside, the "Hot Donuts Now" sign beckons customers to enter and watch donuts being made on the premises. The friendly greeters and the fresh-baked aroma suggest home, but this is no small process—from specially prepared dough shipped in from headquarters to custom donut-making machinery, this is serious donut business. The custom-designed stores are actual production facilities, and shoppers get to see it all. "Donut Theatres" showcase the process of creating these sweet treats—who wouldn't be intrigued by the "glaze waterfall" and the conveyor belts moving the donuts from dough to serving tray? The final act is the sampling and purchasing of fresh donuts, and many shoppers are offered a free taste—truly a shopping experience!

Will the experience last? Will customers tire of it? Will the mystique and multi-sensory experience translate into the same brand following for Krispy Kreme in Canada as has been the case for the company in the U.S.? Or can the competition upstage them?

These questions remain to be answered, but Krispy Kreme continues its march across Canada, now with stores in British Columbia, Alberta, Ontario, and Quebec. Roly Morris, president and CEO of KremeKo, which has the rights to develop the brand in central and eastern Canada, thinks that the Canadian donut landscape allows for 50 Krispy Kreme operations across the country. Sounds like a lot? Canada already has 3,200 donut shops. But Krispy Kreme is banking on strong growth potential in all its markets, using a proven business concept, experienced franchisees, a high-quality premium-priced product supported by a vertically integrated production and supply process, and a uniquely orchestrated shopping experience.

Krispy Kreme relies heavily on public relations to promote their stores, and they are very successful in creating a media buzz and major excitement around new store openings. Free donuts on street corners, boxes of the goodies to the key media outlets, and celebrities professing their love for the donuts all have contributed to the opening day lineups and the loyal fans. While these tactics have worked in Canada, Americans are much more responsive to this kind of promotion; the donut divas discovered that they had to refine their approach for it to work north of the border.

How is Tim Hortons reacting to all this activity? Confident that Canadians will tire of all the hoopla surrounding Krispy Kreme donuts, it has concentrated on expanding its menu and rapidly adding many stores in a variety of different formats. Some argue the two brands don't even compete!

Will changing attitudes toward healthy foods and increasing concern about obesity affect the marketplace for both companies? Undoubtedly, yes! Who will fare worst: one reliant almost totally on donuts or the other that is now targeting meals as opposed to just donuts? Krispy Kreme donuts are sweeter, but Tim Hortons have half the fat. Krispy Kreme donuts are more expensive, but Tim's offers a wider selection of food—and the list goes on. Retail competition can be a tough ball game.

But when it comes down to true love, what governs the heart: the mind or sweet desire? Are these donuts a passion, or just a simple, inexpensive indulgence? Please pass me a donut, or, better still, make that a *box* of donuts.

Questions

1 Consider someone who wants to open a Krispy Kreme store, recognizing that the stores are franchises. What criteria should a franchisee use to evaluate and choose between various franchise opportunities?

2 What are the advantages and disadvantages of a food-related franchise over a clothing store franchise or an automotive brake and muffler franchise?

3 What environmental factors and trends are most likely to have an impact on the future success of Krispy Kreme in Canada?

4 What could Tim Hortons do to create a "shopping experience" to compete with that currently offered by Krispy Kreme? Is it in Tim Hortons' best interest to try to compete this way?

5 Tim Hortons has a stellar record of supporting youth with various corporate initiatives. Suggest something that Krispy Kreme could to do enhance its corporate image as a socially responsible organization.

Integrated Marketing Communications and Interactive Marketing

- Explain the communication process and its elements.

- Understand the promotional mix and the characteristics of each component.

- Understand the promotional strategies that are appropriate for each stage of the product life cycle.

- Explain the use of push and pull strategies.

- Understand the concept of integrated marketing communications, and how to use it.

- Understand what interactive marketing is and how it creates customer value, customer relationships, and customer experiences in the new marketspace.

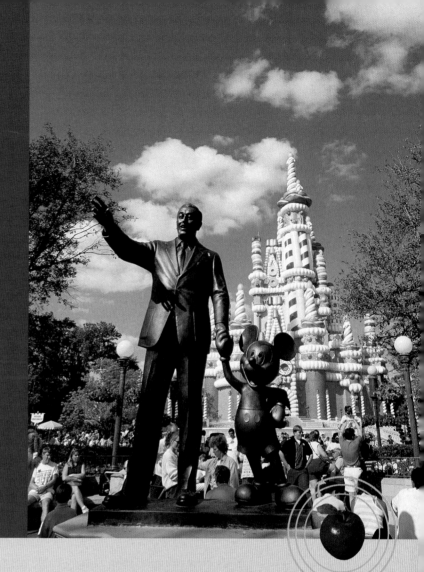

PROMOTIONAL MAGIC AT DISNEY!

Marketing executives at Disney used their expertise at integrating many forms of communication to help people remember—and celebrate—the 100th anniversary of the birth of the company's founder, Walt Disney. The plan called for a US$250 million budget during a 15-month campaign, which included advertising, partnerships with other companies, direct marketing, Internet promotions, and many other ways of getting its message to Disney fans.

The TV advertising included four versions, targeted at families, children, parents, and grandparents. The partnerships included agreements with McDonald's, Coca-Cola, American Express, Kellogg, and Hallmark Cards to run joint promotions. Direct marketing activities included special offers mailed to many of the 31 million households in Disney's database. The website, DisneyWorld.com, provided information about the events associated with the celebration and allowed consumers to make reservations and travel plans. The campaign also included an anthem—"Then the dream began to grow and come alive . . . Touching every one of us, lighting up the skies"—and an in-park promotion called "100 Years of Magic!"

Disney applies a similar, integrated approach to the marketing of all its products, services, and events. Other promotional activities include advertising on Radio Disney, sponsorship of documentaries on the ABC Television network, Internet-linked kiosks to allow potential customers to check for location and availability of products at its stores, and contests and giveaways. Another component of Disney's promotion plan is a membership program called Disney Club, which currently has 300,000 members who pay US$39.95 annually to receive unique merchandise offers, VIP treatment at special events, and discounts. Disney also uses "cross-media" deals, co-branding agreements, and joint ventures. A deal with Toys "Я" Us, for example, includes a US$30 million multimedia promotion plan for magazine, newspaper, movie, radio, and television promotion. Ads will appear on Disney

THE MARKETING PROCESS

WHERE IN THE MARKETING PROCESS ARE WE GOING IN THIS CHAPTER?

Chapter 15 opens a three-chapter discussion of promotion, setting the stage for the overall promotion process—the promotion P of the 4Ps that make up the marketing mix.

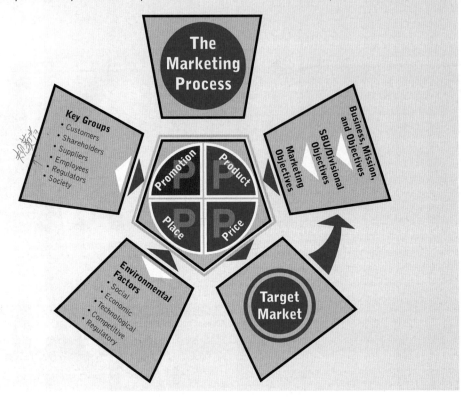

Kids Network and Toon Disney cable network and in a newspaper supplement reaching 50 million homes.[1]

Promotion represents the fourth element in the marketing mix. The promotional element is made up of a mix of tools called the promotional mix, which consists of advertising, personal selling, sales promotion, public relations, and direct marketing. All of these elements can be used to inform prospective buyers about the product, persuade them to try it, and remind them later about the product. This chapter gives an overview of the communication process and the promotional tools used in marketing and then discusses the significance of personal channels of communications, specifically word of mouth. Chapter 16 covers advertising, sales promotion, and public relations, and Chapter 17 discusses personal selling and direct marketing.

THE COMMUNICATION PROCESS

Communication is the process of conveying a message to others and requires six elements: a source, a message, a channel of communication, a receiver, and the processes of encoding and decoding[2] (Figure 15–1). The **source** may be a company or person who has information to share. The information sent, such as a description of a new cellular telephone, forms the **message**. The message is conveyed by means of a **channel of communication**, such as a salesperson, advertising media, or public relations tools. Consumers who read, hear, or see the message are the **receivers**.

communication
Process of conveying a message to others

source
Company or person who has information to share

message
Information sent by a source to a receiver

channel of communication
The means of conveying a message to a receiver

receivers
Consumers who read, hear, or see the message sent by a source

Encoding and Decoding

encoding
Process whereby the sender transforms an idea into symbolic form, using words, pictures, symbols, and sounds

decoding
Process whereby the receiver takes a set of symbols and transforms them into an idea

Encoding and decoding are essential to communication. **Encoding** is the process of having the sender transform an idea into symbolic form, using words, pictures, symbols, and sounds. **Decoding** is the reverse, or the process of having the receiver take a set of symbols, the message, and transform them back to an idea. Look at the accompanying automobile advertisement: Who is the source, and what is the message?

Decoding is performed by the receivers according to their own frame of reference: their attitudes, values, and beliefs.[3] In the ad shown here, Hummer is the source and the message is this advertisement, which appeared in *Outside* magazine (the channel). How would you interpret (decode) this advertisement? The picture and the text in the advertisement show that the source's intention is to generate interest in a vehicle that is "like nothing else"— a statement the source believes will appeal to the readers of the magazine.

The process of communication is not always a successful one. Errors in communication can happen in several ways. The source may not adequately transform the idea into an effective set of symbols, a properly encoded message may be sent through the wrong channel and never make it to the receiver, the receiver may not properly transform the set of symbols into the intended idea, or finally, feedback may be so delayed or distorted that it is of no use to the sender. Although communication appears easy to perform, truly effective communication can be very difficult.

field of experience
The experiences, perceptions, attitudes, and values that senders and receivers of a message bring to a communication situation

For the message to be communicated effectively, the sender and receiver must have a mutually shared **field of experience**—similar understanding and knowledge. Figure 15–2 shows two circles representing the fields of experience of the sender and receiver, which overlap. Some of the better-known communication problems have occurred when companies have taken their messages to cultures with different fields of experience. Imagine this: It is the middle of Stanley Cup hockey playoffs and the Montreal Canadiens are playing against the Toronto Maple Leafs. You ask a student who recently arrived in Canada from India and has never even heard of hockey, "How are the Leafs doing?" The student may think you are talking about a tree! His field of experience does not overlap with yours in this area.

FIGURE 15–1
The communication process

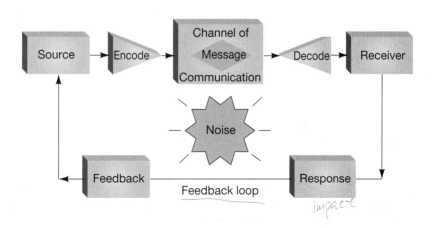

FIGURE 15–2
Fields of experience

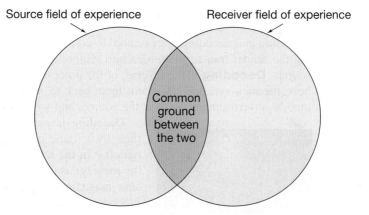

Source field of experience   **Receiver field of experience**

Common ground between the two

response
Impact the message had on the receiver's knowledge, attitudes, or behaviours

feedback
Communication flow from receiver back to the sender that helps the sender know whether the message was decoded and understood as intended

noise
Factors that can work against effective communication by distorting a message or the feedback received

Feedback

Figure 15–1 shows a line labelled *feedback loop*, which consists of a response and feedback. A **response** is the impact the message had on the receiver's knowledge, attitudes, or behaviours. **Feedback** is the sender's interpretation of the response and indicates whether the message was decoded and understood as intended. Chapter 16 reviews approaches called *pretesting* that determine whether or not messages are decoded properly.

Noise

Noise includes extraneous factors that can work against effective communication by distorting a message or the feedback received (Figure 15–1). At each stage of the communication process, factors can interfere with the message reaching its target as anticipated. Sometimes this occurs at the point where the receiver receives the message. Advertising clutter, where a large number of ads confront the receiver at one time, is a major cause of noise. Noise can be a simple error, such as a printing mistake that affects the meaning of a newspaper advertisement, or using words or pictures that fail to communicate the message clearly. Noise can also occur when a salesperson's message is misunderstood by a prospective buyer, such as when a salesperson's accent, use of slang terms, or communication style make hearing and understanding the message difficult.

Concept Check

1. What are the elements required for communication to occur?

2. A difficulty for companies advertising in international markets is that the audience does not share the same _____.

THE PROMOTIONAL MIX

To communicate with consumers, a company can use one or more of five promotional alternatives: advertising, personal selling, public relations, sales promotion, and direct marketing. Figure 15–3 summarizes the distinctions among these five elements. Three of these elements—advertising, sales promotion, and public relations—often employ *mass marketing* to reach very large groups of prospective customers. In contrast, personal selling uses customized interaction between a seller and a prospective buyer. Personal selling activities include face-to-face, telephone, and interactive electronic communication. Direct marketing also uses messages customized for specific customers.

Advertising

advertising
Any paid form of nonpersonal communication about an organization, good, service, or idea by an identified sponsor

Advertising is any paid form of nonpersonal communication about an organization, good, service, or idea by an identified sponsor. The *paid* aspect of this definition is important because the space for the advertising message normally must be bought. An occasional exception is the public service announcement, where the advertising time or space is donated, usually for a non-profit organization or for community service. Advertising can be very expensive. A full-page, four-colour ad in *Maclean's* magazine, for example, costs $32,600.[4] The *nonpersonal* component of advertising is also important. Advertising involves mass media (such as TV, radio, and magazines), which are nonpersonal and do

FIGURE 15-3
The promotional mix

PROMOTIONAL TOOL	TARGET AUDIENCE	COSTS	STRENGTHS	WEAKNESSES
Advertising	Mass	Fees paid for space or time	• Efficient means for reaching large numbers of people • Can use visual, audio, and motion	• High cost • Difficult to receive good feedback • High clutter
Personal selling	Customized	Salespeople paid salary and/or commissions	• Immediate feedback • Very persuasive • Can customize message • Can target audience • Can provide complex information	• Extremely expensive per customer reached • May not have consistent message between salespeople
Public relations	Mass	No direct payment to media	• Often the most credible source in consumers' minds • Many tactics to choose from	• Message may not be controllable • May be difficult to get media cooperation • May be difficult to relate public relations to product sales
Sales promotion	Mass	Wide range of fees paid, depending on type of promotion selected	• Effective at changing behaviour in the short run • Very flexible • Results are measurable	• Easily abused • Can lead to promotion wars • Easily duplicated by competitors • Can train consumers to wait for a sales promotion to buy
Direct marketing	Customized	Cost of mail pieces, telemarketing campaigns, or other communication routes	• Messages can be targeted and customized • Facilitates relationship with customer • Can be measured to determine effectiveness	• Increasing negative customer reaction • Clutter • Requires a database to be done properly, which is expensive

not have an immediate feedback loop as does personal selling. So before the message is sent, marketing research plays a valuable role; for example, it determines that the target market will actually see the medium chosen and that the message will be understood.

There are several advantages to a firm using advertising in its promotional mix. It can be attention-getting and also can communicate specific product benefits to prospective buyers. By paying for the advertising space, a company can control *what* it wants to say and, to some extent, to *whom* the message is sent. If an electronics company wants college students to receive its message about CD players, advertising space is purchased in a college campus newspaper. Advertising also allows the company to decide *when* to send its message, and how often. The nonpersonal aspect of advertising also has its advantages. Once the message is created, the same message is sent to all receivers in a market segment.

Advertising has some disadvantages. As shown in Figure 15–3 and discussed in depth in Chapter 16, the costs to produce and place a message are significant, and the lack of direct feedback makes it difficult to know how well the message was received.

Personal Selling

personal selling
Two-way flow of communication between a buyer and seller, often in a face-to-face encounter, designed to influence a person's or group's purchase decision

The second major promotional alternative is **personal selling**, defined as the two-way flow of communication between a buyer and seller, designed to influence a person's or group's purchase decision. Unlike advertising, personal selling is usually face-to-face communication between the sender and receiver, although telephone and electronic sales are growing. Why do companies use personal selling?

There are important advantages to personal selling, as summarized in Figure 15–3. A salesperson can control to *whom* the presentation is made. The personal component of selling has an advantage over advertising in that the seller can see or hear the potential buyer's reaction to the message. If the feedback is unfavourable, or if there are questions, the salesperson can attempt to determine why, and then modify the message.

The flexibility of personal selling can also be a disadvantage. Different salespeople can change the message so that no consistent communication is given to all customers. The high cost of personal selling is probably its major disadvantage. On a cost-per-contact basis, it is generally the most expensive of the five promotional elements.

Public Relations

public relations
Form of communication management that seeks to influence the feelings, opinions, or beliefs held by customers, potential customers, stockholders, suppliers, employees, and others about a company and its products or services

publicity
Communication about an organization that is non-personal and not paid for directly by the organization

Public relations is a form of communication management that seeks to influence the feelings, opinions, or beliefs held by customers, prospective customers, stockholders, suppliers, employees, and others about a company and its products or services.[5] Many tools such as special events, lobbying efforts, annual reports, and image management may be used by a public relations department, although publicity often plays the most important role.

Publicity is another public relations tool, and the one that is probably most often used. We describe it as a non-personal form of communication that is not paid for directly by the organization. How does it work? A company may prepare a news story, an editorial, or a product release, and then uses it to attract media attention. The goal is for the media to run a favourable story about the item or the company, which sometimes happens, but sometimes the story that is run actually has a negative result for the company. Another situation occurs when the media become aware of an event and run a news item on it. Two examples illustrate this:

- When mad cow disease was found on a farm in Alberta, the media made it headline news. The news triggered a drop in beef sales and led the U.S. and other countries that buy Canadian beef to stop purchasing it. This had a very negative effect on cattle farmers, causing them to lose millions of dollars.

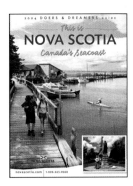

- In 2003, the city of Vancouver won the right to host the 2010 Winter Olympics. The subsequent media coverage has led to increased awareness of Vancouver as a tourist destination and will continue to do so up until the event takes place.

An advantage of publicity is credibility. When you read a positive story about a company's product, you tend to believe it, maybe more than you would believe an advertisement on TV for that product. The Nova Scotia Department of Tourism and Culture produces a travel planner to send to those interested in visiting the province; the planner is also posted on www.novascotia.com. The planner lists restaurants and hotels in the province—invaluable publicity to these establishments. The businesses mentioned in the planner do not pay to be included in it, and they are listed because the tourism department staff has determined through their research that they are good establishments to recommend to visitors to the province. A business can purchase an ad in the publication, but this may not have the same impact as the listing does. In recent years, tourism in the province of Nova Scotia has increased substantially, as has the promotion of it, and the businesses listed have benefited as well. The province won an award for their "right here, right now" promotional campaign, and the media have responded very positively by giving the province a lot of publicity.[6]

Publicity has a downside, too. The company has no control over what is published. A manufacturer can invite a news team to its headquarters to preview its revolutionary new exercise equipment and hope that it is featured on the 6:00 P.M. newscast, but there is no guarantee that this will happen. Also, a media reporter may find an item newsworthy and plan to use it in an upcoming newscast, but if a more newsworthy event comes up (say, a missing child story or a celebrity arrest), the item may be dropped.

Companies often have public relations staff who build relationships with the media and prepare information packages and press releases. Still, despite how well they attempt to influence and handle the media, they ultimately have no control on what the media report, or even if they do report it.

Sales Promotion

sales promotion
A short-term offer designed to arouse interest in buying a good or service

A fourth promotional element is **sales promotion**, a short-term offer of value designed to arouse interest in buying a good or service. Sales promotions are used in conjunction with advertising, personal selling, and, increasingly, as part of direct marketing. They are also offered to intermediaries as well as to final consumers. Coupons, rebates, samples, and sweepstakes are just a few examples of the many types of sales promotions available.

The advantage of sales promotion is that the short-term nature of these programs, such as a coupon or sweepstakes with an expiration date, often increases sales for their duration. Offering value to the consumer in terms of a cents-off coupon or rebate may increase store traffic from consumers who are not store-loyal.[7] However, sales promotions cannot be the only basis for a campaign because gains are often temporary and sales drop off when the deal ends.[8] Advertising support is needed to convert the customer who tried the product because of a sales promotion into a repeat customer.[9] If sales promotions are conducted continuously, they lose their effectiveness. Customers begin to delay purchase until a coupon is offered, or they question the product's value. Some aspects of sales promotions also are regulated by the federal government. Sales promotions are reviewed in detail later in Chapter 16.

Direct Marketing

direct marketing
Promotional element that uses direct communication with consumers to generate a response in the form of an order, a request for further information, or a visit to a retail outlet

Another promotional alternative, **direct marketing**, uses direct communication with consumers to generate a response in the form of an order, a request for further information, or a visit to a retail outlet.[10] The communication can take many forms, including face-to-face selling, direct mail, catalogues, telemarketing, direct response advertising (on television and radio and in print), and online marketing. Like personal selling, direct marketing often consists of interactive communication. It also has the advantage of being customized to match the needs of specific target markets. Messages can be developed and adapted quickly to facilitate one-to-one relationships with customers.

While direct marketing has been one of the fastest-growing forms of promotion, it poses several challenges. First, most forms of direct marketing require a comprehensive and up-to-date database with information about the target market. Developing and maintaining the database can be expensive and time consuming. In addition, growing concern about privacy has led to a decline in response rates among some customer groups. Companies with successful direct marketing programs are sensitive to these issues and often use a combination of direct marketing alternatives together, or direct marketing combined with other promotional tools, to increase value for customers. Direct marketing is discussed in detail in Chapter 17.

Concept Check

1. Explain the difference between advertising and publicity when both appear on television.

2. Which promotional element should be offered only on a short-term basis?

3. Cost per contact is highest with which tool of the promotional mix?

INTEGRATED MARKETING COMMUNICATIONS— DEVELOPING THE PROMOTIONAL MIX

promotional mix
Combination of one or more of the promotional tools—advertising, personal selling, public relations, sales promotion, and direct marketing—a firm uses to communicate with consumers

A firm's **promotional mix** is the combination of one or more of the promotional tools it chooses to use. In putting together the promotional mix, a marketer must consider several issues. Should advertising be emphasized more than personal selling? Should a promotional rebate be offered? Would public relations activities be effective? In other words, the combination of tools to be used and the importance placed on them has to be determined. Several factors affect such decisions: the type of product, the target audience for the promotion,[11] the stage of the product's life cycle, and the channel of distribution. Second, because the various promotional elements are often the responsibility of different departments, coordinating a consistent promotional effort is necessary. A promotional planning process designed to ensure integrated marketing communications can help achieve this goal.

Integrated Marketing Communications

integrated marketing communications
Concept of designing marketing communications programs that coordinate all promotional activities to provide a consistent message across all audiences

In the past, the promotional elements were regarded as separate functions handled by experts in separate departments. The sales force designed and managed its activities independently of the advertising department, and sales promotion and public relations were often the responsibility of outside agencies or specialists. The result was often an overall communication effort that was uncoordinated and, in some cases, inconsistent. Today, the concept of designing marketing communications programs that coordinate all promotional activities—advertising, personal selling, sales promotion, public relations, and direct marketing—to provide a consistent message across all audiences is referred to as **integrated marketing communications** (IMC).

The key to developing successful IMC programs is to create a process that makes it easier to design and use them. Once the IMC process is put in place, most organizations want to assess its benefits. The tendency is to try to determine which element of promotion "works" better. In an integrated program, however, media advertising might be used to build awareness, sales promotion to generate an inquiry, direct mail to provide additional information to individual prospects, and a personal sales call to complete the transaction. The tools are used for different reasons, and their combined use creates a synergy that should be the focus of the assessment.[12]

The Target Audience

Promotional programs are directed to the ultimate consumer, to a business buyer, or to an intermediary (retailer, wholesaler, or industrial distributor). Promotional programs directed to buyers of consumer products often use mass media because the number of potential buyers is large. Personal selling is used at the place of purchase, generally the retail store. Direct marketing may be used to encourage first-time or repeat purchases. Combinations of many media alternatives are a necessity for some target audiences today. The Marketing NewsNet describes how Generation Y consumers give media only partial attention but can be reached through integrated programs.[13]

Advertising directed to business buyers is used selectively in trade publications, such as *Canadian Grocer*, a publication targeted towards business people employed in the grocery trade in Canada. Because business buyers often have specialized needs or technical questions, personal selling is particularly important. The salesperson can provide information and the necessary support after sales.

Intermediaries are often the focus of promotional efforts. As with business buyers, personal selling is the major promotional tactic. The salespeople assist intermediaries in

---

MARKETING NEWSNET

Cross Functional

COMMUNICATING WITH GEN Y . . . 29.8 HOURS PER DAY!

Recent research indicates that consumers have created 29.8-hour days by using more than one communication medium at the same time—a behaviour often called "multitasking." Generation Y seems to be particularly good at this new phenomenon. For example, it would not be unusual for a college student to log onto the Internet while listening to the radio and checking out web addresses in a magazine. One reason is that media is pervasive—the average student may be exposed to 5,000 messages each day—but another reason is the desire to be informed and to "keep in touch." As a result, this group of consumers probably doesn't give its full attention to any single message. Instead, it uses continuous partial attention to scan the media.

Marketers can still communicate with Gen Y by utilizing a variety of promotional tools—from advertising to packaging to word-of-mouth communication—with an integrated message. Which media work particularly well with Gen Y? The most popular television channel is MTV. The most popular magazines are *Sports Illustrated* and

Seventeen. Favorite websites include anything with content related to their interests: celebrities, music, sports, and videogames. Another tactic growing in popularity is viral, or "buzz," marketing. Volkswagen, for example, holds contests on college campuses to see how many people can fit into a Volkswagen Beetle (the current record is 26). The participants and the observers end up experiencing and talking about the product for at least part of their 29.8-hour day.

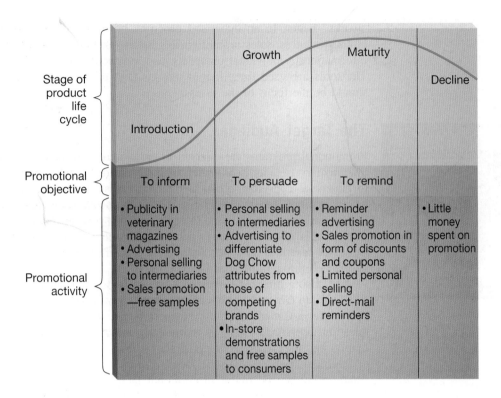

FIGURE 15–4
Promotional tools used over the product life cycle of Purina Dog Chow

making a profit by coordinating promotional campaigns sponsored by the manufacturer and by providing marketing advice and expertise.

The Product Life Cycle

All products have a product life cycle (see Chapter 11), and the composition of the promotional mix changes over the four life-cycle stages:

Purina Dog Chow: a product in the maturity stage of its life cycle.

- *Introduction stage.* Informing consumers in an effort to increase their level of awareness about a new product is the primary promotional objective in the introduction stage of the product life cycle. In general, all the promotional mix elements are used at this time.
- *Growth stage.* The primary promotional objective of the growth stage is to persuade the consumer to buy the product over a competitor's. Advertising is used to communicate brand differences, and personal selling is used to solidify the channel of distribution.
- *Maturity stage.* In the maturity stage the need is to retain existing buyers. Advertising's role is to remind buyers of the brand's and product's existence. Sales promotion, in the form of discounts and coupons, is important in maintaining loyal buyers.
- *Decline stage.* The decline stage of the product life cycle is usually a period of phase-out for the product, and little money is spent in the promotional mix.

Figure 15–4 shows how the promotional mix for Purina Dog Chow might change through the product life cycle.

Channel Strategies

Chapter 13 discussed the movement of goods through the channel from producer to intermediaries to consumer. Achieving control of the channel is often difficult for the manufacturer, and promotional strategies can assist in moving a product through the

channel of distribution. This is where a manufacturer has to make an important decision about whether to use a push strategy, pull strategy, or both in its channel of distribution.[14]

Push Strategy   Figure 15–5A shows how a manufacturer uses a **push strategy**, directing the promotional mix to channel members to gain their cooperation in ordering, stocking, and selling the product. In this approach, personal selling and sales promotions play major roles. Salespeople call on wholesalers to encourage orders and provide sales assistance. Sales promotions to intermediaries, such as case discount allowances (20 percent off the regular case price), are offered to stimulate demand. By pushing the product through the channel, the goal is to get channel members to promote it to their customers.

Pull Strategy   In some instances, manufacturers face resistance from channel members who do not want to order a new product or increase inventory levels of an existing brand. As shown in Figure 15–5B, a manufacturer may then elect to implement a **pull strategy** by directing its promotional mix at ultimate consumers to encourage them to ask the retailer for the product. Seeing demand from ultimate consumers, retailers order the product from wholesalers, and thus the item is pulled through the intermediaries. Pharmaceutical companies, for example, now spend more than $1.2 billion annually to advertise prescription drugs directly to consumers.[15] The strategy is designed to encourage consumers to ask their physicians for a specific drug by name—pulling it through the channel. Successful campaigns such as Pfizer Canada's ads for Viagra, the erectile dysfunction (ED) medication, can have dramatic effects on the sales success of a product. *Strategy* magazine voted Toronto's Taxi ad agency the 2003 Agency of the Year; one of the agency's winning campaigns was for Viagra. This campaign was a change from past advertising for sensitive products. It promoted not only the product but also the openness with which they should discuss their condition with their doctor.[16]

push strategy
Directing the promotional mix to channel members to encourage them to order, stock, and sell a product

pull strategy
Directing the promotional mix at ultimate consumers to encourage them to ask the retailer for the product

FIGURE 15–5
A comparison of push and pull promotional strategies

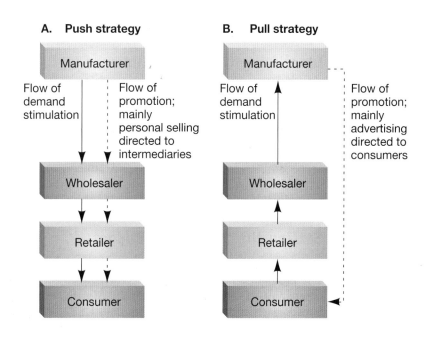

1. Which promotional mix elements are used during the introduction stage of the product life cycle?
2. Explain the differences between a push strategy and a pull strategy.
3. What is the primary benefit of integrated marketing communications programs?

DEVELOPING THE PROMOTION PROGRAM

Because media costs are high, promotion decisions must be made carefully, using a systematic approach. Like the planning, implementation, and control steps described in the strategic marketing process (Chapter 2), the promotion decision process is divided into developing, executing, and evaluating the promotion program (Figure 15–6).

Specifying Promotion Objectives

hierarchy of effects
Sequence of stages a potential buyer goes through: awareness, interest, evaluation, trial, and adoption

First, a decision must be reached on what the promotion should accomplish. Consumers are said to respond in terms of a **hierarchy of effects**, which is the sequence of stages a prospective buyer goes through from initial awareness of a product to eventual action, either trial or adoption of the product.[17]

- *Awareness.* The consumer's ability to recognize and remember the product or brand name.
- *Interest.* An increase in the consumer's desire to learn about some of the features of the product or brand.
- *Evaluation.* The consumer's appraisal of the product or brand on important attributes.
- *Trial.* The consumer's actual first purchase and use of the product or brand.
- *Adoption.* Through a favourable experience on the first trial, the consumer's repeated purchase and use of the product or brand.

For a totally new product, such as hand-held personal digital assisstants (PDAs), the sequence applies to the entire product category. For a new brand competing in an established product category, such as HP digital cameras, it applies to the brand itself. In either case, the hierarchy of effects can serve as a guideline for developing promotion objectives.

Identifying the Target Audience

The second decision in developing the promotion program is identifying the *target audience*, the group of prospective buyers toward which a promotion program is directed. To the extent that time and money permit, the target audience for the promotion program is the same as the target market for the firm's product, which is identified from marketing research and market segmentation studies. The more a firm knows about its target audience's profile—including their lifestyle, attitudes, and values—the easier it is to develop a promotion program. If a firm wanted to reach you with television and magazine ads, for example, it would need to know what TV shows you watch and what magazines you read.

Setting the Promotion Budget

After setting the promotion objectives, a company must decide on how much to spend. The promotion budgets needed to reach North American households are enormous. Six companies—General Motors, Philip Morris, Procter & Gamble, Ford, Pfizer, and Pepsi—each spend a total of more than US$2 billion dollars annually on promotion.[18]

FIGURE 15-6

The promotion decision
process

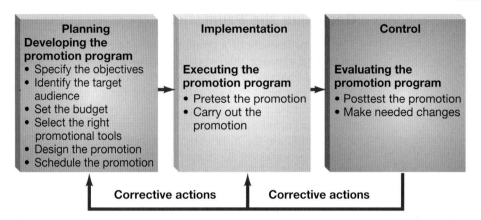

Determining the ideal amount for the budget is difficult because there is no precise way to measure the exact results from the promotion dollars spent. However, there are several methods used to set the promotion budget.[19]

- *Percentage of sales.* In the percentage of sales budgeting approach, the amount of money spent on promotion is a percentage of past or anticipated sales. A common budgeting method,[20] this approach is often stated in terms such as "our promotion budget for this year is 3 percent of last year's gross sales."
- *Competitive parity.* Competitive parity budgeting matches the competitor's absolute level of spending or the proportion per point of market share.[21]
- *All you can afford.* Common to many small businesses, the all-you-can-afford budgeting method allows money to be spent on promotion only after all other budget items—such as manufacturing costs—are covered.
- *Objective and task.* The best approach to budgeting is objective and task budgeting, whereby the company determines its promotion objectives, outlines the tasks to accomplish these objectives, and determines the promotion cost of performing these tasks and sets the budget accordingly.[22]

Of the various methods, only the objective and task method takes into account what the company wants to accomplish and requires that the objectives be specified.[23]

Selecting the Right Promotional Tools

Once a budget has been determined, the combination of the five basic IMC tools—advertising, personal selling, public relations, sales promotion, and direct marketing—can be specified. While many factors provide direction for selection of the appropriate mix, the large number of possible combinations of the promotional tools means that many combinations can achieve the same objective. Therefore, an analytical approach and experience are particularly important in this step of the promotion decision process. The specific mix can vary from a simple program using a single tool to a comprehensive program using all forms of promotion. The Olympics have become a very visible example of a comprehensive integrated communication program. Because the Games are held every two years, the promotion is almost continuous. Included in the program are advertising campaigns, personal selling efforts by the Olympic committee and organizers, sales promotion activities such as product tie-ins and sponsorships, public relations programs managed by the host cities, and direct marketing efforts targeted at a variety of audiences including governments, organizations, firms, athletes, and individuals.[24] It is also important to assess the relative importance of the various tools. While it may be desirable to use several forms of promotion, one may deserve emphasis. The Olympics, for example, emphasize public relations and publicity.

Designing the Promotion

The key component of a promotion program is the message. Many considerations go into creating a message that works: what information to convey, whether or not to use pictures and imagery, what music should accompany the promotional material, and how the message can be used across the tools of the promotional mix. The design of the promotion requires a creative strategy followed by the development of creative tactics. Part of the design includes deciding on how to appeal to the target consumers; fear, humour, sex, and emotion are the most common appeals used. Think of some ads you may have seen. An ad that warns of the dangers of drinking and driving by showing a serious car accident is using a fear appeal. Labatt has won many awards for its humorous ads for the Budweiser brand. Many fragrance ads show attractive models, sometimes male and female models together, and use sex as their appeal. The famous Molson Canadian ad, "The Rant," with its very nationalistic message is clearly an emotional appeal. It is important to design a message that works well in all of the promotional media that will be used in the campaign, and to ensure that the message is consistent through all of the tools.

Scheduling the Promotion

Once the design of each of the promotional program elements is complete, it is important to determine the most effective timing of their use. The promotion schedule describes the order in which each promotional tool is introduced and the frequency of its use during the campaign. New Line Cinema, for example, developed one of the longest promotion schedules on record for its *Lord of the Rings* movie trilogy, released in 2001, 2002, and 2003. To generate interest in the first movie months before its release, a movie "trailer" was shown on the television season premiere of *Angel*. Stickers and other products were then released to stores, followed by a global marketing program at Burger King's 10,000 restaurants.[25] Overall, the scheduling of the various promotions was designed to generate interest, bring consumers into theatres, and then encourage additional purchases after seeing the movie.

Several factors such as seasonality and competitive promotion activity can also influence the promotion schedule. Businesses such as ski resorts, airlines, and professional sports teams are likely to reduce their promotional activity during the "off" season. Similarly, restaurants, retail stores, and health clubs are likely to increase their promotional activity when new competitors enter the market.

EXECUTING AND EVALUATING THE PROMOTION PROGRAM

As shown earlier in Figure 15–6, the ideal execution of a promotion program involves pretesting each design before it is actually used to allow for changes and modifications that improve its effectiveness. Similarly, posttests are recommended to evaluate the impact of each promotion and the contribution of the promotion toward achieving the program objectives. The most sophisticated pretest and posttest procedures have been developed for advertising and are discussed in Chapter 16. Testing procedures for sales promotion and direct marketing efforts currently focus on comparisons of different designs or responses of different segments. To fully benefit from IMC programs, companies must create and maintain a test-result database that allows comparisons of the relative impact of the promotional tools, and their implementation options, in varying situations. Information from the database will allow informed design and implementation decisions and provide support for IMC activities during internal reviews by financial or administrative personnel. The Montreal Expos baseball team, for example, developed a database of information relating attendance to its integrated campaign using a new logo, special events, merchandise sales, and a loyalty program.

Carrying out the promotion program can be expensive and time consuming. One researcher estimates that "an organization with sales less than $10 million can successfully implement an IMC program in one year, one with sales between $200 million and $500 million will need about three years, and one with sales between $2 billion and $5 billion will need five years." There are integrated marketing communications agencies in operation to help companies make the transition. In addition, some of the largest advertising agencies are adopting approaches that embrace "total communications solutions." J. Walter Thompson, for example, now has a Total Solutions Group that is responsible for designing integrated programs such as the diamond campaign for the Diamond Trading Company (better known by its old name of De Beers). The campaign has appeared in 23 countries on television, in print, and in other media and is supported by an extensive range of public relations, point-of-sale, and educational materials. While most agencies still have departments dedicated to promotion, direct marketing, and other specialties, the trend today is clearly toward a long-term perspective in which all forms of promotion are integrated.[26]

Concept Check

1. What are the stages of the hierarchy of effects?
2. What are common approaches to setting the promotion budget?
3. How have advertising agencies changed to help companies develop IMC programs?

INTERACTIVE MARKETING

Internet/Web technology has had a major impact on the dynamics of the marketplace. Consumers are empowered to seek information, evaluate alternatives, and make purchase decisions, and they can do this on their own terms and conditions. At the same time, this technology has also challenged marketers to deliver to consumers *more* (selection, service, quality, enjoyment, convenience, and information) for *less* (money, time, and effort). The result? The Web's promise of immediacy and interactivity quickly transformed itself into a customer-value standard and marketing mantra: anytime, anywhere, any way!

Today, consumers expect to shop and buy their favourite products and services anytime, anywhere, and any way without constraints. Marketers have responded by engaging in interactive and multichannel marketing. Let's talk about how companies design and implement marketing programs that take advantage of the unique value-creation capabilities of Internet/Web technology. We begin by explaining how this technology can create customer value, build customer relationships, and produce customer experiences in novel ways.[27]

Customer-Value Creation in Marketspace

Despite the widespread interest in online marketspace, its economic significance remains small compared with the traditional marketplace. Electronic commerce is expected to represent less than 20 percent of total North American consumer and business goods and services expenditures in 2005, and less than 9 percent of global expenditures.[28] Why then has the new marketspace captured the eye and imagination of marketers?

Marketers believe that, over time, the possibilities for customer-value creation are greater in marketspace than in the traditional marketplace. We talked in Chapter 1 about marketing creating time, place, form, information, and possession utilities for customers, thereby providing value. In marketspace, providing direct, on-demand information is possible from marketers *anywhere* to customers *anywhere at any time*. Why? Operating hours and geographical constraints do not exist in marketspace. For example, some online retailers report that 35 percent of their orders are placed between 10 P.M. and 7 A.M., long after and before retail stores are open for business. This is not surprising. About 58 percent of Internet/Web users prefer to shop and buy in their night clothes or pajamas![29] Think about place: an online consumer can access Marks & Spencer, the well-known British department store, to shop for clothing as easily as a person living near their flagship store in London's Piccadilly Circus. Possession utility—getting a product or service to consumers so that they can own or use it—is accelerated, especially when combined with overnight courier service. Airline, car rental, and lodging electronic reservation systems such as Travelocity and Expedia, and even some airlines, allow comparison shopping for the lowest fares, rentals, and rates and almost immediate access to and confirmation of travel arrangements and accommodations.

The greatest marketspace opportunity for marketers is its potential for creating form and information utility. Interactive two-way Internet/Web-enabled communication capabilities in marketspace invite consumers to tell marketers exactly what their requirements are, making it possible to customize a product or service to fit the buyer's exact needs. Bluefly.com, an apparel company, encourages customers to develop their own catalogue, free of unwanted items. Consumers can specify the brands, clothing category, and sizes right for their needs. Holt Renfrew, an upscale clothing store, will do all your personal and gift shopping on a regular basis if you give them enough information online to create a profile.[30]

Interactivity, Individuality, and Customer Relationships in Marketspace

Marketers also benefit from two unique capabilities of Internet/Web technology that promote and sustain customer relationships: *interactivity* and *individuality*.[31] Both capabilities are important building blocks for buyer–seller relationships. For these relationships to occur, companies need to interact with their customers by listening and responding to their needs. Marketers must also treat customers as individuals, by empowering them to influence the timing and extent of the buyer–seller interaction and letting them have a say in the kind of products and services they buy, the information they receive, and, in some cases, the prices they pay.

Internet/Web technology allows for interaction, individualization, and customer relationship-building to be carried out on a scale never before available, and it makes interactive marketing possible. **Interactive marketing** involves two-way buyer–seller electronic communication in a computer-mediated environment in which the buyer controls the kind and amount of information received from the seller. Interactive marketing today is characterized by sophisticated choiceboard and personalization systems that transform information supplied by customers into customized responses to their individual needs.

interactive marketing
Two-way buyer–seller electronic communications in a computer-mediated environment in which the buyer controls the kind and amount of information received from the seller

choiceboard
Interactive, Internet/Web-enabled system that allows individual customers to design their own products and services

collaborative filtering
Process that automatically groups people with similar buying intentions, preferences, and behaviours and predicts future purchases

- *Choiceboards*. A **choiceboard** is an interactive, Internet/Web-enabled system that allows individual customers to design their own products and services by answering a few questions and choosing from a menu of product or service attributes, prices, and delivery options.[32] Customers today can design their own computers with Dell Computer's online configurator, create their own athletic shoe at www.niketown.com, and even design their own rugs and carpets at www.northernrugs.com. Because choiceboards collect precise information about the preferences and behaviour of individual buyers, a company becomes more knowledgeable about the customer and better able to anticipate and fulfill that customer's needs.
- *Collaborative filtering*. Most choiceboards are essentially transaction devices. However, companies such as Dell Computer have expanded the functionality of choiceboards using collaborative filtering technology. **Collaborative filtering** is a process that

automatically groups people with similar buying intentions, preferences, and behaviours and predicts future purchases. Think of it as customer segmentation on a website. For example, if two people who have never met buy a few of the same books over time, collaborative filtering software is programmed to reason that these two buyers might have similar reading tastes. If one buyer likes a particular book or author, then the other will like it as well. The outcome? Collaborative filtering gives marketers the ability to make an on-target sales recommendation to a buyer in *real time*!

- *Personalization.* Choiceboards are *marketer*-initiated efforts to provide customized responses to the needs of individual buyers. Personalization systems are typically *buyer*-initiated efforts. **Personalization** is the consumer-initiated practice of generating content on a marketer's web site that is custom-tailored to their personal specific needs and preferences. For example, phone companies such as Telus allow customers to create personalized "myTelus" pages. Customers can add or delete different types of information from their personal pages, including specific stock quotes, weather conditions in various cities across Canada, and professional hockey team schedules. In turn, the phone companies can use the customer profile data entered when users register at the site to tailor e-mail messages, advertising, and content to the individual.

personalization
Consumer-initiated practice of generating content on a marketer's website that is tailored to an individual's specific needs and preferences

An aspect of personalization is a buyer's willingness to have tailored communications brought to his or her attention. Obtaining this approval is called **permission marketing**, the request for a consumer's consent (called "opt-in") to receive e-mail and advertising based on personal data supplied by the consumer. Permission marketing is a proven vehicle for building and maintaining customer relationships, provided it is properly used. Companies that successfully employ permission marketing use three rules.[33]

permission marketing
Asking for a consumer's consent (called "opt-in") to receive e-mail and advertising based on personal data supplied by the consumer

First, they make sure opt-in customers only receive information that is relevant and meaningful to them. Second, their customers are given the option of opting out or changing the kind, amount, or timing of information sent to them. Finally, their customers are assured that their name or buyer-profile data will not be sold or shared with others. In an online world, where spam is an increasing problem, permission marketing is a way for marketers to ensure that they capture the customer's attention.

Creating an Online Customer Experience

Designing and executing marketing programs that make good use of the unique and evolving customer-value-creation capabilities of Internet/Web technology is a continuing challenge for companies. Simply applying Internet/Web technology to create time, place, form, information, and possession utility is not enough to claim a meaningful marketspace presence. Today, the quality of the customer experience produced by a company is the standard by which a meaningful marketspace presence is measured.

customer experience
The sum total of interactions that a customer has with a company's website

From an interactive marketing perspective, **customer experience** is defined as the sum total of the interactions that a customer has with a company's website, from the first look at a home page through the entire purchase-decision process.[34] Companies produce a customer experience through seven website design elements: context, content, community, customization, communication, connection, and commerce, each of which is summarized in Figure 15-7. Let's look at how each of these elements contributes to customer experience:

- *Context* refers to a website's visual appeal and functional look and feel reflected in site layout and design. A functionally oriented website focuses largely on the company's offerings—products, services, information. For example, travel websites like that of Cheap Flights Canada (www.cheapflights.ca) tend to be functionally oriented with an emphasis on destinations, scheduling, and prices.
- *Content* includes all digital information included on a website, including the presentation form, text, video, audio, and graphics. Content quality and presentation along with

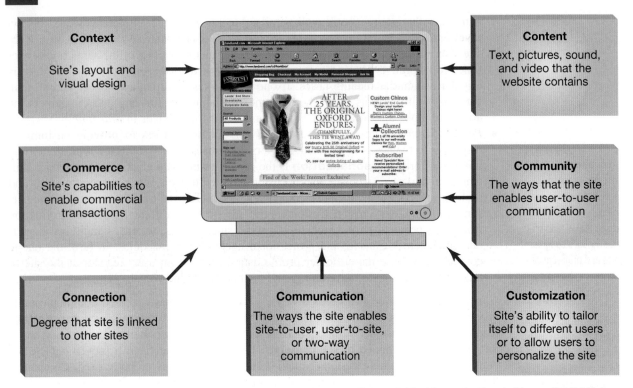

SOURCE: Rafi A. Mohammed, Robert J. Fisher, Bernard J. Jaworski, and Aileen M. Cahill, Internet Marketing: Building Advantage in a Networked Economy (New York: McGraw-Hill/Irwin, 2002), p. 623.

FIGURE 15–7

Web design elements that drive customer experience

Harley-Davidson pays close attention to creating a favourable customer experience at its website.

context dimensions combine to engage a website visitor and provide a platform for the five remaining design elements. Check out the website of leading video games producer Electronic Arts (www.ea.com). As you would expect, it really engages you by allowing you to test out games online.

- Website *customization* is the ability of a site to modify itself to, or be modified by, each individual user. This design element is prominent in websites that offer personalized content, such as My eBay. Another by Bell Mobility (www.bellmobility.ca) personalizes your interaction via the use of computer files called "cookies" – check out the Marketing NewsNet, "WebSpeak for the Interactive Marketer," to find out more about cookies.

- The *connection* element in website design is the network of formal linkages between a company's site and other sites. These links are embedded in the website; appear as highlighted words, a picture, or graphic; and allow a user to effortlessly visit other sites with a mouse click. Websites of automobile manufacturers have links to their dealerships across Canada, model catalogues, parts catalogues, owners' clubs, and more. Check out the Lexus Canada website (www.lexus.ca).

- *Communication*, closely allied to customization, refers to the dialogue that unfolds between the website and its users. Consumers—particularly those who have registered at a site—now expect that communication will be interactive and individualized in real time, much like a personal conversation. Notice how your bank or credit union website acknowledges you by name once you have logged in.

- *Community* refers to the virtual communities created by those company websites that encourage user-to-user communications. This design element is growing in popularity because it has been shown to enhance customer experience and build favorable buyer–seller relationships. An example of a community is the Harley Owners Group (H.O.G.) sponsored by Harley-Davidson (www.harley-davidson.com).

- *Commerce* is the website's ability to complete sales transactions for products and services. Online transactions are quick and simple in well-designed websites. Mountain Equipment Co-op (www.mec.ca), a leading sporting goods retailer, has an interesting website that is easy to use. For example, merchandise ordered online can be shipped direct or made available for pick up at any of their stores across Canada.

All websites do not include all design elements. Although every website has context and content, they differ in the use of the remaining five elements. Why? Websites have different purposes. For example, only websites that emphasize the actual sale of products

MARKETING NEWSNET

WEBSPEAK FOR THE INTERACTIVE MARKETER

Technology & E-commerce

Internet and interactive technology has spawned a whole new vocabulary, and it is evolving at breakneck speed. Every day a new term is coined. For "computer geeks," there are many high-tech words and terms that make techspeak sound like a foreign language. For marketers, there are also a few key terms that pepper their conversations, including these that relate to our coverage of interactive marketing. Make sure that your lexicon includes these, and if you want to build your nettalk, visit www.netlingo.com or www.webopedia.com.

- *Web communities.* Websites that allow people to meet online and exchange views on topics of common interest. The site iVillage.com is a web community for women and includes topics such as career management, personal finances, parenting, relationships, beauty, and health.

- *Spam.* Communication can take the form of electronic junk mail or unsolicited e-mail. The prevalence of spam has prompted some online services such as Hotmail to institute policies and procedures to prevent spammers from spamming their subscribers, and many jurisdictions have antispamming laws.

- *Buzz.* A popular term for word-of-mouth behaviour in marketspace. In marketspace, the scope and speed of word of mouth has increased fourfold on average because of consumer chat rooms, instant messaging,

and product and service review websites such as www.epinions.com and www.consumerreview.com.[35]

- *Viral marketing.* An Internet/Web-enabled promotional strategy that encourages individuals to forward marketer-initiated messages to others via e-mail.

- *Portals.* Electronic gateways to the World Wide Web that supply a broad range of news and entertainment, information resources, and shopping services. Well-known portals include Yahoo!, America Online, and MSN.com.

- *Cookies.* Computer files that a marketer can download onto the computer of an online shopper who visits the marketer's website. Cookies allow the marketer's website to record a user's visit, track visits to other websites, and store and retrieve this information in the future. Cookies also contain information provided by visitors, such as expressed product preferences, personal data, and financial information, including credit card numbers.

- *Blogs.* A web page where an individual posts personal information in a journal style, usually a reflection of the author's personality. Often a blog is updated daily.

- *Bots.* Derived from "robot," an electronic shopping agent that combs websites, to compare prices and product or service features.

- *Customerization.* Customizing not only a product or service, but also customizing the marketing and shopping experience for each customer.

and services include the commerce element, and websites that are used primarily for advertising and promotion purposes emphasize the communication element; this is the distinction between transactional and promotional websites.

Interactive and Internet marketing are dynamic and exciting tools in the savvy marketer's arsenal of promotional considerations. In the next few years, we will see them increase in importance and usage. Consumers and marketers are locked in a dance of more technology, more service, more expectations. Consumers become ever more demanding; they want it right now—a perfect product/service at a good price—with no hassles. Consumers cannot be taken for granted or easily manipulated; they are savvy, selective, critical, and skeptical. Customer loyalty is elusive. Marketers continue in their frantic race for the best interactive experience and the most engaging stimuli. The real challenge for the marketer is meeting and exceeding the ever-bigger expectations of a very demanding consumer from any corner of the globe.

Concept Check

1. What kind of utility can online marketers best create for their customers?

2. What are the different elements that companies use to produce a unique customer experience online?

PERSONAL CHANNELS OF COMMUNICATION

Two or more people communicating directly constitute a personal channel of two-way communication. Communication may be face to face or via print or electronic media such as telephone or Internet. A distinguishing feature of these channels is that they permit personalization and interaction, as opposed to a regular advertisement, which is a one-way communication. Marketers, and more often salespeople, use these channels to communicate directly with customers because they are very effective.

There are, however, others who communicate with customers about firms and products. These would include impartial experts, friends, neighbours, work colleagues, and even family. Importantly, these people are not paid to communicate with customers, and the commentary they offer is based on their opinions and experience. Quite often they are very knowledgeable about specific products.

People influencing each other during conversations is called word of mouth (described previously in Chapter 5). Word-of-mouth communications are viewed by the recipient as credible and trustworthy and, when positive, are considered the most powerful form of promotion. Marketers take special care to identify and influence those they believe will exert positive word-of-mouth communications about the firm and its products. Increasingly, marketers also seek referrals from satisfied customers and develop programs to involve friends and associates.

SUMMARY

1 Communication is the process of conveying a message to others and requires a source, a message, a channel of communication, a receiver, and the processes of encoding and decoding.

2 For effective communication to occur, the sender and receiver must have a shared field of experience. The receiver's response provides feedback to the sender and helps determine whether decoding has occurred or noise has distorted the message.

3 The promotional tools consist of advertising, personal selling, sales promotion, public relations, and direct marketing. These tools vary according to whether they use mass communication or customized interaction.

4 In selecting the appropriate promotional mix, marketers must consider the products, the target audience, the stage of the product's life cycle, and the channel of distribution.

5 The target for promotional programs can be the ultimate consumer, an intermediary, or both. Ultimate consumer programs rely more on advertising, whereas personal selling is more important in reaching business buyers and intermediaries.

6 The emphasis on the promotional tools varies with a product's life cycle. In introduction, awareness is important. During growth, creating brand preference is essential. Advertising is more important in the former stage and personal selling in the latter. Sales promotion helps maintain buyers in the maturity stage.

7 When a push strategy is used, personal selling and sales promotions directed to intermediaries play major roles. In a pull strategy, advertising and sales promotions directed to ultimate consumers are important.

8 Integrated marketing communications programs coordinate all promotional activities to provide a consistent message across all audiences.

9 The promotion decision process involves developing, implementing, and evaluating the promotion program.

10 Setting promotion objectives is based on the hierarchy of effects: awareness, interest, evaluation, trial, and adoption.

11 Budgeting methods often used are percentage of sales, competitive parity, and the all-you-can-afford approaches. The best budgeting approach is based on the objectives set and tasks required.

12 Selecting, designing, and scheduling promotional elements requires experience and creativity because of the large number of possible combinations of the promotion mix.

13 Consumers and companies populate two market environments today: the traditional marketplace and the new online marketspace. A company's marketspace success hinges largely on designing and executing a marketing program that capitalizes on the unique customer-value-creation capabilities of Internet/Web technology.

14 Internet/Web technology creates time, place, form, information, and possession utility in novel ways, resulting in customer value.

15 Marketers benefit from two unique capabilities of Internet/Web-enabled technology that create customer relationships: interactivity and individuality. Both capabilities make interactive marketing possible. Interactive marketing, in turn, is characterized by choiceboard and personalization systems that transform information supplied by customers into customized responses to their individual needs.

16 Customer experience is the standard by which a meaningful marketspace presence is measured and produced through seven website elements: context, content, community, customization, communication, connection, and commerce.

KEY TERMS AND CONCEPTS

advertising p. 353
channel of communication p. 350
choiceboard p. 364
collaborative filtering p. 364
communication p. 350
customer experience p. 365
decoding p. 351
direct marketing p. 355
encoding p. 351
feedback p. 352
field of experience p. 351
hierarchy of effects p. 360
interactive marketing p. 364
integrated marketing communications p. 356

message p. 350
noise p. 352
permission marketing p. 365
personal selling p. 354
personalization p. 365
promotional mix p. 356
publicity p. 354
public relations p. 354
pull strategy p. 359
push strategy p. 359
receivers p. 350
response p. 352
sales promotion p. 355
source p. 350

QUESTIONS: APPLYING MARKETING CONCEPTS AND PERSPECTIVES

1 After listening to a recent sales presentation, Mary Smith signed up for membership at the local health club. On arriving at the facility, she learned there was an additional fee for racquetball court rentals. "I don't remember that in the sales talk; I thought they said all facilities were included with the membership fee," complained Mary. Describe the problem in terms of the communication process.

2 Develop a matrix to compare the strengths and weaknesses of the five elements of the promotional mix.

3 Explain how the promotional tools used by an airline would differ if the target audience were (a) consumers who travel for pleasure and (b) corporate travel departments that select the airlines to be used by company employees.

4 Suppose you introduced a new consumer food product and invested heavily both in national advertising (pull strategy) and in training and motivating your field sales force to sell the product to food stores (push strategy). What kinds of feedback would you expect from both the advertising and your sales force? How could you increase both the quality and quantity of each?

5 Fisher-Price Company, long known as a manufacturer of children's toys, has introduced a line of clothing for children. Outline a promotional plan to get this product introduced in the marketplace.

6 Imagine that you are the marketing director for a new food company that manufactures a line of barbeque sauces. You know that you have to launch a promotional campaign to get your product out into the market; specifically, you are trying to get into the Sobeys, Loblaws, and Safeway chains. How would you create a budget for your campaign? What are the alternative methods you could use?

7 Identify the sales promotion tools that might be useful for (a) Tastee Yogourt, a new brand introduction, (b) 3M self-sticking Post-it notes, and (c) Wrigley's Spearmint Gum.

8 Design an integrated marketing communications program—using each of the five promotional elements—for an online music store.

DISCUSSION FORUM

You are the marketing director of a new private college operating in Montreal. Your target market is new immigrants to Canada and international students who want to become proficient in English and French.

1 Identify the problems that may occur in the communications process with your target market.

2 Specify how you would deal with these problems.

3 Select the promotional mix and indicate the importance to be placed on each element.

4 Explain and justify an integrated marketing communications approach.

5 Discuss how you will make your marketing interactive.

INTERNET EXERCISE

Several large advertising agencies have described shifts in their philosophies to include IMC approaches to communication. In many cases, the outcome has been campaigns that use a combination of the five promotional elements. Go to J. Walter Thompson's website at www.jwt.com, and review its integrated campaigns.

www.mcgrawhill.ca/college/thecore

1 Describe the promotional elements of one of the campaigns. Why were these elements selected? How are they integrated?

2 How would you evaluate the effectiveness of each of the promotional elements used? How would you evaluate the effectiveness of the entire campaign?

VIDEO CASE 15

AIRWALK INC.: USING IMC TO REACH ITS TARGET MARKETS

"To effectively communicate with the youth audience," observed Sharon Lee, "It is important to earn their respect by knowing what they think and how they think. You must stay one step ahead of them by constantly studying what they are reading, doing, listening to, playing, and watching."

Sharon Lee spoke from experience. She was an account director at The Lambesis Agency, the California advertising agency whose integrated marketing communications (IMC) program launched Airwalk shoes into the stratosphere. Lee's job was to be the key link between Airwalk and Lambesis. Her special insights into the youth market helped make Airwalk's past success possible.

EARLY DAYS: THE STRUGGLE

George Yohn founded the company in 1986, searching for a piece of the fast-growing athletic shoe craze headed by Nike and Reebok. His first efforts marketing an aerobic shoe hit the wall, so he had to find a new product and marketing strategy. Then one of his designers found a sport that other sneaker manufacturers hadn't yet discovered: skateboarding. Yohn watched skateboarders drag their feet to turn and brake, so he developed a special athletic shoe that had extra layers of leather, more rubber in the sole, and double-stitching to add longer life. Watching skateboarders do a popular trick of popping the board into the air, he named his new company Airwalk.

The colourful skateboard shoes almost jumped off the shelves in the surf and skate shops stocking them, so Airwalk moved into other freestyle segments such as snowboarding and BMX bike riding. Industry sources estimated that there were 10 million skateboarders, 3.5 to 5 million snowboarders, and 3.7 million BMX participants in the United States alone. Airwalk sales quickly hit US$20 million.

REPOSITIONING AIRWALK: TARGETING MAINSTREAM YOUTHS

At this point, Yohn got his great insight: if basketball shoes aren't worn only by basketball players, why should skateboarding shoes be worn only by skateboarders? This gave Yohn his new challenge: reposition Airwalk to bring its hot-dogger image to mainstream youths who were looking for stylish shoes but weren't into skateboarding.

While this repositioning looked great on paper, making it actually happen was a tall order. Although Airwalk was well known among action-sport enthusiasts, the brand name was almost unknown among mainstream youths. It was at this point that Airwalk introduced its active/casual line of sneakers targeted at these youths, mainly teens.

RESEARCH: FINDING WHAT'S COOL!

Looking back, we find some key elements that led to Airwalk's early success. One was the huge effort it put into "trend spotting" research, discussed earlier in Chapter 8. Dee Gordon, a nationally known expert in trend spotting, was on the staff of Lambesis. She authored the *L Report*, published

quarterly by Lambesis, which surveyed 18,000 trendsetter and mainstream respondents from ages 14 to 30 on every aspect of their lives. Gordon's research gave other Lambesis employees like Sharon Lee, and its clients, in-depth insights into what the trendsetters and cool kids were thinking, doing, and buying. Dee Gordon also studied trends around the world as a foundation for global marketing strategies developed by Lambesis clients.

MAKING IT HAPPEN: THE IMC STRATEGY

Airwalk and Lambesis recognized that much of Nike's and Reebok's success was that they recognized their business was no longer simply about selling shoes—it was about creating a cool image for their shoes. Mastering the marketing of the hard-to-define concept known as "cool" was the task that Airwalk dropped in the lap of Lambesis when Airwalk launched its first active/casual footwear line, targeted at the youth market.

The special challenge for Lambesis was to expand the market for Airwalk shoes by reaching the new, broader cool segments for its shoes without diluting their image among the existing core segments. Chad Farmer, the creative director at Lambesis charged with coming up with ideas for Airwalk ads, saw an opportunity to position Airwalk to the youth market as the harbinger of style in casual footwear. At the same time, Airwalk's integrated marketing communications program needed to retain its shoes' reputation for quality and durability while featuring their original designs and colours.

Chad Farmer's IMC program illustrated the diversity of media and strategies available to creative agencies and clients trying to break through the media clutter. This clutter was reflected in youths often seeing about 5,000 advertising messages in a typical day. Airwalk's TV commercials and print ads were alive with humour, irreverence, and unrestrained attitude. In many of the 14 countries where Airwalks were sold, youths stole its outdoor posters to hang in their rooms.

Airwalk's IMC strategy didn't stop with conventional media. Airwalk team "riders" included the best competitive skateboarders, snowboarders, mountain-bike riders, and surfers who represented the company in major competitions globally. Bands and musicians such as the Beastie Boys, Green Day, Pearl Jam, and R.E.M. wore Airwalks and provided great visibility for the brand. Lambesis got product placement everywhere from movies and music videos to skateboard/BMX camps and fashion magazine photos.

What has resulted from all of this? Sales increased 400 percent in a single year, eventually topping more than US$300 million. Then the air came out of Airwalk's ride—and fast!

WHAT HAPPENED AND WHAT TO DO?

According to industry analysts, the brands (Airwalk and a companion brand Andy Mac) lost their appeal. "They tried to be everywhere and everything and they lost their identity," said one analyst. The company that owned Airwalk was subsequently acquired by another firm. It was renamed and new management was put into place. Their task—a big one—was to revive the sagging fortunes of Airwalk. The new CEO, Bruce Pettet, commented that, "You have to be in touch with the 12- to 24-year-old consumers who change their tastes and preferences quickly." His biggest challenge is likely to be keeping up with the ever-changing fads in the competitive $10-billion action-sports retail sector. He sees a growing demand for "classic retro" styles and feels he can reintroduce retro Airwalk into the Japanese market. In another bold strategy, he has launched a new etura line targeted to a 17- to 34-year-old demographic. Andrew Shaddy, a category manager for Airwalk's footwear admits this target market is "advertising weary." Will an IMC strategy once again have the folks at Airwalk walking on air?

Questions

1 What were the promotional objectives for Airwalk's IMC program when it decided to target mainstream youths with its line of shoes?

2 Airwalk developed what it called a "tripod" strategy to stress three simple one-word concepts in its IMC program to successfully communicate to the youth it targeted. From reading the case and from what you know about the youth market, what might these be?

3 Describe how Airwalk might use the following media or promotional elements in their IMC strategy to target the notoriously difficult-to-reach target market of youths: *(a)* TV, *(b)* billboards, *(c)* product placements in movies, *(d)* special events, and *(e)* website. Explain your answers.

4 What media would you recommend Airwalk use to effectively communicate with the "advertising weary" 17- to 34-year-old market? Justify your choices.

5 As Airwalk sells its shoes around the world, it has chosen to use a global marketing strategy, as defined in Chapter 7. *(a)* What are the advantages and disadvantages for Airwalk of this strategy? *(b)* For example, in print ads how might Airwalk take advantage of this strategy?

Advertising,
Sales Promotion, and
Public Relations

G®OSS, BUT G®EAT!

One guy always has six books on the go, doesn't read magazines, loves movies and music, and is a creative genius—some say the ultimate artist. The other guy is a channel-hopping, self-professed pop-culture junkie who loves magazines, always has a book on the go, catches a movie at least once a week, and is an aggressive salesperson—some say the ultimate persuader. Sound like a winning combo? Their clients and their successful ad campaigns leave no doubt about it—these guys at the ad agency Rethink are good.

One of Rethink's most successful award-winning series of campaigns was for Playland, an amusement park in Vancouver. Using an integrated campaign of print, radio, outdoor, transit, and television ads, Rethink literally managed to gross out just about everyone over the age of 18. And that is exactly what they wanted to do. A primary target market for the park is teenagers, and what teenager would not be attracted to ads that their parents and older siblings disliked. The print ad above depicts one of the most famous rides at Play-land—notice the small toilet sign. The implication is that you will need to visit the toilet after, if not during, the ride. A companion radio ad takes place in an elevator with two men and a woman apparently returning to work after the weekend. The first guy begins vomiting after starting to tell the others that he took the family to Playland over the weekend. This of course sets off the other two who also begin throwing up. How gross is that?

Rethink's successful run with the Playland account ended in 2003. While the agency was saddened to lose the account, according to co-founder Ian Grais (the ultimate artist), who worked with the account for 10 years (including time at another agency before bringing it over to Rethink), "It was a great opportunity to stretch ourselves creatively." It was indeed; according to Chris Staples (the ultimate persuader), the Playland campaigns over the years garnered more than 300 awards and became famous all over the world. How is that for a ride?

THE MARKETING PROCESS

WHERE IN THE MARKETING PROCESS ARE WE GOING IN THIS CHAPTER?

Chapter 16 delves into three of the key promotional tools: advertising, sales promotion, and public relations. They are part of the promotion P of the 4Ps that make up the marketing mix.

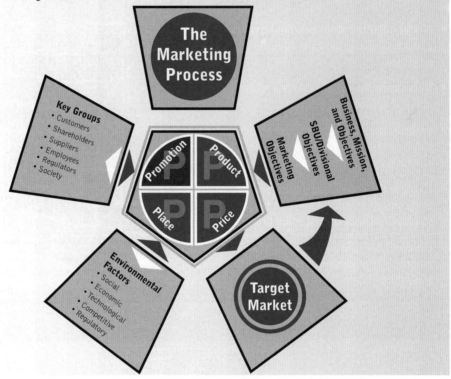

advertising
Any paid form of nonpersonal communication about an organization, good, service, or idea by an identified sponsor

Chapter 15 described **advertising** as any *paid* form of *nonpersonal* communication about an organization, good, service, or idea by an identified sponsor. This chapter explains the role and purpose of advertising, how to develop an advertising campaign and select appropriate media, why and how to use sales promotion in its various forms, and the use and development of public relations initiatives.

Print ads for Rethink's Playland campaign, obviously showing the after-effects of a Playland ride.

ROLE AND SCOPE OF ADVERTISING

Advertising is everywhere! Think of all the ads that reach you every day. We have come to expect ads on television, and we know that most magazines will be full of advertising; we may even purchase the magazine to see ads that interest us. But advertising has become much more pervasive than this. A sticker on a banana, a poster in a washroom stall, a city bus painted with a product message, and a logoed paper coffee cup are all advertisements. Where will they think of next to plant an advertising message? Is there any eyespace we can look at that is immune from carrying a promotion? Some in the advertising world say that we are "hit" by some 5,000 promotional messages in a day. If this is true, most of us are in promotion overload. In this climate, how do advertisers get through to us? How do they make their message be the one that is remembered out of the day's 5,000? It is a challenge. And in Canada, it is a $10-billion industry, growing every year.[1]

Organizations use advertising to convey a message to people, a message designed to influence thinking about the organization and its products, and, ultimately, to influence the behaviour of the people receiving the message. Ideally, the advertiser wants the target market to purchase a product, to support a cause, or to pursue some other course of action. And it doesn't stop there—there is a long-term purpose to advertisements, too: to get customers to continue to do all of these things over time. As we observed in Chapters 5 through 7, the decision to purchase a product involves several stages, and advertising can be employed to help move buyers through each of those stages of the process. Advertising fulfills a number of tasks, including creating awareness, stimulating demand, conveying positioning and differentiation strategies, reassuring the purchaser, and building brand loyalty. Rarely is advertising used alone. Sales promotion, personal selling, direct marketing, and public relations initiatives often accompany advertising to build on the effect and to reinforce the message.

When we think of advertising, we often think about product ads; however, it is also used to convey messages about organizations themselves and can be used effectively for both consumers and organizational buyers.

DEVELOPING THE ADVERTISING PROGRAM

Effective advertising requires careful planning and management. Over the next few pages we talk about the development, implementation, and evaluation of advertising, and the considerations a marketing executive makes in the process.

Setting Advertising Objectives

An important first step in planning an advertising program is setting objectives. Many different people work on an advertising program, and objectives describe what they aim to achieve and how they will measure the results of their efforts. Well-crafted objectives communicate goals and help to coordinate the work among the various players. Advertising objectives must be set to reflect the overall marketing objectives, as an advertising campaign is established to achieve some marketing purpose.

A meaningful objective communicates a specific goal to be achieved in a specific time frame and relates to a specific target market. In 2003, McDonald's launched the new "I'm lovin' it" campaign, its first "borderless approach to marketing."[2] The objective is for the campaign to unify the fast-food giant's upcoming marketing and advertising efforts over the next two years. McDonald's wants to cultivate a cool reputation[3] and plans to reach target markets in more than 100 countries. Larry Light, McDonald's global chief marketing officer, described the new creative direction as the "strategic glue for local marketing adaptations around the world."[4] That is quite an objective!

Identifying the Target Audience

A key consideration in advertising planning is to determine the target audience for the ads. Understanding the target consumers—their lifestyles, their attitudes, their demographics, and their characteristics—is essential to developing advertising that will attract the attention and interest of the intended market. When Rethink Breast Cancer, a national charitable organization dedicated to fighting the disease, launched its very successful and novel marketing campaign, the target market was defined as women and men ages 18 to 34. This may sound strange to you, but the idea was for men to be aware of the disease and to encourage the women in their life to take a proactive approach to it.[5] Even scheduling depends on the target audience to be reached. Rethink Breast Cancer television ads played on MuchMusic, and the organization partnered with The Gap and Pattison Outdoor (the billboard company) to reach the target groups.

Types of Advertisements

As you look through any magazine, watch television, listen to the radio, or browse the Web, the variety of advertisements you see or hear may give you the impression that they have few similarities. Advertisements are prepared for different purposes, but they basically consist of two types: product and institutional.

product advertisements
Advertisements that focus on selling a good or service; forms include pioneering (informational), persuasive (competitive), and reminder

Advertisements serve different purposes. Which ad would be considered pioneering, persuasive, and a reminder?

Product Advertisements
Focused on selling a good or service, **product advertisements** take three forms: pioneering (or informational), persuasive (or competitive), and reminder. Look at the ads by Lotto Super 7, Xerox, and Modèle, and determine the type and objective of each ad.

Used in the introductory stage of the life cycle, *pioneering* advertisements tell people what a product is, what it can do, and where it can be found. The key objective of a pioneering advertisement, such as the ad for Jeep's new Liberty, is to inform the target market. Informative ads have been found to be interesting, convincing, and effective.[6]

Advertising that promotes a specific brand's features and benefits is *persuasive*. The objective of these messages is to persuade the target market to select the firm's brand rather than that of a competitor. An increasingly common form of *competitive* advertising is *comparative* advertising, which shows one brand's strengths relative to those of competitors.[7] The Xerox ad, for example, highlights the competitive advantage of Xerox over its primary com-

Dial soap uses reinforcement ads to encourage consumers to keep using the product.

institutional advertisements
Advertisements designed to build goodwill or an image for an organization, rather than promote a specific good or service

petitor Hewlett-Packard. Studies indicate that comparative ads attract attention and may increase the perceived quality of the advertiser's brand.[8] Firms that use comparative advertising need market research to support claims made in the ads.[9]

Reminder advertising is used to reinforce previous knowledge of a product. The Lotto Super 7 ad shown on the preceding page reminds consumers about an event: Friday's lottery draw. Reminder advertising is good for products that have achieved a well-recognized position and are in the mature phase of their product life cycle. Another type of reminder ad, *reinforcement*, is used to assure current users they made the right choice. One example: "Aren't you glad you use Dial? Don't you wish everybody did?"

Institutional Advertisements   The objective of **institutional advertisements** is to build goodwill or an image for an organization, rather than promote a specific good or service. Institutional advertising has been used by companies such as Canadian Tire, Pfizer, and IBM to build confidence in the company name.[10] Often this form of advertising is used to support the public relations plan or respond to negative publicity. Four alternative forms of institutional advertisements are often used:

1. *Pioneering institutional* advertisements are similar to pioneering ads for products—they may focus on what the company does, what it is, or where it is located. Recent Bayer ads stating "We cure more headaches than you think" are intended to inform consumers that the company produces more products than just the popular aspirin brand.
2. *Advocacy* advertisements state the position of a company on a particular issue or situation. Labatt was the first brewery in Canada to embark on a responsible drinking program.[11] Molson now also has a similar program.
3. *Competitive institutional* advertisements promote the advantages of one class of products over another, and they are used in markets where different product classes compete for the same buyers. The Steel Alliance, for example, made up of major North American steel producers including Stelco, Dofasco, and IPSCO, spends millions of dollars on advertising that promotes steel's advantages over alternative products such as wood, plastic, and aluminum.
4. *Reminder institutional* advertising, like reminder product advertising, simply brings the company's name to the attention of the market again. The Canadian government runs ads about the Canadian armed forces, reminding people who may be interested in joining the armed forces, about the organization.

Concept Check

1. What is the difference between pioneering and competitive ads?
2. What is the purpose of an institutional advertisement?

Setting the Advertising Budget

Advertising can be very expensive. For example, the cost of placing a 30-second ad during the Super Bowl is over $2.5 million—and that does not include actually making the ad. However, if you consider that over 100 million people watch the game, the cost per viewer is not very high. The ads have become as big a feature as the football game itself, and advertisers often showcase a new and extraordinary ad at this venue.[12]

Advertising spending is a huge industry; in 2002, the world's biggest advertisers spent over US$74 billion. Leading them is Procter & Gamble, spending US$4.5 billion, Unilever spent US$3.3 billion; and third-ranked General Motors spent US$3.2 billion. GM is Canada's largest advertiser, estimated to have spent US$227.4 million on advertising in 2000—this is 4 percent of the US$5.2 billion spent in Canada in total in that year.[13]

Before advertisers begin to design advertisements, they must set a budget. There are several different approaches to this budgeting process:

- *Percentage of sales method.* Companies set a certain percentage of sales revenue to be spent on advertising, using their current year's sales or a forecast of what they think their sales will be for the coming year to make their computation. This method is easy to apply, but if sales fall, less is spent on advertising when more advertising is really needed.
- *Competitive parity method.* Advertisers look at the amount being spent by their competitors advertising a competing product and set their spending to match. Two problems with this approach: Do the competitors know the optimal amount to advertise? Are the companies and their promotional needs the same?
- *All-you-can-afford method.* Some companies, particularly smaller ones, estimate the amount of money they feel they can afford and that becomes their advertising budget. Often, they calculate all of their other expenditures first, and little is left for advertising. Using this method also ignores the effect of advertising on sales.
- *Objective and task method.* The best method of setting an advertising budget is to consider the advertising tasks the company wants to undertake, identify the costs associated with them, and then set the total cost as the advertising budget. This method relates spending to objectives, and ensures that, each year, the company's expenditures are tied to the promotional results it expects to achieve.

Designing the Advertisement

In today's world, with so much advertising clutter, it is increasingly difficult to get the attention of the target audience. If an advertisement does not attract attention or convey a clear message, it will not be effective. Consider this familiar slogan: "It tastes awful. And it works." Buckley's, the Canadian-produced cough remedy, has attracted consumer attention with a unique feature—a terrible taste. And yes, this advertising works! An advertising message usually focuses on the key benefits of the product that are important to a prospective buyer.

The message depends on the general form or appeal used in the ad and the actual words included in the ad.

Message Appeal   Most advertising messages are made up of both informational and persuasional elements. Information and persuasive content can be combined in the form of an appeal to provide a basic reason for the consumer to act. Although the marketer can use many different types of appeals, common advertising appeals include fear appeals,[14] sex appeals, and humorous appeals.

Fear appeals suggest to the consumer that he or she can avoid some negative experience through the purchase and use of a product or through a change in behaviour. Insurance companies often try to show the negative effects of premature death on the relatives of those who don't carry enough life or mortgage insurance. Food producers encourage the purchase of low-fat, high-fibre products as a means of reducing cholesterol levels and the possibility of a heart attack.[15] When using fear appeals, the advertiser must be sure that the appeal is strong enough to get the audience's attention and concern, but not so strong that it will lead them to tune out the message.

In contrast, *sex appeals* suggest to the audience that the product will increase the attractiveness of the user. Sex appeals can be found in almost any product category, from automobiles to toothpaste. The contemporary women's clothing store bebe, for example, designs its advertising to "attract customers who are intrigued by the playfully sensual and evocative imagery of the bebe lifestyle." Similarly, Diet Coke used this form of advertising when its advertising agency designed a campaign "to capture the sexual energy between men and women, and explore the traits that make them attractive to one another." Unfortunately, many commercials that use sex appeals are only successful at gaining the attention of the audience; they have little impact on how consumers think, feel, or act. Some advertising experts even argue that such appeals get in the way of successful communication by distracting the audience from the purpose of the ad.

Humorous appeals imply either directly or more subtly that the product is more fun or exciting than competitors' offerings. As with fear and sex appeals, the use of humour is widespread in advertising and can be found in many product categories. Of 32 awards recently given in *Advertising Age's* Best Awards advertising competition, 23 were to ads using humour appeals. You may have a favorite humorous ad character such as the Energizer battery bunny. Unfortunately for the advertiser, humour tends to wear out quickly, eventually boring the consumer. Another problem with humorous appeals is that their effectiveness may vary across cultures if used in a global campaign.[16]

Creating the Actual Message   Copywriters are responsible for creating the text portion of the messages in advertisements. Translating a copywriter's ideas into an actual advertisement is a complex process. Designing quality artwork, layout, and production for the advertisements is costly and time-consuming. A high-quality 30-second TV commercial typically costs about $270,000 to produce, a task done by commercial production companies. One reason for the high costs is that as companies have developed global campaigns, the need to shoot commercials in "exotic" locations has increased. Audi recently filmed commercials in Australia and Morocco. Actors are expensive also. The Screen Actors Guild reports that an actor in a typical network TV car ad would earn between $12,000 and $15,000.[17]

Award-winning advertising agency Taxi, an upstart Toronto-based firm, has won a string of industry kudos, 2001 Agency of the Year (*Marketing* magazine), 2002 and 2003 Agency of the Year (*Strategy* magazine), and an impressive number of awards for their advertising and strategy campaigns. Check them out at www.taxi.ca. In an industry that has seen a lot of small firms bought up by major multinationals, Taxi is the largest privately owned, independent Canadian agency. Campaigns that Taxi has done that you may

be familiar with include Telus Mobility, Viagra, Mini, Mark's Work Wearhouse, Covenant House, and The Movie Network. Jane Hope, Taxi's co-founder, describes the firm's credo: "Doubt the conventional, create the exceptional."[18] Taxi is an acknowledged leader in the advertising industry, not only for outstanding and creative ads but also for the firm's advertising strategy.

What do you think when you see the accompanying ad for Viagra? Taxi's creative campaign extended from television and magazines to transit and professional sports events. During Taxi's campaign for The Movie Network, awareness was measured at 85 percent and subscribers increased by 5 percent.[19]

Concept Check

1. What are the most common ways of setting an advertising budget?
2. Describe three common forms of advertising appeals.

Selecting the Right Media

Every advertiser must select the advertising media in which to place its ads. Examples of media options include newspapers, magazines, radio, and TV. This media selection decision is related to the target audience, type of product, nature of the message, campaign objectives, available budget, and the costs of the alternative media. Figure 16–1 shows the distribution of the monies spent on advertising among the many media alternatives.

In deciding where to place advertisements, a company has several media to choose from and a number of alternatives, or vehicles, within each medium. Often advertisers use a mix of media forms and vehicles to maximize the exposure of the message to the target audience while at the same time minimizing costs. These two conflicting goals of maximizing exposure and minimizing costs are of central importance to media planning.

Because advertisers try to maximize the number of individuals in the target market exposed to the message, they must be concerned with reach. **Reach** is the number of

reach
Number of different people or households exposed to an advertisement

Canadian advertising expenditures by medium, as a percentage of total ad spending

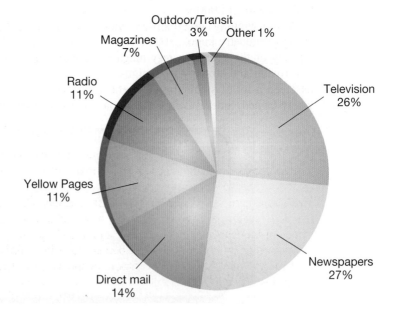

Television 26%
Newspapers 27%
Direct mail 14%
Yellow Pages 11%
Radio 11%
Magazines 7%
Outdoor/Transit 3%
Other 1%

different people or households exposed to an advertisement. The exact definition of reach sometimes varies among alternative media. Newspapers often describe reach in terms of their total circulation or the number of different households that buy the paper. Television and radio stations describe their reach using the term **rating**—the percentage of households in a market that are tuned to a particular TV show or radio station. In general, advertisers try to maximize reach in their target market at the lowest cost.

Although reach is important, advertisers are also interested in exposing their target audience to a message more than once. This is because consumers often do not pay close attention to advertising messages, some of which contain large amounts of relatively complex information. When advertisers want to reach the same audience more than once, they are concerned with **frequency**, the average number of times a person in the target audience is exposed to a message or advertisement. Like reach, greater frequency is generally viewed as desirable.[20] Studies indicate that with repeated exposure to advertisements consumers respond more favourably to brand extensions.[21]

When reach (expressed as a percentage of the total market) is multiplied by frequency, an advertiser will obtain a commonly used reference number called **gross rating points** (GRPs). To obtain the appropriate number of GRPs to achieve an advertising campaign's objectives, the media planner must balance reach and frequency. The balance will also be influenced by cost. **Cost per thousand** (CPM) refers to the cost of reaching 1,000 individuals or households with the advertising message in a given medium (*M* is the Roman numeral for 1,000).

Different Media Alternatives

Figure 16–2 summarizes the advantages and disadvantages of the major advertising media, which are described in more detail below. Direct mail will be discussed in Chapter 17.

Television   Television is a valuable medium because it communicates with sight, sound, and motion. Print advertisements alone could never give you the sense of a sports car cornering at high speed or communicate Ford's excitement about its new Thunderbird. In addition, network television is the only medium that can reach 99 percent of the homes in Canada.[22]

Television's major disadvantage is cost: the price of a prime-time, 30-second ad run on *Friends* is US$455,700 and the average price for all prime-time programs is US$115,799.[23] Because of these high charges, many advertisers choose less expensive "spot" ads, which run between programs in 10-, 15-, 30, or 60-second lengths. Shorter ads reduce costs but severely restrict the amount of information and emotion that can be conveyed. Research indicates, however, that two different versions of a 15-second commercial, run back-to-back, will increase recall over long intervals.[24]

Another popular form of television advertising is the infomercial. **Infomercials** are program-length (30-minute) advertisements that take an educational approach to communication with potential customers. Today more than 90 percent of all TV stations air infomercials, and more than 25 percent of all consumers have purchased a product as a result of seeing an infomercial.

Radio   There are 941 radio stations in Canada. The major advantage of radio is that it is a segmented medium. There are, for example, news stations, ethnic radio, campus stations, all-talk shows, and hard rock stations, all listened to by different market segments. Among teens ages 12 to 17, 82.6 percent tune in to FM radio every week, and 14.7 percent to AM, making radio an important media consideration for advertisers wanting to reach this market.[25]

---

rating
Percentage of households in a market that are tuned to a particular TV show or radio station

frequency
Average number of times a person in the target audience is exposed to a message or advertisement

gross rating points
Reference number for advertisers, created by multiplying reach (expressed as a percentage of the total market) by frequency

cost per thousand
Cost of reaching 1,000 individuals or households with an advertising message in a given medium

infomercials
Program-length (30-minute) advertisements that take an educational approach to communication with potential customers

MEDIUM	ADVANTAGES	DISADVANTAGES
Television	Reaches extremely large audience; uses picture, print, sound, and motion for effect; can target specific audiences	High cost to prepare and run ads; short exposure time and perishable message; difficult to convey complex information
Radio	Low cost; can target specific local audiences; ads can be placed quickly; can use sound, humour, and intimacy effectively	No visual element; short exposure time and perishable message; difficult to convey complex information
Magazines	Can target specific audiences; high-quality colour; long life of ad; ads can be clipped and saved; can convey complex information	Long advance time needed to place ad; relatively high cost; competes for attention with other magazine features
Newspapers	Excellent coverage of local markets; ads can be placed and changed quickly; ads can be saved; quick consumer response; low cost	Ads compete for attention with other newspaper features; short life span; poor color
Internet	Video and audio capabilities; animation can capture attention; ads can be interactive and link to advertiser	Animation and interactivity require large files and more time to "load"; effectiveness is still undetermined
Outdoor	Low cost; local market focus; high visibility; opportunity for repeat exposures	Message must be short and simple; low selectivity of audience; criticized as a traffic hazard
Direct mail	High selectivity of audience; can contain complex information and personalized messages; high-quality graphics	High cost per contact; poor image (junk mail)

SOURCES: William F. Arens, *Contemporary Advertising*, 8th ed. (New York: McGraw-Hill/Irwin, 2002), p. 291; and William G. Nickels, James M. McHugh, and Susan M. McHugh, *Understanding Business*, 6th ed. (Burr Ridge, IL: McGraw-Hill/Irwin, 2002), p. 493.

FIGURE 16–2

Advantages and disadvantages of major advertising media

The disadvantage of radio is that it has limited use for products that must be seen. Another problem is the ease with which consumers can tune out a commercial by switching stations. Radio is also a medium that competes for people's attention as they do other activities such as driving, working, or relaxing. Peak radio listening time is during the drive times before and after work (6 to 10 A.M. and 4 to 7 P.M.).

Magazines   Magazines have become a very specialized medium, primarily because there are currently more than 5,000 magazines, and new magazines such as *O at Home, An Oprah Magazine; CosmoGirl; eCompany Now; Revolution;* and *Elle Girl* are introduced each year. The marketing advantage of this medium is the great number of special-interest publications that appeal to narrowly defined segments. Runners read *Runner's World*, sailors buy *Yachting*, gardeners subscribe to *Canadian Gardening*, and teenagers look at *Teen People*. More than 675 publications focus on computers and technology, 669 are dedicated to travel, and 500 magazine titles are related to music.[26] Each magazine's readers often represent a unique profile. The *Rolling Stone* reader tends to listen to music more than most people — so Sony knows an ad for its new MP3 audio player in Rolling Stone is reaching the desired target audience. In addition to the distinct audience profiles of magazines, good color production is an advantage that allows magazines to create strong images.[27]

The high cost of advertising in national magazines is a disadvantage, but many national publications publish regional and even metro editions, which reduce the absolute cost and wasted coverage. Time publishes well over 400 different editions, including Latin American, Canadian, Asian, South Pacific, European, and U.S. editions.

Newspapers   Newspapers are an important local medium with excellent reach potential. Because of the daily publication of most papers, they allow advertisements to focus on specific current events, such as a "24-hour sale." Local retailers often use newspapers as their sole advertising medium. Newspapers are rarely saved by the purchaser, however, so companies are generally limited to ads that call for an immediate customer response, although customers can clip and save ads they select. Companies also cannot depend on newspapers for colour reproduction as good as that in most magazines.

National advertising campaigns can use this medium in conjunction with local distributors of their products. In these instances, both parties often share the advertising costs using a cooperative advertising program, which is described later in this chapter. Another exception is the use of newspapers such as *The Globe and Mail* and the *National Post*, which have national distribution.

Internet   The Internet represents a relatively new medium for advertisers, although it has already attracted a wide variety of industries. Online advertising is similar to print advertising in that it offers a visual message. It has additional advantages, however, because it can also use the audio and video capabilities of the Internet. Sound and movement may simply attract more attention from viewers, or they may provide an element of entertainment to the message. Online advertising also has the unique feature of being interactive. Called *rich media*, these interactive ads have drop-down menus, built-in games, or search engines to engage viewers. Although online advertising is relatively small compared to other traditional media, it offers an opportunity to reach younger consumers who have developed a preference for online communication.[28]

One disadvantage of online advertising is that because the medium is new, technical and administrative standards for the various formats are still evolving. This situation makes it difficult for advertisers to run national online campaigns across multiple sites. The Internet Advertising Bureau provides some guidance for online advertising standards and makes recommendations for new formats. Another disadvantage to online advertising is the difficulty of measuring impact. Online advertising lags behind radio, TV, and print in offering advertisers proof of effectiveness.

Viral Marketing   **Viral marketing** is an Internet/Web-enabled promotional strategy that encourages individuals to forward marketer-initiated messages to others via e-mail—spreading like a virus! There are three approaches to viral marketing:

1. Marketers can embed a message in the product or service so that customers hardly realize they are passing it along. You are probably familiar with Hotmail, which was one of the first companies to provide free, Web-based e-mail. Each outgoing e-mail message has this tagline: Get Your Private, Free Email from MSN Hotmail at www.hotmail.com. Today, Hotmail has over 100 million users.

2. Marketers can also make the website content so compelling that viewers want to share it with others. The Diamond Company (previously known as De Beers) has done this at www.adiamondisforever.com where users can design their own rings and show them to friends and family. One out of five website visitors e-mail their ring design to friends and relatives, who can then visit the site. eBay reports that more than half its visitors were referred by other visitors.

3. Finally, marketers can offer incentives (discounts, sweepstakes, or free merchandise) for referrals. Procter & Gamble did this for its Physique shampoo. People who referred

viral marketing
Internet/Web-enabled promotional strategy that encourages users to forward market-initiated messages to others via e-mail

10 friends to the shampoo's website received a free, travel-sized styling spray and were entered in a sweepstakes to win a year's supply of the shampoo. The response? The promotion generated 2 million referrals and made Physique the most successful new shampoo ever launched by Proctor & Gamble!

Promotional Websites In Chapter 13, we discussed the difference between transactional and promotional websites. Here, we look at promotional websites in detail. Their function is to advertise and promote a company's products and services and provide information on how items can be used and where they can be purchased. They engage the visitor in an interactive experience involving games, contests, and quizzes, with electronic coupons and other gifts as prizes. Procter & Gamble maintains separate websites for its leading brands, including Pringles potato chips, Vidal Sassoon hair products, Scope mouthwash, and Pampers diapers. Promotional sites are effective in generating interest in and trial of a company's products and services (see Figure 16-3).[29]

General Motors reports that 80 percent of the people visiting a Saturn store first visited the brand's website and 70 percent of Saturn leads come from its website. Visit the Saturn website and find out what they offer that is so compelling (www.saturn.com).

Promotional websites also are used to support a company's traditional marketing channel and build customer relationships. Clinique is a division of Estée Lauder Companies, which markets cosmetics through department stores. Clinique reports that 80 percent of current customers who visit its website later purchase a Clinique product at a department store, and 37 percent of non-Clinique buyers make a Clinique purchase after visiting the company's website. Impressive results like these are expected to become the norm for companies using promotional websites as part of their promotional and channel strategies.[30]

Outdoor A very effective medium for reminding consumers about products is outdoor advertising, such as the Harvey's ad shown on the next page. The most common form of outdoor advertising, called billboards, often results in good reach and frequency and has been shown to increase purchase rates.[31] The visibility of this medium is good supplemental reinforcement for well-known products, and it is a relatively low-cost, flexible alternative. A company can buy space just in the desired geographical market. A disadvantage to billboards, however, is that the message has to be very short. Also, a good billboard site depends on traffic patterns and sight lines. In many areas, municipal laws limit the use of this medium.

FIGURE 16-3

Promotional websites as part of channel strategies

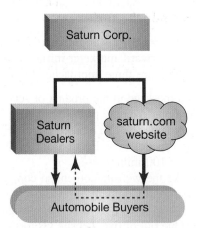

- 70% of Saturn leads come from its website.
- 80% of people visiting a Saturn dealer first visited its website.

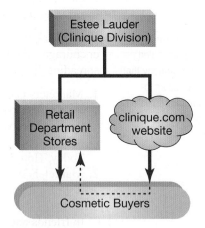

- 80% of current Clinique buyers who visit its website later purchase a Clinique product at a store.
- 37% of non-Clinique buyers make a Clinique purchase after visiting its website.

Outdoor advertising for Harvey's, created by the advertising agency John St.

In 2001, Harvey's took stock of declining sales and identified its competitive advantage: the only fast-food restaurant that grills its burgers. Harvey's ad agency, John St., created a campaign that featured "Long live the grill" as its message. A billboard campaign was one element; other elements included TV, radio, tray liners, new packaging, and in-restaurant ads.[32]

If you have ever lived in a metropolitan area, chances are you might have seen another form of outdoor advertising, transit advertising. This medium includes messages on the interior and exterior of buses, subway cars, and taxis. As use of mass transit grows, transit advertising may become increasingly important. Selectivity is available to advertisers, who can buy space by neighbourhood or bus route. One disadvantage to this medium is that during the heavy travel times, when the audiences are the largest, people may find it difficult to read advertising copy. They are standing shoulder to shoulder, hoping not to miss their transit stop, and paying little attention to the advertising.

Captivate TV Network offers "TV in Elevators."

Other Media   As traditional media have become more expensive and cluttered, advertisers have been attracted to a variety of nontraditional advertising options, called *place-based media*. Messages are placed in locations that attract a specific target audience such as airports, doctors' offices, health clubs, and theatres (where ads are played on the screen before the movies are shown), and even in bathrooms of bars, restaurants, and nightclubs, on video screens on gas pumps and ABMs, and in elevators![33] Aerial advertising can often be seen over major metropolitan areas such as Toronto, Montreal, and Vancouver. Small airplanes or helicopters tow banners or giant billboards. Airports offer other opportunities for alternate types of media: indoor walls, parking lots, walkways, feature advertising displays, and back-lit posters.

Scheduling the Advertising

There is no one correct schedule for advertising a product, but three factors must be considered. First is the issue of *buyer turnover*, which is how often new buyers enter the market to buy the product. The higher the buyer turnover, the greater is the amount of advertising required. A second issue in scheduling is the *purchase frequency*; the more frequently the product is purchased, the less repetition is required. Finally, companies must consider the *forgetting rate*, the speed with which buyers forget the brand if advertising is not seen.

Setting schedules requires an understanding of how the market behaves. Most companies tend to follow one of three basic approaches (see Figure 16-4):

1. *Continuity (steady) schedule.* When seasonal factors are unimportant, advertising is run at a continuous or steady schedule throughout the year.
2. *Flighting (intermittent) schedule.* Periods of advertising are scheduled between periods of no advertising to reflect seasonal demand.
3. *Pulsing (burst) schedule.* A flighting schedule is combined with a continuous schedule because of increases in demand, heavy periods of promotion, or introduction of a new product.

For example, products such as dry breakfast cereals have a stable demand throughout the year and would typically use a continuous schedule of advertising. In contrast, products such as snow skis and suntan lotions have seasonal demands and receive flighting-schedule advertising during the seasonal demand period. Some products such as toys or automobiles require pulse-schedule advertising to facilitate sales throughout the year and during special periods of increased demand (such as holidays or new car introductions).

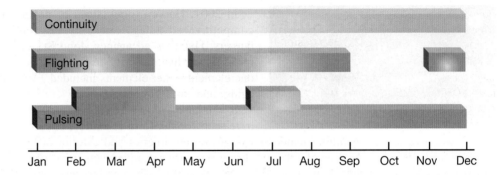

Concept Check

1. You see the same ad in *Time* and *Maclean's* magazines and on billboards and TV. Is this an example of reach or frequency?

2. Why has the Internet become a popular advertising medium?

3. Describe three approaches to scheduling advertising.

EXECUTING THE ADVERTISING PROGRAM

Executing the advertising program involves pretesting the advertising copy and actually carrying out the advertising program. John Wanamaker, the founder of Wanamaker's Department Store in Philadelphia, remarked, "I know half my advertising is wasted, but I don't know what half." By evaluating advertising efforts marketers can try to ensure that their advertising expenditures are not wasted.[34] Evaluation is done usually at two separate times: before and after the advertisements are run in the actual campaign. Several methods used in the evaluation process at the stages of idea formulation and copy development are discussed below. Posttesting methods are reviewed in the section on evaluation.

Pretesting the Advertising

pretests
Tests conducted before an advertisement is placed to determine whether it communicates the intended message or to select among alternative versions of an advertisement

To determine whether the advertisement communicates the intended message or to select among alternative versions of the advertisement, **pretests** are conducted before the advertisements are placed in any medium.

Portfolio Tests   Portfolio tests are used to test copy alternatives. The test ad is placed in a portfolio with several other ads and stories, and consumers are asked to read through the portfolio. Afterward subjects are asked for their impressions of the ads on several evaluative scales, such as from "very informative" to "not very informative."

Jury Tests   Jury tests involve showing the ad copy to a panel of consumers and having them rate how they liked it, how much it drew their attention, and how attractive they thought it was. This approach is similar to the portfolio test in that consumer reactions are obtained. However, unlike the portfolio test, a test advertisement is not hidden within other ads.

Theatre Tests   Theatre testing is the most sophisticated form of pretesting. Consumers are invited to view new television shows or movies in which test commercials are also shown. Viewers register their feelings about the advertisements either on hand-held electronic recording devices used during the viewing or on questionnaires afterward.

full-service agency
Advertising agency providing the most complete range of services, including market research, media selection, copy development, artwork, and production

limited-service agency
Specializes in one aspect of the advertising process such as providing creative services to develop the advertising copy or buying previously unpurchased media space

in-house agency
Company's own advertising staff, which may provide full services or a limited range of services

posttests
Tests conducted after an advertisement has been shown to the target audience to determine whether it has accomplished its intended purpose

Carrying Out the Advertising Program

The responsibility for actually carrying out the advertising program can be handled in one of three types of agencies. The **full-service agency** provides the most complete range of services, including market research, media selection, copy development, artwork, and production. Agencies that assist a client by both developing and placing advertisements have traditionally charged a commission of 15 percent of media costs. As corporations have introduced integrated marketing approaches, however, most advertisers have switched from paying commissions to paying incentives or fees based on performance. The most common performance criteria used are sales, brand and ad awareness, market share, and copy test results. A **limited-service agency** specializes in one aspect of the advertising process such as providing creative services to develop the advertising copy or buying previously unpurchased media space. Limited-service agencies that deal in creative work are compensated by a contractual agreement for the services performed. Finally, an **in-house agency** made up of the company's own advertising staff may provide full services or a limited range of services.

EVALUATING THE ADVERTISING PROGRAM

The advertising decision process does not stop with executing the advertising program. The advertisements should be posttested to determine whether they are achieving their intended objectives, and results may indicate that changes should be made in the advertising program.

Posttesting the Advertising

An advertisement may go through **posttests** after it has been shown to the target audience to determine whether it accomplished its intended purpose. Five approaches common in posttesting are discussed here.[35]

Aided Recall (Recognition-Readership)
After being shown an ad, respondents are asked whether their previous exposure to it was through reading, viewing, or listening. The Starch test shown in the accompanying photo uses aided recall to determine the percentage of those who remember seeing a specific magazine ad (*noted*), who saw or read any part of the ad identifying the product or brand (*seen-associated*), and who read at least half of the ad (*read most*). Elements of the ad are then tagged with the results, as shown in the picture.

Starch scores an advertisement.

Unaided Recall
A question such as "What ads do you remember seeing yesterday?" is asked of respondents without any prompting to determine whether they saw or heard advertising messages.

Attitude Tests
Respondents are asked questions to measure changes in their attitudes after an advertising campaign, such as whether they have a more favourable attitude toward the product advertised.[36]

Inquiry Tests
Additional product information, product samples, or premiums are offered to an ad's readers or viewers. Ads generating the most inquiries are presumed to be the most effective.

Sales Tests
Sales tests allow a manufacturer, a distributor, or an advertising agency to manipulate an advertising variable (such as schedule or copy) and observe subsequent sales effects by monitoring data collected from checkout scanners in supermarkets.[37]

Concept Check

1. Explain the difference between pretesting and posttesting advertising copy.

2. What is the difference between aided and unaided recall posttests?

SALES PROMOTION

The Importance of Sales Promotion

Sales promotion has become a key element of the promotional mix, which now accounts for more than $100 billion in annual expenditures. In a recent survey by the Promotion Marketing Association, marketing professionals reported that approximately 53 percent of their budgets was spent on advertising, 23 percent on consumer promotion, 18 percent on trade promotion, and 6 percent on public relations and customer service.[38] The distribution of marketing expenditures reflects the trend toward integrated promotion programs that include a variety of promotion elements. Selection and integration of the many promotion techniques require a good understanding of the advantages and disadvantages of each kind of promotion.[39]

Consumer-Oriented Sales Promotions

consumer-oriented sales promotions
Sales tools, such as coupons, sweepstakes, and samples, used to support a company's advertising and personal selling efforts directed to ultimate consumers

Directed to ultimate consumers, **consumer-oriented sales promotions**, or simply consumer promotions, are sales tools used to support a company's advertising and personal selling. Consumer-oriented sales promotion tools include coupons, deals, premiums, contests, sweepstakes, samples, continuity programs, point-of-purchase displays, rebates, and product placement.

Coupons   Coupons are sales promotions that usually offer a discounted price to the consumer, which encourages trial. Are you a coupon user? Many Canadians are. In 2003, 2.6 billion coupons were distributed in Canada, and 97 million of them were redeemed—a 4 percent redemption rate. The average value of the coupons that were distributed was $1.23, and consumers saved an estimated $105 million through coupon use. Over the past five years, the coupon industry has changed. Magazine coupons, free-standing inserts, and event and professional couponing increased, while instantly redeemable (on-pack) coupons and shelf pack coupons decreased. The number of coupons requiring the consumer to make multiple-product purchases increased, and marketers issuing coupons for pet foods and infant care tended to make their coupon offers lower in value. Most marketers used Internet coupons in 2003, but as a medium, the Internet accounts for less than 1 percent of all couponing. Retail sales increase directly with the use of coupons, and for this reason it is felt to be "an important and effective marketing tool."[40]

Coupons are often far more expensive than the face value of the coupon; a 25-cent coupon can cost three times that after paying for the advertisement to deliver it, dealer handling, clearinghouse costs, and redemption. In addition, misredemption, or paying the face value of the coupon even though the product was not purchased, should be added to the cost of the coupon. See the accompanying Ethics and Social Responsibility Alert for additional information about misredemption.[41]

Deals   Deals are short-term price reductions, commonly used to increase trial among potential customers or to retaliate against a competitor's actions. For example, if a

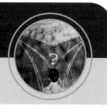

ETHICS AND SOCIAL RESPONSIBILITY ALERT

COUPON SCAMS COST MANUFACTURERS $500 MILLION EACH YEAR

Coupon fraud has become a serious concern for consumer goods manufacturers. How serious? The Coupon Information Center estimates that companies pay out coupon refunds of more than $500 million a year to retailers and individuals who don't deserve them. That adds a huge cost to promotions designed to help consumers.

The methods used by the cheaters are becoming very sophisticated. For example,

- Some scam artists set up a fake store and send coupons to manufacturers for payment.
- Coupon collectors often sell coupons to retailers who are paid full face value by manufacturers, even though the products were not sold.
- Retailers increase their refunds by adding extra coupons to those handed in by shoppers.

- Counterfeiters print rebate forms and proofs of purchase to collect big cash rebates without buying the products.

One of the newest forms of coupon fraud is the result of Internet coupon sites that allow coupons to be printed at home. The coupon bar code, value, or even the offer can be manipulated and copied with now-common computer equipment and skills.

Some of the steps being taken to reduce coupon and rebate fraud include requiring handwritten redemption requests and requesting a proof of purchase.

What are your reactions to misredemption? Should action be taken against coupon fraud?

---

rival manufacturer introduces a new cake mix, the company responds with a "two packages for the price of one" deal. This short-term price reduction builds up the stock on the kitchen shelves of cake mix buyers and makes the competitor's introduction more difficult.

Premiums   A promotional tool often used with consumers is the premium, which consists of either merchandise offered free or merchandise offered at a significant savings over its retail price. The second type of premium is called self-liquidating because the cost charged to the consumer covers the cost of the item. Milk-Bone dog biscuits used a self-liquidating premium when it offered a ball toy for $8.99 and two proofs of purchase.[42] By offering a premium, companies encourage customers to return frequently or to use more of the product.

Contests   A fourth sales promotion, the contest, is where consumers apply their skill or analytical or creative thinking to try to win a prize. For example, Tim Hortons' "Roll Up the Rim to Win" contest gives away million of prizes. Specially marked cups show an arrow directing the consumer to roll up the rim of the cup; they may find a "play again" message, or they may win one of the millions of prizes available. The accompanying television ads promote the contest, which has become very popular across Canada.[43] Have you played?

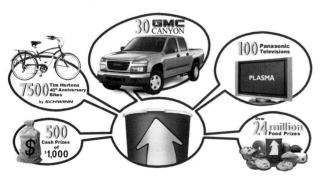

Sweepstakes   Reader's Digest and Publisher's Clearing House are two of the better-promoted sweepstakes. These sales promotions require participants to submit some kind of entry form but are purely games of chance requiring no analytical or creative effort by the consumer. The approach is very effective—*Time* magazine obtained 1.4 million new subscribers in one year through sweepstakes promotions.[44]

Canada has federal and provincial rules covering sweepstakes, contests, and games to regulate their fairness, ensure that the chance for winning is represented honestly, and guarantee that the prizes are actually awarded.

Samples   Another common consumer sales promotion is sampling, which is offering the product free or at a greatly reduced price. Often used for new products, sampling puts the product in the consumer's hands. A trial size is generally offered that is smaller than the regular package size. If consumers like the sample, it is hoped they will remember and buy the product. When Mars changed its Milky Way Dark to Milky Way Midnight it gave away more than 1 million samples to college students at night clubs, several hundred campuses, and popular spring break locations. Awareness of the candy bar rose to 60 percent, trial rose 166 percent, and sales rose 25 percent! Overall, companies invest billions in sampling programs each year.[45]

Continuity Programs   Continuity programs are a sales promotion tool used to encourage and reward repeat purchases by acknowledging each purchase made by a consumer and offering a premium as purchases accumulate. The most popular continuity programs today are the frequent flyer and frequent traveler programs used by airlines, hotels, and car rental services to reward loyal customers. Canadian Tire money is indisputably the most successful and the most popular loyalty program in Canada. It all started over 45 years ago with a cash bonus coupon, and now the company estimates that $30 million in Canadian Tire money is floating around. Check your wallet—do you have any? Imagine the power of this campaign. Customers are given Canadian Tire money each time they make a cash purchase at a Canadian Tire store. They can use it for any later purchase, and 90 percent of them are redeemed. Nine out of every ten Canadian adults shop at a Canadian Tire store at least twice a year. That suggests that 90 percent of the adult population may be storing a few of these little gems in their wallet or car, and every time they look at them, they are reminded of Canadian Tire. Canadian Tire money is a "cornerstone" of the company's marketing mix, as well as a key competitive advantage.[46]

Point-of-Purchase Displays   In a store aisle, you often encounter a sales promotion called a point-of-purchase display. These product displays take the form of advertising signs, which sometimes actually hold or display the product, and are often located in high-traffic areas near the cash register or the end of an aisle. The accompanying picture shows a point-of-purchase display for Nabisco's annual back-to-school program. The display is designed to maximize the consumer's attention to lunch box and after-school snacks, and to provide storage for the products. A recent survey of retailers found that 87 percent plan to use more point-of-purchase materials in the future, particularly for products that can be purchased on impulse.[47]

Rebates   Another consumer sales promotion, the cash rebate, offers the return of money based on proof of purchase. This tool has been used heavily by car manufacturers facing increased competition. When the rebate is offered on lower-priced items, the time and trouble of mailing in a proof of purchase to get the rebate cheque often means that many buyers never take advantage of it. However, this "slippage" is less likely to occur with frequent users of rebate promotions.[48] In addition, online consumers are more likely to take advantage of rebates.

product placement
Using a brand-name product in a movie, television show, video, or commercial for another product

Product Placement   A final consumer promotion, **product placement**, involves the use of a brand-name product in a movie, television show, video, or a commercial for

Can you identify these product placements?

another product. It was Steven Spielberg's placement of Hershey's Reese's Pieces in *E.T.* that first brought a lot of interest to the candy. Similarly, when Tom Cruise wore Bausch and Lomb's Ray-Ban sunglasses in *Risky Business* and its Aviator sunglasses in *Top Gun*, sales skyrocketed from 100,000 pairs to 7,000,000 pairs in five years. More recently you might remember seeing participants in the television show *Survivor* eating Doritos and drinking Mountain Dew, actors in the movie *Bandits* driving a Chrysler PT Cruiser, or women in the cast of *Ally McBeal* wearing bebe clothing. And after driving a BMW in his last three movies, James Bond is driving Aston Martin's V12 Vanquish once again, the only car he drove in the first 16 Bond movies. Another form of product placement uses new digital technology that can make "virtual" placements in any existing program. Reruns of *Seinfeld*, for example, could insert a Pepsi on a desktop, a Lexus parked on the street, or a box of Tide on the countertop.[49]

Trade-Oriented Sales Promotions

trade-oriented sales promotions
Sales tools used to support a company's advertising and personal selling efforts directed to wholesalers, distributors, or retailers

Trade-oriented sales promotions, or simply trade promotions, are sales tools used to support a company's advertising and personal selling directed to wholesalers, retailers, or distributors. Some of the consumer sales promotions we just reviewed are used for this purpose, but there are three other common approaches targeted uniquely to these intermediaries: allowances and discounts, cooperative advertising, and training of distributors' sales forces.

Allowances and Discounts   Trade promotions often focus on maintaining or increasing inventory levels in the channel of distribution. An effective method for encouraging such increased purchases by intermediaries is the use of allowances and discounts. However, overuse of these "price reductions" can lead to retailers changing their ordering patterns in the expectation of such offerings. Although there are many variations that manufacturers can use with discounts and allowances, three common approaches include the merchandise allowance, the case allowance, and the finance allowance.[50]

Reimbursing a retailer for extra in-store support or special featuring of the brand is a *merchandise allowance*. A *case allowance* is a discount on each case ordered during a specific time period. A *finance allowance* involves paying retailers for financing costs or financial losses associated with consumer sales promotions.

cooperative advertising
Advertising programs where a manufacturer pays a percentage of the retailer's local advertising expense for advertising the manufacturer's products

Cooperative Advertising   Resellers often perform the important function of promoting the manufacturer's products at the local level. One common sales promotional activity is to encourage both better quality and greater quantity in the local advertising efforts of resellers through **cooperative advertising**. These are programs where a manufacturer pays a percentage of the retailer's local advertising expense for advertising the manufacturer's products.

Training of Distributors' Sales Forces   One of the many functions the intermediaries perform is customer contact and selling for the producers they represent. Both retailers and wholesalers employ and manage their own sales personnel. It is in the best interest of the manufacturer to help train the reseller's sales force. Because the reseller's sales force is often less sophisticated and knowledgeable about the products than the manufacturer might like, training can increase their sales performance. Training activities include producing manuals and brochures to educate the reseller's sales force.

PUBLIC RELATIONS

In Chapter 15, we discussed public relations, a form of communication management that seeks to analyze and influence the image of an organization and its products and services. Public relations efforts may utilize a variety of tools and may be directed at many distinct audiences. While public relations personnel usually focus on communicating positive aspects of the business, they may also be called on to minimize the negative impact of a problem or crisis. Firestone, for example, recalled millions of tires after receiving complaints from consumers about product safety. Debates with Ford about the tire failures created a difficult situation for the Firestone public relations department.[51]

Organizations manage and plan public relations, and often large organizations will have public relations staff. The result of public relations is publicity, or news that is generated by the media and broadcast or placed in print media.

Public Relations Audiences

There are many different audiences, or "publics," with an interest or influence on a firm. Internal publics consist of employees, distributors, suppliers, shareholders, and customers. External publics include the media, government (at several levels), potential customers, potential shareholders, and the general public. Different issues require the firm to direct their efforts at different groups of their publics.

ETHICS AND SOCIAL RESPONSIBILITY ALERT
PUBLIC RELATIONS: WHAT SHOULD WE BELIEVE?

Many organizations realize that most consumers view public relations, particularly news-oriented publicity, as more credible than advertising per se. As such, many organizations have turned to well-managed public relations programs in order to influence the perceptions that relevant publics have toward them or their causes. Many organizations disseminate information that will cast them only in the best possible light or to ensure that their view on a particular issue is conveyed to the public. There is a growing concern about the public relations battle being waged between PETA (People for the Ethical Treatment of Animals) and the Canadian Cattlemen's Association. PETA is using a public relations campaign to persuade men to stop eating meat. Their message: eating meat causes impotence. But doctors claim that while there may be some truth in the claim, it's only a small part of the story. The Canadian Cattlemen's Association, which represents beef producers, dismisses PETA's claims as "ludicrous." This campaign by PETA follows on the heels of another campaign titled "Jesus Was a Vegetarian," that encourages Christians to give up meat.

What are the dangers when organizations with conflicting views on an issue market their positions via public relations activities? What roles do the media have in this situation?

Public Relations Tools

In developing a public relations campaign, several tools and tactics are available to the marketer. The most frequently used public relations tool is a news release, which is an announcement written by the organization and sent to the media for them to use if they find it newsworthy and relevant. The news (or press) release usually is some form of a presentation of an organization, good, or service, often an announcement regarding changes in the company or the product line. The objective of a *news release* is to inform a newspaper, radio station, or other medium of an idea for a story. A study found that more than 40 percent of all free mentions of a brand name occur during news programs.[52]

A second common publicity tool is the *news conference*. Representatives of the media are invited to an informational meeting, and advance materials regarding the content are sent. This tool is often used when negative publicity—as in the cases of the Tylenol poisonings and the Martha Stewart obstruction of justice issue—requires a company response.[53]

Nonprofit organizations rely heavily on publicity to spread their messages. *Public service announcements* (PSAs), where free space or time is donated by the media, is a common use of publicity for these organizations. The Canadian Red Cross, for example, depends on PSAs on radio and television to announce their needs.

A growing area of public relations involves the creation, or support, and publicizing of *special events* such as company-sponsored seminars, conferences, sports competitions, entertainment events, or other celebrations. The goal of event sponsorship is to create a forum to disseminate company information or to create brand identification to members of the target audience. Sports events such as the CIS (Canadian Interuniversity Sport) hockey and football championships are sponsored by Coca-Cola and General Motors, while AT&T Canada is the official sponsor of the Calgary Stampede and the Canadian Senior Golf Championship. DaimlerChrysler, Petro-Canada, and others have sponsored the development of the Trans Canada Trail.[54]

Another public relations tool is for the organization to engage in *public service activities* such as establishing or supporting community-based initiatives that benefit the well-being of society. For example, Ciba-Geigy Canada sponsors Health Canada's Quit 4 Life program, which encourages teens to quit smoking.

Finally, the development of *collateral materials* such as annual reports, brochures, newsletters, or video presentations about the company and its products are also basic public relations tools. These materials provide information to target publics and often generate publicity.

Public service ad campaign for Covenant House dramatizes the contrast between street kids who need help and average Canadian teenagers. This campaign won an award as it demonstrated the need for donations.

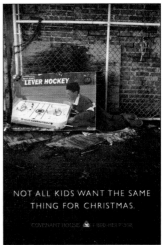

NOT ALL KIDS WANT THE SAME THING FOR CHRISTMAS.

As a promotional tool, public relations has a number of important strengths. Because the messages are usually delivered by the media, they tend to have more credibility than advertising, as they are seen as being impartial. The cost of public relations is quite low in comparison to other promotional tools, and the exposure is often better, as there is less clutter. Targeting specific groups can be done quite easily, and different approaches can be taken with different publics. As a tool for creating and enhancing a firm's image, public relations can be very effective. It does, however, have some drawbacks. The firm cannot control the content of messages put out by the media. If a positive article or news item comes out about a firm, it can be worth thousands or even millions of dollars in promotional value. If the spin is negative, the opposite is true. It can take a long time and involve significant costs to counteract negative publicity in the minds of the public. Media do not always publish the key ideas the firm would like to see, and the timing of publicity is at the discretion of the media, which may not be the optimal timing for the firm.

Good public relations activities should be planned and made part of an organization's integrated marketing communications effort. However, public relations activities must be used wisely and in an ethical and socially responsible manner (see the preceding Ethics and Social Responsibility Alert).[55]

Concept Check

1. Which sales promotional tool is most common for new products?
2. Which trade promotion is used to encourage local advertising efforts of resellers?
3. What is a news release?

SUMMARY

1 Advertising may be classified as either product or institutional. Product advertising can take three forms: pioneering, persuasive, or reminder. Institutional ads are one of these three, or advocacy.

2 The promotion decision process described in Chapter 15 can be applied to each of the promotional elements such as advertising.

3 Copywriters and art directors have the responsibility of identifying the key benefits of a product and communicating them to the target audience with attention-getting advertising. Common appeals include fear, sex, and humour.

4 In selecting the right medium, there are distinct trade-offs among television, radio, magazines, newspapers, direct mail, outdoor, and other media. The decision is based on media habits of the target audience, product characteristics, message requirements, and media costs.

5 In determining advertising schedules, a balance must be made between reach and frequency. Scheduling must take into account buyer turnover, purchase frequency, and the rate at which consumers forget.

6 Advertising is evaluated before and after the ad is run. Pretesting can be done with portfolio, jury, or theatre tests. Posttesting is done on the basis of aided recall, unaided recall, attitude tests, inquiry tests, and sales tests.

7 To execute an advertising program, companies can use several types of advertising agencies. These firms can provide a full range of services or specialize in creative or placement activities. Some firms have their own in-house services.

8 Almost equal amounts of money are spent on sales promotion and advertising. Selecting sales promotions requires a good understanding of the advantages and disadvantages of each option.

9 There is a wide range of consumer-oriented sales promotions: coupons, deals, premiums, contests, sweepstakes, samples, continuity programs, point-of-purchase displays, rebates, and product placements.

10 Trade-oriented promotions consist of allowances and discounts, cooperative advertising, and training of distributors' sales forces. These are used at all levels of the channel.

11 The most frequently used public relations tool is publicity—a nonpersonal, indirectly paid presentation of an organization, good, or service conducted through new releases, news conferences, special events, or public service announcements.

KEY TERMS AND CONCEPTS

advertising p. 376
consumer-oriented sales promotions p. 390
cooperative advertising p. 393
cost per thousand p. 383
frequency p. 383
full-service agency p. 389
gross rating points p. 383
infomercials p. 383
in-house agency p. 389
institutional advertisements p. 379

limited-service agency p. 389
posttests p. 389
pretests p. 388
product advertisements p. 378
product placement p. 393
rating p. 383
reach p. 382
trade-oriented sales promotions p. 393
viral marketing p. 385

QUESTIONS: APPLYING MARKETING CONCEPTS AND PERSPECTIVES

1 How does competitive product advertising differ from competitive institutional advertising?

2 Suppose you are the advertising manager for a new line of children's fragrances. Which media would you use for this new product?

3 You have recently been promoted to be director of advertising for the Timkin Tool Company. In your first meeting with Mr. Timkin, he says, "Advertising is a waste! We've been advertising for six months now and sales haven't increased. Tell me why we should continue." Give your answer to Mr. Timkin.

4 A large life insurance company has decided to switch from using a strong fear appeal to a humorous approach. What are the strengths and weaknesses of such a change in message strategy?

5 Which medium has the lowest cost per thousand?

MEDIUM	COST	AUDIENCE
TV show	$5,000	25,000
Magazine	2,200	6,000
Newspaper	4,800	7,200
FM radio	420	1,600

6 Some national advertisers have found that they can have more impact with their advertising by running a large number of ads for a period and then running no ads at all for a period. Why might such a flighting schedule be more effective than a steady schedule?

7 Each year managers at Bausch and Lomb evaluate the many advertising media alternatives available to them as they develop their advertising program for contact lenses. What advantages and disadvantages of each alternative should they consider? Which media would you recommend to them?

8 What are two advantages and two disadvantages of the advertising posttests described in the chapter?

9 Federated Bank is interested in consumer-oriented sales promotions that would encourage senior citizens to direct deposit their Old Age Pension cheques with the bank. Evaluate the sales promotion options, and recommend two of them to the bank.

10 How can public relations be used by Firestone and Ford following investigations into complaints about tire failures?

11 Maybe you have seen those envelopes that come in the mail, unaddressed, with 15 or 20 coupons in them. Some people go through these envelopes and decide which ones to use, and others throw them out without opening them. How effective do you think this type of sales promotion is? Do you think there is a specific target market that uses coupons like this? How can they be made more attractive to people who now do not open them?

12 Assume that you work at a sports clothing store, and the Nike representative for your province comes in and offers a bonus of a pair of runners to the first salesperson who sells $500 worth of a new line of workout wear. Is this a push or a pull strategy? What other promotions would you think that Nike may use at the same time for their new line?

13 A baby car seat manufacturer has had to recall 100,000 of last fall's new model, because the seat belt buckle kept opening while the vehicle was moving. How would you suggest handling public relations for this situation?

DISCUSSION FORUM

To do this activity, you will need some magazines and newspapers. Find at least five magazines, all with different subject matter and different target markets, and one or two newspapers (ideally a local newspaper and a national one). Make sure that you have a mix of consumer and business magazines. Then find three ads, all for different products and services, in each, and consider them all from these perspectives:

1 Is this a product or a service ad?

2 What are the advantages and disadvantages of running it in this particular publication?

3 Is this a consumer- or trade-oriented ad? What changes would you make to change it to the opposite orientation?

4 How would you design a sales promotion to work in concert with this ad?

5 What public relations activities would work well with this ad?

6 What advertising technique is used in the ad to convey the message?

Now pick the ad you like best of those you selected and sketch out the process you think might have been used to develop the advertising program the ad comes from.

When you are finished this activity, and this chapter, you may see advertising, sales promotion, and public relations a bit differently from how the average consumer sees them.

INTERNET EXERCISE

There are many forms of print advertising available today. If you were to advise your university to advertise in magazines, which magazines would you recommend? Most magazines provide advertising information on their web page as a "media kit" or under "advertising rates." For example, *Time* magazine advertising information is available at www.time-planner.com/planner/rates. Select four magazines and answer these questions, recording your

www.mcgrawhill.ca/college/thecore

information in the chart provided.

1 What is the monthly rate for a full page ad in each of the magazines?

2 Describe the profile of the audience for each of the magazines.

3 Calculate the CPM for each magazine.

4 Provide the same data for the Canadian edition.

MAGAZINE	FULL-PAGE RATE	AUDIENCE PROFILE	CPM
1.			
2.			
3.			
4.			

VIDEO CASE 16

RETHINK: NOT YOUR AVERAGE AD AGENCY

Does creativity fall victim to the politics and hierarchical structures often found in larger ad agencies? Chris Staples of Rethink, a small Vancouver ad agency, certainly thinks so. And that's the reason he and his two partners, Ian Grais and Tom Shepansky, left their former employer, Palmer Jarvis DDB, one of Canada's largest and most successful ad agencies—that is, of course, if you measure success based on revenues. Staples would prefer to measure success based on the effect that ads have on people.

After working more than 10 years for the conventional ad agency, the creative trio broke away to form their own company, Rethink, in October 1999. The small agency immediately began drawing media attention and clients, including large companies such as A&W and A&P/Dominion. And while it may seem surprising that such a small ad agency has managed to lure clients away from larger firms, it would appear that some of these clients are looking for new ideas and more exciting advertising.

The reason is that advertising is everywhere. Consumers are bombarded by hundreds of ads every day and people are getting bored with the same old advertising. Companies such as Labatt North America have grown tired of the traditional ad agency structure and approach and have dropped their lead agencies. Many favour smaller ad agencies because of their refreshing new approach to advertising, which includes more time spent on thinking and creating and less time on planning and strategy.

There is nothing traditional about Rethink. The founders have no business plan and don't believe in market research. Instead, they have a one-word philosophy: "Rethink." Believing that large agencies are trying to be everything to everybody, like big department stores, Rethink wants instead to be fabulous at just a few things, spending all of its creative energy thinking up unique ads. So, in this sense, Rethink is not a full-service agency like the larger firms. Rather, it has carved out a niche for itself that appeals to companies that are bored with their current advertising and are looking for something bold and daring.

So far, Rethink has not needed to do much to attract new clients. Mostly, the partners have just had to pick up the telephone and propose an idea. The creative trio has a great reputation in the industry, having won a Cannes Lion award. Many clients have come knocking at their door, but Rethink won't take on just anybody; it's very picky about the companies it chooses. There must be chemistry, a passion for the product, and, above all, creative carte blanche. Staples, Grais, and Shepansky want the freedom to create, to be different, to stand out from the rest. They won't tolerate a lot of interference from clients. And rather than having a traditional agency-client relationship, Rethink prefers to think of itself as a part of the client's business.

As masters of self-promotion, the founders have been able to draw a lot of attention to their young company. Rethink's approach has been described as dynamic, refreshing, and unorthodox—and it works. Only four months after opening, the small ad agency had already picked up some large clients and $15 million in new business. The agency has also won numerous awards for its ads.

Rethink is more than just the name of the company; it is a brand that the founders intend to build. As Staples explains, many traditional ad agencies are named after "dead white guys." He means, of course, their founders, who are no longer alive. Staples wants Rethink to be a brand rather than a person's name, so that the brand will outlive its partners and take on an identity of its own. And they are building their brand by creating products that will carry the Rethink name. Their first such venture was beer.

After months of developing their product in cooperation with Tree Breweries, a British Columbia microbrewery, the agency launched its own Rethink beer in 2000. The beer even came in a cool, new package rather than in the traditional cardboard box. The idea behind Rethink beer was that the new product would provide free advertising for the agency. Despite many obstacles and delays in bringing Rethink beer to the market, it served its purpose. The buzz around the beer turned out to be great promotion for the small ad agency. The beer was also meant to show prospective clients that Rethink can do more than just advertise—it can think up products.

Rethink is not a small agency by necessity; it's small by choice, at the founders' insistence. Otherwise, it will risk losing its identity, its creativity, and its focus. Staples calls Rethink an ideas company, positioning itself as an agency that puts creativity first. It claims that it is not in it for the money. To prove this, Rethink tells its clients that if they are not satisfied, Rethink does not get paid all of its fees. The agency's goal is to earn its fees in performance. It gets involved with clients, rather than just treating them as clients. In fact, many small firms complain that when they go to the larger ad agencies, their accounts are often given to "B" teams. They know they are not a priority for the bigger ad agencies that have much larger clients. Smaller ad agencies like Rethink are therefore more appealing to these companies.

Is Rethink changing the face of advertising? Or is it simply carving out a niche that appeals to a certain type of client? Certainly, the partners' in-your-face attitude and their criticism of the larger agencies have elicited negative responses from the advertising industry. But their attitude and their philosophy is also the reason that major clients have signed on with them. Rethink brings refreshing ideas and clever advertising to clients; these clients need to stick out in an increasingly competitive market. Rethink has succeeded in standing out and in making many of its clients stand out with outlandish ads.

Questions

1 How has Rethink positioned itself in the competitive advertising industry?

2 What are the advantages for an ad agency to stay small?

3 Are smaller ad agencies more creative than their larger counterparts?

4 Does Rethink's advertising style fit with every prospective client? Why or why not?

Direct Marketing and Personal Selling

AFTER READING THIS CHAPTER YOU SHOULD BE ABLE TO:

- Explain the value of direct marketing to both consumers and sellers.

- Understand the technical, global, and ethical issues associated with direct marketing.

- Recognize the different approaches to personal selling.

- Describe the stages in the personal selling process.

- Specify the functions and tasks involved in sales force management.

- Describe recent trends in sales force organization, automation. and customer relationship management.

SELLING THE WAY CUSTOMERS WANT TO BUY

The right person for the job! As president and chief executive officer at Xerox, Anne Mulcahy has a tough assignment. In the midst of successfully directing one the greatest feats in the annals of recent business history—restoring Xerox's legendary marketing and financial vitality—she is already producing amazing results.

Mulcahy (shown above) took the helm in 2001 and said in her opening commentary, "As CEO of Xerox, I am ready and privileged to lead a team of dedicated employees who are as sharply focused and committed as I am in the successful turnaround of our company, transforming it to the realities of the digital age and putting Xerox back on a growth trajectory." With a broad range of products and services at competitive prices offered via direct, indirect, Web, and telephone sales and customer support, she said, "We will win back market share one customer at a time, one sale at a time. We'll do that by providing greater value than our competitors—and that means selling the way they want to buy."

Ideally suited to the task, Mulcahy has been with Xerox for more than 25 years. She began her career with Xerox as a field sales representative and was promoted to management and executive positions with increasing responsibility. These included chief staff officer, president of Xerox's General Markets Operations, and her most recent as president and chief operating officer of Xerox. As CEO, she has had to muster the knowledge and experience gained from this varied background. Not surprisingly, her exposure to marketing and her sales background has played a pivotal role as she leads Xerox to position itself to conduct business successfully in the twenty-first century.[1]

This chapter examines the scope and significance of direct marketing, personal selling, and aspects of salesforce management. It discusses direct marketing, highlights the many forms of personal selling, and outlines the selling process. Sales force management is then described, including recent trends in the way the sales forces are organized along with advances in sales force automation and customer relationship management.

WHERE IN THE MARKETING PROCESS ARE WE GOING IN THIS CHAPTER?

Chapter 17 continues the theme of promotional tools; direct marketing and personal selling are featured here. Like the topics of Chapter 16, they are part of the promotion P of the 4Ps that make up the marketing mix.

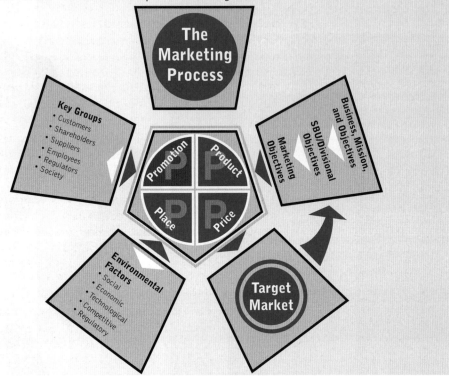

DIRECT MARKETING

Direct marketing is a promotional tool that uses direct communication with consumers to encourage them to place an order, request more information, or visit a store. Direct marketing has many forms and utilizes a variety of media. Several forms of direct marketing—direct mail and catalogues, television, telemarketing, and direct selling—were discussed as methods of nonstore retailing in Chapter 14. In addition, although advertising is discussed in Chapter 16, a form of advertising—direct response advertising—is an important form of direct marketing. In this section the growth of direct marketing, its benefits, and key global, technological, and ethical issues are discussed.

The Growth of Direct Marketing

The increasing interest in customer relationship management is reflected in the dramatic growth of direct marketing. The ability to customize communication efforts and create one-to-one interactions is appealing to most marketers, particularly those with IMC programs. While direct marketing methods are not new, the ability to design and use them effectively has increased with the availability of databases. In recent years, direct marketing growth—in terms of spending, revenue generated, and employment—has outpaced total economic growth. Direct marketing in Canada has grown in expenditures, sales, and employment. The Canadian Marketing Association reports that, in 2001, $2 billion was spent in direct mail advertising and $3 billion in telephone marketing. Sales from direct response advertising in 2001 rang in at $55 billion and are forecast to be $82 billion by 2005. Employment in the industry has remained relatively steady over the past few years; direct marketing employs thousands of people across the country.[2]

The Value of Direct Marketing

One of the most telling indicators of the power of direct marketing is how it is used by consumers. Over half of the Canadian population has ordered merchandise or services by phone or mail, and millions have purchased from television direct marketing offers. The Internet is also having a major impact, and catalogue shopping is also popular, with about 20 percent of adults making a purchase from a catalogue each year.[3]

Consumers report many benefits, including the following: they don't have to go to a store, they can usually shop 24 hours a day, buying direct saves time, they avoid hassles with salespeople, they can save money, it's fun and entertaining, and direct marketing offers more privacy than in-store shopping. Many consumers also believe that direct marketing provides excellent customer service.[4] Toll-free telephone numbers, customer service representatives with access to information regarding purchasing preferences, overnight delivery services, and unconditional guarantees all help create value for direct marketing customers. At Landsend.com, when customers need assistance they can click a "help" icon and a sales rep will take control of their browser until the correct product is found. "It's like we were walking down the aisle in a store," says one Lands' End customer![5]

The value of direct marketing for sellers can be described in terms of the responses it generates.[6] **Direct orders** are the result of offers that contain all the information necessary for a prospective buyer to make a decision to purchase and complete the transaction. Club Med, for example, uses direct e-mail offers to sell "last-minute specials" to people in its database. The messages, which are sent midweek, describe rooms and air transportation available at a 30 to 40 percent discount if the customer can make the decision to travel on such short notice.[7] **Lead generation** is the result of an offer designed to generate interest in a product or service and a request for additional information. America Online announced a contest with direct advertising and used a direct-mail trial offer to generate interest in its latest release.[8] Finally, **traffic generation** is the outcome of an offer designed to motivate people to visit a business. Mitsubishi recently mailed a sweepstakes offer to 1 million prospective buyers to encourage them to visit a Mitsubishi dealer and test drive the new Galant. The names of prospects who took test drives were entered in the sweepstakes, which included a Galant, a trip to Hawaii, and large-screen TVs as prizes.[9]

Technological, Global, and Ethical Issues in Direct Marketing

The information technology and databases described in Chapter 8 are key elements in any direct marketing program. Databases are the result of organizations' efforts to collect demographic, media, and purchase profiles of customers so that direct marketing tools— such as catalogues—can be directed at specific customers. For example, PEI's Padinox Inc. started its very successful Paderno cookware business in 1979, selling quality stainless steel cookware in selected stores in Canada. Now, the firm sells its products across North America, and in some very interesting and profitable ways. Twice a year Padinox holds a sale at 400 selected stores across Canada, a four-day event that is advertised via direct mail to customers on the company's database. Only 150 of these stores carry Paderno cookware at other times than during these sales. Padinox also has 22 factory stores across the country. The firm's catalogue, KitchenWear, was started many years ago, and it has grown from just a few pages to a glossy, 40-page edition, a key tool for contacting customers, selling products, and announcing new products to their customers. The cookware can also be purchased from the website www.paderno.com, although web sales account for only 5 percent of total sales. Paderno pots come with a 25-year guarantee, so there is a distinct advan-

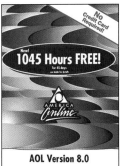

AOL Version 8.0

direct orders
The result of direct marketing offers that contain all the information necessary for a potential buyer to make a decision to purchase and complete the transaction

lead generation
Result of direct marketing offer designed to create interest in a product or a service and a request for additional information

traffic generation
Outcome of direct marketing offer designed to motivate people to visit a business

ETHICS AND SOCIAL RESPONSIBILITY ALERT

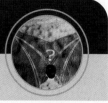

HOW DO YOU LIKE YOUR E-MAIL? "OPT-OUT" OR "OPT-IN" ARE YOUR CHOICES

More than 1 billion e-mail messages are sent each day in North America. You've probably noticed that many of them are direct-marketing messages—personalized offers from companies such as Pepsi, Victoria's Secret, Toyota, and Expedia.ca. In fact, e-mail advertisers spend more than US$2 billion annually on their campaigns. One reason is that e-mail offers one-to-one conversations with each prospective consumer. Another reason is that the average cost per e-mail message is less than $.01 compared to $0.75 to $2.00 for direct mail and $1 to $3 for telemarketing.

Some consumers have complained that they receive too many unsolicited messages, or "spam." Marketers believe that better management of e-mail campaigns will improve the value of e-mail advertising for cus-

tomers. Two general approaches to managing e-mail are being discussed. The "opt-out" system allows recipients to decline future messages after the first contact. The "opt-in" system requires advertisers to obtain e-mail addresses from registration questions on websites, business-reply cards, and even entry forms for contests or sweepstakes. Surveys indicate that about 77 percent of the unsolicited e-mails are deleted without being read, while only 2 percent of the e-mails received with the consumer's permission are deleted.

The European Union's Committee for Citizens' Freedoms and Rights recently debated the issue and gave a preliminary ruling in favour of an opt-out policy. Some companies, however, have adopted opt-in policies. What is your opinion? Why?

tage for customers to register their purchase—this is one route to building Padinox's database. Clearly the marketing database is a key strategic tool in communicating with customers.[10]

Technology may also prove to be important in the global growth of direct marketing. Compared with Canada and the United States, most other countries' direct marketing systems are undeveloped. The mail and telephone systems in many countries are likely to improve, however, creating many new direct marketing opportunities. In Argentina, for example, mail service is very slow, telephone service is poor, and response to some forms of direct marketing such as coupons is negligible. The country is the first, however, to fully deregulate its postal service and expects rapid improvement from the private company, Correo Argentino. In Mexico, direct marketing activities are more advanced. Pond's recently mailed 20,000 direct-mail offers within Mexico and was surprised by a 33 percent response.[11] Another issue for global direct marketers is payment. Outside of North America, fewer consumers have credit cards, alternatives such as C.O.D. (cash on delivery) and bank deposits are needed. Developments in international marketing research and database management will also increase global growth.

Global and domestic direct marketers both face challenging ethical issues today. Of course, there has been considerable attention given to some direct marketing activities such as telephone solicitations during dinner and evening hours. Concerns about privacy, however, have led to various attempts to provide guidelines that balance consumer and business interests. The European Union recently passed a consumer privacy law, called the Data Protection Directive, and the Canadian government established the Office of the Privacy Commissioner of Canada, as well as the Personal Information Protection and Electronic Documents Act (www.privcom.gc.ca) as a way of protecting the privacy of Canadians. Industry associations including the Canadian Marketing Association (www.the-cma.org) have also developed guidelines for their members with regard to consumer privacy.[12] The issue of e-mail advertising has also received increased attention from consumers and marketers. The accompanying Ethics and Social Responsibility Alert discusses the issue of e-mail advertising and options for controlling this most recent form of direct-marketing communication.[13]

1. What technologies have helped to increase the design and use of direct marketing?

2. What are the three types of responses generated by direct marketing activities?

SCOPE AND SIGNIFICANCE OF PERSONAL SELLING AND SALES FORCE MANAGEMENT

Chapter 15 described personal selling and management of the sales effort as being part of the firm's promotional mix. Although it is important to recognize that personal selling is a useful means of communicating with present and potential buyers, it is much more.

Nature of Personal Selling and Sales Force Management

personal selling
The two-way flow of communication between a buyer and seller, often in a face-to-face encounter, designed to influence a person's or group's purchase decision

Personal selling involves the two-way flow of communication between a buyer and seller, often in a face-to-face encounter, designed to influence a person's or group's purchase decision. However, with advances in telecommunications, personal selling also takes place over the telephone, through video teleconferencing and Internet/Web-enabled links between buyers and sellers.

Personal selling remains a highly human-intensive activity despite the use of technology. Accordingly, the people involved must be managed. **Sales force management** involves planning the selling program and implementing and controlling the personal selling effort of the firm. The tasks involved in managing personal selling include setting objectives; organizing the sales force; recruiting, selecting, training, and compensating salespeople; and evaluating the performance of individual salespeople.

sales-force management
Planning the selling program and implementing the personal selling effort of the firm

Selling Happens Almost Everywhere

"Everyone lives by selling something," wrote author Robert Louis Stevenson a century ago. His observation still holds true today. In Canada, more than 4 million people are employed in sales- and service-related positions.[14] Included in this number are manufacturing sales personnel, real estate brokers, stockbrokers, and salesclerks who work in retail stores. In reality, however, virtually every occupation that involves customer contact has an element of personal selling. For example, lawyers, accountants, bankers, and company personnel recruiters perform sales-related activities, whether or not they acknowledge it. Many executives in major companies, like Anne Mulcahy at Xerox, have held sales positions at some time in their careers. Selling often serves as a stepping-stone to top management, as well as being a career path in itself.

Personal Selling in Marketing

Personal selling serves three major roles in a firm's overall marketing effort. First, salespeople are the critical link between the firm and its customers. This role requires that salespeople match company interests with customer needs to satisfy both parties in the exchange process. Second, salespeople *are* the company in a consumer's eyes. They represent what a company is or attempts to be and are often the only personal contact a customer has with the company. For example, the "look" projected by Gucci salespeople is an important factor in communicating the style of the company's apparel line. Third, personal selling may

Could this be a salesperson in the operating room? Read the text to find why Medtronic salespeople visit hospital operating rooms.

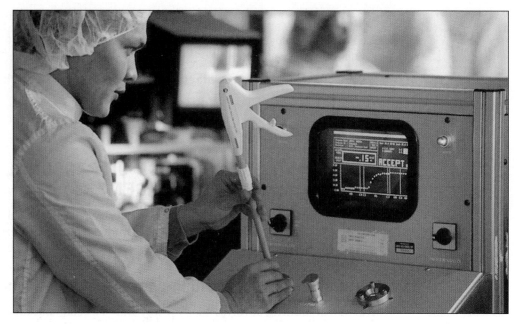

play a dominant role in a firm's marketing program. Avon, for example, spends almost 40 percent of its total sales dollars on selling expenses.

Creating Customer Value through Salespeople: Relationship and Partnership Selling

As the critical link between the firm and its customers, salespeople can create customer value in many ways. For instance, by being close to the customer, salespeople can identify creative solutions to customer problems. Salespeople at Medtronic, Inc., the world leader in the heart pacemaker market, are in the operating room for more than 90 percent of the procedures performed with their product and are on call, wearing pagers, 24 hours a day. "It reflects the willingness to be there in every situation, just in case a problem arises—even though nine times out of ten the procedure goes just fine," notes a satisfied customer.[15] Salespeople can create value by easing the customer buying process.

relationship selling
Practice of building ties to customers based on a salesperson's attention and commitment to customer needs over time

Customer value creation is made possible by **relationship selling**, the practice of building ties to customers based on a salesperson's attention and commitment to customer needs over time. Relationship selling involves mutual respect and trust among buyers and sellers. It focuses on creating long-term customers, not a one-time sale.[16] A recent survey of 300 senior sales executives revealed that 96 percent consider "building long-term relationships with customers" to be the most important activity affecting sales performance. Companies such as Bell Canada, National Bank, IBM Canada, and Kraft Canada have made relationship building a core focus of their sales effort.[17]

Relationship selling represents another dimension of customer relationship management. It emphasizes the importance of learning about customer needs and wants and tailoring solutions to customer problems as a means of creating customer value.

Concept Check

1. What is personal selling?
2. What is involved in sales force management?

THE MANY FORMS OF PERSONAL SELLING

Personal selling assumes many forms based on the amount of selling done and the amount of creativity required to perform the sales task. Broadly speaking, two types of personal selling exist: order taking and order getting. While some firms use only one of these types of personal selling, others use a combination of both.

Order Taking

order taker
Salesperson who processes routine orders or reorders

Typically, an **order taker** processes routine orders or reorders for products that were previously sold by the company to existing customers. The primary responsibility of order takers is to preserve an ongoing relationship with existing customers and maintain sales.

Two types of order takers exist. *Outside order takers* visit customers, arrange displays, and replace inventory stocks of resellers, such as retailers or wholesalers. For example, Frito-Lay salespeople call on supermarkets, neighbourhood grocery stores, and other establishments to ensure that the company's line of snack products is in adequate supply. *Inside order takers*, also called *order clerks* or *salesclerks*, typically answer simple questions, take orders, and complete transactions with customers. Many retail clerks are inside order takers. Inside order takers are often employed by companies that use *inbound telemarketing*, the use of telephone numbers that customers can call to obtain information about products or services and make purchases.

Order takers generally do little selling in a conventional sense and engage in only modest problem solving with customers. They often represent products that have few options, such as confectionery items, magazine subscriptions, and highly standardized industrial products. Inbound telemarketing is also an essential selling activity for more customer-service-driven firms, such as Dell Computer. At these companies, order takers undergo extensive training so that they can better assist callers with their purchase decisions.

Order Getting

order getter
Salesperson who sells in a conventional sense and identifies prospective customers, provides customers with information, persuades customers to buy, closes sales, and follows up on customers' use of a product or service

An **order getter** sells in a conventional sense and identifies prospective customers, provides customers with information, persuades customers to buy, closes sales, and follows up on customers' use of a product or service. Like order takers, order getters can be inside

A Frito-Lay salesperson takes inventory of snacks for the store manager to sign. In this situation, the manager will make a straight rebuy decision.

FIGURE 17–1

How outside order-getting salespeople spend their time each week

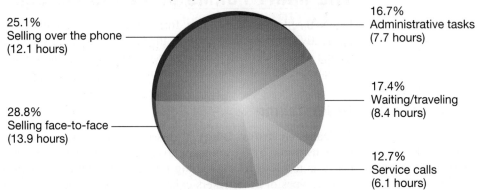

How salespeople spend their time each week

25.1%
Selling over the phone
(12.1 hours)

16.7%
Administrative tasks
(7.7 hours)

17.4%
Waiting/traveling
(8.4 hours)

28.8%
Selling face-to-face
(13.9 hours)

12.7%
Service calls
(6.1 hours)

(an automobile salesperson) or outside (a Xerox salesperson). Order getting involves a high degree of creativity and customer empathy. This type of personal selling is typically required for complex or technical products with many options, so extensive product knowledge and sales training are necessary. An order getter acts as a problem solver who identifies how a particular product may satisfy a customer's need. Similarly, in the purchase of a service, such as insurance, a Metropolitan Life insurance agent can provide a mix of plans to satisfy a buyer's needs depending on income, stage of the family's life cycle, and investment objectives.

Order getting is not a 40-hour-per-week job. Industry research indicates that outside order getters, or field service representatives, work about 48 hours per week. As shown in Figure 17–1, 54 percent of their time is spent selling and another 13 percent is devoted to customer service calls. The remainder of their work is occupied by getting to customers and performing numerous administrative tasks.[18]

Order getting by outside salespeople is also expensive. It is estimated that the average cost of a single field sales call is almost $170, factoring in salespeople compensation, benefits, and travel-and-entertainment expenses.[19] This cost illustrates why outbound telemarketing is so popular today. *Outbound telemarketing* is the practice of using the telephone rather than personal visits to contact customers. A significantly lower cost per sales call (in the range of $20 to $25) and little or no field expense are the reasons for its widespread appeal. Outbound telemarketing has grown significantly over the past decade, despite legislative controls aimed at setting standards for its use and growing opposition by consumer groups.[20]

We mentioned at the beginning of this section that many firms employ both order takers and order getters. If we view this as a continuum, some sales people will be strictly order takers, and this means that they will be at one end of the continuum; other sales people will be at the opposite end, as they will be strictly order getters. Most sales jobs require both activities, and, depending on the percentage of each, they would place on the continuum somewhere between the two extremes.

Concept Check

1. What is the main difference between an order taker and an order getter?
2. What percentage of an order-getting salesperson's time is spent selling?

THE PERSONAL SELLING PROCESS: BUILDING RELATIONSHIPS

Selling, and particularly order getting, is a complicated activity that involves building buyer–seller relationships. Although the salesperson–customer interaction is essential to personal selling, much of a salesperson's work occurs before this meeting and continues after the sale itself. The **personal selling process** consists of six stages: prospecting, preapproach, approach, presentation, close, and follow-up (Figure 17–2).

personal selling process
Sales activities occurring before and after the sale itself, consisting of six stages: prospecting, preapproach, approach, presentation, close, and follow-up

Prospecting

Personal selling begins with *prospecting*—searching for and qualifying potential customers. For some products that are infrequent purchases such as home alarm systems, continual prospecting is necessary to maintain sales. There are three types of prospects. A *lead* is the name of a person who may be a possible customer. A *prospect* is a customer who wants

FIGURE 17–2
Stages and objectives of the personal selling process

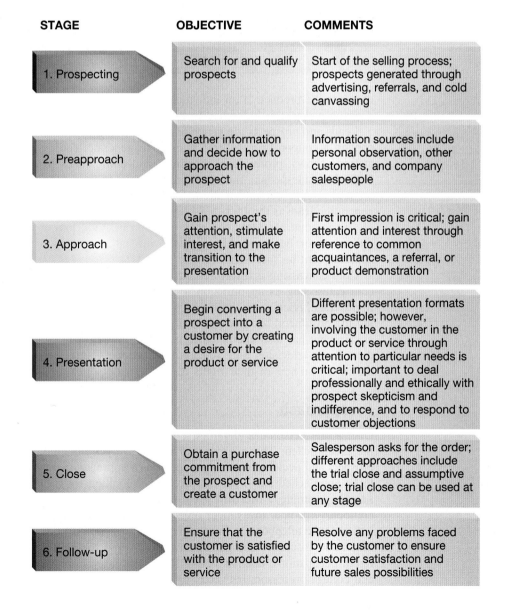

STAGE	OBJECTIVE	COMMENTS
1. Prospecting	Search for and qualify prospects	Start of the selling process; prospects generated through advertising, referrals, and cold canvassing
2. Preapproach	Gather information and decide how to approach the prospect	Information sources include personal observation, other customers, and company salespeople
3. Approach	Gain prospect's attention, stimulate interest, and make transition to the presentation	First impression is critical; gain attention and interest through reference to common acquaintances, a referral, or product demonstration
4. Presentation	Begin converting a prospect into a customer by creating a desire for the product or service	Different presentation formats are possible; however, involving the customer in the product or service through attention to particular needs is critical; important to deal professionally and ethically with prospect skepticism and indifference, and to respond to customer objections
5. Close	Obtain a purchase commitment from the prospect and create a customer	Salesperson asks for the order; different approaches include the trial close and assumptive close; trial close can be used at any stage
6. Follow-up	Ensure that the customer is satisfied with the product or service	Resolve any problems faced by the customer to ensure customer satisfaction and future sales possibilities

or needs the product. If an individual wants the product, can afford to buy it, and is the decision maker, this individual is a *qualified prospect*.

Leads and prospects are generated using several sources. For example, advertising may contain a coupon or a toll-free number to generate leads. Some companies use exhibits at trade shows, professional meetings, and conferences to generate leads or prospects. Staffed by salespeople, these exhibits are used to attract the attention of prospective buyers and to give out information. Others use lists and directories. Another approach for generating leads is through *cold canvassing* in person or by telephone. This approach simply means that a salesperson may open a directory, pick a name, and visit or call that individual or business. Although the refusal rate is high with cold canvassing, this approach can be successful.

Cold canvassing is also often criticized by Canadian consumers. Many consumers see cold canvassing as an intrusion to their privacy, and many find it simply distasteful.[21] Many trade associations have codes of ethics for dealing with this issue, such as adhering to consumers' "do not call," "do not mail," or "do not visit" requests. The Canadian government has also attempted to more closely regulate cold canvassing, with the Canadian Radio-television and Telecommunications Commission requiring telemarketers to inform consumers of their rights regarding such solicitations.[22]

Preapproach

Once a salesperson has identified a qualified prospect, preparation for the sale begins with the preapproach. The *preapproach* stage involves obtaining further information on the prospect and deciding on the best method of approach. Knowing how the prospect prefers to be approached and what the prospect is looking for in a product or service is essential. For example, a Merrill Lynch stockbroker will need information on a prospect's discretionary income, investment objectives, and preference for discussing brokerage services over the telephone or in person. Identifying the best time to contact a prospect is also important. Insurance companies have discovered the best times to call on people in different occupations: dentists before 9:30 A.M., lawyers between 11:00 A.M. and 2:00 P.M., and college professors between 7:00 and 8:00 P.M.

Successful salespeople recognize that the preapproach stage should never be short-changed. Their experience, coupled with research on customer complaints, indicates that failure to learn as much as possible about the prospect is unprofessional and can be the ruin of a sales call.[23]

Approach

The *approach* stage involves the first meeting between the salesperson and prospect, where the objectives are to gain the prospect's attention, stimulate interest, and build the foundation for the sales presentation itself and the basis for a working relationship. The first impression is critical at this stage, and it is common for salespeople to begin the conversation with a reference to common acquaintances, a referral, or even the product or service itself. Which tactic is taken will depend on the information obtained in the prospecting and preapproach stages.

The approach stage is very important in international settings. In many societies outside of Canada, much time is devoted to nonbusiness talk designed to establish a friendly basis for developing a relationship between buyers and sellers. For instance, in the Middle East and Asia, it is common for two or three meetings to occur before business matters are discussed. Gestures are also very important. The first meeting between a salesperson and a prospect in Canada customarily begins with a firm handshake. Handshakes also apply in France, but they are gentle, not firm. Forget the handshake in Japan. A bow is appropriate. What about business cards? Business cards should be printed in English on one side and the language of the prospective customer on the other. Knowledgeable salespeople know that their business cards should be handed to Asian customers using both hands, with the name facing the receiver. In Asia, anything involving names demands respect.[24]

Presentation

The *presentation* is at the core of the order-getting selling process, and its objective is to convert a prospect into a customer by uncovering or creating a desire for the product or service. Three major presentation formats exist: stimulus-response format, formula selling format, and need-satisfaction format.

Stimulus-Response Format

The *stimulus-response presentation* format assumes that given the appropriate stimulus by a salesperson, the prospect will buy. With this format the salesperson tries one appeal after another, hoping to hit the right button. A counter clerk at McDonald's is using this approach when he or she asks whether you'd like an order of french fries or a dessert with your meal. The counter clerk is engaging in what is called *suggestive selling*. Although useful in this setting, the stimulus-response format is not always appropriate, and for many products a more formalized format is necessary.

Formula Selling Format

A more formalized presentation, the *formula selling presentation* format, is based on the view that a presentation consists of information that must be provided in an accurate, thorough, and step-by-step manner to inform the prospect. A popular version of this format is the *canned sales presentation*, which is a memorized, standardized message conveyed to every prospect. Used frequently by firms in telephone and door-to-door selling of consumer products (for example, Electrolux vacuum cleaners), this approach treats every prospect the same, regardless of differences in needs or preference for certain kinds of information. Canned sales presentations can be advantageous when the differences between prospects are unknown or with novice salespeople who are less knowledgeable about the product and selling process than experienced salespeople. Although it guarantees a thorough presentation, it often lacks flexibility and spontaneity and, more important, does not provide for feedback from the prospective buyer—a critical component in the communication process and the start of a relationship.

Need-Satisfaction Format   The stimulus-response and formula selling formats share a common characteristic: The salesperson dominates the conversation. By comparison, the *need-satisfaction presentation* format emphasizes probing and listening by the salesperson to identify needs and interests of prospective buyers. Once these are identified, the salesperson tailors the presentation to the prospect and highlights product benefits that may be valued by the prospect. The need-satisfaction format, which emphasizes problem solving, is the most consistent with the marketing concept and relationship building.

Two selling styles are associated with the need-satisfaction format.[25] **Adaptive selling** involves adjusting the presentation to fit the selling situation, such as knowing when to offer solutions and when to ask for more information. Sales research and practice show that knowledge of the customer and sales situation are key ingredients for adaptive selling. Many consumer service firms such as brokerage and insurance firms and consumer product firms like home renovation and repair effectively apply this selling style. **Consultative selling** focuses on problem identification, where the salesperson serves as an expert on problem recognition and resolution. With consultative selling, problem solution options are not simply a matter of choosing from an array of existing products or services. Rather, novel solutions often arise, thereby creating unique value for the customer. Consultative selling is prominent in business-to-business marketing. Johnson Controls, IBM Canada, and DHL Worldwide Express are often cited for their consultative selling style.

Handling Objections   A critical concern in the presentation stage is handling objections. *Objections* are reasons for not making a purchase commitment or decision. Some objections are valid and are based on the characteristics of the product or service or price. However, many objections reflect prospect skepticism or indifference. Whether valid or not, experienced salespeople know that objections do not put an end to the presentation. Rather, techniques can be used to deal with objections in a courteous, ethical, and professional manner. The following six techniques are the most common:[26]

1. *Acknowledge and convert the objection.* This technique involves using the objection as a reason for buying. For example, a prospect might say, "The price is too high." The reply: "Yes, the price is high because we use the finest materials. Let me show you. . . ."
2. *Postpone.* The postpone technique is used when the objection will be dealt with later in the presentation: "I'm going to address that point shortly. I think my answer would make better sense then."
3. *Agree and neutralize.* Here a salesperson agrees with the objection, then shows that it is unimportant. A salesperson would say, "That's true and others have said the same. However, they concluded that issue was outweighed by the other benefits."
4. *Accept the objection.* Sometimes the objection is valid. Let the prospect express such views, probe for the reason behind it, and attempt to stimulate further discussion on the objection.
5. *Denial.* When a prospect's objection is based on misinformation and clearly untrue, it is wise to meet the objection head on with a firm denial.
6. *Ignore the objection.* This technique is used when it appears that the objection is a stalling mechanism or is clearly not important to the prospect.

Each of these techniques requires a calm, professional interaction with the prospect and is most effective when objections are anticipated in the preapproach stage. Handling objections is a skill requiring a sense of timing, appreciation for the prospect's state of mind, and good communication. Objections also should be handled ethically. Lying or misrepresenting product or service features is an extremely unethical practice.

Close

The *closing* stage in the selling process involves obtaining a purchase commitment from the prospect. This stage is the most important and the most difficult because the salesperson must determine when the prospect is ready to buy. Telltale signals indicating a readiness to buy include body language (prospect re-examines the product or contract closely), statements ("This equipment should reduce our maintenance costs"), and questions ("When could we expect delivery?").

The close itself can take various forms. Several closing techniques are used when a salesperson believes a buyer is about ready to make a purchase: trial close, assumptive close, urgency close, and final close. A *trial close* involves asking the prospect to make a decision on some aspect of the purchase: "Would you prefer the blue or grey model?" The use of a trial close is very common and it can occur at any stage in the selling process. An *assumptive close* involves asking the prospect to consider choices concerning delivery, warranty, or financing terms under the assumption that a sale has been finalized. An *urgency close* is used to commit the prospect quickly by making reference to the timeliness of the purchase: "The low-interest financing ends next week," or "That is the last model we have in stock." Of course, these statements should be used only if they accurately reflect the situation; otherwise, such claims would be unethical. When a prospect is clearly ready to buy, the *final close* is used, and a salesperson asks for the order.

Follow-Up

The selling process does not end with the closing of a sale. Rather, professional selling requires customer follow-up. One marketing authority equated the follow-up with courtship and marriage by observing, "the sale merely consummates the courtship. Then the marriage begins. How good the marriage is depends on how well the relationship is managed."[27] The *follow-up* stage includes making certain the customer's purchase has been properly delivered and installed. Any difficulties experienced with the use of the item are addressed. Attention to this stage of the selling process solidifies the buyer–seller relationship. Moreover, the cost and effort to obtain repeat sales from a satisfied customer is significantly less than that necessary to gain a sale from a new customer.[28] In short, today's satisfied customers become tomorrow's best customers and source of referrals.

Concept Check

1. What are the stages in the personal selling process?
2. Which presentation format is most consistent with the marketing concept? Why?

THE SALES FORCE MANAGEMENT PROCESS

Selling must be managed if it is going to contribute to a firm's overall objectives. Although firms differ in the specifics of how salespeople and the selling effort are managed, the sales force management process is similar across firms. There are three primary functions, as shown in Figure 17-3: sales plan formulation, sales plan implementation, and sales force evaluation.

FIGURE 17-3

The sales force
management process

FIGURE 17-3

The sales force
management process

Sales Plan Formulation

sales plan
Statement describing what
is to be achieved and
where and how the selling
effort of salespeople is to
be directed

Formulating the sales plan is the most basic of the three sales management functions. According to the vice president of the Harris Corporation, a global communications company, "If a company hopes to implement its marketing strategy, it really needs a detailed sales planning process."[29] The **sales plan** is a statement describing what is to be achieved and where and how the selling effort of salespeople is to be directed.

As with any plan, the first step is always to set objectives, including what the overall organization is striving to achieve and down through to what each individual sales group and person are expected to achieve as their contribution to the plan. Objectives include dollar and unit sales, profitability, new accounts to be created, and activities to be performed as part of the plan.

Organizing to implement the plan is a key task. Companies organize sales forces on the basis of geography, by type of customer, by product, and by selling task. Each approach has its merits and limitations; as a result, increasingly today, many firms elect to organize by some combination of these.

major account management
Practice of using team
selling to focus on
important customers so as
to build mutually beneficial,
long-term, cooperative
relationships; also called
key account management

Another trend in sales force organizational structure **major account management**, or *key account management*, the practice of using team selling to focus on important customers so as to build mutually beneficial, long-term, cooperative relationships. Major account management involves teams of sales, service, and often technical personnel who work with purchasing, manufacturing, engineering, logistics, and financial executives in customer organizations. This approach, which often assigns company personnel to a customer account, results in "customer specialists" who can provide exceptional service. Procter & Gamble uses this approach with Wal-Mart as does Black & Decker with Home Depot. Other companies have embraced this practice as described in the accompanying Marketing NewsNet.[30]

In short, there is no one best sales organization for all companies in all situations. Rather, the organization of the sales force should reflect the marketing strategy of the firm. Each year about 10 percent of firms change their sales organizations to implement new marketing strategies.

Sales Plan Implementation

Most managers will agree that the best of plans will not succeed without the right people to implement them, and conversely, even poor plans can be made to work with the right calibre of people. Accordingly, sales force recruitment and selection are considered one of the most crucial tasks of the sales plan implementation stage. Training, compensation, motivation, and supervision are other key tasks in managing the sales force.

Sales Force Evaluation

The final function in the sales management process is evaluating the success of the plan, the work of the sales force, and the activities of individual salespeople. Not only are results an important measure, but the effort that went into achieving the results can be equally important. Techniques that measure both *inputs* (as in activities and efforts) and *outputs* (as in results) are used. Increasingly, with the trend towards relationship selling, an important "output" measure is customer satisfaction. As described in the following section, technology is helping to develop, maintain, and measure customer satisfaction.

MARKETING NEWSNET

CREATING AND SUSTAINING CUSTOMER VALUE THROUGH CROSS-FUNCTIONAL TEAM SELLING

Cross Functional

The day of the lone salesperson calling on a customer is rapidly becoming history. Many companies today are using cross-functional teams of professionals to work with customers to improve relationships, find better ways of doing things, and, of course, create and sustain value for their customers.

Xerox and IBM pioneered cross-functional team selling, but other firms were quick to follow as they spotted the potential to generate value for their customers. Recognizing that corn growers needed a herbicide they could apply less often, a Du Pont team of chemists, sales and marketing executives, and regulatory specialists created just the right product that recorded sales of US$57 million in its first year. Pitney Bowes, Inc., which produces sophisticated computer systems that weigh, rate, and track packages for firms such as UPS and Federal Express, also uses sales teams to meet customer needs. These teams consist of sales personnel, "carrier management specialists," and engineering and administrative executives who continually find ways to improve the technology of shipping goods across town and around the world.

Efforts to create and sustain customer value through cross-functional team selling have become a necessity as customers seek greater value for their money. According to the vice president for procurement of a Fortune 500 company, "Today, it's not just getting the best price but getting the best value—and there are a lot of pieces to value."

Sales Force Automation and Customer Relationship Management

Personal selling and sales force management are undergoing a technological revolution with the integration of sales force automation into customer relationship management processes. In fact, the convergence of computer, information, communication, and Internet/Web technologies has transformed the sales function in many companies and made the promise of customer relationship management a reality. **Sales force automation** is the use of these technologies to make the sales function more effective and efficient. Sales force automation applies to a wide range of activities, including each stage in the personal selling process and management of the sales force itself.

sales force automation
Use of technology to make the sales function more effective and efficient

Sales Force Computerization
Computer technology has become an integral part of field selling. For example, salespeople for Godiva Chocolates use their laptop computers to process orders, plan time usage, forecast sales, and communicate with Godiva personnel and customers. In a department store candy buyer's office, such as The Bay, a salesperson can calculate the order cost (and discount), transmit the order, and obtain a delivery date within minutes from Godiva's order processing department.[31]

Toshiba America Medical System salespeople now use laptop computers with built-in CD-ROM capabilities to provide interactive presentations for their computerized tomography (CT) and magnetic resonance imaging (MRI) scanners. In it the customer sees

Toshiba America Medical System salespeople have found computer technology to be an effective sales tool and training device.

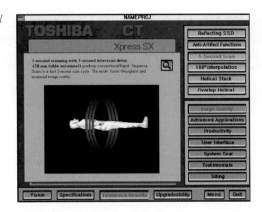
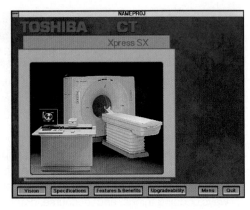

elaborate three-dimensional animations, high-resolution scans, and video clips of the company's products in operation as well as narrated testimonials from satisfied customers. Toshiba has found this application to be effective both for sales presentations and for training its salespeople.[32]

Sales Force Communication

Technology also has changed the way salespeople communicate with customers, other salespeople and sales support personnel, and management. Fax, e-mail, and voice mail are three common communication technologies used by salespeople today. Cellular phone technology, which now allows salespeople to exchange data as well as voice transmissions, is equally popular. Whether traveling or in a customer's office, these technologies provide information at the salesperson's fingertips to answer customer questions and solve problems.

Advances in communication and computer technologies have made possible the mobile and home sales office. Some salespeople now equip minivans with a fully functional desk, swivel chair, light, computer, printer, fax machine, cellular phone, and a satellite dish. If a prospect cannot see the salesperson right away, he or she can go outside and work in the mobile office until the prospect is available. Home offices are now common. A fully equipped home office for a salesperson costs about $8,000 and includes a notebook computer, fax/copier, cellular phone, two phone lines, and office furniture.[33]

Computer and communication technologies have made it possible for salespeople to work out of their homes.

Perhaps the greatest impact on sales force communication is the application of Internet/Web-based technology. Today, salespeople are using their company's intranet for a variety of purposes. They can access their company's intranet to download client material, marketing content, account information, technical papers, and competitive profiles.

Sales force automation is clearly changing how selling is done and how salespeople are managed. As applications increase, sales force automation has the potential to transform selling and sales management in the twenty-first century.

Concept Check

1. What are the primary functions involved in sales force management?
2. What is the link between customer satisfaction and sales force automation?

SUMMARY

1 Direct marketing offers consumers convenience, entertainment, privacy, time savings, low prices, and customer service. Sellers benefit from direct orders, lead generation, and traffic generation.

2 Global opportunities for direct marketing will increase as mail and telephone systems improve worldwide. Consumers' concerns about privacy will be a key issue for direct marketers in the future.

3 Personal selling involves the two-way flow of communication between a buyer and a seller, often in a face-to-face encounter, designed to influence a person's or group's purchase decision. Sales management involves planning the sales program and implementing and controlling the personal-selling effort of the firm.

4 Personal selling plays a major role in a firm's marketing effort. Salespeople occupy a boundary position between buyers and sellers; they *are* the company to many buyers and account for a major cost of marketing in a variety of industries; and they can create value for customers.

5 Two types of personal selling exist: order taking and order getting. They differ in terms of actual selling done and the amount of creativity required to perform the job.

6 The personal selling process, particularly for order getters, is a complex activity involving six stages: prospecting, preapproach, approach, presentation, close, and follow-up.

7 The sales management process consists of three interrelated functions: sales plan formulation, sales plan implementation, and sales force evaluation.

8 A sales plan is a statement describing what is to be achieved and where and how the selling effort of salespeople is to be deployed. Sales planning involves setting objectives, organizing the sales force, and developing account management policies.

9 Effective sales force recruitment and selection efforts, sales training that emphasizes selling skills and product knowledge, and motivation and compensation practices are necessary to successfully implement a sales plan.

10 Salespeople are evaluated using input/output measures that are linked to selling objectives and the sales plan.

11 Sales force automation involves the use of technology designed to make the sales function more effective and efficient.

KEY TERMS AND CONCEPTS

adaptive selling p. 412
consultative selling p. 412
direct orders p. 403
lead generation p. 403
major account management p. 414
order getter p. 407
order taker p. 407

personal selling p. 405
personal selling process p. 409
relationship selling p. 406
sales force automation p. 415
sales force management p. 405
sales plan p. 414
traffic generation p. 403

QUESTIONS: APPLYING MARKETING CONCEPTS AND PERSPECTIVES

1 BMW recently introduced its first sport-utility vehicle, the X5, to compete with other popular 4x4 vehicles such as the Mercedes-Benz M-class and Jeep Grand Cherokee. Design a direct marketing program to generate *(a)* leads, *(b)* traffic in dealerships, and *(c)* direct orders.

2 Develop a privacy policy for database managers that provides a balance of consumer and seller perspectives. How would you encourage voluntary compliance with your policy? What methods of enforcement would you recommend?

3 Jane Dawson is a new sales representative for Scotia McLeod, a leading financial-services provider. In searching for clients, Jane purchased a mailing list of subscribers to the *National Post* and called them all regarding their interest in discount brokerage services. She asked if they have any stocks and if they have a regular broker. Those people without a regular broker were asked their investment needs. Two days later Jane called back with investment advice and asked if they would like to open an account. Identify each of Jane Dawson's actions in terms of the steps of selling.

4 For the first 50 years of business, the Montreal Carpet Company produced carpets for residential use. The sales force was structured geographically. In the past five years, a large percentage of carpet sales has been to industrial users, hospitals, schools, and architects. The company also has broadened its product line to include area rugs, Oriental carpets, and wall-to-wall carpeting. Is the present sales-force structure appropri-ate, or would you recommend an alternative?

5 Where would you place each of the following sales jobs on the order-taker/order-getter continuum shown below, and why? *(a)* Burger King counter clerk, *(b)* automobile insurance salesperson, *(c)* IBM computer salesperson, *(d)* life insurance salesperson, and *(e)* shoe salesperson.

Order taker   Order getter

6 Listed below are two different firms. Which compensation plan would you recommend for each firm, and what reasons would you give for your recommendations? *(a)* A newly formed company that sells lawn care equipment on a door-to-door basis directly to consumers; and *(b)* Maple Leaf Foods Inc., which sells heavily advertised products in supermarkets by having the sales force call on these stores and arrange shelves, set up displays, and make presentations to store buying committees.

7 Suppose someone said to you, "The only real measure of a salesperson is the amount of sales produced." How might you respond?

8 A not-for-profit organization that has traditionally raised funds by going door to door decides to begin using other forms of direct marketing. Suggest what forms they should use, some reasons why this may be a good decision, and what benefits it may bring to the organization.

DISCUSSION FORUM

Imagine that you are the president of a small chain (30 stores) of electronics outlets. You decide to set up a training program for all of your new sales staff, and you want to make sure that you not only teach them good selling skills, but that you also motivate them to represent your company well and have fun at the same time.

1 Outline the information you would present to them in describing the steps of the selling process, and explain why each step is important.

2 Sales sometimes is not regarded as a good career, and salespeople sometimes are not thought of in a positive light. Suggest why this may be some people's perspective, and how you will make sure that your sales team does not hold this view.

3 Identify what your salespeople can do to ensure that they are respected by their customers.

4 Suggest what professional organizations (Sales & Marketing & Executives International, Canadian Marketing Association) can do to raise the profile and the respect of the sales profession.

INTERNET EXERCISE

A unique resource for the latest developments in personal-selling and sales management is the Sales Marketing Network (SMN) at www.info-now.com. SMN provides highly readable reports on a variety of topics including many discussed in this chapter, such as telemarketing, motivation, sales training, and sales management. These reports contain concise overviews, definitions, statistics, and reviews of critical issues. They also include references to additional information and links to related

www.mcgrawhill.ca/college/thecore

material elsewhere on the SMN site. Registration (at no cost) is required to view some of the reports.

Visit the SMN site and do the following:

1 Select a chapter topic, and update the statistics for, say, sales-training costs or the popularity of different sales force incentives.

2 Select a topic covered in the chapter, such as telemarketing, and summarize the critical issues identified for this practice.

VIDEO CASE 17

REEBOK: RELATIONSHIP SELLING AND CUSTOMER VALUE

"I think face-to-face selling is the most important and exciting part of this whole job. It's not writing the sales reports. It's not analyzing trends and forecasting. It's the two hours that you have to try to sell the buyer your products in a way that's profitable for both you and the retailer," relates Robert McMahon, key account sales representative for Reebok. McMahon's job encompasses a myriad of activities, from supervising other sales representatives to attending companywide computer training sessions to monitoring competitors' activities. But it's the actual selling that is most appealing to McMahon. "That's the challenging, stimulating part of the job. Selling to the buyer is a different challenge every day. Every sales call, as well as you may have pre-planned it, can change based on shifts and trends in the market. So you need to be able to react to those changes and really think on your feet in front of the buyer."

REEBOK—HOT ON NIKE'S HEELS IN THE ATHLETIC SHOEAND APPAREL MARKET

Reebok, with global sales of close to US$3.5 billion, is the second-largest athletic-shoe and sports-apparel manufacturer after the market leader, Nike. There are dozens of other competitors, but none come close in terms of sales or size of product lines. In addition to its own brand of shoes and apparel, Reebok also sells the Greg Norman line of casual wear and accessories; Ralph Lauren and Polo athletic and fashion footwear; Rockport casual, dress, and performance footwear; and Weebok shoes and apparel for infants and toddlers. The Reebok sporting goods line remains the flagship brand, though, and distinguishes itself in the market through the DMX cushioning technology in its footwear, which it features in its Classic, Rbk, and Vector premium collections. Reebok concentrates its resources on getting its footwear and sporting goods gear into a diversified mix of distribution channels such as athletic footwear specialty stores, department stores, and large sporting goods stores. Reebok is unique in that it emphasizes relationships with the retailers as an important part of its marketing strategy. As an employee at MVP Sports, one of Reebok's major retailers, puts it, "Reebok is the only company that comes in on a regular basis and gives us information. Nike comes in once in a great while. New Balance comes in every six months. Saucony has come in twice. That's been it. Reebok comes in every month to update us on new information and new products. They tell us about the technology so we can tell the customers." Says Laurie

Sipples, Vector representative for Reebok, "There's a partnership that exists between Reebok and an account like MVP Sports that sets us apart. That relationship is a great asset that Reebok has because the retailer feels more in touch with us than other brands."

THE SELLING PROCESS AT REEBOK

Selling at Reebok includes three elements—building trust between the salesperson and the retailer, providing enough information to the retailer for them to be successful selling Reebok products, and finally supporting the retailer after the sale. Sean Neville, senior vice president and general manager of Reebok North America, explains, "Our goal is not to sell to the retailer; our goal is ultimately to sell to the consumer, and so we use the retailer as a partner. The salespeople are always keeping their eyes open and thinking like the retailer and selling to the consumer."

Reebok sells in teams that consist of the account representatives, who do the actual selling to the retailer, and the Vector representatives, who spend their time in the stores training the store salespeople and reporting trends back to the account manager. The selling teams are organized geographically so that the salespeople live and work in the area they are selling in. This allows the sales team to understand the consumer intuitively. Neville suggests that if you have someone from one city fly to another and try to tell someone on the streets of that city what is happening from a trends standpoint and what products to purchase, it is very difficult.

On average, Reebok salespeople spend 70 percent of their time preparing for a sale and 30 percent of their time actually selling. The sales process at Reebok typically follows the six steps of the personal selling process identified in Figure 17–2: (1) Reebok identifies the outlets it would like to carry its athletic gear; (2) the sales force prepares for the presentation by familiarizing themselves with the store and its customers; (3) a Reebok representative approaches the prospect and suggests a meeting and presentation; (4) as the presentation begins, the salesperson summarizes relevant market conditions and consumer trends to demonstrate Reebok's commitment to a partnership with the retailer, states what he or she hopes to get out of the sales meeting, explains how the products work, and reinforces the benefits of Reebok products; (5) the salesperson engages in an action close (gets a signed document or a firm confirmation of the sale); and (6) later, various members of the sales force

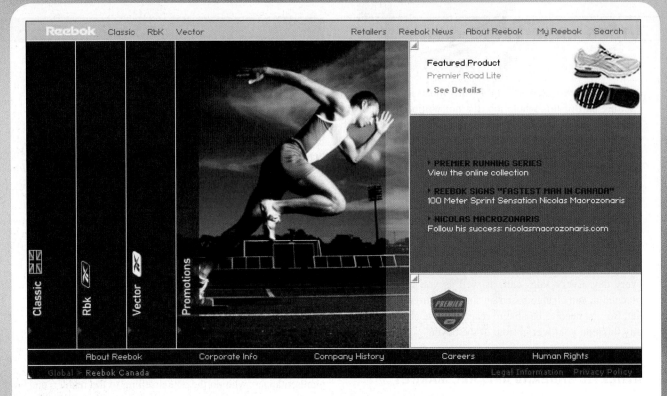

Reebok   Classic   RbK   Vector   Retailers   Reebok News   About Reebok   My Reebok   Search

Featured Product
Premier Road Lite
▸ See Details

▸ PREMIER RUNNING SERIES
View the online collection

▸ REEBOK SIGNS "FASTEST MAN IN CANADA"
100 Meter Sprint Sensation Nicolas Macrozonaris

▸ NICOLAS MACROZONARIS
Follow his success: nicolasmacrozonaris.com

Classic   Rbk   Vector   Promotions

About Reebok   Corporate Info   Company History   Careers   Human Rights

Global ▸ Reebok Canada   Legal Information   Privacy Policy

frequently visit the retailer to provide assistance and monitor consumer preferences.

THE SALES MANAGEMENT PROCESS AT REEBOK

The sales teams at Reebok are organized on the basis of Reebok's three major distribution channels: athletic specialty stores, sporting goods stores, and department stores. The smaller stores have sales teams assigned to them according to geographical location. The sales force is then further broken down into footwear and apparel teams. The sales force is primarily organized by distribution channel because this is most responsive to customer needs and wants. The salespeople are compensated on both a short-term and long-term basis. In the short term, salespeople are paid based on sales results and profits for the current quarter as well as forecasting. In the long term, they are compensated based on their teamwork and team-building efforts. As Neville explains, "Money is typically fourth or fifth on the list of pure motivation. Number one is recognition for a job well done. And that drives people to succeed." Management at Reebok is constantly providing feedback to the sales force acknowledging their success, not just during annual reviews, and Neville feels this is the key to the high level of motivation, energy, and excitement that exists in the sales force at Reebok.

WHAT'S NEW ON THE HORIZON FOR THE SALES FORCE AT REEBOK?

Reebok has issued laptop computers to its entire sales force that enable the salespeople to check inventories in the warehouses, make sure orders are being shipped on time, and even enter orders while they're out in the field. Reebok is also focusing more on relationship selling. McMahon describes his relationship with a major buyer as "one of trust and respect. It's gotten to the point now where we're good friends. We go to a lot of sporting events together, which I think really helps." Another recent innovation is for the sales force to incentivize the stores' sales clerks. For instance, whoever sells the most pairs of Reebok shoes in a month will get tickets to a concert or a football game.

Questions

1   How does Reebok create customer value for its major accounts through relationship selling?

2   How does Reebok utilize team selling to provide the highest level of customer value possible to its major accounts?

3   Is Reebok's sales force organized based on geography, customer, or product?

4   What are some ways Reebok's selling processes are changing due to technical advancements?

Postscript

A Look Back and a View Forward

We have covered the spectrum of marketing as we worked through Chapters 1 through 17. In this Postscript, we review what we studied, and look at how the marketer pulls all of this together to make the marketing function work efficiently and effectively. And then we take a glimpse at the shape of marketing in the future.

Describing the Marketing World

Chapter 1 was our introduction to marketing: we looked at an overview of marketing, we identified basic marketing concepts, and we introduced a marketing model to help explain the marketing process as well as how the various elements interact. Today, marketing goes beyond merely satisfying customer needs and wants—every firm tries to do that. Marketing is not only satisfying customers; with marketing, firms try to wow them. Keys to success lie in delivering value, doing it better than competitors, *and* building long-term relationships with customers—relationships that are mutually beneficial both to customers and to the firm. At the same time, the firm has to deliver value to the other key groups in its business environment, and do so in an ethical and socially responsible manner. All this is happening in a constantly changing business environment—both inside the firm and the outside marketing environment. The stage is set for marketing details!

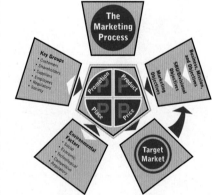

That All-Important Planning Process

Successful businesses plan and operate using carefully crafted strategies, and marketing is a key component of these plans. Chapter 2 introduced the concept of strategy and explained how strategies are formulated as a part of the strategic marketing process. Three phases—planning, implementation, and control—were detailed. A company has to have a clear idea of why it is in business, and what it wants to achieve. The importance and role of a business mission, as well as vision and value statements, were outlined. We also discussed how companies organize themselves and evaluate their various business units, using techniques such as portfolio and market-product analysis. Then we talked about linking marketing objectives, marketing strategies, and marketing plans, and their fit within the corporate planning process. Good marketers are good planners!

Bringing all of this together as a cohesive and compressive strategy is covered in Appendix A, which lays out the steps for preparing a marketing plan.

The Marketing Climate

Chapter 3 dealt with the marketing environment and how marketers must read, interpret, and act on the information they collect. Success in business has been compared to surfing in the ocean: We need good waves to surf properly, and the trick is to choose the right waves; we need more than one wave to keep surfing; and we need to be ready for the waves when they are upon us.

The external marketing environment goes well with the surfing analogy. Waves are like changes: some are enormous and others never make it through, but the important thing is that there are always waves, and many of them. Some waves are useful, so we regard them as opportunities, and others are potentially dangerous and should be considered threats. Business waves come in many forms: from society in general in the form of demands, from groups of customers whose wants and needs are changing, from the competition (both local and global), from legislation at all levels of government (both at home and in other countries).

Then there are economic considerations. Economic forces are having an increasing impact, and not just changes to the local or home country economy, but changes in other markets and other regions of the world that affect the Canadian marketplace and firms. In the past, some firms could exist and comfortably do business just in local markets, facing competition from local or perhaps larger North American firms. But today's reality—including the growth of technology—presents us with generally stronger and more intense global competition. Technology has a dual impact both in how companies employ it, and in the readiness and willingness of consumers to accept and purchase it.

Doing it Right

Marketing is very much in the public eye, and part of the image a company creates is reflected by the company's ethics and how socially responsible it is. Society values companies that are good corporate citizens, that is, companies that "give back" to society. Consumers, too, have ethical and moral responsibilities in the marketplace.

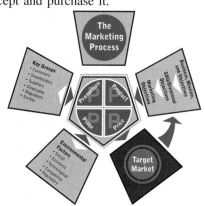

Who Is Marketing Aimed At?

In order to satisfy customer wants and needs, marketers need to know what makes them tick! Understanding what influences and drives those needs and wants is important. It is also necessary to be able to follow, help and influence customers at various stages of the purchase decision process that they go through. Consumers have different needs and wants from organizational or business customers; these two distinct groups function in very different business environments. These aspects were covered in depth in Chapters 5 and 6. As the world becomes more globalized, new marketing thinking is required. We talked about how companies approach and respond to market opportunities in the global arena outside of Canada in Chapter 7.

Information Time!

Marketers are continually faced with challenges, opportunities, threats, and uncertainties; collecting and analyzing information helps them understand a situation and aids in minimizing risk.

To be able to understand customers and the market environment in which they exist requires that information (marketing research) be collected in a planned and systematic manner—this was the message in Chapter 8.

Targeting the Market

It's time to be selective and specific. The marketer has to make a difficult choice, deciding what customers to target and serve better than the competition, and doing so well enough to achieve the objectives set out in the marketing plan. There are many opportunities for any good or service; the challenge is to find those customers that need and would prefer the products. Next question: can the company fulfill these needs with company resources, that is, facilities, technology, finances, people, and partners (suppliers and channel intermediaries)? All this has to be done with an eye to being consistent with the company's mission, values, and corporate objectives—not an easy task! Most firms select several target markets to pursue with a portfolio of products—a single product never meets all the needs of the mass market. Target marketing, market segmentation, and market-product grids as explained in Chapter 9 are key tools for the marketer. After selecting the target markets, and using the marketing research collected, the challenge is to find a way to win over customers. This is referred to as "position-

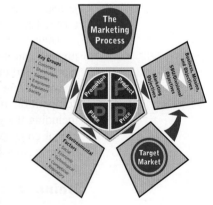

ing" the product in the minds of customers so that they would purchase it over a competing product. Differentiation—setting products apart from the competition—is closely related to positioning.

Knowing the customer, and how to position and differentiate the products, allows the firm to begin the detailed planning to get the right *product*, at the right *price* and the right time and *place*, *promoted* the right way to customers. These four elements—known as the marketing mix—change over time, from the moment the product is introduced in the market, to when market demand grows and matures, to when demand eventually tapers off. Product, place, price, and promotion have to work together and be carefully synchronized in order for the company to succeed. We segment a market to determine what parts of the market can best be served; for the target markets we select, each one warrants its own specific marketing mix.

Managing the Marketing Mix

Details on developing each component of the marketing mix are covered in Chapters 10 through 17. Marketing strategies and marketing mixes vary according to whether the firm is planning new market entries, entering existing growth markets, or pursuing mature and declining markets. Perhaps the biggest challenge facing most firms as we move forward is developing marketing strategies for the new, changing economy.

What Is Marketed?

Product is the generic term we used throughout the text to refer to both goods and services. As services play an increasing role in our economy and they become an integral part of the satisfaction solutions offered by firms, marketers need to understand the very important differences between goods and services, and the changes in marketing strategy required for each. Back to our surfing example, many of the waves that the firm decides to go after invariably require a change in strategy. Firms will usually have a range of products that they offer to their various markets. Developing new products and improving others is key to a company's future, no product lives forever, and the marketer cannot expect to survive without new developments. Coming up with a new successful product takes time, employs lots of resources, and requires research and a systematic new product development process. Beginning with

idea generation, and ending with a detailed marketing plan to launch the product, is a difficult task. As a result, many firms simply resort to product modifications, hoping their existing concepts will live a little longer. The product life cycle shows us how a particular type of product evolves, and how the other components of the marketing mix are modified and blended as the product moves through its life cycle. Branding plays a pivotal role in a product's success, and branding strategies form part of the firm's overall marketing strategies. Nowhere is branding more visible than on packaging, and in today's fiercely competitive business environment, packaging itself can be critical to success. Global brands of yesteryear are still in the forefront in today's markets, testimony to the power of good branding.

Generating Revenues

Pricing is always a challenge for marketers. Many factors must be considered when setting prices. The business environment is dynamic and always in a state of change, so pricing must be continually examined to find out whether there is a need for change. How a change in pricing impacts the overall marketing strategy must also be considered. Chapter 12 covers these aspects in detail.

Getting the Product to the Consumer

Chapters 13 and 14 detail how to develop a distribution strategy and introduce us to the modern world of retailing in both in-store and nonstore. Nowhere is the changing face of marketing more visible to consumers than in retailing. Increasing use of technology is making retailing more convenient and tailored to consumer lifestyles, and is creating an exciting shopping experience. Behind the scenes, how products are moved from producer to consumers is undergoing equally radical change. Computer, communications, and Internet technology are allowing products to move faster and more efficiently to market via multiple distribution channels. We just have to look at the incredible growth of courier services and companies such FedEx and UPS to see this happening.

Getting the Word Out

A lot of people seem to think that marketing is advertising, as advertising is one of the most visible parts of the marketing toolkit, but it is only one of the tools. Promotion—encompassing all of the ways that a company communicates about the product—is covered in depth in Chapters 15 through 17. Here we see radical change with the convergence of marketing channels and distribution channels. We see the power of technology and changing consumer acceptance and demands. The dominance of traditional media such as print, broadcast, and outdoor is being challenged as new forms of media evolve. In many cases we see these media being used as part of an integrated marketing communications strategy designed to step consumers through their purchase decision process and to keep them as loyal and active customers. Interactivity is becoming a key tool for marketers and a key demand by customers. Management's need for measurable results is driving a shift in emphasis towards database marketing as a means to drive customized promotional efforts. With today's technology it is possible to measure both the extent and speed of the results of specific marketing tactics—a major step ahead from the usual debate over how effective conventional advertising really is. The role of personal selling and public relations is still important. But their roles, too, are changing, as they become part of an integrated marketing communications strategy. Integrated communications is the direction for promotion's future.

Summing It All Up

Marketing is a complex field. To do it successfully, the marketer needs to be part analyst, part innovator, part organizer, and part fortune teller. Planning, organizing, and controlling work is a continuous loop. Marketers are involved in a dynamic and constantly changing world of thought and action. What is a marketer to do to keep ahead of his/her game? Understand well, plan incisively, do (and do well), monitor carefully, evaluate and re-evaluate honestly, and keep eyes and ears open.

THE FUTURE

Where is marketing going in the future? How far into the future can we see? What will be the key directions to take? Ask a group of senior executives what they see as the future of marketing, key issues and trends, and you will likely get a variety of responses. There will be some ideas common to all, but when it comes to specifics, those will, driven by interest and industry environment, be very subjective and very different. We cannot accurately predict the future, but we can try.

Marketing's Position in the Business Galaxy

Marketing has not always been well represented in companies at the senior management level, that is, it does not always play a major role in management. Marketers often interact very little with their colleagues in finance, engineering, or even sales. Contrast this with the fact that marketing, done well, is part of the vision that leads a company.

So marketing should be the responsibility of the whole organization, not just a few people in the department with the name "Marketing." Good, solid marketing is insightful, strategic, accountable, and dynamic. Marketing in the future needs to be an integral part of all workings of the organization, and the marketing people will interact with and work in concert with colleagues from product development, research, finance, and technology. Senior management will include more and more marketing faces as part of their team, as marketing moves to a new prominence and legitimacy. You will be able to see and feel the passion, the excitement and the vision of marketing, throughout the organization.

The specific case of the business-to-business (B2B) market suggests that the future will see even more change than will happen in the consumer market. In the B2B arena, marketing is less of a visible force—practised more by default than by purposeful action. Brand and product managers are few and spread thin in the B2B world. They will learn from the experience of the consumer market, and marketing will become more established as part of each business's planning processes.

Marketing Tools in Practice

Smarter marketing will evolve with better use of some of the available tools. Understanding consumers is an important route to serving them better, and knowing them is part science, part art. On the science side, using analytical tools to analyze and predict customer behaviour and to evaluate new potential customers is powerful, and not as complex as it seems. Marketers will see these tools as strategic advantages and use them to their benefit.

Research can take many different forms and can be quite costly. Finding consumers to study—and securing their cooperation—is an ongoing challenge. At the same time, the results of research are growing in importance. Research techniques will change and adapt. Customer insights that companies once got from focus groups may be available through offering online product forums where customers can participate in weblogs or chat with other customers.

Marketers often set a price for a product without a solid rationale for doing so. Pricing models will increasingly allow marketers to determine the best price, considering all of the key aspects and factors that are related. Predicting the future is an imprecise and risky activity. But savvy marketers will not only produce forecasts of what they expect to do and how they anticipate the market will respond, but they will also come back and evaluate their performance against their plans. This is in sharp contrast to the current situation, where the forecasts are rarely compared with what actually happened.

Marketing plans may seem like academic tools that fall under the nice-to-do-but-not-essential category. Diligent and focused marketers will have not only a clear, but brief, marketing plan, but they will also think of contingencies and fallback procedures in case the first initiatives prove unworkable. Communication of the plan throughout the organization secures the buy-in and cooperation of all!

Developments in Marketing Media

The media used for communications are growing in number, and the use of media is evolving. TiVo (interactive television), the consumer pursuit of other interactive media experiences, and the growth in the magazine market are forces we can expect to see more of in the future.

Without a doubt, the Internet is one of the most powerful and notable forces on the media landscape. With it come many changes. Branding products and services is different via the Internet than it is with traditional media. Marketers are forced to think differently when marketing online—and watch for more change in the future. What exactly is so unique about the Internet as a marketing tool? No one would argue that it is a mass medium, but one that operates very distinctly from television or other mass formats. We can not describe it as a broadcast medium, partly because it is interactive. It is a service medium, and using it for advertising is not working particularly well so far. Marketers will learn to use it more effectively as the Internet tells them what works—in the form of results—what does not work, and when to change the approach. Print media became truly effective many decades after it was first introduced, and so did television and radio. For the Internet, it could take 10 years or more for it to be used to its full potential as a promotional forum.

Wireless technology is a hot topic among marketers, and it will evolve into a more powerful marketing venue. The key challenge is to engage customers and to be relevant to them. Here's the climate marketers are working in: A million promotional messages hit the average North American every year. Can a consumer process and assimilate even 10 percent of this mindclutter? Wireless technology is predicted to be one route to breaking through the clutter and noise. We think of it currently as cellular telephones and PDAs, but wireless will be much more as it begins to establish links to automobiles, home appliances, checkout counters in stores, and machines in the work environment, as well as tracking and following us around the globe!

Changing Customer Perspectives

We have gone through the stages of "The customer is king," "The customer is always right," and "Give the customer whatever s/he wants, when, how, and where s/he wants it." This thinking is undergoing a change. Marketing's focus on one-to-one marketing is very narrow and not feasible for most companies—it is simply uneconomic and hugely complicated. Consumers have been viewed as product-hungry creatures, consuming more and more of the market's offerings every year, and eager to spend, spend, spend. We are about to see an evolution in this thinking, as consumers decide that more is not necessarily better. Life balance is a becoming a key goal; being stressed, stretched, time-poor, and overworked is forcing many to re-evaluate their priorities. Marketing to the materialists is giving way to marketing to the reflective and mindful. This shift in values should open some marketer's eyes and alter the way they promote products.

Consumers like to provide input, and they like to be involved. They have a unique window on products targeted to them. In the future, marketers will engage them more as part of the development process. Asking customers for their feedback, insights, preferences, and suggestions will provide a rich source of information. Putting customers in touch with other customers will foster dialogue and an exchange of ideas; the marketer will analyze the interaction and information flow for nuggets of useable data and ideas.

Ethnic marketing has been in the marketing spotlight for many years; target markets are evolving, and the ethnic concept is changing. The cultural mosaic that is Canada suggests that our nation no longer has a definable mainstream market. We will strive to attract well-defined market segments. These segments may have ethnicity as one of their defining characteristics, but it will be one of many. Marketers will learn to target with more precision and analysis. Good targeting and razor-sharp segmentation equals cost efficiency, and money talks!

Marketing Strategy

A lot of marketing we see is tactical, not strategic. When a company runs a new ad simply because the competitor is running new ads, this is a gut reaction—a desperation tactic—as opposed to a strategic move. At best, the tactic works in the very short run, but it is not a profit generator, nor a wise move. Marketers will learn the strategy game, and the moves to make it *their* game. They will think long term, be proactive, coordinate, plan, and strategize—they will not act reactively and at the spur-of-the-moment.

Part of the strategy game is having partners, that is, companies with complementary products or target markets, or with some synergistic offering. Even huge multinational firms develop strategic partners to their mutual benefit. The marketer of the future will see the wisdom in generating liaisons with firms with a similar vision and similar interests.

Promoting a great product without an infrastructure is like diving off a diving board without knowing how to swim. Marketers are moving towards ensuring that all the pieces of the organizational puzzle are in place—company structure, research, financing, promotion, feedback, targeting, and the list goes on—so that products have a strong launch pad from which to be commercialized. A product that is someone's brainchild, with no backdrop of support, will not become the market darling.

Integration—making all the messages from the company tell the same story and present the same mental photo—reinforces consumer mindshare. Marketers are moving towards integrated marketing communications (IMC)—having a theme that runs through all of its promotional vehicles. And just what are those promotional vehicles? Ads, posters, signs on company trucks, coupons, flyers, and brochures—these may be obvious. Salespeople's messages, websites, packaging, and others are also tools to carry the consistent story. IMC is a new mantra for the wise marketer.

Promotion is a marketing strategy, and it should be a prominent force. Some of the new, hot, and powerful tactics must include guerrilla marketing, viral marketing, buzz marketing, experiential marketing, offline events, and ideas to generate word-of-mouth. Winning promotional twists include ideas to stretch brands and expand distribution, which help a product line to grow and benefit from proven past successes. Engaging the interest and buy-in of young people is an excellent long-term strategy; it harnesses the strength of establishing buying power early and stamps the company and brand name indelibly on the impressionable minds of younger consumers.

Canada—A Global Marketing Force?

We, in Canada, have the 35th-largest population in the world—relatively small, considering the physical size of the country and our capabilities as an affluent and advanced society. Here's the problem: We as Canadians are not particularly savvy marketers. Why? The relative size of the population is one reason why we are not the best marketers. There are other reasons, too. Many more sophisticated markets—for example, England, Japan, and the U.S.—have more of a marketing machine in process and have created a global image for both their country and the products that they offer.

In Canada, many international businesses pepper the landscape. Yes, we do have some flagship Canadian firms, and some with international acclaim. We also have some excellent marketers; many have been showcased in this book. In general, Canadians are modest and conservative self-promoters, and this tends not to register on the international radar screen. True, a significant chunk of business is conducted from head offices located in other countries. Many of the global firms that are Canadian are not of the scale of the major multinationals. Here's an opportunity for Canada, and one that may be exploited in the near future—or it may not—this is hard to call.

We operate in an experience economy—70 percent of the jobs in this country are in the service sector, and this figure is projected to rise to 80 percent in the next 10 years. Marketing is uniquely positioned to work in a service context. Canada used to be a resource-driven economy, exporting more natural resources than finished goods. As a well-educated society, we do have expertise and skills that we can market globally. The reality of declining non-renewable resources and higher manufacturing costs leaves us little choice. Canada needs to become a well-marketed, service-driven economy in order to maintain its high standard of living.

Are Marketers Listening?

We live in complex times. They will increasingly become more complex and cluttered in the next few years. Change is the only predictable force. Keeping aware of trends, customer outlooks, and competitor strategies and activities keeps a company operating with eyes wide open. Listening to the market is a must. Listening to customers ranks up there, too. Firms that encourage feedback, are responsive to criticism, and act on customer comments will be seen as trustworthy and ethical, and will gain loyalty, as well as the benefit of good word-of-mouth promotion. Marketers increasingly realize that a customer who takes the time to complain is a force that likely can be converted into a fan; it is the quiet ones, spreading their negative sentiments to friends and family, who damage the marketer's image. Solution? Listen, welcome criticism, and create several ways to encourage and capture information shared by customers.

Measuring Up

For some marketing activities, it is difficult to determine and quantify the value delivered in comparison to the dollars spent. Sales are one—but only one—measure of success. Now we are moving towards a world where practitioners have to supply more proof that marketing expenditures pay off. In the accountable future, it will not be only sales that are used as a success indicator. Financial managers and CEOs will want to see the return on financial investment, and along with it an indication of the process undertaken to get there. Quantifiable results will be linked to future budgets.

Marketers are measuring the value of their brands, and assigning them a dollar value just like they would a building or a piece of machinery. In the next five years, we can expect to see brand equity appear as an item on the balance sheet. It is already a common practice in Europe.

Marketing Themes

The next generation of marketing executions will sport some of these directions and themes:

- Firms will market not only to external targets but also to internal ones; a pumped employee walking around as an advocate of a product is a powerful marketing agent.
- Marketing is a well-organized discipline. The fundamentals work, if the marketers use them properly—and if they keep it simple.
- It is impossible to be all things to all people. Winners don't confuse their audience; they do fewer things, for specific groups, and they do them well.
- Consider what the company has to offer as concepts and benefits, not as physical products—this is a key to understanding and satisfying customers.
- Different marketing solutions work for different companies—regardless of how powerful a tool is, it may not be appropriate for some applications. Marketers will have to make sure their efforts are planned and executed in the context of the industry and firm they are marketing in.
- In a very complex and crowded world, good market segmentation and research-fuelled product development get top marks.
- Building and maintaining trust forges solid bonds with customers.
- Three key words to guide marketing activities: plan, implement, control.
- Everything the marketer puts out must pass the ethics test; good marketing corporate citizens breed loyalty.
- Convergence—logical integration of technologies and media—will bring unprecedented change.

- Innovation and invention will be fast and nimble; the failed product graveyard is full of great ideas that never took off or were not well executed. Continual innovation is the food of the future for successful companies.
- To be heard and to be relevant, marketers will talk consumers' language, using their lexicon and talking in casual, intimate, direct, and personal speak.
- To achieve customer response, marketing offers will be compelling and relevant. Meaningful themes include: make the world better, improve quality of life, be a good corporate citizen, understand the customer, create a truly better future, make the customer feel good about what they are and what they buy, and connect with their passions.

Your Future in Marketing

Marketing is growing as an industry, and it offers exciting, interesting, and fulfilling careers. We have offered a glimpse into some of the drivers of the future. Watch how it unfolds!

If you have not already considered a career in marketing, perhaps it is time to do so. Sustained success in any business is not possible without effective marketing, so why not be a part of the team that will ensure success and become a proactive marketer.

GLOSSARY

above-, at-, or below-market pricing Pricing based on market price.

accelerated development The second stage of the retail life cycle, characterized by rapid increases in market share and profitability.

adaptive selling A need-satisfaction sales presentation that involves adjusting the presentation to fit the selling situation.

administered vertical marketing systems Achieve coordination at successive stages of production and distribution by the size and influence of one channel member rather than through ownership.

adoption Through a favourable experience on the first trial, a consumer's repeated purchase and use of the product or brand.

advertising Any paid form of nonpersonal communication about an organization, good, service, or idea by an identified sponsor.

advertising media Any media in which advertising can be placed, including newspapers, magazines, radio, television, and the Internet.

advocacy advertisements Institutional advertisements that state the position of a company on an issue.

agent An intermediary who serves primarily as the independent selling arm of producers and represents a producer to users.

allowances Reductions from list or quoted prices to buyers for performing some activity.

all-you-can-afford budgeting Allocating funds to promotion only after all other budget items are covered.

anchor stores Well-known national or regional stores located in regional shopping centres.

approach stage In the personal selling process, the initial meeting between the salesperson and prospect, where the objectives are to gain the prospect's attention, stimulate interest, and build the foundation for the sales presentation itself and the basis for a working relationship.

aspiration group Consumer reference group that a person wishes to be a member of or wishes to be identified with, such as a professional society.

assumptive close Involves asking the prospect to consider choices concerning delivery, warranty, or financing terms under the assumption that a sale has been finalized.

atmosphere A store's ambiance or setting.

attitude Tendency to respond to something in a consistently favourable or unfavourable way.

average revenue The average amount of money received for selling one unit of a product.

awareness The consumer's ability to recognize and remember the product or brand name.

baby boomers The generation of children born between 1946 and 1964.

back translation Retranslating a word or phrase into the original language by a different interpreter to catch errors.

backward integration Practice in the corporate vertical marketing system in which a retailer also owns a manufacturing operation.

bait-and-switch advertising An advertising practice in which a company shows a product that it has no intention of selling to lure the customer into the store and sell him a higher-priced item.

barter The practice of exchanging goods and services for other goods and services rather than for money.

behavioural learning The process of developing automatic responses to a situation built up through repeated exposure to it.

beliefs A consumer's perception of how a product or brand performs on different attributes; these are based on personal experience, advertising, and discussions with other people.

blanket branding (see *multiproduct branding*)

brand equity The added value a given brand name gives to a product beyond the functional benefits provided.

brand extension The practice of using a current brand name to enter a completely different product class.

branding Activity in which an organization uses a name, phrase, design, or symbols, or combination of these to identify its products and distinguish them from those of competitors.

brand loyalty Favourable attitude toward and consistent purchase of a single brand over time.

brand name Any word, "device" (design, shape, sound, or color), or combination of these used to distinguish a seller's goods or services.

brand personality A set of human characteristics associated with a brand name.

breadth of product line The variety of different items a store carries.

break-even analysis A technique that analyzes the relationship between total revenue and total cost to determine profitability at various levels of output.

break-even chart A graphic presentation of the break-even analysis.

break-even point (BEP) Quantity at which total revenue and total cost are equal and beyond which profit occurs.

brokers Independent firms or individuals whose main function is to bring buyers and sellers together to make sales.

build-to-order (BTO) Manufacturing a product only when there is an order from a customer.

bundle pricing The marketing of two or more products in a single "package" price.

business analysis Involves specifying the features of the product and the marketing strategy needed to commercialize it and making necessary financial projections.

business analysis stage Step 4 of the new-product process, which involves specifying the product features and marketing strategy and making necessary financial projections to commercialize a product.

business culture Comprises the effective rules of the game, the boundaries between competitive and unethical behaviour, and the codes of conduct in business dealings.

business firm A privately owned organization that serves its customers in order to earn a profit.

business goods Products that are purchased by organizations, and that are used for resale, as inputs for further production or in the operation of the organization.

business marketing The marketing of products to companies, governments, or not-for-profit organizations for use in the creation of goods and services that they then produce and market to others.

business plan A road map for the entire organization for a specific future period of time, such as one year or five years.

business portfolio analysis Analysis of a firm's strategic business units (SBUs) as though they were a collection of separate investments.

business unit An organization that markets a set of related products to a clearly defined group of customers.

business unit goal A performance target the business unit seeks to reach to achieve its mission.

business unit level Level at which business unit managers set the direction for their products and markets.

buy classes Three types of organizational buying situations: new buy, straight rebuy, and modified rebuy.

buyers Role in the buying centre with formal authority and responsibility to select the supplier and negotiate the terms of the contract.

buyer turnover How often new buyers enter the market to buy a product.

buying centre The group of people in an organization who participate in the buying process and share common goals, risks, and knowledge important to a purchase decision.

buying committee A very formal buying centre often found in large multi-store chain resellers such as Sears, 7-Eleven, or Safeway; see *buying centre*.

buying criteria The factors buying organizations use when evaluating a potential supplier and what it wants to sell.

buying situation Variables-such as benefits sought or usage—used to segment consumer markets.

buzz Word-of-mouth behaviour in market space.

canned sales presentation A memorized, standardized message conveyed to every prospect.

capacity management Integrating the service component of the marketing mix with efforts to influence consumer demand.

case allowance A trade-oriented sales promotion giving a discount on each case ordered during a specific time period.

cash and carry wholesaler A limited-service merchant wholesaler that takes title to merchandise but sells only to buyers who call on it, pay cash for merchandise, and furnish its own transportation for merchandise.

cash discount Price reduction to encourage retailers to pay their bills quickly.

category killers Specialty discount outlets that focus on one type of product, such as electronics or business supplies, at very competitive prices. They often dominate the market.

cause-related marketing Occurs when the charitable contributions of a firm are tied directly to the customer revenues produced through the promotion of one of its products.

caveat emptor The legal concept of "let the buyer beware" that was pervasive in business culture before the 1960s.

central business district The oldest retail setting, the community's downtown area.

channel captain A marketing channel member that coordinates, directs, and supports other channel members; may be a producer, wholesaler, or retailer.

channel conflict Arises when one channel member believes another channel member is engaged in behaviour that prevents it from achieving its goals.

channel of communication The means (e.g., a salesperson, advertising media, or public relations tools) of conveying a message to a receiver.

channel partnership Agreements and procedures among channel members for ordering and physically distributing a producer's product through the channel to the ultimate consumer.

choiceboard An interactive, Internet/Web-enabled system that allows individual customers to design their own products and services by answering a few questions and choosing from a menu of product or service attributes (or components), prices and delivery options.

click-and-mortar Online consumer lifestyle segment consisting of female homemakers who tend to browse retailer websites, but actually buy products in traditional retail outlets.

closed-end question Requires respondents to select one or more response options from a set of predetermined choices.

closing stage The stage in the personal selling process that involves obtaining a purchase commitment from a prospect.

code of ethics A formal statement of ethical principles and rules of conduct.

cognitive learning Making connections between two or more ideas or simply observing the outcomes of others' behaviours and adjusting your own accordingly.

cold canvassing Generating leads in person or by telephone from a directory.

collaborative filtering A process that automatically groups people with similar buying intentions, preferences, and behaviours and predicts future purchases.

combination compensation plan A compensation plan whereby a salesperson is paid a specified salary plus a commission based on sales or profit generated.

commerce A website's ability to conduct sales transactions for products and services.

commercialization Positioning and launching a new product in full-scale production and sales.

commercial online services Companies that offer electronic information and marketing services to subscribers who are charged a monthly fee.

communication The process of conveying a message to others, which requires six elements: a source, a message, a channel of communication, a receiver, and the processes of encoding and decoding.

community Website design element encouraging user-to-user communications hosted by the company to create virtual communities.

community shopping centre A retail location that typically has one primary store (usually a department store branch) and 20 to 40 smaller outlets, serving a population of consumers who are within a 2– to 5–kilometre drive.

company forecast (see *sales forecast*)

comparative advertisements Show one brand's strengths relative to those of competitors.

competencies An organization's special capabilities, including skills, technologies, and resources that distinguish it from other organizations.

competition The alternative firms that could provide a product to satisfy a specific market's needs.

competitive advantages Those characteristics of a product or service that make it superior to competing substitutes.

competitive advertisements The objective of these messages is to persuade the target market to select the firm's brand rather than that of a competitor.

competitive parity budgeting Matching the competitors' absolute level of spending or the proportion per point of market share.

complexity The technical sophistication of the product and hence the amount of understanding required to use it.

concept A picture or verbal description of an idea about a product; designed to convey to consumers what is planned for development.

concept tests External evaluations of a product idea that consist of preliminary testing of the new product idea (rather than the actual product) with consumers.

conference selling A form of team selling where a salesperson and other company resource people meet with buyers to discuss problems and opportunities.

connection Website design element that is the network of formal linkages between a company's site and other sites.

consolidated metropolitan statistical area (CMSA) The largest designation in terms of geographical area and market size, made up of several primary metropolitan statistical areas (PMSAs) that total at least 1 million people.

constraints The restrictions, such as time and money, placed on potential solutions by the nature and importance of the problem.

consultative selling Focuses on problem definition, where the salesperson serves as an expert on problem recognition and resolution.

consumer behaviour Actions a person takes in purchasing and using products and services.

consumer goods Products purchased by the ultimate consumer.

consumerism A grassroots movement started in the 1960s to increase the influence, power, and rights of consumers in dealing with institutions.

consumer-oriented sales promotion Sales tools used to support a company's advertising and personal selling efforts directed to ultimate consumers; examples include coupons, sweepstakes, and samples.

consumer socialization The process by which people acquire the skills, knowledge, and attitudes necessary to function as consumers.

content All digital information included on a website, including the presentation form - text, video, audio, and graphics.

contest A sales promotion in which consumers apply their skill or analytical or creative thinking to win a prize.

context A website's aesthetic appeal and functional look and feel reflected in site layout and design.

continuity programs Sales promotions used to encourage and reward repeat purchases by acknowledging each purchase made by a consumer and offering a premium as purchases accumulate.

continuous innovations No new behaviours must be learned to use these new products.

continuous schedule When seasonal factors are unimportant, advertising is run at a continuous schedule throughout the year; also called steady scheduling.

contracting A strategy used during the decline stage of the product life cycle in which a company contracts the manufacturing or marketing of a product to another firm.

contractual system Independently owned stores that band together to act like a chain.

contractual vertical marketing system Independent production and distribution firms integrate their efforts on a contractual basis to obtain greater functional economies and marketing impact than they could achieve alone.

control group A group not exposed to the experimental variable in an experiment.

convenience goods Items that the consumer purchases frequently and with a minimum of shopping effort.

cooperative advertising Advertising programs by which a manufacturer pays a percentage of the retailer's local advertising expense for advertising the manufacturer's products.

copyright law Gives the author of a literary, dramatic, musical, or artistic work the exclusive right to print, perform, or otherwise copy that work.

corporate chain A form of retail ownership with multiple outlets under common ownership.

corporate culture A system of shared attitudes and behaviours held by the employees that distinguish an organization from others.

corporate goals Strategic performance targets that the entire organization must reach to pursue its vision.

corporate level Level at which top management directs overall strategy for the entire organization.

corporate philosophy The values and "rules of conduct" for running an organization.

corporate vertical marketing system The combination of successive stages of production and distribution under a single ownership.

corporate vision A clear word picture of the organization's future, often with an inspirational theme.

corrective advertising FTC action requiring a company to spend money on advertising to correct previous misleading ads.

cost focus strategy Involves controlling expenses and, in turn, lowering prices, in a narrow range of market segments.

cost of goods sold Total value of the products sold during a specified time period.

cost per thousand (CPM) The cost of reaching 1,000 individuals or households with an advertising message in a given medium. (M is the Roman numeral for 1,000.)

cost-plus fixed-fee pricing A pricing method where a supplier is reimbursed for all costs, regardless of what they turn out to be, but is allowed only a fixed fee as profit that is independent of the final cost of the project.

cost-plus percentage-of-cost pricing A fixed percentage is added to the total unit cost.

cost-plus pricing The practice of summing the total unit cost of providing a product or service and adding a specific amount to the cost to arrive at a price.

coupons Sales promotions that usually offer a discounted price to consumers, which encourages trial.

cross-cultural analysis Study of similarities and differences among consumers in two or more societies.

cross-docking Practice of unloading products from suppliers, sorting products for individual stores, and quickly reloading products onto trucks for a particular store.

cross-functional teams A small number of people from different departments in an organization who are mutually accountable to a common set of performance goals.

cross-tabulation Method of presenting and relating data having two or more variables to analyze and discover relationships in the data.

cue A stimulus or symbol perceived by consumers.

cultural ethnocentricity The belief that aspects of one's culture are superior to another's.

cultural symbols Objects, ideas, or processes that represent a particular group of people or society.

culture The set of values, ideas, and attitudes that are learned and shared among the members of a group.

cumulative quantity discounts Apply to the accumulation of purchases of a product over a given time period, typically a year.

currency exchange rate The price of one country's currency expressed in terms of another country's currency.

customary pricing A method of pricing based on tradition, a standardized channel of distribution, or other competitive factors.

customer characteristics Variables - such as region, lifestyle, and household size-used to segment consumer markets.

customer experience The sum total of interactions that a customer has with a company's website.

customer relationship management (CRM) The process of identifying prospective buyers, understanding them intimately, and developing favourable long-term perceptions of the organization and its offerings so that buyers will choose them in the marketplace.

customer service The ability of logistics management to satisfy users in terms of time, dependability, communication, and convenience.

customer value The unique combination of benefits received by targeted buyers that includes quality, price, convenience, on-time delivery, and both before-sale and after-sale service.

customization The ability of a website to modify itself to - or be modified by - each user.

customized interaction Promotional element used in personal selling between a seller and a prospective buyer.

customs Norms and expectations about the way people do things in a specific country or culture.

data The facts and figures related to the problem, comprised of primary and secondary data.

data mining The extraction of hidden predictive information from large databases.

deal A sales promotion that offers a short-term price reduction.

deceptive pricing A practice by which prices are artificially inflated and then marked down under the guise of a sale.

decider Role in buying centre with the formal or informal power to select or approve the supplier that receives the contract.

decision A conscious choice from among two or more alternatives.

decision making The act of consciously choosing from alternatives.

decline stage The fourth and last stage of the product life cycle when sales and profits begin to drop.

decoding The process of having the receiver take a set of symbols, the message, and transform them back to an idea.

deletion Dropping a product from the company's product line.

delivered pricing A pricing method where the price the seller quotes includes all transportation costs.

demand curve Graph relating quantity sold and price, which shows how many units will be sold at a given price.

demand factors Factors that determine consumers' willingness and ability to pay for goods and services.

demographics Describing a population according to selected characteristics such as age, gender, ethnicity, income, and occupation.

department Group at the functional level where specialists create value for the organization.

depth interview Detailed individual interview with someone relevant to the project that often uses a lengthy free-flowing conversational style.

depth of product line The size of the assortment of each item a store carries.

derived demand Demand for industrial products and services driven by, or derived from, demand for consumer products and services.

desk jobber (see *drop shipper*)

development Turning the idea on paper into a prototype.

diffusion of innovation The process by which a product diffuses, or spreads, through the population.

direct channel A marketing channel where a producer and ultimate consumer deal directly with each other.

direct exporting A firm selling its domestically produced goods in a foreign country without intermediaries.

direct forecast Estimating the value to be forecast without any intervening steps.

direct investment A domestic firm actually investing in and owning a foreign subsidiary or division.

direct marketing Promotional element that uses direct communication with consumers to generate a response in the form of an order, a request for further information, or a visit to a retail outlet.

direct orders The result of direct marketing offers that contain all the information necessary for a potential buyer to make a decision to purchase and complete the transaction.

discontinuous innovations Make the consumer learn entirely new consumption patterns in order to use the product.

discounts Reductions from list price that a seller gives a buyer as a reward for some buyer activity favourable to the seller.

discretionary income Money that consumers have left after paying taxes and paying for necessities such as food and shelter; used for spending on luxuries and non-essential items.

disintermediation Channel conflict that arises when a channel member bypasses another member and sells or buys products direct.

disposable income Balance of income left after paying taxes that is used for spending and savings.

dissociative group Consumer reference group that a person wishes to maintain a distance from because of differences in values or behaviours.

diversification A strategy of developing new products and selling them in new markets.

downsizing Reducing the content of packages without changing package size and maintaining or increasing the package price.

drive A need that moves an individual to action.

drop shipper A merchant wholesaler that owns the merchandise it sells but does not physically handle, stock, or deliver; also called a desk jobber.

dual distribution An arrangement by which a firm reaches different buyers by employing two or more different types of channels for the same basic product.

dumping When a firm sells a product in a foreign country below its domestic price or below its actual cost.

durable good An item that usually lasts over an extended number of uses.

dynamically continuous innovations Only minor changes in behaviour are required to use these new products.

early adopters The 13.5 percent of the population who are leaders in their social setting and act as an information source on new products for other people.

early growth The first stage of the retail life cycle, when a new outlet emerges as a sharp departure from competitive forms.

early majority The 34 percent of the population who are deliberate and rely on personal sources for information on new products.

economic espionage The clandestine collection of trade secrets or proprietary information about a company's competitors.

economic infrastructure A country's communications, transportation, financial, and distribution systems.

economy Income, expenditures, and resources that affect the cost of running a business or a household.

80/20 rule A concept that suggests 80 percent of a firm's sales are obtained from 20 percent of its customers.

elastic demand A situation where a 1 percent decrease in price produces more than a 1 percent increase in quantity demanded, thereby actually increasing sales revenue.

electronic commerce Any activity that uses some form of electronic communication in the inventory, exchange, advertisement, distribution, and payment of goods and services.

electronic marketing channels Employ the Internet to make goods and services available for consumption or use by consumers or industrial buyers.

e-marketplaces Online trading communities that bring together buyers and supplier organizations.

encoding Process whereby the sender transforms an idea into symbolic form, using words, pictures, symbols, and sounds.

environmental factors Uncontrollable factors involving social, economic, technological, competitive, and regulatory forces.

environmental scanning Process of continually acquiring information on events occurring outside the organization to identify and interpret potential trends.

ethics The moral principles and values that govern the actions and decisions of an individual or group.

euro-branding The strategy of using the same brand name for the same product across all countries in the European Union.

evaluation The consumer's appraisal of the product or brand on important attributes.

evaluative criteria Factors that represent both the objective attributes of a brand and the subjective ones a consumer uses to compare different products and brands.

everyday fair pricing Retail strategy to try to create value for customers through service and the total buying experience.

everyday low pricing (1) The practice of replacing promotional allowances with lower manufacturer list prices. (2) Retailing strategy that emphasizes consistently low prices and eliminates most markdowns.

evoked set The group of brands that a consumer would consider acceptable from among all the brands in the product class of which he or she is aware.

exchange Trade of things of value between buyer and seller so that each is better off.

exclusive dealing An arrangement a manufacturer makes with a reseller to handle only its products and not those of competitors.

exclusive distribution Only one retail outlet in a specific geographical area carries the firm's products.

exclusive territorial distributorship A manufacturer grants a distributor the sole rights to sell a product in a specific geo-graphic area.

experiment Obtaining data by manipulating factors under tightly controlled conditions to test cause and effect.

experimental group A group exposed to the experimental variable in an experiment.

exporting Producing goods in one country and selling them in another country.

external search In the consumer purchase decision process, occurs when a consumer gathers information from outside sources such as friends, product-rating organizations, or advertising.

extranet Internet-based technology that permits communication between a company and its suppliers, distributors, and other partners (such as advertising agencies).

exurbs The remote suburbs to which the population began to shift in the 1990s.

fad A product that experiences rapid sales on introduction and then an equally rapid decline.

family branding Manufacturer's branding strategy that uses one name for all products; also called multiproduct branding.

family life cycle A family's progression from formation through to retirement, with each phase bringing distinct needs and purchasing behaviours.

fashion product A product that is introduced, declines, and then seems to return. Life cycles may last years or decades.

fast prototyping A "do it, try it, fix it" approach to new products used in software development, encouraging continuing improvements even after the initial design.

fear appeals Advertising messages suggesting to the consumer that he or she can avoid some negative experience through the purchase and use of a product.

feedback The communication flow from receiver back to the sender that helps the sender know whether the message was decoded and understood as intended.

feedback loop Consists of a response and feedback.

field experiment A test of marketing variables in actual store or buying settings.

field of experience The experiences, perceptions, attitudes, and values that senders and receivers of a message bring to a communication situation.

final close Occurs when the prospect is actually ready to purchase.

finance allowance A trade-oriented sales promotion paying retailers for financing costs or financial losses associated with consumer sales promotions.

fixed cost The sum of expenses of the firm that are stable and do not change with the quantity of product that is produced and sold.

flexible-price policy Setting different prices for products and services depending on individual buyers and purchase situations. Also called dynamic pricing.

flighting schedule Periods of advertising are scheduled between periods of no advertising to reflect seasonal demand. Also called intermittent schedule.

FOB (free on board) Refers to the point at which the seller stops paying transportation costs.

FOB origin pricing A method of pricing where the title of goods passes to the buyer at the point of loading.

focus group A research technique where a small group of people (usually six to ten) meet for a few hours (two to three) with a trained moderator to discuss important issues related to a product, service, or image of a company or some other marketing challenge.

follow-up stage Making certain the customer's purchase has been properly delivered and installed and difficulties experienced with using the product are addressed.

forgetting rate The speed with which buyers forget a brand if advertising is not seen.

form of ownership Distinguishes retail outlets based on whether individuals, corporate chains, or contractual systems own the outlet.

formula selling presentation Providing information in an accurate, thorough, and step-by-step manner to inform the prospect.

form utility The value to consumers that comes from production or alteration of a good or service.

forward integration Practice in corporate vertical marketing system in which a producer also owns retail shops.

four Is of service Four unique elements to services: intangibility, inconsistency, inseparability, and inventory.

four Ps (see *marketing mix*)

franchising Contractual arrangement between a parent company (a franchiser) and an individual or firm (a franchisee) that allows the franchise to operate a certain type of business under an established name and according to specific rules.

frequency The average number of times a person in the target audience is exposed to a message or advertisement.

full-service agency An advertising agency providing the most complete range of services, including market research, media selection, copy development, artwork, and production.

functional discounts (see *trade discounts*)

functional level Level at which groups of specialists actually create value for the organization.

gatekeeper Role that controls the flow of information in the buying centre.

General Agreement on Tariffs and Trade (GATT) An international treaty intended to limit trade barriers and promote world trade through the reduction of tariffs.

generalized life cycle The product life cycle that most, but not all, products show.

general merchandise stores Stores that carry a broad product line with limited depth.

general merchandise wholesaler A full-service merchant wholesaler that carries a broad assortment of merchandise and performs all channel functions.

generational marketing The use of marketing programs designed for the distinct attitudes and consumer behaviour of the cohorts, or generations, that make up the marketplace.

Generation X The 15 percent of the population born between 1965 and 1976.

Generation Y Canadians born after 1976, the year that many baby boomers began having children.

generic brand A no-name product with no identification other than a description of contents.

global competition Exists when firms originate, produce, and market their products and services worldwide.

global consumers Customer groups living in many different countries who have similar needs or seek similar features and benefits from products or services.

global marketing strategy The practice of standardizing marketing activities when there are cultural similarities and adapting them when cultures differ.

goals Targets of performance to be achieved within a specific time frame.

government units The federal, state, and local agencies that buy goods and services for the constituents they serve.

green marketing Marketing efforts to produce, promote, and reclaim environmentally sensitive products.

grey market A situation where products are sold through unauthorized channels of distribution; also called parallel importing.

gross domestic product The monetary value of all goods and services produced in a country during one year.

gross income The total amount of money made in one year by a person, household, or family unit.

gross margin Net sales minus cost of goods sold.

gross rating points (GRPs) A reference number for advertisers, created by multiplying reach (expressed as a percentage of the total market) by frequency.

growth stage The second stage of the product life cycle characterized by rapid increases in sales and by the appearance of competitors.

harvesting When a company retains the product but reduces marketing support costs.

hierarchy of effects The sequence of stages a prospective buyer goes through from initial awareness of a product to eventual action (either trial or adoption of the product). The stages include awareness, interest, evaluation, trial, and adoption.

high learning product A product for which significant education of the customer is required and there is an extended introductory period.

hooked, online, and single Online consumer lifestyle segment consisting of young, affluent, and single consumers who bank, play games, and spend more time online than any other segment.

horizontal conflict Disagreements between intermediaries at the same level in a marketing channel.

horizontal price fixing When two or more competitors explicitly or implicitly set prices.

humorous appeals Advertising messages implying either directly or more subtly that a product is more fun or exciting than competitors' offering.

hunter-gatherers Online consumer lifestyle segment consisting of married baby boomers with children at home who use the Internet like a consumer magazine to compare products and prices.

hypermarket A large store (over 200,000 square feet) offering a mix of 40 percent food products and 60 percent general merchandise.

hypothesis A conjecture or idea about the relationship of two or more factors or what might happen in the future.

hypothesis evaluation Research to test ideas discovered in the hypothesis generation stage to help recommend marketing actions.

hypothesis generation A search for ideas that can be evaluated in later research.

idea generation Developing a pool of concepts as candidates for new products.

idle production capacity When the service provider is available but there is not demand.

inbound telemarketing The use of toll-free telephone numbers that customers can call to obtain information about products or services and make purchases.

inconsistency A unique element of services—because services depend on the people who provide them, their quality varies with each person's capabilities and day-to-day job performance.

indirect channel A marketing channel where intermediaries are inserted between the producer and consumers and perform numerous channel functions.

indirect exporting A firm selling its domestically produced goods in a foreign country through an intermediary.

individual branding Manufacturer's branding strategy that gives each product a distinct name; also called *multibranding*.

individual interviews A single researcher asks questions of one respondent.

industrial distributor Performs a variety of marketing channel functions, including selling, stocking, delivering a full product assortment, and financing.

industrial firm An organizational buyer that in some way reprocesses a good or service it buys before selling it again to the next buyer.

industrial goods Products that assist directly or indirectly in providing products for resale (also called B2B goods, business goods, or organizational goods).

industry A group of firms offering products that are close substitutes for each other.

inelastic demand A situation where a 1 percent decrease in price produces less than a 1 percent increase in quantity demanded.

influencer Role in the buying centre that affects the buying decision, usually by helping define the specifications for what is bought.

information technology Designing and managing computer and communication networks to provide a system to satisfy an organization's needs for data storage, processing, and access.

infomercials Program-length (30-minute) advertisements that take an educational approach to communication with potential customers.

in-house agency A company's own advertising staff, which may provide full services or a limited range of services.

innovators The 2.5 percent of the population who are venturesome and highly educated, use multiple information sources, and are the first to adopt a new product.

inseparability A unique element of services - the consumer cannot (and does not) separate the deliverer of the service from the service itself.

inside order takers Typically answer simple questions, take orders, and complete transactions with customers. Also called salesclerks.

installations Support goods, consisting of buildings and fixed equipment.

institutional advertisements Advertisements designed to build goodwill or an image for an organization, rather than promote a specific good or service.

intangibility A unique element of services—services cannot be held, touched, or seen before the purchase decision.

integrated marketing communications The concept of designing marketing communications programs that coordinate all promotional activities—advertising, personal selling, sales promotion, public relations, and direct marketing—to provide a consistent message across all audiences.

intensive distribution A firm tries to place its products or services in as many outlets as possible.

interactive marketing Two-way buyer-seller electronic communications in a computer-mediated environment in which the buyer controls the kind and amount of information received from the seller.

interest An increase in the consumer's desire to learn about some of the features of the product or brand.

intermediaries Individuals or firms performing a role in the marketing channel, involved in making a product available.

internal search In the consumer purchase decision process, occurs when a consumer begins to search for information.

international firm Markets its existing products and services in other countries the same way it does at home.

Internet An integrated global network of computers that gives users access to information and documents.

intertype competition Competition between very dissimilar types of retail outlets.

intranet Internet/Web-based network used within the boundaries of an organization.

introductory stage The first stage of the product life cycle in which sales grow slowly and profit is minimal.

inventory (1) Physical material purchased from suppliers, which may or may not be reworked for sale to customers. (2) A unique element of services-the need for and cost of having a service provider available.

involvement The personal, social, and economic consequences of the purchase to the consumer.

job analysis A study of a particular sales position, including how the job is to be performed and the tasks that make up the job.

job description Written document that describes job relationships and requirements that characterize each sales position.

joint venture An arrangement in which a foreign company and a local firm invest together to create a local business, sharing ownership, control, and profits of the new company.

jury of executive opinion forecast Asking knowledgeable executives inside the firm about likely sales during a coming period.

jury test A pretest in which a panel of customers is shown an advertisement and asked to rate its attractiveness, how much they like it, and how much it draws their attention.

just-in-time (JIT) concept An inventory supply system that operates with very low inventories and requires fast, on-time delivery.

label An integral part of the package that typically identifies the product or brand, who made it, where and when it was made, how it is to be used, and package contents and ingredients.

laggards The 16 percent of the market who have fear of debt, use friends for information sources, and accept ideas and products only after they have been long established in the market.

late majority The 34 percent of the population who are skeptical, below average in social status, and rely less on advertising and personal selling for information than do innovators or early adopters.

laws Society's values and standards that are enforceable in the courts.

lead The name of a person who may be a possible customer.

lead generation Result of direct marketing offer designed to create interest in a product or a service and a request for additional information.

lead time Lag from ordering an item until it is received and ready for use or sale. Also called order cycle time or replenishment time.

learning Behaviours that result from repeated experience or reasoning.

level of service The degree of service provided to the customer by self-, limited-, and full-service retailers.

licensing A contractual agreement whereby a company allows another firm to use its brand name, patent, trade secret, or other property for a royalty or fee.

lifestyle A mode of living that is identified by how people spend their time and resources (activities), what they consider important in their environment (interests), and what they think of themselves and the world around them (opinions).

limited-service agency Specializes in one aspect of the advertising process such as providing creative services to develop the advertising copy or buying previously unpurchased media space.

linear trend extrapolation Occurs when trend extrapolation is described with a straight line; see *trend extrapolation*.

line extension The practice of using a current brand name to enter a new market segment in its product class.

logistics Those activities that focus on getting the right amount of the right products to the right place at the right time at the lowest possible cost.

logistics management The practice of organizing the cost-effective flow of raw materials, in-process inventory, finished goods, and related information from point of origin to point of consumption to satisfy customer requirements.

logo "Device" (design, sound, shape, or color) or other brand name that cannot be spoken.

loss-leader pricing Deliberately selling a product below its customary price to attract attention to it.

lost-horse forecast Starting with the last known value of the item being forecast, listing the factors that could affect the forecast, assessing whether they have a positive or negative impact, and making the final forecast.

low learning product A product for which sales begin immediately because little learning is required by the consumer and the benefits of purchase are readily understood.

maintained markup The difference between the final selling price and retailer cost; also called gross margin.

major account management The practice of using team selling to focus on important customers so as to build mutually beneficial, long-term, cooperative relationships. Also called key account management.

manufacturer branding The producer dictates the brand name using either a multiproduct or multibranding approach.

manufacturer's agents Work for several producers and carry noncompetitive, complementary merchandise in an exclusive territory; also called manufacturer's representatives.

manufacturer's branch office Carries a producer's inventory and performs the functions of a full-service merchant wholesaler.

manufacturer's sales office Does not carry inventory, typically performs only a sales function, and serves as an alternative to agents and brokers.

markdown Discounting a product when it does not sell at the original price and an adjustment is necessary.

market People with both the desire and the ability to buy a specific product.

market development Selling existing products to new markets.

market growth rate The annual rate of growth of the specific market or industry in which a firm or SBU is competing; often used as the vertical axis in business portfolio analysis.

marketing The process of planning and executing the conception, pricing, promotion, and distribution of ideas, goods, and services to create exchanges that satisfy individual and organizational objectives.

marketing channel The set of individuals or firms involved in the process of making a product available.

marketing concept Idea that an organization should strive to satisfy the needs of consumers while also trying to achieve the organization's goals.

marketing mix The marketing manager's controllable factors-product, price, promotion, and place - that can be taken to solve a marketing problem.

marketing orientation When an organization focuses its efforts on continuously collecting information about customers' needs, sharing this information across departments, and using it to create customer value.

marketing plan A road map for the marketing activities of an organization for a specified future period of time.

marketing program A plan that integrates the marketing mix to provide a good, service, or idea to prospective buyers.

marketing research The process of defining a marketing problem and opportunity, systematically collecting and analyzing information, and recommending actions to improve an organization's marketing activities.

marketing strategy The means by which a marketing goal is to be achieved.

marketing tactics Detailed day-to-day operational decisions essential to the overall success of marketing strategies.

market modification Strategy in which a company tries to find new customers, increase a product's use among existing customers, or create new use situations.

market orientation Focusing organizational efforts on continuously collecting information about customers' needs and competitors' capabilities.

market penetration A strategy of increasing sales of present products in their existing markets.

market-product grid Framework to relate the segments of a market to products offered or potential marketing actions by the firm.

market segmentation Considering prospective buyers in terms of groups that have common needs and will respond similarly to a marketing action.

market segments The groups that result from the process of market segmentation; these groups ideally have common needs and will respond similarly to a marketing action.

market share The ratio of the sales revenue of one firm to the total sales revenue of all firms in the industry including the firm itself.

market space Information- and communication-based electronic exchange environment mostly occupied by sophisticated computer and telecommunication technologies and digitized offerings.

market testing Exposing actual products to prospective consumers under realistic purchase conditions to see if they will buy.

markup The difference between selling price and cost.

mass customization Tailoring goods or services to the tastes of individual customers on a high-volume scale.

mass selling Promotional elements used with groups of prospective buyers: advertising, sales promotion, and public relations.

maturity stage The third stage of the product or retail life cycle in which sales increase at a declining rate and profit declines.

measures of success Criteria used in evaluating proposed solutions to a problem.

membership group Consumer reference group to which a person actually belongs, such as fraternities/sororities, social clubs, and the family.

merchandise allowance A trade-oriented sales promotion reimbursing a retailer for extra in-store support or special featuring of the brand.

merchandise line How many different types of products a store carries and in what assortment.

merchant wholesalers Independently owned firms that take title to the merchandise they handle.

message The information sent by a source to a receiver in the communication process.

methods The approaches that can be used to solve all or part of a problem.

metropolitan statistical area (MSA) A city having a population of at least 50,000; an urbanized area with a population in excess of 50,000 with a total metropolitan population of at least 100,000.

mission   Statement of the organization's purpose and direction.

mixed branding A firm markets products under its own name and that of a reseller because the segment attracted by the reseller is different from its own market.

modified rebuy A buying situation in which the users, influencers, or deciders in the buying centre want to change the product specifications, price, delivery schedule, or supplier.

monopolistic competition A competitive setting in which many sellers compete with their products on a substitutable basis.

monopoly A competitive setting in which only one firm sells the product.

moral idealism A personal moral philosophy that considers certain individual rights or duties as universal, regardless of the outcome.

motivation The energizing force that stimulates behaviour to satisfy a need.

multibranding See *individual branding*.

multichannel marketing Blending of different communication and delivery channels that are mutually reinforcing in attracting, retaining, and building relationships with customers.

multichannel retailers Use a combination of traditional store formats and nonstore formats such as catalogues, television, and online retailing.

multidomestic marketing strategy A multinational firm's offering as many different product variations, brand names, and advertising programs as countries in which it does business.

multinational firm Views the world as consisting of unique parts and markets to each part differently; see *multidomestic marketing strategy*.

multiproduct branding See *family branding*.

national character A distinct set of personality characteristics common among people of a country or society.

need That which occurs when a person feels deprived of food, clothing, or shelter.

need-satisfaction presentation A selling format that emphasizes probing and listening by the salesperson to identify needs and interests of prospective buyers.

negative reinforcement Occurs when a consumer's experience in responding to a stimulus is unpleasant.

new buy The first-time purchase of a product or service, involving greater potential risk.

new-product concept A tentative description of a product or service a firm might offer for sale.

new-product process The stages a firm goes through to identify business opportunities and convert them to a salable good or service.

new-product strategy development Defining the role for a new product in terms of the firm's overall corporate objectives.

news conference A publicity tool consisting of an informational meeting with representatives of the media who are sent advance materials on the content.

news release A publicity tool consisting of an announcement regarding changes in the company or the product line.

noise Extraneous factors that can work against effective communication by distorting a message or the feedback received.

noncumulative quantity discounts Price reductions based on the size of an individual purchase order.

nondurable good An item consumed in one or a few uses.

North American Industry Classification System (NAICS) Provides common industry definitions for Canada, Mexico, and the United States, which makes easier the measurement of economic activity in the three member countries of NAFTA.

not-for-profit organization A nongovernmental organization that serves its customers but does not have profit as an organizational goal.

objections Excuses for not making a purchase commitment or decision.

objective and task budgeting A budgeting approach whereby the company determines its promotion objectives, outlines the tasks to accomplish these objectives, and determines the promotion cost of performing these tasks.

objectives Targets of performance to be achieved within a specific time frame.

observational data Facts and figures obtained by watching, either mechanically or in person, how people actually behave.

odd-even pricing Setting prices a few dollars or cents under an even number, such as $19.95.

off-peak pricing Charging different prices during different times of the day or days of the week to reflect variations in demand for the service.

off-price retailing Selling brand-name merchandise at lower than regular prices.

oligopoly A competitive setting in which a few companies control the majority of industry sales.

one-price policy Setting one price for all buyers of a product or service. Also called fixed pricing.

online consumers The subsegment of all Internet/Web users who employ this technology to research products and services and make purchases.

opinion leaders Individuals who have social influence over others.

order getter A salesperson who sells in a conventional sense and identifies prospective customers, provides customers with information, persuades customers to buy, closes sales, and follows up on customers' use of a product or service.

order taker Salesperson who processes routine orders or reorders.

organizational buyers Units such as manufacturers, retailers, or government agencies that buy goods and services for their own use or for resale.

organizational buying behaviour The decision-making process that organizations use to establish the need for products and services and identify, evaluate, and choose among alternative brands and suppliers.

organizational buying criteria The objective attributes of the supplier's products and services and the capabilities of the supplier itself.

organizational goals Specific objectives a business or not-for-profit unit seeks to achieve and by which it can measure its performance.

organizational goods See *industrial goods*.

original markup The difference between retailer cost and initial selling price.

outbound telemarketing Using the telephone rather than personal visits to contact customers.

out-of-home TV Reaches 20 million viewers in bars, hotels, offices, and campuses each week.

outside order takers Visit customers and replenish inventory stock of resellers, such as retailers or wholesalers.

packaging Any container in which a product is offered for sale and on which label information is conveyed.

panel A sample of consumers or stores from which researchers take a series of measurements.

parallel development An approach to new product development that involves cross-functional team members who conduct the simultaneous development of both the product and the production process, staying with the product from conception to production.

patent Exclusive rights to the manufacture of a product or related technology granted to a company for 17 years.

patent law Gives inventors the right to exclude others from making, using, or selling products that infringe the patented invention.

penetration pricing Setting a low initial price on a new product to appeal immediately to the mass market.

perceived risk The anxieties felt because the consumer cannot anticipate the outcomes of a purchase but believes that there may be negative consequences.

percentage of sales budgeting Allocating funds to advertising as a percentage of past or anticipated sales, in terms of either dollars or units sold.

perception The process by which an individual selects, organizes, and interprets information to create a meaningful picture of the world.

perceptual map A means of displaying or graphing in two dimensions the location of products or brands in the minds of consumers.

permission marketing The solicitation of a consumer's consent (called "opt-in") to receive e-mail and advertising based on personal data supplied by the consumer.

personality A person's consistent behaviours or responses to recurring situations.

personalization The consumer-initiated practice of generating content on a marketer's website that is custom tailored to an individual's specific needs and preferences.

personal selling The two-way flow of communication between a buyer and seller, often in a face-to-face encounter, designed to influence a person's or group's purchase decision.

personal selling process Sales activities occurring before and after the sale itself, consisting of six stages: prospecting, preapproach, approach, presentation, close, and follow-up.

physiological needs An individual's needs that are basic to survival and must be satisfied first, such as food and shelter.

pioneering advertisements   Tell people what a product is, what it can do, and where it can be found.

place Means of getting the product to the consumer.

place-based media Advertising messages in locations that attract a specific target audience such as airports, doctor's offices, and health clubs.

place utility The value to consumers of having a good or service available where needed.

planning gap The difference between the projection of the path to reach a new goal and the projection of the path of the results of a plan already in place.

point-of-purchase displays Product displays taking the form of advertising signs, which sometimes actually hold or display the product, and are often located in high-traffic areas near the cash register on the end of an aisle.

points of difference Those characteristics of a product that make it superior to competitive substitutes.

portfolio test A pretest in which a test ad is placed in a portfolio with other ads and consumers are questioned on their impressions of the ads.

possession utility The value of making an item easy to purchase through the provision of credit cards or financial arrangements.

posttests Tests conducted after an advertisement has been shown to the target audience to determine whether it has accomplished its intended purpose.

power centre A large shopping strip with multiple anchor stores, a convenient location, and a supermarket.

preapproach stage The stage of the personal selling process that involves obtaining further information about the prospect and deciding on the best method of approach.

precycling Efforts by manufacturers to reduce waste by decreasing the amount of packaging they use.

predatory pricing Charging a very low price for a product with the intent of driving competitors out of business.

premium A sales promotion that consists of merchandise offered free or at significant savings over its retail price.

presentation stage The core of the personal selling process; its objective is to convert the prospect into a customer by creating a desire for the product or service.

prestige pricing Setting a high price so that status-conscious consumers will be attracted to the product and buy it.

pretests Tests conducted before an advertisement is placed to determine whether it communicates the intended message or to select among alternative versions of an advertisement.

price The money or other considerations (including other goods and services) exchanged for the ownership or use of a product.

price discrimination The practice of charging different prices to different buyers for goods of like trade and quality.

price elasticity of demand The percentage change in quantity demanded relative to a percentage change in price.

price fixing A conspiracy among firms to set prices for a product.

pricing constraints Factors that limit range of price a firm may set.

pricing objectives Expectations that specify the role of price in an organization's marketing and strategic plans.

primary data Facts and figures that are newly collected for the project.

primary demand Desire for the product class rather than for a specific brand.

primary metropolitan statistical area (PMSA) An area that is part of a larger consolidated metropolitan statistical area that has a total population of 1 million or more.

private branding (labelling) When a company manufactures products but sells them under the brand name of a wholesaler or retailer (often called reseller branding).

problem recognition The initial step in the purchase decision process; occurs when a person realizes that the difference between what s/he has and what s/he would like to have is big enough to actually do something about it.

product A good, service, or idea consisting of a bundle of tangible and intangible attributes that satisfies consumers and is received in exchange for money or some other unit of value.

product adaptation Changing a product in some way to make it more appropriate for a country's climate or consumer preferences; examples include Gerber's Vegetable and Rabbit flavour in Poland and its Freeze-Dried Sardines and Rice in Japan.

product advertisements Advertisements that focus on selling a good or service and take three forms: (1) pioneering (or informational), (2) competitive (or persuasive), and (3) reminder.

product class The entire product category or industry.

product development A strategy of selling a new product to existing markets.

product differentiation A strategy of a firm's using different marketing mix activities, such as product features and advertising, to help consumers perceive the product as being different and better than competing products.

product extension Selling virtually the same product in other countries; examples include Coca-Cola and Levi's jeans.

product form Variations of a product within the product class.

product invention Occurs when a company invents totally new products designed to satisfy common needs across countries, such as Black & Decker's Snake Light.

production goods Items used in the manufacturing process that become part of the final product.

product item A specific product as noted by a unique brand, size, or price.

product life cycle The stages a new product goes through in the marketplace: introduction, growth, maturity, and decline.

product line A group of products that are closely related because they satisfy a class of needs, are used together, are sold to the same customer group, are distributed through the same type of outlets, or fall within a given price range.

product mix The number of product lines offered by a company.

product modification Altering a product's characteristics, such as its quality, performance, or appearance, to try to increase and extend the product's sales.

product placement Using a brand-name product in a movie, television show, video, or a commercial for another product.

product positioning The place an offering occupies in consumers' minds on important attributes relative to competitive offerings.

profit The excess of revenues over costs, the reward to a business for the risk it undertakes in offering a product for sale.

profitability analysis A means of measuring the profitability of the firm's products, customer groups, sales territories, channels of distribution, and order sizes.

profiteering Occurs when a company makes excessive profits, usually by taking advantage of a shortage of supply to charge extremely high prices.

profit equation Profit = Total revenue – Total cost; or Profit = (Unit price x Quantity sold) – Total cost.

profit responsibility he view that companies have a simple duty - to maximize profits for their owners or stockholders.

promotion Means of communication between the seller and buyer.

promotional allowance Cash payment or extra amount of "free goods" awarded sellers in the channel of distribution for undertaking certain advertising or selling activities to promote a product.

promotional mix Combination of one or more of the promotional tools—advertising, personal selling, public relations, sales promotion, and direct marketing—a firm uses to communicate with consumers.

promotional websites Advertise and promote a company's products and services and provide information on how items can be used and where they can be purchased.

prospect A customer who wants or needs the product.

prospecting stage In the personal selling process, the search for and qualification of potential customers.

protectionism The practice of shielding one or more industries within a country's economy from foreign competition, usually through the use of tariffs or quotas.

protocol A statement that, before product development begins, identifies a well-defined target market; specific customers' needs, wants, and preferences; and what the product will be and do.

prototype Full-scale operating model of the product under development.

psychographics The analysis of consumer lifestyles (activities, interests, and opinions).

publicity Communication about an organization that is non-personal and not paid for directly by the organization.

public relations A form of communication management that seeks to influence the feelings, opinions, or beliefs held by customers, prospective customers, stockholders, suppliers, employees, and other publics about a company and its products or services.

public service announcement (PSA) A publicity tool that uses free space or time donated by the media.

pull strategy Directing the promotional mix at ultimate consumers to encourage them to ask the retailer for the product.

pulse schedule A flighting schedule is combined with a continuous schedule because of increases in demand, heavy periods of promotion, or introduction of a new product. Also called burst schedule.

purchase decision process The stages a buyer passes through in making choices about which products and services to buy.

purchase frequency The frequency of purchase of a specific product.

pure competition A competitive setting in which every company has a similar product.

pure monopoly One seller who sets the price for a unique product.

push strategy Directing the promotional mix to channel members to encourage them to order, and stock, and sell a product.

qualified prospect An individual who wants a product, can afford to buy it, and is the decision maker.

quality Those features and characteristics of a product that influence its ability to satisfy customer needs.

quantity discounts Reductions in unit costs for a larger order.

questionnaire data Facts and figures obtained by asking people about their attitudes, awareness, intentions, and behaviours.

quota A restriction placed on the amount of a product allowed to enter or leave a country.

rack jobber A merchant wholesaler that furnishes racks or shelves to display merchandise in retail stores, performs all channel functions, and sells on consignment to retailers.

rating (TV or radio) The percentage of households in a market that are tuned to a particular TV show or radio station.

reach The number of different people or households exposed to an advertisement.

rebate A sales promotion in which money is returned to the consumer based on proof of purchase.

receivers Consumers who read, hear, or see the message sent by a source in the communication process.

reciprocity An industrial buying practice in which two organizations agree to purchase each other's products and services.

recycling The use of technological developments to allow products to go through the manufacturing cycle several times.

reference groups People to whom an individual looks as a basis for self-appraisal or as a source of personal standards.

regional rollouts Introducing a new product sequentially into geographical areas to allow production levels and marketing activities to build up gradually.

regional shopping centres Consist of 50 to 150 stores that typically attract customers who live within a 5– to 15–kilometre range, often containing two or three anchor stores.

regulation Restrictions that municipal, provincial, and federal laws place on business.

reinforcement A reward that strengthens a response.

reinforcement advertisement Used to assure current users they made the right choice.

relationship marketing Linking the organization to its individual customers, employees, suppliers, and other partners for their mutual long-term benefits.

relationship selling The practice of building ties to customers based on a salesperson's attention and commitment to customer needs over time.

relative market share The sales of a firm or SBU divided by the sales of the largest firm in the industry; often used as the horizontal axis in business portfolio analysis.

reminder advertisements Used to reinforce previous knowledge of a product.

reminder institutional advertisements Simply bring a company's name to the attention of the target market again.

repeat purchasers People who tried the product, were satisfied, and bought again.

repositioning Changing the place an offering occupies in a consumer's mind relative to competitive offerings.

requirement contract A contract that requires a buyer to purchase all or part of its needs for a product from one seller for a period of time.

resale price maintenance (see *vertical price fixing*)

reseller A wholesaler or retailer that buys physical products and resells them again without any processing.

reseller branding (see *private branding*)

response The impact the message had on the receiver's knowledge, attitudes, or behaviours.

retailer-sponsored cooperative Small, independent retailers form an organization that operates a wholesaler facility cooperatively.

retailing All activities involved in selling, renting, and providing goods and services to ultimate consumers for personal, family, or household use.

retailing mix In retailing strategy, the goods and services, physical distribution, and communications tactics chosen by a store.

retail life cycle The process of growth and decline that retail outlets, like products, experience.

return on investment (ROI) The ratio of after-tax net profit to the investment used to earn that profit.

reverse auction A buyer communicates a need for a product or service and would-be suppliers are invited to bid in competition with each other.

reverse marketing The deliberate effort by organizational buyers to build relationships that shape suppliers' products, services, and capabilities to fit a buyer's needs and those of its customers.

rich media Online promotion, such as banner advertising, that utilizes the audio, video, and interactive capabilities of the Internet to attract more attention from viewers and to provide an element of entertainment to the message.

sales-force automation The use of technology to make the sales function more effective and efficient.

sales-force management Planning the selling program and implementing the personal selling effort of the firm.

sales-force survey forecast Asking the firm's salespeople to estimate sales during a coming period.

sales forecast The total sales of a product that a firm expects to sell during a specified time period under specified environmental conditions and its own marketing efforts (also called company forecast).

sales management Planning the selling program and implementing and controlling the personal selling effort of the firm.

sales plan A statement describing what is to be achieved and where and how the selling effort of salespeople is to be deployed.

sales promotion A short-term offer of value offered to arouse interest in buying a good or service.

samples Some elements taken from the population or universe; a sales promotion offering the product free or at a greatly reduced price.

sampling The process of selecting elements from a population; the process manufacturers use of giving away free samples to introduce a new product.

scrambled merchandising Offering several unrelated product lines in a single retail store.

screening and evaluation The third stage of the new product process which involves internal and external evaluations of the new-product ideas to eliminate those that warrant no further effort.

seasonal discounts Price reductions to encourage buyers to stock inventory earlier than their normal demand would require.

secondary data Facts and figures that have already been recorded before the project at hand.

selective comprehension Interpreting information so that it is consistent with your attitude and beliefs.

selective demand Demand for a specific brand within the product class.

selective distribution A firm selects a few retail outlets in a specific geographical area to carry its products.

selective exposure Occurs when people pay attention to messages that are consistent with their attitudes and beliefs and ignore messages that are inconsistent.

selective perception A filtering of exposure, comprehension, and retention.

selective retention The tendency to remember only part of all the information one sees, reads, or hears, even minutes after exposure to it.

self-concept The way people see themselves and the way they believe others see them.

self-liquidating premium Merchandise offered at a significant cost savings over its retail price, self-liquidating because the cost charged to the consumer covers the cost of the items.

self-regulation An alternative to government control where an industry attempts to police itself.

selling agent Represents a single producer and is responsible for the entire marketing function of that producer.

service continuum A range from tangible to the intangible or goods-dominant to service-dominant offerings available in the marketplace.

services Intangible activities, benefits, or satisfactions that an organization provides to consumers in exchange for money or something else of value.

sex appeals Advertising messages suggesting to the audience that the product will increase the attractiveness of the user.

share points Percentage points of market share; often used as the common basis of comparison to allocate marketing resources effectively.

shopping goods Items for which the consumer compares several alternatives on criteria such as price, quality, or style.

shrinkage Breakage and theft of merchandise by customers and employees.

single-source data Information provided by a single firm on household demographics and lifestyle, purchases, TV viewing behaviour, and responses to promotions like coupons and free samples.

situation analysis Taking stock of where a firm or product's past performance, where it is now, and where it is headed.

situational influences The purchase situation affects the purchase decision process through five situational influences: (1) the purchase task, (2) social surroundings, (3) physical surroundings, (4) temporal effects, and (5) antecedent states.

skimming pricing The highest initial price that customers really desiring the product are willing to pay.

slotting fee Payment manufacturer makes to place a new item on a retailer's shelf.

social audit A systematic assessment of a firm's objectives, strategies, and performance in terms of social responsibility.

social forces Demographic characteristics, lifestyles, cultural values, and beliefs.

social responsibility Idea that organizations are part of a larger society and are accountable to that society for their actions.

societal marketing concept View that organizations should satisfy the needs of consumers in a way that provides for society's well-being.

societal responsibility Obligations that organizations have to the preservation of the ecological environment and to the general public.

solution The best alternative that has been identified to solve the problem.

source A company or person who has information to convey.

specialty goods Items that a consumer makes a special effort to search out and buy.

specialty merchandise wholesaler A full-service merchant wholesaler that offers a relatively narrow range of products but has an extensive assortment within the product lines carried.

specialty outlet Limited- and single-line stores that carry depth of product line, either in related items or in one primary line of merchandise.

stakeholder responsibility The concept of social responsibility that focuses on the obligations an organization has to those who can affect achievement of its objectives.

stakeholders Individuals or groups, either within or outside an organization, that relate to it in what it does and how well it performs.

standard markup pricing Adding a fixed percentage to the cost of all items in a specific product class.

statistical inference Drawing conclusions about a population from a sample taken from that population.

stimulus discrimination A person's ability to perceive differences in stimuli.

stimulus generalization When a response elicited by one stimulus (cue) is generalized to another stimulus.

stimulus-response presentation A selling format that assumes the prospect will buy if given the appropriate stimulus by a salesperson.

stock keeping unit (SKU) A unique identification number that defines an item for ordering or inventory purposes.

straight commission compensation plan A compensation plan where the salesperson's earnings are directly tied to the sales or profit generated.

straight rebuy Reordering an existing product or service from the list of acceptable suppliers, probably without checking with users or influencers.

straight salary compensation plan A compensation plan where the salesperson is paid a fixed fee per week, month, or year.

strategic business unit (SBU) A decentralized profit centre of a large firm that is treated as though it were a separate, independent business; see also business unit.

strategic channel alliances A practice whereby one firm's marketing channel is used to sell another firm's products.

strategic marketing process Approach whereby an organization allocates its marketing mix resources to reach its target markets and achieve its goals.

strategy A plan of action to achieve specific goals.

strip location A cluster of stores serving people who live within a 5- to 10-minute drive.

subbranding Combines a family brand with a new brand.

subcultures Subgroups within the larger, or national, culture with unique values, ideas, and attitudes.

subliminal perception Means that you see or hear messages without being aware of them.

suggestive selling Sales format that assumes, given the appropriate stimulus by a salesperson, the prospect will buy; such as when a fast-food clerk asks if you would like fries with your order.

supercentres Combine a typical merchandise store (typically 70,000 square feet) with a full-size grocery.

supplies Support goods similar to consumer convenience goods, consisting of products such as stationery, paperclips, and brooms.

supply chain A series of firms that perform activities required to create and deliver a good or service to consumers or industrial users.

supply chain management The integration and organization of information and logistic activities across firms in a supply chain for the purpose of creating and delivering goods and services that provide value to customers.

supply partnership A relationship that exists when a buyer and its supplier adopt mutually beneficial objectives, policies, and procedures for the purpose of lowering the cost and/or increasing the value of products and services delivered to the ultimate consumer.

support goods Items used to assist in producing other goods and services.

survey of buyers' intentions forecast Asking prospective customers whether they are likely to buy the product during some future time period.

survey of experts forecast Asking experts on a topic to make a judgment about some future event.

sustainable development Conducting business in a way that protects the natural environment while making economic progress.

sweepstakes Sales promotions consisting of a game of chance requiring no analytical or creative effort by the consumer.

SWOT analysis An organization's appraisal of its internal strengths and weaknesses and its external opportunities and threats.

synergy Increased effectiveness achieved through planned interaction of two or more marketing actions, where results exceed the sum of the effects of the individual actions.

tangibles Dimension of service quality - appearance of physical facilities, equipment, personnel, and communication materials.

target audience Portion of the target market to which advertising is directed.

target market Specific group of existing and potential consumers toward which an organization directs its marketing plan.

target pricing Manufacturer deliberately adjusting the composition and features of a product to achieve the target price to consumers.

target profit pricing Setting an annual target of a specific dollar volume of profit.

target return-on-investment pricing Setting a price to achieve a return-on-investment (ROI) target.

target return-on-sales pricing Setting a price to achieve a profit that is a specified percentage of the sales volume.

tariff A tax on goods or services entering a country.

technology Inventions or innovations from applied science or engineering research.

telemarketing Using the telephone to interact with and sell directly to consumers.

test marketing The process of offering a product for sale on a limited basis in a defined area to gain consumer reaction to the actual product and to examine its commercial viability and the marketing program.

theatre test A pretest in which consumers view test ads in new television shows or movies and report their feelings on electronic recording devices or questionnaires.

time poverty Situation where number of tasks is expanding and time to do them is shrinking.

time utility The value to consumers of having a good or service available when needed.

total cost The total expense incurred by a firm in producing and marketing a product. Total cost is the sum of fixed cost and variable cost.

total logistics cost Expenses associated with transportation, materials handling and warehousing, inventory, stockouts, order processing, and return goods handling.

total revenue The total money received from the sale of a product equal to the unit prices times the quantity sold.

trade (functional) discounts Price reductions to reward wholesalers or retailers for marketing functions they will perform in the future.

trade-in allowance A price reduction given when a used product is part of the payment on a new product.

trademark Identifies that a firm has legally registered its brand name or trade name so the firm has its exclusive use.

trade name A commercial, legal name under which a company does business.

trade-oriented sales promotions Sales tools used to support a company's advertising and personal selling efforts directed to wholesalers, distributors, or retailers. Three common approaches are allowances and discounts, cooperative advertising, and sales force training.

trading down Reducing the number of features, quality, or price.

trading up Adding value to a product (or line) through additional features or higher-quality materials.

traditional auction A seller puts an item up for sale and would-be buyers are invited to bid in competition with each other.

traffic generation The outcome of a direct marketing offer designed to motivate people to visit a business.

transactional websites Electronic storefronts.

transnational firm Views the world as one market and emphasizes universal consumer needs and wants more than differences among cultures; see global marketing strategy.

trend extrapolation Extending a pattern observed in past data into the future.

trial The consumer's actual first purchase and use of the product or brand.

trial close Involves asking the prospect to make a decision on some aspect of the purchase such as the color or model.

truck jobber Small merchant wholesalers who have a small warehouse from which they stock their trucks for distribution to retailers. They handle products such as bakery items, dairy products, and meat.

tying arrangement A seller requires the purchaser of one product also to buy another item in the line.

ultimate consumers The people who use the goods and services purchased for a household.

uncontrollable factors (see *environmental factors*)

uniform delivered pricing The price the seller quotes includes all transportation costs.

unit variable cost Variable cost expressed on a per unit basis.

universal product code (UPC) A number assigned to identify each product, represented by a series of bars of varying widths for scanning by optical readers.

unsought goods Items that the consumer either does not know about or knows about but does not initially want.

urgency close Used to commit the prospect quickly by making reference to the timeliness of the purchase.

usage rate Quantity consumed or patronage—store visits—during a specific period; varies significantly among different customer groups.

users People in the organization who actually use the product or service purchased by the buying centre.

utilitarianism A moral philosophy that focuses on the "greatest good for the greatest number" by assessing the costs and benefits of the consequences of ethical behaviour.

utility Benefits or customer value received by users of the product.

value Specifically, value can be defined as the ratio of perceived benefits to price (Value 5 Perceived benefits/Price).

value added Dimension of the retail positioning matrix that refers to elements such as location, product reliability, or prestige.

value analysis A systematic appraisal of the design, quality, and performance of a product to reduce purchasing costs.

value consciousness The concern for obtaining the best quality, features, and performance of a product or service for a given price.

value-pricing The practice of simultaneously increasing service and product benefits and maintaining or decreasing price.

values Personally or socially preferable modes of conduct or states of existence that tend to persist over time.

variable cost The sum of the expenses of the firm that vary directly with the quantity of product that is produced and sold.

vending machines Make it possible to serve customers when and where stores cannot.

vendor-managed inventory An inventory management system whereby the supplier determines the product amount and assortment a customer (such as a retailer) needs and automatically delivers the appropriate items.

venture teams Multidisciplinary groups of marketing, manufacturing, and R&D personnel who stay with a new product from conception to production.

vertical conflict Disagreement between different levels in a marketing channel.

vertical marketing systems Professionally managed and centrally coordinated marketing channels designed to achieve channel economies and maximum marketing impact.

vertical price fixing The practice whereby sellers are required not to sell products below a minimum retail price. Also called resale price maintenance.

viral marketing Internet/Web-enabled promotional strategy that encourages users to forward market-initiated messages to others via e-mail.

want A need that is shaped by a person's knowledge, culture, and individual characteristics.

warehouse A location, often decentralized, that a firm uses to store, consolidate, age, or mix stock; house product-recall programs; or ease tax burdens.

warehouse clubs Large retail stores (over 100,000 square feet) that require a yearly fee to shop at the store.

warranty A statement indicating the liability of the manufacturer for product deficiencies.

wasted coverage People outside a company's target audience who see, hear, or read the company's advertising.

wheel of retailing A concept that describes how new retail outlets enter the market as low-status, low-margin stores and gradually add embellishments that raise their prices, and status. They now face a new low-status, low-margin operator, and the cycle starts to repeat itself.

whistle-blowers Employees who report unethical or illegal actions of their employers.

wholesaler-sponsored voluntary chain A wholesaler that develops a contractual relationship with small, independent retailers to standardize and coordinate buying practices, merchandising programs, and inventory management efforts.

word of mouth People influencing each other during conversations.

World Trade Organization Institution that sets rules governing trade between its members through panels of trade experts who decide on trade disputes between members and issue binding decisions.

World Wide Web Part of the Internet that supports a retrieval system (browser) that formats information and documents into Web pages.

yield management pricing The charging of different prices to maximize revenue for a set amount of capacity at any given time.

CHAPTER NOTES

CHAPTER 1

1. Data in Figure 1-1 are based on sports participation statistics published by the National Sporting Goods Association and the Sporting Goods Manufacturers Association (www.nsga.org and www.sgma.com).
2. See the website of the American Marketing Association, www.marketingpower.com.
3. Personal interview with Jeremy Stonier, American Marketing Association website, www.marketingpower.com/live/content.php?Item_ID=4620, February 5, 2003.
4. E. Jerome McCarthy, *Basic Marketing: A Managerial Approach* (Homewood, IL: Richard D. Irwin, 1960); and Walter van Waterschoot and Christophe Van den Bulte, "The 4P Classification of the Marketing Mix Revisited," *Journal of Marketing*, October 1992, pp. 83 - 93.
5. James Surowiecki, "The Return of Michael Porter," *Fortune*, February 1999, pp. 135 - 38; and Kathleen M. Eisenhardt and Shona L. Brown, "Time Pacing: Competing in Markets That Won't Stand Still," *Harvard Business Review*, March - April 1998, pp. 59 - 69.
6. Leigh Muzlay, "Shoes That Morph from Sneakers to Skates Are Flying Out of Stores," *The Wall Street Journal*, July 26, 2001, p. B1; and The SGMA Report 2000, "The U.S. Athletic Footwear Market Today," published by the Sporting Goods Manufacturers Association.
7. The material on Rollerblade's current marketing strategy is based on personal interviews with Jeremy Stonier and Nicholas Skally on February 5, 2003, and on information from the Rollerblade website and Rollerblade sales materials.
8. *Annual Report* (New York: General Electric Company, 1952), p. 21.
9. John C. Narver, Stanley F. Slater, and Brian Tietje, "Creating a Market Orientation," *Journal of Market Focused Management*, no. 2 (1998), pp. 241 - 55; Stanley F. Slater and John C. Narver, "Market Orientation and the Learning Organization," *Journal of Marketing*, July 1995, pp. 63 - 74; and George S. Day, "The Capabilities of Market-Driven Organizations," *Journal of Marketing*, October 1994, pp. 37 - 52.
10. The definition of customer relationship management is adapted from Rajendra K. Srivastava, Tasadduq A. Shervani, and Liam Fahey, "Marketing, Business Processes, and Shareholder Value: An Embedded View of Marketing Activities and the Discipline of Marketing," *Journal of Marketing*, special issue, 1999, pp. 168 - 79.
11. Michael E. Porter and Claas van er Linde, "Green and Competitive Ending the Stalemate," *Harvard Business Review*, September - October 1995, pp. 120 - 34; Jacquelyn Ottman, "Edison Winners Show Smart Environmental Marketing," *Marketing News*, July 17, 1995, pp. 16, 19; and Jacquelyn Ottman, "Mandate for the '90s: Green Corporate Image," *Marketing News*, September 11, 1995, p.8.

Rollerblade: This case is based on personal interviews with Jeremy Stonier and Nicholas Skally and on Rollerblade materials.

CHAPTER 2

1. www.benjerry.com.
2. Blair S. Walker, "Good-Humored Activist Back to the Fray," *USA Today*, December 8, 1992, pp. 1B - 2B.
3. Jim Castelli, "Finding the Right Fit: Are You Weird Enough?" *HR Magazine*, September 1990, pp. 38 - 39.
4. Unilever Annual Report, 2002, p. 28.
5. www.benjerry.com/our_company/our_mission.
6. Ibid.
7. Roger A. Kerin, Vijay Mahajan, and P. Rajan Varadarajan, *Contemporary Perspectives on Strategic Marketing Planning* (Boston: Allyn & Bacon, 1990), chap. 1; and Orville C. Walker, Jr., Harper W. Boyd, Jr., and Jean-Claude Larreche, *Marketing Strategy* (Burr Ridge, IL: Richard D. Irwin, 1992), chaps. 1 and 2.
8. Theodore Levitt, "Marketing Myopia," *Harvard Business Review*, July - August 1960, pp. 45 - 56.
9. Kenneth E. Goodpaster and Thomas E. Holloran, "Anatomy of Spiritual and Social Awareness: The Case of Medtronic, Inc." Third International Symposium on Catholic Social Thought and Management Education, Goa, India, 1999, p. 9.
10. George Stalk, Phillip Evans, and Lawrence E. Shulman, "Competing on Capabilities. The New Rules of Corporate Strategy," *Harvard Business Review*, March - April 1992, pp. 57 - 69.
11. Roger A. Kerin and Robert A. Peterson, *Strategic Marketing Problems: Cases and Comments*, 8th ed. (Englewood Cliffs, NJ: Prentice Hall), pp. 2 - 3; and Derek F. Abell, *Defining the Business* (Englewood Cliffs, NJ: Prentice Hall, 1980), p. 18.
12. Christopher Meyer, *Fast Cycle Time* (New York: Free Press, 1993); and Michael E. Porter, *Competitive Advantage* (New York: Free Press, 1985).
13. "Lands' End Debuts at All 870 Sears Full-Line Stores," Sears corporate press release, August 25, 2003.
14. Michael Totty, "Making the Sale," *The Wall Street Journal*, September 24, 2001, p. R6.
15. Adapted from "The Experience Curve Reviewed, IV. The Growth Share Matrix of the Product Portfolio" (Boston: The Boston Consulting Group, 1973).
16. Kerin, Mahajan, and Vardarajan, *Contemporary Perspectives*, p. 52.
17. Linda Swenson and Kenneth E. Goodpaster, *Medtronic in China (A)* (Minneapolis, MN: University of St. Thomas, 1999), pp. 4 - 5.
18. "Kodak to focus on digital," *The Globe and Mail*, August 22, 2003, p. B5.
19. Mark Maremont, "Kodak's New Focus," *Business Week*, January 30, 1995, pp. 63 - 68.
20. Daniel Eisenberg, "Kodak's Photo Op," *Time*, April 30, 2001, pp. 46 - 47.
21. Michael Ryan, "Kodak's Big Moment," *Smartbusinessmay.com*, July 2001, pp. 79 - 84.
22. Ibid.
23. Mike Musgrove, " 'Y' Factor: A Camera That Tapes and Plays," *Washington Post*, March 24, 2001, p. E1.
24. "Kodak to focus on digital," *The Globe and Mail*, August 22, 2003, p. B5.
25. "Kodak Realigns Operations and Leadership Team to Pursue Growth Opportunities in Commercial and Consumer Markets," Kodak corporate press release, August 21, 2003.

Specialized Bicycle Components, Inc.: This case is based on an e-mail interview with Aaron Moulton of Specialized and on Specialized website materials.

CHAPTER 3

1. David Kirkpatrick, "In Napster's Void: You've Got Misery!" *Fortune*, April 2, 2001, pp. 144 - 46; and Devin Leonard, "Don't Call Them Napster," *Fortune*, June 25, 2001, p. 44.

2. Vito Pilieci, "Ottawa company plans to wipe out Net music piracy," *The Gazette* (Montreal), July 23, 2003, p. B12.

3. Glenn Gamboa, "Music: Get your favourite songs on-line for less than a buck," *The Vancouver Sun*, August 21, 2003, p. C7.

4. Chris Taylor, "More Pain for Napster," *Time*, April 16, 2001, p. 43; Monica Roman, "Napster Gets Some Big Buddies," *Business Week*, June 18, 2001, p. 46; Joseph Menn and Jon Healey, "Napster founder pursues legitimate venture," *The Vancouver Sun*, July 8, 2003, p. D5; and Nick Wingfield, *The Wall Street Journal*, July 28, 2003, p. A3.

5. "2001 Census of Canada," Statistics Canada, www12.statcan.ca/english/census01/release/index.cfm.

6. "Metropolitan Outlook — Spring 2003," Conference Board of Canada.

7. Statistics Canada Catalogue # 97F0003XCB01002.

8. Statistics Canada Catalogue # 97F0003XCB01001.

9. "Projected population, by age group and sex, Canada, provinces and territories, July 1, 2000–2026, annual," Statistics Canada Cansim table # 052-0001.

10. "Money and the Canadian Family," The Vanier Institute, www.vifamily.ca.

11. "Historical Statistics of Canada, Second Edition," Statistics Canada, Series B1-14, Catalogue No. 84F0210XPB.

12. Statistics Canada Catalogue # 97F0003XCB01002.

13. "Money and the Canadian Family," The Vanier Institute, www.vifamily.ca.

14. Statistics Canada, Market Research Handbook, 63-224.

15. Statistics Canada Catalogue # 97F0003XCB01001.

16. David K. Foot, *Boom, Bust & Echo: How to Profit from the Coming Demographic Shift* (Toronto: Macfarlane Walter & Ross, 1996).

17. "Getting Inside Gen Y," *American Demographics*, September 2001, p. 44.

18. Statistics Canada Catalogue # 97F0003XCB01001.

19. Statistics Canada Catalogue # 97F0003XCB01002.

20. "United Nations - Population Division - Department of Economic and Social Affairs - February 2001," Statistics Canada, http://geodepot.statcan.ca/Diss/Highlights/Page2/Chart3_e.cfm.

21. Statistics Canada catalogue 97F0001XCB2001002.

22. "Population and Dwelling Counts, for Census Metropolitan Areas and Census Agglomerations, 2001 and 1996 Censuses," Statistics Canada, www12.statcan.ca/english/census01/products/standard/popdwell/Table-CMA-N.cfm.

23. "Provincial and territorial population changes: A century of populations growth," Statistics Canada, http://geodepot.statcan.ca/Diss/Highlights/Page3/Page3_e.cfm.

24. "Canada's ethnocultural portrait: The changing mosaic," Statistics Canada, www12.statcan.ca/english/census01/Products/Analytic/companion/etoimm/canada.cfm.

25. Ibid.

26. Ibid.

27. Ibid.

28. Ibid.

29. Statistics Canada catalogue 97F0007XCB01007.

30. "Selected Birth and Fertility Statistics," Statistics Canada, catalogue #82-553, Series B1-14.

31. "Labour force and participation rates by sex and age group," Statistics Canada, www.statcan.ca/english/Pgdb/labor05.htm.

32. Statistics Canada Daily, August 12, 2003.

33. Statistics Canada Daily, May 30, 2003.

34. "1971 Census of Canada," Statistics Canada, Catalogue 93-710; Statistics Canada Catalogue 95F0437XCB014004; and "Consumer price index (CPI), 2001 basket content, annual," Statistics Canada, CANSIM Table 326-0002.

35. Elizabeth Corcoran, "The Next Small Think," *Forbes*, July 23, 2001, pp. 96 - 106; Michael J. Mandel and Robert D. Hof, "Rethinking the Internet," *Business Week*, March 26, 2001, pp. 117 - 22; Catherine Arnst, "The Birth of a Cancer Drug," *Business Week*, July 9, 2001, pp. 95 - 102; and Clint Willis, "25 Cool Things You Wish You Had and Will," *Forbes ASAP*, June 1, 1998, pp. 49 - 60.

36. Neil Gross, Peter Coy, and Otis Post, "The Technology Paradox," *Business Week*, March 6, 1995, pp. 76 - 84.

37. Leon Jaroff, "Smart's the Word in Detroit," *Time*, February 6, 1995, pp. 50 - 52.

38. Willis, "25 Cool Things You Wish You Had and Will."

39. "All Plastic Bottle Collection program increases yields," Canadian Plastics Industry Association, March 11, 2004, www.cpia.ca/newsroom/details.php?ID=431.

40. Jim Carlton, "Recycling Redefined," *The Wall Street Journal*, March 6, 2001, pp. B1, B4; Stephanie Anderson, "There's Gold in Those Hills of Soda Bottles," *Business Week*, September 11, 1995, p. 48; Maxine Wilkie, "Asking Americans to Use Less Stuff," *American Demographics*, December 1994, pp. 11 - 12; and Jacquelyn Ottman, "New and Improved Won't Do," *Marketing News*, January 30, 1995, p. 9.

41. International Trade Administration definition reported in A. J. Campbell, "Ten Reasons Why Your Company Should Use Electronic Commerce," *Business America*, May 1998, p. 12; Andrew Urbaczewski, Leonard M. Jessup, and Bradley C. Wheeler, "A Manager's Primer on Electronic Commerce," *Business Horizons*, September - October 1998, pp. 5 - 16; and Ravi Kalakota and Andrew B. Whinston, *Electronic Commerce: A Manager's Guide* (Reading, MA: Addison-Wesley, 1997).

42. John Wilke, Ted Bridis, and Nick Wingfield, "Microsoft Scores a Big Legal Victory," *The Wall Street Journal*, June 29, 2001, pp. B1, B3; and Steve Hamm, Amy Cortese, and Susan B. Garland, "Microsoft's Future," *Business Week*, January 19, 1998, pp. 59 - 68.

Flyte Time Productions, Inc.: This case was written by William Rudelius based on personal interviews with Jimmy Jam and Terry Lewis and the following sources: Jon Bream, "Flyte Tyme Is Still Ticking after 20 Years of Hits," *Star Tribune*, April 29, 2001, pp. F1, F7; and "Jimmy Jam and Terry Lewis Make Flyte Tyme Studios No. 1," *Business Wire*, August 21, 2001.

CHAPTER 4

1. www.vancity.com/community.

2. "Just How Honest Are You?" *Inc.*, February 1995, p. 104.

3. Ray O. Werner, "Marketing and the Supreme Court in Transition, 1982 - 1984," *Journal of Marketing*, Summer 1985, pp. 97 - 105; and Jane Bryant Quinn, "Computer Program Deceives Consumers," *Dallas Morning News*, March 2, 1998, p. B3.

4. Ann Carroll and Aaron Derfel, "Surgery patients warned of HIV: Infected doctor operated on 2,614 over 13 years," *Calgary Herald*, January 23, 2004, p. A5.

5. Jim Bronskill, "Scandals have 'shaken our trust' in corporate Canada, poll finds," *Ottawa Citizen*, December 26, 2002, p. A1.

6. "The Rot at the Top," *National Post*, April 24, 2002, p. A21.

7. Dan T. Swartwood and Richard J. Hefferman, *Trends in Intellectual Property Loss, Survey Report* (Alexandria, VA: American Society for Industrial Security, 1998).

8. "Five Years: $59.2 Billion Lost," Software & Information Industry Association press release, May 2000.

9. Vern Terpstra and Kenneth David, *The Cultural Environment of International Business*, 3rd ed. (Cincinnati: South-Western, 1991), p. 12.

10. Competition Bureau website, http://cb-bc.gc.ca/epic/internet/incb-bc.nsf/en/home.

11. Consumers' Association of Canada website, www.consumer.ca/1625.

12. "Carnivore in the Cabbage Patch," *U.S. News and World Report*, January 20, 1997, p. 69.

13. "P&G Expected to Get about $120 Million in Settlement of Chewy-Cookie Lawsuit," *The Wall Street Journal*, September 11, 1989, p. B10.

14. www.transparency.de, downloaded August 9, 2002.

15. "KPMG Ethics Survey 2000: Managing for Ethical Practice," KPMG LLP, www.kpmg.ca/en/services/forensic/documents/EthicsSurvey2000.pdf.

16. ZENON Environmental website, www.zenonenv.com.

17. *The 2000 National Business Ethics Survey* (Washington, DC: Ethics Resource Center, 2000).

18. "KPMG Ethics Survey 2000: Managing for Ethical Practice," KPMG LLP, www.kpmg.ca/en/services/forensic/documents/EthicsSurvey2000.pdf.

19. "50 Best Corporate Citizens," Corporate Knights Inc., www.corporateknights.ca/best50/index.asp.

20. Tamara Gignac, "Ethical lapses keep on coming," *Calgary Herald*, June 6, 2003, p. D1; and conversation with Jerry Lemmon, Razorquest.

21. Harvey S. James and Farhad Rassekh, "Smith, Friedman, and Self-Interest in Ethical Society," *Business Ethics Quarterly*, July 2000, pp. 659 - 74.

22. "Beating the Odds in Biotech," *Newsweek*, October 12, 1992, p. 63.

23. "Perrier - Overresponding to a Crisis," in Robert F. Hartley, *Marketing Mistakes and Successes*, 8th ed. (New York: John Wiley & Sons, 2001), pp. 127 - 37.

24. Harvey Meyer, "The Greening of Corporate America," *Journal of Business Strategy*, January - February 2000, pp. 38 - 43; and Irina Maslennikova and David Foley, "Xerox's Approach to Sustainability," *Interfaces*, May - June 2000, pp. 226 - 33.

25. Just Cause Marketing website, www.justcause.ca/clients.html; and CIBC website, www.cibc.com/ca/inside-cibc/cibc-your-community/sponsorship.html.

26. "Saving the Earth, One Click at a Time," *American Demographics*, January 2001, pp. 30 - 34; "The Socially Correct Corporation"; and "The Wider Benefits of Backing a Good Cause."

27. These steps are adapted from J. J. Carson and G. A. Steiner, *Measuring Business Social Performance: The Corporate Social Audit* (New York: Committee for Economic Development, 1974). See also, Sandra Waddock and Neil Smith, "Corporate Responsibility Audits: Doing Well by Doing Good," *Sloan Management Review*, Winter 2000, pp. 75 - 84.

28. "A World of Sweatshops," *Business Week*, November 6, 2000, pp. 84 - 86.

29. "Who's Responsible?" *American Demographics*, December 1999, p. 17; Meyer, "The Greening of Corporate America"; and Waddock and Smith, "Corporate Responsibility Audits."

30. "Poll rates corporate Canada on CSR," *Marketing Magazine*, October 6–13, 2003, p. 26.

31. Saskatchewan Justice website, www.saskjustice.gov.sk.ca/cpb/rightsrespon.shtml.

32. "Factoids," *Research Alert*, December 1, 2000, p. 4; Paul Bernstein, "Cheating: The New National Pastime?" *Business*, October - December 1995, pp. 24 - 33; and "Penny for Your Thoughts," *American Demographics*, September 2000, pp. 8 - 9.

33. "A Lighter Shade of Green," *American Demographics*, February 2000, p. 24.

34. "Schism on the Green," *Brandweek*, February 26, 2001, p. 18.

35. Paul Hanley, "Green cars gain global advantage," *The StarPhoenix* (Saskatoon), December 2, 2003, p. C2.

Pharmaceutical pricing: [TK – need citation from Berkowitz 5CE chapter notes for chapter 4]

CHAPTER 5

1. Ted Latumus, "Cars That Women Love: Automakers Reckon with Female Buying Power," *Western Driver*, November 2001.

2. Ibid.

3. "Women in the Automotive Industry" and "He Said, She Said," www.womanmotorist.com, downloaded August 28, 2001; "Selling Cars to Women: Make & Model, Experience at Dealership Matter More," www.diversity.com, downloaded May 7, 2001; and "A Sweet Deal," *American Demographics*, January 2000, pp. 10 - 11.

4. Toyota Canada website, www.toyota.ca.

5. James F. Engel, Roger D. Blackwell, and Paul Miniard, *Consumer Behavior*, 9th ed. (Fort Worth, TX: Dryden Press, 1998).

6. For thorough descriptions of consumer expertise, see Joseph W. Alba and J. Wesley Hutchinson, "Knowledge Calibration: What Consumers Know and What They Think They Know," *Journal of Consumer Research*, September 2000, pp. 123 - 56.

7. For in-depth studies on external information search patterns, see Sridhar Moorthy, Brian T. Ratchford, and Debabrata Tulukdar, "Consumer Information Search Revisited: Theory and Empirical Analysis," *Journal of Consumer Research*, March 1997, pp. 263 - 77; and Joel E. Urbany, Peter R. Dickson, and William L. Wilkie, "Buyer Uncertainty and Information Search," *Journal of Consumer Research*, March 1992, pp. 452 - 63.

8. For an extended discussion on evaluative criteria, see Del J. Hawkins, Roger J. Best, and Kenneth A. Coney, *Consumer Behavior*, 8th ed. (New York: Irwin/McGraw-Hill, 2001), pp. 566 - 83.

9. John A. Howard, *Buyer Behavior in Marketing Strategy*, 2nd ed. (Englewood Cliffs, NJ: Prentice Hall, 1994), pp. 101, 128 - 89.

10. Jagdish N. Sheth, Banwari Mitral, and Bruce Newman, *Consumer Behavior* (Fort Worth, TX: Dryden Press, 1999), p. 22.

11. Frederick F. Reichheld and Thomas Teal, *The Loyalty Effect* (Boston: Harvard Business School Press, 1996); "What's a Loyal Customer Worth?" *Fortune*, December 11, 1995, p. 182; and Patricia Sellers, "Keeping the Buyers You Already Have," *Fortune*, Autumn - Winter 1993, p. 57. For an in-depth examination of this topic, see Werner J. Reinartz and V. Kumar, "On the Profitability of Long-Life Customers in a Noncontractual Setting: An Empirical Investigation and Implications for Marketing," *Journal of Marketing*, October 2000, pp. 17 - 35.

12. Rahul Jacob, "The Struggle to Create an Organization for the 21st Century," *Fortune*, April 3, 1995, pp. 90 - 99.

13. Lands' End website, www.landsend.com/cd/fp/help/0,1452,1_36877_36883_37024__,00.html?sid=6752072684971181040.

14. For an overview of research on involvement, see John C. Mowen and Michael Minor, *Consumer Behavior*, 6th ed. (Upper Saddle River, NJ: Prentice Hall, 2001), pp. 64 - 68; and Frank R. Kardes, *Consumer Behavior* (Reading, MA: Addison-Wesley, 1999), pp. 256 - 58.

15. For an overview on the three problem-solving variations, see Hawkins, Best, and Coney, *Consumer Behavior*, pp. 506 - 7; and Howard, *Buyer Behavior*, pp. 69 - 162.

16. Russell Belk, "Situational Variables and Consumer Behavior," *Journal of Consumer Research*, December 1975, pp. 157 - 63.

17. A. H. Maslow, *Motivation and Personality* (New York: Harper & Row, 1970).

18. Arthur Koponen, "The Personality Characteristics of Purchasers," *Journal of Advertising Research*, September 1960, pp. 89 - 92; Joel B. Cohen, "An Interpersonal Orientation to the Study of Consumer Behavior," *Journal of Marketing Research*, August 1967, pp. 270 - 78; and Rena Bartos, *Marketing to Women around the World* (Cambridge, MA: Harvard Business School, 1989).

19. Myron Magnet, "Let's Go for Growth," *Fortune*, March 7, 1994, p. 70.

20. Michael R. Solomon, *Consumer Behavior*, 5th ed. (Upper Saddle River, NJ: Prentice Hall, 2002), p. 61.

21. BMW website, www.bmw.com/generic/com/en/services/service/index.html?content=service_overview.html.

22. Martin Fishbein and I. Aizen, *Belief, Attitude, Intention and Behavior: An Introduction to Theory and Research* (Reading, MA: Addison-Wesley, 1975), p. 6.

23. Richard J. Lutz, "Changing Brand Attitudes through Modification of Cognitive Structure," *Journal of Consumer Research*, March 1975, pp. 49 - 59; "Pepsi's Gamble Hits Freshness Dating Jackpot," *Advertising Age*, September 19, 1994, p. 50; and "Every Which Way to Color, Whiten, Brighten," *Brandweek*, June 17, 2002, p. 558.

24. www.future.sri.com, downloaded January 3, 2002; Eric Arnould, Linda Price, and George Zinkham, *Consumers* (Burr Ridge, IL: McGraw-Hill/Irwin, 2002), pp. 285 - 90.

25. See, for example, Lawrence F. Feick and Linda Price, "The Market Maven: A Diffuser of Marketplace Information," *Journal of Marketing*, January 1987, pp. 83 - 97.

26. "Maximizing the Market with Influentials," *American Demographics*, July 1995, p. 42; also see, "I'll Have What He's Having," *American Demographics*, July 2000, p. 22.

27. Representative recent work on positive and negative word of mouth can be found in Robert E. Smith and Christine A. Vogt, "The Effects of Integrating Advertising and Negative Word-of-Mouth Communications on Message Processing and Response," *Journal of Consumer Psychology* 4 (1995), pp. 133-51; Paula Bone, "Word-of-Mouth Effects on Short-Term and Long-Term Product Judgments," *Journal of Business Research* 32 (1995), pp. 213-23; Chip Walker, "Word of Mouth," *American Demographics*, July 1995, pp. 38-45; and Dale F. Duhan, Scott D. Johnson, James B. Wilcox, and Gilbert D. Harrell, "Influences on Consumer Use of Word-of-Mouth Recommendation Sources," *Journal of the Academy of Marketing Science*, Fall 1997, pp. 283-95.

28. For an extended discussion on reference groups, see Wayne D. Hoyer and Deborah J. MacInnis, *Consumer Behavior*, 2nd ed. (Boston: Houghton Miffin, 2001), chap. 15.

29. For an extensive review on consumer socialization of children, see Deborah Roedder John, "Consumer Socialization of Children: A Retrospective Look at Twenty-Five Years of Research," *Journal of Consumer Research*, December 1999, pp. 183-213.

30. This discussion is based on "The American Family in the 21st Century," *American Demographics*, August 2001, p. 20; and J. Paul Peter and Jerry C. Olson, *Consumer Behavior and Marketing Strategy*, 5th ed. (New York: Irwin/McGraw-Hill, 1999), pp. 341 - 43.

31. "Household Type, in Private Households, 2001 Counts, for Canada, Provinces and Territories," Statistics Canada, www12.statcan.ca/english/census01/products/highlight/PrivateHouseholds/Page.cfm?Lang=E&Geo=PR&Code=0&View=1a&Table=1&StartRec=1&Sort=2&B1=Counts.

32. Diane Crispell, "Dual-Earner Diversity," *American Demographics*, July 1995, pp. 32 - 37.

33. "There She Is . . . ." *American Demographics*, August 2001, p. 6; "Wearing the Pants," *Brandweek*, October 20, 1997, pp. 20, 22; and "Look Who's Shopping," *Progressive Grocer*, January 1998, p. 18.

34. "Call It 'Kid-fluence,'" *U.S. News & World Report*, July 30, 2001, pp. 32 - 33; "Special Report: Superstars of Spending," *Advertising Age*, February 20, 2001, pp. S1, S10; and Teen Research Unlimited, www.teenresearch.com, downloaded September 4, 2001.

35. Statistics Canada Catalogue # 97F0007XCB01007.

36. [TK: Pick up Berkowitz footnote 52 from somewhere around pp. 139-140]

37. "Canada's ethnocultural portrait: The changing mosaic," Statistics Canada, www12.statcan.ca/english/census01/products/analytic/companion/etoimm/contents.cfm.

The Consumer on the Couch: [TK – need citation from Berkowitz 5CE chapter notes for chapter 4]

CHAPTER 6

1. Gerry Bellett, "LED firm sets out to shake up the world," *Vancouver Sun*, December 15, 2003, p. D7.

2. TIR Systems website, www.tirsys.com/technology/technology_ssl.asp.

3. TIR Systems website, www.tirsys.com/corporate/corporate_our_vision.asp.

4. Peter LaPlaca, "From the Editor," *Journal of Business and Industrial Marketing*, Summer 1992, p. 3.

5. This figure is based on Statistical Abstract of the United States: 2002, 122nd ed. (Washington, DC: U.S. Census Bureau, 2002).

6. Nortel Networks website, www.nortelnetworks.com/corporate/technology/olh/index.html.

7. "FAA Announces Contract for New Workstations," *Dallas Morning News*, April 30, 1999, p. 16H; and "Canada's Manley Says Government Spending C$5 Bln Under Budget," Bloomberg.com, September 29, 2003.

8. "List of Canadian registered charities," Canada Revenue Agency website, www.cra-arc.gc.ca/tax/charities/online_listings/canreg_interim-e.html.

9. *2002 NAICS United States Manual* (Washington, DC: Office of Management and Budget, January 2002).

10. This listing and portions of the following discussion are based on F. Robert Dwyer and John F. Tanner, Jr., *Business Marketing*, 2nd ed. (Burr Ridge, IL: McGraw-Hill/Irwin, 2002); and Edward G. Brierty, Robert W. Eckles, and Robert R. Reeder, *Business Marketing*, 3rd ed. (Upper Saddle River, NJ: Prentice Hall, 1998).

11. "Latin Trade Connection," *Latin Trade*, June 1997, p. 72; and "Canadian firm wins contract to upgrade Cingular Wireless," *Amarillo Globe News*, March 7, 2002, http://amarillonet.com/stories/030702/tex_toupgrade.shtml.

12. "Rumble over Tokyo," *Business Week*, April 2, 2001, pp. 80 - 82; "FedEx Chooses Airbus 380," www.airwise.com, January 16, 2001; "Qatar Opts for Super Jumbo," www.airwise.com, March 1, 2001; and "Understanding the Next 20 Years," www.airbus.com/products/A380_Market, downloaded April 22, 2001.

13. This discussion is based on James C. Anderson and James A. Narus, *Business Market Management* (Upper Saddle River, NJ: Prentice Hall, 1999); and Joseph P. Cannon and Christian Homburg, "Buyer - Supplier Relationships and Customer Firm Costs," *Journal of Marketing*, January 2001, pp. 29 - 43.

14. Thomas V. Bonoma, "Major Sales: Who Really Does the Buying?" *Harvard Business Review*, May - June 1982, pp. 11 - 19.

15. Ibid.

16. These definitions are adapted from Frederick E. Webster, Jr., and Yoram Wind, *Organizational Buying Behavior* (Englewood Cliffs, NJ: Prentice Hall, 1972), p. 6.

17. "Can Corning Find Its Optic Nerve?" *Fortune*, March 19, 2001, pp. 148 - 50.

18. Representative studies on the buy-class framework that document its usefulness include Erin Anderson, Wujin Chu, and Barton Weitz, "Industrial Purchasing: An Empirical Exploration of the Buy-Class Framework," *Journal of Marketing*, July 1987, pp. 71 - 86; Morry Ghingold, "Testing the 'Buy-Grid' Buying Process Model," *Journal of Purchasing and Materials Management*, Winter 1986, pp. 30 - 36; P. Matthyssens and W. Faes, "OEM Buying Process for New Components: Purchasing and Marketing Implications," *Industrial Marketing Management*, August 1985, pp. 147 - 57; and Thomas W. Leigh and Arno J. Ethans, "A Script-Theoretic Analysis of Industrial Purchasing Behavior," *Journal of Marketing*, Fall 1984, pp. 22 - 32. Studies not supporting the buy-class framework include Joseph A. Bellizi and Philip McVey, "How Valid Is the Buy-Grid Model?" *Industrial Marketing Management*, February 1983, pp. 57 - 62; and Donald W. Jackson, Janet E. Keith, and Richard K. Burdick, "Purchasing Agents' Perceptions of Industrial Buying Center Influences: A Situational Approach," *Journal of Marketing*, Fall 1984, pp. 75 - 83.

19. "Evolution, Not Revolution," *Forbes*, May 21, 2001, pp. 38 - 39; "Business Connections: The Wired Way We Work," *Newsweek*, April 30, 2001, p. 59; and "Behind the Crystal Ball," *The Industry Standard*, March 26, 2001, pp. 81 - 83.

20. This discussion is based on Mark Roberti, "General Electric's Spin Machine," *The Industry Standard*, January 22 - 29, 2001, pp. 74 - 83; "Smart Business 50," *Smart Business*, November 2000, pp. 121 - 50; and "Grainger Lightens Its Digital Load," *Industrial Distribution*, March 2001, pp. 77 - 79.

21. "Internet Trading Exchanges: E-Marketplaces Come of Age," *Fortune*, April 15, 2001, special section; "Private Exchanges May Allow B-to-B Commerce to Thrive after All," *The Wall Street Journal*, March 16, 2001, pp. B1, B4; and Steven Kaplan and Mohanbir Sawhney, "E-Hubs: The New B2B Marketplaces," *Harvard Business Review*, May - June, 2000, pp. 97 - 103.

22. Quadrem website, www.quadrem.com.

23. A major portion of this discussion is based on Robert J. Dolan and Youngme Moon, "Pricing and Market Making on the Internet," *Journal of Interactive Marketing*, Spring 2000, pp. 56 - 73; and "Auctions Have Taken the Internet by Storm," *Dallas Morning News*, January 25, 2001, pp. 1F, 9F.

24. Bob Tedeschi, "GE Has a Bright Idea," *Smart Business*, June 2001, pp. 86 - 91.

25. Sandy Jap, "Going, Going, Going," *Harvard Business Review*, November - December, 2000, p. 30.

Lands' End: This case is based on information available on the company website (www.landsend.com) and the following sources: Robert Berner, "A Hard Bargain at Lands' End?" *Business Week* (May 28, 2001), p. 14; Rebecca Quick, "Getting the Right Fit-Hips and All-Can a Machine Measure You Better Than Your Tailor?" *The Wall Street Journal* (October 18, 2000), p. B1; Stephanie Miles, "Apparel E-tailers Spruce Up for Holidays," *The Wall Street Journal* (November 6, 2001), p. B6; Dana James, "Custom Goods Nice Means for Lands' End," *Marketing News* (August 14, 2000), p. 5.

CHAPTER 7

1. Cervélo website, www.cervelo.com.

2. "U.S. and World Population Clocks – POPClocks," U.S. Census Bureau, www.census.gov/main/www/popclock.html.

3. "GDP – purchasing power parity," GeographyIQ, www.geography-iq.com/ranking/ranking_GDP_purchasing_power_parity_dall.htm.

4. "A Fruit Peace," *The Economist*, April 21, 2001, pp. 75 - 76; and Gary C. Hufbauer and Kimberly A. Elliott, *Measuring the Cost of Protection in the United States* (Washington, DC: Institute for International Economics, 1994).

5. Joe McLaughlin, "The head of a lobby group defending American lumbermen says the latest offer to resolve the longstanding soft-wood lumber dispute with Canada is their final offer," *Red Deer Advocate*, December 11, 2003; and "Legal Proceedings in the Countervailing Duty Investigation," British Columbia Ministry of Forests, www.for.gov.bc.ca/HET/Softwood/Legal.htm.

6. "Levels of Tariff Rate Quotas for Agricultural Products," Department of Foreign Affairs and International Trade, Serial No. 509, May 15, 1995, www.dfait-maeci.gc.ca/trade/eicb/notices/ser509-en.asp.

7. This discussion is based on information provided by the World Trade Organization, at www.wto.org, downloaded September 4, 2002.

8. Gilbert Gagne, "The Canada–U.S. softwood lumber dispute: a test case for the development of international trade rules," *International Journal*, summer 2003.

9. "Regional Trade Agreements: Facts and Figures," World Trade Organization, www.wto.org/english/tratop_e/region_e/regfac_e.htm#top.

10. Ibid.

11. "GATT and the Goods Council," World Trade Organization, www.wto.org/english/tratop_e/gatt_e/gatt_e.htm.

12. For an excellent overview of different types of global companies and marketing strategies, see Warren J. Keegan, *Global Marketing Management*, 7th ed. (Upper Saddle River, NJ: Prentice Hall, 2002).

13. "Global Companies Don't Work; Multinationals Do," *Advertising Age*, April 18, 1994, p. 23; and David Benady, "Unilever in Global Ad Shake-Up," *Marketing Week*, February 11, 1999, p. 7.

14. Elissa Moses, *The $100 Billion Allowance: Accessing the Global Teen Market* (New York: John Wiley & Sons, 2000); Jim Landers, "The Tempest Abroad," *Dallas Morning News*, November 21, 2000, pp. D1, D4; "MTV Returns to Japan," *AdAge Global*, September 2000, p. 10; and "Benetton Bounces Back," *Brandweek*, February 12, 2001, pp. 1, 8.

15. This discussion is based on "Behind the Crystal Ball," *The Industry Standard*, March 26, 2001, pp. 81 - 83; and "The World's Online Populations," www.cyberatlas.com, downloaded September 2, 2002.

16. For comprehensive references on cross-cultural aspects of market-ing, see Paul A. Herbig, *Handbook of Cross-Cultural Marketing* (New York: Halworth Press, 1998); and Jean-Claude Usunier, *Marketing across Cultures*, 2nd ed. (London: Prentice Hall Europe, 1996). Unless otherwise indicated, examples found in this section appear in these excellent sources.

17. "McDonald's Adapts Mac Attack to Foreign Tastes with Expansion," *Dallas Morning News*, December 7, 1997, p. 3H; and "Taking Credit," *The Economist*, November 2, 1996, p. 75.

18. Patricia Adams, "Foreign aid corruption case puts Canada on trial," *National Post*, August 20, 1999.

19. These examples appear in Del I. Hawkins, Roger J. Best, and Kenneth A. Coney, *Consumer Behavior*, 8th ed. (Burr Ridge, IL: McGraw-Hill/Irwin, 2001), chap. 2.

20. "Greeks Protest Coke's Use of Parthenon," *Dallas Morning News*, August 17, 1992, p. D4.

21. "Global Thinking Paces Computer Biz," *Advertising Age*, March 6, 1995, p. 10.

22. This discussion is based on "Rubles? Who Needs Rubles?" *Business Week*, April 13, 1998, pp. 45 - 46; and "Betting on a New Label: Made in Russia," *Business Week*, April 12, 1999, p. 122.

23. TK.

24. Chip Walker, "The Global Middle Class," *American Demographics*, September 1995, pp. 40 - 47.

25. This discussion is based on "Mattel Plans to Double Sales Abroad," *The Wall Street Journal*, February 11, 1998, pp. A3, A11; Philip R. Cateora and John L. Graham, *International Marketing*, 11th ed. (Burr Ridge, IL: McGraw-Hill/Irwin, 2002), p. 560; and "Honda Takes Currency Hit in Europe," *The Wall Street Journal*, March 28, 2001, p. A16.

26. "EU Turning into Battleground over More Curbs on Marketing," *Advertising Age*, September 18, 2000, p. 60; "Europe Forges Ahead with Web Innovations," *Marketing News*, August 14, 2000, p. 8; and "Will East Asia Slam the Door?" *The Economist*, September 12, 1998, p. 88.

27. For an extensive and recent examination of these market-entry options and examples, see Johny K. Johansson, Global Marketing: Foreign Entry, Local Marketing, and Global Management, 3rd ed. (Burr Ridge, IL: McGraw-Hill/Irwin, 2003); Keegan, Global Marketing Management; Masaaki Kotabe and Kristiaan Helsen, Global Marketing Management, 2nd ed. (New York: Wiley, 2001), p. 440; and Philip R. Cateora and John L. Graham, *International Marketing*, 11th ed. (Burr Ridge, IL: McGraw-Hill/Irwin, 2002), p. 560.

28. Conversation with Bob Lyons, president of Terrapin Communications Inc., February 12, 2004; and www.safetyturtle.com.

29. Bombardier website, www.bombardier.com/index.jsp?id=0_0&lang=en&file= /en/0_0/0_0_1_6_1.html.

30. McDonald's website, www.mcdonalds.com/corp/about.html and www.mcdonalds.com/corp/franchise.html.

31. Toyota website, www.toyota.com/about/operations/manufactur-ing/manu_location/captin.html.

32. "Honda of Canada mfg. achieves milestone; produces its three-mil-lionth vehicle," January 12, 2004, Honda press release, http://world.honda.com/news/2004/4040112.html.

33. The examples in this section are found in "The Color of Beauty," *Forbes*, November 22, 2000, pp. 170 - 76; "It's Goo, Goo, Goo, Goo Vibrations at the Gerber Lab," *The Wall Street Journal*, December 4, 1996, pp. A1, A6; Donald R. Graber, "How to Manage a Global Product Development Process," *Industrial Marketing Management*, November 1996, pp. 483 - 98; and Herbig, *Handbook of Cross-Cultural Marketing*.

34. "McDonald's® Unveils 'i'm lovin' it™' Worldwide Brand Campaign," September 2, 2003, McDonalds press release, www.mcdonalds.com/corp/news/corppr/pr09022003.html.

35. Jagdish N. Sheth and Atul Parvatiyar, "The Antecedents and Consequences of Integrated Global Marketing," *International Marketing Review* 18, no. 1 (2001), pp. 16 - 29.

36. "Stores Told to Lift Prices in Germany," *The Wall Street Journal*, September 11, 2000, pp. A27, A30.

37. "Rotten Apples," *Dallas Morning News*, April 7, 1998, p. 14A.

38. "When Grey Is Good," *The Economist*, August 22, 1998, p. 17; and Neil Belmore, "Parallel Imports and Grey Market Issues," The Canadian Institute, December 5–6, 2001.

CNS Breathe Right Strips: This case was prepared by Giana Eckardt based on the following sources: CNS, Inc., 1997 Annual Report (Minneapolis: CNS, Inc., 1998); and personal interview with Dr. Daniel E. Cohen, chief executive officer of CNS, June 1998.

CHAPTER 8

1. John Horn, "Studios Play Name Games," *Star Tribune*, August 10, 1997, p. F11.

2. *2000 US Economic Review*, Worldwide Market Research Department, Motion Picture Association of America, pp. 14, 16.

3. Helene Diamond, "Lights, Camera . . . Research!" *Marketing News*, September 11, 1989, pp. 10 - 11; and "Killer!" *Time*, November 16, 1987, pp. 72 - 79.

4. For an expanded definition, consult the American Marketing Association's website at www.marketingpower.com/live/content.php?item_ID-4620; for a researcher's comments on this and other definitions of marketing research, see Lawrence D. Gibson, "Quo Vadis, Marketing Research?" *Marketing Research*, Spring 2000, pp. 36 - 41.

5. Conversation with John Vavrik, director of the B.C. Centre for Strategic Management of Risk in Transportation.

6. Transport Canada website, www.tc.gc.ca/roadsafety/rssrinfo/aboutrs.htm.

7. Lawrence D. Gibson, "Defining Marketing Problems," *Marketing Research*, Spring 1998, pp. 4 - 12.

8. Cyndee Miller, "Kiddi Just Fine in the UK, But Here It's Binky," *Marketing News*, August 28, 1995, p. 8.

9. Michael J. McCarthy, "Ford Companies Hunt for a 'Next Big Thing' but Few Can Find One," *The Wall Street Journal*, May 8, 1997, pp. A1, A6.

10. "Focus on Consumers," General Mills Midyear Report, Minneapolis, MN: January 8, 1998, pp. 2–3.

11. Michael J. McCarthy, "Stalking the Elusive Teenage Trend Setter," *The Wall Street Journal*, November 19, 1998, pp. B1, B10.

12. Roy Furchgott, "For Cool Hunters, Tomorrow's Trend is the Trophy," *The New York Times*, June 28, 1998, p. 10; and Emily Nelson, "The Hunt for Hip: A Trend Scout's Trail," *The Wall Street Journal*, December 9, 1998, pp, B1, B6.

13. "What TV Ratings Really Mean," Nielsen Media Research web-site, pp. 1 - 8. See www.nielsenmedia.com/ whatratingsmean.

14. "Nielsen Media Research Estimates 106.7 Million TV Households in the U.S.," Nielsen Media Research news release, August 28, 2002, p. 1.

15. Mark Maremont, "New Toothbrush Is Big-Ticket Item," *The Wall Street Journal*, October 27, 1998, pp. B1, B6; and Emily Nelson, "P&G Checks Out Real Life," *The Wall Street Journal*, May 17, 2001, pp. B1, B4.

16. Joshua Grossnickle and Oliver Raskin, "What's Ahead on the Internet," *Marketing Research*, Summer 2001, pp. 9 - 13; and Gordon A. Wyner, "Life (on the Internet) Imitates Research," *Marketing Research*, Summer 2000, pp. 38 - 39.

17. Wendy Zellner, "Look Out, Supermarkets - Wal-Mart Is Hungry," *Business Week*, September 14, 1998, pp. 98 - 100; Richard McCattery, "Wal-Mart Rumbles in the Supermarket Jungle," *The Motley Fool*, March 7, 1998, www.fool.com/news/foth/2000/foth000307.htm; and "Our 1,000 Supercenter," Wal-Mart news release, August 22, 2001.

18. Much of the step 4 discussion was written by Tere Carral of Tony's Pizza.

19. Laurence N. Gold, "High Technology Data Collection for Measurement and Testing," *Marketing Research*, March 1992, pp. 29 - 38; and information obtained from the websites of Information Resources, Inc. (www.infores.com) and AC Nielsen (www.acnielsen.com).

20. Joe Schwartz, "Back to the Source," *American Demographics*, January 1989, pp. 22 - 26; and Felix Kessler, "High-Tech Shocks in Ad Research," *Fortune*, July 7, 1986, pp. 58 - 62.

21. Mark A. Moon, John T. Mentzer, Carlo D. Smith, and Michael S. Garver, "Seven Keys to Better Forecasting," *Business Horizons*, September - October 1998, pp. 44 - 52.

22. Interview with Bill McKee, manager of Corporate Communications/Public Relations, Xerox Corporation, and annual reports available at www2.xerox.com/go/xix/about_xerox/T_archive.jsp?view=annual-reports.

Source: http://www.cbc.ca/consumers/market/files/food/sugar/index.html

CHAPTER 9

1. Material on sneakers is based on the SGMA Report 2002, "The U.S. Athletic Footwear Market Today," which is published annually by the Sporting Goods Manufacturers Association (www.sgma.com) based on a study by the NPD Group (www.npd.com), which polls 35,000 consumers weekly and collects data from over 3,500 retailers to provide this information; and April Y. Pennington, "Heeling Art," *Entrepreneur Magazine*, May 2002, www.entrepreneur.com.

2. "Heeling Sports buys Soap shoe brand," *Dallas Business Journal*, October 23, 2002, http://dallas.bizjournals.com/dallas/stories/2002/10/21/daily37.html.

3. Heelys website, www.heelys.com.

4. SGMA Report 2002, "The U.S. Athletic Footwear Market Today"; and Pennington, "Heeling Art."

5. Information obtained from press releases from www.reebok.com, www.nike.com, www.vans.com, www.footlocker-inc.com, and www.cmax.com, as well as Terry Lefton, "Mike Likes Spite for Nike's New Jordan Line," *Business Journal - Portland*, July 29, 2002, www.portland.bizjournals.com.

6. Matt Forney, "Harry Potter, Meet 'Ha-li Bo-te,'" *The Wall Street Journal*, September 21, 2000, p. B1; Gerry Khermouch, "Buzzzz Marketing," *Business Week*, July 30, 2001, pp. 50 - 56; and "Potter Back on Top," February 2, 2002, BBC News, www.news.bbc.lo.uk.

7. "Special Report on Mass Customization: A Long March," *The Economist*, July 14, 2001, pp. 63 - 65.

8. Goldfarb Consultants, Toronto, February, 1999.

9. Example provided by Allison Scoleri, Goldfarb Consultants, Toronto, February 1, 1999.

10. Ibid.

11. Chris Daniels, "Wild for Wildness," www.marketingmag.ca, June 4, 2001.

12. Sanjoy S. Mehta and Gurinderjit B. Mehta, "Development and Growth of the Busines Class: Strategic Implications for the Airline Industry," *Journal of Customer Service in Marketing and Management*, vol. 3, no. 1 (1997), pp. 59–78.

13. *National Consumer Survey Choices 3 Crosstabulation Report: Fast-Food Restaurants* (New York: Simmons Market Research Bureau, Spring, 2001).

14. Jennifer Ordonez, "Taco Bell Chef Has New Tactic: Be Like Wendy's," *The Wall Street Journal*, February 23, 2001, pp. B1, B4; and Jennifer Ordonez, "An Efficiency Drive: Fast-Food Lanes Are Getting Even Faster," *The Wall Street Journal*, May 18, 2000, pp. A1, A10.

15. Dennis Sellers, "Business Journal: Digital Hub Plan Just Might Work," *MacCentral*, January 16, 2001, Mac Publishing, LLC.

16. Rebecca Winters, "Chocolate Milk," *Time*, April 30, 2001, p. 20.

Nokia: This case was written by Michael Vessey and Steven Hartley based on information available on the company website (www.nokia.com); correspondence with Keith Nowak; a personal interview with Paul Dittner of Gartner Dataquest; Ari Bensinger, "Weaker Signals for Mobile Phone Firms," *Business Week Online*, April 6, 2001; "The Cellular Telecommunications & Internet Association's Wireless Industry Survey," www.wow-com.com; "Nokia's First Imaging Phone Marks Start of Multimedia Messaging Era," Nokia press release, November 19, 2001; "New Nokia 6340 Handset to Enable Roaming Across TDMA, GSM Networks," Nokia press release, January 7, 2002; "Nokia Unveils a New Active Category for Mobile Phones," Nokia press release, November 19, 2001; and "Users Say 'No Thanks' to Mobile Advertising Unless Vendors Take Right Approach," In-Stat Group press release, October 31, 2001, www.instat.com; "Global FY Handset Shipments Seen Up 1.8% - IDC," Ananova.com press release; "Gartner Dataquest Says Fourth Quarter Sales Lead Mobile Phone Market to 6 Percent Growth in 2002," Gartner Dataquest press release; Sue Marek, "Handsets: Catching Customers with Color," January 1, 2003, *Wireless Week* (see www.wirelessweek.com).

CHAPTER 10

1. Personal interview with Kenneth M. Hart, Ph.D., 3M, 2002.

2. Ibid.

3. Terry Fiedler, "3M Innovation to Be Tested," *Star Tribune*, December 10, 2000, pp. D1, D11.

4. Definitions within this section are adapted from Peter D. Bennett, *Dictionary of Marketing Terms*, 2nd ed. (Lincolnwood, IL: NTC Publishing Group, 1995); and Committee on Definitions, *Marketing Definitions: A Glossary of Marketing Terms* (Chicago: American Marketing Association, 1985).

5. General Mills corporate website, www.generalmills.com.

6. "Gross Domestic Product (GDP) at basic prices, by NAICS," Cansim series V2036138, Statistics Canada; "Gross Domestic Product (GDP) at basic prices, special industry aggregations," Cansim series V2044341, Statistics Canada; and "Gross Domestic Product (GDP) at basic prices, special industry aggregations," Cansim series V2044342, Statistics Canada.

7. Christopher H. Lovelock, *Services Marketing*, 4th ed. (Upper Saddle River, NJ: Prentice-Hall, 2001).

8. Robert Berner, "Why P&G's Smile Is So Bright," *Business Week*, August 12, 2002, pp. 58 - 60.

9. Morgan L. Swink and Vincent A. Mabert, "Product Development Partnerships: Balancing Needs of OEMs and Suppliers," *Business Horizons*, May - June 2000, pp. 59 - 68.

10. Alec Klein, "The Techies Grumbled, but Polaroid's Pocket Turned into a Huge Hit," *The Wall Street Journal*, May 2, 2000, pp. A1, A10.

11. Dennis Berman, "Now Tennis Balls Are Chasing Dogs," *Business Week*, July 23, 1998, p. 138.

12. Jonathan Eig, "General Mills Intends to Reshape Doughboy in Its Own Image," *The Wall Street Journal*, July 18, 2000, pp. A1, A8; Julie Forster, "The Lucky Charm of Steve Sanger," *Business Week*, March 26, 2001, pp. 75 - 76; 2000 General Mills Annual Report, pp. 1 - 13; Joseph L. Bower, "Not All MAs Are Alike - and That Matters," *Harvard Business Review*, March 2001, pp. 92 - 101.

13. 2000 General Mills Annual Report, pp. 8 - 13.

14. Gary Hammel, "Innovation's New Math," *Fortune*, July 9, 2001, pp. 130 - 31.

15. Bill Vlasic, "When Air Bags Aren't Enough," *Business Week*, June 8, 1998, pp. 84 - 86; and Arthur J. Cummins, "Detroit Faces Crunch Time: Designing Gentler SUV's," *The Wall Street Journal*, February 25, 1998, pp. B1, B9.

16. Tom Molson and George Sproles, "Styling Strategy," *Business Horizons*, September-October 2000, pp. 45 - 52.

17. Christopher Ryan, "Virtual reality in marketing," *Direct Marketing*, April 2001, p. 57.

18. Jennifer Ordonez, "How Burger King Got Burned in Quest to Make the Perfect Fry," *The Wall Street Journal*, January 16, 2001, pp. A1, A8.

19. Greg A. Stevens and James Burley, "3,000 Raw Ideas 5 1 Commercial Success!" *Research-Technology Management*, May - June 1997, pp. 16 - 27.

20. R. G. Cooper and E. J. Kleinschmidt, "New Products - What Separates Winners from Losers?" *Journal of Product Innovation Management*, September 1987, pp. 169 - 84; Robert G. Cooper, *Winning at New Products*, 2nd ed. (Reading, MA: Addison-Wesley, 1993), pp. 49 - 66; and Thomas D. Kuczmarski, "Measuring Your Return on Innovation," *Marketing Management*, Spring 2000, pp. 25 - 32.

21. Greg Burns, "Has General Mills Had Its Wheaties?" *Business Week*, May 8, 1995, pp. 68 - 69.

22. John Gilbert, "To Sell Cars in Japan, U.S. Needs to Offer More Right-Drive Models," *Star Tribune*, May 27, 1995, p. M1.

23. "Sonic Sinker," *The Economist*, November 23, 2002, p. 58.

24. Marcia Mogelonsky, "Product Overload?" *American Demographics*, August 1998, pp. 5 - 12.

25. Family Time Store website, www.familytimestore.com/monster-spray.cfm; and e-mail communication with Erin Torres, customer service, OUT! International.

Palm Inc.: This case was written by Michael Vessey and Steven W. Hartley.

CHAPTER 11

1. "The Jones Soda Story," Jones Soda Co. website, www.jonessoda.com/stockstuff/story.html.

2. Beverly Cramp, "Reinventing Cool," *Profit*, December 2001/January 2002, pp. 41 - 44; and "The Jones Soda Story."

3. Glenn Rifkin, "Mach 3: Anatomy of Gillette's Latest Global Launch," *Strategy & Business*, 2nd Quarter 1999, pp. 34 - 41.

4. "There's No Replacement - Not Even E-Mail," *Purchasing Online*, downloaded June 15, 2001; "Fax Is Still a Favorite, Despite the Alternatives," *Computing Canada*, June 25, 1999, pp. 62 - 65; and "We've All Got Mail," *Newsweek*, May 15, 2000, p. 73k.

5. "Why Coke Indulges (the Few) Fans of Tab," *The Wall Street Journal*, April 13, 2001, pp. B1, B4.

6. "Gillette's Edge," *Brandweek*, May 28, 2001, p. 5.

7. "How to Separate Trends from Fads," *Brandweek*, October 23, 2000, pp. 30, 32.

8. Everett M. Rogers, *Diffusion of Innovations*, 4th ed. (New York: Free Press, 1995).

9. Jagdish N. Sheth, Banwasi Mitral, and Bruce Newman, *Consumer Behavior* (Fort Worth, TX: Dryden Press, 1999).

10. CoverGirl website, www.covergirl.com.

11. "When Free Samples Become Saviors," *The Wall Street Journal*, August 14, 2001, pp. B1, B4.

12. "Haggar, Farah, Levi's Iron Out the Wrinkles," *Advertising Age*, March 6, 1995, p. 12.

13. "Mass-Market Brands See More Upscale Heads," *Advertising Age*, September 25, 2000, p. S16.

14. Arm & Hammer website, www.armandhammer.com/myhome.

15. Sandy Allen and Ashok Chandrashekar, "Outsourcing Services: The Contract Is Just Beginning," *Business Horizons*, March-April 2000, pp. 25-34.

16. Dan R. E. Thomas, "Strategy Is Different in Service Businesses," *Harvard Business Review*, July-August 1978, pp. 158-65.

17. Haim Oren, "Branding Financial Services Helps Consumers Find Order in Chaos," *Marketing News*, March 29, 1993, p. 6; and Leonard L. Berry, Edwin F. Lefkowith, and Terry Clark, "In Services, What's in a Name?" *Harvard Business Review*, September-October 1998, pp. 28-30.

18. Frederick H. deB. Harris and Peter Peacock, "Hold My Place, Please," *Marketing Management*, Fall 1995, pp. 34-46.

19. Kent B. Monroe, "Buyer's Subjective Perceptions of Price," *Journal of Marketing Research*, February 1973, pp. 70-80; and Jerry Olson, "Price as an Informational Cue: Effects on Product Evaluation," in A. G. Woodside, J. N. Sheth, and P. D. Bennett, eds., *Consumer and Industrial Buying Behavior* (New York: Elsevier North-Holland, 1977), pp. 267-86.

20. Robert E. Hite, Cynthia Fraser, and Joseph A. Bellizzi, "Professional Service Advertising: The Effects of Price Inclusion, Justification, and Level of Risk," *Journal of Advertising Research* 30 (August-September 1990), pp. 23-31; William R. George and Leonard L. Berry, "Guidelines for the Advertising of Services," *Business Horizons*, July-August 1981, pp. 52-56; and Eugene M. Johnson, Eberhard E. Scheuing, and Kathleen A. Gaida, *Profitable Service Marketing* (Homewood, IL: Dow Jones-Irwin, 1986).

21. Kathleen Mortimer, "Services Advertising: The Agency Viewpoint," *Journal of Services Marketing*, no. 2 (2001), pp. 131-46; and Sak Onkvisit and John J. Shaw, "Service Marketing: Image, Branding, and Competition," *Business Horizons*, January-February 1989, pp. 13-18.

22. "Blond Ambition," *ABA Journal*, January 1996, p. 12.

23. Joe Adams, "Why Public Service Advertising Doesn't Work," *Ad Week*, November 17, 1980, p. 72.

24. This discussion is based on Kevin Lane Keller, *Strategic Brand Management*, 2nd ed. (Upper Saddle River, NJ: Prentice Hall, 2003); and Jennifer L. Aaker, "Dimensions of Brand Personality," *Journal of Marketing Research*, August 1997, pp. 347 - 56. See also, Susan Fournier, "Consumers and Their Brands: Developing Relationship Theory in Consumer Research," *Journal of Consumer Research*, March 1998, pp. 343 - 73.

25. For an extended treatment of brand equity, see David A. Aaker, *Building Strong Brands* (New York: Free Press, 1996).

26. This discussion is based on Kevin Lane Keller, "Building Customer-Based Brand Equity," *Marketing Management*, July - August 2001, pp. 15 - 19.

27. This discussion is based on Roger A. Kerin and Raj Sethuraman, "Exploring the Brand Value - Shareholder Value Nexus for Consumer Goods Companies," *Journal of the Academy of Marketing Science*, Winter 1998, pp. 260 - 73; "P&G Sells to Cadbury Hawaiian Punch Label in $203 Million Accord," *The Wall Street Journal*, April 16, 1999, p. B2; and "Will Triarc Make Snapple Crackle?" *Business Week*, April 28, 1997, p. 64. See also, "The Best Global Brands," *Business Week*, August 6, 2001, pp. 50 - 64.

28. "The Best Global Brands," Interbrand website, www.interbrand.com/best_brands_2004.asp; and "The 100 Top Brands," *BusinessWeek*, August 2, 2004, pp. 68 - 71.

29. "The Best of Canada's Brands," Timothy Woolstencroft and Jeannette Hanna, *Marketing Magazine*, June 14, 2004, p. 13.

30. Rob Osler, "The Name Game: Tips on How to Get It Right," *Marketing News*, September 14, 1998, p. 50; and Keller, *Strategic Brand Management*. See also Pamela W. Henderson and Joseph A. Cote, "Guidelines for Selecting or Modifying Logos," *Journal of Marketing*, April 1998, pp. 14 - 30; and Chiranjeev Kohli and Douglas W. LaBahn, "Creating Effective Brand Names: A Study of the Naming Process," *Journal of Advertising Research*, January - February 1997, pp. 67 - 75.

31. Paul Thurrott, "The Fun Never Stops: Microsoft vs. MikeRoweSoft," *Windows IT Pro*, January 20, 2004, www.winnetmag.com/Article/ArticleID/41510/41510.html.

32. "A Survey of Multinationals," *The Economist*, June 24, 1995, p. 8.

33. "When Brand Extension Becomes Brand Abuse," *Brandweek*, October 26, 1998, pp. 20, 22.

34. www.pez.com, downloaded August 30, 2001; "The National Peztime," *Dallas Morning News*, October 9, 1995, pp. 1C, 2C; David Welch, *Collecting Pez* (Murphysboro, IL: Bubba Scrubba Publications, 1995); and "Pez Dispense with Idea It's Just for Kids," *Brandweek*, September 26, 1996, p. 10.

35. "Just the Facts," *Research Alert*, July 2002, p. 5.

36. "L'eggs Hatches a New Hosiery Package," *Brandweek*, January 1, 2001, p. 6.

BMW: This case was written by Giana Eckhardt based on company interviews.

CHAPTER 12

1. "More Canadians Look to the Internet to Book Travel Plans," Ipsos press release, August 28, 2003, www.ipsos-na.com/news/pressrelease.cfm?id=1890.

2. www.lamborghini.com and www.kbb.com.

3. Roger A. Kerin and Robert A. Peterson, "Throckmorten Furniture (A)," *Strategic Marketing Problems: Cases and Comments*, 9th ed. (Englewood Cliffs, NJ: Prentice Hall, 1998), pp. 235 - 45.

4. "Nintendo GameCube Set at Mass Market Price of $199.95"; "Dedicated Gameplay System Launches November 5, 2001, with Six First-Party Titles Priced at $49.95," Nintendo of America, Inc., press release, May 21, 2001.

5. For the classic description of skimming and penetration pricing, see Joel Dean, "Pricing Policies for New Products," *Harvard Business Review*, November - December 1976, pp. 141 - 53. See also, Reed K. Holden and Thomas T. Nagle, "Kamikaze Pricing," *Marketing Management*, Summer 1998, pp. 31 - 39.

6. Jean-Noel Kapferer, "Managing Luxury Brands," *Journal of Brand Management*, July 1997, pp. 251 - 60.

7. "Why That Deal Is Only $9.99," *Business Week*, January 10, 2000, p. 36. For further reading on odd-even pricing, see Robert M. Schindler and Thomas M. Kilbarian, "Increased Consumer Sales Response through Use of 99-Ending Prices," *Journal of Retailing*, Summer 1996, pp. 187 - 99; Mark Stiving and Russell S. Winer, "An Empirical Analysis of Price Endings with Scanner Data," *Journal of Consumer Research*, June 1997, pp. 57 - 67; and Robert M. Schindler, "Patterns of Rightmost Digits Used in Advertised Prices: Implications for Nine-Ending Effects," *Journal of Consumer Research*, September 1997, pp. 192 - 201.

8. For an overview on target pricing, see Stephan A. Butscher and Michael Laker, "Market Driven Product Development," *Marketing Management*, Summer 2000, pp. 48 - 53.

9. Thomas T. Nagle and Reed K. Holden, *The Strategy and Tactics of Pricing*, 3rd ed. (Englewood Cliffs, NJ: Prentice Hall, 2002), pp. 243 - 49.

10. www.airbus.com and www.boeing.com.

11. Peter M. Noble and Thomas S. Gruca, "Industrial Pricing: Theory and Managerial Practice," *Marketing Science* 18, no. 3 (1999), pp. 435 - 54.

12. George E. Belch and Michael A. Belch, *Introduction to Advertising and Promotion*, 5th ed. (New York: Irwin/McGraw-Hill, 2001), p. 93.

13. "Retailers Using Cut-Rate Videos as Lures," *Dallas Morning News*, October 4, 1995, p. 5H.

14. Frank Bruni, "Price of Newsweek? It Depends," *Dallas Times Herald*, August 14, 1986, pp. S1, S20.

15. Bruce Orwall, "Hollywood's Costs Rose 8% in 2000 to a Record High," *The Wall Street Journal*, March 7, 2001, p. B6; and Bruce Orwall, "Theater Consolidation Jolts Hollywood Power Structure," *The Wall Street Journal*, January 21, 1998, pp. B1, B2.

16. Darren Rovell, "Jerseys from old-timers' game on the block," ESPN.com, December 4, 2003, http://espn.go.com/sportsbusiness/news/2003/1204/1678438.html.

17. "How Dell Fine-Tunes Its PC Pricing to Gain Edge in a Slow Market," *The Wall Street Journal*, June 8, 2001, pp. A1, A8.

18. For an extensive discussion on discounts, see Kent B. Monroe, *Pricing: Making Profitable Decisions*, 2nd ed. (New York: McGraw Hill, 1990), chaps. 14 and 15.

Washburn International: The case is based on information and materials provided by the company.

CHAPTER 13

1. www.avoncompany.com, downloaded January 20, 2002; Rochelle Kass, "Experimental Beauty," *The Journal News*, July 21, 2001, pp. 1D, 2D; Nanette Byrnes, "Avon: The New Calling," *Fortune*, September 18, 2000, pp. 136 - 48; "Retail Makeover," *Dallas Morning News*, May 9, 2001, p. 2D; and "Cosmetic Firms Try Change of Face," *Dallas Morning News*, September 19, 2000, p. 4D.

2. See Peter D. Bennett, ed., *Dictionary of Marketing Terms*, 2nd ed. (Chicago: American Marketing Association, 1995).

3. PepsiCo, Inc., Annual Report 1997.

4. This discussion is based on Bert Rosenbloom, *Marketing Channels: A Management View*, 6th ed. (Fort Worth: Dryden Press, 1999), pp. 452 - 58.

5. Johny K. Johansson, "International Alliances: Why Now?" *Journal of the Academy of Marketing Science*, Fall 1995, pp. 301 - 4.

6. General Mills, Inc., Annual Report 2000.

7. Howard Solomon, "Customers in the Crosshairs," *eBusiness Journal*, January 2002, p. 4.

8. "Eddie Bauer's Banner Time of Year," *Advertising Age*, October 1, 2001, p. 55.

9. Michael Krantz, "Click Till You Drop," *Time*, July 20, 1998, pp. 34 - 39.

10. *Multi-Channel Integration — The New Retail Battleground* (Columbus, OH: PricewaterhouseCoopers, March 2001).

11. "Don't Cut Back Now," *Business Week e-biz*, October 1, 2001, p. EB34.

12. *Fighting Fire with Water — From Channel Conflict to Confluence* (Cambridge, MA: Bain & Company, July 1, 2000).

13. For an overview of vertical marketing systems, see Lou Pelton, David Strutton, and James R. Lumpkin, *Marketing Channels*, 2nd ed. (Burr Ridge, IL: McGraw-Hill/Irwin, 2003), chap. 14.

14. Petcetera website, www.petcetera.ca.

15. "5 Down 95 to Go," www.apple.com, downloaded August 1, 2001; Apple Computer, press release, May 21, 2001; "Apple to Open Its First Retail Store in New York City," www.apple.com, downloaded July 20, 2002.

16. For an extensive discussion on channel conflict, see Anne T. Coughlan, Erin Anderson, Louis W. Stern, and Adel I. El-Ansary, *Marketing Channels*, 6th ed. (Upper Saddle River, NJ: Prentice Hall, 2001).

17. "Black Pearls Recast for Spring," *Advertising Age*, November 13, 1995, p. 49.

18. For an extensive discussion on power and influence in marketing channels, see Coughlan et al., *Marketing Channels*.

19. *What's It All About?* (Oakbrook, IL: Council of Logistics Management, 1993).

20. This example is described in David Sinchi-Levi, Philip Kaminsky, and Edith Sinchi-Levi, *Designing and Managing the Supply Chain* (Burr Ridge, IL: McGraw-Hill/Irwin, 2000), p. 5.

21. This discussion is based on Robyn Meredith, "Harder than the Hype," *Forbes*, April 16, 2001, pp. 188 - 94; Robert M. Monczka and Jim Morgan, "Supply Chain Management Strategies," *Purchasing*, January 15, 1998, pp. 78 - 85; and Robert B. Handfield and Earnest Z. Nichols, *Introduction to Supply Chain Management* (Upper Saddle River, NJ: Prentice Hall, 1998), chap. 1.

22. Major portions of this discussion are based on Sunil Chopra and Peter Meindl, *Supply Chain Management: Strategy, Planning, and Operations* (Upper Saddle River, NJ: Prentice Hall, 2001), chaps. 1 - 3; and Marshall L. Fisher, "What Is the Right Supply Chain for Your Product?" *Harvard Business Review*, March - April 1997, pp. 105 - 17.

23. For an extensive listing and description of total logistics costs, see James R. Stock and Douglas M. Lambert, *Strategic Logistics Management*, 4th ed. (Burr Ridge, IL: McGraw-Hill/Irwin, 2001).

24. Michael Levy and Barton A. Weitz, *Retailing Management*, 4th ed. (Burr Ridge, IL: McGraw-Hill/Irwin, 2001), pp. 335 - 36.

25. Fisher, "What Is the Right Supply Chain for Your Product?"

Creston Vineyards: The case is based on information and materials provided by the company.

CHAPTER 14

1. Canadian Tire website, www2.canadiantire.ca/CTenglish/corpidx.html; and "Ten Marketers That Mattered," *Marketing* magazine, December 16/23, 2002, p. 7.

2. Kenneth Cline, "The Devil in the Details," *Banking Strategies*, November - December 1997, p. 24; and Roger Trap, "Design Your Own Jeans," *The Independent*, October 18, 1998, p. 22.

3. Bank of Montreal website, www.bmo.com.

4. "Retail — The Heart of Every Community," Retail Council of Canada, www.retailcouncil.org/research/data/il/structure/jacobson/rcc_profile_2001.pdf.

5. *Retail Trade*, Statistics Canada, December 2003.

6. R. Gomez-Insausti, "Canada's Leading Retailers: Latest Trends and Strategies – 2002" (Toronto: Centre for the Study of Commercial Activity, Ryerson University).

7. *Retail Trade*, Statistics Canada, December 2003.

8. "A Brief History of the Hudson's Bay Company," Province of Manitoba, Hudson's Bay Company Archives, www.gov.mb.ca/chc/archives/hbca/about/the_bay.html.

9. "Retail — The Heart of Every Community."

10. "2004 Global Powers of Retailing," Deloitte Touche Tohmatsu, January 2004, www.stores.org/pdf/GlobalRetail04.pdf.

11. "Retail Trade - Establishments, Employees, and Payroll," *Statistical Abstract of the United States*, 120th ed. (Washington, DC: U.S. Department of Commerce, Bureau of the Census, October 2000); and Gene Koretz, "Those Plucky Corner Stores," *Business Week*, December 5, 1994, p. 26.

12. "Franchise 500," *Entrepreneur*, January 2001; and Scott Shane and Chester Spell, "Factors for New Franchise Success," *Sloan Management Review*, Spring 1998, pp. 43 - 50.

13. "Holt Renfrew... One of the World's Leading Fashion and Lifestyle Shopping Experiences Benchmarked against the Best," Holt Renfrew website, www.holtrenfrew.com/english/history.

14. Francis J. Mulhern and Robert P. Leon, "Implicit Price Bundling of Retail Products: A Multiproduct Approach to Maximizing Store Profitability," *Journal of Marketing*, October 1991, pp. 63 - 76.

15. Gwen Ortmeyer, John A. Quelch, and Walter Salmon, "Restoring Credibility to Retail Pricing," *Sloan Management Review*, Fall 1991, pp. 55 - 66.

16. William B. Dodds, "In Search of Value: How Price and Store Name Information Influence Buyers' Product Perceptions," *Journal of Consumer Marketing*, Spring 1991, pp. 15 - 24.

17. Neil Gross, "On beyond Shoplifting Prevention," *Business Week*, October 2, 2000, p. 170; and "A Time to Steal," *Brandweek*, February 16, 1999, p. 24.

18. Barry Brown, "Edmonton Makes Size Pay Off in Down Market," *Advertising Age*, January 27, 1992, pp. 4 - 5.

19. James R. Lowry, "The Life Cycle of Shopping Centers," *Business Horizons*, January - February 1997, pp. 77 - 86; Eric Peterson, "Power Centers! Now!" *Stores*, March 1989, pp. 61 - 66; and "Power Centers Flex Their Muscle," *Chain Store Age Executive*, February 1989, pp. 3A, 4A.

20. Ranjay Gulati and Janson Garino, "Getting the Right Mix of Bricks and Clicks," *Harvard Business Review*, May - June 2000, pp. 107 - 14; Marshall L. Fisher, Ananth Raman, and Anna Sheen McClelland, "Rocket Science Retailing Is Almost Here: Are You Ready?" *Harvard Business Review*, July - August 2000, pp. 115 - 24; Charla Mathwick, Naresh Malhotra, and Edward Rigdon, "Experiential Value: Conceptualization, Measurement and Application in the Catalog and Internet Shopping Environment," *Journal of Retailing*, Spring 2001, pp. 39 - 56; Lawrence M. Bellman, "Bricks and Mortar: 21st Century Survival," *Business Horizons*, May - June 2001, pp. 21 - 28; Zhan G. Li and Nurit Gery, "E-Tailing - for All Products?" *Business Horizons*, November - December 2000, pp. 49 - 54; and Bill Hanifin, "Go Forth and Multichannel: Loyalty Programs Need Knowledge Base," *Marketing News*, August 27, 2001, p. 23.

21. Ginny Parker, "Vending the Rules," *Time*, May 7, 2001, p. 24.

22. Julie Mitchell, "Electronic Payment Services Move beyond Tollbooths," *Investor's Business Daily*, August 30, 2001, p. 10; and Steve Scrupski, "Tiny 'Brains' Seen for Vending Machines," *Electronic Design*, December 1, 1998, p. 64F.

23. "Joe Namath, Franco Harris, Boomer Esiason, and Tim Brown Appear on Home Shopping Network during Super Bowl Week," *PR Newswire*, January 23, 2001; "Cover Girls Queen Latifah and Molly Sims Brush Up on Youth Volunteerism," *PR Newswire*, August 22, 2001; Carole Nicksin, "QVC Opens Up in Mall Space," *HFN*, August 20, 2001, p. 6; and Chris Wynn and Tim Adler, "Battle for UK Home-Shopping Viewers Hots Up as QVC Gets Heavyweight Rival," *New Media Markets*, May 11, 2001.

24. Edward Nash, "The Roots of Direct Marketing," *Direct Marketing*, February 1995, pp. 38 - 40; and Edith Hipp Updike and Mary Kurtz, "Japan Is Dialing 1 800 BUYAMERICA," *Business Week*, June 12, 1995, pp. 61 - 64.

25. Lee Valley website, www.leevalley.com.

26. Donna Bursey, "Targeting Small Businesses for Telemarketing and Mail Order Sales," *Direct Marketing*, September 1995, pp. 18 - 20; "Inbound, Outbound Telemarketing Keeps Ryder Sales in Fast Lane," *Direct Marketing*, July 1995, pp. 34 - 36; "Despite Hangups, Telemarketing a Success," *Marketing News*, March 27, 1995, p. 19; Kelly Shermach, "Outsourcing Seen as a Way to Cut Costs, Retain Service," *Marketing News*, June 19, 1995, pp. 5, 8; and Greg Gattuso, "Marketing Vision," *Direct Marketing*, February 1994, pp. 24 - 26.

27. Canadian Marketing Association website, www.the-cma.org.

28. Nanette Byrnes, "The New Calling," *Business Week*, September 18, 2000, pp. 137 - 48.

29. Bill Vlasic and Mary Beth Regan, "Amway II: The Kids Take Over," *Business Week*, February 1, 1998, pp. 60 - 70.

30. Mathew Schifrin, "Okay, Big Mouth," *Forbes*, October 9, 1995, pp. 47 - 48; Veronica Byrd and Wendy Zellner, "The Avon Lady of the Amazon," *Business Week*, October 24, 1994, pp. 93 - 96; and Ann Marsh "Avon Is Calling on Eastern Europe," *Advertising Age*, June 20, 1994, p. 116.

31. Heather Green, "Where Did All the Surfers Go?" *Business Week*, August 6, 2001, p. 35; Steve Hamm, David Welch, Wendy Zellner, Faith Keenan, and Peter Engardio, "E-Biz: Down but Hardly Out," *Business Week*, March 26, 2001, pp. 126 - 30; Lewis Braham, "E-Tailers Are Clicking," *Business Week*, July 23, 2001, p. 73; "Will Wal-Mart Get It Right This Time?" *Business Week*, November 6, 2000, p. 104; and Raymond R. Burke, "Do You See What I See? The Future of Virtual Shopping," *Journal of the Academy of Marketing Science*, Fall 1997, pp. 352 - 60.

32. "My Virtual Model Inc. Acquires EZsize," *PR Newswire*, June 21, 2001; Steve Casimiro, "Shop Till You Crash," *Fortune*, December 21, 1998, pp. 267 - 70; and De' Ann Weimer, "Can I Try (Click) That Blouse (Drag) in Blue?" *Business Week*, November 9, 1998, p. 86.

33. "Usability Study of PC and TV-Based Web Platforms Reveals Online Shopping Tasks Confuse, Frustrate Users," *PR Newswire*, September 5, 2001.

34. "What's so new about the 'New Economy'? Glad you asked," *Business 2.0*, August – September 2001, p. 84.

35. This discussion is based on "By the Numbers: Buying Breakdown," *The Wall Street Journal*, September 24, 2001, p. R4; "Factoids," *Research Alert*, November 17, 2000, p. 4; and Weiss, "Online America."

36. "NPD e-Visory Report Shows Offline Sales Benefit from Online Browsing," NPD Group, July 17, 2001.

37. This discussion is based on "Statistics: U.S. Online Shoppers," www.shop.org, downloaded September 14, 2001; "The Clicks-and-Bricks Way to Buy That Car," *Business Week*, May 7, 2001, pp. 128 - 30; and *The Next Chapter in Business-to-Consumer E-Commerce* (Boston: The Boston Consulting Group, March 2001).

38. "The 90/20 Rule of e-Commerce: Nearly 90% of Online Sales Accounted for by 20% of Consumers," Cyber Dialogue, press release, September 25, 2000.

39. This discussion is based on Hyokjin Kwak, Richard J. Fox, and George M. Zinkhan, "What Products Can Be Successfully Promoted via the Internet?" *Journal of Advertising Research*, January - February 2002, pp. 23 - 38; "A Hard Sell Online? Think Again," *Business Week*, July 12, 1999, pp. 142 - 43; and Forrester Research estimates reported in "Briefing Business to Customers," *Red Herring*, June 1, 2001, p. 54.

40. William R. Davidson, Albert D. Bates, and Stephen J. Bass, "Retail Life Cycle," *Harvard Business Review*, November - December 1976, pp. 89 - 96.

Krispy Kreme: This case is based on "The Krispy Cult," by Angela Kryhul, *Marketing* magazine, January 28, 2002.

CHAPTER 15

1. "Best Promoted Brands of 2001," *PROMO*, September 2001, pp. 55 - 62; "Daring Disney," *Advertising Age*, March 26, 2001, p. 20; Wayne Friedman, "Disney's Twist on Film Promo," *Advertising Age*, March 19, 2001, p. 3; Wayne Friedman, "Disney Sets $250 Mil Birthday Bash," *Advertising Age*, July 2, 2001, p. 1; Bob Garfield, "Disney's Quest for Boomers Shows a Bit of Imagineering," *Advertising Age*, August 13, 2001, p. 29; Stephanie Thompson, "The Mouse in the Food Aisle," *Advertising Age*, September 10, 2001, p. 73; Lorraine Calvacca, "Mouse Trapping," *PROMO*, May 2001, p. 47; Stephanie Thompson, "A Disney Assist," *Advertising Age*, July 30, 2001, p. 39; Wayne Friedman, "Disney, Toys 'R' Us Sign Cross-Media Deal," *Advertising Age*, June 18, 2001, p. 3; Chester Dawson, "Will Tokyo Embrace Another Mouse?" *Business Week*, September 10, 2001, p. 65; and David Jackson, "How to Build a Better Mousetrap," *Time*, February 19, 2001, pp. 40 - 42.

2. Wilbur Schramm, "How Communication Works," in Wilbur Schramm, ed., *The Process and Effects of Mass Communication* (Urbana, IL: University of Illinois Press, 1955), pp. 3 - 26.

3. E. Cooper and M. Jahoda, "The Evasion of Propaganda," *Journal of Psychology* 22 (1947), pp. 15 - 25; H. Hyman and P. Sheatsley, "Some Reasons Why Information Campaigns Fail," *Public Opinion Quarterly* 11 (1947), pp. 412 - 23; and J. T. Klapper, *The Effects of Mass Communication* (New York: Free Press, 1960), chap. VII.

4. Canadian Media Directors' Council, *2002 - 2003 Media Digest*, p. 46.

5. Adapted from *Dictionary of Marketing Terms*, 2nd ed., Peter D. Bennett, ed. (Chicago: American Marketing Association, 1995), p. 231.

6. Nova Scotia Department of Tourism website, www.novascotia.com; and e-mail communication with Peggy Tibbo-Cameron, Tourism Partnership Council.

7. Kusum L. Ailawadi, Scott A. Neslin, and Karen Gedenk, "Pursuing the Value-Conscious Consumer: Store Brands versus National Brand Promotions," *Journal of Marketing*, January 2001, pp. 71 - 89.

8. B. C. Cotton and Emerson M. Babb, "Consumer Response to Promotional Deals," *Journal of Marketing* 42 (July 1978), pp. 109 - 13.

9. Robert George Brown, "Sales Response to Promotions and Advertising," *Journal of Advertising Research* 14 (August 1974), pp. 33 - 40.

10. Adapted from *Economic Impact: U.S. Direct Marketing Today* (New York: Direct Marketing Association, 1998), p. 25.

11. Siva K. Balasubramanian and V. Kumar, "Analyzing Variations in Advertising and Promotional Expenditures: Key Correlates in Consumer, Industrial, and Service Markets," *Journal of Marketing*, April 1990, pp. 57 - 68.

12. Don Schultz, "Objectives Drive Tactics in IMC Approach," *Marketing News*, May 9, 1994, pp. 14, 18; and Neil Brown, "Redefine Integrated Marketing Communications," *Marketing News*, March 29, 1993, pp. 4 - 5.

13. Don E. Schultz, "Consumer Marketing Changed by Advent of 29.8/7 Media Week," *Marketing News*, September 24, 2001, pp. 13, 15; Pamela Paul, "Getting Inside Gen Y," *American Demographics*, September 2001, pp. 43 - 49; Charles Pappas, "Ad Nauseam," *Advertising Age*, July 10, 2000, pp. 16 - 18; Dan Lippe, "It's All in Creative Delivery," *Advertising Age*, June 25, 2001, pp. S8, S9; and Kate Fitzgerald, "Viral Marketing Breaks Through," *Advertising Age*, June 25, 2001, p. S10.

14. James M. Olver and Paul W. Farris, "Push and Pull: A One-Two Punch for Packages Products," *Sloan Management Review*, Fall 1989, pp. 53 - 61.

15. Fusun F. Gonul, Franklin Carter, Elina Petrova, and Kannan Srinivasan, "Promotion of Prescription Drugs and Its Impact on Physicians' Choice Behavior," *Journal of Marketing*, July 2001, pp. 79 - 90.

16. *Strategy* Magazine Agency of the Year winners, 2003, www.strategymag.com/aoy/2003/taxi/viagara.html.

17. Robert J. Lavidge and Gary A. Steiner, "A Model for Predictive Measurement of Advertising Effectiveness," *Journal of Marketing*, October 1961, p. 61.

18. "45th Annual Report: 100 Leading National Advertisers," *Advertising Age*, September 24, 2001, pp. S1 - S26.

19. Don E. Schultz and Anders Gronstedt, "Making Marcom an Investment," *Marketing Management*, Fall 1997, pp. 41 - 49; and J. Enrique Bigne, "Advertising Budget Practices: A Review," *Journal of Current Issues and Research in Advertising*, Fall 1995, pp. 17 - 31.

20. John Philip Jones, "Ad Spending: Maintaining Market Share," *Harvard Business Review*, January - February 1990, pp. 38 - 42; and Charles H. Patti and Vincent Blanko, "Budgeting Practices of Big Advertisers," *Journal of Advertising Research* 21 (December 1981), pp. 23 - 30.

21. James A. Schroer, "Ad Spending: Growing Market Share," *Harvard Business Review*, January - February 1990, pp. 44 - 48.

22. James E. Lynch and Graham J. Hooley, "Increasing Sophistication in Advertising Budget Setting," *Journal of Advertising Research* 30 (February - March 1990), pp. 67 - 75.

23. Jimmy D. Barnes, Brenda J. Muscove, and Javad Rassouli, "An Objective and Task Media Selection Decision Model and Advertising Cost Formula to Determine International Advertising Budgets," *Journal of Advertising* 11, no. 4 (1982), pp. 68 - 75.

24. Don E. Schultz, "Olympics Get the Gold Medal in Integrating Marketing Event," *Marketing News*, April 27, 1998, pp. 5, 10.

25. "The Fellowship of the New Line," *PROMO*, September 2001, p. 84; and "Sneak Preview of Trailer for New Line Cinema's 'The Lord of the Rings: The Fellowship of the Ring,'" *PR Newswire*, September 21, 2001.

26. Kate Fitzgerald, "Beyond Advertising," *Advertising Age*, August 3, 1998, pp. 1, 14; Curtis P. Johnson, "Follow the Money: Sell CFO on Integrated Marketing's Merits," *Marketing News*, May 11, 1998, p. 10; and Laura Schneider, "Agencies Show That IMC Can Be Good for Bottom Line," *Marketing News*, May 11, 1998, p. 11.

27. Rafi A. Mohammed, Robert J. Fisher, Bernard J. Jaworski, and Aileen M. Cahill, *Internet Marketing: Building Advantage in a Networked Economy* (Burr Ridge, IL: McGraw-Hill/Irwin, 2002); and Yoram Wind, Vijay Mahajan, and Robert Gunther, *Convergence Marketing* (Upper Saddle River, NJ: Prentice Hall, 2002).

28. "The Five-Year Forecast," *The Industry Standard*, March 26, 2001, pp. 82 - 83.

29. Michael Weiss, "Online America," *American Demographics*, March 21, 2001, pp. 53 - 60.

30. Holt Renfrew website, www.holtrenfrew.com/english/personalservices/index.asp.

31. Mohammed et al., *Internet Marketing*.

32. Adrian J. Slywotzky, "The Age of the Choiceboard," *Harvard Business Review*, January - February 2000, pp. 40 - 41.

33. Alan Rosenspan, "Participation Marketing," *Direct Marketing*, April 2001, pp. 54 - 66.

34. This discussion is drawn from Jeffrey F. Rayport and Bernard J. Jaworski, *E-Commerce* (Burr Ridge, IL: McGraw-Hill/Irwin MarketspaceU, 2001); and Mohammed et al., *Internet Marketing*.

35. For references on buzz and viral marketing, see "Buzz Marketing," *Business Week*, July 30, 2001, pp. 50 - 56; and Renée Dye, "The Buzz on Buzz," *Harvard Business Review*, November - December 2000, pp. 139 - 46.

Airwalk, Inc.: The case was written by Michael Vessey and Steven Hartley based on a video from George Belch and Michael Belch, *Advertising and Promotion* (New York: McGraw-Hill, 1998).

CHAPTER 16

1. Canadian Media Directors' Council, *2003 - 2004 Media Digest*, p. 10.

2. Lesley Young, "McDonald's lovin' it," *Marketing* magazine, June 23, 2003.

3. *Nation's Restaurant News*, June 23, 2003, p. 1.

4. Ibid.

5. "Ten Marketers That Mattered," *Marketing* magazine, December 16/23, 2002, p. 20.

6. David A. Aaker and Donald Norris, "Characteristics of TV Commercials Perceived as Informative," *Journal of Advertising Research* 22, no. 2 (April - May 1982), pp. 61 - 70.

7. Larry D. Compeau and Dhruv Grewal, "Comparative Price Advertising: An Integrative Review," *Journal of Public Policy & Marketing*, Fall 1998, pp. 257 - 73; and William Wilkie and Paul W. Farris, "Comparison Advertising: Problems and Potentials," *Journal of Marketing*, October 1975, pp. 7 - 15.

8. Jennifer Lawrence, "P&G Ads Get Competitive," *Advertising Age*, February 1, 1993, p. 14; Jerry Gotlieb and Dan Sorel, "The Influence of Type of Advertisement, Price, and Source Credibility on Perceived Quality," *Journal of the Academy of Marketing Science*, Summer 1992, pp. 253 - 60; and Cornelia Pechman and David Stewart, "The Effects of Comparative Advertising on Attention, Memory, and Purchase Intentions," *Journal of Consumer Research*, September 1990, pp. 180 - 92.

9. Bruce Buchanan and Doron Goldman, "Us vs. Them: The Minefield of Comparative Ads," *Harvard Business Review*, May - June 1989, pp. 38 - 50; Dorothy Cohen, "The FTC's Advertising Substantiation Program," *Journal of Marketing*, Winter 1980, pp. 26 - 35; and Michael Etger and Stephen A. Goodwin, "Planning for Comparative Advertising Requires Special Attention," *Journal of Advertising* 8, no. 1 (Winter 1979), pp. 26 - 32.

10. Lewis C. Winters, "Does It Pay to Advertise to Hostile Audiences with Corporate Advertising?" *Journal of Advertising Research*, June - July 1988, pp. 11 - 18; and Robert Selwitz, "The Selling of an Image," *Madison Avenue*, February 1985, pp. 61 - 69.

11. Labatt corporate website, www.labatt.com/english/lbc_responsible/lbc_main.htm.

12. David Kaplan, "Expect bigger, better Super Bowl ads this year," *Houston Chronicle*, January 30, 2004, www.chron.com/cs/CDA/ssistory.mpl/business/2377942.

13. "FactPack 2002 Edition: A Handy Guide to the Advertising Business," *Advertising Age*, September 9, 2002, www.adage.com/images/random/FactPack2002.pdf.

14. Michael S. LaTour and Herbert J. Rotfeld, "There Are Threats and (Maybe) Fear-Caused Arousal: Theory and Confusions of Appeals to Fear and Fear Arousal Itself," *Journal of Advertising*, Fall 1997, pp. 45 - 59.

15. Bob Garfield, "Allstate Ads Bring Home Point about Mortgage Insurance," *Advertising Age*, September 11, 1989, p. 120; and Judann Dagnoli, "'Buy or Die' Mentality Toned Down in Ads," *Advertising Age*, May 7, 1990, p. S12.

16. Anthony Vagnoni, "Best Awards," *Advertising Age*, May 28, 2001, pp. S1 - 18; Dana L. Alden, Wayne D. Hoyer, and Chol Lee, "Identifying Global and Culture-Specific Dimensions of Humor in Advertising: A Multinational Analysis," *Journal of Marketing*, April 1993, pp. 64 - 75; and Johny K. Johansson, "The Sense of 'Nonsense': Japanese TV Advertising," *Journal of Advertising*, March 1994, pp. 17 - 26.

17. Jean Halliday, "Exotic Ads Get Noticed," *Advertising Age*, April 9, 2001, p. S4.

18. Taxi website, www.taxi.ca; and "Permission to be great," *Strategy* Magazine Agency of the Year winners, 2003, www.strategymag.com/aoy/2003/aoygold.html.

19. *Strategy* Magazine Agency of the Year winners, 2003, www.strategymag.com/aoy/2003/taxi/movie.html.

20. Giles D'Souza and Ram C. Rao, "Can Repeating an Advertisement More Frequently than the Competition Affect Brand Preference in a Mature Market?" *Journal of Marketing*, April 1995, pp. 32 - 42.

21. Vicki R. Lane, "The Impact of Ad Repetition and Ad Content on Consumer Perceptions of Incongruent Extensions," *Journal of Marketing*, April 2000, pp. 80 - 91.

22. Canadian Media Directors' Council, *2003 - 2004 Media Digest*, p. 13.

23. David Goetzl and Wayne Friedman, "'Friends' Tops Ad Price List," *Advertising Age*, September 30, 2002, pp. 1, 58.

24. Surendra N. Singh, Denise Linville, and Ajay Sukhdial, "Enhancing the Efficacy of Split Thirty-Second Television Commercials: An Encoding Variability Application," *Journal of Advertising*, Fall 1995, pp. 13 - 23; Scott Ward, Terence A. Oliva, and David J. Reibstein, "Effectiveness of Brand-Related 15-Second Commercials," *Journal of Consumer Marketing*, no. 2 (1994), pp. 38 - 44; and Surendra N. Singh and Catherine Cole, "The Effects of Length, Content, and Repetition on Television Commercial Effectiveness," *Journal of Marketing Research*, February 1993, pp. 91 - 104.

25. Canadian Media Directors' Council, *2003 - 2004 Media Digest*, p. 32.

26. "Change in Number of Magazine Titles," *Marketing News*, July 2, 2001, p. 11; R. Craig Endicott, "Past Performance Is Not a Guarantee of Future Returns," *Advertising Age*, June 18, 2001, pp. S1, S6; and George R. Milne, "A Magazine Taxonomy Based on Customer Overlap," *Journal of the Academy of Marketing Science*, Spring 1994, pp. 170 - 79.

27. Julia Collins, "Image and Advertising," *Harvard Business Review*, January - February 1989, pp. 93 - 97.

28. Sandeep Krishnamurthy, "Deciphering the Internet Advertising Puzzle," *Marketing Management*, Fall 2000, pp. 35 - 39; Judy Strauss and Raymond Frost, *Marketing on the Internet: Principles of Online Marketing* (Englewood Cliffs, NJ: Prentice Hall, 1999), pp. 196 - 249; and Maricris G. Briones, "Rich Media May Be Too Rich for Your Blood," *Marketing News*, March 29, 1999, p. 4.

29. Tom Duncan, *IMC: Using Advertising and Promotion to Build Brands* (New York: McGraw-Hill, 2002); and Larry Chiagouris and Brandt Wansley, "Branding on the Internet," *Marketing Management*, Summer 2000, pp. 35 - 38.

30. *The Next Chapter in Business-to-Consumer E-Commerce.*

31. Arch G. Woodside, "Outdoor Advertising as Experiments," *Journal of the Academy of Marketing Science* 18 (Summer 1990), pp. 229 - 37.

32. *Strategy* Magazine Agency of the Year winners, 2003, www.strategymag.com/aoy/2003/aoyfinalist1.html.

33. Ed Brown, "Advertisers Skip to the Loo," *Fortune*, October 26, 1998, p. 64; John Cortex, "Growing Pains Can't Stop the New Kid on the Ad Block," *Advertising Age*, October 12, 1992, pp. 5 - 28; Allen Banks, "How to Assess New Place-Based Media," *Advertising Age*, November 30, 1992, p. 36; and John Cortex, "Media Pioneers Try to Corral On-the-Go Consumers," *Advertising Age*, August 17, 1992, p. 25.

34. Rob Norton, "How Uninformative Advertising Tells Consumers Quite a Bit," *Fortune*, December 26, 1994, p. 37; and "Professor Claims Corporations Waste Billions on Advertising," *Marketing News*, July 6, 1992, p. 5.

35. The discussion of posttesting is based on William F. Arens, *Contemporary Advertising*, 6th ed. (Burr Ridge, IL: Richard D. Irwin, 1996), pp. 181 - 82.

36. David A. Aaker and Douglas M. Stayman, "Measuring Audience Perceptions of Commercials and Relating Them to Ad Impact," *Journal of Advertising Research* 30 (August - September 1990), pp. 7 - 17; and Ernest Dichter, "A Psychological View of Advertising Effectiveness," *Marketing Management* 1, no. 3 (1992), pp. 60 - 62.

37. David Kruegel, "Television Advertising Effectiveness and Research Innovation," *Journal of Consumer Marketing*, Summer 1988, pp. 43 - 51; and Laurence N. Gold, "The Evolution of Television Advertising Sales Measurement: Past, Present, and Future," *Journal of Advertising Research*, June - July 1988, pp. 19 - 24.

38. "A Cautionary Tale," *PROMO's 9th Annual Sourcebook*, 2002, pp. 12 - 14.

39. Magid M. Abraham and Leonard M. Lodish, "Getting the Most out of Advertising and Promotion," *Harvard Business Review*, May - June 1990, pp. 50 - 60; Steven W. Hartley and James Cross, "How Sales Promotion Can Work for and against You," *Journal of Consumer Marketing*, Summer 1988, pp. 35 - 42; Robert D. Buzzell, John A. Quelch, and Walter J. Salmon, "The Costly Bargain of Trade Promotion," *Harvard Business Review*, March - April 1990, pp. 141 - 49; and Mary L. Nicastro, "Break-Even Analysis Determines Success of Sales Promotions," *Marketing News*, March 5, 1990, p. 11.

40. "Coupon Distribution Grows in Changing Market," Watts NCH Promotional Services Ltd., March 2004, www.couponscanada.org/SR0104e.pdf.

41. Michael Scroggie, "Online Coupon Debate," *PROMO*, April 2000; "Coupon Fraud Indicted," *PROMO*, June 2000, p. 16; "Experts Warn about E-Coupon Fraud," *Brandmarketing*, June 2000, p. 38; "Nine Steps to a Fraud-Proof Rebate Form," *PROMO*, December 1994, p. 16; Kerry Smith, "The Promotion Gravy Train," *PROMO*, August 1995, pp. 50 - 52; Christopher Power, "Coupon Scams Are Clipping Companies," *Business Week*, June 15, 1992, pp. 110 - 11; and Kerry J. Smith, "Coupon Scam Uncovered in Detroit," *PROMO*, December 1992, pp. 1, 45.

42. Carrie MacMillan, "Creature Features," *PROMO*, October 2001, p. 11; Dan Hanover, "Not Just for Breakfast Anymore," *PROMO*, September 2001, p. 10.

43. Tim Hortons website, www.timhortons.com.

44. Lorraine Woellert, "The Sweepstakes Biz Isn't Feeling Lucky," *Business Week*, March 22, 1999, p. 80.

45. "Best Activity Generating Brand Awareness/Trial," *PROMO*, September 2001, p. 51; and "Brand Handing," *PROMO's 9th Annual Sourcebook*, 2002, p. 32.

46. "On a Roll," *Marketing* magazine, July 1, 2002; and "Hey, Big Spender," *Marketing* magazine, January 14, 2002.

47. Cyndee Miller, "P-O-P Gains Followers as 'Era of Retailing' Dawns," *Marketing News*, May 14, 1990, p. 2.

48. Marvin A. Jolson, Joshua L. Wiener, and Richard B. Rosecky, "Correlates of Rebate Proneness," *Journal of Advertising Research*, February - March 1987, pp. 33 - 43.

49. Paula Lyon Andruss, "Survivor Packages Make Real-Life Money," *Marketing News*, March 26, 2001, p. 5; Wayne Friedman, "Eagle-Eye Marketers Find Right Spot, Right Time," *Advertising Age*, January 22, 2001, p. S2; David Goetzl, "TBS Tries Virtual Advertising," *Advertising Age*, May 21, 2001, p. 8; James Poniewozik, "This Plug's for You," *Time*, June 18, 2001, pp. 76 - 77; and "Never Say Never Again," *PROMO*, October 2001, p. 16.

50. This discussion is drawn particularly from John A. Quelch, *Trade Promotions by Grocery Manufacturers: A Management Perspective* (Cambridge, MA: Marketing Science Institute, August 1982).

51. "Safetyforum.com and Public Citizen Report: NHTSA Forces Firestone to Recall Defective Tires, Expand Wilderness Ats Recall," *PR Newswire*, October 5, 2001; Cindy Skrzycki and Frank Swoboda, "Firestone Refuses Voluntary Recall," Safetyforum.com, July 20, 2001; Jim Suhr, "Tire Recall Response Time Defended," Safetyforum.com, August 10, 2000.

52. Scott Hue, "Free 'Plugs' Supply Ad Power," *Advertising Age*, January 29, 1990, p. 6.

53. Mike Harris, "Earnhardt's Lap Belt Was Broken," Safetyforum.com, February 23, 2001; and Marc Weinberger, Jean Romeo, and Azhar Pircha, "Negative Product Safety News: Coverage, Responses, and Effects," *Business Horizons*, May - June 1991, pp. 23 - 31.

54. Trans Canada Trail website, www.tctrail.ca.

55. Martin O'Hanlon, "Meat Lovers Not Complete Lovers," *The Chronicle-Herald*, August 11, 1999, pp. A1, A2.

Rethink: This case was based on the following material: "The Princes of Pitch," CBC's *Venture*, July 24, 2001; Eve Lazarus, "True Believers," *Marketing Online*, November 26, 2001; "Agency Report: Scouting Canada's Agencies 2000 - Part Three," *Marketing Online*, December 4, 2000; Mark Etting, "Mark Etting's Street Talk: Private-Label Chris," *Marketing Online*, November 8, 1999; Mark Etting, "Mark Etting's Street Talk: Re-thinking Rethink," *Marketing Online*, October 25, 1999; Eve Lazarus, "Rethinking ropes in $15M in business," *Marketing Online*, January 17, 2000; and Eve Lazarus, "The Young Turks...." *Marketing Online*, February 15, 2001.

CHAPTER 17

1. Kathleen Cholewka, "Xerox's Savior?" *Sales & Marketing Management*, April 2001, pp. 36 - 42; "Anne Mulcahy Named Xerox Chief Executive Officer," www.xerox.com, downloaded July 26, 2001; "She's Here to Fix the Xerox," *Business Week*, August 6, 2001, pp. 47 – 48; Donna Fuscaldo and Sue Golf, *The Wall Street Journal*, April 26, 2004, p. B8; and Nancy Dillon, Knight Ridder Tribune Business News, Washington, January 28, 2004, p. 1.

2. *Canadian Marketing Association Fact Book*, 2001.

3. Eric Berkowitz, et al., *Marketing*, 5th Canadian Ed. (Whitby, ON: McGraw-Hill Ryerson, 2003).

4. *Statistical Fact Book '98* (New York: The Direct Marketing Association, 1998).

5. Robert Berner, "Going that Extra Inch," *Business Week*, September 18, 2000, p. 84.

6. Adapted from *Economic Impact: U.S. Direct Marketing Today* (New York: Direct Marketing Association, 1998), pp. 25 - 26.

7. Carol Krol, "Club Med Uses E-Mail to Pitch Unsold, Discounted Packages," *Advertising Age*, December 14, 1998, p. 40.

8. "Rising to the Top," *PROMO*, September 2001, pp. 46 - 62.

9. Jean Halliday, "Taking Direct Route," *Advertising Age*, September 7, 1998, p. 17.

10. This discussion is based on a telephone conversation with Scott Chandler, Padinox Inc., May 4, 2004; and "Kitchenwear," Paderno 2004 kitchen and housewares catalogue.

11. Alan K. Gorenstein, "Direct Marketing's Growth Will Be Global," *Marketing News*, December 7, 1998, p. 15; Don E. Schultz, "Integrated Global Marketing Will Be the Name of the Game," *Marketing News*, October 26, 1998, p. 5; and Mary Sutter and Andrea Mandel-Campbell, "Customers Are Eager, Infrastructure Lags," *Advertising Age International*, October 5, 1998, p. 12.

12. Canadian Marketing Association website, www.the-cma.org.

13. Douglas Wood and David Brosse, "Mulling E-Mail Options," *PROMO*, September 2001, p. 18; Kathleen Cholewka, "Making E-Mail Matter," *Sales and Marketing Management*, September 2001,

pp. 21, 22; "$2.1 Billion Will Be Spent on E-Mail Marketing by Year-End 2001," *Direct Marketing*, August 2001, p. 7; Arlene Weintraub, "When E-Mail Ads Aren't Spam," *Business Week*, October 16, 2000, p. 112; "Opting Out of E-Mail Ads Isn't So Easy to Do," *Business Week*, November 6, 2000, p. 20; and "With E-Mail Marketing, Permission Is Key," *eStatNews*, www.emarketer.com, September 2001.

14. "Labour force survey estimates (LFS), by full- and part-time students during school months, sex and age group, annual," Statistics Canada, Table 282-0095, May 2003.

15. "America's 25 Best Sales Forces," *Sales & Marketing Management*, July 2000, pp. 57 - 85.

16. For recent representative research on and commentary on relationship selling, see James Boles, Thomas Brashear, Danny Bellenger, and Hiram Barksdale, Jr., "Relationship Selling Behaviors: Antecedents and Relationship with Performance," *Journal of Business & Industrial Marketing* 15, no. 2/3 (2000), pp. 141 - 53; and Barton A. Weitz and Kevin D. Bradford, "Personal Selling and Sales Management: A Relationship Marketing Perspective," *Journal of the Academy of Marketing Science*, Spring 1999, pp. 241 - 54.

17. David W. Cravens, "The Changing Role of the Sales Force," *Marketing Management*, Fall 1995, pp. 49 - 57.

18. Christen Heide, *Dartnell's 31st Sales Force Compensation Survey 2000* (Chicago: The Dartnell Corporation, 2000), p. 176.

19. "What a Sales Call Costs," *Sales & Marketing Management*, August 2002, p. 80.

20. "Keep Calling!" *Sales & Marketing Report*, May 2001, p. 3.

21. "Don't Call Laws Raise False Hope for Peace, Quiet," *The Wall Street Journal*, December 22, 2000, pp. B1, B4.

22. James Pollock, "In Pursuit of Privacy," *Marketing* magazine, June 4, 1993, pp. 1, 4.

23. "What Do Customers Hate about Salespeople?" *Sales & Marketing Management*, June 2001, pp. 43 - 51.

24. "Japanese Business Etiquette," *Smart Business*, August 2000, p. 55.

25. See Barton Weitz, Stephen B. Castleberry, and John F. Tanner, Jr., *Selling: Building Partnerships*, 4th ed. (Burr Ridge, IL: McGraw-Hill/Irwin, 2001), chap. 6.

26. For an extensive discussion of objections, see Charles M. Futrell, *Fundamentals of Selling* (New York: Irwin/McGraw-Hill, 2002), chap. 10.

27. Theodore Levitt, *The Marketing Imagination* (New York: Free Press, 1983), p. 111.

28. "Focus on the Customer," *Fortune*, September 7, 1998, special advertising section.

29. *Management Briefing: Sales and Marketing* (New York: Conference Board, October 1996), pp. 3 - 4.

30. Neil Rackham, Lawrence Friedman, and Richard Ruff, *Getting Partnering Right* (New York: McGraw-Hill, 1996), pp. 47 - 48; and "The Selling Game," *The Wall Street Journal*, March 29, 1994, p. A1.

31. Cravens, "The Changing Role of the Sales Force."

32. Robert L. Lindstrom, "Training Hits the Road, Part 2," *Sales & Marketing Management*, June 1995, pp. 10 - 14.

33. "Supercharged Sell," *Inc. Tech*, November 1998, pp. 42 - 50.

Reebok International Ltd.: This case was written by Giana Eckardt.

CREDITS

Chapter 1

p. 5 Courtesy of Rollerblade, Inc.; p. 8 (left) Courtesy Rollerblade, Inc.; p. 8 (right) Courtesy of Rollerblade, Inc.; p. 10 Taxi/Getty Images; p. 12 (left) Courtesy of Wal-Mart Stores, Inc.; p. 12 (right) The Hudson's Bay Company (HBC); p. 14 (left) Courtesy of Rollerblade, Inc.; p. 14 (right) Courtesy of Rollerblade, Inc.; p. 17 MADD Canada; p. 20 Courtesy of Rollerblade, Inc.

Chapter 2

p. 23 Ben & Jerry's Homemade Holdings, Inc.; p. 27 Courtesy of Medtronic; p. 29 Courtesy of Rick Armstrong; p. 31 (top) Courtesy of Fujitsu PC Corporation; p. 31 (bottom) Courtesy of Aurora Foods; p. 33 (left) Courtesy of Unilever United States, Inc.; p. 33 (right top) Courtesy of Unilever United States, Inc.; p. 33 (right bottom) Courtesy of Unilever United States, Inc.; p. 36 Courtesy of Medtronic;

Chapter 3

p. 42 Apple Computer, Inc.; p. 55 (left) © The Proctor & Gamble Company. Used by permission; p. 55 (right) Rogers Communications Inc.; p. 63 (left) Courtesy of Zenith Electronics Corporation; p. 63 (right) Courtesy of EchoStar Communications; p. 64 (left) Resource Recycling: North America's Recycling and Composting Journal; p. 64 (right) Courtesy of the Lever Brothers Company; p. 66 Courtesy of Lotus Development Corporation, an IBM Company; p. 72 Courtesy of Flyte Tyme.; p. 73 Courtesy of Flyte Tyme.

Chapter 4

p. 75 VanCity Credit Union; p. 76 VanCity Credit Union; p. 87 Tony Stone; p. 88 Courtesy of McDonald's Corporation.

Chapter 5

p. 95 Canadian Press/Jill Connelly; p. 95 Canadian Press/Carlos Osorio; p. 95 Canadian Press/Rich Buchan; p. 102 Courtesy of Inscape for Time Warner Interactive; p. 103 (left) FRESH STEP ® is a registered trademark of The Clorox Pet Products Company. Used with permission; p. 103 (right) © Mary Kay, Inc.; Photos by: Grace Huang/for Sarah Laird; p. 105 (left) Courtesy of Colgate-Palmolive Company; p. 105 (right) The Bayer Company; p. 109 (left) Canadian Press/Robert Borea; p. 109 (right) Canadian Press/Edmonton Sun (Aaron Whitfield); p. 111 Courtesy of Haggar Clothing Co.; p. 112 Canadian Press/Nick Procaylo.

Chapter 6

p. 120 (top) Viacom Canada Inc.; p. 120 (bottom) TIR Systems Ltd.; p. 126 Courtesy of Airbus; p. 127 Intel Corporation; p. 129 Dan Bosler/Tony Stone; p. 132 (top) Courtesy of Covisint, L.L.C.; p. 132 (bottom) Quadrem International Ltd.

Chapter 7

p. 140 Peter Donato; p. 144 Courtesy of ALMA/BBDO São Paulo; p. 145 Photo: O. Toscani; Courtesy United Colours of Benetton; p. 147 Courtesy of Nestlé S.A.; p. 149 (left) Travelpix/FPG International; p. 149 (right) Antonio Rosario/The Image Bank; p. 151 Courtesy of The Coca-Cola Company; p. 154 Terrapin Communications; p. 155 (left) Courtesy of McDonald's Corporation; p. 155 (right) Courtesy of McDonald's Corporation; p. 157 (left) Courtesy of The Gillette Company; p. 157 (centre) Courtesy of The Gillette Company; p. 157 (right) Courtesy of The Gillette Company.

Chapter 8

p. 165 "Two Towers" Copyright 2003, New Line Productions, Inc. All rights reserved; Poster appears courtesy of New Line Productions, Inc.; All rights reserved; p. 166 "Lord of the Rings" Copyright 2001; New Line Productions, Inc. All rights reserved; p. 168 Canadian Press/St. Catherines Standard (Denis Cahill); p. 175 Courtesy of Teen Research Unlimited; p. 179 Courtesy of Nielsen Media Research; p. 180 (left) Courtesy of The Gillette Company; p. 180 (centre) Courtesy of 3M; p. 180 (right) Courtesy of Skechers USA; p. 182 Joerg Sarbach/AP/Wide World Photos; p. 186 Courtesy of Wilson Sporting Goods Co.

Chapter 9

p. 193 Heeling Sports Ltd.; p. 195 (left) © M. Hruby; p. 195 (centre) © M. Hruby; p. 195 (right) Courtesy Heelys™, Heeling Sports Limited; p. 197 © M. Hruby; p. 202 Courtesy Xerox Corporation; p. 203 DILBERT reprinted by permission of United Features Syndicate, Inc.; p. 205 Canadian Press/Rich Buchan; p. 206 Courtesy Apple Computer; p. 207 Courtesy of Apple Computer; p. 212 Courtesy of Nokia.

Chapter 10

p. 217 Courtesy of 3M; p. 220 Photo: Stuart Hamilton for General Motors/Hummer; p. 223 Canadian Press/Richard Lappas; p. 226 Courtesy of Hewlitt-Packard Company; p. 227 Polaroid Corporation; p. 228 Courtesy of Frito-Lay, Inc.; p. 229 © M. Hruby; p. 230 Jose Azel/Aurora; p. 232 © M. Hruby; p. 234 (left) © Laura Johansen; p. 234 (right) © Kim Kulish/Corbis SABA; p. 235 New Product Showcase and Learning Center, Inc.; Photography by Robert Haller; p. 237 Courtesy of the Original Pet Drink Co.; p. 237 (left/centre) Courtesy of Palm, Inc.; p. 237 (right/centre) Quick-Books ®

2002; Courtesy of Intuit; p. 237 (right) Courtesy of Swatch USA; p. 238 Courtesy of NewProductWorks; p. 240 Courtesy of New ProductWorks; p. 241 Courtesy of Palm, Inc.

Chapter 11

p. 245 Jones Soda Co.; p. 250 (left) Courtesy of American Honda Motor Co.; Agency: Rubin Postaer & Associates; p. 250 (right) © Toshiba America Consumer Products; p. 255 © Andrew Simpson; p. 259 (left) Courtesy of Advanced Research Labs; p. 259 (right) © Kim Brewster; p. 261 Canadian Press/Toronto Star (Boris Spremo); p. 264 (left) Courtesy of Black & Decker (U.S.), Inc.; p. 264 (right) Courtesy of DeWalt Industrial Tool Company; p. 265 Courtesy of Pez Candy, Inc.; p. 266 Sheer Energy package courtesy of Sara Lee Hosiery; p. 269 © 2001 BMW of North America. Used with permission. The BMW name and logo are registered trademarks.

Chapter 12

p. 271 Expedia, Inc.; p. 272 Courtesy of Automobili Lamborghini S.p.A.; p. 274 Courtesy The Sharp Electronics Corporation; p. 275 © Reuters 2001; p. 275 Sears Roebuck and Co.; p. 278 Courtesy the Caplow Company; p. 280 © M. Hruby; p. 286 Canadian Press/Edmonton Sun (Aaron Whitfield); p. 289 © Kim Brewster; p. 290 Photo by James Leynse/Corbis SABA; p. 291 Courtesy of The Toro Company.

Chapter 13

p. 300 Courtesy of Avon Products; p. 306 Courtesy Nestlé S.A.; p. 308 (left) Darren Hick; p. 308 (right) Darren Hick; p. 311 Courtesy of Apple Computer, Inc.; p. 316 (left) Courtesy Dell Computer; p. 316 (right) Courtesy of Wal-Mart Stores, Inc.

Chapter 14

p. 323 Canadian Press/Steve White; p. 323 Canadian Press/Boris Spremo; p. 325 Courtesy of Levi Strauss USA; p. 330 (top) Reprinted with permission of Tandy Corporation; p. 330 (bottom) Gregory Smith/AP Wide World; p. 335 Courtesy of Marconi Commerce Systems; p. 336 (top) The Shopping Channel; p. 336 (centre) Lee Valley Tools Ltd.; p. 336 (bottom) L.L. Bean, Inc.

Chapter 15

p. 350 Network Aspen; p. 351 Photo: Tim Simmons for General Motors/Hummer; p. 355 Nova Scotia Department of Tourism, Culture and Heritage; p. 357 Reprinted with permission of *Canadian Grocer* and Tomas Kraus, photographer; p. 357 Photo/Volkswagen contest; Courtesy Volkswagen of America, Inc.; p. 358 © Darren Hick; p. 359 Taxi; p. 371 (left) Courtesy of Items International, Inc., p. 371 (right) Courtesy of Items International, Inc.

Chapter 16

p. 375 Rethink Communications Inc.; p. 376 Rethink Communications Inc.; p. 378 (left) British Columbia Lottery Corporation; p. 378 (centre) Courtesy of Xerox Corporation; p. 378 (right) Reprinted with permission of the Jeep® Brand, a Division of Daimler-Chrysler; p. 379 Courtesy of DDB Needham Worldwide and The Dial Corporation; p. 379 Labatt Breweries ; p. 380 Buckley's; p. 381 Taxi; p. 383 Courtesy of Ford Motor Company; p. 384 Courtesy Teen People Magazine, A Division of Time, Inc., p. 387 (top) John St. / TM – Cara Operations Limited; p. 387 (bottom) Courtesy Captivate Network, Inc.; p. 389 Courtesy Starch™; p. 392 (top) © Darren Hick; p. 393 (left) © Shooting Star; p. 393 (right) Time Photo Illustration; Leave It To Beaver: Photofest; p. 395 Taxi; p. 399 Rethink Communications Inc.

Chapter 17

p. 402 Courtesy of Xerox Corporation; p. 406 © John Madere; p. 407 Mitch Kezar/Stone; p. 410 Enzig Photography; p. 411 CB Productions/Corbis Stock Market; p. 415 Courtesy of Xerox Corporation; p. 416 (top) Courtsy of Toshiba America Medical Systems and Interactive Media; p. 416 (bottom) Jose Peleaz/The Stock Market; p. 420 Reebock Canada, Ltd.

NAME INDEX

COMPANY/PRODUCT INDEX

SUBJECT INDEX

Ch. 12